MICHIGAN
RAILROAD
LINES

MICHIGAN RAILROAD LINES

VOLUME 1

GRAYDON M. MEINTS

MICHIGAN STATE UNIVERSITY PRESS · EAST LANSING

♾ The paper used in this publication meets the minimum requirements
of ANSI/NISO Z39.48-1992 (R 1997) (Permanence of Paper).

Michigan State University Press
East Lansing, Michigan 48823-5245

Printed and bound in the United States of America.

10 09 08 07 06 05   1 2 3 4 5 6 7 8 9 10

LIBRARY OF CONGRESS CATALOGING-IN-PUBLICATION DATA
Meints, Graydon M.
Michigan railroad lines / Graydon M. Meints.
p. cm.
Includes index.
ISBN 0-87013-693-3 (cloth : alk. paper)
1. Railroads—Michigan. I. Title.
TF24.M5M44 2004
385'.09774—dc22

Michigan State University Press is a member of the Green Press Initiative and is committed to
developing and encouraging ecologically responsible publishing practices. For more information
about the Green Press Initiative and the use of recycled paper in book publishing, please visit
www.greenpressinitiative.org.

Book design by Sharp Des!gns, Lansing, MI
Cartograpy by Nick Korstange

Visit Michigan State University Press on the World Wide Web at *www.msupress.msu.edu*

FOR SAM BRECK

MAY ALL YOUR SIGNALS BE WHITE

CONTENTS

INTRODUCTION

More than 150 years have elapsed since the first railroad train ran in Michigan. As the years have passed details about construction particularly before 1875, have slipped into obscurity. The names of companies, what they built, and when they built, have become confused and inaccuracies have accumulated. This book attempts to put a sound footing under the construction and abandonment of Michigan's railroad network.This compilation details the railroad lines of Michigan, but there are important limitations to this statement. First, this work includes all the common-carrier "steam" railroads of Michigan. These consist of railroads with operations for use by the general public, for freight, for passengers, or for all three. Second, this embraces all companies that were formed under one of the state's General Railway Acts for incorporating railroads. Therefore, privately owned railroads are excluded. In Michigan this also excludes lines that were facilities of lumbering and mining companies. Also excluded are industrial or "plant" railroads operated within or by a company for its own convenience.

A separate chapter details the electric interurban and city street car lines. These were largely unregulated by the state until the twentieth century. Documentation, particularly of the early city street railway lines, has been difficult to locate. The lines of companies incorporated under the state's Train Railway Acts are included with either the "steam" or the electric railroads, as their operations dictate.

Chapter 1 is a narrative and tabulation of Michigan's railroad line construction between 1836, when the first line began operations, and 1875, when the Michigan Railroad Commissioner's annual reports on the state's railroad system began reporting this information. The chapter concludes with a complete list of sources for the information.

Chapter 2 is a year-by-year company-by-company table of Michigan's railroad mileage.

Chapter 3 is an index of all companies mentioned in chapters 4, 5, and 6.

Chapter 4 is a list, company by company, of the railroad lines of track in the Lower Peninsula of Michigan. Chapter 5 lists the lines in the Upper Peninsula; and chapter 6 lists the electric lines, both interurban and city lines. A detailed key to the data presented in chapters 4, 5 and 6 is in Appendix 1.

Chapter 7 is a set of maps showing the rail lines in each of Michigan's 83 counties. There are a number of more detailed maps for some of Michigan's larger cities.

The work concludes with a bibliography and several appendices. Appendix 1 explains the detail shown in chapters 4, 5 and 6. Appendix 2 discusses the logic that governs mileage.

ABBREVIATIONS

Ann Arbor	A.A.
Avenue	Ave.
Benton Harbor	Ben. Hbr.
Canada/Canadian	Can.
Central	Cent.
Chicago	Chi.
Cincinnatti	Cinci.
City	Cty
Cleveland	Cleve.
Crystal Falls	Cr.Fa.
Detroit	Det.
Directional words	N, S, E, W
Escanaba	Esc.
Exposition	exp.
Fort Wayne	Ft. Wyn.
Grand Haven	Gr. Hav.
Grand Ledge	Gr. Ledge
Grand Rapids	Gr. Rpds.
Grand Trunk	Gr. Trunk
Great Western	Gr. We.
Houghton	Hough.
Illinois	IL
Indiana	IN
Iron Mountain	Iron Mtn.
Ishpeming	Ish.
Jeffersonville	Jeff.
junction	Jct.
Kalamazoo	Kal.
Keewenaw	Kew.
Lake Shore	Lk. Sh.
Lake	Lk.
Lansing	Lans.
Luddington	Lud.
Mackinaw	Mack.
Marenisco	Mare.
Marine City	Mar. Cty.
Mary Charlotte	Ma. Ch.
Marquette	Marq.
Martin's Landing	Mar. Lan.
Menominee	Men.
Metropolitan	Metro.
Michigammi	Michi.
Michigan (state)	MI
Michigan (city, avenue, lake, etc.)	Mich.
Michigan Department of Transportation	MDOT
Milwaukee	Milw.
Minneapolis	Mnpls.
Mount Clemens	Mt. Clem.
Mount Pleasant	Mt. Pl.
Muskegon	Musk.
New Richmond	New Ri.
Northwestern	Nwest.
Ohio	OH
Ontario	ON
Ontonogon	Ont.
Port Huron	Pt. Hur.
Quinnesec	Quin.
River	Riv.
Rolling Mill	R. Mil.
Saginaw	Sag.
Saint Clair	St. Clair
Sault Ste. Marie	S.S. Marie
South Bend	S. Bend
Stephenson	Steph.
Street	St.
Sunday Lake	Sun. Lk.
Thompsonville	Thom.
Tittabawasee	Ttb.
Traverse	Trav.
Watersmeet	Wtrs.
Wisconsin	Wis.
Youngstown	Yngs.
Ypsilanti	Ypsi.

RAILROAD CONSTRUCTION, 1836–1875

1836

DATE	COMPANY	FROM–TO	MILEAGE	NOTE
2 Nov.	Erie & Kal.	Toledo–Adrian	21.3	5
		CUMULATIVE MILES	21.3	
		COMMISSIONER MILES	0	

Railroads came to Michigan in 1836. The Detroit & St. Joseph held the oldest active charter, dated 29 June 1832. The federal government had surveyed a route for it in 1834. It was not until 1835 that stock subscriptions began to pay in enough money to begin construction. By early 1836 contracts were let for grubbing and clearing the first part of the line.[1] The grubbing was finished between Detroit and Ypsilanti by November, and ten miles had been graded from Detroit west.[2] On 25 April 1836, contracts were awarded for grubbing the first fifteen miles of the Detroit & Pontiac.[3]

It is difficult to establish when construction began on the Erie & Kalamazoo Railroad. It appears that the work was financed to a considerable extent by notes issued by the company's bank at Adrian. The bank opened in 1836.[4] The difficulties of the Michigan–Ohio boundary dispute, and the hostilities of the Toledo War in 1835, no doubt impeded progress. Construction probably began in 1835, with a substantial part of the work completed in 1836.

The Erie & Kalamazoo was the first railroad to operate trains in Michigan. The company was named to reflect its goal of connecting Lake Erie with some point on the Kalamazoo River. Although it never reached that goal, it did begin service between Toledo and Adrian on Wednesday, 2 November 1836.[5] In Michigan the road extended 21.3 miles, from the Ohio state line near Sylvania to Adrian at the intersection of Maple and Winter Streets. Of this length, 14.2 miles are still in use and formerly were operated by the New York Central as its Old Road. This section extends from the Ohio border to the east end of the curve east of Palmyra at the Driggs Road crossing, a point originally named Palmyra Junction. The original line between Palmyra Junction and Adrian has been abandoned.

1837

No lines were put in service during 1837, although construction was underway on several. The State of Michigan began to implement its internal improvement program and, on 22 April 1837, purchased the franchise and work of the Detroit & St. Joseph.[6] The State also looked at the Detroit & Pontiac with an eye to buying it, but instead lent it some money to help it along.[7] The State also considered buying the Erie & Kalamazoo. This road channeled its traffic into a "foreign" city—Toledo, Ohio—and Michigan most certainly was not going to help a company that favored anything in Ohio.

1838

DATE	COMPANY	FROM–TO	MILEAGE	NOTE
3 Feb.	State of Mich.	Det.–Ypsi.	29.6	8
19 May	Det. & Pontiac	Det.–Royal Oak	12.0	
4 July	Det. & Pontiac	In Royal Oak	0.3	9
9 Aug.	Palmyra & Jackson	Palmyra Jct.–Tecumseh	11.6	10
no date	Riv. Raisin & L.E.	In Monroe	2.9	11
		YEAR'S MILEAGE	56.4	
		BROUGHT FORWARD	21.3	
		CUMULATIVE MILES	77.7	
		COMMISSIONER MILES	63	

The state's "Central" line depot for Detroit was at the southeast corner of Michigan and Griswold, at the site of the old City Hall.[12] The line ran on Michigan Avenue from Griswold to about 20th Street, where it curved over to the present right-of-way.

The city gave the state permission to extend tracks down Woodward Avenue from the station to Atwater Street, and to build 1000 feet in each direction on Atwater. This track, 0.7 miles in length, was put in service in the Spring, and remained in service until March 1844.[13] Horses were used to move the cars throughout this time. Given its short duration, this line is not counted in the mileage summary.

The Detroit & Pontiac extended from the intersection of Jefferson and Dequindre in Detroit to near Main Street in Royal Oak. The July construction extended the line to just north of 11 Mile Road. Horses were used to pull D&P trains until 1839.

The Palmyra & Jacksonburgh, a subsidiary of the Erie & Kalamazoo, built a line from a connection with the E&K at Palmyra Junction, through Lenawee Junction to Tecumseh. There is evidence that this line extended to Clinton, another 4.5 miles.[14] The Clinton section very probably was built and horses used for motive power, but the line operated for only a year or two before its use was discontinued. The Board of Internal Improvement's annual report for 1845 refers to the line and asks the Legislature for an appropriation for repairs and iron and to use the Clinton segment.[15] Since the Clinton extension was so short-lived, only the part as far as Tecumseh is included in 1838 mileage.

The River Raisin & Lake Erie constructed a line between downtown Monroe and LaPlaisance Bay, to its warehouses on the bay, but the precise length is difficult to determine. This construction probably coincided with the beginning of work in Spring 1838, on the State's "Southern" line which was to extend west from Monroe.[16]

1839

DATE	COMPANY	FROM–TO	MILEAGE	NOTE
16 Aug.	Det. & Pontiac	Royal Oak–Birmingham	5.3	17
17 Oct.	State of Mich.	Ypsi.–A.A.	7.5	18
		YEAR'S MILEAGE	12.8	
		BROUGHT FORWARD	77.7	
		CUMULATIVE MILEAGE	90.5	
		COMMISSIONER MILES	71	

The line of the Detroit & Pontiac was along the east side of Washington Street and Woodward Avenue. The Railroad Commissioner gives the completion date as Spring, 1841.[19]

The State of Michigan's "Central" route was entirely south of the Huron River, approximately on the route of Huron River Drive.

The State of Michigan completed a part of its "Southern" line, between Monroe and Petersburg. It did not open to public service, and is not included in 1839 construction for that reason.[20]

Also to be considered in the construction for the year was the line built by the Shelby & Detroit. It was originally chartered in 1834 to build a 23–mile line from Shelby, through Utica, to Detroit. According to Farmer it completed part of the line in September, 1839, "from Utica to within five miles of Gratiot Road."[21] Only horse-drawn cars were utilized, and the company ended operations in 1844. The line appears to have followed the present route of the Michigan Central Bay City Branch.[22] The distance from the Utica depot to Eight Mile Road is twelve miles. A point five miles north of Gratiot Road, on Mt. Elliott Road, would place the southern terminus at about Seven Mile Road—one additional mile—for a total of 13 miles. The company did not come back to life after 1844, despite several charter amendments and a new name. Given the uncertainty of some of the facts about the company, and its short duration, it has not been included in the mileage table.

1840

DATE	COMPANY	FROM–TO	MILEAGE	NOTE
23 Nov.	State of Mich.	Monroe–Adrian	32.6	23
No date	State of Mich.	In Monroe	0.4	24

YEAR'S MILEAGE		33.0	
BROUGHT FORWARD		90.5	
CUMULATIVE MILES		123.5	
COMMISSIONER MILES		104	

The 0.4–mile segment in Monroe was built to connect the "Southern" line with the River Raisin & Lake Erie line. The state purchased the River Raisin line on 14 September.[25]

1841

DATE	COMPANY	FROM–TO	MILEAGE	NOTE
30 June	State of Mich.	A.A.–Dexter	10.8	26
31 Dec.	State of Mich.	Dexter–Jackson	28.6	27
		YEAR'S MILEAGE	39.4	
		BROUGHT FORWARD	123.5	
		CUMULATIVE MILES	162.9	
		COMMISSIONER MILES	147	

The "Central" line, as originally constructed, was entirely south of the Huron River between Ann Arbor and Dexter. The extension to Jackson was completed at the date given, but was not ready for regular operations until Spring 1842.[28]

1842

DATE	COMPANY	FROM–TO	MILEAGE	NOTE
Summer	State of Mich.	Adrian–Clayton	11.0	29
No date	Det. & Pontiac	In Det.	1.2	30
		YEAR'S MILEAGE	12.2	
		BROUGHT FORWARD	162.9	
		CUMULATIVE MILES	175.1	
		COMMISSIONER MILES	147	

The Detroit & Pontiac construction shown was a line on Gratiot Avenue to Farmer Street. Detroiters eventually objected to the poor maintenance of the street by the railroad company, and disrupted service several times.[31]

1843

DATE	COMPANY	FROM–TO	MILEAGE	NOTE
27 May	State of Mich.	Clayton–Hudson	6.5	32
4 July	Det. & Pontiac	Birmingham–Pontiac	7.8	33
25 Sept.	State of Mich.	Hudson–Hillsdale	15.8	34
		YEAR'S MILEAGE	30.1	
		BROUGHT FORWARD	175.1	
		CUMULATIVE MILES	205.2	
		COMMISSIONER MILES	180	

1844

DATE	COMPANY	FROM–TO	MILEAGE	NOTE
25 June	State of Mich.	Jackson–Albion	20.4	35
12 Aug.	State of Mich.	Albion–Marshall	11.7	36

YEAR'S MILEAGE	32.1
BROUGHT FORWARD	205.2
CUMULATIVE MILES	237.3
COMMISSIONER MILES	220

The original line in Marshall curved more sharply to the northwest from a point east of Marshall Street, curved to the west between Madison and Jefferson Streets just north of Spruce Street, and joined the present line near Cherry Street.

1845

DATE	COMPANY	FROM–TO	MILEAGE	NOTE
25 Nov.	State of Mich.	Marshall–Battle Creek	13.0	37
		YEAR'S MILEAGE	13.0	
		BROUGHT FORWARD	237.3	
		CUMULATIVE MILES	250.3	
		COMMISSIONER MILES	233	

The distance shown is to the original Battle Creek station on the east side of Monroe Street.

1846

DATE	COMPANY	FROM–TO	MILEAGE	NOTE
2 Feb.	State of Mich.	Battle Creek–Kal.	23.0	38
No date	State of Mich.	In Monroe	–2.5	
		YEAR'S MILEAGE	20.5	
		BROUGHT FORWARD	250.3	
		CUMULATIVE MILES	270.8	
		COMMISSIONER MILES	279	

It appears that at or before the sale of the "Southern" line to the Michigan Southern, a substantial part of the former River Raisin & Lake Erie line to LaPlaisance Bay was abandoned.

Summary to 1846

By the end of 1846 the State of Michigan had sold its "Central" and "Southern" lines to the Michigan Central and the Michigan Southern, respectively. It had also done some grading on the "Northern" line but had not laid tracks.

At the end of 1846 the Michigan Central extended from the intersection of Michigan and Griswold Avenues in Detroit to Kalamazoo, a distance of 144.6 miles. The Michigan Southern extended from a point 1.5 miles east of Eastchester Street in Monroe, through Adrian, to Hillsdale, a distance of 66.7 miles. The Michigan Southern owned a branch from Palmyra Junction to Tecumseh that was 11.6 miles long. It is not certain that it operated the section between Palmyra Junction and Lenawee Junction, since the Erie & Kalamazoo was an independent company at this time and the two roads probably were not on particularly good terms. The Erie & Kalamazoo owned 21.3 miles in Michigan of a line extending from Toledo to Adrian. The Detroit & Pontiac ran 26.6 miles from Detroit to Pontiac.

These four companies owned a total of 270.8 miles of line. The Commissioner of Railroads gives a total of 279 miles at the end of 1846—8.2 miles more than developed here. Using only the Commissioner's figures, the progress of construction appears to be as follows:

YEAR	RR	POINTS	BUILT	TOTAL
1838	MC	Det.–Ypsi.	30 miles	
	MS	Palmyra Jct.–Clinton	16	
	MS	Riv. Raisin & Lake Erie line	4	
	D&P	Det.–Royal Oak	13	63 miles
1839	MC	Ypsi.–A.A.	8 miles	71 miles
1840	MS	Monroe–Adrian	33 miles	104 miles
1841	MC	A.A.–Jackson	38 miles	
	D&P	Royal Oak–Birmingham	5	147 miles
1843	MS	Adrian–Hillsdale	33 miles	180 miles
1844	MC	Jackson–Marshall	32 miles	
	D&P	Birmingham–Pontiac	8	220 miles
1845	MC	Marshall–Battle Creek	13 miles	233 miles
1846	MC	Battle Creek–Kal.	23 miles	
	E&K	To adjust Toledo–Adrian	23	279 miles
		GRAND TOTAL TO 1846		279 miles

The Commissioner appears to have overlooked the discontinuation of 4.5 miles of the line between Tecumseh and Clinton. Other adjustments are minor, and part of the discrepancy might be in rounding the numbers.

1848

DATE	COMPANY	FROM–TO	MILEAGE	NOTE
30 May	Mich. Cent.	To Det. old station	−1.9	39
30 May	Mich. Cent.	To Det. 3rd St. station	1.7	40
28 June	Mich. Cent.	Kal.–Lawton	16.4	41
1 Oct.	Mich. Cent.	Lawton–Niles	31.3	42
No date	Mich. Cent.	alter Ypsi–A.A.	0.3	
No date	Mich. Cent.	alter A.A.–Dexter	−1.2	
		YEAR'S MILEAGE	46.6	
		BROUGHT FORWARD	270.8	
		CUMULATIVE MILES	317.4	
		COMMISSIONER MILES	326	

The line built between approximately one mile west of Kalamazoo and Mattawan was on a route through Oshtemo, south of the present route. The mileage shown above is accurate for the route constructed, which was 0.8 miles shorter than the present route.

The Michigan Central main line was altered substantially between Ypsilanti and Dexter. The rebuilt route straightened the original circuitous line and was 0.9 miles shorter.

1849

DATE	COMPANY	FROM–TO	MILEAGE	NOTE
23 Apr.	Mich. Cent.	Niles–New Buffalo	26.7	43
		YEAR'S MILEAGE	26.7	
		BROUGHT FORWARD	317.4	
		CUMULATIVE MILES	344.1	
		COMMISSIONER MILES	353	

This segment probably was somewhat longer than stated here, since it extended to a pier on Lake Michigan to allow access to the MC's Chicago-bound steamships. Given the short duration of that service, the extension is not included.

1850

DATE	COMPANY	FROM–TO	MILEAGE	NOTE
Sept.	Mich. Southern	Hillsdale–Jonesville	4.5	44
29 Oct.	Mich. Central	New Buffalo–Mich. Cty. IN	3.8	45
10 Dec.	Mich. Southern	Jonesville–Coldwater	18.0	46
		YEAR'S MILEAGE	26.3	
		BROUGHT FORWARD	344.1	
		CUMULATIVE MILES	370.4	
		COMMISSIONER MILES	380	

Ringwalt, reporting federal Bureau of Census data, gives state mileage as 342.0, or 28.4 miles less than given here. Since the Census was taken in April it is possible that the Bureau did not count the 26.3 miles completed later in 1850, which would account for all but 2.1 miles of the difference.

1851

DATE	COMPANY	FROM–TO	MILEAGE	NOTE
March	Mich. Southern	Coldwater–Sturgis	23.7	47
July	Mich. Southern	Sturgis–Wh. Pi.	11.8	48
4 Oct.	Mich. Southern	Wh. Pi.–S. Bend	4.0	49
		YEAR'S MILEAGE	39.5	
		BROUGHT FORWARD	370.4	
		CUMULATIVE MILES	409.9	
		COMMISSIONER MILES	421	

1852

DATE	COMPANY	FROM–TO	MILEAGE	NOTE
no date	Mich. Southern	Wh. Pi.–Constantine	3.9	50
no date	Det. & Pontiac	In Det.	0.9	51
no date	Det. & Pontiac	In Det.	−1.2	52
		YEAR'S MILEAGE	3.6	
		BROUGHT FORWARD	409.9	
		CUMULATIVE MILES	413.5	
		COMMISSIONER MILES	425	

The Michigan Southern segment between White Pigeon and Constantine apparently was built to satisfy the company's charter requirements to touch a point on the St. Joseph River. The alteration on the Detroit & Pontiac is the construction along the present route between Gratiot and Jefferson Streets and the abandonment of the line on Gratiot Avenue to downtown Detroit at Farmer Street.

Summary to 1854

No construction was completed during 1853 and 1854. The Commissioner of Railroads reports total mileage in Michigan at the end of 1854 as 425 miles. This included the Michigan Central in operation from Third Street in Detroit to the Indiana state line near Grand Beach, a total of 221.7 miles. The Michigan Southern owned 33.4 miles from Monroe to Adrian, 11.6 miles from Palmyra Jct. to Tecumseh, 95.3 miles from Adrian to the Indiana state line west of White Pigeon, 3.9 miles from White Pigeon to Constantine, and a lease of 21.3 miles of the Erie & Kalamazoo between Adrian and the Ohio state line east of Ottawa Lake. This is a total of 144.2 miles for the Michigan Southern. The Detroit & Pontiac extended 26.3 miles from Detroit to Pontiac. This is a total of 413.5 miles, which is 11.5 miles less than the Commissioner's total.

1855

DATE	COMPANY	FROM–TO	MILEAGE	NOTE
2 Oct.	Det. & Milw.	Pontiac–Fenton	24.4	53
25 Dec.	Det. Monroe & Toledo	Det.–Monroe	37.2	54
no date	Mich. Southern & Northern Ind.	Tecumseh–Manchester	12.3	55
no date	St. Joseph Valley	Constantine–Three Rivers	7.5	56
		YEAR'S MILEAGE	81.4	
		BROUGHT FORWARD	413.5	
		CUMULATIVE MILES	494.9	
		COMMISSIONER MILES	462	

The Detroit, Toledo & Monroe construction extended from D & M Junction, at Mile Post 3.2 on the Detroit & Milwaukee, in Detroit. The company also held trackage rights over D&M tracks into the Brush Street station in Detroit.

1856

DATE	COMPANY	FROM–TO	MILEAGE	NOTE
1 July	Det. & Milw.	Fenton–Owosso	27.8	57
July	Det. Monroe & Toledo	Monroe–Toledo	14.0	58
		YEAR'S MILEAGE	41.8	
		BROUGHT FORWARD	494.9	
		CUMULATIVE MILES	536.7	
		COMMISSIONER MILES	530	

1857

DATE	COMPANY	FROM–TO	MILEAGE	NOTE
14 Jan.	Det. & Milw.	Owosso–St. Johns	19.6	59
July	Mich. Southern & Northern Ind.	Manchester–Jackson	20.8	60
12 Aug.	Det. & Milw.	St. Johns–Ionia	26.1	61
August	Iron Mtn.	Marq.–Ish.	16.3	62
no date	Iron Mtn.	Cleve. Lk. Mine br.	1.0	
		YEAR'S MILEAGE	83.8	
		BROUGHT FORWARD	536.7	
		CUMULATIVE MILES	620.5	
		COMMISSIONER MILES	579	

The Iron Mountain was the Upper Peninsula's first railroad. Sources are unclear as to the end points of the construction. The 16.3 miles shown here is from the first Marquette ore dock to the Lake Superior Mine at Ishpeming. *Aids, Gifts, Grants* states construction was 16.25 miles from Front Street in Marquette to the Lake Superior Mine, which includes the distance to the ore dock. Ringwalt divides the construction between 15.0 miles in 1857 and 1.87 in 1858.[63]

1858

DATE	COMPANY	FROM–TO	MILEAGE	NOTE
4 July	Det. & Milw.	Ionia–Gr. Rpds.	33.3	64
30 Aug.	Det. & Milw.	Gr. Rpds.–Spring Lk.	28.9	65
22 Nov.	Det. & Milw.	Spring Lk.–Gr. Hav.	2.3	66
no date	Amboy, Lans. & Trav. Bay	Owosso–Laingsburg	11.8	67

YEAR'S MILEAGE	76.3
BROUGHT FORWARD	620.5
CUMULATIVE MILES	696.8
COMMISSIONER MILES	703

The Detroit & Milwaukee's line into Grand Rapids was the first rail service to that city. The D&M station for Grand Haven was on the north side of the Grand River, approximately opposite the station at the foot of Washington Street.

1859

DATE	COMPANY	FROM–TO	MILEAGE	NOTE
21 Nov.	Chi., Det. & C.G.T.J	W. Det.–Fort Gratiot	59.5	68
no date	Amboy, Lans. & Trav. Bay	Laingsburg–Bath	7.1	69
		YEAR'S MILEAGE	66.6	
		BROUGHT FORWARD	696.8	
		CUMULATIVE MILES	763.4	
		COMMISSIONER MILES	770	

Summary to 1860

No new construction was completed in 1860. At this time the mileage of the individual railroads was:

Amboy, Lansing & Traverse Bay	18.9 miles
Detroit & Milwaukee	188.7
Grand Trunk Railway of Canada, which owned	
Chicago, Detroit & Canada Grand Trunk Junction	59.5
Iron Mountain	17.3
Michigan Central	21.7
Michigan Southern & Northern Indiana	173.4
Detroit, Monroe & Toledo (owned by MS&NI)	51.2
Erie & Kalamazoo (leased by MS&NI)	21.3
St. Joseph Valley	7.5
leased from Michigan Southern & Northern Indiana	3.9
TOTAL	763.4

1861

DATE	COMPANY	FROM–TO	MILEAGE	NOTE
4 Sept.	Amboy, Lans. & Trav. Bay	Bath–N. Lans.	7.1	70
		YEAR'S MILEAGE	7.1	
		BROUGHT FORWARD	763.4	
		CUMULATIVE MILES	770.5	
		COMMISSIONER MILES	777	

The south end of the Amboy's construction was at Grand River Avenue in Lansing.

1862

DATE	COMPANY	FROM–TO	MILEAGE	NOTE
20 Jan.	Flint & Pere Marq.	Sag.–Mt. Morris	26.1	71
Fall	Bay de Noquet & Marq.	Ish.–Winthrop Mine	2.9	72
		YEAR'S MILEAGE	29.2	
		BROUGHT FORWARD	770.5	
		CUMULATIVE MILES	799.5	
		COMMISSIONER MILES	811	

1863

DATE	COMPANY	FROM–TO	MILEAGE	NOTE
25 Aug.	Amboy, Lans. & Trav. Bay	N. Lans.–Lans.	1.0	73
8 Dec.	Flint & Pere Marq.	Mt. Morris–Flint	7.2	74
		YEAR'S MILEAGE	8.2	
		BROUGHT FORWARD	799.5	
		CUMULATIVE MILES	807.7	
		COMMISSIONER MILES	812	

1864

DATE	COMPANY	FROM–TO	MILEAGE	NOTE
Sept.	Peninsula	Esc.–Jackson Mine	62.7	75
1 Nov.	Flint & Holly	Flint–Holly	16.8	76
		YEAR'S MILEAGE	79.5	
		BROUGHT FORWARD	807.7	
		CUMULATIVE MILES	887.2	
		COMMISSIONER MILES	891	

Both the opening date and the length of the line of the Peninsula are open to some uncertainty. Kenneth D. Lafayette's *Flaming Brands* states the opening date was 22 December 1864, but the first ore shipment was not made until 12 May 1865. The most commonly given distance is 62 miles, although Stennett gives 61. Lafayette puts the north end of the line at the Jackson Mine. The mileage given here is from the intersection of 1st Street North and 3rd Street in Escanaba to the Jackson Mine. The line built used the more direct route between Mineral Branch and the east end of Palmer Street in Negaunee.

1865

DATE	COMPANY	FROM–TO	MILEAGE	NOTE
July	Marq. & Ont.	Winthrop Jct.–Lk. Michi.	19.6	77
Dec.	Jackson, Lans. & Sag.	Jackson–Mason	24.6	78
no date	Mich. Cent.	alter in Marshall	−0.1	79
no date	Chi. & North Western	Negaunee–Ish.–Holmes Mine	4.5	80
		YEAR'S MILEAGE	48.6	
		BROUGHT FORWARD	887.2	
		CUMULATIVE MILES	935.8	
		COMMISSIONER MILES	931	

The Marquette & Ontonagon construction extended from Winthrop Junction westward on the present line as far as Mile Post 185, just east of Champion. The line extended west from that point to the shore of Lake Michigammi in the southeast quarter of section 9. The M&O main line toward Ontonagon originally was to be built around the south shore of Lake Michigammi.

The Chicago & North Western construction in this period is difficult to recreate. The opening and closing years of the iron mines helped to establish dates. The extension to the Lake Angeline Mine is given in *Aids, Gifts, Grants* as built in 1870. Inasmuch as the New York, Holmes, and Lake Angeline Mines all opened in or about 1864, the date of construction has been moved to 1865.

1866

DATE	COMPANY	FROM–TO	MILEAGE	NOTE
25 June	Jackson, Lans. & Sag.	Mason–Lans.	12.1	81
		YEAR'S MILEAGE	12.1	
		BROUGHT FORWARD	935.8	
		CUMULATIVE MILES	947.9	
		COMMISSIONER MILES	943	

The north end of the JL&S construction was at Michigan Avenue in Lansing at a connection with the Amboy, Lansing & Traverse Bay.

1867

DATE	COMPANY	FROM–TO	MILEAGE	NOTE
3 May	Kal. & Wh. Pi.	Kal.–Three Rivers	25.1	82
Sept.	Paw Paw	Paw Paw–Lawton	3.8	83
11 Oct.	Jackson, Lans. & Sag.	Owosso–St. Charles	21.8	84
1 Nov.	Bay Cty. & E. Sag.	Sag.–Bay Cty.	12.5	85
1 Dec.	Flint & Pere Marq.	Sag.–Midland	20.0	86
6 Dec.	Jackson, Lans. & Sag.	St. Charles–Bay Cty.	27.6	87
25 Dec.	Gr. Rpds. & Ind.	Gr. Rpds.–Cedar Springs	20.1	88
no date	Chi. & North Western	Iron Mtn. Mine Br.	5.4	89
		YEAR'S MILEAGE	136.3	
		BROUGHT FORWARD	947.9	
		CUMULATIVE MILES	1,084.2	
		COMMISSIONER MILES	1,066	

Railroad construction through October 1867, completed a total of 998.3 miles of line in Michigan. The opening of the Bay City & East Saginaw company's line of 12.5 miles marked the completion of the first thousand miles of railroad in Michigan—nearly 31 years to the day after the first trains of the Erie & Kalamazoo began running. The distance given for the BC&ES line is to the 4th Street station, approaching it via Jefferson Street from the south.

The end of the Jackson, Lansing & Saginaw line in Bay City was in the vicinity of West Main Street, in an area then called Wenona. This use of the name Wenona should not be confused with its later use by the Michigan Central for its classification yard north of Bay City.

The Grand Rapids & Indiana terminus in Grand Rapids was located at West Bridge Street.

1868

DATE	COMPANY	FROM–TO	MILEAGE	NOTE
4 July	Gr. Riv. Valley	Rives Jct.–Eaton Rapids	13.6	90
15 Aug.	Gr. Riv. Valley	Eaton Rapids–Charlotte	10.7	91
20 Oct.	Flint & Pere Marq.	Midland–Averill	5.8	92
Oct.	Hecla & Torch Lake	Calumet–Torch Lake	4.5	93
23 Nov.	Kal., Allegan & Gr. Rpds.	Kal.–Allegan	25.3	94
no date	Gr. Rpds. & Ind.	In Gr. Rpds.	2.4	95
no date	Chi. & North Western	Barnum Mine Spur	0.5	96

YEAR'S MILEAGE	62.8	
BROUGHT FORWARD	1,084.2	
CUMULATIVE MILES	1,147.0	
COMMISSIONER MILES	1,124	

The location of the south end of the Grand Rapids & Indiana construction has not been determined with certainty. The company was required to build from Bridge Street, across the Grand River, to the downtown area to be eligible for municipal aid. The track probably ends about halfway between Hall and Franklin Streets, the original site of South Yard. The company already had begun constructing its line south of Grand Rapids to Fort Wayne, Indiana.

1869

DATE	COMPANY	FROM–TO	MILEAGE	NOTE
26 Jan.	Gr. Riv. Valley	Charlotte–Nashville	14.9	97
22 Feb.	Gr. Riv. Valley	Nashville–Hastings	11.6	98
1 Mar.	Kal., Allegan & Gr. Rpds.	Allegan–Gr. Rpds.	33.2	99
21 June	Gr. Rpds. & Ind.	Cedar Springs–Morley	19.2	100
18 Nov.	Ionia & Lans.	N. Lans.–Portland	23.1	101
22 Nov.	Ft. Wyn., Jackson & Sag.	Jackson–Reading	35.4	102
Nov.	Pt. Hur. & Lk. Mich.	Pt. Hur.–Emmett	17.6	103
9 Dec.	Mich. Air Line Ry.	Ridgeway–Romeo	14.2	104
Dec.	Ionia & Lans.	Portland–Ionia	14.0	105
Dec.	Mich. Lk. Shore	Ferrysburg–Musk.	13.0	106
	YEAR'S MILEAGE		196.2	
	BROUGHT FORWARD		1,147.0	
	CUMULATIVE MILES		1,343.2	
	COMMISSIONER MILES		1,362	

The Grand River Valley construction ended near State and East Streets in Hastings, at a point which later was named Hastings Freight House.

The line of the Kalamazoo, Allegan & Grand Rapids extended north of its Grand Rapids station at Fulton Street, to Bridge Street where it made a connection with the Grand Rapids & Indiana.

The mileage shown for the Fort Wayne, Jackson & Saginaw extends from the line's connection with the Michigan Central at East Avenue in Jackson. The Fort Wayne company ran on 0.5 miles of MC tracks to reach the MC's Jackson station. The line was built on a direct line between Fort Wayne Junction and Bankers, and passed west of Hillsdale.

The Ferrysburg–Muskegon line of the Michigan Lake Shore was the first rail line into Muskegon. It extended north from a connection with the Detroit & Milwaukee at Ferrysburg. The road's original Muskegon station was at Third Street, 0.3 miles north of the present station, and this is used as the northern terminus. One source reports a branch to Lake Michigan, but does not locate the line or give a completion date.[107]

1870

DATE	COMPANY	FROM–TO	MILEAGE	NOTE
1 Jan.	Gr. Riv. Valley	Hastings–Gr. Rpds.	33.0	108
1 Jan.	Peninsular	Battle Creek–Bellevue	13.4	109
17 Jan.	Ft. Wyn., Jackson & Sag.	Reading–Angola IN	8.9	110
2 Feb.	Chi. & Mich. Lk. Shore	St. Joseph–New Buffalo	26.9	111
14 Feb.	Peninsular	Bellevue–Charlotte	3.2	112
10 Mar.	Kal. & S. Haven	Kal.–Kendall	14.6	113
8 June	Pt. Hur. & Lk. Mich.	Emmett–Capac	8.6	114
13 June	Peninsular	Charlotte–Lans.	18.5	115

22 June	Gr. Rpds. & Ind.	Ft. Wyn. IN–Sturgis	2.7	116
4 July	Kal. & S. Haven	Kendall–Bloomingdale	8.2	117
28 July	Pt. Hur. & Lk. Mich.	Capac–Imlay Cty.	7.3	118
no date	Det. & Milw.	Ferrysburg–Gr. Hav.	1.3	119
no date	Det. & Milw.	Ferrysburg–Gr. Hav. (old)	−1.7	120
Summer	Mich. Air Line RR	Jackson Jct.–Homer	23.8	121
12 Aug.	Gr. Rpds. & Ind.	Morley–Paris	21.0	122
29 Aug.	Mich. Lk. Shore	Allegan–Gr. Hav.	44.0	123
Aug.	Gr. Rpds. & Ind.	Sturgis–Kal.	36.3	124
13 Sept.	Gr. Rpds. & Ind.	Kal.–Gr. Rpds.	47.3	125
Sept.	Ionia & Lans.	Ionia–Greenville	18.6	126
15 Oct.	Peninsular	Battle Creek–Climax	10.4	127
Autumn	Mich. Air Line RR	Homer–Three Rivers	45.8	128
Nov.	Flint & Pere Marq.	Averill–Clare	24.6	129
29 Dec.	Flint & Pere Marq.	Clare–Lake	12.1	130
Dec.	Pt. Hur. & Lk. Mich.	Imlay Cty.–Attica	4.7	131
no date	Chi. & Mich. Lk. Shore	Nunica–North Yard	15.7	132
	YEAR'S MILEAGE		459.2	
	BROUGHT FORWARD		1,343.2	
	CUMULATIVE MILES		1,802.4	
	COMMISSIONER MILES		1,739	

The end of the Grand River Valley's line in Grand Rapids was at its Williams Street passenger station.

The Chicago & Michigan Lake Shore's line ended at the Michigan Central station in New Buffalo. Its original route between New Buffalo and Union Pier was close to the present Riviera Road.

The Michigan Air Line route between 2 miles west of Concord and 28 Mile Road east of Homer was north of the current grade. It crossed 30 Mile Road about 0.6 miles north of N Drive South. Between Haires and Bridge St. in Jackson, the road shared tracks with the Fort Wayne, Jackson & Saginaw with the MAL owning the north main track and the Fort Wayne line the southerly.

The Detroit & Milwaukee built a new line on the south side of the Grand River to a new station on Washington Avenue in Grand Haven. It appears that a part of the old line may have been retained for industrial service.

The Michigan Lake Shore obtained rights to use the D&M's Grand River drawbridge as part of its route. In Holland it crossed the Chicago & Michigan Lake Shore just north of the 8th Street passenger station, ran along the north side of 7th Street, turned north and crossed the Black River east of Central Avenue, and joined the present line at Cronje. The Allegan terminus was at a connection with the Kalamazoo, Allegan & Grand Rapids east of Main Street.

That part of the Peninsular's line from Angell Street in Battle Creek nearly to Renton Road was on a route through Kellogg Airfield. It crossed Columbia Avenue just east of Stone Jug Road. A short piece of the east end of the old line remains in use for industrial service.

Two sources indicate an extension of the Chicago & North Western from Negaunee to the Saint Lawrence Mine. This work has been included in the construction given for 1865.[133]

1871

DATE	COMPANY	FROM–TO	MILEAGE	NOTE
2 Jan.	Kal. & S. Haven	Bloomingdale–S. Haven	16.6	134
31 Jan.	Jackson, Lans. & Sag.	Bay Cty.–Kawkawlin	5.3	135
28 Feb.	Chi. & Mich. Lk. Shore	St. Joseph–Grand Jct.	34.1	136
Feb.	Mich. Air Line RR	Three Rivers–Niles	33.9	137
25 May	Pt. Hur. & Lk. Mich.	Attica–Davison	18.1	138
30 May	Holly, Wayne & Monroe	Wayne–Northville	11.7	139
30 June	Detroit, Lansing & Lake Michigan	W. Det.–Plymouth	19.4	140
30 June	Chi. & Mich. Lk. Shore	Grand Jct.–Waverly	29.3	141

30 June	Chi. & Mich. Lk. Shore	North Yard–Montague	14.4	142
30 June	Chi. & Mich. Lk. Shore	Waverly–Nunica	19.9	143
June	Peninsular	Climax–Cassopolis	42.1	144
31 July	Det., Lans. & Lk. Mich.	Plymouth–Brighton	20.6	145
31 July	Det., Lans. & Lk. Mich.	Lans.–Williamston	14.0	146
July	Det., Hillsdale & Ind.	Ypsi.–Saline	10.7	147
31 Aug.	Det., Lans. & Lk. Mich.	Brighton–Williamston	28.2	148
31 Aug.	Jackson, Lans. & Sag.	Kawkawlin–Standish	23.0	149
23 Sept.	Det., Hillsdale & Ind.	Saline–Manchester	13.3	150
30 Sept.	Det., Lans. & Lk. Mich.	Greenville–Gowen	6.1	151
Sept.	Flint & Pere Marq.	Lake–Evart	13.4	152
Sept.	Mansfield, Coldwater & Lk. Mich.	Allegan–Montieth	11.2	153
6 Nov.	Holly, Wayne & Monroe	Northville–Holly	28.4	154
30 Nov.	Det., Lans. & Lk. Mich.	Gowen–Howard Cty.	13.5	155
Nov.	Flint & Pere Marq.	Evart–Reed Cty.	13.3	156
13 Dec.	Pt. Hur. & Lk. Mich.	Davison–(N.) Flint	9.0	157
31 Dec.	Jackson, Lans. & Sag.	Standish–Wells	12.1	158
Dec.	Gr. Rpds. & Ind.	Paris–Cadillac	36.4	159
no date	Chi. & North Western	Cascade Jct.–Winthrop Jct.	13.6	160
no date	Chi. & North Western	Salisbury Mine Spur	0.8	161
no date	Chi. & North Western	Rolling Mill Mine Spur	0.7	162
		YEAR'S MILEAGE	513.1	
		BROUGHT FORWARD	1,802.4	
		CUMULATIVE MILES	2,315.5	
		COMMISSIONER MILES	2,298	

The Detroit, Lansing & Lake Michigan line began at West Detroit where it connected with the Michigan Central, and had trackage rights to reach that road's Detroit passenger station. The line also used Jackson, Lansing & Saginaw tracks between Lansing and North Lansing.

The Mansfield, Coldwater & Lake Michigan connected with the Grand Rapids & Indiana at Montieth which was located 1.0 miles south of Martin.

1872

DATE	COMPANY	FROM–TO	MILEAGE	NOTE
1 Jan.	Chi. & Mich. Lk. Shore	Waverly–Gr. Rpds.	24.5	163
1 Jan.	Chi. & Mich. Lk. Shore	Montague–Pentwater	26.8	164
1 Jan.	Holly, Wayne & Monroe	Wayne–Monroe	24.0	165
7 Jan.	Northern Cent. Mich.	Jonesville–Albion	21.7	166
Jan.	Det., Hillsdale & Ind.	Manchester–Hillsdale	37.6	167
9 May	Gr. Rpds., Newaygo & Lk. Shore	Gr. Rpds.–Sparta	14.0	168
June	Gr. Rpds., Newaygo & Lk. Shore	Sparta–Casnovia	7.6	169
4 July	Chi. & Can. Southern	Grosvenor–Fayette OH	20.5	170
8 Sept.	Mineral Range	Hancock–Highway	8.1	171
11 Sept.	Gr. Rpds., Newaygo & Lk. Shore	Casnovia–Newaygo	13.7	172
30 Sept.	Northern Cent. Mich.	Albion–Eaton Rapids	20.1	173
Sept.	Gr. Rpds & Ind.	Cadillac–Fife Lake	26.0	174
Sept.	Marquette, Hou. & Ont.	Humboldt Jct.–Republic Mine	9.5	175
Fall	Det., Lans. & Lk. Mich.	Kidd–Belding	1.7	176
Fall	Peninsular	Cassopolis–S. Bend IN	11.8	177
8 Oct.	Flint Riv.	Horton–Otter Lk.	14.4	178
31 Oct.	Det. & Bay Cty.	Bay Cty. Jct.–Oxford	41.0	179
15 Nov.	Trav. Cty.	Walton Jct.–Trav. Cty.	26.0	180
30 Nov.	Det. & Bay Cty.	Oxford–Lapeer	17.2	181

Nov.	Det., Hillsdale & Ind.	Hillsdale–Bankers	2.8	182
31 Dec.	Det. & Bay Cty.	Lapeer–Otter Lk.	13.2	183
Dec.	Marq., Hough. & Ont.	Champion Jct.–L'Anse	33.0	184
Dec.	Chi. & North Western	Men.–Esc.	65.6	185
no date	Chi. & North Western	adjust lines in Esc.	−1.8	186
no date	Mich. Air RR	Niles–S. Bend IN	5.5	187
no date	Lapeer & Northern	Lapeer–end of line	3.7	188
no date	Marq., Hough. & Ont.	Old Champion Mine Branch	1.9	189
no date	Marq., Hough. & Ont.	Champion Mine–Lk. Michi.	−5.8	190
no date	Marq., Hough. & Ont.	Rolling Mill Mine Br.	1.5	191
no date	Marq., Hough. & Ont.	Sag. Mine Br.	2.5	192
no date	Chi. & North Western	Smith Mine Br.	5.5	193
no date	Chi. & North Western	Allen Mine Spur	0.6	194
no date	Chi. & North Western	McComber Mine Spur	1.5	195
		YEAR'S MILEAGE	495.9	
		BROUGHT FORWARD	2,315.5	
		CUMULATIVE MILES	2,811.4	
		COMMISSIONER MILES	2,822	

The Chicago & Michigan Lake Shore's line ended at Ottawa and Fulton Streets in Grand Rapids.

The Holly, Wayne & Monroe line ended at a junction with the Detroit, Monroe & Toledo (Lake Shore & Michigan Southern) 1.5 miles north of Monroe.

The Detroit, Hillsdale & Indiana original line through Hillsdale apparently was in a general northeast–southwest direction crossing Broad Street a short distance north of the fairgrounds. The grade has been obscured.

The Detroit, Lansing & Lake Michigan received the Belding–Kidd segment as a donation. It may have been operated with horses before conveyance.

The Mineral Range station in Hancock was near the foot of Tezcuco Street.

In 1873 the newly-appointed Commissioner of Railroads issued his first annual report. This first statement of railroad mileage is less than helpful since it has duplicate reports of some track and shows as completed some work that other sources report as not yet finished. The individual road totals do not sum to the 2,822 miles that he reports for end of the year 1872.

1873

DATE	COMPANY	FROM–TO	MILEAGE	NOTE
1 Jan.	Saginaw Valley & St. Louis	Paines–St. Louis	28.6	196
13 Jan.	Northern Cent. Mich.	Eaton Rapids–N. Lans.	18.8	197
Feb.	Det., Lans. & Lk. Mich.	Haynor–Stanton	20.0	198
31 Mar.	Det. & Bay Cty.	Otter Lake–Vassar	12.6	199
May	Jackson, Lans. & Sag.	Wells–Otsego Lake	72.0	200
21 July	Chi. & Mich. Lk. Shore	Berry–Big Rapids	51.1	201
31 July	Det. & Bay Cty.	Vassar–Bay City E.S.	22.7	202
July	Jackson, Lans. & Sag.	Otsego Lake–Gaylord	7.4	203
Sept.	Can. Southern Bridge	Slocum Jct.–Grosse Ile	3.1	204
1 Sept.	Toledo, Can. Southern & Det.	Det.–Toledo OH	46.8	205
11 Oct.	Mineral Range	Highway–Calumet	4.4	206
13 Nov.	Chi. & Can. Southern	Slocum Jct.–Grosvenor	41.9	207
7 Dec.	Mich. Midland & Can.	St. Clair Springs–Lenox	14.0	208
no date	Lapeer & Northern	extension of line	0.5	209
no date	Marq., Hough. & Ont.	Eagle Mills–Morgan Furnace	1.1	210
no date	Marq., Hough. & Ont.	Branch to McComber Mine	0.7	211
no date	Chi. & North Western	Winthrop Jct.–Sag. Mine	3.1	212
no date	Chi. & North Western	Branch to Foster Mine	4.6	213

DATE	COMPANY	FROM–TO	MILEAGE	NOTE
no date	Chi. & North Western	Branch to Excelsior Mine	2.0	214
no date	Chi. & North Western	Smith Mine Br. reduction	−0.5	215
no date	Marq., Hough. & Ont.	extend Champion Mine Br.	0.3	216
no date	Marq., Hough. & Ont.	extend Sag. Mine Br.	0.5	217
no date	Det. & Milw.	Corunna Mine Br.	2.0	218
		YEAR'S MILEAGE	357.7	
		BROUGHT FORWARD	2,811.4	
		CUMULATIVE MILES	3,169.1	
		COMMISSIONER MILES	3,252	

The Saginaw Valley & St. Louis held running rights over the Jackson, Lansing & Saginaw between Paines and Saginaw.

The Detroit end of the Toledo, Canada Southern & Detroit ended at a connection with the Michigan Central just east of West Detroit, near Clark Street. It used MC tracks to reach the MC's Detroit station.

In Calumet the Mineral Range line extended to the east side of the village, north of First Street and a block west of Calumet Street.

The Detroit & Milwaukee's Corunna Mine Branch's principal function was to provide coal for company use.

1874

DATE	COMPANY	FROM–TO	MILEAGE	NOTE
May	Gr. Rpds. & Ind.	Fife Lake–Petoskey	67.0	219
1 Dec.	Flint & Pere Marq.	Reed City–Lud.	48.4	220
no date	Glencoe, Pinconning & Lake Shore	Glencoe–Pinconning	10.5	221
no date	Lapeer & Northern	Extension	0.5	222
no date	Marq., Hough. & Ont.	Br. to Kloman Mine	1.8	223
no date	Marq., Hough. & Ont.	Br. to Carp Furnace	1.9	224
no date	Marq., Hough. & Ont.	Extend Morgan Furnace Br.	1.6	225
no date	Marq., Hough. & Ont.	Reduce at Republic Mine	−0.4	226
no date	Chi. & North Western	Cambria Mine Br.	1.2	227
		YEAR'S MILEAGE	132.5	
		BROUGHT FORWARD	3,169.1	
		CUMULATIVE MILES	3,301.6	
		COMMISSIONER MILES	3,313	

The distance given for the Flint & Pere Marquette to the Ludington docks on the assumption that a water connection was made.

The Glencoe, Pinconning & Lake Shore was one of Michigan's first chartered lumbering railroads. It extended from a point named Glencoe, which can no longer be located with certainty but appears to have been in the extreme southwest corner of Mount Forest Township, in Bay County.

There may have been other construction by the Chicago & North Western, for a total increase of 11.1 miles for the year, but the segments could not be determined.

1875

DATE	COMPANY	FROM–TO	MILEAGE	NOTE
15 Aug.	Chi., Sag. & Can.	St. Louis–Riverdale	12.6	228
24 Sept.	Gr. Rpds., Newaygo & Lk. Shore	Newaygo–White Cloud	11.1	229
1 Dec.	Chi., Sag. & Can.	Riverdale–Cedar Lake	7.7	230
no date	Erie & Kal.	In Adrian	−1.6	231
no date	Det. & Milw.	Pontiac State Hospital Br.	0.7	232

YEAR'S MILEAGE	30.5
BROUGHT FORWARD	3,301.6
CUMULATIVE MILES	3,332.1
COMMISSIONER MILES	3,347

The Erie & Kalamazoo change reports the abandonment of that part of the line west of its crossing with the Lake Shore & Michigan Southern in Adrian and on the city streets to its original downtown terminal.

The annual report of the Chicago & North Western to the Commissioner of Railroads reports a 1.1 mile increase in trackage, but the report does not identify the track built; this work has not been included herein.

For further discussion of the variance in mileage between the reports of the Commissioner of Railroads and this study, see Appendix 2.

SOURCES & NOTES

The starting point for any study of early Michigan railroads has to be the *Annual Reports* of the Commissioner of Railroads. The report for the year 1875 (published in 1876) has a compilation of dates of openings arranged by companies. A chief fault of the Commissioner's reports is his complete reliance on data submitted by the railroad companies which, in turn, were unbelievably casual. Discrepancies also exist between the 1876 compilation and the data in the statements of the individual companies.

Edmund A. Calkins, statistician to the Michigan Railroad Commission, modestly named himself as "Compiler" of a 1919 yeoman project entitled *Aids, Gifts, Grants and Donations to Railroads including Outline of Development and Successions in Titles to Railroads in Michigan*. It represents the most complete and only comprehensive treatment to date of the growth of the Michigan rail network. Calkins tends also to rely on dates and mileages used by the Commissioner, at least for the period treated herein, but does note dates derived from alternate sources.

J. L. Ringwalt's *Development of Transportation Systems in the United States*, cited as Ringwalt, *Development of Transportation Systems*, reports the growth in mileage by company. It appears that he works with mileage in effect at the time of writing. This in turn causes him to ignore line relocations and abandonments. Further limiting the usefulness of this work is that no figures are given by state per year—a very real drawback when the route crossed state boundaries.

The *Annual Reports* of the Board of Internal Improvement of the State of Michigan shed some light on the projects undertaken by the State prior to 1847. The reports completely ignore any privately-financed construction except that of the Palmyra & Jacksonburgh.

The county histories published between 1880 and 1910 cover, enthusiastically if not always accurately, the development of early rail projects in Michigan. Valuable is Silas Farmer's *History of Detroit and Wayne County* (1890; reprint, Detroit: Gale Research, 1969). Farmer is one of the more reliable county historians. Also used were Talcott E. Wing's *History of Monroe County* (New York, 1890), Richard I. Bonner's *Memoirs of Lenawee County* (Madison, Wisc.: Western Historical Association, 1909), and Albert Baxter's *History of the City of Grand Rapids* (New York: Munsell & Company, 1891).

Willis Dunbar's history of Michigan railroading, *All Aboard!* (Grand Rapids, Mich.: Eerdmans, 1969) remains a generally readable account. It is not particularly detailed about construction after the early years. Dunbar does rely heavily on the original sources cited above.

Paul Wesley Ivey's *The Pere Marquette Railroad Company* (1919, reprint; Grand Rapids, Mich.: Black Letter, 1970), Alvin F. Harlow's *The Road of the Century* (New York: Creative Age Press, 1947), and George H. Burgess and Miles C. Kennedy's *Centennial History of the Pennsylvania Railroad* (Philadelphia: Pennsylvania Railroad, 1949), all are readable histories of their subject companies, but shed little light on the subject covered by this work. Better is William H. Stennett's treatment of the Chicago & North Western in *Yesterday and Today* (Chicago: Chicago & North Western Railway, 1910), but he leaves a curious gap in the early 1870s.

FOOTNOTES

1. Following chartering and incorporating the company, work usually proceeded in the following steps: 1. Surveying a proposed route, 2. Acquiring the right of way, 3. Clearing the route of trees and underbrush

("grubbing"), 4. Grading, 5. Track-laying the wooden superstructure and possibly installing strap iron the stringers. At the completion of track-laying the road is ready to be opened to public use.

2. Farmer, *Detroit and Wayne County*, 895–96.

3. Ibid., 893.

4. Dunbar, *All Aboard!*, 25.

5. Bonner, *Memoirs of Lenawee County*, 140 and Mrs. Frank P. Dodge, "Marking the Terminus of the Erie and Kalamazoo Railroad," *Michigan Pioneer & Historical Collections* XXXVIII (1912), 491, give 2 November 1836, but cite no source for the date. Michigan Railroad Commission, *Aids, Gifts, Grants*, 98n b also mentions this although he gives 20 June 1837, as the probable completion date. Farmer, *Detroit and Wayne County*, 901, dates completion as 1 October 1836. Contemporary newspapers support the November date. Wing, *History of Monroe County*, 216, has 1836, as do Dunbar, *All Aboard!*, 20; Harlow, *Road of the Century*, 247; and George N. Fuller, *Michigan Centennial History* (Chicago: Lewis, 1939), 1:281; all of whom appear to rely on the earlier sources. A number of other sources, among them *Aids, Gifts, Grants*, give dates in 1837, varying from January to August. These dates appear to reflect the replacement of horses with steam locomotives. *Aids, Gifts, Grants* uses this same premise for initial dates of the Detroit & Pontiac.

6. *Aids, Gifts, Grants*, 89.

7. Farmer, *Detroit and Wayne County*, 894.

8. Farmer, *Detroit and Wayne County*, 896; Board of Internal Improvement, *Annual Reports*, 1838, *House Documents No. 17*, (Lansing: 1839), 289. Commissioner of Railroads, *Annual Reports*, 1875, xxvi has 5 February, as does *Aids, Gifts, Grants*, 89. Farmer also says "as early as January, 1838, the road was in operation to Dearborn."

9. Farmer, *Detroit and Wayne County*, 893. *Aids, Gifts, Grants*, 35 and Commissioner of Railroads, *Annual Reports*, 1875, xxii have Autumn 1838.

10. *Aids, Gifts, Grants*, 99; Bonner, *Memoirs of Lenawee County*, 142.

11. *Aids, Gifts, Grants*, 99.

12. Farmer, *Detroit and Wayne County*, 898.

13. Ibid.

14. Dunbar, *All Aboard!*, 26.

15. Board of Internal Improvement, *Annual Reports*, 1845, 5–6.

16. Wing, *History of Monroe County*, 221. Farmer, *Detroit and Wayne County*, 902 says construction began 14 May 1838.

17. Farmer, *Detroit and Wayne County*, 893.

18. Commissioner of Railroads, *Annual Reports*, 1875, xxvi; *Aids, Gifts, Grants*, 89; Farmer, *Detroit and Wayne County*, 897.

19. Commissioner of Railroads, *Annual Reports*, 1875, xxii; *Aids, Gifts, Grants*, 35.

20. *Aids, Gifts, Grants*, 99.

21. Farmer, *Detroit and Wayne County*, 890.

22. *Aids, Gifts, Grants*, 93.

23. Commissioner of Railroads, *Annual Reports*, 1875, xxv; *Aids, Gifts, Grants*, 99; Board of Internal Improvement, *Annual Reports*, 1840, 157.

24. Board of Internal Improvement, *Annual Reports*, 1840, 204. Also Farmer, *Detroit and Wayne County*, 902; Commissioner of Railroads, *Annual Reports*, 1875, xxv.

25. *Aids, Gifts, Grants*, 99 says 1841, but this year is assumed given the completion of the adjoining segment.

26. Commissioner of Railroads, *Annual Reports*, 1875, xxvi; *Aids, Gifts, Grants*, 89; Farmer, *Detroit and Wayne County*, 897. Board of Internal Improvement, *Annual Reports*, 184, 191 gives the date as 4 July 1841.

27. Commissioner of Railroads, *Annual Reports*, 1875, xxvi; *Aids, Gifts, Grants*, 89; Farmer, *Detroit and Wayne County*, 897.

28. Board of Internal Improvements, *Annual Report*, 1842, 154.

29. *Aids, Gifts, Grants*, 99.

30. Farmer, *Detroit and Wayne County*, 894.

31. Ibid.

32. *Aids, Gifts, Grants,* 99; Wing, *History of Monroe County,* 226.

33. Farmer, *Detroit and Wayne County,* 893. Commissioner of Railroads, *Annual Reports,* 1875, xxii says Autumn of 1844; *Aids, Gifts, Grants,* 35 says September 1844.

34. Commissioner of Railroads, *Annual Reports,* 1875, xxv; *Aids, Gifts, Grants,* 99. Board of Internal Improvement, *Annual Reports,* 1843, 9 reports the work completed in early October.

35. Commissioner of Railroads, *Annual Reports,* 1875, xxvi; *Aids, Gifts, Grants,* 89; Farmer, *Detroit and Wayne County,* 897. The original station in Marshall was on Hart St. between Eagle and Jefferson.

36. Commissioner of Railroads, *Annual Reports,* 1875, xxvi; *Aids, Gifts, Grants,* 89; Farmer, *Detroit and Wayne County,* 897.

37. Commissioner of Railroads, *Annual Reports,* 1875, xxvi; *Aids, Gifts, Grants,* 89; Farmer, *Detroit and Wayne County,* 897.

38. Commissioner of Railroads, *Annual Reports,* 1875, xvii; *Aids, Gifts, Grants,* 89; Farmer, *Detroit and Wayne County,* 897.

39. Farmer, *Detroit and Wayne County,* 898.

40. Ibid.

41. Farmer, *Detroit and Wayne County,* 899.

42. Farmer, *Detroit and Wayne County,* 899. Commissioner of Railroads, *Annual Reports,* 1875, xxvi, and *Aids, Gifts, Grants,* 97 have Autumn 1848 for completion to Niles.

43. Farmer, *Detroit and Wayne County,* 899. Commissioner, xxvi, and *Aids, Gifts, Grants,* 97 have Spring 1849.

44. Commissioner of Railroads, *Annual Reports,* 1875, xxv; *Aids, Gifts, Grants,* 99.

45. Farmer, *Detroit and Wayne County,* 899. *Aids, Gifts, Grants,* 97 has Autumn 1850.

46. Harlow, *Road of the Century,* 253. *Aids, Gifts, Grants,* 99 has December 1850.

47. Commissioner of Railroads, *Annual Reports,* 1875, xxv; *Aids, Gifts, Grants,* 97.

48. Commissioner of Railroads, *Annual Reports,* 1875, xxv; *Aids, Gifts, Grants,* 97.

49. Commissioner of Railroads, *Annual Reports,* 1875, xxv; *Aids, Gifts, Grants,* 97.

50. Commissioner of Railroads, *Annual Reports,* 1875, xxv; *Aids, Gifts, Grants,* 99.

51. Farmer, *Detroit and Wayne County,* 894.

52. Ibid.

53. Commissioner of Railroads, *Annual Reports,* 1875, xxii; *Aids, Gifts, Grants,* 35; Farmer, *Detroit and Wayne County,* 895.

54. *Aids, Gifts, Grants,* 100; Farmer, *Detroit and Wayne County,* 902; Wing, *History of Monroe County,* 232. Commissioner of Railroads, *Annual Reports,* 1875, xxiii has the wrong year.

55. Commissioner of Railroads, *Annual Reports,* 1875, xxv; *Aids, Gifts, Grants,* 99.

56. Commissioner of Railroads, *Annual Reports,* 1875, xxv; *Aids, Gifts, Grants,* 99.

57. Commissioner of Railroads, *Annual Reports,* 1875, xxii; *Aids, Gifts, Grants,* 35; Farmer, *Detroit and Wayne County,* 895.

58. Farmer, *Detroit and Wayne County,* 902; Wing, *History of Monroe County,* 232; Commissioner of Railroads, *Annual Reports,* 1875, xxiii and *Aids, Gifts, Grants,* 101 have the wrong year.

59. Farmer, *Detroit and Wayne County,* 895. *Aids, Gifts, Grants,* 35 has 16 January.

60. Commissioner of Railroads, *Annual Reports,* 1875, xxv; *Aids, Gifts, Grants,* 101.

61. Farmer, *Detroit and Wayne County,* 895. *Aids, Gifts, Grants,* 35 has September.

62. *Aids, Gifts, Grants,* 81. Ralph D. Williams, *The Honorable Peter White* (Cleveland: Penton, 1907), 146 gives September as the completion date, but a trial run was made in August.

63. Ringwalt, *Development of Transportation Systems,* 142–43.

64. Farmer, *Detroit and Wayne County,* 895. *Aids, Gifts, Grants,* 35 has 12 July to Grand Rapids.

65. Farmer, *Detroit and Wayne County,* 895.

66. Commissioner of Railroads, *Annual Reports,* 1875, xxii.

67. Commissioner of Railroads, *Annual Reports,* 1875, xxiv. *Aids, Gifts, Grants,* 89 has November 1860.

68. Farmer, *Detroit and Wayne County,* 904.

69. Commissioner of Railroads, *Annual Reports,* 1875, xxiv. *Aids, Gifts, Grants,* 89 has 24 December 1860.

70. Commissioner of Railroads, *Annual Reports,* 1875, xxiv. *Aids, Gifts, Grants,* 89 has 19 November 1862.

71. Commissioner of Railroads, *Annual Reports,* 1875, xxiii.

72. Certificate of completion of 20.03 miles was filed 20 November 1862, to obtain the state land grant (*Aids, Gifts, Grants,* 81n. ≠). It included the Iron Mountain's line. The distance from Front Street in

Marquette to the Winthrop Mine is 18.5 miles, and 0.7 miles additional to the Lake Superior Mine, for a total of 19.2 miles. Another 0.8 miles would put the end of the line near the center of section 28, in the vicinity of the Shenango Mine. The distance here is only to the Winthrop Mine.

73. *Aids, Gifts, Grants,* 89. Commissioner of Railroads, *Annual Reports,* 1875, xxiv gives only 1863.

74. *Aids, Gifts, Grants,* 41; Ivey, *Pere Marquette Railroad,* 215. Commissioner, xxiii has date one year earlier. The end of track in Flint probably was at the Thread River; mileage given is to Flint station.

75. Commissioner of Railroads, *Annual Reports,* 1875, xxii. *Aids, Gifts, Grants,* 65 has 1864.

76. Commissioner of Railroads, *Annual Reports,* 1875, xxiii; *Aids, Gifts, Grants,* 41; Ivey, *Pere Marquette Railroad,* 216.

77. *Aids, Gifts, Grants,* 81. Commissioner of Railroads, *Annual Reports,* 1875, xxvi has June.

78. *Aids, Gifts, Grants,* 89; Commissioner of Railroads, *Annual Reports,* 1875, xxiv. The line used Michigan Central tracks from Pearl Street to reach the Jackson station.

79. The date of this alteration is not certain, but appears to be at about the time the passenger station in Marshall was built (1865).

80. The date of this construction could not be determined accurately, but it appears reasonable given the activity of the iron mines served.

81. *Aids, Gifts, Grants,* 89. Commissioner of Railroads, *Annual Reports,* 1875, xxiv has only June.

82. *Aids, Gifts, Grants,* 101; Commissioner of Railroads, *Annual Reports,* 1875, xxv.

83. *Aids, Gifts, Grants,* 53. Commissioner of Railroads, *Annual Reports,* 1875, xxvii has October.

84. *Aids, Gifts, Grants,* 89.

85. *Aids, Gifts, Grants,* 41; Commissioner of Railroads, *Annual Reports,* 1875, xxiii.

86. *Aids, Gifts, Grants,* 41; Commissioner of Railroads, *Annual Reports,* 1875, xxiii.

87. *Aids, Gifts, Grants,* 89; Commissioner of Railroads, *Annual Reports,* 1875, xxiv.

88. Baxter, *Grand Rapids,* 532. *Aids, Gifts, Grants,* 115 and Commissioner of Railroads, *Annual Reports,* 1875, xxiv have 23 December.

89. The date of this construction could not be determined accurately, but it appears reasonable given the activity of the iron mines served.

90. *Aids, Gifts, Grants,* 89; Commissioner of Railroads, *Annual Reports,* 1875, xxiv.

91. Commissioner of Railroads, *Annual Reports,* 1875, xxiv. S. W. Durant, *History of Ingham and Eaton Counties* (Philadelphia: D. W. Ensign & Co., 1880), 380 has 15 August. *Aids, Gifts, Grants,* 89 has Autumn.

92. *Aids, Gifts, Grants,* 41; Commissioner of Railroads, *Annual Reports,* 1875, xxiii. Ivey, *Pere Marquette Railroad,* 218 has 25 October.

93. Ringwalt, *Development of Transportation Systems,* 174–77. Dunbar, *All Aboard!,* 187 has 1866. Commissioner of Railroads, *Annual Reports,* 1875, xxiv has October 1868. The company's annual reports to the Commissioner have October 1868.

94. Commissioner of Railroads, *Annual Reports,* 1875, xxv; Henry F. Thomas, *A Twentieth Century History of Allegan County* (Chicago: Waterman, Watkins & Co., 1907), 118. *Aids, Gifts, Grants,* 101 has the wrong year.

95. *Aids, Gifts, Grants,* 115.

96. The date of this construction could not be determined accurately, but it appears reasonable given the activity of the iron mines served.

97. Ensign, *Allegan and Barry Counties,* 80.

98. Ensign, *Allegan and Barry Counties,* 80. Commissioner of Railroads, *Annual Reports,* 1875, xxiv and *Aids, Gifts, Grants,* 91 say Spring.

99. *Aids, Gifts, Grants,* 101; Commissioner of Railroads, *Annual Reports,* 1875, xxv; Baxter, *Grand Rapids,* 530. Regular service did not begin until 22 May.

100. Baxter, *Grand Rapids,* 533; Commissioner of Railroads, *Annual Reports,* 1875, xxiv. *Aids, Gifts, Grants,* 115 has 22 June.

101. *Aids, Gifts, Grants,* 47; Commissioner of Railroads, *Annual Reports,* 1875, xxiii.

102. *Aids, Gifts, Grants,* 101; Commissioner of Railroads, *Annual Reports,* 1875, xxiii.

103. *Aids, Gifts, Grants,* 37; Commissioner of Railroads, *Annual Reports,* 1875 xxi. *Aids, Gifts, Grants,* 37 has 16.02 miles, which ignores the distance between the Military Street passenger station and Court Street, the site of the original Port Huron & Lake Michigan station.

104. *Aids, Gifts, Grants*, 39. Commissioner of Railroads, *Annual Reports*, 1875, xxvi has December. *Aids, Gifts, Grants*, 38n, d repeats the Commssioner's statement that the line was completed to a total of 20.8 miles to Shelby, but was operated only as far west as Romeo. The western segment was not put in service until 1879.

105. *Aids, Gifts, Grants*, 47.

106. *Aids, Gifts, Grants*, 51, which also gives the distance as 15.0 miles.

107. *Aids, Gifts, Grants*, 51.

108. Commissioner of Railroads, *Annual Reports*, 1875, xxiv. *Aids, Gifts, Grants*, 91 gives 1 January based on Baxter, *Grand Rapids*, 535.

109. *Aids, Gifts, Grants*, 37n. x.

110. Commissioner of Railroads, *Annual Reports*, 1875, xxiii; *Aids, Gifts, Grants*, 101. Commissioner of Railroads, *Annual Reports*, 1875, xxiii reports the line was completed to Fort Wayne on 1 December.

111. *Aids, Gifts, Grants*, 49; Franklin Ellis, *History of Berrien and Van Buren Counties* (Philadelphia: D.W. Ensign & Co., 1880), 56. Commissioner of Railroads, *Annual Reports*, 1875, xxii has 1 February.

112. *Aids, Gifts, Grants*, 37n, x.

113. Ellis, *Berrien and Van Buren Counties*, 53

114. *Aids, Gifts, Grants*, 37.

115. Ibid., 37n. x.

116. Commissioner of Railroads, *Annual Reports*, 1875, xxiii; *Aids, Gifts, Grants*, 115.

117. Ellis, *Berrien and Van Buren Counties*, 53.

118. *Aids, Gifts, Grants*, 37.

119. Percival, "Railroads in Ottawa County," 274.

120. Ibid.

121. Commissioner of Railroads, *Annual Reports*, 1875, xxiv; *Aids, Gifts, Grants*, 91.

122. Commissioner of Railroads, *Annual Reports*, 1875, xxiv; *Aids, Gifts, Grants*, 115.

123. *Aids, Gifts, Grants*, 51. Commissioner of Railroads, *Annual Reports*, 1875, xxvi has 1 July.

124. *Aids, Gifts, Grants*, 115. Commissioner of Railroads, *Annual Reports*, 1875, xxiii has "August or September, 1870."

125. Baxter, *Grand Rapids*, 533. *Aids, Gifts, Grants*, 115 gives October 1; and Commissioner of Railroads, *Annual Reports*, 1875, xxiv has October. These may refer to the operation of the first through train from Fort Wayne to Paris on 1 October.

126. Commissioner of Railroads, *Annual Reports*, 1875, xxiii; *Aids, Gifts, Grants*, 47.

127. *Aids, Gifts, Grants*, 37n, x.

128. Commissioner of Railroads, *Annual Reports*, 1875, xxiv; *Aids, Gifts, Grants*, 93.

129. Commissioner of Railroads, *Annual Reports*, 1875, xxiii; *Aids, Gifts, Grants*, 41.

130. Commissioner of Railroads, *Annual Reports*, 1875, xxiii; *Aids, Gifts, Grants*, 41.

131. Commissioner of Railroads, *Annual Reports*, 1875, xxii; *Aids, Gifts, Grants*, 37.

132. *Aids, Gifts, Grants*, 49.

133. *Aids, Gifts, Grants*, 65; Stennett, *Yesterday and Today*, 164.

134. Commissioner of Railroads, *Annual Reports*, 1875, xxv; *Aids, Gifts, Grants*, 93. Ellis, *Berrien and Van Buren Counties*, 53 has December 17 as the date construction was completed.

135. *Aids, Gifts, Grants*, 91.

136. Commissioner of Railroads, *Annual Reports*, 1875, xxii; *Aids, Gifts, Grants*, 49.

137. Commissioner of Railroads, *Annual Reports*, 1875, xxvi; *Aids, Gifts, Grants*, 93.

138. *Aids, Gifts, Grants*, 37.

139. Commissioner of Railroads, *Annual Reports*, 1875, xxiii; *Aids, Gifts, Grants*, 41.

140. *Aids, Gifts, Grants*, 47.

141. Commissioner of Railroads, *Annual Reports*, 1875, xxii; *Aids, Gifts, Grants*, 49.

142. Commissioner of Railroads, *Annual Reports*, 1875, xxii; *Aids, Gifts, Grants*, 49.

143. Commissioner of Railroads, *Annual Reports*, 1875, xxii; *Aids, Gifts, Grants*, 49.

144. Alfred Mathews, *History of Cass County* (Chicago: Waterman, Watkins & Co., 1882), 177.

145. *Aids, Gifts, Grants*, 47.

146. Ibid.

147. Ibid., 101.

148. Ibid., 47.

149. Ibid., 91.
150. Ibid., 101.
151. *Aids, Gifts, Grants*, 47. Commissioner of Railroads, *Annual Reports*, 1875, xxiii has August.
152. Commissioner of Railroads, *Annual Reports*, 1875, xxiii; *Aids, Gifts, Grants*, 41.
153. Commissioner of Railroads, *Annual Reports*, 1875, xxv; *Aids, Gifts, Grants*, 103, 115.
154. Commissioner of Railroads, *Annual Reports*, 1875, xxiii; *Aids, Gifts, Grants*, 41.
155. *Aids, Gifts, Grants*, 47. Commissioner of Railroads, *Annual Reports*, 1875, xxiii has August.
156. Commissioner of Railroads, *Annual Reports*, 1875 xxiii; *Aids, Gifts, Grants*, 41.
157. Commissioner of Railroads, *Annual Reports*, 1875, xxii; *Aids, Gifts, Grants*, 37. The mileage herein is to its intersection with the Flint & Pere Marquette in downtown Flint.
158. *Aids, Gifts, Grants*, 91.
159. Commissioner of Railroads, *Annual Reports*, 1875, xxiv; *Aids, Gifts, Grants*, 115.
160. This year is assumed from the opening dates of the mines served.
161. This year is assumed from the opening dates of the mines served.
162. This year is assumed from the opening dates of the mines served.
163. Commissioner of Railroads, *Annual Reports*, 1875, xxii; *Aids, Gifts, Grants*, 49.
164. Commissioner of Railroads, *Annual Reports*, 1875, xxii; *Aids, Gifts, Grants*, 49.
165. Commissioner of Railroads, *Annual Reports*, 1875, xxiii; *Aids, Gifts, Grants*, 41.
166. Commissioner of Railroads, *Annual Reports*, 1875, xxvii; *Aids, Gifts, Grants*, 101.
167. Commissioner of Railroads, *Annual Reports*, 1875, xxvii; *Aids, Gifts, Grants*, 101.
168. Commissioner of Railroads, *Annual Reports*, 1875, xxiv; *Aids, Gifts, Grants*, 51.
169. Commissioner of Railroads, *Annual Reports*, 1875, xxiv; *Aids, Gifts, Grants*, 51.
170. Bonner, *Memoirs of Lenawee County*, 146.
171. Commissioner of Railroads, *Annual Reports*, 1875, xxvi; *Aids, Gifts, Grants*, 87.
172. Commissioner of Railroads, *Annual Reports*, 1875, xxiv; *Aids, Gifts, Grants*, 51.
173. Commissioner of Railroads, *Annual Reports*, 1875, xxvii; *Aids, Gifts, Grants*, 101.
174. Commissioner of Railroads, *Annual Reports*, 1875, xxiv; *Aids, Gifts, Grants*, 115.
175. *Aids, Gifts, Grants*, 83.
176. Ibid., 47.
177. Commissioner of Railroads, *Annual Reports*, 1875, xxii; *Aids, Gifts, Grants*, 37.
178. Commissioner of Railroads, *Annual Reports*, 1875, xxiii; *Aids, Gifts, Grants*, 41.
179. Commissioner of Railroads, *Annual Reports*, 1875, xxii; *Aids, Gifts, Grants*, 93.
180. Page, *The Traverse Region*, 54. *Aids, Gifts, Grants*, 115 and Commissioner of Railroads, *Annual Reports*, 1875, xxvii have December.
181. Commissioner of Railroads, *Annual Reports*, 1875, xxii; *Aids, Gifts, Grants*, 93.
182. Commissioner of Railroads, *Annual Reports*, 1875, xxvii; *Aids, Gifts, Grants*, 101.
183. Commissioner of Railroads, *Annual Reports*, 1875, xxii; *Aids, Gifts, Grants*, 93.
184. Commissioner of Railroads, *Annual Reports*, 1875, xxvi; *Aids, Gifts, Grants*, 83.
185. Commissioner of Railroads, *Annual Reports*, 1875, xxii. This construction provided a new main line through Escanaba. The southerly 1.8 miles of the original construction by the Peninsula is reclassified as yard trackage.
186. Ibid.
187. *Aids, Gifts, Grants*, 93.
188. Ibid.
189. Ibid., 83.
190. Ibid.
191. Ibid.
192. Ibid.
193. This work is inferred from Commissioner of Railroads, *Annual Reports*, 1872.
194. This work is inferred from Commissioner of Railroads, *Annual Reports*, 1872.
195. This work is inferred from Commissioner of Railroads, *Annual Reports*, 1872.
196. Commissioner of Railroads, *Annual Reports*, 1875, xxvii; *Aids, Gifts, Grants*, 47.
197. Commissioner of Railroads, *Annual Reports*, 1875, xxvii. *Aids, Gifts, Grants*, 101 says it was finished 8 December 1872, but not open for public use.
198. Commissioner of Railroads, *Annual Reports*, 1875, xxiii; *Aids, Gifts, Grants*, 47.

199. Commissioner of Railroads, *Annual Reports,* 1875, xxii; *Aids, Gifts, Grants,* 93.
200. Commissioner of Railroads, *Annual Reports,* 1875, xxiv; *Aids, Gifts, Grants,* 91; M. A. Leeson, *History of Saginaw County* (Chicago: Charles C. Chapman & Co., 1881), 450.
201. Commissioner of Railroads, *Annual Reports,* 1875, xxii; *Aids, Gifts, Grants,* 49.
202. Commissioner of Railroads, *Annual Reports,* 1875, xxii; *Aids, Gifts, Grants,* 93.
203. Commissioner of Railroads, *Annual Reports,* 1875, xxiv; *Aids, Gifts, Grants,* 91.
204. *Aids, Gifts, Grants,* 95.
205. Commissioner of Railroads, *Annual Reports,* 1875, xxvii; *Aids, Gifts, Grants,* 95.
206. Commissioner of Railroads, *Annual Reports,* 1875, xxvi; *Aids, Gifts, Grants,* 87.
207. *Aids, Gifts, Grants,* 101.
208. Commissioner of Railroads, *Annual Reports,* 1875, xxvi; *Aids, Gifts, Grants,* 95.
209. *Aids, Gifts, Grants,* 93.
210. Ibid., 83.
211. This work is inferred from Commissioner of Railroads, *Annual Reports* 1873.
212. This work is inferred from Commissioner of Railroads, *Annual Reports* 1873.
213. This work is inferred from Commissioner of Railroads, *Annual Reports* 1873.
214. This work is inferred from Commissioner of Railroads, *Annual Reports* 1873.
215. This work is inferred from Commissioner of Railroads, *Annual Reports* 1873.
216. This work is inferred from Commissioner of Railroads, *Annual Reports* 1873.
217. This work is inferred from Commissioner of Railroads, *Annual Reports* 1873.
218. Ringwalt, *Development of Transportation Systems,* 212–214.
219. Commissioner of Railroads, *Annual Reports,* 1875, xxiv; *Aids, Gifts, Grants,* 115; Baxter, *Grand Rapids,* 533.
220. Commissioner of Railroads, *Annual Reports,* 1875, xxiii; *Aids, Gifts, Grants,* 41; Ivey, *Pere Marquette Railroad,* 221.
221. Ibid., 91.
222. Ibid., 93.
223. Ibid., 83.
224. Ibid.
225. Ibid.
226. This work is inferred from Commissioner of Railroads, *Annual Reports* 1874.
227. This work is inferred from Commissioner of Railroads, *Annual Reports* 1874.
228. Commissioner of Railroads, *Annual Reports,* 1875, xxii; *Aids, Gifts, Grants,* 47.
229. Commissioner of Railroads, *Annual Reports,* 1875, xxiv; *Aids, Gifts, Grants,* 51.
230. Commissioner of Railroads, *Annual Reports,* 1875, xxii; *Aids, Gifts, Grants,* 47.
231. This adjustment appears to taken place at about this time.
232. Ringwalt, *Development of Transportation Systems,* 212–214.

TABLE OF MICHIGAN RAILROAD MILEAGE, 1836–1999

Railroad Mileage, 1836–1839

LOWER PENINSULA

	1836	1837	1838	1839
Det. & Pontiac			12.3	17.6
Erie & Kal.	21.3	21.3	21.3	21.3
Palmyra & Jacksonburgh			11.6	11.6
Mich., State of				
Cent. line			29.6	37.1
Riv. Raisin & Lk. Erie			2.9	2.9
MICH. YEAR TOTAL	21.3	21.3	77.7	90.5
MICH. YEAR CHANGE	21.3	0.0	56.4	12.8
COMMR. YEAR TOTAL			63.0	71.0
COMMR. YEAR CHANGE			+63.0	8.0

Railroad Mileage, 1840–1849

LOWER PENINSULA

	1840	1841	1842	1843	1844	1845	1846	1847	1848	1849
Det. & Pontiac	17.6	17.6	18.8	26.6	26.6	26.6	26.6	26.6	26.6	26.6
Erie & Kal.	21.3	21.3	21.3	21.3	21.3	21.3	21.3	21.3	21.3	
Palmyra & Jacksonburgh	11.6	11.6	11.6	11.6						
Mich., State of										
Cent. line	37.1	76.5	76.5	76.5	108.6	121.6				
Southern line	35.9	35.9	46.9	69.2	80.8	80.8				
Mich. Cent.							144.6	144.6	191.2	217.9
Mich. Southern							78.3	78.3	78.3	78.3
Erie & Kal.										21.3
MICH. YEAR TOTAL	123.5	162.9	175.1	205.2	237.3	250.3	270.8	270.8	317.4	344.1
MICH. YEAR CHANGE	33.0	39.4	12.2	30.1	32.1	13.0	20.5	0.0	46.6	26.7
COMMR. YEAR TOTAL	104.0	147.0	147.0	180.0	220.0	233.0	279.0	279.0	326.0	353.0
COMMR. YEAR CHANGE	33.0	43.0	0.0	33.0	40.0	13.0	46.0	0.0	47.0	27.0

Railroad Mileage, 1850–1859

LOWER PENINSULA

	1850	1851	1852	1853	1854	1855	1856	1857	1858	1859
Amboy, Lans. & Trav. Bay									11.8	18.9
Chi., Det. & Can. Gr. Trunk Jct.										59.5
Det. & Milw.						50.7	78.5	124.2	188.7	188.7
Det. & Pontiac	26.6	26.6	26.3	26.3	26.3					
Mich. Cent.	221.7	221.7	221.7	221.7	221.7	221.7	221.7	221.7	221.7	221.7
Mich. Southern	100.8	140.3	144.2	144.2	144.2					
Erie & Kal.	21.3	21.3	21.3	21.3	21.3					
Mich. Southern & Northern Ind.						156.5	156.5	177.3	177.3	177.3
Det., Monroe & Toledo						37.2	51.2	51.2	51.2	51.2
Erie & Kal.						21.3	21.3	21.3	21.3	21.3
St. Joseph Valley						7.5	7.5	7.5	7.5	7.5

	1850	1851	1852	1853	1854	1855	1856	1857	1858	1859
L. P. YEAR TOTAL	370.4	409.9	413.5	413.5	413.5	494.9	536.7	603.2	679.5	746.1
L. P. YEAR CHANGE	26.3	39.5	3.6	0.0	0.0	81.4	41.8	66.5	76.3	66.6

UPPER PENINSULA

	1850	1851	1852	1853	1854	1855	1856	1857	1858	1859
Bay de Noquet & Marq.									17.3	17.3
Iron Mtn.								17.3	0.0	
U. P. YEAR TOTAL	0.0	0.0	0.0	0.0	0.0	0.0	0.0	17.3	17.3	17.3
U. P. YEAR CHANGE	0.0	0.0	0.0	0.0	0.0	0.0	0.0	17.3	0.0	0.0
MICH. YEAR TOTAL	370.4	409.9	413.5	413.5	413.5	494.9	536.7	620.5	696.8	763.4
MICH. YEAR CHANGE	26.3	39.5	3.6	0.0	0.0	81.4	41.8	83.8	76.3	66.6
COMMR. YEAR TOTAL	380.0	421.0	425.0	425.0	425.0	462.0	530.0	579.0	703.0	770.0
COMMR. YEAR CHANGE	27.0	41.0	4.0	0.0	0.0	37.0	68.0	49.0	124.0	67.0
STUDY LESS COMMR.	–9.6	–11.1	–11.5	–11.5	–11.5	32.9	6.7	41.5	–6.2	–6.6

Railroad Mileage, 1860–1869

LOWER PENINSULA

	1860	1861	1862	1863	1864	1865	1866	1867	1868	1869
Amboy, Lans. & Trav. Bay	18.9	26.0	26.0	27.0	27.0	27.0				
Bay Cty. & E. Sag.								12.5		
Det. & Milw.	188.7	188.7	188.7	188.7	188.7	188.7	188.7	188.7	188.7	188.7
Flint & Holly					16.8	16.8	16.8	16.8		
Flint & Pere Marq.			26.1	33.3	33.3	33.3	33.3	53.3	75.9	75.9
Bay Cty. & E. Sag.									12.5	12.5
Ft. Wyn., Jackson & Sag.										35.4
Gr. Rpds. & Ind.								20.1	22.5	41.7
Grand Riv. Valley									24.3	50.8
Gr. Trunk Ry–Can.										
Chi., Det. & Can. Gr. Trunk Jct.	59.5	59.5	59.5	59.5	59.5	59.5	59.5	59.5	59.5	59.5
Ionia & Lans.										37.1
Kal., Allegan & Gr. Rpds.									25.3	
Kal. & Schoolcraft								13.1	13.1	
Jackson, Lans. & Sag.						24.6	63.7	113.1	113.1	113.1
Lk. Shore & Mich. Southern										173.4
Det., Monroe & Toledo										51.2
Erie & Kal.										21.3
Kal., Allegan & Gr. Rpds.										58.5
Kal. & White Pigeon										36.5
Mich. Air Line RR										14.2
Mich. Cent.	221.7	221.7	221.7	221.7	221.7	221.6	221.6	221.6	221.6	221.6
Mich. Lk. Shore										13.0
Mich. Southern & No. Ind.	177.3	177.3	177.3	177.3	173.4	173.4	173.4	173.4	173.4	
Det., Monroe & Toledo	51.2	51.2	51.2	51.2	51.2	51.2	51.2	51.2	51.2	
Erie & Kal.	21.3	21.3	21.3	21.3	21.3	21.3	21.3	21.3	21.3	
Paw Paw								3.8	3.8	3.8
Pt. Hur. & Lk. Mich.										17.6
St. Joseph Valley	7.5	7.5	7.5	7.5	11.4	11.4	11.4	11.4	11.4	
Schoolcraft & Three Rivers								12.0	12.0	

L. P. YEAR TOTAL	746.1	753.2	779.3	787.5	804.3	828.8	840.9	971.8	1029.6	1225.8
L. P. YEAR CHANGE	0.0	7.1	26.1	8.2	16.8	24.5	12.1	130.9	57.8	196.2

UPPER PENINSULA

	1860	1861	1862	1863	1864	1865	1866	1867	1868	1869
Bay de Noquet & Marq.	17.3	17.3	20.2	20.2	20.2	39.8	39.8	39.8	39.8	39.8
Chi. & N. Western					62.7	67.2	67.2	72.6	73.1	73.1
Hecla & Torch Lk.									4.5	4.5
U. P. YEAR TOTAL	17.3	17.3	20.2	20.2	82.9	107.0	107.0	112.4	117.4	117.4
U. P. YEAR CHANGE	0.0	0.0	2.9	0.0	62.7	24.1	0.0	5.4	5.0	0.0
MICH.YEAR TOTAL	763.4	770.5	799.5	807.7	887.2	935.8	947.9	1084.2	1147.0	1343.2
MICH. YEAR CHANGE	0.0	7.1	29.0	8.2	79.5	48.6	12.1	136.3	62.8	196.2
COMMR. YEAR TOTAL	770.0	777.0	811.0	812.0	891.0	931.0	943.0	1066.0	1124.0	1362.0
COMMR. YEAR CHANGE	0.0	7.0	34.0	1.0	79.0	40.0	12.0	123.0	58.0	238.0
STUDY LESS COMMR.	−6.6	−6.5	−11.5	−4.3	−3.8	4.8	4.9	18.2	23.0	−18.8

Railroad Mileage, 1870–1879

LOWER PENINSULA

	1870	1871	1872	1873	1874	1875	1876	1877	1878	1879
Bear Lk. Train Ry							5.0	5.0	5.0	5.0
Can. Southern										
Can. So. Bridge				3.1	3.1	3.1	3.1	3.1	3.1	3.1
Chi. & Can. So.			20.5	62.4	62.4	62.4	62.4	62.4	62.4	
Toledo, C. S. & Det.				46.8	46.8	46.8	46.8	46.8	46.8	46.8
Chi. & Northeastern								49.3	49.3	49.3
Chi. & Lk. Huron									174.7	174.7
Chi. & Mich. Lk. Sh.	42.6	140.3	191.6	242.7	242.7	242.7	242.7	242.7		
Chi. & W. Mich.									242.7	242.7
Chi., Sag. & Can.						20.3	20.3	20.3	23.1	34.1
Det. & Bay Cty.			71.4	106.7	106.7	106.7	106.7	106.7	119.3	135.2
Lapeer & N.ern			3.7	4.2	4.7	4.7	7.7	7.7	7.7	7.7
Det. & Milw.	188.3	188.3	188.3	190.3	190.3	191.0	191.0	191.0		
Det., Gr. Haven & Milw.									191.0	191.0
Det., Hillsdale & Ind.		24.0	64.4	64.4	64.4					
Det., Hillsdale & Southwestern							64.4	64.4	64.4	64.4
Det., Lans. & Lk. Mich.		157.5	159.2	179.2	179.2	179.2				
Det., Lans. & N.ern							179.2	179.2	188.6	198.0
Sag. Valley & St. Louis										28.6
Sag. & Gr. Rpds.										3.7
Flint & Pere Marq.	112.6	139.3	230.3	230.3	278.7	278.7	278.7	278.7	278.7	278.7
Bay Cty. & E. Sag.	12.5	12.5								
Sag. & Clare County										8.9
Sag. & Mt. Pl.										14.7
Ft. Wyn. & Jackson										44.3
Ft. Wayne, Jackson & Sag.	44.3	44.3	44.3	44.3	44.3	44.3	44.3	44.3	44.3	
Glencoe, Pinconning & Lk. Sh.					10.5	10.5	12.8	12.8	15.3	
Gr. Hav.								57.0	57.0	57.0
Gr. Rpds. & Ind.	149.0	185.4	211.4	211.4	278.4	278.4	279.4	279.4	279.4	279.4
Allegan & Southeastern								11.2	11.2	11.2

Trav. Cty.		26.0	26.0	26.0	26.0	26.0	26.0	26.0	26.0
Gr. Rpds., Newaygo & Lk. Sh.		35.3	35.3	35.3	46.4	46.4	46.4	46.4	46.4
Gr. Trunk Ry–Can.									
Chi., Det. & Can. Gr. Trunk Jct. 59.5	59.5	59.5	59.5	59.5	59.5	59.5	59.5	59.5	59.5
Mich. Air Line Ry					14.2	14.2	14.2	14.2	26.3
Hobart & Manistee Riv.									9.2
Holly, Wayne & Monroe	40.1								
Ionia & Lans. 55.7									
Lk George & Musk. Riv.							9.3	14.3	21.3
Lk. Huron & Southwestern								22.8	22.8
Lk. Sh. & Mich. Southern 173.4	173.4	173.4	173.4	173.4	173.4	173.4	173.4	173.4	173.4
Chi. & Can. Southern									
Det., Monroe & Toledo 51.2	51.2	51.2	51.2	51.2	51.2	51.2	51.2	51.2	51.2
Erie & Kal. 21.3	21.3	21.3	21.3	21.3	19.7	19.7	19.7	19.7	19.7
Kal., Allegan & Gr. Rpds. 58.5	58.5	58.5	58.5	58.5	58.5	58.5	58.5	58.5	58.5
Kal. & White Pigeon 36.5	36.5	36.5	36.5	36.5	36.5	36.5	36.5	36.5	36.5
Northern Cent. Mich.		41.8	60.6	60.6	60.6	60.6	60.6	60.6	60.6
Mansfield, Coldwater & Lk. Mich.	11.2	11.2	11.2	11.2	11.2	11.2			
Mich. Air Line Ry 14.2	14.2								
Mich. Cent. 221.6	221.6	221.6	221.6	221.6	221.6	221.6	221.6	221.6	221.6
Grand Riv. Valley 83.8	83.8	83.8	83.8	83.8	83.8	83.8	83.8	83.8	83.8
Jackson, Lans. & Sag. 113.1	153.5	153.5	232.9	232.9	232.9	232.9	232.9	232.9	232.9
Kal. & S. Haven 22.8	39.4	39.4	39.4	39.4	39.4	39.4	39.4	39.4	39.4
Mich. Air Line RR 69.6	103.5	109.0	109.0	109.0	109.0	109.0	109.0	109.0	109.0
Mich. Lk. Sh. 57.0	57.0	57.0	57.0	57.0	57.0	57.0			
Mich. Midland & Can.		14.0	14.0	14.0	14.0	14.0	14.0	14.0	14.0
Musk. & Rose Lk.								7.5	7.5
Paw Paw 3.8	3.8	3.8	3.8	3.8	3.8	3.8	3.8	3.8	3.8
Peninsular 55.5	97.6	109.4	109.4	109.4	109.4	109.4	109.4		
Pinconning									14.5
Pt. Hur. & Lk. Mich. 38.2	65.3	65.3	65.3	65.3	65.3	65.3	65.3		
Pt. Hur. & N.western									26.6
Sag. Valley & St. Louis		28.6	28.6	28.6	28.6	28.6	28.6		
St. Clair & Chi. Air Line		14.2	14.2	14.2					
Toledo & A.A.								39.9	39.9
Toledo & S. Haven							8.3	14.7	14.7
L. P. YEAR TOTAL 1685.0	2183.0	2556.8	2898.3	3024.7	3055.2	3066.5	3133.4	3242.3	3297.6
L. P. YEAR CHANGE 459.2	498.0	373.8	341.5	126.4	30.5	11.3	66.9	108.9	55.3

UPPER PENINSULA

	1870	1871	1872	1873	1874	1875	1876	1877	1878	1879
Bay de Noquet & Maquette	39.8									
Chi. & N. Western	73.1	88.2	159.6	168.8	170.0	170.0	170.0	170.0	170.0	170.0
Men. Riv.								27.1	27.1	27.1
Hecla & Torch Lk.	4.5	4.5	4.5	4.5	4.5	4.5	4.5	4.5	4.5	4.5
Marq. & Ont.		39.8								
Marq., Hough. & Ont.			82.4	85.0	89.9	89.9	89.9	89.9	89.5	86.8
Mineral Range			8.1	12.5	12.5	12.5	12.5	12.5	12.5	12.5
U. P. YEAR TOTAL	117.4	132.5	254.6	270.8	276.9	276.9	276.9	304.0	303.6	300.9
U. P. YEAR CHANGE	0.0	15.1	122.1	16.2	6.1	0.0	0.0	27.1	−0.4	−2.7
MICH. YEAR TOTAL	1802.4	2315.5	2811.4	3169.1	3301.6	3332.1	3343.4	3437.4	3545.9	3598.5
MICH. YEAR CHANGE	459.2	513.1	495.9	357.7	132.5	30.5	11.3	94.0	108.5	52.6

COMMR. YEAR TOTAL	1739.0	2298.0	2822.0	3252.0	3313.0	3347.0	3410.0	3455.0	3564.0	3657.0
COMMR. YEAR CHANGE	377.0	559.0	524.0	430.0	61.0	34.0	63.0	45.0	109.0	93.0
STUDY LESS COMMR.	63.4	17.5	−10.6	−82.9	−11.4	−14.9	−66.6	−17.6	−18.1	−58.5

Railroad Mileage, 1880–1889

LOWER PENINSULA

	1880	1881	1882	1883	1884	1885	1886	1887	1888	1889
Allegan & Lk. Sh.						5.0	5.0	5.0		
Arcadia & Betsey Riv. Train Ry				11.0	11.0	11.0	11.0	11.0	11.0	11.0
Battle Creek & Sturgis										41.6
Bay Cty. & Alpena			32.1							
Bay Cty. & Battle Creek										18.0
Bear Lk. & Eastern			12.5	12.5	12.5	12.5	16.0	18.0	18.0	18.0
Bear Lk. Train Ry	5.0	5.0								
Buckley & Douglas		8.0	8.0	8.0	8.0	8.0	8.0	8.0	8.0	
Can. & St. Louis									4.4	
Can. Southern										
Can. So. Bridge	3.1	3.1								
Toledo., C. S. & Det.	46.8	46.8								
Chi. & W. Mich. RR	259.0									
White Riv.	4.9									
Chi. & W. Mich. Ry		344.5	348.6	339.6	369.9	369.9	369.9	369.9	364.4	364.4
White Riv.		13.2	14.4	30.4						
Chi., Kal. & Sag.										43.9
Chi., Sag. & Can.	35.1	35.1	35.1							
Cinci., Jackson & Mack.								132.9	155.2	155.2
Cinci., Wabash & Mich.			33.4	33.4	33.4	33.4	33.4	33.4	33.4	33.4
Colfax & Big Rapids								5.5	5.5	
Crawford & Manistee Riv.						9.5	9.5	9.5	9.5	12.5
Det. & Bay Cty.	135.2									
Lapeer & Northern	7.7									
Det., Bay Cty. & Alpena				56.8	59.4	80.0	163.3	188.8	195.4	195.9
Det., Gr. Hav. & Milw.	188.3	188.3								
Det., Hillsdale & Southwestern	64.4									
Det., Lans. & Northern	222.6	222.6	222.6	227.8	227.8	227.8	227.8	227.8	227.8	227.8
Gr. Rpds., Lans. & Det.									54.6	54.6
Sag. & Western				30.7	30.7	30.7	41.5	41.5	41.5	41.5
Sag. Valley & St. Louis	28.6	28.6	28.6	28.6	28.6	28.6	28.6	28.6	28.6	28.6
Sag. & Gr. Rpds.	3.7	3.7	3.7	4.7	4.7	4.7	4.7	4.7	4.7	4.7
Det. Union RR Depot & Sta.			3.2	3.2	3.2	3.2	3.2	3.2	3.2	3.2
Flint & Pere Marq.	285.1	290.3	287.1	287.1	287.1	287.1	287.1	287.1	365.9	604.0
Sag. & Clare County	15.5	15.5	15.5	29.9	29.9	29.9	29.9	32.4		
Sag. & Mt. Pl.	14.7	14.7	14.7	14.7	29.9	14.7	14.7	14.7		
Manistee		23.9	23.9	23.9	23.9	23.9	23.9	23.9		
Ft. Wyn. & Jackson	44.3	44.3								
Gr. Hav.	57.0									
Gr. Rpds. & Ind.	279.4	279.4	306.5	314.3	347.2	354.2	355.0	355.0	362.0	356.2
Allegan & Southeastern	11.2	11.2	11.2							
Bay View, Lit. Trav. & Mack.			7.0	7.0	7.0	7.0	7.0	7.0		
Gr. Rpds., Ind. & Mack.			32.9	32.9						
Musk., Gr. Rpds. & Ind.							36.9	36.9	36.9	36.9
Trav. Cty.	26.0	26.0	26.0	26.0	26.0	26.0	26.0	26.0	26.0	26.0

Gr. Rpds., Newaygo & Lk. Sh.	46.4									
Gr. Trunk Ry–Can.										
Chi. & Gr. Trunk	224.0	224.0	224.0	224.0	224.0	224.0	224.0	224.0	224.0	224.0
Chi., Det. & Can. G. T. Jct.	59.5	59.5	59.5	59.5	59.5	59.5	59.5	59.5	59.5	59.5
Det., Gr. Haven & Milw.			188.3	188.3	188.3	188.3	188.3	188.3	188.3	188.3
Mich. Air Line Ry	35.3	35.3	35.3	59.0	105.9	105.9	105.9	105.9	105.9	105.9
Tol., Sag. & Musk.									96.0	96.0
Grass Lk. & Manistee Riv.							9.5	9.5	13.5	13.5
Hobart & Manistee Riv.	9.2	9.2	9.2	9.2	9.2	9.2	9.2	9.2	9.2	9.2
Ithaca & Alma			6.7	6.7	6.7	6.7	6.7	6.7	6.7	6.7
Lk. County	3.8	6.0	8.0	8.0	8.0	8.0	8.0	11.0	11.0	11.0
Lk. George & Musk. Riv.	20.0	21.8	0.0							
Lk. Sh. & Mich. Southern	173.4	173.4	173.4	173.4	173.4	173.4	173.4	173.4	173.4	173.4
Chi. & Can. Southern	62.4	62.4	62.4	62.4	62.4	62.4	62.4	62.4		
Det. & Chi.									62.4	62.4
Det., Hillsdale & Southwest.		65.2	65.2	65.2	65.2	65.2	65.2	65.2	65.2	65.2
Det., Monroe & Toledo	51.2	51.2	51.2	51.2	51.2	51.2	51.2	51.2	51.2	51.2
Erie & Kal.	19.7	19.7	19.7	19.7	19.7	19.7	19.7	19.7	19.7	19.7
Ft. Wyn. & Jackson			44.3	44.3	44.3	44.3	44.3	44.3	44.3	44.3
Kal., Allegan & Gr. Rapids	58.5	58.5	58.5	58.5	58.5	58.5	58.5	58.5	58.5	58.5
Kal. & White Pigeon	36.5	36.5	36.5	36.5	36.5	36.5	36.5	36.5	36.5	36.5
Northern Cent. Mich.	60.6	60.6	60.6	60.6	60.6	60.6	60.6	60.6	60.6	60.6
Sturgis, Goshen & St. Louis										3.4
Lowell & Hastings								13.0	13.0	13.0
Manistee & N.eastern									33.4	36.2
Mason & Oceana								21.3	27.2	27.2
Mecosta				9.5	9.5	4.0	15.0	10.0		
Mich. & Ohio				132.9	132.9	132.9	132.9			
Mich. Cent.	221.6	221.6	221.6	221.6	221.6	221.6	221.6	221.6	221.6	221.6
Can. Southern										
Can. So. Bridge			3.1	3.1	3.1	3.1	3.1	3.1	3.1	3.1
Mich. Midland & Can.			14.0	14.0	14.0	14.0	14.0	14.0	14.0	14.0
Toledo, C. S. & Det.			46.8	46.8	46.8	46.8	46.8	46.8	46.8	46.8
Det. & Bay Cty.		135.9	135.9	135.9	135.9	135.9	135.9	135.9	135.9	135.9
Lapeer & Northern		7.7	7.7	7.7	7.7	7.7	7.7	7.7		
Grand Riv. Valley	83.8	83.8	83.8	83.8	83.8	83.8	83.8	83.8	83.8	83.8
Jackson, Lans. & Sag.	232.9	296.0	296.3	296.3	307.8	323.7	337.9	351.4	351.4	351.4
Kal. & S. Haven	39.4	39.4	39.4	39.4	39.4	39.4	39.4	39.4	39.4	39.4
Mich. Air Line RR	109.0	109.0	109.0	109.0	109.0	109.0	109.0	109.0	109.0	109.0
Sag. Bay & Northwestern				46.7	58.5	75.2	76.8	97.8	99.5	101.6
Mich. Midland & Can.	14.0	14.0								
Musk. Riv. & Rose Lk.	7.5									
Muskrat Lk. & Clam Riv.			8.0	8.0	8.0	8.0				
N. Branch & Sauble Riv.									10.0	10.0
Paris & Pere Marq. Riv.				16.0	16.0	16.0	16.0	16.0		
Paw Paw	3.4	3.4	3.4	3.4	3.4	3.4	3.4			
Pontiac, Oxford & N.ern										99.7
Pontiac, Oxford & Port Austin				99.7	99.7	99.7	99.7	99.7	99.7	
Pt. Hur. & Northwestern	70.5	129.4	214.9	214.9	214.9	214.9	214.9	214.9	214.9	
Potts Logging Ry							59.9	59.9	59.9	59.9
Sag. Bay & Northwestern	29.3	32.4	46.7							
Sag., Tuscola & Huron			37.0	37.0	46.0	46.0	65.3	65.3	65.3	65.3
St. Joseph Valley		10.0	10.0	10.0	10.0	10.0	10.0	10.0	10.0	10.0
Tawas & Bay County	22.8	32.1								
Toledo & S. Haven	14.7	14.7	14.7	14.7	14.7	14.7	14.7	30.0	33.4	33.4

Toledo, A.A. & Gr. Trunk	39.9	54.1	54.1	54.1					
Toledo, A.A. & Northern Mich.					93.1	139.8	168.5	172.7	236.2	303.2
Toledo, Sag. & Mack.									39.2	39.2
Toledo, Sag. & Musk.								18.9		
Wabash, St. Louis & Pacific		78.3	78.3	78.3	78.3	78.3	78.3			
Wabash										78.3
Wabash Western								78.3	78.3	
L. P. YEAR TOTAL	3486.9	3749.3	3994.5	4304.8	4467.7	4568.4	4839.9	4977.2	5282.9	5448.7
L. P. YEAR CHANGE	189.3	262.4	245.2	310.3	162.9	100.7	271.5	137.3	305.7	165.8

UPPER PENINSULA

	1880	1881	1882	1883	1884	1885	1886	1887	1888	1889
Chi. & N. Western	172.0	172.0	301.1	310.6	370.8	375.3	380.7	392.9	392.5	476.6
Iron Range									35.7	
Iron Riv.								41.2	41.2	
Men. Riv.	44.5	47.2								
Det., Mackinac & Marq.	19.5	151.6	151.6	151.6	151.6	151.6				
Duluth, So. Shore & Atlantic							151.6	153.8	198.7	198.7
Marq., Hough. & Ont.								175.5	234.3	235.0
Marq. & Western								21.5	21.5	20.8
Negaunee & Palmer									6.2	6.2
Gogebic & Montreal Riv.								13.4		
Hermansville & Western				4.5	4.5	9.1	12.7	12.7	12.7	12.7
Ingalls, White Riv. & No.								15.0	15.0	15.0
Marq. & Western					22.0					
Marq., Hough. & Ont.	91.8	92.9	100.3	134.8	134.8	133.2	132.1			
Marq. & Western					22.0	22.0	22.0			
Men. Branch					1.4	1.4				
Milw. & Northern							1.4	65.6	65.6	65.6
Milw., Lk. Sh. & Western				8.7	68.7	73.1	77.8	87.4	87.4	87.4
Mineral Range	12.5	12.5	12.5	12.5	12.5	14.0	17.2	17.2	17.2	17.2
Hancock & Calumet						16.9	16.9	20.3	20.3	20.3
Mpls. St. Paul & S. S. Marie									191.9	191.9
Sault Ste. Marie Bridge									0.5	0.5
Wisconsin Cent.										
Gogebic & Montreal Riv.									13.4	19.9
Ont. & Brule Riv.			19.5	19.5	19.5	19.5	19.5	19.5	19.5	46.0
U. P. YEAR TOTAL	340.3	476.2	585.0	642.2	807.8	816.1	831.9	1036.0	1373.6	1413.8
U. P. YEAR CHANGE	39.4	135.9	108.8	57.2	165.6	8.3	15.8	204.1	337.6	40.2
MICH. YEAR TOTAL	3827.2	4225.5	4579.5	4947.0	5275.5	5384.5	5671.8	6013.2	6656.5	6862.5
MICH. YEAR CHANGE	228.7	398.3	354.0	367.5	328.5	109.0	287.3	341.4	643.3	206.0
COMMR. YEAR TOTAL	3823.0	4252.0	4609.0	4966.0	5120.0	5247.0	5577.0	5768.0	6411.0	6760.0
COMMR. YEAR CHANGE	166.0	429.0	357.0	357.0	154.0	127.0	330.0	191.0	643.0	349.0
STUDY LESS COMMR.	4.2	−26.5	−29.5	−19.0	155.5	137.5	94.8	245.2	245.5	102.5

Railroad Mileage, 1890–1899

LOWER PENINSULA

	1890	1891	1892	1893	1894	1895	1896	1897	1898	1899
Alpena & Northern				28.4	54.1					
A.A.						298.6	296.2	288.0	288.0	288.0
Arcadia & Betsey Riv.						17.8	21.0	21.0	21.0	21.0
Arcadia & Betsey Riv. Train Ry	11.0	11.0	11.0	11.0	11.0					
Au Sable & N.western		98.3	104.0	104.0	104.0	104.0	104.0	71.1	64.6	60.6
Bay Cty. Belt Line		5.4	5.4	5.4	5.4	5.4	5.4	5.4		
Bear Lk. & Eastern	18.0	18.0	18.0	18.0	18.0	18.0	18.0	18.0	18.0	18.0
Ben. Hbr., Coloma & P. P. L.							2.7	2.7	2.7	2.7
Boyne Cty. & Southeastern				7.2	13.0	13.0	15.0	19.0	24.0	31.0
Chi. & W. Mich.	444.7	444.7	444.7	444.7	444.7	448.0	448.0	448.0	448.0	
Chi. & N. Mich.			93.2	93.2	93.2	93.2	93.2	93.2	93.2	
Chi., Kal. & Sag.	43.9	43.9	43.9	43.9	43.9	43.9	43.9	43.9	43.9	43.9
Cinci., Jackson & Mack.	155.2	155.2	155.2	155.2	155.2	155.2	155.2			
Cinci. Northern								22.3	39.9	39.9
Det., Toledo & Milw.										132.9
Cinci., Wabash & Mich.	33.4	33.4								
Cleve., Cinci., Chi. & St. Louis										
Cinci., Wabash & Mich.			33.4	33.4	33.4	33.4	33.4	33.4	33.4	33.4
Crawford & Manistee Riv.	12.5	12.5	12.5	12.5	12.5	12.5	12.5	12.5	12.5	12.5
Det. & Mack.					201.7	237.1	236.1	226.6	249.4	249.4
Erie & Mich. Ry & Nav.								4.7	4.7	4.7
Det. & Lima N.ern								38.4	56.2	56.2
Det., Bay Cty. & Alpena	195.9	192.1	192.1	201.7						
Det., Gr. Rpds. & Western							251.9	381.3	381.3	
Gr. Rpds., Lans. & Det.							54.6			
Sag. & Western							41.5			
Sag. Valley & St. Louis							28.6			
Sag. & Gr. Rpds.							4.7			
Det., Lans. & N.ern	227.8	227.8	227.8	227.8	251.9	251.9				
Gr. Rpds., Lans. & Det.	54.6	54.6	54.6	54.6	54.6	54.6				
Sag. & Western	41.5	41.5	41.5	41.5	41.5	41.5				
Sag. Valley & St. Louis	28.6	28.6	28.6	28.6	28.6	28.6				
Sag. & Gr. Rpds.	4.7	4.7	4.7	4.7	4.7	4.7				
Det., Toledo & Milw.								132.9	132.9	
Det. Union RR Depot & Sta.	3.2	3.2	3.2	3.2	3.2	3.2	3.2	3.2	3.2	3.2
Epworth League							1.2	1.2	1.2	1.2	1.2
Flint & Pere Marq.	604.0	696.3	701.1	703.2	688.7	681.4	672.2	690.6	645.0	
Bay Cty. Belt Line									5.4	
Monroe & Toledo							18.4			
Fort St. Union Depot				1.2	1.2	1.2	1.2	1.2	1.2	1.2
Gr. Rpds. & Ind.	372.1	376.2	380.1	380.1	380.1	380.1	377.0	374.2	377.6	371.8
Musk., Gr. Rpds. & Ind	36.9	36.9	36.9	36.9	36.9	36.9	36.9	36.9	36.9	36.9
Trav. Cty.	26.0	26.0	26.0	26.0	26.0	26.0	26.0	26.0	26.0	26.0
Gr. Rpds., Belding & Sag.										13.0
Gr. Rpds., Kalkaska & Southeastern										40.4
Gr. Trunk Ry–Can.										
Chi. & Gr. Trunk	224.0	224.0	222.8	222.8	222.8	222.8	222.8	222.8	222.8	222.8
Chi., Det. & Can. G. T. Jct.	59.5	59.5	55.6	55.6	55.6	55.6	55.6	55.6	55.6	55.6
Cinci., Sag. & Mack.	58.9	58.9	58.9	58.9	58.9	58.9	58.9	58.9	58.9	58.9
Det., Gr. Haven & Milw.	188.3	188.3	188.3	188.3	188.3	188.3	188.3	188.3	188.3	188.3
Mich. Air Line Ry	105.9	105.9	105.9	105.9	105.9	105.9	105.9	105.9	105.9	105.9

St. Clair Tunnel			1.1	1.1	1.1	1.1	1.1	1.1	1.1	1.1
Tol., Sag. & Musk.	96.0	96.0	96.0	96.0	96.0	96.0	96.0	96.0	96.0	96.0
Grass Lk. & Manistee Riv.	13.5	13.5								
Ithaca & Alma	6.7	6.7	6.7	6.7	6.7	6.7	6.7			
Jackson & Ohio							17.6	17.6		
Lk. County	11.0	11.0	10.8	10.8	0.0					
Lk. Sh. & Mich. Southern	173.4	173.4	173.4	173.4	173.4	173.4	173.4	173.4	173.4	173.4
Det. & Chi.	62.4	62.4	62.4	56.9	56.9	56.9	56.9	20.5	20.5	20.5
Det., Hillsdale & Southwest.	65.2	65.2	65.2	65.2	65.2	65.2	65.2	65.2	65.2	65.2
Det., Monroe & Toledo	51.2	51.2	51.2	51.2	51.2	51.2	51.2	51.2	51.2	51.2
Erie & Kal.	14.2	14.2	14.2	14.2	14.2	14.2	14.2	14.2	14.2	14.2
Ft. Wyn. & Jackson	44.3	44.3	44.3	44.3	44.3	44.3	44.3	44.3	44.3	44.3
Kal., Allegan & Gr. Rapids	58.5	58.5	58.5	58.5	58.5	58.5	58.5	58.5	58.5	58.5
Kal. & White Pigeon	36.5	36.5	36.5	36.5	36.5	36.5	36.5	36.5	36.5	36.5
Northern Cent. Mich.	60.6	60.6	60.6	60.6	60.6	60.6	60.6	60.6	60.6	60.6
Sturgis, Goshen & St. Louis	10.6	10.6	10.6	10.6	10.6	10.6	10.6	10.6	10.6	10.6
Lewiston & Southeastern							13.0	13.0	13.0	17.5
Lima Northern						5.6	5.6			
Lowell & Hastings	13.0	13.0	13.0	13.0	13.0	13.0	13.0	13.0	13.0	
Manistee & Gr. Rpds.			28.6	28.6	28.6	31.2	44.7	44.7	44.7	44.7
Manistee & N.eastern	59.5	59.5	80.6	85.1	88.1	88.1	88.1	92.1	105.5	104.8
Mason & Oceana	27.2	27.2	27.2	27.2	27.2	27.2	27.2	27.2	27.2	27.2
Mich. Cent.	221.6	221.6	221.6	221.6	221.6	221.6	221.6	221.6	221.6	221.6
Battle Creek & Sturgis	34.4	34.4	34.4	34.4	34.4	34.4	34.4	34.4	34.4	34.4
Bay Cty. & Battle Creek	18.0	18.0	18.0	18.0	18.0	18.0	18.0	18.0	18.0	18.0
Can. Southern										
Can. So. Bridge	3.1	3.1	3.1	3.1	3.1	3.1	3.1	3.1	3.1	3.1
Mich. Midland & Can.	14.0	14.0	14.0	14.0	14.0	14.0	14.0	14.0	14.0	14.0
Toledo, Can. Southern & Det.	46.8	46.8	46.8	46.8	46.8	46.8	46.8	46.8	46.8	46.8
Det. & Bay Cty.	135.9	135.9	135.9	135.9	135.9	135.9	135.9	135.9	135.9	135.9
Det., Delray & Dearborn						4.8	4.8	4.8	4.8	4.8
Grand Riv. Valley	83.8	83.8	83.8	83.8	83.8	83.8	83.8	83.8	83.8	83.8
Grayling, Twin Lks. & NE			27.4	27.4	27.4	38.4	48.0	48.0	48.0	48.0
Jackson, Lans. & Sag.	369.2	364.5	355.3	355.3	355.3	355.3	364.5	371.7	371.7	371.7
Kal. & S. Haven	39.4	39.4	39.4	39.4	39.4	39.4	39.4	39.4	39.4	39.4
Mich. Air RR	109.0	109.0	109.0	109.0	109.0	109.0	109.0	109.0	109.0	109.0
Sag. Bay & NW	101.6	99.5	97.4	92.4	92.4	92.4	95.3	94.9	94.9	95.1
Milw., Bent. Hbr. & Columbus								26.1	26.1	26.1
N. Branch & Sauble Riv.	10.0	10.0	10.0	10.0	10.0	10.0				
Pere Marq. RR										1567.5
Pontiac, Oxford & N.ern	99.7	99.7	99.7	99.7	99.7	99.7	99.7	99.7	99.7	99.7
Potts Logging Ry	59.9	0.0								
St. Joseph Valley	10.0	10.0	10.0	10.0	10.0	10.0	10.0			
S. Haven & Eastern										
Terre Haute & Ind.										
Ind. & Lk. Mich.	25.3	25.3	25.3	25.3	25.3	25.3	25.3	25.3	25.3	
St. Joseph, S. Bend & Southern										25.3
Toledo & S. Haven	3.4	33.4	33.4	33.4						
Tol., A.A. & N. Mich.	303.2	295.6	296.7	300.2	299.9					
Wabash	78.3	78.3	78.3	78.3	78.3	78.3	78.3	78.3	78.3	78.3
L. P. year total	5521.0	5673.0	5829.8	5875.8	5875.4	5883.4	5949.8	5921.7	5932.0	5968.2
L. P. year change	72.3	152.0	156.8	46.0	−0.4	8.0	66.4	−28.1	10.3	36.2

UPPER PENINSULA

	1890	1891	1892	1893	1894	1895	1896	1897	1898	1899
Chi. & N. Western	436.1	385.1	432.8	514.5	512.7	511.5	511.9	510.9	510.9	510.9
Esc., Iron Mtn. & W..		50.5	50.5	50.5	50.5	50.5	50.5	50.5	50.5	50.5
Men. Riv.	43.9	46.6								
Milw., Lk. Sh. & Western		79.3	79.3							
Chi., Milw. & St. Paul		4.1	4.1	164.1	164.1	165.9	165.9	165.9	165.9	165.9
Milw. & Northern	111.6	111.6	111.6							
Copper Range										41.5
Duluth, So. Shore & Atlantic	462.6	463.9	463.9	463.9	465.3	452.7	455.7	455.7	450.5	450.5
Hermansville & Western	12.7	12.7	12.7	12.7	12.7	12.7	12.7	12.7	12.7	12.7
Ingalls, White Riv. & No.	15.0	15.0	15.0	15.0	15.0	0.0				
Lk. Superior & Ish.							20.6	22.5	22.5	22.5
Manistique & Northwestern								34.8	49.4	55.4
Milw., Lk. Sh. & Western	79.3									
Mineral Range	17.2	17.2	17.2	23.3	23.7	23.7	17.2	17.2	25.2	29.2
Hancock & Calumet	20.3	21.6	21.6	31.2	31.2	34.2	35.3	35.9	32.9	35.5
Mpls., St. Paul & S. S. Marie	191.9	191.9	191.9	197.9	197.9	197.9	197.9	197.9	207.6	231.9
Sault Ste. Marie Bridge	0.5	0.5	0.5	0.5	0.5	0.5	0.5	0.5	0.5	0.5
Munising Ry								38.4	45.4	47.9
Wisconsin & Mich.					22.6	27.6	28.1	28.1	29.9	29.9
Wisconsin Cent.										
Gogebic & Montreal Riv.	19.9	19.9	19.9	19.9	19.9	19.9	19.9	19.9	19.9	19.9
U. P. YEAR TOTAL	1411.0	1419.9	1421.0	1493.5	1516.1	1497.1	1516.2	1590.9	1623.8	1704.7
U. P. YEAR CHANGE	−2.8	8.9	1.1	72.5	22.6	−19.0	19.1	74.7	32.9	80.9
MICH. YEAR TOTAL	6932.0	7092.9	7250.8	7369.3	7391.5	7380.5	7466.0	7512.6	7555.8	7672.9
MICH. YEAR CHANGE	69.5	160.9	157.9	118.5	22.2	−11.0	85.5	46.6	43.2	117.1
COMMR. YEAR TOTAL	6957.0	7275.0	7447.0	7512.0	7513.0	7609.0	7759.0	7817.0	7826.0	7929.0
COMMR. YEAR CHANGE	197.0	318.0	172.0	65.0	1.0	96.0	150.0	58.0	9.0	103.0
STUDY LESS COMMR.	−25.0	−182.1	−196.2	−142.7	−121.5	−228.5	−293.0	−304.4	−270.2	−256.1

Michigan Electric Lines Mileage, 1890–1899

	1890	1891	1892	1893	1894	1895	1896	1897	1898	1899
A.A. & Ypsi. Electric							7.9			
A.A. & Ypsi. St.		7.9	7.9	7.9	7.9	7.9				
Det. & N.western										8.4
Det. & Pontiac								16.7	16.7	16.7
Det. & Riv. St. Clair									27.7	27.7
Det., Lk. Sh. & Mt. Clem.									14.2	14.2
Det., Mt. Clem. & Marine Cty.										2.8
Det., Plymouth & Northville										14.5
Det., Ypsi. & A.A.								7.9	32.0	32.0
Esc. Electric St. Ry			3.3	3.3	3.3	5.8	5.8	5.8	5.8	5.8
Grand Riv. Electric									4.3	
Holland & Lk. Mich.									6.5	6.5
InterUrban								8.6	8.6	8.6
Mt. Clemens & Lakeside Trac.									2.8	
Negaunee & Ish. St.				3.6	3.6	3.6	3.6	3.6	3.6	3.6

Pontiac & Sylvan Lk.						1.8	1.8	1.8	1.8	
Rapid Ry.						15.5	15.5	15.5	15.5	15.5
Sag. Valley Trac. InterUrban										8.6
Saugatuck, Douglas & L. S.										10.1
Twin Cty. General Electric				8.0	8.0	8.0	8.0	8.0	8.0	8.0
Wyandotte & Det. Riv.			1.5	10.6	10.6	10.6	10.6	10.6	10.6	10.6
Ypsi. & Saline Electric										10.1
MICH. YEAR TOTAL	0.0	7.9	12.7	33.4	33.4	53.2	61.8	78.5	158.1	195.1
MICH. YEAR CHANGE		7.9	4.8	20.7	0.0	19.8	8.6	16.7	79.6	37.0

Railroad Mileage, 1900–1909

LOWER PENINSULA

	1900	1901	1902	1903	1904	1905	1906	1907	1908	1909
A.A.	288.0	288.0	288.0	288.0	288.0	288.0	288.0	288.0	288.0	288.0
Arcadia & Betsey Riv.	21.0	21.0	21.0	21.0	21.0	21.0	21.0	21.0	21.0	21.0
AuSable & Northwestern	64.4	64.4	64.4	64.4	64.4	64.4	64.4	51.1	55.5	61.5
Bear Lk. & Eastern	18.0	18.0								
Bent. Hbr., Coloma & P. P. L.	2.7	2.7	2.7							
Boyne Cty. & Southeastern	32.0	35.7	35.7	42.2	36.3					
Boyne Cty., Gaylord & Alpena						69.0	73.3	73.3	75.9	75.9
Chi., Kal. & Sag.	43.9	43.9	55.0	55.0	55.0	55.0	55.0	55.0	55.0	45.5
Cinci. Northern	39.9									
Det., Toledo & Milw.	132.9									
Cleve., Cinci., Chi. & St. Louis										
Cinci. Northern		39.9	39.9	39.9	39.9	39.9	39.9	39.9	39.9	39.9
Det., Toledo & Milw.		132.9								
Cinci., Wabash & Mich.	33.4	33.4	33.4	33.4	33.4	33.4	33.4	33.4	33.4	33.4
Crawford & Manistee Riv.	12.5	12.5	12.5	12.5						
Det. & Charlevoix		49.9	49.9	49.9	49.9	49.9	49.9			
Det. & Lima Northern	56.2									
Det. & Mackinac	305.1	314.8	314.8	294.2	324.7	329.9	329.9	331.1	339.1	355.0
Erie & Mich. Ry & Nav.	4.7	4.7	4.7	4.7	4.7	4.7	4.7	4.7	4.7	4.7
Det. & Toledo Shore Line				43.8	43.8	43.8	43.8	43.8	43.8	43.8
Det. Southern		64.8	64.8	64.8	64.8					
Det., Toledo & Ironton						64.8	64.8	64.8	64.8	64.8
Det., Toledo & Milw.			132.9	132.9	132.9	132.9	132.9	132.9	132.9	132.9
Det. Union RR Depot & Sta.	3.2	3.2	3.2	3.2	3.2	3.2	3.2	3.2	3.2	3.2
E. Jordan & Southern		18.6	18.6	18.6	18.6	18.6	18.6	18.6	18.6	18.6
Empire & S. Eastern	11.2	11.2	11.2	11.2	11.2	14.3	14.3	14.3	14.3	14.3
Epworth League	1.2									
Fort St. Union Depot	1.2	1.2	1.2	1.2	1.2	1.2	1.2	1.2	1.2	1.2
Gr. Rpds. & Ind.	373.3	377.8	377.8	377.8	361.2	368.8	369.2	368.8	365.3	378.6
Musk., Gr. Rpds. & Ind.	36.9	36.9	36.9	36.9	36.9	36.9	36.9	36.9	36.9	36.9
Trav. Cty.	26.0	26.0	26.0	26.0	26.0	26.0	26.0	26.0	26.0	26.0
Gr. Rpds., Kalkaska & SE	40.4	40.4	40.4							
Gr. Trunk Ry–Can.										
Chi., Det. & Can. G.T. Jct.	55.6	55.6	55.6	55.6	55.6	55.6	55.6	55.6	55.6	55.6
Cinci., Sag. & Mack.	58.9	58.9	58.9	58.9	58.9	58.9	58.9	58.9	58.9	58.9
Det., Gr. Haven & Milw.	188.3	188.3	188.3	188.3	188.3	188.3	188.3	188.3	188.3	188.3
Gr. Rpds. Terminal							1.5	1.5	1.5	1.5
Gr. Trunk Western	222.8	222.8	222.8	222.8	222.8	222.8	222.8	222.8	222.8	222.8

Mich. Air Line Ry	105.9	105.9	105.9	105.9	105.9	105.9	105.9	105.9	105.9	105.9
Pontic, Oxford & N.ern										99.7
St. Clair Tunnel	1.1	1.1	1.1	1.1	1.1	1.1	1.1	1.1	1.1	1.1
Tol., Sag. & Musk.	96.0	96.0	96.0	96.0	96.0	96.0	96.0	96.0	96.0	96.0
Ind., Illinois & Iowa		1.6	1.6	1.6	1.6					
St. Joseph, S. Bend & So.	25.3	25.3	25.3	25.3	25.3					
Kal., Lk. Sh. & Chi.								49.4	49.4	49.4
Lk. Sh. & Mich. Southern	173.4	173.4	173.4	173.4	173.4	173.4	173.4	173.4	173.4	173.4
Det. & Chi.	20.5	20.5	20.5	20.5	20.5	20.5	20.5	20.5	20.5	20.5
Det., Hillsdale & Southwest.	65.2	65.2	65.2	65.2	65.2	65.2	65.2	65.2	65.2	65.2
Det., Monroe & Toledo	51.2	51.2	51.2	51.2	51.2	51.2	51.2	51.2	51.2	51.2
Erie & Kal.	14.2	14.2	14.2	14.2	14.2	14.2	14.2	14.2	14.2	14.2
Ft. Wyn. & Jackson	44.3	44.3	44.3	44.3	44.3	44.3	44.3	44.3	44.3	44.3
Kal., Allegan & Gr. Rpds.	58.5	58.5	58.5	58.5	58.5	58.5	58.5	58.5	58.5	58.5
Kal. & White Pigeon	36.5	36.5	36.5	36.5	36.5	36.5	36.5	36.5	36.5	36.5
N.ern Cent. Mich.	60.6	60.6	60.6	60.6	60.6	60.6	60.6	60.6	60.6	60.6
Sturgis, Goshen & St. Louis	10.6	10.6	10.6	10.6	10.6	10.6	10.6	10.6	10.6	10.6
Lewiston & Southeastern	17.5	8.0	8.0	15.0	15.0	15.0	15.0	15.0	15.0	18.0
Lud. & Northern		4.6	4.6	4.6	4.6	5.6	5.6	5.6	5.6	
Manistee & Gr. Rpds.	68.9	72.0	63.1	63.1	63.1	63.1	77.0	77.0	77.0	77.0
Manistee & Northeastern	108.8	102.2	112.9	124.3	123.3	123.3	123.3	123.3	123.3	160.5
Mason & Oceana	27.2	27.2	31.0	31.0	37.0	37.0	31.0	31.0	27.2	0.0
Mich. Cent.	221.6	222.4	222.4	222.7	222.7	222.7	222.7	222.7	222.7	222.7
Battle Creek & Sturgis	34.4	34.4	34.4	34.4	34.4	34.4	34.4	34.4	34.4	34.4
Bay Cty. & Battle Creek	18.0	18.0	18.0	18.0	18.0	18.0	18.0	18.0	18.0	18.0
Can. Southern										
Can. So. Bridge	3.1	3.1	3.1	3.1	3.1	3.1	3.1	3.1	3.1	3.1
Mich. Midland & Can.	14.0	14.0	14.0	14.0	14.0	14.0				
St. Clair & Western							14.0	14.0	14.0	14.0
Toledo, C. S. & Det.	46.8	46.8	46.8	46.8	46.8	46.8	46.8	46.8	46.8	46.8
Chi., Ind. & S.–part							1.6	1.6	1.6	1.6
Det. & Bay Cty.	135.9	135.9	135.9	135.9	135.9	135.9	135.9	135.9	156.8	156.8
Caro & Lk. Huron		20.9	20.9	20.9	20.9	20.9	20.9	20.9		
Det. & Charlevoix								49.9	49.9	49.9
Det., Delray & Dearborn	4.8	4.8	4.8	4.8	4.8	4.8	5.7	5.7	5.7	5.7
Grand Riv. Valley	83.8	83.8	83.8	83.8	83.8	83.8	83.8	83.8	83.8	83.8
Grayling, Twin Lks. & NE	59.8									
Ind., Ill. & Iowa–part						1.6				
Jackson, Lans. & Sag.	355.6	476.1	476.1	476.1	502.3	502.3	502.3	529.5	525.7	525.7
Kal. & S. Haven	39.4	39.4	39.4	39.4	39.4	39.4	39.4	39.4	39.4	39.4
Mich. Air Line RR	109.0	109.5	109.5	109.5	109.5	109.5	109.5	109.5	109.5	109.5
Sag. Bay & NW	68.1									
St. Joseph, S. Bend & So.						25.3	25.3	25.3	25.3	25.3
Milw., Bent. Hbr. & Columbus	26.1	26.1	26.1							
Pere Marq. RR	1587.3	1594.6	1595.0	1769.7	1769.7	1752.6	1744.4	1741.7	1741.7	1741.7
Bay Cty. Belt Line	5.4	5.4	5.4	0.0						
Gr. Rpds., Belding & Sag.	28.9	28.9	28.9	0.0						
Gr. Rpds., Kalkaska & SE				40.4	40.4	40.4	40.4	40.4	40.4	40.4
Huron & Western				11.3	11.3	11.3	11.3	11.3	11.3	11.3
Sag., Tuscola & Huron	65.3	65.3	65.3							
Pontiac, Oxford & N.ern	99.7	99.7	99.7	99.7	99.7	99.7	99.7	99.7	99.7	
Pt. Hur. & Southern		2.8	2.8	2.8	2.8	2.8	2.8	2.8	2.8	2.8
S. Haven & Eastern	33.4	33.4	33.4							
Trav.Cy., Leelanau & Manistique								23.2	23.8	23.8	23.8
Wabash	78.3	78.3	78.3	78.3	78.3	78.3	78.3	78.3	78.3	78.3

	1900	1901	1902	1903	1904	1905	1906	1907	1908	1909
L. P. YEAR TOTAL	6178.1	6290.0	6289.1	6361.7	6388.4	6420.9	6450.9	6512.9	6516.8	6549.9
L. P. YEAR CHARGE	209.9	111.9	−0.9	72.6	26.7	32.5	30.0	62.0	3.9	33.1

UPPER PENINSULA

	1900	1901	1902	1903	1904	1905	1906	1907	1908	1909
Blaney & Southern			7.2	7.2	7.2	7.2	7.2	7.2	7.2	7.2
Chi. & N. Western	537.0	543.4	543.4	539.9	547.6	547.6	550.1	554.4	556.5	563.4
Esc., Iron Mtn. & W..	50.5	50.5	50.5	50.5	50.5	50.5	50.5	50.5	50.5	50.5
Chi., Milw. & St. Paul	182.1	184.8	185.6	184.2	184.2	184.4	184.4	186.3	186.7	198.4
Copper Range	41.5	62.1	65.4	84.0	84.0	84.0	84.0	84.0	84.0	85.3
Duluth, So. Shore & Atlantic	447.9	450.5	447.0	448.9	448.9	447.6	445.5	446.5	448.6	448.0
Mineral Range	66.6	66.6	66.6	70.8	70.8	71.8	71.8	71.8	71.8	71.8
Hancock & Calumet	35.5	32.5	32.5	29.2	31.9	35.0	35.0	34.3	34.3	34.3
Mohawk Mining Co.				17.0	17.0	17.0	17.0	17.0	17.0	17.0
Esc. & Lk. Superior	63.5	75.7	99.4	104.0	104.0	115.1	115.1	115.1	115.1	124.2
Hermansville & Western	12.7	12.7	12.7	12.7	12.7	12.7	12.7	12.7	5.4	5.4
Keweenaw Cent.							7.1	20.4	28.9	34.4	34.4
Lk. Superior & Ish.	22.5	22.5	22.5	27.6	27.6	31.3	31.3	31.3	31.5	30.3
Manistique, Marq. & No.			58.4	56.4	56.4	56.4	56.4	54.6		
Manistique & Lk. Superior										54.6
Manistique & Northern									54.6	
Manistique & Northwestern	58.4	58.4								
Marq. & Southeastern				26.8	26.8	50.5	50.5	50.5	50.5	50.5
Mpls., St. Paul & S. S. Marie	231.9	231.3	239.0	250.5	250.5	250.5	248.2	248.2	248.5	247.1
Sainte Marie Union Depot			0.5	0.5	0.5	0.5	0.5	0.5	0.5	0.5
Sault Ste. Marie Bridge	0.5	0.5	0.5	0.5	0.5	0.5	0.5	0.5	0.5	0.5
Wisconsin Cent.										0.2
Gogebic & Montreal Riv.										19.9
Munising Ry	47.9	47.9	62.2	62.2	62.2	75.9	75.9	76.4	77.6	77.6
Wisconsin & Mich.	29.9	29.9	24.9	41.6	48.2	54.8	54.8	54.8	54.8	58.7
Quinnesec & Western					6.6					
Wisconsin Cent.		0.2	0.2	0.2	0.2	0.2	0.2	0.2	0.2	
Gogebic & Montreal Riv.	19.9	19.9	19.9	19.9	19.9	19.9	19.9	19.9	19.9	
U. P. YEAR TOTAL	1828.4	1869.3	1918.3	2014.5	2038.1	2100.4	2111.8	2125.5	2130.0	2179.8
U. P. YEAR CHANGE	123.7	40.9	49.0	96.2	23.6	62.3	11.4	13.7	4.5	49.8
MICH. YEAR TOTAL	8006.5	8159.3	8207.4	8376.2	8426.5	8521.3	8562.7	8638.4	8646.8	8729.7
MICH. YEAR CHANGE	333.6	152.8	48.1	168.8	50.3	94.8	41.4	75.7	8.4	82.9
COMMR. YEAR TOTAL	7946.0	8133.0	8366.0	8483.0	8507.0	8794.0	8902.0	8976.0	9011.0	9059.0
COMMR. YEAR CHANGE	17.0	187.0	233.0	117.0	24.0	287.0	108.0	74.0	35.0	48.0
STUDY LESS COMMR.	60.5	26.3	−158.6	−106.8	−80.5	−272.7	−339.3	−337.6	−364.2	−329.3

Michigan Electric Lines Mileage, 1900–1909

	1900	1901	1902	1903	1904	1905	1906	1907	1908	1909
Benton Hbr.–St. Joe Ry & L.							12.6	12.6	12.6	12.6
Det. & Northwestern	36.1									
Det. & Pontiac	16.7									
Det. & Pt. Hur. Shore Line										
Det. & Lk. St. Clair	14.2									

Mt. Clemens & Mar. Cy.	34.6									
Pt. Huron, St. Clair & Mar. Cy.	17.8									
Rapid Ry	15.5									
Det., Flint & Sag.				11.8	11.8	11.8	11.8			
Det., Monroe & Toledo Sh. L.		14.8	27.3	45.6	45.6					
Det., Plymouth & Northville	14.5	14.5	14.5	14.5	14.5	14.5				
Det., Lk. Orion & Flint	39.1									
Det. United Ry.		134.4	134.4	134.4	134.4	134.4	134.4	134.4	134.4	134.4
Det. & Pt. Hur. Shore L.										
Det. & Lk. St. Clair		14.2	14.2	14.2	14.2	14.2	14.2	14.2	14.2	14.2
Det., Mt. Clemens & Mar. Cty.		34.6	34.6	34.6	34.6	34.6	34.6	34.6	34.6	34.6
Pt. Huron, St. Clair & M. C.		17.8	27.3	27.3	27.3	27.3	27.3	27.3	27.3	27.3
Rapid Ry.		15.5	15.5	15.5	15.5	15.5	15.5	15.5	15.5	15.5
Det., Jackson & Chi.								94.6	94.6	94.6
Det., Monroe & Tol. Sh. L.							45.6	45.6	45.6	45.6
Det., Ypsi. & A.A.	32.0									
Det., Ypsi., A. A. & Jackson		42.1	80.1	80.1	80.1	80.1	80.1			
Esc. Electric St. Ry.	5.8	5.8	5.8	5.8	5.8	5.8	5.8	5.8	5.8	
Esc. Traction										5.8
Gr. Rpds., Gr. Hvn. & Musk.			41.0	41.0	41.0	41.0	41.0	41.0	41.0	41.0
Gr. Rpds., Holland & Chi.				42.3	42.3	42.3	42.3	42.3	42.3	42.3
Gr. Rpds., Holland & Lk. Mich.	18.6	42.3	42.3	42.3						
Grand Riv. Electric	36.1									
Hough. Co. St. Ry.	8.1	23.5	23.5	23.5	23.5	23.5	23.5			
Hough. Co. Traction								28.1	28.1	28.1
Jackson & Battle Creek Tr.				40.2	40.2	40.2				
Jackson & Suburban		8.6	8.6	8.6						
Jackson, A.A. & Det.							14.5			
Jackson Consol. Traction					12.3	12.3	12.3			
Lans. & Suburban Tr.					18.5	18.5				
Marq. Co. Gas & Electric							3.8	3.8	3.8	3.8
Marq. Co. Gas Light & Tr.					3.8	3.8				
Mich. Suburban										
Lans, St. Johns & St. Louis			18.5	18.5						
Mich. Traction		26.4	26.4	26.4	26.4	26.4				
Mich. United Rys							85.1	85.1	97.4	131.6
Jackson Consol. Traction								12.3		
Negaunee & Ish. St.	3.8	3.8	3.8	3.8						
N. Det. Electric	6.7									
Sag. & Flint									11.8	31.7
Sag. Valley Traction										
InterUrban	8.6	8.6	8.6	8.6	8.6	8.6	8.6	8.6	8.6	8.6
S. Bend & So. Mich.				5.2	5.2	5.2				
Southern Mich. Ry.							27.3	27.3	27.3	27.3
Toledo & Monroe		14.8								
Toledo & Western		18.7	23.2	23.4	23.4	23.4	23.4	23.4	23.4	23.4
Toledo, Ottawa Beach & No.							7.2	7.2	7.2	7.2
Twin Cty. General Electric	8.0	8.0	8.0	8.0	8.0	8.0	8.0	8.0	8.0	8.0
Wyandotte & Det. Riv.	10.6									
Ypsi. & Saline Electric	10.1									
MICH. YEAR TOTAL	336.9	433.6	545.1	603.2	637.0	637.0	678.9	683.5	683.5	737.6
MICH. YEAR CHANGE	141.8	96.7	111.5	58.1	33.8	0.0	41.9	4.6	0.0	54.1

Railroad Mileage, 1910–1919

LOWER PENINSULA

	1910	1911	1912	1913	1914	1915	1916	1917	1918	1919
A.A.	288.0	288.0	288.0	288.0	288.0	288.0	288.0	288.0	288.0	288.0
Arcadia & Betsey Riv.	21.0	21.0	21.0	21.0	21.0	21.0	21.0	21.0	21.0	21.0
Au Sable & Northwestern	63.6	63.6								
Boyne Cty., Gaylord & Alpena	75.9	75.9	75.9	51.3	77.2	73.0	59.8	59.8	92.8	92.8
Chi., Kal. & Sag.	44.2	44.2	44.2	44.2	44.2	44.2	44.2	44.2	44.2	44.2
Cleve., Cinci., Chi. & St. Louis				33.4	33.4	33.4	33.4	33.4	33.4	33.4
Cinci. Northern	39.9	39.9	39.9	39.9	39.9	39.9	39.9	39.9	39.9	39.9
Cinci., Wabash & Mich.	33.4	33.4	33.4							
Det. & Mackinac	355.0	368.6	367.3	367.3	367.3	398.3	386.7	386.7	386.7	386.7
Au Sable & Northwestern			66.5	66.5	69.1					
Erie & Mich. Ry & Nav.	4.7	4.7	4.7	4.7	4.7	4.7	4.7	4.7	4.7	4.7
Det. & Toledo Shore Line	43.8	43.8	43.8	43.8	43.8	43.8	43.8	43.8	43.8	43.8
Det., Bay Cty. & Western	64.8	64.8	64.8	64.8	64.8	64.8	64.8	64.8	64.8	64.8
Det. Terminal			13.7	14.1	17.9	18.0	18.0	18.0	18.0	18.0
Det., Toledo & Ironton	64.8	64.8	64.8	64.8	64.8	64.8	64.8	64.8	64.8	64.8
Toledo–Det.							19.7	19.7	19.7	19.7
Det., Toledo & Milw.	132.9	132.9	132.9	90.4	90.4	90.4	90.4	90.4	90.4	90.4
Det. Union RR Depot & Sta.	3.2	3.2	3.2	3.2	3.2	3.2	3.2	3.2	3.2	3.2
E. Jordan & Southern	18.6	18.6	18.6	18.6	18.6	18.6	18.6	18.6	18.6	18.6
Empire & S. Eastern	14.3	14.3	14.3	14.3	14.3	14.3	11.2	11.2	11.2	11.2
Fort St. Union Depot	1.2	1.2	1.2	1.2	1.2	1.2	1.2	1.2	1.2	1.2
Gr. Rpds. & Ind.	374.5	374.5	374.5	364.7	362.1	362.1	362.1	423.6	423.5	423.5
Musk., Gr. Rpds. & Ind.	36.9	36.9	36.9	36.9	36.9	36.9	36.9			
Trav. Cty.	26.0	26.0	26.0	26.0	26.0	26.0	26.0			
Gr. Trunk Ry–Can.										
Bay Cty. Terminal				1.2	1.2	1.2	1.2	1.2	1.2	1.2
Chi. & Kal. Terminal	11.3	11.3	11.3	11.3	11.3	11.3	11.3	11.3	11.3	11.3
Chi., Det. & Can. Gr. Trunk Jct.	55.6	55.6	55.6	55.6	55.6	55.6	55.6	55.6	55.6	55.6
Chi., Kal. & Sag.	9.5	9.5	9.5	9.5	9.5	9.5	9.5	9.5	9.5	9.5
Cinci, Sag. & Mack.	58.9	58.9	58.9	58.9	58.9	58.9	58.9	58.9	58.9	58.9
Det. & Huron				18.3	18.3	18.3	18.3	18.3	18.3	18.3
Det., Gr. Haven & Milw.	188.3	188.3	188.3	188.3	188.3	188.3	188.3	188.3	188.3	188.3
Gr. Rpds. Terminal	1.5	1.5	1.5	1.5	1.5	1.5	1.5	1.5	1.5	1.5
Gr. Trunk Western	213.7	213.7	213.7	213.7	213.7	213.7	213.7	213.7	213.7	213.7
Mich. Air Line Ry	105.9	105.9	105.9	105.9	105.9	105.9	105.9	105.9	105.9	105.9
Pontiac, Oxford & Northern	99.7	99.7	99.7	99.7	99.7	99.7	99.7	99.7	99.7	99.7
St. Clair Tunnel	1.1	1.1	1.1	1.1	1.1	1.1	1.1	1.1	1.1	1.1
Tol., Sag. & Musk.	96.0	96.0	96.0	96.0	96.0	96.0	96.0	96.0	96.0	96.0
Kal., Lk. Sh. & Chi.	49.4	54.4	54.4	54.4	49.4	49.4	16.0	16.0	16.0	16.0
Lk. Sh. & Mich. Southern	173.4	173.4	173.4	173.4	173.4					
Det. & Chi.	20.5	20.5	20.5	20.5	20.5					
Det., Hillsdale & Southwest.	65.2	65.2	65.2	65.2	65.2					
Det., Monroe & Toledo	51.2	51.2	51.2	51.2	51.2					
Erie & Kal.	14.2	14.2	14.2	14.2	14.2					
Ft. Wyn. & Jackson	44.3	44.3	44.3	44.3	44.3					
Kal., Allegan & Gr. Rpds.	58.5	58.5	58.5	58.5	58.5					
Kal. & White Pigeon	36.5	36.5	36.5	36.5	36.5					
Northern Cent. Mich.	60.6	60.6	60.6	60.6	60.6					
Sturgis, Goshen & St. Louis	10.6	10.6	10.6	10.6	10.6					
Lud. & Northern	7.6	7.6	7.6	7.6	7.6	7.6	7.6	7.6	7.6	3.4
Manistee & Gr. Rpds.	77.0	77.0	77.0							

	1910	1911	1912	1913	1914	1915	1916	1917	1918	1919
Manistee & Northeastern	178.2	178.2	178.2	178.2	178.2	178.2	178.2	178.2	178.2	178.2
Leelanau Transit										23.8
Mich. Cent.	222.7	221.5	221.5	221.5	221.5	221.5	1202.8	1205.4	1197.1	1190.6
Battle Creek & Sturgis	34.4	34.4	34.4	34.4	34.4	34.4	34.4	34.4	34.4	34.4
Bay Cty. & Battle Creek	18.0	18.0	18.0	18.0	18.0	18.0				
Can. Southern										
Can. So. Bridge	3.1	3.1	3.1	3.1	3.1	3.1	3.1	3.1	3.1	3.1
Det.Riv.Tunnel	1.4	1.4	1.4	1.4	1.4	1.4	1.4	1.4	1.4	1.4
St. Clair & Western	14.0	14.0	14.0	14.0	14.0	14.0	14.0	14.0	14.0	14.0
Toledo, C. S. & Det.	46.8	46.8	46.8	46.8	46.8	46.8				
Chi., Ind. & S–part	1.6	1.6	1.6	1.6	1.6	1.6				
Det. & Bay Cty.	156.8	156.8	156.8	156.8	156.8	156.8				
Det. & Charlevoix	49.9	49.9	49.9	49.9	49.9	49.9				
Det., Delray & Dearborn	5.7	5.7	5.7	5.7	5.7	5.7				
Grand Riv. Valley	83.8	83.8	83.8	83.8	83.8	83.8				
Jackson, Lans. & Sag.	527.4	527.4	422.2	523.3	523.3	523.7				
Kal. & S. Haven	39.4	39.4	39.4	39.4	39.4	39.4				
Mich. Air Line RR	109.5	109.5	109.5	109.5	109.5	109.5				
New York Cent.–part							1.6	1.6	1.6	1.6
St. Joseph, S. Bend & So.	25.3	25.3	25.3	25.3	25.3	25.3	25.3	25.3	25.3	25.3
Mich. E. & W.			77.0	77.0	72.0	72.0	72.0	72.0	72.0	72.0
New York Cent.						352.8	352.8	352.8	352.8	352.8
Det., Hillsdale & SW						65.2	65.2	65.2	65.2	65.2
Erie & Kal.						14.2	14.2	14.2	14.2	14.2
Ft. Wyn. & Jackson						44.3	44.3	44.3	44.3	44.3
Kal., Allegan & Gr. Rpds.						58.5	58.5	58.5	58.5	58.5
Pere Marq. RR	1706.9	1695.8	1695.8	1695.8	1695.8	1693.1	1717.2			
Gr. Rpds., Kalkaska & SE	40.4	40.4	40.4	40.4	40.4	32.9	32.9			
Huron & Western	11.3	11.3	11.3	11.3	11.3	11.3	11.3			
Pere Marq. Ry								1717.2	1717.2	1717.2
Gr. Rpds., Kalkaska & SE								19.2	19.2	19.2
Huron & Western								11.3	11.3	11.3
Pt. Hur. & Det.									15.7	15.7
Pt. Hur. Southern	2.8	2.8	2.8	2.8	2.8	2.8	2.8	2.8	2.8	2.8
Toledo–Det.			14.2	14.2	19.7					
Trav. Cty., Leelanau & Manistique	23.8	23.8	23.8	23.8	23.8	23.8	23.8	23.8	23.8	
Wabash	78.3	78.3	78.3	78.3	78.3	78.3	78.3	78.3	78.3	78.3
L. P. YEAR TOTAL	6598.7	6605.0	6515.1	6573.4	6598.1	6546.6	6457.1	6444.6	6484.9	6474.2
L. P. YEAR CHANGE	48.8	6.3	–89.9	58.3	24.7	–51.5	–89.5	–12.5	40.3	–10.7

UPPER PENINSULA

	1910	1911	1912	1913	1914	1915	1916	1917	1918	1919
Blaney & Southern	7.2	7.2	7.2	7.2	7.2	7.2	7.2	7.2	7.2	7.2
Chi. & N. Western	563.4	565.3	568.7	565.0	565.7	554.5	551.5	553.1	559.2	554.6
Esc., Iron Mtn. & W..	50.5	50.5	50.5	50.5	50.5	50.5	50.5	50.5	50.5	50.5
Chi., Milw. & St. Paul	197.7	197.7	197.7	193.6	208.5	206.9	206.3	220.2	220.2	219.3
Copper Range	85.3	85.3	85.3	86.2	86.2	86.2	86.2	104.9	104.9	104.9
Duluth, So. Shore & Atlantic	447.0	447.0	447.0	447.0	447.0	444.0	441.5	441.5	441.5	441.5
Mineral Range	71.8	71.8	71.8	68.3	68.3	66.3	66.3	66.3	76.2	76.2
Hancock & Calumet	34.3	34.3	34.3	34.3	34.3	34.3	34.3	31.9	31.9	31.9
Mohawk Mining Co.	17.0	17.0	17.0	17.0	17.0	17.0	17.0	0.0		
Esc. & Lk. Superior	124.2	124.2	124.2	124.2	124.2	142.0	143.2	146.0	146.0	146.0
Garden Bay						13.7	13.7			

Hermansville & Western	5.4	5.4	5.4	5.4	5.4	5.4	5.4	5.4	5.4	5.4
Keweenaw Cent.	34.4	34.4	34.4	34.4	34.4	34.4	34.4	34.4	0.0	
Lk. Superior & Ish.	30.3	30.3	43.8	43.8	43.8	41.6	41.6	41.6	41.6	
Manistique & Lk. Superior	56.6	60.3	60.3	60.3	60.3	60.3	60.3	60.3	54.3	54.3
Marq. & Southeastern	50.5									
Munising, Marq. & Southeastern		138.0	138.0	138.0	138.9	138.9	138.9	138.9	138.9	138.9
Mpls., St. Paul & S. S. Marie	238.1	237.8	237.8	237.8	237.8	236.3	236.3	236.3	236.3	236.3
Sainte Marie Union Depot	0.5	0.5	0.5	0.5	0.5	0.5	0.5	0.5	0.5	0.5
Sault Ste. Marie Bridge	0.5	0.5	0.5	0.5	0.5	0.5	0.5	0.5	0.5	0.5
Wisconsin Cent.	0.2	0.2	0.2	0.2	0.2	0.2	0.2	0.2	0.2	0.2
Gogebic & Montreal Riv.	19.9	19.9	19.9	19.9	19.9	19.9	19.9	19.9	19.9	19.9
Munising Ry	50.5									
Wisconsin & Mich.	56.4	56.4	56.4	56.4	55.3	55.3	55.3	55.3	37.8	32.0
U. P. YEAR TOTAL	2141.7	2184.0	2200.9	2190.5	2205.9	2215.9	2211.0	2214.9	2173.0	2120.1
U. P. YEAR CHANGE	−38.1	42.3	16.9	−10.4	15.4	10.0	−4.9	3.9	−41.9	−52.9
MICH. YEAR TOTAL	8740.4	8789.0	8716.0	8763.9	8804.0	8762.5	8668.1	8659.5	8657.9	8594.3
MICH. YEAR CHANGE	10.7	48.6	−73.0	47.9	40.1	−41.5	−94.4	−8.6	−1.6	−63.6
COMMR. YEAR TOTAL	9021.0	8943.0	8921.0	8998.0	8934.0	8862.0	8885.0	8925.0	8888.0	8770.0
COMMR. YEAR CHANGE	−38.0	−78.0	−22.0	77.0	−64.0	−72.0	23.0	40.0	−37.0	−118.0
STUDY LESS COMMR.	−280.6	−154.0	−205.0	−234.1	−130.0	−99.5	−216.9	−265.5	−230.1	−175.7

Michigan Electric Lines Mileage, 1910–1919

	1910	1911	1912	1913	1914	1915	1916	1917	1918	1919
Benton Hbr.–St. Joe Ry. & L.	27.5	37.5	37.5	37.5	37.5	37.5	37.5	37.5	37.5	37.5
Det. United Ry	134.4	134.4	134.4	134.4	134.4	134.4	134.4	134.4	134.4	134.4
Det., Almont & Noerthern					9.3	16.9	16.9	16.9	16.9	19.5
Det. & Pt. Hur. Shore L.										
Det. & Lk. St. Clair	14.2	14.2	14.2	14.2	14.2	14.2	14.2	14.2	14.2	14.2
Det., Mt. Clem. & Mar. Cy.	34.6	34.6	34.6	34.6	34.6	34.6	34.6	34.6	34.6	34.6
Pt. Huron, St. Clair & M. C.	27.3	27.3	27.3	27.3	27.3	27.3	27.3	27.3	27.3	27.3
Rapid Ry.	15.5	15.5	15.5	15.5	15.5	15.5	15.5	15.5	15.5	15.5
Det., Jackson & Chi.	94.6	94.6	94.6	94.6	94.6	94.6	94.6	94.6	94.6	94.6
Det., Monroe & Tol. Sh. L.	45.6	45.6	45.6	45.6	45.6	45.6	45.6	45.6	45.6	45.6
Esc. Traction	5.8	11.6	11.6	11.6	11.6	11.6	11.6	11.6	11.6	11.6
Gogebic & Iron Counties	8.0									
Gr. Rpds., Gr. Hav., & Musk.	41.0	41.0	41.0	41.0	41.0	41.0	41.0	41.0	41.0	41.0
Gr. Rpds., Holland & Chi.	42.3	42.3	42.3	42.9	42.9	42.9				
Hough. Co. Traction	28.0	28.0	28.0	28.0	28.0	28.0	28.0	28.0	28.0	28.0
Iron Riv., Stam. & Cr. Falls				3.9	3.9	3.9	3.9	3.9	3.9	3.9
Ironwood & Bessemer		8.0	8.0	8.0	8.0	8.0	8.0	8.0	8.0	8.0
Marq. County Electric								3.6	3.6	3.6
Marq. Co. Gas & Electric	3.6	3.6	3.6	3.6	3.6	3.6	3.6			
Mich. & Chi.				38.6						
Mich. RR										135.4
Gr. Rpds., Holland & Chi.										42.9
Sag.–Bay Cty.										8.6
Mich. Ry					81.1	133.9	133.9	133.9	135.4	
Gr. Rpds., Holland & Chi.							42.9	42.9	42.9	
Mich. United Rys							156.0	156.0	156.0	156.0

Sag.–Bay Cty.					8.6	8.6	8.6	8.6	8.6	
Mich. United Rys	131.6	131.6								
Lans. & Northeastern		29.5								
Mich. United Traction			131.6	131.6	131.6	161.1				
Lans. & Northeastern			29.5	29.5	29.5					
Mich. United Rys			46.5	46.5	46.5					
Sag.–Bay Cty.	8.6	8.6	8.6	8.6						
Sag. & Flint	31.7	31.7	31.7	31.7						
Southern Mich. Ry.	27.3	27.3	27.3	27.3	27.3	27.3	27.3	27.3	27.3	27.3
Toledo & Western	23.4	23.4	23.4	23.4	23.4	23.4	23.4	23.4	23.4	23.4
Toledo, Ottawa Beach & No.	7.2	7.2	7.2	7.2	7.2	7.2	7.2	7.2	7.2	7.2
MICH. YEAR TOTAL	752.2	797.5	844.0	887.1	907.2	921.1	916.0	916.0	917.5	920.1
MICH. YEAR CHANGE	14.6	45.3	46.5	43.1	20.1	13.9	−5.1	0.0	1.5	2.6

Railroad Mileage, 1920–1929

LOWER PENINSULA

	1920	1921	1922	1923	1924	1925	1926	1927	1928	1929
A.A.	288.0	288.0	288.0	288.0	288.0	288.0	288.0	288.0	288.0	288.0
Arcadia & Betsey Riv.	17.8	17.8	17.8	17.8	17.8	17.8	17.8	17.8	17.8	17.8
Boyne Cty., Gaylord & Alpena	92.8	92.8	92.8	92.8	92.8	92.8	92.8	92.8	92.8	92.8
Can. National										
Gr. Trunk Western									790.8	791.6
Chi., Kal. & Sag.									9.5	9.5
Cinci., Sag. & Mack.									57.3	57.3
Musk. Ry & Nav.									5.5	5.5
St. Clair Tunnel									1.1	1.1
Chesapeake & Ohio										
Pere Marq. Ry										1645.0
Flint Belt										8.2
Gr. Rpds., Kalkaska & SE										19.2
Huron & Western										11.3
Chi., Kal. & Sag.	44.2	44.2	44.2	44.2	44.2	44.2	44.2	44.2	44.2	44.2
Cleve., Cinci., Chi. & St. Louis	33.4	33.4	33.4	33.4	33.4	33.4	33.4	33.4	33.4	33.4
Cincinnati Northern	39.9	39.9	39.9	39.9	39.9	39.9	39.9	39.9	39.9	39.9
Det. & Mackinac	386.7	386.7	386.7	376.6	377.4	384.1	382.7	321.6	306.2	282.5
Erie & Mich. Ry & Nav.	4.7	4.7	4.7	4.7	4.7	4.7	4.7	4.7	4.7	4.7
Det. & Toledo Shore Line	43.8	43.8	43.8	43.8	43.8	43.8	43.8	43.8	43.8	43.8
Det., Bay Cty. & Western	97.9	97.9	97.9	97.9	97.9					
Det., Caro & Sandusky						97.9	48.5	48.5	48.5	48.5
Det. Terminal	18.0	18.0	18.0	18.0	18.0	18.0	18.0	18.0	18.0	18.0
Det., Toledo & Ironton	64.8	64.8	64.8	64.8	64.8	64.8	90.6	90.6	90.6	90.2
Det. & Ironton				13.6	15.3	15.3	15.3	15.3	15.3	15.3
Toledo–Det.	19.7	19.7	19.7	19.7	19.7	19.7	19.7	19.7	19.7	19.7
Det., Toledo & Milw.	90.4	90.4	90.4	90.4	90.4	90.4	90.4			
Det. Union RR Depot & Sta.	3.2	3.2	3.2	3.2	3.2	3.2	3.2	3.2	3.2	3.2
E. Jordan & Southern	18.6	18.6	18.6	18.6	18.6	18.6	18.6	18.6	18.6	18.6
Empire & S. Eastern	11.2	11.2	11.2	0.0						
Fort St. Union Depot	1.2	1.2	1.2	1.2	1.2	1.2	1.2	1.2	1.2	1.2
Gr. Trunk Ry–Can.										
Bay Cty. Terminal	1.2	1.2	1.2	1.2	1.2	1.2	1.2	1.2		
Chi. & Kal. Terminal	11.3	11.3	11.3	11.3	11.3	11.3	11.3	11.3		
Chi., Det. & Can. Gr. Trunk Jct.	55.6	55.6	55.6	55.6	55.6	55.6	55.6	55.6		

Chi., Kal. & Sag.	9.5	9.5	9.5	9.5	9.5	9.5	9.5	9.5		
Cinci, Sag. & Mack.	58.9	58.9	58.9	58.9	58.9	58.9	58.9	58.9		
Det. & Huron	18.3	18.3	18.3	18.3	18.3	18.3	18.3	18.3		
Det., Gr. Hav. & Milw.	188.3	188.3	188.3	188.3	188.3	188.3	188.3	188.3		
Gr. Rpds. Terminal	1.5	1.5	1.5	1.5	1.5	1.5	1.5	1.5		
Gr. Trunk Western	213.7	213.7	213.7	213.7	213.7	213.7	213.7	213.7		
Mich. Air Line Ry	105.9	105.9	105.9	105.9	105.9	105.9	105.9	105.9		
Musk. Ry. & Nav.							5.5	5.5		
Pontiac, Oxford & Northern	99.7	99.7	99.7	99.7	99.7	99.7	99.7	99.7		
St. Clair Tunnel	1.1	1.1	1.1	1.1	1.1	1.1	1.1	1.1		
Tol., Sag. & Musk.	96.0	96.0	96.0	96.0	96.0	96.0	96.0	96.0		
Kal., Lk. Sh. & Chi.	16.0	16.0	16.0	16.0	0.0					
Lud. & Northern	3.4	3.4	3.4	3.4	3.4	3.4	3.4	3.4	3.4	3.4
Manistee & Northeastern	178.2	161.4	161.4	161.4	161.4	86.7	86.7	86.7	86.7	86.7
Leelanau Transit	23.8	23.8	23.8	23.8	23.8	23.8	23.8	23.8	23.8	23.8
Mich. Cent.	1190.6	1184.3	1184.3	1176.4	1164.2	1137.6	1131.9	1107.6	1106.8	1082.2
Battle Creek & Sturgis	34.4	34.4	34.4	34.4	34.4	34.4	34.4	34.4	34.4	34.4
Can. Southern										
Can. So. Bridge	3.1	3.1	3.1	3.1	3.1	3.1	3.1	3.1	3.1	0.0
Det. Riv. Tunnel	1.4	1.4	1.4	1.4	1.4	1.4	1.4	1.4	1.4	1.4
St. Clair & Western	14.0	14.0	14.0	14.0	14.0	14.0	14.0	14.0	14.0	14.0
New York Cent.–part	1.6	1.6	1.6	1.6	1.6	1.6	1.6	1.6	1.6	1.6
St. Joseph, S. Bend & So.	25.3	25.3	25.3	25.3	25.3	25.3	25.3	25.3	25.3	25.3
Mich. E. & W.	72.7	0.0								
Musk. Ry. & Nav.			5.5	5.5	5.5					
New York Cent.	352.8	352.8	352.8	352.8	352.8	352.8	352.8	352.8	352.8	352.8
Det., Hillsdale & SW	65.2	65.2	65.2	65.2	65.2	65.2	65.2	65.2	65.2	65.2
Erie & Kal.	14.2	14.2	14.2	14.2	14.2	14.2	14.2	14.2	14.2	14.2
Ft. Wyn. & Jackson	44.3	44.3	44.3	44.3	44.3	44.3	44.3	44.3	44.3	44.3
Kal., Allegan & Gr. Rpds.	58.5	58.5	58.5	58.5	58.5	58.5	58.5	58.5	58.5	58.5
Pennsylvania			20.7	20.7	20.7	20.7	20.7	20.7	20.7	20.7
Gr. Rpds. & Ind.	423.5	423.5	423.5	423.5	423.5	423.5	423.5	420.5	419.5	419.5
Pere Marq. Ry	1717.2	1717.2	1717.2	1717.2	1717.2	1717.2	1717.2	1717.2	1717.2	
Flint Belt				8.2	8.2	8.2	8.2	8.2	8.2	
Gr. Rpds., Kalkaska & SE	19.2	19.2	19.2	19.2	19.2	19.2	19.2	19.2	19.2	
Huron & Western	11.3	11.3	11.3	11.3	11.3	11.3	11.3	11.3	11.3	
Pt. Hur. & Det.	15.7	15.7	15.7	18.5	18.5	18.5	18.5	18.5	18.5	18.5
Pt. Hur. Southern	2.8	2.8	2.8							
Wabash	78.3	78.3	78.3	78.3	78.3	78.3	78.3	78.3	78.3	78.3
L. P. YEAR TOTAL	6504.8	6409.0	6429.7	6427.8	6402.1	6307.5	6276.8	6098.0	6078.5	5955.3
L. P. YEAR CHANGE	30.6	−95.8	20.7	−1.9	−25.7	−94.6	−30.7	−178.8	−19.5	−123.2

UPPER PENINSULA

	1920	1921	1922	1923	1924	1925	1926	1927	1928	1929
Blaney & Southern	7.2	7.2	7.2	7.2	7.2	0.0				
Chi. & N. Western	554.8	554.8	547.6	550.7	549.9	561.3	567.3	567.0	567.0	574.4
Esc., Iron Mtn. & W..	50.5	50.5	50.5	50.5	50.5	50.5	50.5	50.5	50.5	50.5
Chi., Milw. & St. Paul	219.3	219.3	218.5	218.5	218.5	216.7	216.3	215.3		
Chi., Milw., St. Paul & Pac.									214.1	214.1
Copper Range	104.9	104.9	104.9	104.9	104.9	104.9	104.9	104.9	104.2	104.2
Duluth, So. Shore & Atlantic	439.0	439.5	436.0	436.0	436.0	436.0	438.5	437.5	426.4	429.2
Mineral Range	75.0	75.0	65.6	55.7	55.7	55.7	55.7	55.7	46.5	46.5
Hancock & Calumet	29.9	29.9	29.9	29.9	29.9	29.9	29.9	19.5	19.5	19.5
Esc. & Lk. Superior	143.9	143.9	143.9	143.9	143.9	67.0	67.0	67.0	67.0	67.0

Hermansville & Western	5.4	5.4	5.4	5.4	5.4	0.0				
Lk. Superior & Ish.	41.6	41.6	41.6	41.6	180.0	180.0	180.0	180.0	176.3	176.3
Manistique & Lk. Superior	51.8	51.8	51.8	51.8	51.8	48.3	48.3	48.3	48.3	48.3
Munising, Marq. & Southeastern	138.9	138.9	138.9	138.9						
Mpls., St. Paul & S. S. Marie	236.3	236.3	236.3	236.3	236.3	236.3	236.3	236.3	236.3	236.3
Sainte Marie Union Depot	0.5	0.5	0.5	0.5	0.5	0.5	0.5	0.5	0.5	0.5
Sault Ste. Marie Bridge	0.5	0.5	0.5	0.5	0.5	0.5	0.5	0.5	0.5	0.5
Wisconsin Cent.	0.2	0.2	0.2	0.2	0.2	0.0	0.0	0.0	0.0	0.0
Gogebic & Montreal Riv.	19.9	19.9	19.9	19.9	19.9	12.4	12.0	12.0	12.0	12.0
Wisconsin & Mich.	44.0	44.0	44.0	44.0	44.0	44.0	44.0	44.0	44.0	44.0
U. P. YEAR TOTAL	2163.6	2164.1	2143.2	2136.4	2135.1	2044.0	2051.7	2039.0	2013.1	2023.3
U. P. YEAR CHANGE	43.5	0.5	−20.9	−6.8	−1.3	−91.1	7.7	−12.7	−25.9	10.2
MICH. YEAR TOTAL	8668.4	8573.1	8572.9	8564.2	8537.2	8351.5	8328.5	8137.0	8091.6	7978.6
MICH. YEAR CHANGE	74.1	−95.3	−0.2	−8.7	−27.0	−185.7	−23.0	−191.5	−45.4	−113.0
COMMR. YEAR TOTAL	8734.0	8601.0	8549.0	8544.0	8500.0	8349.0	8356.0	8261.0	8209.0	8155.0
COMMR. YEAR CHANGE	−36.0	−133.0	−52.0	−5.0	−44.0	−151.0	7.0	−95.0	−52.0	−54.0
STUDY LESS COMMR.	−65.6	−27.9	23.9	20.2	37.2	2.5	−27.5	−124.0	−117.4	−176.4

Michigan Electric Lines Mileage, 1920–1929

	1920	1921	1922	1923	1924	1925	1926	1927	1928	1929
Benton Hbr.–St. Joe Ry. & L.	37.5	37.5	37.5	37.5	37.5	37.5	37.5	37.5	0.0	
Det. United Ry	134.4	134.4	124.3	124.3	124.3	124.3	119.2	109.9	0.0	
Det., Almont & Northern	19.5	24.4	24.4	24.4	24.4	24.4	24.4	7.5	6.4	6.4
Det. & Pt. Hur. Shore L.										
Det. & Lk. St. Clair	14.2	14.2	14.2	14.2	14.2	14.2	14.2	14.2		
Det., Mt. Clem. & Mar. Cy.	34.6	34.6	34.6	34.6	34.6	34.6	34.6	34.6		
Pt. Huron, St. Clair & M. C.	27.3	27.3	27.3	27.3	27.3	27.3	27.3	27.3		
Rapid Ry.	15.5	15.5	12.2	12.2	12.2	12.2	12.2	12.2		
Det., Jackson & Chi.	94.6	94.6	94.6	94.6	94.6	84.5	84.5	70.0		
Det., Monroe & Tol. Sh. L.	45.6	45.6	45.6	45.6	45.6	45.6	45.6	45.6		
Eastern Mich.									96.1	96.1
Det. & Pt. Hur. Shore L.										
Det. & Lk. St. Clair									14.2	0.0
Det., Mt. Clem. & Mar. Cy.									34.6	0.0
Pt. Huron, St. Clair & M. C.									27.3	27.3
Rapid Ry.									11.1	11.1
Eastern Mich.–Toledo									45.6	45.6
Esc. Traction	11.6	11.6	11.6	11.6	11.6	11.6	11.6	11.6	11.6	11.6
Gr. Rpds., Gr. Hav., & Musk.	41.0	41.0	41.0	41.0	41.0	41.0	41.0	41.0	0.0	
Gr. Rpds., Holland & Chi.					42.9	42.9	5.9	0.0		
Hough. Co. Traction	28.0	28.0	28.0	28.0	28.0	28.0	28.0	28.0	28.0	28.0
Iron Riv., Stam. & Cr. Fa.	3.9	0.0								
Ironwood & Bessemer	8.0	8.0								
Lk. Superior Dist. Power			8.0	8.0	8.0	8.0	8.0	8.0	8.0	8.0
Marq. Co. Electric	3.6	3.6	3.6	3.6	3.6	3.6	3.6	0.0		
Mich. Electric			156.0	153.8	153.8	153.8	146.4	84.9		
Mich. Electric Shares										13.2
Mich. RR	135.4	135.4	130.3	130.3	130.3	130.3	130.3	130.3	53.3	
Gr. Rpds., Holland & Chi.	42.9	42.9	42.9	42.9						

Sag.–Bay Cty.	8.6	8.6	8.6	0.0						
Mich. Ry										
Mich. United Rys	156.0									
Mich. United Rys		156.0	156.0							
Southern Mich. Ry.	27.3	27.3	27.3	27.3	27.3	27.3	27.3	27.3	27.3	27.3
Toledo & Western	23.4	23.4	23.4	23.4	23.2	23.2	23.2	23.2	23.2	23.2
Toledo, Ottawa Beach & No.	7.2	7.2	7.2	7.2	7.2	7.2	7.2	0.0		
United Suburban								5.9	5.9	5.9
MICH. YEAR TOTAL	920.1	921.1	902.6	894.0	891.6	881.5	839.4	780.5	477.5	303.7
MICH. YEAR CHANGE	0.0	1.0	–18.5	–8.6	–2.4	–10.1	–42.1	–58.9	–303.0	–173.8

Railroad Mileage, 1930–1939

LOWER PENINSULA

	1930	1931	1932	1933	1934	1935	1936	1937	1938	1939
A.A.	288.0	288.0	288.0	288.0	288.0	288.0	288.0	288.0	288.0	288.0
Arcadia & Betsey Riv.	17.8	17.8	17.8	17.8	17.8	17.8				
Boyne Cty.							7.2	7.2	7.2	7.2	7.2
Boyne Cty., Gaylord & Alpena	92.8	92.8	92.8	92.8	92.8					
Canadian National										
Gr. Trunk Western	791.3	791.0	791.0	791.0	791.0	791.0	791.0	791.0	791.0	791.0
Chi., Kal. & Sag.	9.5	9.5	9.5	9.5	9.5	9.5	9.5	9.5	9.5	9.5
Cinci., Sag. & Mack.	54.5	54.5	54.5	54.5	54.5	54.5	54.5	54.5	54.5	54.5
Musk. Ry & Nav.	5.5	5.5	5.5	5.5	5.5	5.5	5.5	5.5	5.5	5.5
St. Clair Tunnel	1.1	1.1	1.1	1.1	1.1	1.1	1.1	1.1	1.1	1.1
Chesapeake & Ohio										
Pere Marq. Ry	1645.0	1645.0	1645.0	1625.0	1588.6	1582.0	1582.0	1582.0	1582.0	1582.0
Flint Belt	8.2	8.2	8.2	8.2	8.2	8.2	8.2	8.2	8.2	8.2
Huron & Western	11.3	11.3	11.3	11.3	11.3	11.3	11.3	11.3	11.3	11.3
Manistee & Northeastern	86.4	86.4	86.4	86.4	46.9	46.9	46.9	46.9	46.9	46.9
Leelanau Transit	23.8	23.8	23.8	23.8	23.8	23.8	23.8	23.8	23.8	23.8
Det. & Mackinac	241.3	241.3	241.3	241.3	241.3	241.3	241.3	241.3	241.3	241.3
Erie & Mich. Ry & Nav.	4.7	4.7	4.7	4.7	4.7	4.7	4.7	4.7	4.7	4.7
Det. & Toledo Shore Line	43.8	43.8	43.8	43.8	43.8	43.8	43.8	43.8	43.8	43.8
Det., Caro & Sandusky	48.5	48.5	48.5	48.5	48.5	48.5	48.5	42.1	42.1	42.1
Det. Terminal	18.0	18.0	18.0	18.0	18.0	18.0	18.0	18.0	18.0	18.0
Det., Toledo & Ironton	85.9	113.8	113.8	113.8	113.8	113.8	113.8	113.8	113.8	113.8
Det. & Ironton	15.3									
Toledo–Det.	12.6									
Det. Union RR Depot & Sta.	3.2	3.2	3.2	3.2	3.2	3.2	3.2	3.2	3.2	3.2
E. Jordan & Southern	18.6	18.6	18.6	18.6	18.6	18.6	18.6	18.6	18.6	18.6
Fort St. Union Depot	1.2	1.2	1.2	1.2	1.2	1.2	1.2	1.2	1.2	1.2
Lud. & Northern	3.4	3.4	3.4	3.4	3.4	3.4	3.4	3.4	3.4	3.4
New York Cent.	352.8	352.8	352.8	352.8	352.8	346.1	346.1	346.1	346.1	346.1
Chi., Kal. & Sag.	57.4	57.4	57.4	57.4	57.4	57.4	57.4	30.9	30.9	30.9
Clev., Cinci., Chi., & St. L.	33.4	33.4	33.4	33.4	33.4	33.4	33.4	33.4	73.3	73.3
Cinci. N.ern	39.9	39.9	39.9	39.9	39.9	39.9	39.9	39.9		
Det., Hillsdale & SW	65.2	65.2	65.2	65.2	65.2	65.2	65.2	65.2	65.2	65.2
Det., Toledo & Milw.	90.4	90.4	1.6	1.6	1.6	1.6	1.6			
Erie & Kal.	14.2	14.2	14.2	14.2	14.2	14.2	14.2	14.2	14.2	14.2
Ft. Wyn. & Jackson	44.3	44.3	44.3	44.3	44.3	44.3	44.3	44.3	44.3	44.3
Kal., Allegan & Gr. Rpds.	58.5	58.5	58.5	58.5	58.5	58.5	58.5	58.5	58.5	58.5
Mich. Cent.	1076.8	1063.0	1063.0	1024.2	1024.2	1020.2	1020.2	1007.3	1007.3	1007.3
Battle Creek & Sturgis	34.4	34.4	34.4	34.4	34.4	0.0				

Can. Southern										
Det. Riv. Tunnel	1.4	1.4	1.4	1.4	1.4	1.4	1.4	1.4	1.4	1.4
St. Clair & Western	14.0	14.0	0.0							
New York Cent.–part	1.6	1.6	1.6	1.6	1.6	1.6	1.6	1.6	1.6	1.6
St. Joseph, S. Bend & So.	25.3	25.3	25.3	25.3	25.3	25.3	25.3	25.3	25.3	25.3
Ohio & Morenci				2.4	2.4	2.4	2.4	2.4	2.4	2.4
Blissfield						19.6	0.0			
Pennsylvania	20.7	20.7	20.7	20.7	20.7	20.7	20.7	20.7	20.7	20.7
Gr. Rpds. & Ind.	413.3	413.3	413.3	413.3	413.3	413.3	413.3	413.3	403.0	403.0
Pt. Hur. & Det.	18.5	18.5	18.5	18.5	18.5	18.5	18.5	18.5	18.5	18.5
Wabash	78.3	78.3	78.3	78.3	78.3	78.3	78.3	78.3	78.3	78.3
L. P. YEAR TOTAL	5972.1	5958.0	5855.2	5798.8	5722.9	5605.2	5567.8	5520.4	5510.1	5510.1
L. P. YEAR CHANGE	16.8	−14.1	−102.8	−56.4	−75.9	−117.7	−37.4	−47.4	−10.3	0.0

UPPER PENINSULA

	1930	1931	1932	1933	1934	1935	1936	1937	1938	1939
Chi. & N. Western	568.6	559.6	559.6	540.5	540.5	540.5	537.8	521.9	521.9	520.1
Esc., Iron Mtn., & W.	50.5	50.5	50.5	50.5	50.5	50.5	50.5	50.5	50.5	50.5
Chi., Milw., St. Paul & Pac.	214.1	214.1	214.1	200.7	200.7	193.6	193.6	192.4	192.4	192.4
Copper Range	103.0	103.0	103.0	103.0	103.0	103.0	103.0	103.0	103.0	99.4
Duluth, So. Shore & Atlantic	413.3	413.3	414.2	414.2	414.2	414.2	414.2	415.6	415.6	415.6
Mineral Range	46.5	44.6	44.6	44.6	44.6	54.7	43.5	43.5	43.5	43.5
Hancock & Calumet	10.1	10.1	10.1	10.1	10.1	0.0				
Esc. & Lk. Superior	67.0	67.0	67.0	67.0	67.0	67.0	67.0	67.0	67.0	67.0
Lk. Superior & Ish.	176.3	176.3	176.3	176.3	176.3	176.3	176.3	176.3	176.3	176.3
Manistique & Lk. Superior	38.3	38.3	38.3	38.3	38.3	38.3	38.3	38.3	38.3	38.3
Mpls., St. Paul & S. S. Marie	233.9	233.9	233.9	233.9	233.9	233.9	233.9	233.9	233.9	233.9
Sainte Marie Union Depot	0.5	0.5	0.5	0.5	0.5	0.5	0.5	0.5	0.5	0.5
Sault Ste. Marie Bridge	0.5	0.5	0.5	0.5	0.5	0.5	0.5	0.5	0.5	0.5
Wisconsin Cent.	0.0	0.0	0.0	0.0	0.0	0.0	0.0	0.0	0.0	0.0
Gogebic & Montreal Riv.	12.0	12.0	12.0	12.0	12.0	12.0	12.0	12.0	12.0	12.0
Wisconsin & Mich.	44.0	44.0	44.0	44.0	44.0	44.0	44.0	44.0	44.0	0.0
U. P. YEAR TOTAL	1978.6	1967.7	1968.6	1936.1	1936.1	1929.0	1915.1	1899.4	1899.4	1850.0
U. P. YEAR CHANGE	−44.7	−10.9	0.9	−32.5	0.0	−7.1	−13.9	−15.7	0.0	−49.4
MICH. YEAR TOTAL	7950.7	7925.7	7823.8	7734.9	7659.0	7534.2	7482.9	7419.8	7409.5	7360.1
MICH. YEAR CHANGE	−27.9	−25.0	−101.9	−88.9	−75.9	−124.8	−51.3	−63.1	−10.3	−49.4
COMMR. YEAR TOTAL	8072.0	8020.0	7832.0	7726.0	7647.0	7498.0	7444.0	7438.0	7352.0	7338.0
COMMR. YEAR CHANGE	−83.0	−52.0	−188.0	−106.0	−79.0	−149.0	−54.0	−6.0	−86.0	−14.0
STUDY LESS COMMR.	−121.3	−94.3	−8.2	8.9	12.0	36.2	38.9	−18.2	57.5	22.1

Michigan Electric Lines Mileage, 1930–1939

	1930	1931	1932	1933	1934	1935	1936	1937	1938	1939
Eastern Mich.	96.1	6.4	6.4	6.4	0.0					
Eastern Mich.–Toledo	45.6	45.6	0.0							
Esc. Traction	11.6	11.6	0.0							
Hough. Co. Traction	28.0	28.0	0.0							
Ironwood & Bessemer	8.0	8.0	0.0							
Southern Mich. Ry.	27.3	27.3	27.3	27.3	0.0					

Toledo & Western	23.2	23.2	23.2	18.7	18.7	0.0				
United Suburban	5.9	5.9								
MICH. YEAR TOTAL	245.7	156.0	56.9	52.4	18.7	0.0	0.0	0.0	0.0	0.0
MICH. YEAR CHANGE	−58.0	−89.7	−99.1	−4.5	−33.7	−18.7	0.0	0.0	0.0	0.0

Railroad Mileage, 1940–1949

LOWER PENINSULA

	1940	1941	1942	1943	1944	1945	1946	1947	1948	1949
A.A.	288.0	288.0	288.0	288.0	288.0	288.0	288.0	288.0	288.0	288.0
Boyne Cty.	7.2	7.2	7.2	7.2	7.2	7.2	7.2	7.2	7.2	7.2
Canadian National										
Gr. Trunk Western	791.0	789.8	789.8	844.8	844.8	790.1	790.1	790.1	788.6	788.6
Chi., Kal. & Sag.	9.5	9.5	9.5	9.5	9.5	9.5	9.5	9.5	9.5	9.5
Cinci., Sag. & Mack.	54.5	54.5	54.5							
Musk. Ry & Nav.	5.5	5.5	5.5	5.5	5.5	5.5	5.5	5.5	5.5	5.5
St. Clair Tunnel	1.1	1.1	1.1	1.1	1.1	1.1	1.1	1.1	1.1	1.1
Chesapeake & Ohio								1435.1	1435.1	1435.1
Pere Marq. Ry	1582.0	1582.0	1536.9	1465.9	1452.9	1435.1	1435.1			
Flint Belt	8.2	8.2	8.2	8.2	8.2	8.2	8.2	8.2	8.2	8.2
Huron & Western	11.3									
Manistee & Northeastern	46.9	46.9	46.9	46.9	35.6	35.6	35.6	35.6	35.6	35.6
Leelanau Transit	23.8	23.8	23.8	23.8	23.8	23.8	23.8	23.8	23.8	23.8
Det. & Mackinac	241.3	241.3	241.3	229.5	229.5	229.5	229.5	229.5	229.5	229.5
Erie & Mich. Ry & Nav.	4.7	4.7	4.7	4.7	4.7	4.7	4.7	4.7	4.7	4.7
Det. & Toledo Shore Line	43.8	43.8	43.8	43.8	43.8	43.8	43.8	43.8	43.8	43.8
Det., Caro & Sandusky	42.1	42.1	42.1	42.1	42.1	42.1	42.1	42.1	31.1	31.1
Det. Terminal	18.0	18.0	18.0	18.0	18.0	18.0	18.0	18.0	18.0	18.0
Det., Toledo & Ironton	113.8	113.8	113.8	113.8	113.8	113.8	113.8	113.8	113.8	113.8
Det. Union RR Depot & Sta.	3.2	3.2	3.2	3.2	3.2	3.2	3.2	3.2	3.2	3.2
E. Jordan & Southern	18.6	18.6	18.6	18.6	18.6	18.6	18.6	18.6	18.6	18.6
Fort St. Union Depot	1.2	1.2	1.2	1.2	1.2	1.2	1.2	1.2	1.2	1.2
Lud. & Northern	3.4	3.4	3.4	3.4	3.4	3.4	3.4	3.4	3.4	3.4
New York Cent.	346.1	316.1	316.1	301.1	301.1	301.1	301.1	301.1	301.1	301.1
Chi., Kal. & Sag.	30.9	30.9	22.4	22.4	22.4	22.4	22.4	22.4	22.4	22.4
Clev., Cinci., Chi., & St. L.	73.3	73.3	66.3	66.3	66.3	66.3	66.3	66.3	66.3	66.3
Det., Hillsdale & SW	65.2	65.2	65.2	65.2	65.2	65.2	65.2	65.2	65.2	65.2
Erie & Kal.	14.2	14.2	14.2	14.2	14.2	14.2	14.2	14.2	14.2	14.2
Ft. Wyn. & Jackson	43.6	43.6	43.6	43.6	43.6	43.6	43.6	43.6	43.6	43.6
Kal., Allegan & Gr. Rpds.	58.5	58.5	58.5	58.5	58.5	58.5	58.5	58.5	58.5	58.5
Mich. Cent.	1003.3	1003.3	997.7	965.6	965.6	965.6	965.6	965.6	965.6	965.6
Can. Southern										
Det. Riv. Tunnel	1.4	1.4	1.4	1.4	1.4	1.4	1.4	1.4	1.4	1.4
New York Cent.–part	1.6	1.6	1.6	1.6	1.6	1.6	1.6	1.6	1.6	1.6
St. Joseph, S. Bend & So.	25.3	25.3	25.3	11.4	11.4	11.4	11.4	11.4	11.4	11.4
Ohio & Morenci	2.4	2.4	2.4	2.4	2.4	2.4	2.4	2.4	2.4	2.4
Blissfield										
Pennsylvania	20.7	20.7	20.7	20.7	20.7	20.7	20.7	20.7	20.7	20.7
Gr. Rpds. & Ind.	403.0	403.0	403.0	403.0	403.0	403.0	403.0	403.0	403.0	403.0
Pt. Hur. & Det.	18.5	18.5	18.5	18.5	18.5	18.5	18.5	18.5	18.5	18.5
Wabash	78.3	78.3	78.3	78.3	78.3	78.3	78.3	78.3	78.3	78.3
L. P. YEAR TOTAL	5505.4	5462.9	5396.7	5253.4	5229.1	5156.6	5156.6	5156.6	5144.1	5144.1
L. P. YEAR CHANGE	−4.7	−42.5	−66.2	−143.3	−24.3	−72.5	0.0	0.0	−12.5	0.0

UPPER PENINSULA

	1940	1941	1942	1943	1944	1945	1946	1947	1948	1949
Chi. & N. Western	517.9	486.4	486.4	485.1	460.7	444.0	444.0	494.5	494.2	494.2
Esc., Iron Mtn. & W.	50.5	50.5	50.5	50.5	50.5	50.5	50.5			
Chi., Milw., St. Paul & Pac.	192.4	192.4	192.4	192.4	192.4	190.9	190.3	187.8	187.8	187.8
Copper Range	99.4	99.4	99.4	99.4	99.4	99.4	99.4	99.4	99.4	99.4
Duluth, So. Shore & Atlantic	414.5	414.5	414.5	414.5	414.5	414.5	414.5	414.5	414.5	414.5
Mineral Range	43.5	27.6	27.6	27.6	27.6	26.0	26.0	26.0	26.0	0.0
Esc. & Lk. Superior	67.0	67.0	67.0	67.0	67.0	67.0	67.0	67.0	67.0	67.0
Lk. Superior & Ish.	176.3	176.3	168.6	170.5	170.5	170.5	170.5	171.2	164.2	168.5
Manistique & Lk. Superior	38.3	38.3	38.3	38.3	38.3	38.3	38.3	38.3	38.3	38.3
Mpls., St. Paul & S. S. Marie	222.7	225.0	225.0	225.0	225.0	225.0	225.0	225.0	225.0	225.0
Sainte Marie Union Depot	0.5	0.5	0.5	0.5	0.5	0.5	0.5	0.5	0.5	0.5
Sault Ste. Marie Bridge	0.5	0.5	0.5	0.5	0.5	0.5	0.5	0.5	0.5	0.5
Wisconsin Cent.	0.0	0.0	0.0	0.0	0.0	0.0	0.0	0.0	0.0	0.0
Gogebic & Montreal Riv.	12.0	12.0	12.0	12.0	12.0	12.0	12.0	12.0	12.0	12.0
U. P. YEAR TOTAL	1835.5	1790.4	1782.7	1783.3	1758.9	1739.1	1738.5	1736.7	1729.4	1707.7
U. P. YEAR CHANGE	−14.5	−45.1	−7.7	0.6	−24.4	−19.8	−0.6	−1.8	−7.3	−21.7
MICH. YEAR TOTAL	7340.9	7253.3	7179.4	7036.7	6988.0	6895.7	6895.1	6893.3	6873.5	6851.8
MICH. YEAR CHANGE	−19.2	−87.6	−73.9	−142.7	−48.7	−92.3	−0.6	−1.8	−19.8	−21.7
COMMR. YEAR TOTAL	7303.0	7256.0	7455.0	7653.0	6984.0	6954.0	6899.0	6900.0	6808.0	6807.0
COMMR. YEAR CHANGE	−35.0	−47.0	199.0	198.0	−669.0	−30.0	−55.0	1.0	−92.0	−1.0
STUDY LESS COMMR.	37.9	−2.7	−275.6	−616.3	4.0	−58.3	−3.9	−6.7	65.5	44.8

Railroad Mileage, 1950–1959

LOWER PENINSULA

	1950	1951	1952	1953	1954	1955	1956	1957	1958	1959
A.A.	288.0	288.0	288.0	288.0	288.0	288.0	288.0	288.0	288.0	288.0
Boyne Cty.	7.2	7.2	7.2	7.2	7.2	7.2	7.2	7.2	7.2	7.2
Canadian National									1.1	1.1
Gr. Trunk Western	788.6	770.3	770.3	770.3	770.3	775.8	775.8	775.8	775.8	775.8
Chi., Kal. & Sag.	9.5	9.5	9.5	9.5	9.5	9.5	9.5	9.5	9.5	9.5
Musk. Ry & Nav.	5.5	5.5	5.5	5.5	5.5					
St. Clair Tunnel	1.1	1.1	1.1	1.1	1.1	1.1	1.1	1.1		
Chesapeake & Ohio	1432.6	1432.6	1432.6	1432.6	1432.6	1465.7	1429.4	1429.4	1429.4	1429.4
Flint Belt	8.2	8.2	8.2	8.2	8.2					
Manistee & Northeastern	35.6	35.6	35.6	35.6	27.2					
Leelanau Transit	23.8	23.8	23.8	23.8	23.8	23.8	23.8	23.8	23.8	23.8
Det. & Mackinac	229.5	229.5	229.5	229.5	229.5	229.5	229.5	229.5	229.5	229.5
Erie & Mich. Ry & Nav.	4.7	4.7	4.7	4.7	4.7	4.7	4.7	4.7	4.7	4.7
Det. & Toledo Shore Line	43.8	43.8	43.8	43.8	43.8	43.8	43.8	43.8	43.8	43.8
Det., Caro & Sandusky	31.1	31.1	31.1							
Det. Terminal	18.0	18.0	18.0	18.0	18.0	18.0	18.0	18.0	18.0	18.0
Det., Toledo & Ironton	113.8	113.8	113.8	113.8	113.8	113.8	113.8	113.8	105.2	105.2
Det. Union RR Depot & Sta.	3.2	3.2	3.2	3.2	3.2	3.2	3.2	3.2	3.2	3.2
E. Jordan & Southern	18.6	18.6	18.6	18.6	18.6	18.6	18.6	18.6	18.6	18.6
Fort St. Union Depot	1.2	1.2	1.2	1.2	1.2	1.2	1.2	1.2	1.2	1.2
Lud. & Northern	3.4	3.4	3.4	3.4	3.4	3.4	3.4	3.4	3.4	3.4
New York Cent.	301.1	301.1	301.1	291.6	291.6	291.6	291.6	291.6	293.6	293.6

Chi., Kal. & Sag.	22.4	22.4	22.4	22.4	22.4	22.4	22.4	22.4	22.4	22.4
Clev., Cinci., Chi., & St. L.	66.3	66.3	66.3	66.3	66.3	66.3	66.3	66.3	66.3	66.3
Det., Hillsdale & SW	65.2	65.2	65.2	65.2	65.2	65.2	65.2	65.2	65.2	65.2
Erie & Kal.	14.2	14.2	14.2	14.2	14.2	14.2	14.2	14.2	14.2	14.2
Ft. Wyn. & Jackson	43.6	43.6	43.6	43.6	43.6	43.6	43.6	43.6	43.6	43.6
Kal., Allegan & Gr. Rpds.	58.5	58.5	58.5	58.5	58.5	58.5	58.5	58.5	58.5	58.5
Mich. Cent.	977.0	977.0	977.0	977.0	977.0	979.3	979.3	979.3	966.6	966.6
Can. Southern										
Det. Riv. Tunnel	1.4	1.4	1.4	1.4	1.4	1.4	1.4	1.4	1.4	1.4
New York Cent.–part	1.6	1.6	1.6	1.6	1.6	1.6	1.6	1.6	1.6	1.6
Ohio & Morenci	0.0									
Pennsylvania	20.7	20.7	20.7	20.7	20.7	20.7	20.7	20.7	20.7	20.7
Gr. Rpds. & Ind.	403.0	403.0	403.0	403.0	403.0	403.0	403.0	403.0	403.0	403.0
Pt. Hur. & Det.	18.5	18.5	18.5	18.5	18.5	18.5	18.5	18.5	18.5	18.5
Wabash	78.3	78.3	78.3	78.3	78.3	78.3	78.3	78.3	78.3	78.3
L.P. year total	5139.2	5120.9	5120.9	5080.3	5071.9	5071.9	5035.6	5035.6	5016.3	5016.3
L.P. year change	−4.9	−18.3	0.0	−40.6	−8.4	0.0	−36.3	0.0	−19.3	0.0

UPPER PENINSULA

	1950	1951	1952	1953	1954	1955	1956	1957	1958	1959
Chi. & N. Western	484.7	484.7	491.3	490.2	490.2	485.0	483.5	481.7	481.7	475.5
Chi., Milw., St. Paul & Pac.	187.8	187.8	187.8	187.8	187.8	191.3	189.2	189.2	189.2	189.2
Copper Range	99.4	99.4	99.4	99.4	99.4	99.4	99.4	99.4	99.4	99.4
Duluth, So. Shore & Atlantic	411.7	409.6	412.0	423.2	423.2	423.2	423.2	423.2	423.2	423.2
Esc. & Lk. Superior	67.0	67.0	67.0	67.0	67.0	67.0	67.0	67.0	67.0	67.0
Lk. Superior & Ish.	163.5	163.5	176.3	176.3	176.3	176.3	172.1	187.8	187.8	187.8
Manistique & Lk. Superior	38.3	38.3	38.3	38.3	38.3	38.3	38.3	38.3	38.3	38.3
Mpls., St. Paul & S. S. Marie	222.7	222.7	223.2	223.2	223.2	223.2	223.2	223.2	223.2	223.2
Sainte Marie Union Depot	0.5	0.5	0.0							
Sault Ste. Marie Bridge	0.5	0.5	0.5	0.5	0.5	0.5	0.5	0.5	0.5	0.5
Wisconsin Cent.	0.3	0.3	0.3	0.3	0.3	0.3	0.3	0.3	0.3	0.3
Gogebic & Montreal Riv.	12.0	12.0	12.0	12.0	12.0	12.0	12.0	12.0	12.0	12.0
U. P. YEAR TOTAL	1688.4	1686.3	1708.1	1718.2	1718.2	1716.5	1708.7	1722.6	1722.6	1716.4
U. P. YEAR CHANGE	−19.3	−2.1	21.8	10.1	0.0	−1.7	−7.8	13.9	0.0	−6.2
MICH. YEAR TOTAL	6827.6	6807.2	6829.0	6798.5	6790.1	6788.4	6744.3	6758.2	6738.9	6732.7
MICH. YEAR CHANGE	−24.2	−20.4	21.8	−30.5	−8.4	−1.7	−44.1	13.9	−19.3	−6.2
COMMR. YEAR TOTAL	6803.0	6776.0	6783.0	6776.0	6731.0	6680.0	6674.0	6692.0	6675.0	6665.0
COMMR. YEAR CHANGE	−4.0	−27.0	7.0	−7.0	−45.0	−51.0	−6.0	18.0	−17.0	−10.0
STUDY LESS COMMR.	24.6	31.2	46.0	22.5	59.1	108.4	70.3	66.2	63.9	67.7

Railroad Mileage, 1960–1969

LOWER PENINSULA

	1960	1961	1962	1963	1964	1965	1966	1967	1968	1969
A.A.	288.0	288.0	288.0	288.0	288.0	288.0	288.0	288.0	288.0	294.4
Boyne Cty.	7.2	7.2	7.2	7.2	7.2	7.2	7.2	7.2	7.2	7.2
Cadillac & Lk. Cty.					21.1	21.1	21.1	21.1	21.1	21.1
Canadian National	1.1	1.1	1.1	1.1	1.1	1.1	1.1	1.1	1.1	1.1
Gr. Trunk Western	775.8	775.8	775.8	775.8	775.8	775.8	775.8	775.8	775.8	775.8

Chi., Kal. & Sag.	9.5	9.5	9.5	9.5	9.5	9.5	9.5	9.5	9.5	9.5
Chesapeake & Ohio	1429.4	1429.4	1429.4	1419.4	1419.4	1419.4	1419.4	1419.4	1419.4	1419.4
Leelanau Transit	23.8	23.8	23.8	23.8	23.8	23.8	23.8	23.8	23.8	23.8
Det. & Mackinac	228.9	228.9	228.9	228.9	228.9	220.6	220.6	218.2	218.2	218.2
Erie & Mich. Ry & Nav.	4.7	4.7	4.7	4.7	4.7	4.7	4.7	4.7	4.7	4.7
Det. & Toledo Shore Line	43.8	43.8	43.8	43.8	43.8	43.8	43.8	43.8	43.8	43.8
Det. Terminal	18.0	18.0	16.8	16.8	16.8	16.8	16.8	16.8	16.8	16.8
Det., Toledo & Ironton	105.2	105.2	105.2	105.2	105.2	93.7	93.7	92.4	92.4	92.4
Det. Union RR Depot & Sta.	3.2	3.2	3.2	3.2	3.2	3.2	3.2	3.2	3.2	3.2
E. Jordan & Southern	18.6									
Fort St. Union Depot	1.2	1.2	1.2	1.2	1.2	1.2	1.2	1.2	1.2	1.2
Lud. & N.ern	3.4	3.4	3.4	3.4	3.4	3.4	3.4	3.4	3.4	3.4
New York Cent.	269.6	269.6	259.5	259.5	251.1	251.1	251.1	244.6		
Chi., Kal. & Sag.	22.4	17.9	17.9	17.9	17.9	17.9	17.9	17.9		
Clev., Cinci., Chi., & St. L.	66.3	66.3	66.3	66.3	66.3	66.3	66.3	66.3		
Det., Hillsdale & SW	65.2	35.4	35.4	35.4	35.4	35.4	35.4	29.1		
Erie & Kal.	14.2	14.2	14.2	14.2	14.2	14.2	14.2	14.2		
Ft. Wyn. & Jackson	43.6	43.6	43.6	43.6	43.6	43.6	43.6	43.6		
Kal., Allegan & Gr. Rpds.	58.5	58.5	58.5	58.5	58.5	58.5	58.5	58.5		
Mich. Cent.	966.6	966.6	931.0	931.0	931.0	931.0	931.0	931.0		
Can. Southern										
Det. Riv. Tunnel	1.4	1.4	1.4	1.4	1.4	1.4	1.4	1.4		
New York Cent.–part	1.6	1.6	1.6	1.6	1.6	1.6	1.6	1.6		
Norfolk & Western										
Wabash					78.3	78.3	78.3	78.3	78.3	78.3
Penn Cent.									233.4	233.4
Chi., Kal. & Sag.									17.9	17.9
Clev., Cinci., Chi., & St. L.									66.3	66.3
Det., Hillsdale & SW									29.1	29.1
Erie & Kal.									14.2	14.2
Ft. Wyn. & Jackson									43.6	43.6
Gr. Rpds. & Ind.									368.7	368.7
Kal., Allegan & Gr. Rpds.									58.5	58.5
Mich. Cent.									931.0	931.0
Can. Southern										
Det. Riv. Tunnel									1.4	1.4
Penn Cent.–part									1.6	1.6
Pennsylvania	20.7	20.7	20.7	20.7	20.7	20.7	20.7	20.7		
Gr. Rpds. & Ind.	403.0	395.6	389.8	389.8	368.7	368.7	368.7	368.7		
Pt. Hur. & Det.	18.5	18.5	18.5	18.5	18.5	18.5	18.5	18.5	18.5	18.5
Wabash	78.3	78.3	78.3	78.3						
L. P. YEAR TOTAL	4991.7	4931.4	4878.7	4868.7	4860.3	4840.5	4840.5	4824.0	4792.1	4798.5
L. P. YEAR CHANGE	−24.6	−60.3	−52.7	−10.0	−8.4	−19.8	0.0	−16.5	−31.9	6.4

UPPER PENINSULA

	1960	1961	1962	1963	1964	1965	1966	1967	1968	1969
Chi. & N. Western	473.9	473.9	465.2	456.2	456.2	449.3	448.0	444.1	443.5	436.6
Chi., Milw., St. Paul & Pac.	189.2	189.2	189.2	189.2	189.2	189.2	189.2	189.2	189.2	157.0
Copper Range	99.4	99.4	99.4	99.4	68.7	68.7	68.7	68.7	68.7	68.7
Duluth, So. Shore & Atlantic	423.2									
Esc. & Lk. Superior	67.0	67.0	67.0	67.0	67.0	67.0	67.0	67.0	67.0	67.0
Lk. Superior & Ish.	187.8	187.8	186.3	162.6	162.6	129.5	129.5	129.5	129.5	116.0
Manistique & Lk. Superior	38.3	38.3	38.3	38.3	38.3	38.3	38.3	38.3	0.0	
Marq. & Huron Mtn.				23.7	23.7	23.7	23.7	8.2	8.2	8.2

Mpls., St. Paul & S. S. Marie	225.0									
Sainte Marie Union Depot	0.5									
Sault Ste. Marie Bridge	0.5									
Wisconsin Cent.	0.3									
Gogebic & Montreal Riv.	12.0									
Soo Line		665.0	665.0	665.0	665.0	657.0	657.0	657.0	655.0	655.0
Sault Ste. Marie Bridge		0.5	0.5	0.5	0.5	0.5	0.5	0.5	0.5	0.5
U. P. YEAR TOTAL	1717.1	1721.1	1710.9	1701.9	1671.2	1623.2	1621.9	1602.5	1561.6	1509.0
U. P. YEAR CHANGE	0.7	4.0	−10.2	−9.0	−30.7	−48.0	−1.3	−19.4	−40.9	−52.6
MICH. YEAR TOTAL	6708.8	6652.5	6589.6	6570.6	6531.5	6463.7	6462.4	6426.5	6353.7	6307.5
MICH. YEAR CHANGE	−23.9	−56.3	−62.9	−19.0	−39.1	−67.8	−1.3	−35.9	−72.8	−46.2
COMMR. YEAR TOTAL	6640.0	6592.0	6520.0	6502.0	6461.0	6408.0	6392.0	6375.0	6303.0	6241.0
COMMR. YEAR CHANGE	−25.0	−48.0	−72.0	−18.0	−41.0	−53.0	−16.0	−17.0	−72.0	−62.0
STUDY LESS COMMR.	68.8	60.5	69.6	68.6	70.5	55.7	70.4	51.5	50.7	66.5

Railroad Mileage, 1970–1979

LOWER PENINSULA

	1970	1971	1972	1973	1974	1975	1976	1977	1978	1979
Amtrak							77.7	77.7	77.7	77.7
A.A.	294.4	294.4	294.4	294.4	294.4	294.4	66.6	66.6	66.6	66.6
Boyne Cty.	7.2	7.2	7.2	7.2	7.2	7.2				
Cadillac & Lk. Cty.	21.1	21.1	12.8	12.8	12.8	4.5	4.5	4.5	4.5	4.5
Can. National	1.1	1.1	1.1	1.1	1.1	1.1	1.1	1.1	1.1	1.1
Gr. Trunk Western	775.8	775.8	775.8	775.6	775.6	740.0	840.3	825.0	825.0	825.0
Chi., Kal. & Sag.	9.5	9.5	9.5	9.5	9.5	9.5				
Conrail							9.5	9.5	9.5	9.5
Chesapeake & Ohio	1410.5	1409.5	1363.7							
Leelanau Transit	23.8	23.8	23.8							
Chessie System										
Chesapeake & Ohio				1350.3	1338.3	1338.3	1338.3	1338.9	1338.9	1314.8
Leelanau Transit				23.8	23.8	23.8	23.8	23.8	23.8	23.8
Consol. Rail–owned							574.2	574.2	574.2	574.2
Can. Southern										
Det. Riv. Tunnel							1.4	1.4	1.4	1.4
Consol. Rail–D. O.										
Det. & Mackinac–owned	218.2	218.2	218.2	218.2	218.2	218.2	291.4	291.4	291.4	291.4
Det. & Mackinac–D.O.							[105.0]	[105.0]	[105.0]	[105.0]
Erie & Mich. Ry & Nav.	4.7	4.7	4.7	4.7	4.7	4.7	4.7	4.7	4.7	4.7
Det. & Toledo Shore Line	43.8	43.8	43.8	43.8	43.8	43.8	43.8	43.8	43.8	43.8
Det. Terminal	16.8	16.8	16.8	16.8	16.8	16.8	16.8	16.8	16.8	16.8
Det., Toledo & Ironton	92.4	90.7	90.7	90.7	90.7	90.7	90.7	90.7	90.7	74.0
Det. Union RR Depot & Sta.	3.2	3.2	3.2	3.2	3.2	3.2	3.2	3.2	3.2	3.2
Fort St. Union Depot	1.2	1.2	0.0							
Hillsdale County–D. O.							[40.0]	[40.0]	[40.0]	[40.0]
Kent–Barry–Eaton Conn.–D. O.										[41.9]
Lenawee County–owned										3.8
Lenawee County–D. O.								[8.1]	[26.7]	[26.7]
Lud. & Northern	3.4	3.4	3.4	3.4	3.4	3.4	3.4	3.4	3.4	3.4
Mich., State of							193.4	193.4	193.4	193.4

	1970	1971	1972	1973	1974	1975	1976	1977	1978	1979
Mich. Interstate–D. O.								[287.3]	[287.3]	[287.3]
Mich. Northern–D. O.							[245.6]	[245.6]	[245.6]	[245.6]
Norfolk & Western										
Wabash	78.3	78.3	78.3	78.3	78.3	78.3	78.3	78.3	78.3	89.4
Penn Cent.	231.7	231.7	227.4	221.3	221.3	221.3	585.4	576.5	560.1	559.4
Chi., Kal. & Sag.	17.6	17.6	17.6	17.6	17.6	17.6				
Clev., Cinci., Chi., & St. L.	66.3	66.3	66.3	66.3	66.3	66.3				
Det., Hillsdale & SW	12.3	12.3	4.4	4.4	4.4	4.4				
Erie & Kal.	14.2	14.2	14.2	14.2	14.2	14.2				
Ft. Wyn. & Jackson	43.6	43.6	43.6	32.4	32.4	32.4				
Gr. Rpds. & Ind.	368.7	368.7	368.7	368.7	368.7	368.7				
Kal., Allegan & Gr. Rpds.	58.5	58.5	48.5	48.5	48.5	48.5				
Mich. Cent.	931.0	931.0	931.0	884.3	884.3	884.3				
Can. Southern										
Det. Riv. Tunnel	1.4	1.4	1.4	1.4	1.4	1.4				
Penn Cent.–part	1.6	1.6	1.6							
Pt. Hur. & Det.	18.5	18.5	18.5	18.5	18.5	18.5	18.5	18.5	18.5	18.5
Tuscola & Sag. Bay–D. O.							0.5	[45.0]	[45.0]	[45.0]
L. P. YEAR TOTAL	4770.8	4768.1	4690.6	4611.4	4599.4	4555.5	4267.5	4243.4	4227.0	4200.4
L. P. YEAR CHANGE	−27.7	−2.7	−77.5	−79.2	−12.0	−43.9	−288.0	−24.1	−16.4	−26.6

UPPER PENINSULA

	1970	1971	1972	1973	1974	1975	1976	1977	1978	1979
Chi. & N. Western	339.5	336.9	336.9	336.9	331.6	326.6	326.6	326.6	325.1	324.2
Chi., Milw., St. Paul & Pac.	157.0	157.0	157.0	157.0	157.0	157.0	149.0	149.0	149.0	149.0
Copper Range	68.7	55.9	55.9	0.0						
Esc. & Lk. Superior	67.0	67.0	67.0	67.0	67.0	67.0	67.0	67.0	67.0	67.0
Lk. Superior & Ish.	116.0	116.0	116.0	116.0	113.6	100.7	100.7	100.7	100.7	43.9
Marq. & Huron Mtn.	8.2	8.2	8.2	8.2	8.2	8.2	8.2	8.2	8.2	8.2
Soo Line	655.0	655.0	655.0	655.0	655.0	655.0	655.0	628.0	614.4	583.6
Sault Ste. Marie Bridge	0.5	0.5	0.5	0.5	0.5	0.5	0.5	0.5	0.5	0.5
U. P. YEAR TOTAL	1411.9	1396.5	1396.5	1340.6	1332.9	1315.0	1307.0	1280.0	1264.9	1176.4
U. P. YEAR CHANGE	−97.1	−15.4	0.0	−55.9	−7.7	−17.9	−8.0	−27.0	−15.1	−88.5
MICH. YEAR TOTAL	6182.7	6164.6	6087.1	5952.0	5932.3	5870.5	5574.5	5523.4	5491.9	5376.8
MICH. YEAR CHANGE	−124.8	−18.1	−77.5	−135.1	−19.7	−61.8	−296.0	−51.1	−31.5	−115.1
COMMR. YEAR TOTAL	6140.0	6111.0	5961.0	5911.0	5891.0	5834.0	5609.0	5569.0	5542.0	5408.0
COMMR. YEAR CHANGE	−101.0	−29.0	−150.0	−50.0	−20.0	−57.0	−225.0	−40.0	−27.0	−134.0
STUDY LESS COMMR.	42.7	53.6	126.1	41.0	41.3	36.5	−34.5	−45.6	−50.1	−31.2

Railroad Mileage, 1980–1989

LOWER PENINSULA

	1980	1981	1982	1983	1984	1985	1986	1987	1988	1989
Alanson & Petoskey										
Penn Cent.									8.9	8.9
Amtrak	77.7	77.7	77.7	77.7	77.7	77.7	77.7	77.7	77.7	77.7
Cadillac & Lk. Cty.	4.5	4.5	4.5	4.5	0.0					
Can. National	1.1	1.1	1.1	1.1	1.1	1.1	1.1	1.1	1.1	1.1
Gr. Trunk Western	825.0	854.6	854.6	883.7	836.8	836.8	753.1	504.7	504.7	504.7

Conrail	9.5	9.5	9.5	9.5	9.5	9.5	9.5	9.5	9.5	9.5
Can.Natl–Can.Pac.										
Can. Southern										
Det. Riv. Tunnel						1.4	1.4	1.4	1.4	1.4
Cent. Mich.								225.4	225.4	188.9
Coe Rail					8.7	8.7	8.7	8.7	8.7	8.7
Consol. Rail	574.2	572.6	435.8	432.4	449.2	447.8	447.8	447.8	447.8	419.0
Can. Southern										
Det. Riv. Tunnel	1.4	1.4	1.4	1.4	1.4	0.0				
Coopersville & Marne										6.4
CSX Corp.										
Chesapeake & Ohio	1314.8	1275.8	1137.6	1121.5	1114.0	1114.0	996.8	0.0		
Leelanau Transit	23.8	23.8								
CSX Transportation								922.8	782.0	753.6
Det. & Mackinac–owned	295.0	295.0	295.0	295.0	295.0	295.0	295.0	275.4	275.4	215.2
Det. & Mackinac–D.O.	[105.0]	[105.0]	[105.0]	[105.0]	[105.0]	[105.0]	[105.0]	[105.0]	[105.0]	[105.0]
Erie & Mich. Ry & Nav	4.7	4.7	4.7	4.7	4.7	4.7	4.7	4.7	4.7	4.7
Det. & Toledo Shore Line	43.8	0.0								
Det. Terminal	16.8	16.8	16.8	16.8						
Det., Toledo & Ironton	74.0	74.0	74.0	0.0						
Hillsdale County–D. O.	[40.0]	[40.0]	[40.0]	[40.0]	[40.0]	[40.0]	[40.0]	[40.0]	[40.0]	[40.0]
Huron & Eastern								81.5	81.5	140.0	140.0
Kal., Lk. Shore & Chi.								13.1	13.1	13.1	13.1
Kent–Barry–Eaton Conn.–D. O.	[41.9]	[41.9]	[9.0]							
Leelanau Transit			23.8	23.8	23.8	23.8	23.8	23.8	23.8	23.8
Lenawee County–owned	3.8	3.8	3.8	3.8	3.8	3.8	3.8	3.8	3.8	3.8
Lenawee County–D. O.	[26.7]	[26.7]	[27.3]	[27.3]	[27.3]	[27.3]	[27.3]	[27.3]	[27.3]	[27.3]
Lud. & N.ern	3.4	3.4	3.4	3.4	3.4	3.4	3.4	3.4	3.4	3.4
Mich., State of–by D. O.s	365.2	365.2	414.3	414.3	691.0	691.0	691.0	678.5	639.3	639.3
Mich., State of–railbanked				62.5	62.5	62.5	92.0	131.2	131.2
Mich. Interstate–D. O.	[287.3]	[287.3]	[48.2]	[48.2]	[48.2]	[48.2]	[48.2]	[48.2]	[48.2]	[48.2]
Mich. Northern–D. O.	[245.6]	[245.6]	[433.3]	[433.3]	[33.8]	[33.8]	[33.8]			
Mich. Southern										30.2
Mid-Mich.								68.8	68.8	68.8
Norfolk & Western										
Wabash	89.4	89.4								
Norfolk Southern										
Norfolk & Western										
Wabash			89.4	89.4	89.4	78.3	78.3	78.3	78.3	78.3
Penn Cent.	449.4	449.4	384.8	375.8	33.8	33.8	33.8	33.8	33.8	33.8
Pt. Hur. & Det.	18.5	18.5	18.5	18.5	0.0					
Southwestern Mich.										
Tuscola & Sag. Bay–owned					12.0	12.0	12.0	12.0	12.0	12.0
Tuscola & Sag. Bay–D. O.	[45.0]	[45.0]	[135.6]	[135.6]	[472.5]	[472.5]	[472.5]	[472.5]	[402.2]	[402.2]
L. P. YEAR TOTAL	4196.0	4141.2	3850.7	3777.3	3717.8	3705.3	3599.0	3568.2	3494.8	3377.5
L. P. YEAR CHANGE	−4.4	−54.8	−290.5	−73.4	−59.5	−12.5	−106.3	−30.8	−73.4	−117.3

UPPER PENINSULA

	1980	1981	1982	1983	1984	1985	1986	1987	1988	1989
Chi. & N. Western	313.4	285.6	178.1	178.1	178.1	178.1	178.1	178.1	178.1	178.1
Chi., Milw., St. Paul & Pac.	4.6	1.6	1.6	1.6	1.6	0.0				
Esc. & Lk. Superior	188.9	191.7	98.6	73.4	73.4	71.3	71.3	71.3	71.3	71.3
Esc. & Lk. Superior–D.O.			[93.1]	[118.3]	[118.3]	[118.3]	[118.3]	[118.3]	[118.3]	[118.3]
Lk. Superior & Ish.	48.1	48.1	48.1	48.1	48.1	48.1	48.1	48.1	48.1	48.1

Marq. & Huron Mtn.	8.2	8.2	0.0							
Mich., State of–by D. O.			93.1	118.3	118.3	118.3	118.3	118.3	118.3	118.3
Mich., State of–railbanked								25.8	25.8	25.8
Soo Line	583.6	516.4	516.4	516.4	516.4	516.4	489.2			
Sault Ste. Marie Bridge	0.5	0.5	0.5	0.5	0.5	0.5	0.5			
Wisconsin Cent. Ltd.								454.1	454.1	454.1
Sault Ste. Marie Bridge								0.5	0.5	0.5
U. P. YEAR TOTAL	1147.3	1052.1	936.4	936.4	936.4	932.7	905.5	896.2	896.2	896.2
U. P. YEAR CHANGE	−29.1	−95.2	−115.7	0.0	0.0	−3.7	−27.2	−9.3	0.0	0.0
MICH. YEAR TOTAL	5343.3	5193.3	4787.1	4713.7	4654.2	4638.0	4504.5	4464.4	4391.0	4273.7
MICH. YEAR CHANGE	−33.5	−150.0	−406.2	−73.4	−59.5	−16.2	−133.5	−40.1	−73.4	−117.3
COMMR. YEAR TOTAL	5370.0	5231.0								
COMMR. YEAR CHANGE	−38.0	−139.0		0.0	0.0	0.0	0.0	0.0	0.0	0.0
STUDY LESS COMMR.	−26.7	−37.7								

Railroad Mileage, 1990–1999

LOWER PENINSULA

	1990	1991	1992	1993	1994	1995	1996	1997	1998	1999
Adrian & Blissfield–D.O.	[19.2]	[19.2]	[19.2]	[19.2]	[19.2]	[19.2]	[19.2]	[19.2]	[19.2]	[19.2]
Alanson & Petoskey										
Penn Cent.	8.9	8.9	0.0							
Amtrak	77.7	77.7	77.7	77.7	77.7	79.5	79.5	79.5	79.5	79.5
Canadian National	1.1	1.1	1.1	1.1	1.1	1.1	1.1	1.1	1.1	1.1
Gr. Trunk Western	504.7	504.7	504.7	504.7	504.7	504.7	504.7	484.1	447.1	447.1
Conrail	9.0	9.0	9.0	9.0	9.0	9.0	9.0	9.0	9.0	
Norfolk Southern										9.0
Can.Natl–Can.Pac.										
Can. Southern										
Det. Riv. Tunnel	1.4	1.4	1.4	1.4	1.4	1.4	1.4	1.4	1.4	1.4
Cent. Mich.	183.4	141.3	141.3	105.1	99.5	99.5	92.9	92.6	92.9	92.9
Coe Rail	8.7	8.7	8.7	8.7	8.7	8.7	8.7	8.7	8.7	8.7
Consol. Rail	419.0	419.0	419.0	398.7	398.7	396.9	396.0	396.0	396.0	25.1
Coopersville & Marne	6.4	6.4	6.4	6.4	6.4	6.4	13.3	13.3	13.3	13.3
CSX Transportation	751.6	751.6	751.6	751.6	751.6	751.6	751.6	741.4	663.7	669.3
Consol. Rail								0.9	0.9	0.9
Norfolk Southern										0.9
Det. & Mack.–owned	219.9	219.9	0.0							
Det. & Mack.–D.O.	[105.0]	[105.0]	0.0							
Gr. Rpds. Eastern										
Hillsdale County–D. O.	[40.0]	[40.0]	[40.0]							
Huron & Eastern–owned	140.0	140.0	140.0	140.0	140.0	140.0	132.5	132.5	132.5	132.5
Huron & Eastern–D. O.		[45.0]	[45.0]	[45.0]	[45.0]	[45.0]	[45.0]	[45.0]	[45.0]	[45.0]
Ind. & Ohio								20.6	20.6	20.6
Ind. Northeastern				[40.0]	[40.0]	[40.0]	[40.0]	[40.0]	[40.0]	[40.0]
Kal., Lk. Shore & Chi.	14.7	14.7	14.7	14.7	14.7	0.0				
Lk. State Rail Corp.–owned			219.9	152.4	152.4	152.4	152.4	152.4	143.0	143.0
Lk. State Rail Corp.–D. O.			[105.0]	[105.0]	[105.0]	[105.0]	[105.0]	[105.0]	[105.0]	[105.0]
Leelanau Transit	23.8	23.8	23.8	23.8	23.8	12.5	0.0			
Lenawee County–owned	3.8	0.0								

Lenawee County–D. O.	[27.3]	[0]								
Lud. & Northern	3.4	3.4	3.4	3.4	3.4	3.4	3.4	0.0		
Mich., State of–by D. O.s	639.3	632.1	632.1	632.1	632.1	633.1	633.1	633.1	633.1	633.1
Mich., State of–railbanked	131.2	22.7	22.7	22.7	0.0					
Mich. Interstate–D. O.	[48.2]	[48.2]	[48.2]	[48.2]	[48.2]	[48.2]	[48.2]	[48.2]	[48.2]	[48.2]
Mich. Southern	30.2	30.2	30.2	44.7	44.7	44.7	44.7	44.7	44.7	44.7
Mid-Mich.	67.8	67.8	67.8	67.8	67.8	67.8	67.8	67.8	67.8	62.2
Norfolk Southern								78.3	78.3	449.2
Norfolk & Western		78.3	78.3	78.3	78.3	78.3	78.3			
Wabash	78.3									
Tuscola & Sag. Bay–owned	12.0	12.0	12.0	12.0	12.0	12.0	12.0	12.0	12.0	12.0
Tuscola & Sag. Bay–D. O.	[402.2]	[357.2]	[357.2]	[357.2]	[357.2]	[357.2]	[357.2]	[357.2]	[357.2]	[357.2]
W. Mich.						14.7	14.7	14.7	14.7	14.7
L. P. YEAR TOTAL	3336.3	3174.7	3165.8	3056.3	3028.0	3017.7	2998.0	2984.1	2860.3	2860.3
L. P. YEAR CHANGE	−41.2	−161.6	−8.9	−109.5	−28.3	−10.3	−19.7	−13.9	−123.8	0.0

UPPER PENINSULA

	1990	1991	1992	1993	1994	1995	1996	1997	1998	1999
Chi. & N. Western	178.1	178.1	178.1	178.1	178.1	0.0				
Esc. & Lk. Superior	71.3	71.3	71.3	71.3	71.3	71.3	71.3	71.3	71.3	71.3
Esc. & Lk. Superior–D.O.	[118.3]	[118.3]	[118.3]	[118.3]	[118.3]	[118.3]	[118.3]	[118.3]	[118.3]	[118.3]
Lk. Superior & Ish.	42.2	42.2	42.2	42.2	42.2	42.2	42.2	42.2	42.2	42.2
Mich., State of–by D. O.	118.3	118.3	118.3	118.3	118.3	118.3	118.3	118.3	118.3	118.3
Mich., State of–railbanked	25.8	25.8	25.8	25.8	25.8	0.0				
Union Pacific										
Chi. & N. Western						178.1	178.1	0.0		
Wisconsin Cent. Ltd.	460.0	460.0	460.0	460.0	460.0	460.0	460.0	460.0	460.0	394.0
Sault Ste. Marie Bridge Co.	0.5	0.5	0.5	0.5	0.5	0.5	0.5	178.6	178.6	178.6
U. P. YEAR TOTAL	896.2	896.2	896.2	896.2	896.2	870.4	870.4	870.4	870.4	804.4
U. P. YEAR CHANGE	0.0	0.0	0.0	0.0	0.0	−25.8	0.0	0.0	0.0	−66.0
MICH. YEAR TOTAL	4232.5	4070.9	4062.0	3952.5	3924.2	3888.1	3868.4	3854.5	3730.7	3664.7
MICH. YEAR CHANGE	−41.2	−161.6	−8.9	−109.5	−28.3	−36.1	−19.7	−13.9	−123.8	−66.0
COMMR. YEAR TOTAL	0.0	0.0	0.0	0.0	0.0	0.0	0.0	0.0	0.0	0.0
COMMR. YEAR CHANGE	0.0	0.0	0.0	0.0	0.0	0.0	0.0	0.0	0.0	0.0

{3}

INDEX OF
RAILROAD COMPANIES

{4}

LOWER PENINSULA
RAILROAD COMPANIES

Adrian & Blissfield

LINE (A&B)

For arrangement of stations, construction record, and prior ownerships, see Lake Shore lines LS-A and LS-F, and Detroit, Toledo & Ironton line DTI-A.

DATE	ACT	A&B–	END POINTS	MP	CHANGE	DES.OPR. MAIN	SOURCE	NOTE
1990/12	C	[LS-A2]	Riga–Lenawee Jct.	315.5–325.5	+10.0			1
12	C	[LS-A3]	Lenawee Jct.–Adrian	325.5–333.0	+7.5			
12	C	[LS-F]	Grosvenor–MP 1.7	0–1.7	+1.7			
12	P	[DTI-A]	In Adrian	45.9–47.0	(+1.1)			2
					TOTAL	19.2		

OWNERSHIP

1990   Ownership of all lines except line DTI-A is by the State of Michigan. Line DTI-A is owned by Adrian & Blissfield.

Act Column Key

C   Operated under Designated Operator contract
P   Purchased from Lenawee County

Notes

1   The trackage between MP 315.5 and MP 318.4 was leased by the State of Michigan to an elevator until 30 September 1992 and switching service provided by A&B from December 1990 until the end of the lease.
2   The ownership of this segment is not clear, but it is assumed to have been purchased from the abandonment of the Lenawee County. Also, it is assumed that that part of line DTI-A south of MP 45.9 was abandoned.

Alanson & Petoskey

MAIN LINE (A&P)

For arrangement of stations, construction record, and prior ownerships, see Grand Rapids & Indiana line GR&I-N.

DATE	ACT	A&P–	END POINTS	MP	CHANGE	MAIN	SOURCE	NOTE
1988 ca.	L	[GR&I-N]	Petoskey–Alanson	426.0–434.9	+8.9	8.9		
1994 ca.	XL	[GR&I-N]	Petoskey–Alanson	426.0–434.9	–8.9	0		

OWNERSHIP

1988   Alanson & Petoskey, leased from Penn Central.

Act Column Key

L   Leased from Penn Central
XL   Lease from Penn Central canceled

Notes

GENERAL   This road was operated as a tourist line and apparently not as a common carrier. The actual dates of lease and lease cancellation could not be determined.

Algonac Transit

MAIN LINE (ATR)

	MILEAGE	COUNTY	CROSSINGS, JUNCTIONS, ETC.
Mar. Cty.	0	St. Clair	J/PH&D 19.1
Broadbridge	1.9	"	
Roberts Landing	3.8	"	
Algonac	7.1	"	

CONSTRUCTION/ABANDONMENT

DATE	ACT	END POINTS	MP	CHANGE	MICHIGAN MAIN	YARD	NOTE
1930/1	P	Line	0–7.1	+7.1	7.1		
1957/10/15	X	Line	0–7.1	–7.1	0		

OWNERSHIP

1930   Algonac Transit Company

Act Column Key

P   Purchased from Detroit & Port Huron Shore Line
X   Abandoned

Allegan & Lake Shore (line not located)

LINE (A&LS)

	MILEAGE	COUNTY	CROSSINGS, JUNCTIONS, ETC.
(Kal. Riv.)	0	Allegan	
(End)	5	"	

CONSTRUCTION/ABANDONMENT

DATE	ACT	END POINTS	MP	CHANGE	MAIN	SOURCE	NOTE
1885/4/15	B	Line	0–5	+5	5.0	1	
1889	X	Line	0–5	–5	0	2	

OWNERSHIP

1885   Allegan & Lake (B)

Act Column Key

B   Built by Allegan & Lake Shore
X   Abandoned

Sources

1.   Michigan, Commissioner of Railroads, *Annual Reports,* 1885.
2.   Michigan, Commissioner of Railroads, *Annual Reports,* 1890.

AMTRAK (National Rail Passenger Corporation) _____

For arrangement of stations, construction record, and prior ownerships, see Michigan Central lines MC-C and MC-W.

ACQUISITION/DISPOSITION RECORD

DATE	ACT	AMK–	END POINTS	CHANGE	MAIN	NOTE
1976/4/1	P1	[MC-C]	MP 145.0–MP 191.9	+46.9		
	P1	[MC-W]	MP 191.9–MP 222.6	+30.8	77.7	
1995/7	P2	[MC-C]	MP 143.2–MP 145.0	+1.8	79.5	

OWNERSHIP

1976   Amtrak (National Rail Passenger Corporation)

Act Column Key

P1   Purchased from Penn Central
P2   Purchased from Conrail

Ann Arbor _____

MAIN LINE, FIRST DISTRICT (AA-A)

	MILEAGE	COUNTY	CROSSINGS, JUNCTIONS, ETC.
Toledo OH (Cherry Street)	0	Lucas OH	
Boulevard	2.5	"	
Hallett	3.7	"	
Alexis OH	4.9	"	
(OH/MI state line)	5.7		
Hawthorn	8.3	Monroe	
Temperance	9.3	"	
Samaria	11.5	"	f. Weeks Sta.
France	14.8	"	
Lulu	16.7	"	
Federman	18.6	"	X/LS-M 12.4, f. Monroe Jct.
Diann	20.5	"	X/DTI-M 40.1
Dundee	22.8	"	X/DTM 0. X/DTI-Z 4.9
Macon	24.7	"	J/AA-YQ 0
Azalia	26.8	"	f. Reeves
Milan	30.9	"	X/WAB 37.3, f. Milan Jct.

Milan (old)	31.5	Washtenaw	
Nora	35	"	
Urania	36.5	"	
(Jct.)	37.4	"	J/AA-YH 0
(Bridge)	39.1	"	B/DUR-S 6.6
Pittsfield	40.4	"	X/LS-Y 7.1 (AA-G) f. Ypsilanti Jct.
Ferry	44.5	"	
A.A.	45.2	"	(old 45.6)
(Bridge)	45.5	"	B/DUR-J 33.6
(Bridge)	46.2	"	B/MC-E 37.7
Bell	46.9	"	
(Jct.)	47.3	"	J/AA-O1 47.3
White Star Track	47.9	"	
Barton	49.0	"	
Osmer	50.9	"	f. Northfield, f. Kirby
(Jct.)	54.5	"	J/AA-O1 56.9
Whitmore Lk.	56.9	"	
Hamburg	59.4	Livingston	
(Crossing)	61.7	"	X/GTW-A 69.9
Lakeland	61.8	"	
Hamburg Jct.	62.2	"	J/GTW-A 70.4
Pettysville	63.3	"	
Chilson	66.9	"	
Ann Pere	72.0	"	X/PM-D 52.3, f. Howell Jct.
Glade	73.4	"	
Howell	73.9	"	
Oak Grove	80.2	"	
(Jct.)	82.7	"	J/AA-03 82.7
Cohoctah	84.5	"	
Byron	88.9	Shiawassee	
Pitt	93.9	"	C/GTW-D 65.5
Emergency	94.8	"	
(Crossing, jct.)	95.2	"	X/GTW-D 66.8, J/AA03 96.5
Durand	95.5	"	X/GTW-C 253.3
(Jct.)	95.6	"	J/GTW-S 0.1
Durand (first sta.)	95.7	"	
York	96.2	"	
Vernon	98.7	"	
(Crossing)	103.5	"	X/GTW-YDC 0.1
Corunna	104.0	"	
San	104.9	"	C/GTW-D 76.5
(Crossing)	106.0	"	X/OWCL-1 1.3
(Jct.)	106.0	"	J/AA-YM 0
Faben	106.7	"	
Owosso	107.1	"	J/AA-B 107.1

CONSTRUCTION/ABANDONMENT

DATE	ACT	END POINTS	MP	CHANGE	MI MAIN	SOURCE	NOTE
1874/8/5	B1	Boulevard–Alexis	2.5–4.9	+2.4	0	2,4	1
1881/8	B2	Alexis–A.A. (first)	4.9–45.6	+40.7	39.9	5	2
1881/8	B3	A.A.–MP 47.3	45.6–47.3	+1.7	41.6	4	3
1885	B4	Hamburg Jct.–MP 82.7	62.2–82.7	+20.5		4	
1885	B4	MP 95.2–Durand (first)	95.2–95.7	+0.5	62.6	4	
1886/10	B4	Durand (first)–Owosso	95.7–107.1	+11.4	74.0	4	6

DATE	ACT	END POINTS	MP	CHANGE	MI MAIN	SOURCE	NOTE
1893	B4	MP 54.5–MP 62.2	54.5–62.2	+7.7	81.7	5	
1895	B4	MP 82.7–MP 95.2	82.7–95.2	+12.5	94.2	5	
1896/Summer	B10	MP 47.3–MP 62.2	47.3–54.5	+7.2	101.4	5	
1897	B10	Cherry St.–Boulevard	0–2.5	+2.5	101.4	5	
1976/4/1	S	Toledo–A.A.	0–47.5	–47.5		3	27
1976/4/1	S	A.A.–Durand	47.5–93.9	–46.4		3	28
1976/4/1	S	Durand–Owosso	93.9–107.1	–13.2	0	3	31

OWNERSHIP

1874	Toledo & State Line (B1)
1878/5/11	Toledo & Ann Arbor (B2), merger of Toledo & State Line
1880/10/14	Toledo, Ann Arbor & Grand Trunk (B3), merger of Toledo & Ann Arbor
1884/5/19	Toledo, Ann Arbor & North Michigan (B4), merger of Toledo, Ann Arbor & Grand Trunk
1895/9/20	Ann Arbor (B10), reorganization of Toledo, Ann Arbor & North Michigan
1976/4/1	State of Michigan purchased MP 0–MP 47.5 as MICH-[AA-A1]
1976/4/1	State of Michigan purchased MP 47.5–MP 93.9 as MICH-[AA-A2]
1976/4/1	Grand Trunk Western purchased MP 93.9–MP 107.1 as GTW-[AA-A]

ORIGINAL MAIN LINE, TOLEDO (AA-T)

	MILEAGE	COUNTY	CROSSINGS, JUNCTIONS, ETC.
Toledo OH (Summit Street)	0	Lucas OH	
Galena Street	0.7	"	
Manhattan	1.7	"	
Boulevard OH	2.7	"	J/AA-A 2.5

CONSTRUCTION/ABANDONMENT

DATE	ACT	END POINTS	MP	CHANGE	MI MAIN	SOURCE	NOTE
1874/8/5	B1	Summit Street–Boulevard	0–2.7	+2.7	0	2,4	1
1976/4/1	S	Summit Street–Boulevard	0–2.7	–2.7	0	3	27

OWNERSHIP

1874	Toledo & State Line (B1)
1878/5/11	Toledo & Ann Arbor, merger of Toledo & State Line
1880/10/14	Toledo, Ann Arbor & Grand Trunk, merger of Toledo & Ann Arbor
1884/5/19	Toledo, Ann Arbor & North Michigan, merger of Toledo, Ann Arbor & Grand Trunk
1895/9/20	Ann Arbor, reorganization of Toledo, Ann Arbor & North Michigan
1976/4/1	State of Michigan purchased as MICH-[AA-T]

ORIGINAL MAIN LINE, VIA LELAND (AA-01)

	MILEAGE [Toledo]	COUNTY	CROSSINGS, JUNCTIONS, ETC.
(Jct.)	47.3	Washtenaw	J/AA-A 47.3
Leland	52.2	"	J/AA-S 52.2
(Jct.)	56.9	"	J/AA-A 54.5
Whitmore Lk. (original)	59.3	"	
(Jct.)	61.1	Livingston	J/GTW-A 67.2

CONSTRUCTION/ABANDONMENT

DATE	ACT	END POINTS	MP	CHANGE	MAIN	SOURCE	NOTE
1881/8	B3	MP 47.3–Leland	47.3–52.2	+4.9	4.9	4	3
1886	B4	Leland–MP 61.1	52.2–61.1	+8.9	13.8	4	7
1893	X	MP 56.9–MP 61.1	56.9–61.1	–4.2	9.6	5	17
1896/Summer	X	MP 47.3–MP 56.9	47.3–56.9	–9.6	0	5	20

OWNERSHIP

1881	Toledo, Ann Arbor & Grand Trunk (B3)
1884/5/19	Toledo, Ann Arbor & North Michigan (B4), merger of Toledo, Ann Arbor & Grand Trunk
1895/9/20	Ann Arbor, reorganization of Toledo, Ann Arbor & North Michigan

SOUTH LYON BRANCH (AA-S)

	MILEAGE [Toledo]	COUNTY	CROSSINGS, JUNCTIONS, ETC.
Leland	52.2	Washtenaw	J/AA-O 52.2
Worden	54.9	"	
South Lyon	59.8	Oakland	

CONSTRUCTION/ABANDONMENT

DATE	ACT	END POINTS	MP	CHANGE	MAIN	SOURCE	NOTE
1881/8	B3	Leland–South Lyon	52.2–59.8	+7.6	7.6	4	3
1891/3/29	X	Leland–South Lyon	52.2–59.8	−7.6	0		14

OWNERSHIP

1881	Toledo, Ann Arbor & Grand Trunk (B3)
1884/5/19	Toledo, Ann Arbor & North Michigan, merger of Toledo, Ann Arbor & Grand Trunk

ORIGINAL MAIN LINE, AT BYRON (AA-03)

	MILEAGE [Toledo]	COUNTY	CROSSINGS, JUNCTIONS, ETC.
(Jct.)	82.7	Livingston	J/AA-A 82.7
Cohoctah (original)	84.4	"	
Byron (original)	90.7	Shiawassee	
(Jct.)	96.5	"	J/AA-A 95.2

CONSTRUCTION/ABANDONMENT

DATE	ACT	END POINTS	MP	CHANGE	MAIN	SOURCE	NOTE
1885	B4	Line	82.7–96.5	+13.8	13.8	4	
1895	X	Line	82.7–96.5	−13.8	0		19

OWNERSHIP

1885	Toledo, Ann Arbor & North Michigan (B4)
1895/9/20	Ann Arbor, reorganization of Toledo, Ann Arbor & North Michigan

MACON QUARRY SPUR (AA-YQ)

	MILEAGE	COUNTY	CROSSINGS, JUNCTIONS, ETC.
(Jct.)	0	Monroe	J/AA-A 24.7
(End of track)	1.6	"	

CONSTRUCTION/ABANDONMENT

DATE	ACT	END POINTS	MP	CHANGE	MAIN	SOURCE	NOTE
1886	B4	Line	0–1.6	[Y]+1.6	0	4	
1892	X	Line	0–1.6	[Y]−1.6	0	4	

OWNERSHIP

1884	Toledo, Ann Arbor & North Michigan (B4)
1895/9/20	Ann Arbor, reorganization of Toledo, Ann Arbor & North Michigan

STATE HOSPITAL SPUR (AA-YH)

	MILEAGE	COUNTY	CROSSINGS, JUNCTIONS, ETC.
(Jct.)	0	Washtenaw	J/AA-A 37.4
(End of track)	0.7	"	

CONSTRUCTION/ABANDONMENT

DATE	ACT	END POINTS	MP	CHANGE	MAIN	SOURCE	NOTE
1930	B10	Line	0–0.7	[Y]+0.7	0		25

OWNERSHIP

1930   Ann Arbor (B10), of segment

SIX MILE MINE SPUR (AA-YM)

	MILEAGE	COUNTY	CROSSINGS, JUNCTIONS, ETC.
(Jct.)	0	Shiawassee	J/AA-A 106.0
Six Mile Mine	7.1	"	

CONSTRUCTION/ABANDONMENT

DATE	ACT	END POINTS	MP	CHANGE	MAIN	SOURCE	NOTE
1895	B4	Line	0–7.1	[Y]+7.1	0		
ca.1951	X	Line	0–7.1	[Y]–7.1	0		

OWNERSHIP

1895   Toledo, Ann Arbor & North Michigan (B4)
1895/9/20   Ann Arbor, reorganization of Toledo, Ann Arbor & North Michigan

MAIN LINE, SECOND DISTRICT (AA-B)

	MILEAGE	COUNTY	CROSSINGS, JUNCTIONS, ETC.
	[Toledo]		
Owosso	107.1	Shiawassee	J/A-AA 107.1
Owosso Jct.	107.8	"	X/MC-S 63.6
(Jct.)	107.9	"	J/C to GTW-D 79.2, 0.1 mis.
King	108.8	"	
Carland	115.7	"	
Elsie	120.3	Clinton	
Bannister	123.8	Gratiot	
Hayes	125.8	"	
Ashley	128.3	"	J/GTW-M 0
Whites	131.2	"	
North Star	133.7	"	f. Douglas
(Jct.)	137.0	"	J/AA-02 0
Rawn	137.8	"	
Ithaca	138.3	"	
(End of purchase)	138.6	"	S end PM-VT
Wright	144.7	"	
(Jct.)	144.9	"	J/PM-VT 0.4
(Crossing)	145.1	"	X/PM-V 39.9
Alma	145.4	"	J/AA-BA 0
(Jct.)	145.9	"	J/PM-V 40.7
(Jct.)	146.3	"	J/AA-02 12.6
Forest Hill	149.8	"	
Parkinsons	150.8	"	
Shepherd	156.2	Isabella	f. Salt River
Burdick	158.4	"	
Brodie	159.9	"	

Taylors	160.8	"	
Mt. Pl.	163.8	"	
Transport	164.2	"	J/PM-LM 14.7
Martha	166.3	"	
Dingmans	168.3	"	
Rosebush	170.5	"	f. Calkinsville
Cowdens	172.5	"	
Doherty	174.0	"	
Burnham	176.1	"	
Clare	178.8	Clare	X/PM-L 50.4
(Crossing)	181.2	"	X/PM-LH(old) 2.5
Farwell	183.7	"	
Clintons	186.8	"	
Summit	189.0	"	
Phelps	190.0	"	
(Jct.)	192.1	"	J/AA-04 192.1
Lake George	194.2	"	
Clarence	197.6	"	
(Jct.)	200.2	"	J/AA-04 200.5
Temple	200.7	"	f. Campbell
Pennocks	203.4	"	
Marion	208.6	Osceola	J/M&GR-A 72.0
Park Lake	212.7	"	
Duroy	212.9	"	
McBain	216.4	Missaukee	
Littlefield		"	
Lucas	220.4	"	
Nelson		"	
Brink Siding		"	
Browns Siding		Wexford	
CN	227.0	"	X/GR&I-N 331.5
Cadillac	227.1	"	J/AA-C 227.1

CONSTRUCTION/ABANDONMENT

DATE	ACT	END POINTS	MP	CHANGE	MAIN	SOURCE	NOTE
1884/6/27	B4	Owosso–MP 137.0	107.9–137.0	+29.1		1	4
1884/6/27	B4	GTW connection in Owosso	0.1	+0.1	29.2	1	
1885	B4	Alma–Shepherd	145.4–156.2	+10.8	40.0	2	
1886/7/1	B6	Shepherd–Mt. Pl.	156.2–163.8	+7.6		1	5
1886/10	B4	Owosso–MP 107.9	107.1–107.9	+0.8	48.4		6
1888/8	B7	Mt. Pl.–MP 192.1	163.8–192.1	+28.3		4	
1888/8	B7	MP 200.2–Cadillac	200.2–227.1	+26.9		4	
1888	S1	GTW connection in Owosso		–0.1	103.5		10
1889	B4	MP 137.0–Ithaca	137.0–138.6	+1.6	105.1	4	
1894	B4	MP 192.1–MP 200.2	192.1–200.2	+8.1	113.2	5	
1897/2/15	P1	Ithaca–MP 144.9	138.6–144.9	+6.3		4	21
1897	B10	MP 144.9–MP 145.4	144.9–145.4	+0.5	120.0		
1976/4/1	S2	Owosso–Ashley	107.1–128.3	–21.2		3	31
1976/4/1	S1	Ashley–Cadillac	128.3–227.1	–98.8	0	3	29

OWNERSHIP

1884	Toledo, Ann Arbor & North Michigan (B4)
1885	Lansing, Alma, Mt. Pleasant & Northern (B5), of segment
1886/5/5	Toledo, Ann Arbor & Mt. Pleasant (B6), renaming of LAMP&N
1886/8/19	Toledo, Ann Arbor & North Michigan, merger of Toledo, Ann Arbor & Mt. Pleasant

1887	Toledo, Ann Arbor & Cadillac (B7)
1887/12/21	Toledo, Ann Arbor & North Michigan, merger of Toledo, Ann Arbor & Cadillac
1895/9/20	Ann Arbor (B10), reorganization of Toledo, Ann Arbor & North Michigan
1976/4/1	Grand Trunk Western purchased MP 107.1–MP 128.3 as GTW-[AA-B]
1976/4/1	State of Michigan purchased MP 128.3–MP 145.4 as MICH-[AA-B1]
1976/4/1	State of Michigan purchased MP 145.4–MP 227.1 as MICH-[AA-B2]

ALMA BRANCH (AA-BA)

	MILEAGE	COUNTY	CROSSINGS, JUNCTIONS, ETC.
Alma	0	Gratiot	J/AA-B 145.4
(Pine Riv.)	1.1	"	

CONSTRUCTION/ABANDONMENT

DATE	ACT	END POINTS	MP	CHANGE	MAIN	SOURCE	NOTE
1885	B5	Line	0–1.1	+1.1	1.1	2	
1897	X	Line	0–1.1	−1.1	0		

OWNERSHIP

1885	Lansing, Alma, Mt. Pleasant & Northern (B5)
1886/5/5	Toledo, Ann Arbor & Mt. Pleasant, renaming of Lansing, Alma, Mt. Pleasant & Northern
1886/8/19	Toledo, Ann Arbor & North Michigan, merger of Toledo, Ann Arbor & Mt. Pleasant
1895/9/20	Ann Arbor, reorganization of Toledo, Ann Arbor & North Michigan

ORIGINAL MAIN LINE, VIA ST. LOUIS (AA-02)

	MILEAGE	COUNTY	CROSSINGS, JUNCTIONS, ETC.
(Jct.)	0	Gratiot	J/AA-B 137.0
Ithaca (original)	0.9	"	
(Crossing, jct.)	8.4	"	X/PM-V 37.0, J/AA-2A 8.4
(Jct.)	9.3	"	J/PM-VO 37.2
Alma (original)	12.3	"	
(Jct.)	12.4	"	J/PM-VO 40.3
(Jct.)	12.6	"	J/AA-B 146.

CONSTRUCTION/ABANDONMENT

DATE	ACT	END POINTS	MP	CHANGE	MAIN	SOURCE	NOTE
1884/6/27	B4	(Jct.–Jct.)	0–8.4	+8.4	8.4	1	4
1887	B4	(Jct.)–(Jct.)	8.4–12.6	+4.2	12.6		8
1897	X	Line	0–12.6	−12.6	0		23

OWNERSHIP

| 1884 | Toledo, Ann Arbor & North Michigan (B4) |
| 1895/9/20 | Ann Arbor, reorganization of Toledo, Ann Arbor & North Michigan |

BRANCH TO ST. LOUIS (AA-02A)

	MILEAGE [Ithaca]	COUNTY	CROSSINGS, JUNCTIONS, ETC.
(Jct.)	8.4	Gratiot	J/AA-2 8.4
(Crossing)	9.0	"	X/PM-VO 36.7
St. Louis	9.8	"	

CONSTRUCTION/ABANDONMENT

DATE	ACT	END POINTS	MP	CHANGE	MAIN	SOURCE	NOTE
1884/6/27	B4	(Jct.)–St. Louis	8.4–9.8	+1.4	1.4	1	4
1897	X	Line	8.4–9.8	−1.4	0		24

OWNERSHIP

1884	Toledo, Ann Arbor & North Michigan (B4)	
1895/9/20	Ann Arbor, reorganization of Toledo, Ann Arbor & North Michigan	

ORIGINAL MAIN LINE, AT LAKE GEORGE (AA-04)

	MILEAGE [Toledo]	COUNTY	CROSSINGS, JUNCTIONS, ETC.
(Jct.)	192.1	Clare	J/AA-B 192.1
Lk. George (original)	192.8	"	
(Jct.)	200.5	"	J/AA-B 200.2

CONSTRUCTION/ABANDONMENT

DATE	ACT	END POINTS	MP	CHANGE	MAIN	SOURCE	NOTE
1888/8	B4	Line	192.1–200.5	+8.4	8.4	4	9
1894	X	Line	192.1–200.5	–8.4	0	5	18

OWNERSHIP

1888	Toledo, Ann Arbor & Cadillac (B7)	
1887/12/21	Toledo, Ann Arbor & North Michigan, merger of Toledo, Ann Arbor & Cadillac	

MAIN LINE, THIRD DISTRICT (AA-C)

	MILEAGE [Toledo]	COUNTY	CROSSINGS, JUNCTIONS, ETC.
Cadillac	227.1	Wexford	J/AA-B 227.1
(Crossing)	228.0	"	J/spurs to Diggins Mill and to GR&I
Selma	228.2	"	f. Cadillac Yard
Bunyea	234.0	"	
Millersville	235.3	"	
Diggins	236.3	"	
Boon	237.7	"	
Williams	239.8	"	
McPherson	240.8	"	
Duforts	242.1	"	
Harrietta	244.1	"	
Pecks Siding		"	
Saunders	246.2	"	
Derrys	246.6	"	
Yuma	249.1	"	
Perues	251.1	"	
Wards Siding		"	
Mesick	254.1	"	f. Sherman
Claggetts	256.3	"	B/M&NE-R 15.1
Bagnall	257.7	"	f. Springville
Arcadia	259.2	"	
Fays	259.6	"	
Harts	260.1	"	
(Jct.)	261.2	Manistee	J/AA-05 261.2
Harland	261.6	"	
(Jct.)	263.3	"	J/AA-05 263.2
Pomona	265.0	"	f. Cleon Center
Copemish	267.6	"	X/M&NE-A 29.4
(Jct.)	268.0	"	J/A&BR 21.0
Beecher	269.7	"	
Thompsonville	270.4	Benzie	X/PM-P 120.9
Willis	270.9	"	

Weldon Bridge	271.3	"		
Weldon Center	273.4?	"		
Welden	276.6	"		
Homestead	277.9	"		
Benzonia	281.5	"	f. Cases?	
Beulah	282.8	"	f. Crystal Cty.	
Lake	283.3	"		
VanDemans	284.0	"		
Gravel Pit	285.8	"		
Bay Point	286.3	"	f. Crystal Lk.	
Jct. Switch	290.3	"	J/AA-F 290.3	
Frankfort	292.2	"		
(End of track)	292.4	"		

CONSTRUCTION/ABANDONMENT

DATE	ACT	END POINTS	MP	CHANGE	MAIN	SOURCE	NOTE
1889/11/17	B6	Cadillac–MP 261.2	227.1–261.2	+34.1		4	11
1889/11/17	B8	MP 263.3–Beecher	263.3–269.7	+6.4		4	
1889/11/25	B9	Frankfort–Beecher	292.2–269.7	+22.5	63.0	4	
1897	B10	MP 261.2–MP 263.3	261.2–263.3	+2.1	65.1		
1980/7	S1	Cadillac–Frankfort	227.1–292.2	−65.1	0	3	30
1994	X	Thompsonville–Frankfort	271.2–292.2	[−21.0]			

OWNERSHIP

1889	Toledo, Ann Arbor & Lake Michigan (B8)
1889	Frankfort & South Eastern (B9)
1890/4/16	Toledo, Ann Arbor & North Michigan, merger of Toledo, Ann Arbor & Lake Michigan
1892/5/15	Toledo, Ann Arbor & North Michigan, purchase of Frankfort & South Eastern
1895/9/20	Ann Arbor, reorganization of Toledo, Ann Arbor & North Michigan
1980/7	State of Michigan purchased as MICH-[AA-C]

LINE TO BOAT LANDING (AA-F)

	MILEAGE [Toledo]	COUNTY	CROSSINGS, JUNCTIONS, ETC.
Jct. Switch	290.3	Benzie	J/AA-C 290.3
Elberta	290.7	"	
Boat Landing	291.8	"	f. S. Frankfort

CONSTRUCTION/ABANDONMENT

DATE	ACT	END POINTS	MP	CHANGE	MAIN	SOURCE	NOTE
1889?	B9	Junction Switch–Elberta	290.3–290.7	+0.4	0.4	4	
1892?	B4	Elberta–Boat Landing	290.7–291.8	+1.1	1.5	5	15
1980/7	S1	Jct. Switch–Boat Landing	290.3–291.8	−1.5	0	3	30
1994	X	Line	290.3–291.8	[−1.5]			

OWNERSHIP

1889	Frankfort & South Eastern (B9)
1892/5/15	Toledo, Ann Arbor & North Michigan (B4), purchase of Frankfort & South Eastern
1895/9/20	Ann Arbor, reorganization of Toledo, Ann Arbor & North Michigan
1980/7	State of Michigan purchased as MICH-[AA-F]

ORIGINAL MAIN LINE, AT HARLAND (AA-05)

	MILEAGE	COUNTY	CROSSINGS, JUNCTIONS, ETC.
	[Toledo]		
(Jct.)	261.2	Manistee	J/AA-C 261.2
Churchills	262.6	"	
(Jct.)	263.2	"	J/AA-C 263.3

CONSTRUCTION/ABANDONMENT

DATE	ACT	END POINTS	MP	CHANGE	MAIN	SOURCE	NOTE
1889/11/17	B8	Line	261.2–263.2	+2.0	2.0	4	
1897	X	Line	261.2–263.2	–2.0	0	4	22

OWNERSHIP

1889	Toledo, Ann Arbor & Lake Michigan (B8)
1890/4/16	Toledo, Ann Arbor & North Michigan, merger of Toledo, Ann Arbor & Lake Michigan
1895/9/20	Ann Arbor, reorganization of Toledo, Ann Arbor & North Michigan

ROSS MILL SPUR (AA-X6)

	MILEAGE	COUNTY	CROSSINGS, JUNCTIONS, ETC.
(Jct.)	0	?	
Ross Mill	1.5	?	

CONSTRUCTION/ABANDONMENT

DATE	ACT	END POINTS	MP	CHANGE	MAIN	SOURCE	NOTE
1890	B4	Line	0–1.5	[Y]+1.5	0	4	12
1897	X	Line	0–1.5	[Y]–1.5	0	4	

OWNERSHIP

1890	Toledo, Ann Arbor & North Michigan (B4)
1895/9/20	Ann Arbor, reorganization of Toledo, Ann Arbor & North Michigan

DIGGINS MILL SPUR (AA-X7)

	MILEAGE	COUNTY	CROSSINGS, JUNCTIONS, ETC.
(Jct.)	0	?	
Diggins Mill	1.3	?	

DATE	ACT	END POINTS	MP	CHANGE	MAIN	SOURCE	NOTE
1890	B4	Line	0–1.3	+1.3	1.3	4	13
1897	X	Line	0–1.3	–1.3	0	4	

OWNERSHIP

1890	Toledo, Ann Arbor & North Michigan (B4), of segment
1895/9/20	Ann Arbor, reorganization of Toledo, Ann Arbor & North Michigan

SALINE BRANCH (AA-G)

	MILEAGE	COUNTY	CROSSINGS, JUNCTIONS, ETC.
(End)	0	Washtenaw	
Pittsfield	2.3	"	J/AA-A 40.4
Saline	6.4	"	

DATE	ACT	END POINTS	MP	CHANGE	MAIN	SOURCE	NOTE
1969	P	Pittsfield–Saline	0–6.4	+6.4	6.4	3	26
1976/4/1	S1	Pittsfield–Saline	0–6.4	–6.4	0	3	27

OWNERSHIP

| 1969 | Ann Arbor. (Also see Lake Shore line LS-Y for prior ownerships) |
| 1976/4/1 | State of Michigan purchased as MICH-[AA-G] |

ACQUISITION/DISPOSITION RECORD

DATE	ACT	AA–	END POINTS		MI CHANGE	MAIN	NOTE
1874/8/5	B1	T,A	Summit St.(Toledo)–Alexis		+5.1	0	1
1878/6/21	B2	A	Alexis–Ann Arbor		+40.7	39.9	2
1881/8	B3	A,01,S	Ann Arbor–South Lyon		+14.2	54.1	3
1884/6/27	B4	B,02,02A	Owosso–St. Louis		+39.0	93.1	4
1885	B4	A,03	Hamburg Jct.–Durand		+34.8		
	B5	B,BA	Alma–Shepherd		+11.9	139.8	7
1886/7/1	B6	B	Shepherd–Mt. Pl.		+7.6		5
10	B4	A,B	Durand–Owosso		+12.2		6
	B4	YQ	Macon Quarry Spur		[Y] +1.6		
	B4	01	Leland–(Hamburg)		+8.9	168.5	7
1887	B4	02	St. Louis–Alma		+4.2	172.7	8
1888/8	B7	B,04	Mt. Pleasant–Cadillac		+63.6		9
	S2	B	In Owosso		–0.1	236.2	10
1889	B4	B	In Ithaca		+1.6		
/11/17	B8	C,05	Cadillac–Beecher		+42.5		11
/11/25	B9	C	Beecher–Frankfort		+22.5		
	B9	F	To Elberta		+0.4	303.2	
1890	B4	X6	Ross Mill Spur		[Y] +1.5		12
	B4	X7	Diggins Mill Spur		[Y] +1.3	303.2	13
1891/3/29	X	S	Leland–South Lyon		–7.6	295.6	4
1892	W	YQ	Macon Quarry Spur		–1.6		
	B4	F	Elberta–Boat Landing		+1.1	296.7	15
1893	B4	A	Whitmore Lk.–Lakeland		+7.7		16
	X	01	Whitmore Lk.–(Hamburg)		–4.2	300.2	17
1894	B4	B	At Lk. George		+8.1		
	X	04	At Lk. George		–8.4	299.9	18
1895	B10	YM	Six Mile Mine Spur		[Y] +7.1		
	B4	A	Cohoctah–Durand		+12.5		
	X	03	Cohoctah–Durand		–13.8	298.6	19
1896/Sum.	B10	A	A.A.–Whitmore Lk.		+7.2		
	X	01	A.A.–Whitmore Lk.		–9.6	296.2	20
1897/2/15	P1	B	Ithaca–Alma		+6.3		21
	B10	B	In Alma		+0.5		
	B10	A	Cherry St.–Boulevard		+2.5		
	B10	C	At Harland		+2.1		
	X	05	At Harland		–2.0		22
	X	X6	Ross Mill Spur		[Y]–1.5		12
	X	X7	Diggins Mill Spur		[Y]–1.3		13
	X	02	Ithaca–Alma		–12.6		23
	X	02A	To St. Louis		–1.4		24
	X	BA	In Alma		–1.1	288.0	
1930	B10	YH	State Hospital Spur		[Y]+0.7	288.0	25
1951?	X	YM	Six Mile Mine Spur		[Y]–7.1	288.0	
1969	P	G	Pittsfield–Saline		+6.4	294.4	26
1976/4/1	S1	A	Toledo–A.A.	MP 0–MP 47.5	–47.5		27[a]
4/1	S1	A	A.A.–Pitt	MP 47.5–MP 93.9	–46.4		28[b]
4/1	S2	A	Pitt–Owosso	MP 93.9–MP 107.1	–13.2		31[c]
4/1	S2	B	Owosso–Ashley	MP 107.1–MP 128.3	–21.2		31[d]

4/1	S1	B	Ashley–Cadillac	MP 128.3–MP 227.1	–98.8		29[e]
4/1	S1	G	Saline Branch	MP 0–MP 6.4	–6.4		27[f]
4/1	X	YH	State Hospital Spur		(–0.7)		
4/1	S	T	Summit St. Main Line		–2.7	66.6	27
1980/7	S1	C	Cadillac–Frankfort	MP227.1–292.2	–65.1		30[g]
7	S1	F	To Boat Landing	MP290.3–MP291.8	–1.5	0	30[h]

In 1980/7 all property had been conveyed to the State of Michigan or Grand Trunk Western, which see for subsequent acts.

1994	X		Thom.–Frankfort	271.2–292.2	[–21.0]
	X		to Boat Landing	290.3–291.8	[–1.5]

Act Column Key

A	Adjust mileage
B1	Built by Toledo & State Line
B2	Built by Toledo & Ann Arbor
B3	Built by Toledo, Ann Arbor & Grand Trunk
B4	Built by Toledo, Ann Arbor Northern Michigan
B5	Built by Lansing, Alma, Mt. Pleasant & Northern
B6	Built by Toledo, Ann Arbor & Mt. Pleasant
B7	Built by Toledo, Ann Arbor & Cadillac
B8	Built by Toledo, Ann Arbor & Lake Michigan
B9	Built by Frankfort & South Eastern
B10	Built by Ann Arbor
P	Purchase from Penn Central
S1	Sale to State of Michigan
S2	Sale to Grand Trunk Western
X	Abandonment
Y	Yard track
Z	Service ended

Sources

1. Ceasar, *Lamp Road.*
2. ICC, Valuation Docket 127.
3. MDOT official records.
4. Michigan Railroad Commission, *Aids, Gifts, Grants.*
5. Riggs, *Ann Arbor Railroad.*

Notes

[a]   to MICH-[AA-A1]
[b]   to MICH-[AA-A2]
[c]   to GTW-[AA-A]
[d]   to GTW-[AA-B]
[e]   to MICH-[AA-B]
[f]   to MICH-[AA-G]
[g]   to MICH-[AA-C]
[h]   to MICH-[AA-F]

1. This segment was constructed by the Pennsylvania Railroad for its owner and leased by it upon completion. It was purchased by J. M. Ashley on 1 May 1878. Summit Street served as the Toledo station until 1896.
2. This segment was built on a grade completed in 1873 by the Toledo, Ann Arbor & Northern. On 9 June 1877, J. M. Ashley purchased the grade from its purchasers in bankruptcy. Source 5 says tracklaying completed 16 May 1878.
3. Source 2 states construction began on this segment in Oct. 1879. Source 5 says construction completed May 1881, and that grading was completed to Pontiac by that time. The grade between South Lyon and Pontiac

was subsequently sold to a subsidiary of the Grand Trunk Western.

4. A graded line for this segment was purchased in 1883 from the Owosso & North Western. Source 4 says segment completed Aug. 1884. Source 2 states construction was begun about Oct. 1883.

5. Source 2 says the segment to Mt. Pleasant was completed in June 1886. The grade was acquired from the Lansing, Alma, Mt. Pleasant & Northern in March 1883 by J. M. Ashley. Source 5 says the segment was completed 1 November 1885; Source 3 appears to be in error.

6. Trackage rights over the Detroit, Grand Haven & Milwaukee were used between 1885 and the completion of this segment.

7. Trackage rights over the Michigan Air Line were acquired between the connection east of Hamburg and Hamburg Jct.

8. Between MP 9.3 and MP 12.4 this segment was on a grade formerly used by the Chicago, Saginaw & Canada and purchased 17 March 1887, from the Saginaw & Western.

9. This segment used a grade formerly used by the Lake George & Muskegon River which was purchased between 25 August 1886, and 20 December 1886, from C. H. Hackley & Company. Source 5 states construction began about July 1886.

10. This sale is assumed given the completion of the Toledo, Saginaw & Muskegon and a grant of trackage rights to the Grand Trunk Railway between MP 107.9 and Ashley that connected the properties.

11. Source 2 states construction was begun about June 1888. Source 5 states segment was completed from Cadillac to Harrietta in 1888.

12. This line has not been located but probably is in Clare County. Source 4 refers to a terminus on the Muskegon River.

13. This line has not been located but probably is in Wexford County.

14. Source 4 states northerly 2.0 miles was abandoned 30 September 1890, and the remainder in 1891. Source 2 states that the segment was sold to the South Lyon & Northern, but this sale appears not to have been consummated.

15. This date is assumed based on the beginning of car ferry operations and is supported inferentially by Source 5.

16. Source 4 gives completion date as 1895.

17. This segment was replaced by present main line AA-A, MP 54.5 to MP 62.2. Trackage rights on Grand Trunk Western ceased at this same time.

18. This segment was replaced by present main line AA-B, MP 192.1 to MP 200.2.

19. This segment was replaced by present main line AA-A, MP 82.7 to MP 95.2.

20. This segment was replaced by present main line AA-A, MP 47.3 to MP 54.5.

21. This segment was completed by the Ithaca & Alma on 28 December 1882, and purchased as part of an agreement for exchange of property dated 15 February 1897.

22. This segment was replaced by present main line AA-A, MP 82.7 to MP 95.2.

23. This segment was replaced by present main line AA-B, MP 137.0 to MP 146.3.

24. This segment was abandoned by the Ann Arbor as shown, but part of it retained by the Pere Marquette in St. Louis. This property was part of an agreement shown in Note 21.

25. This date is assumed given the construction of the hospital.

26. This segment was purchased from Penn Central and was originally completed in 1871. It originally appeared as LS-Y, MP 4.8 to MP 11.2.

27. This segment was provided service under state subsidy agreement beginning 1 April, 1976. Conrail was the designated operator until 30 September 1977, and Michigan Interstate Railway thereafter. State subsidy to Michigan Interstate was ended 1 October 1982.

28. This segment was provided service under state subsidy agreement beginning 1 April, 1976. Conrail was the designated operator until 30 September 1977; Michigan Interstate Railway thereafter until 1 October 1982; Tuscola & Saginaw Bay thereafter.

29. This segment was provided service under state subsidy agreement beginning 1 April, 1976. Conrail was the designated operator until 30 September 1977; Michigan Interstate Railway thereafter until 1 October 1982. Tuscola & Saginaw Bay became the designated operator between Ashley and Alma. Michigan Northern became the designated operator between Alma and Cadillac until 6 May 1984, and the Tuscola & Saginaw Bay thereafter.

30. This segment was provided service under state subsidy agreement beginning 1 April, 1976. Conrail was the designated operator until 30 September 1977; Michigan Interstate Railway thereafter until 1 October 1982.

Michigan Northern became the designated operator until 6 May 1984, and the Tuscola & Saginaw Bay thereafter.

31. The State of Michigan retained trackage rights on Grand Trunk Western tracks between these points.

Arcadia & Betsey River

MAIN LINE (A&BR)

	MILEAGE	COUNTY	CROSSINGS, JUNCTIONS, ETC.
Arcadia	0	Manistee	
State Rd.	1	"	
Sorenson	4.2	"	
Malcolm	6.4	"	
Butwell	8.3	"	J/spur to Timberlands, 1.0 mile
Saile	10.5	"	
Glovers Lk.	12.6	"	f. Glovers
Humphrey	13.8	"	
Springdale	15.0	"	
Henry	17.8	"	X/M&NE-1 4.4, X/PM-P 117.0
(Jct.)	21.0	"	J/AA-C 268.0
(Copemish, via AA-C	21.4)	"	

CONSTRUCTION/ABANDONMENT

DATE	ACT	END POINTS	MP	CHANGE	MAIN	SOURCE	NOTE
1884 ca.	B1	Arcadia–MP 11	0–11.0	+11.0	11.0		
1895/11/15	B2	Arcadia–Henry	0–17.8	+6.8	17.8	1	1,2
1896/12/12	B2	Henry–MP 21.0	17.8–21.0	+3.2	21.0	1	
1918/11/30	X	Henry–MP 21.0	17.8–21.0	–3.2	17.8	2	
1936/12/4	X	Arcadia–Henry	0–17.8	–17.8	0		

OWNERSHIP

1884	Arcadia & Betsey River Train Railway
1895/11/15	Arcadia & Betsey River, bought Arcadia & Betsey River Train Railway

Act Column Key

B1	Built by A&BR Train Ry
B2	Built by A&BR Ry
P	Purchased from A&BR Train Ry
X	Abandonment

Sources

1. Michigan Commissioner of Railroads, *Annual Report,* 1896.
2. Michigan Railroad Commission, *Aids, Gifts, Grants.*

Notes

1. This segment was built, in whole or in part, by the Arcadia & Betsey River Train Railway prior to transfer to this company. The predecessor was incorporated 3 April 1883, but the date it constructed its line is unknown.
2. Source 1 for year 1896 states the branch to Timberlands was 2.5 miles in length; Source 2 states the length as 1.0 miles.

Au Sable & Northwestern

MAIN LINE (ASNW-A)

	MILEAGE	COUNTY	CROSSINGS, JUNCTIONS, ETC.
AuSable	0.0	Iosco	
AuSable Riv. Jct.	0.9	"	X/D&M-S 73.6
Tucker Farm	2.5	"	f. Tucker
(Jct.)	2.9	"	J/D&M-SA 1.3
Foote Dam Jct.	5.7	"	
Seven Mile Hill	7	"	
Doane	9.8	"	
Bisonette	11.9	"	f. Beadle
Cooke Dam	13.3	"	
Fitzpatrick	15	"	
Five Channels Jct.	17.6	"	J/ASNW-A2 0
Bryant	18.5	Alcona	
Lott	21.1	"	f. Batton?
Glennie	23.3	"	f. Vaughn
Chevriers	24.4	"	
Bamfield	27.3	"	
Flat Rock (Lodge)	29.4	"	
Grams (Crossing)	32	"	
Russell	34.0	"	J/ASNW-AO 34.0, f. N. Branch
Hardy	39.8	"	J/ASNW-B 0
McCollum(s)	43.3	Oscoda	
Millen	46.4	"	J/ASNW-2B 10.3
Dew	47.5	"	
Wiggins	49	"	
Comins	51.1	"	J/ASNW-3 0, J/ASNW-4 0, J/ASNW-5 0, f.Pingree?

CONSTRUCTION/ABANDONMENT

DATE	ACT	END POINTS	MP	CHANGE	MAIN	SOURCE	NOTE
1891	B1	Au Sable–Russell	0–34.0	+34.0	34.0		2
1900	B2	Millen–Comins	46.4–51.1	+4.7	38.7		10
1907	B2	Russell–Millen	34.0–46.4	+12.4	51.1		11
1915	X	Au Sable–MP 2.9	0–2.9	−2.9	48.2		13,14
1927	X	Line	2.9–51.1	−48.2	0	1	14

OWNERSHIP

1891	Potts Logging Railway (B1)
1891/7/17	Au Sable & Northwestern, purchase of Potts Logging Railway
1912/6/1	Leased to Detroit & Mackinac
1914/6/1	Detroit & Mackinac, purchase of Au Sable & Northwestern

OLD MAIN LINE (ASNW-AO)

	MILEAGE [AuSable]	COUNTY	CROSSINGS, JUNCTIONS, ETC.
Russell	34.0	Alcona	J/ASNW-A 34.0
Twin Lake Jct.	36.6	Oscoda	J/ASNW-2 1.8
McKinley	38.4	"	J/ASNW-1 0, J/ASNW-2A 0, f. Potts

CONSTRUCTION/ABANDONMENT

DATE	ACT	END POINTS	MP	CHANGE	MAIN	SOURCE	NOTE
1891	B1	Russell–McKinley	34.0–38.4	+4.4	4.4		2
1907 ca.	X	Russell–McKinley	34.0–38.4	−4.4	0		11

OWNERSHIP

1891	Potts Logging Railway (B1)
1891/7/17	Au Sable & Northwestern, purchase of Potts Logging Railway

FIVE CHANNELS BRANCH (ASNW-A2)

	MILEAGE	COUNTY	CROSSINGS, JUNCTIONS, ETC.
Five Channels Jct.	0	Iosco	J/ASNW-A 17.6
Five Channels Dam	4.6	"	
Loud Dam	7.2		

CONSTRUCTION/ABANDONMENT

DATE	ACT	END POINTS	MP	CHANGE	MAIN	SOURCE	NOTE
1912/12/11	B2	Five Ch. Jct.–Five Ch. Dam	0–4.6	+4.6	4.6	2	12
1914	B2	Five Ch. Dam–Loud Dam	4.6–7.2	+2.6	7.2		12,14
1927	X	Line 0–7.2	−7.2		0		14

OWNERSHIP

1912	Au Sable & Northwestern (B2)
1912/6/1	Leased to Detroit & Mackinac
1914/6/1	Detroit & Mackinac, purchase of Au Sable & Northwestern

CURRAN BRANCH (ASNWB)

	MILEAGE	COUNTY	CROSSINGS, JUNCTIONS, ETC.
Hardy	0	Alcona	J/ASNW-A 39.8
Code	2.3	"	f. Marsh
Curran	4.4	"	
Byers	6.5	"	
Beevers	10.8	"	

CONSTRUCTION/ABANDONMENT

DATE	ACT	END POINTS	MP	CHANGE	MAIN	SOURCE	NOTE
1908/3/5	B2	Hardy–Curran	0–4.4	+4.4	4.4	2	
1910/6/18	B2	Curran–Byers	4.4–6.5	+2.1	6.5	2	
1912/12/11	B2	Byers–Beevers	6.5–10.8	+4.3	10.8	2	
1917 ca.	X	Curran–Beevers	4.4–10.8	−6.4	4.4	1	
1927	X	Hardy–Curran	0–4.4	−4.4	0	1	14

OWNERSHIP

1908	Au Sable & Northwestern (B2)
1912/6/1	Leased to Detroit & Mackinac
1914/6/1	Detroit & Mackinac, purchase of Au Sable & Northwestern

SOUTH BRANCH (ASNW-1)

	MILEAGE	COUNTY	CROSSINGS, JUNCTIONS, ETC.
McKinley	0	Oscoda	J/ASNW-AO 38.4, f. Potts
Imlay	7.9	"	
Church	14	"	
Woodrow	20	Ogemaw	
Damon	22.1	"	
Hicks	26	Oscoda	
Big Creek	30.5	"	
Luzerne	35.6	"	
(End of track)	36.5	"	

CONSTRUCTION/ABANDONMENT

DATE	ACT	END POINTS	MP	CHANGE	MAIN	SOURCE	NOTE
1886	B1	McKinley–Luzerne	0–36.5	+36.5	36.5		1
1897	X	McKinley–Luzerne	0–36.5	–36.5	0	2	7

OWNERSHIP

1886	Potts Logging Railway (B1)
1891/7/17	Au Sable & Northwestern, purchase of Potts Logging Railway

NORTH BRANCH (ASNW-2)

	MILEAGE	COUNTY	CROSSINGS, JUNCTIONS, ETC.
	[McKinley]		
Twin Lk. Jct.	1.8	Oscoda	J/ASNW-AO 36.6
(Jct.)	4.5	"	J/ASNW-2A 2.9
(Jct.)	9.6	"	J/ASNW-2B 9.6
Fairview	13.5	"	
Lymburn	15	"	
Townline	18.1	"	
Kane	24	"	
Maple Grove		"	
(Crossing)	24.7	"	X/L&SE-A 8.7 (sec 17 T28N R2E)
Tong	25	"	
Red Oak	ca.28	"	
Lewiston	30.9	Montmorency	f.Twin Lk.
(Crossing)	32.1	"	X/MC-MT5 1.4
Bear Lk.	34.5	"	

CONSTRUCTION/ABANDONMENT

DATE	ACT	END POINTS	MP	CHANGE	MAIN	SOURCE	NOTE
1886	B1	MP 4.5–Tong	4.5–25	+20.5	20.5		1,3
1892 ca.	B2	Tong–Lewiston	25–30.9	+5.9	26.4		5
1892	B2	Twin Lake Jct.–MP 4.5	1.8–4.5	+2.7	29.1		4
1897	B2	Lewiston–Bear Lake	30.9–34.5	+3.6	32.7	2	6
1898	X	Bear Lake–Red Oak	34.5–28	–6.5	26.2	2	8
1899	X	Red Oak–ca.MP24	28–24	–4.0	22.2	2	
1900	X	MP 9.6–MP 24	9.6–24	–14.4	7.8		9
1907	X	MP 9.6–Twin Lk. Jct.	9.6–1.8	–7.8	0		11

OWNERSHIP

1886	Potts Logging Railway (B1)	
1891/7/17	Au Sable & Northwestern (B2), purchase of Potts Logging Railway	

BRANCH (ASNW-2A)

	MILEAGE	COUNTY	CROSSINGS, JUNCTIONS, ETC.
McKinley	0	Oscoda	J/ASNW-AO 38.4, J/ASNW-1 0, f. Potts
(Jct.)	2.9	"	J/ASNW-2 9.6

CONSTRUCTION/ABANDONMENT

DATE	ACT	END POINTS	MP	CHANGE	MAIN	SOURCE	NOTE
1886 ca.	B1	Line	0–2.9	+2.9	2.9		1
1892	X	Line	0–2.9	–2.9	0		11

OWNERSHIP

1886	Potts Logging Railway (B1)	
1891/7/17	Au Sable & Northwestern, purchase of Potts Logging Railway	

BRANCH (ASNW-2B)

	MILEAGE	COUNTY	CROSSINGS, JUNCTIONS, ETC.
(Jct.)	9.6	Oscoda	J/ASNW-2 9.6
Millen	10.3	"	J/ASNW-A 46.4

CONSTRUCTION/ABANDONMENT

DATE	ACT	END POINTS	MP	CHANGE	MAIN	SOURCE	NOTE
1900	B2	Line	9.6–10.3	+0.7	0.7		10
1907	X	Line	9.6–10.3	–0.7	0		11

OWNERSHIP

1900	Au Sable & Northwestern (B2)	

BRANCH (ASNW-3)

	MILEAGE	COUNTY	CROSSINGS, JUNCTIONS, ETC.
Comins	0	Oscoda	J/ASNW-A 51.1
Marsh	1.7	"	
Hills	3.7	"	
(End of track)(Hardy?)	5.7	"	

CONSTRUCTION/ABANDONMENT

DATE	ACT	END POINTS	MP	CHANGE	MAIN	SOURCE	NOTE
1900	B2	Line	0–5.7	+5.7	5.7		10
1907	X	Line	0–5.7	–5.7	0		11

OWNERSHIP

1900	Au Sable & Northwestern (B2)	

BRANCH (ASNW-4)

	MILEAGE	COUNTY	CROSSINGS, JUNCTIONS, ETC.
Comins	0	Oscoda	J/ASNW-A 51.1
(Jct.)	2.1	"	J/ASNW-4A 2.1
Hardy (?)	4.2	"	

CONSTRUCTION/ABANDONMENT

DATE	ACT	END POINTS	MP	CHANGE	MAIN	SOURCE	NOTE
1900	B2	Line	0–4.2	+4.2	4.2		10
1907	X	Line	0–4.2	−4.2	0		11

OWNERSHIP

1900   Au Sable & Northwestern (B2)

BRANCH (ASNW-4A)

	MILEAGE	COUNTY	CROSSINGS, JUNCTIONS, ETC.
(Jct.)	2.1	Oscoda	J/ASNW-4 2.1
Fitzpatrick		"	
LeLone	ca.5	"	

CONSTRUCTION/ABANDONMENT

DATE	ACT	END POINTS	MP	CHANGE	MAIN	SOURCE	NOTE
1900	B2	Line	2.1–5	+2.9	2.9		10
1907	X	Line	2.1–5	−2.9	0		11

OWNERSHIP

1900   Au Sable & Northwestern (B2)

BRANCH (ASNW-5)

	MILEAGE	COUNTY	CROSSINGS, JUNCTIONS, ETC.
Comins	0	Oscoda	J/ASNW-A 51.1
Bonard	6	Montmorency	

CONSTRUCTION/ABANDONMENT

DATE	ACT	END POINTS	MP	CHANGE	MAIN	SOURCE	NOTE
1909/12/10	B2	Line	0–6	+6.0	6.0	2	
ca.1912	X	Line	0–6	−6.0	0		

OWNERSHIP

1909   Au Sable & Northwestern (B2)

ACQUISITION/DISPOSITION RECORD

DATE	ACT	ASNW–	END POINTS	CHANGE	MAIN	NOTE
1886 ca.	B1	1	McKinley–Luzerne	+36.5		2
ca.	B1	2,2A	McKinley–Tong	+23.4	59.9	2
1891 ca.	B1	A	Au Sable–Russell	+34.0		1
ca.	B1	AO	Russell–McKinley	+4.4	98.3	1,3
1892	B2	2	Twin Lk Jct.–MP 4.5	+2.7		4
	X	2A	McKinley–MP 2.9	−2.9		4
	B2	2	Tong–Lewiston	+5.9	104.0	5
1897	B2	2	Lewiston–Bear Lk.	+3.6		6
	X	1	McKinley–Luzerne	−36.5	71.1	7
1898	X	2	Bear Lk.–Red Oak	−6.5	64.6	8
1899	X	2	Red Oak–ca.MP 24	−4.0	60.6	
1900	X	2	ca.MP24–MP 9.6	−14.4		9
	B2	A	Millen–Comins	+4.7		10
	B2	2B	MP 9.6–Millen	+0.7		10

	B2	3	Comins–northwesterly	+5.7		10
	B2	4,4A	Comins–northeasterly	+7.1	64.4	10
1907	B2	A	Russell–Millen	+12.4		11
	X	AO	Russell–McKinley	–4.4		11
	X	2,2B	Twin Lake Jct.–Millen	–8.5		11
	X	3	Comins–northwesterly	–5.7		11
	X	4,4A	Comins–northeasternly	–7.1	51.1	11
1908/3/5	B2	B	Hardy–Curran	+4.4	55.5	
1909/12/10	B2	5	Comins–Bonard	+6.0	61.5	
1910/6/18	B2	B	Curran–Byers	+2.1	63.6	

On June 1912 this company was leased and on 1 June 1914 was sold to Detroit & Mackinaw. The lines conveyed were:

LINE DESIG.	END POINTS	MP	MAIN	SOURCE	NOTE
ASNW-A	AuSable–Comins	0–51.1	51.1		
ASNW-B	Hardy–Byers	0–6.5	6.5		
ASNW-5	Comins–Bonard	0–6	6.0		
	TOTAL		63.6		

DATE	ACT	ASNW-	END POINTS	CHANGE	MAIN	NOTE
1912/12/11	B2	B	Byers–Beevers	+4.3		
	B2	A2	Five Ch. Jct.–Five Ch. Dam	+4.6		12
	X	5	Comins–Bonard	–6.0	66.5	
1914	B2	A2	Channels Dam–Loud Dam	+2.6	69.1	12,14
1915	X	A	Au Sable–MP 2.9	–2.9	66.2	13,14
1917	X	B	Curran–Beevers	–6.4	59.8	14
1927	X	A	MP 2.9–Comins	–48.2		14
	X	A2	Five Ch. Jct.–Loud Dam	–7.2		14
	X	B	Hardy–Curran	–4.4	0	14

Act Column Key

B1   Built by Potts Logging Railway
B2   Built by AS&NW
 P   Purchased from Potts Logging Railway
 X   Abandoned

Sources

1.   ICC, *Finance Dockets*
2.   Michigan Railroad Commision, *Aids, Gifts, Grants.*

Notes

1.   This section was built in 1885–1886 by the J. E. Potts Salt & Lumber Company and subsequently passed to the Potts Logging Railway. It was conveyed to the AS&NW on 17 July 1891.
2.   This section was built in 1891 by the J. E. Potts Salt & Lumber Company and subsequently passed to the Potts Logging Railway. It was conveyed to the AS&NW on 17 July 1891.
3.   Tong (or Tongs) has not been located with certainty.
4.   This work is inferred from data in the 1893 *Michigan Manual* and the June 1893 *Official Guide.*
5.   This work is inferred from data in the June 1893 *Official Guide.* Source A has 1896.
6.   Source 2 reports 20 miles constructed. It is assumed that of the remaining 16.4 miles a part was logging branches and a part included as an adjustment for the completion of the Tong–Lewiston segment.
7.   Source 2 states that the western terminus was Woodrow, but this differs from the location of that point as shown in the June 1893 *Official Guide.*
8.   Source 2 reports 17.0 miles abandoned, but part of this total apparently was in logging branches.
9.   This abandonment is inferred given the start of operations to Comins.
10.   This work may been done in 1899, but Source 2 does not identify it clearly.

11. This work appears to have been done during this year given the realignment stated shown in the 1907 corporate articles.
12. This sequence of construction is assumed given the progress of construction of the two dams.
13. This is inferred given the D&M's construction of a connection from Au Sable Jct., on its main line, to Mile Post 2.9. It was most likely done in connection with the conversion of the line from narrow- to standard-gauge. This alteration eliminated the bridge over the Au Sable River. It is not known if any trackage was retained in Au Sable.
14. This work was done by the D&M which owned the property at the time.

Bear Lake & Eastern

MAIN LINE (BL&E)

	MILEAGE	COUNTY	CROSSINGS, JUNCTIONS, ETC.
Pierport	0	Manistee	(Sec 4 T23N R16W)
Patches		"	
Bear Lk.	5	"	
Saunders	6	"	
Chicken Creek		"	
Biglow		"	
Maple Grove	16	"	

CONSTRUCTION/ABANDONMENT

DATE	ACT	END POINTS	MP	CHANGE	MAIN	SOURCE	NOTE
1876 ca.	B1	Main line	0–5	+5.0			1
1882	B2	Main line	5–12.5	+7.5	12.5	1	
1886/12/2	B2	Extend Main line	12.5–16.0	+3.5	16.0	1	
1887/11/1	B2	Extend Main line	16.0–18.0	+2.0	18.0	1	
1902	X	Entire line	0–18.0	–18.0	0		

OWNERSHIP

1876	Bear Lake Train Railway
1882/1/20	Bear Lake & Eastern Railroad

Act Column Key

B1 Built by Bear Lake Train Railway
B2 Built by Bear Lake & Eastern
X Abandoned

Sources

1. Michigan, Commissioner of Railroads, *Annual Report,* 1887.

Notes

1. This segment was constructed by the Bear Lake Train Railway, probably in the late 1870s, and conveyed to the Bear Lake & Eastern as of its incorporation date. Both companies had the same owners.

Blissfield

MAIN LINE (BLIS)

For arrangement of stations, construction record, and prior ownerships, see Toledo & Western line T&W-A.

CONSTRUCTION/ABANDONMENT

DATE	ACT	END POINTS	MP	CHANGE	MI MAIN	SOURCE	NOTE
1935/6/15	P	Fitch OH–Wabash Subway	5.3–36.1	+30.8	19.6	1	1
1936/11	X	Fitch OH–Colling	5.3–24.7	–19.4		1	2
1936/11	S	Colling–MP 25.5	24.7–25.5	–0.8		1	3
1936/11	X	MP 25.5–Wabash Subway	25.5–36.1	–10.6	0	1	2

OWNERSHIP

1935	Toledo & Blissfield, purchased from Toledo & Western
1936/1/1	Blissfield RR, assumed operations from Toledo & Blissfield

Act Column Key

P   Purchased from Toledo & Western
S   Sold to private owners as private industrial road
X   Abandonment

Sources

1   Sell and Findlay, *The Teeter & Wobble*

Notes

GENERAL   The line was purchased from Toledo & Western, which see for earlier records. Both the Toledo & Blissfield and the Blissfield were controlled by the Joseph Schonthal Company, which also owned the Ohio & Morenci.

1.   The I.C.C. *Finance Docket* authorizing this purchase approved only 12.5 miles of line from the DT&I crossing at Riga to Adrian (Wabash Subway). Joseph Schonthal Co. may have taken title to the entire line and operated only that part authorized by the I.C.C.

2.   The I.C.C. *Finance Docket* authorizing abandonment approved only 12.5 miles of line.

3.   I.C.C. *Finance Docket* 11679 of 30 June 1937 authorized the Ohio & Morenci to acquire 1.7 miles of line, which included industrial tracks as well as 4100 feet of main line from Main Street east.

Boyne City

MAIN LINE (BC-A)

	MILEAGE	COUNTY	CROSSINGS, JUNCTIONS, ETC.
(End)	0.8	Charlevoix	
Boyne City	0	"	
Doyles	4	"	
Cushman	4.4	"	J/BC-2 0, f. Thumb Lk. Jct.
Moore(s)	6.1	"	J/BC-AB 6.1, f. Whites Jct.

(S. Wye)	6.3	"	J/wye to BC-AB 6.3, 0.2 miles
E. Moore	6.6	"	
Project	6.9	"	J/BC-3 0
Spur 3	10.4	Antrim	
Camp 10	?	"	J/BC-4 0
Camp 11	?	"	
Orville	11	"	
Staley	12.5	"	
N. Elmira	13.2	Otsego	B/GR&I-N 401.5
Mosher	14.8	"	
Marion	15.9	"	
Hallock	16.9	"	
Yuill	18.1	"	
Cameron	20.3	"	f. Hamilton
(Crossing)	23.0	"	X/MC-M 119.0
Gaylord	23.2	"	
Sparr	28.8	"	
(Crossing)	31.8	"	X/MC-MB3C 0.1
(Jct.)	32.8	"	J/spur, 1.2 miles
Shultz	33.3	"	
Marl	36	"	
Johnston	36.9	"	
Beeham	38?	"	
Nizer	38.8?	"	J/BC-5A 0, f. Barn Br.
Gibbs	40.2	Montmorency	
Galt	41	"	
Whiting	42.0	"	J/BC-5B 0
Kaybee	43	"	
Camp 21	43.5	"	
Stevens	44.0	"	
Fitzpatrick	45.7	"	
Meaford	46	"	
Camp 25	47	"	
Green	49.5	"	
Anderson	50	"	
Larson	51	"	
Atlanta	52.9	"	
Kingsland	55.5	"	
Watson	56.2	"	
Hemlock	58.1	"	J/BC-5N 0, J/BC-5S 0, f. Hoey?
Dobbins	58.7	"	
Stoddard	58.9	"	
Lutes	61	"	
Rust	62.8	"	
Connors	64.5	"	
Cahoon	65.9	"	
Cedar Spur	68.1	Alpena	
Canfield	69	"	
Fletcher	69.0	"	
Paisley	69.6	"	
Rayburn	71	"	
Spratt	74.4	"	
Stinsons	76.8	"	
Martin	79.8	"	
Herron	80.2	"	

McHarg	81.4	"	
Hillman Crossing	85.5	"	X/D&M-H 5.3
(Crossing)	90.9	"	X/D&M-N 125.2
(Crossing)	91.5	"	X/D&M-Q 0.7
Alpena	93.1	"	

CONSTRUCTION/ABANDONMENT

DATE	ACT	END POINTS	MP	CHANGE	MAIN	SOURCE	NOTE
1893/8/28	B1	Boyne Cty.–Moore	0–6.1	+6.1	6.1	2	
1894	B1	Moore–Project	6.1–6.9	+0.8	6.9	2	
1895	B1	Boyne–(End)	0–0.8	(+0.8)		2	
1905	B2	Project–Gaylord	6.9–23.2	+16.3	23.2	2	
1914/12/7	B2	Gaylord–Atlanta	23.2–52.9	+29.7	52.9	2	
1915/7	B2	Atlanta–Dobbins	52.9-58.7	+5.8	58.7	2	
1918/8/15	B2	Dobbins–Alpena	58.7–93.1	+34.4	93.1	2	
1935	X	Alpena–Moore	93–1–6.1	–87.0	6.1		
———							
1982	X	Boyne City–(End)	0–0.8	(–0.8)			
1982	X	Boyne City–Moore	0–6.1	–6.1	0		

OWNERSHIP

1893	Boyne City & South Eastern (B1)
1905/3/17	Boyne City, Gaylord & Alpena (B2), bought Boyne City & South Eastern
1935/1/15	Boyne City, bought Boyne City, Gaylord & Alpena
1976	Boyne Valley, bought Boyne City

CONNECTION TO BOYNE FALLS (BC-AB)

	MILEAGE	COUNTY	CROSSINGS, JUNCTIONS, ETC.
	[Boyne Cty.]		
Moore(s)	6.1	Charlevoix	J/BC-A 6.1
Boyne Falls	7.2	"	J/GR&I-N 409.0

CONSTRUCTION/ABANDONMENT

DATE	ACT	END POINTS	MP	CHANGE	MAIN	SOURCE	NOTE
1893/8/28	B1	Moore–Boyne Falls	6.1–7.2	+1.1	1.1	2	
———							
1982	X	Moore–Boyne Falls	6.1–7.2	–1.1	0		

OWNERSHIP

1893	Boyne City & South Eastern (B1)
1905/3/17	Boyne City, Gaylord & Alpena (B2), bought Boyne City & South Eastern
1935/1/15	Boyne City, bought Boyne City, Gaylord & Alpena
1976	Boyne Valley, bought Boyne City

THUMB LAKE BRANCH (BC-2)

	MILEAGE	COUNTY	CROSSINGS, JUNCTIONS, ETC.
Cushman	0	Charlevoix	J/BC-A 4.4
Easton	1.4	"	X/GR&I-N 410.3
Guerin		"	
Waggoner	4.0	"	J/BC-2E 0
Van Platen	6.4	"	J/BC-2A 0, J/BC-2D 0, f. Gaylord Jct.
Summit	7	"	
Camp 1	8-1/2	"	
Thumb Lk.	10	"	
(End)	13.7	Otsego	

CONSTRUCTION/ABANDONMENT

DATE	ACT	END POINTS	MP	CHANGE	MAIN	SOURCE	NOTE
1898/5/20	B1	Cushman–Guerin	0–5.0	+5.0	5.0	2	
1899/11/25	B1	Guerin–Thumb Lk.	5.0–10.0	+5.0	10.0	2	
1901	B1	Thumb Lk.–(End)	10.0–13.7	+3.7	13.7	2	
1904	X	East end of line	13.7–11.3	–2.4	11.3	2	
1913	X	MP 11.3–Waggoner	11.3–4.0	–7.3	4.0		
1915	X	Waggoner–Cushman	4.0–0	–4.0	0	2	

OWNERSHIP

1898	Boyne City & South Eastern (B1)	
1905/3/17	Boyne City, Gaylord & Alpena, bought Boyne City & South Eastern	

BRANCH (BC-2A)

	MILEAGE	COUNTY	CROSSINGS, JUNCTIONS, ETC.
Van Platen	0	Charlevoix	J/BC-2 6.4
Camp 2	3.5	"	
(Jct.)	4.5	"	J/BC-2G 0
Branch Lk.	5.0	"	J/BC-2B 0, J/BC-2C 0
Camp 3	6.0	"	

CONSTRUCTION/ABANDONMENT

DATE	ACT	END POINTS	MP	CHANGE	MAIN	SOURCE	NOTE
1903/10/1	B1	Van Platen–Camp 2	0–3.5	+3.5	3.5	2	
1904/6/1	B1	Camp 2–Camp 3	3.5–6.0	+2.5	6.0	2	
1913	X	Camp 3–Van Platen	6.0–0	–6.0	0	2	

OWNERSHIP

1903	Boyne City & South Eastern (B1)	
1905/3/17	Boyne City, Gaylord & Alpena, bought Boyne City & South Eastern	

BRANCH (BC-2B)

	MILEAGE	COUNTY	CROSSINGS, JUNCTIONS, ETC.
Branch Lk.	0	Charlevoix	J/BC-2A 5.0
Camp 4	0.5	"	
(Jct.)	2.7	"	J/BC-2B1 2.7
Camp 6	3.3	"	

CONSTRUCTION/ABANDONMENT

DATE	ACT	END POINTS	MP	CHANGE	MAIN	SOURCE	NOTE
1905	B2	Branch Lk.–Camp 6	0–3.3	+3.3	3.3	2	
1913	X	Branch Lk.–Camp 6	0–3.3	–3.3	0	2	

OWNERSHIP

1905	Boyne City, Gaylord & Alpena (B2)

BRANCH (BC-2B1)

	MILEAGE	COUNTY	CROSSINGS, JUNCTIONS, ETC.
(Jct.)	2.7	Charlevoix	J/BC-2B 2.7
(End)	6.2	"	

CONSTRUCTION/ABANDONMENT

DATE	ACT	END POINTS	MP	CHANGE	MAIN	SOURCE	NOTE
1905	B2	Line	2.7–6.2	+3.5	3.5	2	
1913	X	Line	2.7–6.2	–3.5	0	2	

OWNERSHIP

1905   Boyne City, Gaylord & Alpena (B2)

BRANCH (BC-2C)

	MILEAGE	COUNTY	CROSSINGS, JUNCTIONS, ETC.
Branch Lk.	0	Charlevoix	J/BC-2A 5.0
Camp 5	0.6	"	

CONSTRUCTION/ABANDONMENT

DATE	ACT	END POINTS	MP	CHANGE	MAIN	SOURCE	NOTE
1905	B2	Branch Lk.–Camp 5	0–0.6	+0.6	0.6	2	
1913	X	Branch Lk.–Camp 5	0–0.6	–0.6	0	2	

OWNERSHIP

1905   Boyne City, Gaylord & Alpena (B2)

BRANCH (BC-2D)

	MILEAGE	COUNTY	CROSSINGS, JUNCTIONS, ETC.
Van Platen	0	Charlevoix	J/BC-2 6.4
Camp 8	2.6	"	(section 6)

CONSTRUCTION/ABANDONMENT

DATE	ACT	END POINTS	MP	CHANGE	MAIN	SOURCE	NOTE
1908	B2	Van Platen–Camp 8	0–2.6	+2.6	2.6	2	
1913	X	Van Platen–Camp 8	0–2.6	–2.6	0	2	

OWNERSHIP

1905   Boyne City, Gaylord & Alpena (B2)

BRANCH (BC-2E)

	MILEAGE	COUNTY	CROSSINGS, JUNCTIONS, ETC.
Waggoner	0	Charlevoix	J/BC-2 4.0
Camp 8	1.5	"	(section 19)
(End)	3.0	"	

CONSTRUCTION/ABANDONMENT

DATE	ACT	END POINTS	MP	CHANGE	MAIN	SOURCE	NOTE
1906 ca.	B2	Line	0–3.0	+3.0	3.0		
1915	X	Line	0–3.0	–3.0	0	2	

OWNERSHIP

1905   Boyne City, Gaylord & Alpena (B2)

BRANCH (BC-2G)

	MILEAGE	COUNTY	CROSSINGS, JUNCTIONS, ETC.
(Jct.)	0	Charlevoix	J/BC-2A 4.5
Camp 9	1.3	"	

CONSTRUCTION/ABANDONMENT

DATE	ACT	END POINTS	MP	CHANGE	MAIN	SOURCE	NOTE
1906 ca.	B2	Line	0–1.3	+1.3	1.3		
1913	X	Line	0–1.3	–1.3	0	2	

OWNERSHIP

1905   Boyne City, Gaylord & Alpena (B2)

HEADQUARTERS BRANCH (BC-3)

	MILEAGE	COUNTY	CROSSINGS, JUNCTIONS, ETC.
Project	0	Charlevoix	J/BC-A 6.9
(Jct.)	1.0	"	J/BC-3E 1.0
(Jct.)(Goo?)	2.0	"	J/BC-3A 2.0
(Jct.)(Brown?)	3-1/2?	Antrim	J/BC-3B 0
(Maple Slope?)	4.0	"	
(Jct.)(Dow?)	5.2	"	J/BC-3C 5.2
White Siding	6.0?	"	
(Jct.)(Headquarters?)	7.0	"	J/BC-3D 7.0
(End)(S. End?)	8.6	"	

CONSTRUCTION/ABANDONMENT

DATE	ACT	END POINTS	MP	CHANGE	MAIN	SOURCE	NOTE
1894/11/12	B1	Project–MP 1	0–1.0	+1.0	1.0		
1897/11/20	B1	MP 1.0–Maple Slope	1.0–4.0	+3.0	4.0		
1899/12/30	B1	Maple Slope–White Siding	4.0–6.0	+2.0	6.0		
1900/12/20	B1	White Siding–Headquarters	6.0–7.0	+1.0	7.0		
1905	B2	Headquarters–South End	7.0–8.6	+1.6	8.6		
1916	X	Line	0–8.6	–8.6	0		

OWNERSHIP

1894   Boyne City & South Eastern (B1)
1905/3/17   Boyne City, Gaylord & Alpena (B2), bought Boyne City & South Eastern

BRANCH (BC-3A)

	MILEAGE	COUNTY	CROSSINGS, JUNCTIONS, ETC.
(Jct.)(Goo?)	2.0	Charlevoix	J/BC-3 2.0
(Jct.)	4.0	"	J/BC-3A1 (spur 1.0 miles)

CONSTRUCTION/ABANDONMENT

DATE	ACT	END POINTS	MP	CHANGE	MAIN	SOURCE	NOTE
1903	B1	Line and spur	2.0–4.0+1.0	+3.0	3.0		
1915	X	Line and spur	2.0–4.0+1.0	–3.0	0		

OWNERSHIP

1903   Boyne City & South Eastern (B1)
1905/3/17   Boyne City, Gaylord & Alpena, bought Boyne City & South Eastern

BRANCH (BC-3B)

	MILEAGE	COUNTY	CROSSINGS, JUNCTIONS, ETC.
(Jct.)(Brown?)	0	Charlevoix	J/BC-3 3-1/2
(Brickerville?)	1	"	

CONSTRUCTION/ABANDONMENT

DATE	ACT	END POINTS	MP	CHANGE	MAIN	SOURCE	NOTE
1897/11/20	B1	Line	0–1	+1.0	1.0		
1916	X	Line	0–1	–1.0	0		

OWNERSHIP

1897   Boyne City & South Eastern (B1)
1905/3/17   Boyne City, Gaylord & Alpena, bought Boyne City & South Eastern

BRANCH (BC-3C)

	MILEAGE	COUNTY	CROSSINGS, JUNCTIONS, ETC.
(Jct.)	5.2	Antrim	J/BC-3 5.2
(End)(E. End?)	7.7	"	

CONSTRUCTION/ABANDONMENT

DATE	ACT	END POINTS	MP	CHANGE	MAIN	SOURCE	NOTE
1905	B2	Line	5.2–7.7	+2.5	2.5		
1916	X	Line	5.2–7.7	–2.5	0		

OWNERSHIP

1905　Boyne City, Gaylord & Alpena (B2)

BRANCH (BC-3D)

	MILEAGE	COUNTY	CROSSINGS, JUNCTIONS, ETC.
(Jct.)	7.0	Antrim	J/BC-3 7.0
(End)(Kentucky?)	8.1	"	

CONSTRUCTION/ABANDONMENT

DATE	ACT	END POINTS	MP	CHANGE	MAIN	SOURCE	NOTE
1905	B2	Line	7.0–8.1	+1.1	1.1		
1916	X	Line	7.0–8.1	–1.1	0		

OWNERSHIP

1905　Boyne City, Gaylord & Alpena (B2)

BRANCH (BC-3E)

	MILEAGE	COUNTY	CROSSINGS, JUNCTIONS, ETC.
(Jct.)	1.0	Charlevoix	J/BC-3 1.0
—spurs off BC-3E, 2 miles in length, unlocated			
(End)(Camp 2?)	5.0	"	(sec 23 T32N R6W)

CONSTRUCTION/ABANDONMENT

DATE	ACT	END POINTS	MP	CHANGE	MAIN	SOURCE	NOTE
1894/11/12	B1	Line	1.0–5.0	+4.0	4.0	2	
1896/12/20	B1	Spurs	—	+2.0	6.0		
1904	X	Line and spurs	1.0–5.0	–6.0	0		

OWNERSHIP

1894　Boyne City & South Eastern (B1)

BRANCH (BC-4)

	MILEAGE	COUNTY	CROSSINGS, JUNCTIONS, ETC.
Camp 10	0	Antrim	J/BC-A near MP 10
Springwater	3.8	"	

CONSTRUCTION/ABANDONMENT

DATE	ACT	END POINTS	MP	CHANGE	MAIN	SOURCE	NOTE
1905	B2	Line	0–3.8	+3.8	3.8	2	
1914	X	Line	0–3.8	–3.8	0	2	

OWNERSHIP

1905　Boyne City, Gaylord & Alpena (B2)

BRANCH (BC-5A)

	MILEAGE	COUNTY	CROSSINGS, JUNCTIONS, ETC.
Nizer	0	Otsego	J/BC-A 38.8?
(End)	3.0	"	

CONSTRUCTION/ABANDONMENT

DATE	ACT	END POINTS	MP	CHANGE	MAIN	SOURCE	NOTE
??		Line					11

OWNERSHIP

??	Boyne City, Gaylord & Alpena (B2)

BRANCH (BC-5B)

	MILEAGE	COUNTY	CROSSINGS, JUNCTIONS, ETC.
(Whiting)	0	Montmorency	J/BC-A 41.9
Camp 29	4.0	"	

CONSTRUCTION/ABANDONMENT

DATE	ACT	END POINTS	MP	CHANGE	MAIN	SOURCE	NOTE
??		Line					11

OWNERSHIP

??	Boyne City, Gaylord & Alpena (B2)

BRANCH (BC-5N)

	MILEAGE	COUNTY	CROSSINGS, JUNCTIONS, ETC.
Hemlock	0	Montmorency	J/BC-A 58.1
(Jct.)	1.7	"	J/spur to Camp 30, 0.8 miles
(Jct.)	3.3	"	J/spur, 0.7 miles
(End)	5.3	"	

CONSTRUCTION/ABANDONMENT

DATE	ACT	END POINTS	MP	CHANGE	MAIN	SOURCE	NOTE
??		Line					11

OWNERSHIP

??	Boyne City, Gaylord & Alpena (B2)

BRANCH (BC-5S)

	MILEAGE	COUNTY	CROSSINGS, JUNCTIONS, ETC.
Hemlock	0	Montmorency	J/BC-A 58.1
(Jct.)	5.6	"	J/spur, 1.5 miles
Camp 29	6.1	"	
(End)	7.2	"	

CONSTRUCTION/ABANDONMENT

DATE	ACT	END POINTS	MP	CHANGE	MAIN	SOURCE	NOTE
??		Line					11

OWNERSHIP

??	Boyne City, Gaylord & Alpena (B2)

ACQUISITION/DISPOSITION RECORD

DATE	ACT	BC–	END POINTS	CHANGE	MI MAIN	NOTE
1893/8/28	B1	A,AB	Boyne City–Boyne Falls	+7.2	7.2	
1894/11/12	B1	A	Moore–Project	+0.8		
	B1	3	Project–south	+1.0		
	B1	3E	Branch	+4.0	13.0	
1895	B1	A	In Boyne City	(+0.8)	13.0	
1896/12/20	B1	3E	Spurs off branch	+2.0	15.0	
1897/11/20	B1	3	Extend to Maple Slope	+3.0		
	B1	3B	Branch to Brickerville	+1.0	19.0	
1898/5/20	B1	2	Cushman–Guerin	+5.0	24.0	
1899/11/25	B1	2	Guerin–Thumb Lake	+5.0		
12/30	B1	3	Maple Slope–White Siding	+2.0	31.0	1
1900/12/20	B1	3	White Siding–Headquarters	+1.0	32.0	
1901	B1	2	Thumb Lake–east	+3.7	35.7	
1903	B1	2A	Van Platen–Camp 2	+3.5		
	B1	3A	Branch	+3.0	42.2	
1904/6/1	B1	2A	Camp 2–Camp 3	+2.5		
	X	2	East end of branch	−2.4		
	X	3E	Branch and spurs	−6.0	36.3	
1905	B2	A	Project–Gaylord	+16.3		
	B2	2B	Branch Lake–Camp 6	+3.3		
	B2	2B1	Spur	+3.5		
	B2	2C	Branch Lake–Camp 5	+0.6		
	B2	3	Headquarters–South End	+1.6		2
	B2	3C	Branch	+2.5		
	B2	3D	Branch	+1.1		
	B2	4	Camp 10–Springwater	+3.8	69.0	3
1906 ca.	B2	2E	Waggoner–Camp 8	+3.0		4
	B2	2G	Br. to Camp 9	+1.3	73.3	4
1908	B2	2D	Van Platen–Camp 8	+2.6	75.9	5
1913	X	2	East of Waggoner	−7.3		
	X	2A	Van Platen–Camp 3	−6.0		
	X	2B	Branch Lk.–Camp 6	−3.3		
	X	2B1	Spur	−3.5		
	X	2C	Branch Lk.–Camp 5	−0.6		
	X	2D	Van Platen–Camp 8	−2.6		
	X	2G	Br. to Camp 9	−1.3	51.3	6
1914	X	4	Camp 10–Springwater	−3.8		
	B2	A	Gaylord–Atlanta	+29.7	77.2	7
1915/7	B2	A	Atlanta–Dobbins	+5.8		
	X	2,2E	Cushman–east	−7.0		
	X	3A	Br.	−3.0	73.0	
1916	X	3	Project–S. End	−8.6		
	X	3B	Brown–Brickerville	−1.0		
	X	3C	Branch to E. End	−2.5		
	X	3D	Branch	−1.1	59.8	8
1918/8/15	B2	A	Dobbins–Alpena	+34.4	94.2	
1935	X	A	Alpena–Moore	−87.0	7.2	9
1977	S	A,AB	Boyne Cty.–Boyne Falls	−8.0	0	10

Act Column Key

    B1   Built by Boyne City & South Eastern
    B2   Built by Boyne City, Gaylord & Alpena
    S   Sale to Boyne Valley
    X   Abandonment

Sources

    1.   Michigan, Commissioner of Railroads, *Annual Report,* 1899.
    2.   Michigan Railroad Commission, *Aids, Gifts, Grants.*

Notes

GENERAL   The construction and abandonment records for the Thumb Lake Branch (BC-2) and the spurs from that branch, and for the Headquarters Branch (BC-3) and the spurs from that branch, are fragmentary and in some cases contradictory. These branches were used primarily for lumbering operations of the owner of the railroad. In some cases judgments have been made as to mileage of the various spurs. The location of some of the branches cited in Source 2 have not been located in this research.

1.   Source 1 gives 19.12 miles of main line and 12.88 miles of sidings and spurs.

2.   Source 2 gives 12.10 miles added to line BC-3. This total probably included spurs off that branch.

3.   This branch has not been located.

4.   This construction has been assigned to this year but was not so stated in Source 2.

5.   Source 2 also has an addition to BC-3 of 4.5 miles which has not been included herein.

6.   Source 2 has a total reduction of 20.4 miles, all of which is attributed to BC-2 and spurs from that branch.

7.   Source 2 also has a reduction of 4.0 miles from BC-3 or one of the spurs off that line.

8.   Source 2 states that the company abandoned 21.58 miles, apparently all of it from BC-3 and spurs off that line, and also an adjustment reducing length by 10.63 miles which has not been located for this work.

9.   The ICC authorized abandonment of 83.6 miles. Some trackage in Alpena may have been sold to the Detroit & Mackinac.

10.   The purchasing Boyne Valley Railroad operated the property as a tourist railroad, but apparently did not represent itself to be a common carrier. The property was not used for several years before its removal in 1982.

11.   The date of construction and/or abandonment could not be determined and, therefore, this line is not included in the mileage shown in the Acquisition/Disposition Record.

Buckley & Douglas

LINE (B&D)

	MILEAGE	COUNTY	CROSSINGS, JUNCTIONS, ETC.
(Musk. Riv.)	0	Manistee	(sec 36 T22N R14W)
(End)	8.0	"	(sec 20? T23N R13W)

CONSTRUCTION/ABANDONMENT

DATE	ACT	END POINTS	MP	CHANGE	MAIN	SOURCE	NOTE
1881/6/20	B	Line	0–8.0	+8.0	8.0	1	
1889	X	Line	0–8.0	–8.0	0	1	

OWNERSHIP

    1881   Buckley & Douglas

Act Column Key

    B   Built by Buckley & Douglas
    X   Abandoned

Sources

1. Michigan, Commissioner of Railroads, *Annual Reports,* 1881, 1889.

Cadillac & Lake City

MISSAUKEE JCT.–VENEER JCT. (CLC-[GR&I-K])

CONSTRUCTION/ABANDONMENT

DATE	ACT	END POINTS	MP	CHANGE	MAIN	SOURCE	NOTE
1964	P	Missaukee Jct–Veneer Jct.	0–15.3	+15.3	15.3	1	
1972	X	Sandstown–Veneer Jct.	10.6–15.3	–4.7	10.6	1	
1975	X	Round Lk. Jct.–Sandstown	4.5–10.6	–6.1	4.5	1	
1984	X	Missaukee Jct.–Round Lk. Jct.	0–4.5	–4.5	0	1	1

OWNERSHIP

1964   Cadillac & Lake City

SANDSTOWN–LAKE CITY (CLC-[GR&I-K3])

CONSTRUCTION/ABANDONMENT

DATE	ACT	END POINTS	MP	CHANGE	MAIN	SOURCE	NOTE
1964	P	Sandstown–Lk. Cty.	10.6–11.8	+1.2	1.2	1	
1975	X	Sandstown–Lk. Cty.	10.6–11.8	–1.2	0	1	

OWNERSHIP

1964   Cadillac & Lake City

VENEER JUNCTION–FALMOUTH (CLC-[GR&I-K4])

CONSTRUCTION/ABANDONMENT

DATE	ACT	END POINTS	MP	CHANGE	MAIN	SOURCE	NOTE
1964	P	Veneer Jct.–Falmouth	15.3–19.9	+4.6	4.6	1	
1972	X	Veneer Jct.–Falmouth	15.3–19.9	–4.6	0	1	

OWNERSHIP

1964   Cadillac & Lake City

ACQUISITION/DISPOSITION RECORD

In 1964 this company bought part of Pennsylvania. For the arrangement of stations, construction record, and prior ownership see Grand Rapids & Indiana. The lines acquired were:

	CLC–	END POINTS	MP	MI MAIN	NOTE
	[GR&I-K]	Missaukee Jct.–Veneer Jct.	0–15.3	15.3	
	[GR&I-K3]	Sandstown–Lake City	10.6–11.8	1.2	
	[GR&I-K4]	Veneer Jct.–Falmouth	15.3–19.9	4.6	
		TOTAL		21.1	

DATE	ACT	CLC–	END POINTS	CHANGE	MI MAIN	NOTE
1972	X	K4	Veneer Jct.–Falmouth	–4.6		
	X	K	Sandstown–Veneer Jct.	–4.7	11.8	
1975	X	K3	Sandstown–Lk. Cty.	–1.2		

	X	K	Round Lk. Jct.–Sandstown	−6.1	4.5
1984	X	K	Missaukee Jct.–Round Lk. Jct.	−4.5	0

Act Column Key

  P Purchased from Pennsylvania Railroad.

  X Abandoned

Sources

  1. MDOT official records

Notes

  1. Line was not operated after about 1975 although company held itself out to be active.

Cadillac & Northeastern

MAIN LINE (C&NE)

	MILEAGE	COUNTY	CROSSINGS, JUNCTIONS, ETC.
(Lk. Cadillac)	0	Wexford	
(Crossing)	0.5	"	X/AA-C 228.0
(Crossing)	1.1	"	X/GR&I-N 332.8
(County line)	5.6	"	
Blodgett	6	Missaukee	
(Crossing)	7.5	"	X/GR&I-K 5.6
Becketts Crossing	8	"	
Gerrish	9	"	
Mitchells Crossing	10	"	
Kokomo (Park)	11	"	
Lk. Cty.	13.0	"	

CONSTRUCTION/ABANDONMENT

DATE	ACT	END POINTS	MP	CHANGE	MAIN	SOURCE	NOTE
1884	B1	Lk. Cadillac–Kokomo	0–11.0	+11.0	11.0	1	
1885	B1	Kokomo–Lk. Cty.	11.0–13.0	+2.0	13.0	1	1
1892	X	Line	0–13.0	−13.0	0		2

OWNERSHIP

  1884 Cadillac & Northeastern

Act Column Key

  B1 Built by Cadillac & Northeastern

  X Abandoned

Sources

  1 McGovern, "Cadillac and Northeastern Railway."

Notes

  GENERAL Although this company was not an incorporated railroad company under Michigan law, it conducted its affairs in such a way that it appeared to be a common carrier. The railroad was a wholly-owned operation of the Cummer Lumber Company.

  1. In the fall of 1885 the road built an extension into downtown Cadillac, near Pine and Lake Streets, for its passenger station. Also at this time the company built several logggging branches in Missaukee Company. for which no documentation could be found. This mileage is not included in the mileage record.

2. The abandonment was of the line north of MP 1.1. South of this point the road was retained for private logging road service. That part between MP 0.5 and MP 1.1 eventually was transferred to the Grand Rapids & Indiana as a yard track.

Canada Southern

CHICAGO & CANADA SOUTHERN (CCS)

	MILEAGE [Det.]	COUNTY	CROSSINGS, JUNCTIONS, ETC.
Slocum Jct.	17.1	Wayne	J/MC-T 17.1, J/MC-TG 0
Chandler	17.5	"	X/LS-D 22.4
(Jct.)	17.6	"	J/DTI-M 12.9 (present site)
Flat Rock	23.1	"	
Bryar Hill	26.5	Monroe	
Carleton	28.7	"	
Exeter	34.0	"	now Scofield
Maybee	35.5	"	
N. Raisinville	38.3	"	
(Jct.)	39.3	"	J/DTI-M 34.6 (present site)
Dundee	43.0	"	
Petersburg	47.8	"	
Deerfield	51.8	Monroe	
Corbus	53.5	"	X/LS-M 22.2
Grosvenor	59.0	"	X/LS-A 321.2
—thence via LS-F, for detail which see			
Fayette OH	83.9		

CONSTRUCTION/ABANDONMENT

DATE	ACT	END POINTS	MP	CHANGE	MI MAIN	SOURCE	NOTE
1872/7/4	B	Grosvenor–Fayette OH	59.0–84.2	+25.2	20.5	1	
1873/11/13	B	Slocum Jct.–Grosvenor	17.1–59.0	+41.9	62.4	1	
1893	X	Grosvenor–Corbus	53.5–59.0	−5.5	56.9		1
1897	X	Slocum Jct.–MP 17.6	17.1–17.6	−0.5			2
1897/11/15	S	MP 17.6–MP 39.3	17.6–39.3	−21.7			1
1897/12/5	X	MP 39.3–Corbus	39.3–53.5	−14.2	20.5	1	2
		for subsequent record see Lake Shore & Michigan Southern line LS-F					

OWNERSHIP

1872	Chicago & Canada Southern (B), controlled by Canada Southern
1879/11	Lake Shore & Michigan Southern, leased Chicago & Canada Southern
1888/11/11	Detroit & Chicago, to reorganize Chicago & Canada Southern
	for subsequent ownership see Lake Shore & Michigan Southern line LS-F

CANADA SOUTHERN BRIDGE COMPANY

See Michigan Central line MC-TG for detail of stations

CONSTRUCTION/ABANDONMENT

DATE	ACT	END POINTS	MP	CHANGE	MAIN	SOURCE	NOTE
1873/9	B2	Slocum Jct.–Stony Island	0–3.1	+3.1	3.1	1	
		for subsequent record see Michigan Central line MC-TG					

OWNERSHIP

1873   Canada Southern Bridge Co. (B2), controlled by Canada Southern
for subsequent ownership see Michigan Central line MC-TG

TOLEDO, CANADA SOUTHERN & DETROIT
See Michigan Central line MC-T for detail of stations

CONSTRUCTION/ABANDONMENT

DATE	ACT	END POINTS	MP	CHANGE	MI MAIN	SOURCE	NOTE
1873/9/1	B3	MP 2.7–Toledo OH	2.7–59.2	+56.4	6.8	1	

for subsequent record see Michigan Central line MC-T

OWNERSHIP

1873   Toledo, Canada Southern & Detroit (B3), controlled by Canada Southern
for subsequent ownership see Michigan Central line MC-T

MICHIGAN MIDLAND
See Michigan Central line MC-DM for detail of stations

CONSTRUCTION/ABANDONMENT

DATE	ACT	END POINTS	MP	CHANGE	MAIN	SOURCE	NOTE
1873/12/7	B4	St. Clair Springs–Lenox	0–14.0	+14.0	14.0	1	

for subsequent record see Michigan Central line MC-DM

OWNERSHIP

1873   Michigan Midland & Canada (B4)
1882   Canada Southern, obtained control of stock
for subsequent ownership see Michigan Central line MC-DM

ACQUISITION/DISPOSITION RECORD

DATE	ACT	BELOW	END POINTS	CHANGE	MI MAIN	NOTE
1872/7/4	B1	LS-F	Grosvenor–Fayette OH (MI=20.5)	+25.2	20.5	
1873/9/1	B3	MC-T	W. Det.–Toledo OH (MI=46.8)	+56.5		
9	B2	MC-TG	Slocum Jct.–Stony Island	+3.1		
11/13	B1	CCS	Slocum Jct.–Grosvenor	+41.9		
12/7	B4	MC-DM	St. Clair Springs–Lenox	+14.0	126.3	
1879/11			properties LS-F and CCS leased to Lake Shore & Michigan Southern	−67.1	63.9	
1882/12/12			properties MC-T, MC-TG, and MC-DM assigned to Michigan Central	−73.6	0	

Act Column Key

B1   Built by Chicago & Canada Southern
B2   Built by Canada Southern Bridge Co.
B3   Built by Toledo, Canada Southern & Detroit
B4   Built by Michigan Midland & Canada
S   Sold to Detroit & Lima Northern (later Detroit, Toledo & Ironton)
X   Abandoned

Sources

1.   Michigan Railroad Commission, *Aids, Gifts, Grants.*

Notes

1. The actual date of abandonment is not determinable. Source 1 states it was not used after 1888 and abandoned not later than 1893.
2. This abandonment is inferred given the sale of the line east of Dundee in 1897 and the earlier abandonment of the line west of Corbus.

Central Michigan

For arrangement of stations, construction record, and prior ownerships, see Grand Trunk Western lines as identified below.

ACQUISITION/DISPOSITION RECORD

On 1987/9/4 Central Michigan acquired part of Grand Trunk Western. The lines acquired were:

LINE DESIG.	END POINTS	MP	MI MAIN	SOURCE	NOTE
CMGN-					
GTW-D	Durand–Coopersville	69.0–173.0	106.0		
GTW-S	Durand–Mere.St.Jct.	0–39.0			
	and Mershon–Carrollton	40.6–44.4			
	and Mac–N. Bay Cty.	51.0–56.6	48.4		
GTW-YGR	In Gr. Rpds.	158.2–159.6	(1.4)		
GTW-MR	Muskegon Ry. & Nav.	0–5.5	5.5		
GTW-DM	Penn Jct.–Walker	0–0.8	0.8		
GTW-[GR&I-M]	Walker–Musk.	10.0–39.3	29.3		
GTW-[GR&I-YM]	In Musk.	38.0–39.3	(1.3)		
GTW-Y1M	In Musk.	90.1–95.8	(5.7)		
	(GTW-M 2.4 miles converted to Y and added to GTW-Y1M above)				
GTW-YMA	In Musk.	0–0.4	(0.4)		
GTW-[PM-YI]	In Ionia	24.9–26.1	(1.2)		
GTW-[MC-Y1S]	In Owosso	61.1–64.2	(3.1)		
GTW-[MC-Y2S]	Swan Creek–Sag. Bay Jct.	92.5–101.2	(8.7)		
GTW-[MC-S]	Sag. Bay Jct–Bay Cty. WS	101.2–114.6	13.4		
GTW-[MC-Y1M]	Bay Cty. ES–Bay Cty. WS	0–0.7	(0.7)		
GTW-[MC-M]	Bay Cty. WS–Kawkawlin	0.7–5.0	4.3		
GTW-[MC-L]	BC&BC Jct.–Midland	1.7–18.9	17.2		
GTW-[MC-YM1]	In Midland	0–3.0	(3.0)		
GTW-[MC-YM2]	In Midland	0–0.6	(0.6)		
GTW-[MC-YBN]	Woodside–end	0.4–2.9	(2.5)		
GTW-[MC-Y3B]	Bay Cty. ES–Water St. Jct.	106.1–108.9	(2.8)		
GTW-[MC-YBL]	Water St. Jct.–26th St.	3.0–6.4	(3.1)		
GTW-[MC-YBS]	S. Water St.	1.1–2.7	(1.6)		
GTW-[MC-BS]	Sag. Bay Jct.–MX	20.7–20.2	0.5		
GTW-[MC-Y4B]	MX–Harger	20.2–15.5	(4.7)		
GTW-[AA-YB]	In Owosso	107.1–107.7	(0.6)		
		TOTAL	225.4		

DATE	ACT	LINE	END POINTS	MP	CHANGE	MAIN	NOTE
		CMGN-					
1989/12/14	S1	GTW-D	Marne–Coopersville	166.6–173.0	−6.4		
	X	GTW-DM	Musk. Br. conn.	0–0.8	−0.8		
	X	GTW-[GR&I-M]	Walker–Musk.	10.0–39.3	−29.3		
	X	GTW-Y1M	In Musk.	90.1–91.1	(−1.0)		
	X	GTW-YMA	In Musk.	0–0.4	(−0.4)		
	X	GTW-[GR&I-YM]	In Musk.	38.0–39.3	(−1.3)	188.9	

(continued)

1990/12/12	S2	GTW-MR	MR&N	0–4.0	–4.0		
12/12	S2	GTW-Y1M	In Musk.	91.1–95.8	(–4.7)		
	X	GTW-MR	In Musk.	4.0–5.5	–1.5	183.4	
1991	X	GTW-D	Owosso–Ionia	82.2–123.5	–41.3		1
ca.	X	GTW-S	Mershon–Carrollton	40.6–44.4	–0.8	141.3	
1993/7	S3	GTW-D	Ionia–Fuller	123.5–159.7	–36.2		
	S3	GTW-YGR	In Gr. Rpds.	0–1.4	(–1.4)		
	S3	GTW-[PM-Y1] In Ionia		0–1.2	(–1.2)	105.1	
1994 ca.	X	GTW-[MC-Y1M] Bay Cty. ES–Woodside		0–0.2	(–0.2)		
	X	GTW-[MC-Y3B] Bay Cty. ES–Water St. Jct.		106.1–108.9	(–2.8)		
	X	GTW-S	Mac-MP 54.2	51.0–54.2	–3.2		
	Y	GTW-S	MP 54.2–N. Bay Cty.	54.2–56.6	(2.4)	99.5	
1996	S1	GTW-D	Fuller–Marne	159.7–166.6	–6.9		
				TOTAL		92.6	

OWNERSHIP

1987   Central Michigan

Act Column Key

P   Purchased from Grand Trunk Western

S1   Sold to Coopersville & Marne

S2   Sold to Michigan Shore

S3   Sold to Grand Rapids Eastern

X   Abandoned

Note

1.   This is the date ICC authorized abandonment. Rails were not removed for several years after authorization.

Charlotte Southern

For arrangement of stations, construction record, and prior ownerships, see Michigan Central line MC-G.

ACQUISITION/DISPOSITION RECORD

DATE	ACT	END POINTS	MP	CHANGE	MAIN	SOURCE	NOTE
1999/1	P	[MC-Y1G] Charlotte–east	35.0–32.0	[Y]+3.0	0		

OWNERSHIP

1999   Charlotte Southern, wholly owned subsidiary of Adrian & Blissfield.

Act Column Key

P   Purchased from Grand Trunk Western.

Notes

GENERAL   This company is a terminal switching road and not an intercity carrier. Its mileage is not included the Michigan mileage table in chapter 2.

Chesapeake & Ohio

On 1 April 1947 this company acquired Pere Marquette. For arrangement of stations, construction record, and prior ownerships, see individual Pere Marquette lines. Its Acquisition/Disposition Record is continued in two places: under the name of the former company and under the name of the new company. The lines acquired were:

LINE DESIG.	END POINTS	MP	MAIN	SOURCE	NOTE
C&O-					
[PM-T]	Sag.–Toledo OH	0–130.1	130.1		
[PM-F]	Horton–Otisville	4.7–14.5	9.8		
[PM-FB]	Flint Belt	29.5–37.7	8.2		
[PM-B]	Sag.–Bay Cty.	0–17.0	17.0		
[PM-YBH]	Huron & Western	1.1–2.7	(1.6)		
[PM-YBS]	S. Bay Cty. Spur	0–1.9	(1.9)		
[PM-YBE]	Essexville Spur	0–2.4	(2.4)		
[PM-L]	Sag.–Ludington	0–137.6	137.6		
[PM-YL1]	4th Ward Branch, Lud.	0–2.2	(2.2)		
[PM-YL2]	Development Branch, Lud.	0–2.1	(2.1)		
[PM-M]	Walhalla–Manistee	0–26.8	26.8		
[PM-LM]	Coleman–Mt. Pl.	0–14.7	14.7		
[PM-S]	Sag.–Bad Axe	0–63.9	63.9		
[PM-SB]	Bay Port Branch	0–1.4	1.4		
[PM-SR]	Robert Gage Coal Spur	0–2.2	(2.2)		
[PM-N]	Pt. Hur.–Port Austin	0–86.9	86.9		
[PM-NS]	Poland–Sandusky	0–7.1	7.1		
[PM-NH]	Palms–Harbor Beach	0–26.1	26.1		
[PM-Q]	Sag.–Pt. Hur.	2.6–90.1	87.5		
[PM-YSB]	Sag. Belt Line	0.7–5.4	(4.7)		
[PM-YSL]	Loop Line, Sag.	0–1.3	(1.3)		
[PM-YSZ]	Zilwaukee Spur, Sag.	0–1.4	(1.4)		
[PM-YSW]	W. Side Branch, Sag.	0–1.7 & 2.9–3.1	(1.9)		
[PM-YSS]	S. Sag. Line, Sag.	0–4.2	(4.2)		
[PM-V]	Paines–Lakeview	7.7–71.7	64.0		
[PM-Y1VT]	In Alma	0–0.4	(0.4)		
[PM-D]	Delray–Wealthy St., Gr.Rpds.	4.6–151.8	146.4		
[PM-DW]	W. Det.–Oak	0–7.9	7.9		
[PM-YEL]	In E. Lans.	0–1.5	(1.5)		
[PM-DZ]	Pleasant St.–Sunnyside	151.5–151.9	0.4		
[PM-YDR]	Reeds Lk. Br., Gr. Rpds.	0–1.4	(1.4)		
[PM-G]	Edmore–Elmdale	59.5–110.5	51.0		
[PM-I]	Gr.Ledge–Ionia	0.8–27.6	26.8		
[PM-J]	Edmore–Remus	51.7–74.6	15.9		
[PM-I2]	Lyons Spur	0–1.0	1.0		
[PM-C]	Gr. Rpds.–Porter IN	0–117.9	117.9		
[PM-W]	New Buffalo–LaCrosse IN	34.2–0	1.2		
[PM-H]	S. Haven–Paw Paw	0–30.4	30.4		
[PM-Y1U]	In Ben. Hbr.	0–2.7	(2.7)		
[PM-A]	Allegan–Holland	0–23.0			
	And Cronje–Mears	24.5–92.2	90.1		
[PM-A2]	Waverly–Cronje	23.6–24.5	0.9		
[PM-Y1H]	In Holland	23.0–23.8	(0.8)		
[PM-AM]	Mears–Hart	91.6–95.2	3.6		
[PM-YM1]	S. Horn, Musk.	0–6.0	(6.0)		
[PM-YM2]	In Musk.	31.3–35.6	(4.3)		
[PM-YM3]	N. Horn, Musk.	0–1.0	(1.0)		
[PM-YGH1]	In Gr. Hav.	0–0.6	(0.6)		
[PM-YHG2]	In Gr. Hav.	0–1.3	(1.3)		
[PM-R]	Berry–White Cloud	0–31.0	31.0		
[PM-P]	Sunnyside–Bay View	0–226.2	226.2		
[PM-YTC]	In Trav. Cty.	147.2–148.5	(1.3)		
[PM-PE]	Williamsburg–Elk Rapids	0–9.4	9.4		
		TOTAL	1441.2		

On 30 November 1955 this company acquired Manistee & Northeastern. For arrangement of stations, construction record, and prior ownerships, see individual M&NE lines. Its Acquisition/Disposition Record is continued in two places: under the name of the former company and under the name of the new company. The lines acquired were:

LINE DESIG.	END POINTS	MP	MAIN	SOURCE	NOTE
C&O-					
[M&NE-A]	Manistee–Kaleva and	0–19.9			
	Hatchs–Trav. Cty.	64.6–69.8	25.1		
[M&NE-YM1]	Manistee–Filer Cty.	0–3.5	(3.5)		
[M&NE-YM2]	In Manistee	0–1.5	(1.5)		
[M&NE-N]	Hatchs–Northport	5.5–29.3	23.8		
[M&NE-O]	Onekama Jct.–Onekama	9.8–12.6	2.8		
		TOTAL	51.7		
		1955 YEAR TOTAL	1492.9		

ACQUISITION/DISPOSITION RECORD

DATE	ACT	C&O-	END POINTS	CHANGE	MI MAIN	NOTE
1956	X	[PM-P]	Baldwin–Kaleva	−36.3	1456.6	
1960 ca.	X	[PM-YSB]	In Sag.	(−0.9)	1456.6	
1963	X	[PM-R]	White Cloud–Fremont	−9.2		
	Y	[PM-R]	In White Cloud (as PM-Y1R)	(0.8)	1446.6	
1970 ca.	X	[PM-YGH1]	In Gr. Hav.	(−0.6)		
	Y	[PM-T]	In Flint (as PM-Y1T & Y2T)	(8.2)		
	X	[PM-T]	In Flint	−0.7	1437.7	
1971	X	[PM-H]	S. Haven–Cableton	−1.0		
	X	[PM-ES]	Erieau–Blenheim ON (MI=0)	−7.0	1436.7	
1972	X	[PM-I]	Ionia–Warden	−1.5		
	X	[PM-F]	Horton–Otisville	−9.0		1
	Y	[PM-F]	In Horton (as PM–Y1F)	(0.8)		
	X	[PM-N]	Pt. Hur.–Croswell	−24.6		
	X	[PM-NH]	Port Hope–Harbor Beach	−7.1		
	X	[M&NE-O]	Onekama Jct.–Onekama	−2.8	1390.9	
1973/11/15	X	[PM-A]	Allegan–Hamilton	−12.0		
	Y	[PM-SB]	Bay Port Br. (as PM-Y2SB)	(0.9)		
	X	[PM-SB]	In Bay Port	−0.5	1377.5	
1974	X	[PM-V]	Edmore–Lakeview	−12.0	1365.5	
1977/7/6	P1	[PM-A]	Ferrysburg–Gr. Hav.	+0.6	1366.1	
1979	X	[PM-PE]	Williamsburg–Elk Rapids	−9.4		
	X	[PM-LM]	Coleman–Mt. Pl.	−11.6		
	Y	[PM-LM]	In Mt. Pl. (as PM-Y2LM)	(2.3)		
	Y	[PM-LM]	In Coleman (as PM-Y1LM)	(0.8)	1342.0	
1981	X	[PM-A]	Mears–Montague	−19.9		
	X	[PM-AH]	Mears–Hart	3.6		
	X	[PM-YM3]	N. Horn, Musk.	(−1.0)		
	X	[PM-I]	Edmore–Remus	−15.9	1302.6	
1982/2/19	S2	[PM-P]	Grawn–Williamsburg	−22.7		
2/19	S2	[PM-P]	Charlevoix–Bay View	−16.5		
	S2	[PM-YTC]	In Trav. Cty.	(−1.3)		
	X	[PM-P]	Kaleva–Grawn	−26.3		
	X	[PM-P]	Williamsburg–Charlevoix	−50.6		
	X	[M&NE-A]	Manistee–Kaleva	−19.9		
	X	[M&NE-A]	Hatchs–Trav. Cty.	−5.2		
ca.	XL	[M&NE-N]	Hatchs–Northport	−23.8	1137.6	

1983	X	[PM-P]	In Hamilton		−0.9	
	S3	[PM-I]	In Ionia		−1.2	
	X	[PM-I]	Portland–Ionia		−13.0	
	X	[PM-I2]	Lyons Spur		−1.0	
/1/26	P1	[GTW-YMG]	In Greenville		(+0.6)	1121.5
1984	X	[PM-N]	Port Austin–Kinde		−7.4	
	X	[PM-N]	In Pt. Hur.		−0.1	
/12	P2	[PHD-A]	Pt. Hur.–Mar. Cty.		+18.5	1132.5
1986/3/27	S4	[PM-S]	In Bad Axe		−1.3	
3/27	S4	[PM-N]	Kinde–Croswell		−54.8	
3/27	S4	[PM-NH]	Palms–Harbor Beach		−19.0	
3/27	S4	[PM-NS]	Poland–Sandusky		−7.1	
8/14	S5	[PM-H]	Paw Paw–Hartford		−13.1	
	X	[PM-H]	Cableton–Hartford		−14.3	
ca.	X	[PM-I]	Eagle–Portland		−7.6	
	X	[PM-Y1U]	In Ben. Hbr.		(−2.7)	1015.3

On 2 September 1987 this company was conveyed to CSX Transportation.

Act Column Key

M1	Merge Manistee & Northeastern
P1	Buy from Grand Trunk Western
P2	Buy Port Huron & Detroit
S2	Sold to State of Michigan for operation by other companies
S3	Sold to Grand Trunk Western
S4	Sold to Huron & Eastern
S5	Sold to Kalamazoo, Lake Shore & Chicago
X	Abandoned
XL	Lease canceled
Y	Yard trackage

Notes

1. A portion of this line was conveyed to Genesee County, Michigan for use as part of the line of the Huckleberry Central Railroad.

Chicago, Kalamazoo & Saginaw

MAIN LINE (CK&S-A)

	MILEAGE	COUNTY	CROSSINGS, JUNCTIONS, ETC.
Kal.	0	Kal.	J/CK&S–S 0
(Crossing)	0.1	"	X/KACL–1 0.4
(Crossing)	0.2	"	X/MC–C 143.0
Kal. (old)	0.3	"	
(Jct.)	1.0	"	J/conn. to GR&I–S 186.4, 0.4 miles
(Mosel Ave.)	1.7	"	
(Crossing)	2.2	"	X/MUR–W 2.65
Streeter	3	"	
E. Cooper	4.2	"	
Carrolls	5.9	"	f. Spring Brook, aka Carrolls Pit
Richland Jct.	8.9	"	X/DTM 108.8, f. Flagg (also MUR-WB 18.4)
Cressey	11.1	Barry	
Milo	13.6	"	
Crooked Lk.	16.5	"	

Delton	17.3	"	
Williams Crossing		"	
Wall Lk.		"	
Cloverdale	20.5	"	
Ackers Point	21	"	
Nashs	23	"	
Shultz	24.2	"	
Hastings	30.4	"	
(Crossing)	30.6	"	X/MC–G 61.7
Coats Grove	36.1	"	
Woodland	40.4	"	
Woodbury	44.2	Eaton	J/PM–D 116.2

CONSTRUCTION/ABANDONMENT

DATE	ACT	END POINTS	MP	CHANGE	MAIN	SOURCE	NOTE
1889/9/1	B	Kal.(old)–Woodbury	0.3–44.2	+43.9	43.9	4	1,2
1901/12/1	B	Kal.–Kal.(old)	0–0.3	+0.3	44.2	4	2
1937/6/15	X	Woodbury–MP 30.9	44.2–30.9	–13.3		2	
1937/6/15	Y	Hastings–MP 30.9				2	3
		(to CKS-YH)	30.9–30.0	(0.9)			
1937/6/15	X	Hastings–Delton	30.0–17.7	–12.3	17.7	2	
1942/3/31	X	In Delton	17.7–17.5	–0.2		2	
1942/12/23	X	Delton–Richland Jct.	17.5–9.2	–8.3	9.2	2	
1970/12/16	X	In Kal.	0–0.3	–0.3	8.9	2	
1978	Y	In Kal.					
		(to CK&S-YA)	0.3–1.9	(1.6)			
1978	X	MP 1.9–Richland Jct.	1.9–9.2	–7.3	0		
1982	X	CKS-YH in Hastings	30.0–30.9	(–0.9)	0		
1995 ca.	X	In Kal. (CK&S-YA)	0.3–0.8	(–0.5)	0		

OWNERSHIP

1889	Chicago, Kalamazoo & Saginaw (B)
1906	Control, 60% by Michigan Central and 40% by Lake Shore & Michigan Southern
1930/2/1	New York Central, leased Chicago, Kalamazoo & Saginaw
1968/2/1	Penn Central, lease assigned by New York Central
1976/4/1	Conrail, purchase of part of Penn Central line in Kalamazoo
1999/6/1	Norfolk Southern, purchase of Conrail

RICHLAND–HOOPER LINE (CK&S-[DTM])

	MILEAGE	COUNTY	CROSSINGS, JUNCTIONS, ETC.
Richland	0	Kal.	
Richland Jct.	2.9	"	X/CK&S–A 8.9
Doster	8.7	Barry	
Neely	11.8	"	
Hooper	12.8	"	
(End)	13.2	"	

CONSTRUCTION/ABANDONMENT

DATE	ACT	END POINTS	MP	CHANGE	MAIN	SOURCE	NOTE
1930/7/25	P1	Richland–Hooper	0–13.2	+13.2	13.2	1	6
1961	X	Hooper–Doster	13.2–8.7	–4.5	8.7	3	
1978	X	Richland–Doster	0–8.7	–8.7	0		

PAVILION BRANCH (CK&S-S)

	MILEAGE	COUNTY	CROSSINGS, JUNCTIONS, ETC.
Kal.	0	Kal.	J/CK&S-A 0
(Jct.)	0.1	"	J/conn. to LS-G 36.6, 0.2 miles
(Mill St.)	0.4	"	J/GTW-K 10.4, J/conn. to MC-C 141.8, 0.6 miles
Pavilion Jct. (Lk. St.)	1.3	"	J/GTW-K 9.5, J/CK&S-YK 1.3
(Bridge)	1.4	"	B/MUR-S 66.6
Beckwith	4.0	"	
Kealey	6.0	"	
Pomeroy	9.0	"	
Pavilion	10.8	"	J/GTW-C 157.2

CONSTRUCTION/ABANDONMENT

DATE	ACT	END POINTS	MP	CHANGE	MAIN	SOURCE	NOTE
1901/12/1	B	Kal.–Pavilion	0–10.8	+10.8	10.8	4	
1910/8/1	L	Pavilion Jct.–Pavilion	1.3–10.8	−9.5		4	4
1910/8/1	Y	Kal.–Pavilion					
		(CK&S-YS)	0–1.3	(1.3)	0		
1984 ca.	X	In Kal.	0–1.3	(−1.3)	0		

OWNERSHIP

1901	Chicago, Kalamazoo & Saginaw (B)
1906	Control, 60% by Michigan Central and 40% by Lake Shore & Michigan Southern
1930/2/1	New York Central, leased Chicago, Kalamazoo & Saginaw
1968/2/1	Penn Central, lease assigned by New York Central
1976/4/1	Conrail, purchase of Penn Central and Chicago, Kalamazoo & Saginaw

KALAMAZOO YARD (CK&S-YK)

	MILEAGE	COUNTY	CROSSINGS, JUNCTIONS, ETC.
Pavilion Jct.	1.3	Kal.	J/CK&S-S 1.3
(Bridge)	1.5	"	B/GR&I-S 183.9
(Portage St.)	2.6	"	

CONSTRUCTION/ABANDONMENT

DATE	ACT	END POINTS	MP	CHANGE	MAIN	SOURCE	NOTE
1901 ca.	B	Line	1.3–2.6	(+1.3)			5
1984 ca.	X	Line	1.3–2.6	(−1.3)			

OWNERSHIP

1901	Chicago, Kalamazoo & Saginaw (B), from first date shown
1906	Control, 60% by Michigan Central and 40% by Lake Shore & Michigan Southern
1930/2/1	New York Central, leased Chicago, Kalamazoo & Saginaw
1968/2/1	Penn Central, lease assigned by New York Central
1976/4/1	Conrail, purchase of Penn Central and Chicago, Kalamazoo & Saginaw

ACQUISITION/DISPOSITION RECORD

DATE	ACT	CK&S–	END POINTS	CHANGE	MAIN	NOTE
1889/9/1	B	A	Kal. (old)–Woodbury	+43.9	43.9	1,2
1901/12/1	B	A	Kal.–Kal. (old)	+0.3		2
12/1	B	S	Kal.–Pavilion	+10.8		
	B	YK	In Kal.	(+1.3)	55.0	5
1910/8/1	L	S	Pavilion Jct.–Pavilion	−9.5		

	Y	S	Kal.–Pavilion Jct. (to CK&S-YS)	(1.3)	44.2	4
1930/7/25	P1	DTM	Richland–Hooper	+13.2	57.4	6
1937/6/15	X	A	Woodbury–MP 30.9	−13.3		
6/15	Y	A	MP 30.9–Hastings (to CK&S-YH)	(0.9)		3
6/15	X	A	Hastings–Delton	−12.3	30.9	
1942/3/31	X	A	In Delton	−0.2		
12/23	X	A	Delton–Richland Jct.	−8.3	22.4	
1961	X	DTM	Hooper–Doster	−4.5	17.9	

On 1 February 1968 this company was leased to Penn Central.

1970	X	A	Kal.–MP 0.3	−0.3	17.6	

On 1 April 1976 this company was conveyed to Conrail.

1976	Y	A	In Kal. (to CK&S-YA)	(1.6)	16.0	
1978	X	A	Kal.–Richland Jct.	−7.3		7
	X	DTM	Richland–Doster	−8.7	0	7
1982	X	YH	In Hastings	(−0.9)		8
1984 ca.	X	YK	In Kal.	(−1.3)		
ca.	X	YS	In Kal.	(−1.3)		
1995 ca.	X	YA	In Kal.	(−0.5)		

On 1 June 1999 this company's lines were conveyed to Norfolk Southern.

Act Column Key

B   Built by Chicago, Kalamazoo & Saginaw
L   Leased to Grand Trunk Western
P1   Purchased from Michigan United Railway
X   Abandoned
Y   Converted main line to yard track

Sources

1. ICC, Finance Dockets.
2. Michigan Central Railroad engineering records.
3. MDOT office records.
4. Michigan Railroad Commission, *Aids, Gifts, Grants.*

Notes

1. The road was operated by its construction contractor, the Kalamazoo & Hastings Construction Company, between Kalamazoo and Hastings by late 1888.
2. The original station in Kalamazoo at MP 0.3 was at North Street.
3. This segment in Hastings was retained as yard trackage and operated by Michigan Central.
4. The Pavilion–Pavilion Jct. segment was leased to the Grand Trunk Western for 99 years effective 1 August 1910. The mileages shown for Beckwith, Kealey and Pomeroy do not agree precisely with those shown by Grand Trunk Western. See line GTW-K for those mileages.
5. This segment was constructed about the time shown as part of a project of the CK&S to extend its line to the northeast corner of Cass County to make a connection with the Grand Trunk Western. The segment did extend to the west side of Portage Street for a time, but was reduced a few years later to the east side of Portage Street.
6. This line was originally built by the Michigan & Ohio Railroad, and completed for service on 20 November 1883. On 1 September 1913 it was conveyed by the Detroit, Toledo & Milwaukee to the Michigan & Chicago Railway, later the Michigan Railway, and converted to electric operations. With the demise of that company, the property was purchased by the CK&S and converted to steam operations.
7. This property was operated by Conrail for Penn Central trustees under a subsidy agreement with the State

of Michigan from 1 April 1976 until abandonment.

8.   This property was operated by Conrail, and later by Kent–Barry–Eaton Connecting, for Penn Central trustees under subsidy from the State of Michigan from 1 April 1976 until 3 March 1982.

Cleveland, Cincinnati, Chicago & St. Louis

CINCINNATI NORTHERN (CC-N)

	MILEAGE	COUNTY	CROSSINGS, JUNCTIONS, ETC.
(Jackson, via NYC-W)	0	Jackson	
OD	1.2	"	J/LS–J 41.3, J/MC–A 0.8
Lyonette	4.3	"	
Ackerson Lk.	5.7	"	
Clark Lk.	9.7	"	
Cement Cty.	13.5	Lenawee	
(Bridge)	14.0	"	B/LS–Y 40.7
Kelleys Pit	14	"	
Cowham		"	
Wood	18.0	"	
Addison Jct.	18.8	"	X/DTM 35.9
Abbott	20	"	
Manitou Beach	20.8	"	f. Oak Beach
Townley		"	
Rollin	24.9	"	
Clay	25.9	"	
(Bridge)	29.8	"	B/LS–A 346.1
Hudson	29.9	"	
Prattville	35.7	Hillsdale	
Waldron	39.5	"	
(MI/OH state line)	41.1		
Alvordton OH	43.9	Williams OH	X/WB
W. Unity	49.0	"	
(Crossing)	49.6	"	X/WB
Pulaski	55.9	"	
DV	58.5	"	X/NYC–T
Bryan	59.5	"	
Ney	66.0	Defiance OH	
Moats	69.4	"	
Sherwood	73.1	"	X/BO
Cecil	78.8	Paulding OH	X/WB
Gill	80.8	"	f. N. Paulding
Paulding	84.9	"	
Gasco	86.0	"	
Latty	88.5	"	X/NKP
Dague	90.4	"	
Folmer	92.4	"	
Haviland	93.1	"	
Scott	95.1	VanWert OH	
Cavett	98.1	"	
Van Wert Yard	102.2	"	
CN	103.3	"	X/PRR
Van Wert	103.3	"	
Stumps	106.3	"	
Ohio Cty.	110.6	"	X/ER, X/NKP

Shaffers	114.0	"	
Shanes Crossing	115.6	Mercer OH	
Rockford	116.3	"	
Tama	120.6	"	
S. Tama	121.5	"	
Celina OH	126.9	"	
(Crossing)	127.2	"	X/NKP
Coldwater	132.4	"	
Philothea	134.5	"	
St. Henry	137.0	"	
Gilberts	141.5	"	
New Weston	142.5	Darke OH	
Martins	143.5	"	
Rossburg	146.6	"	
Ansonia	151.3	"	X/CC
Meekers	154.0	"	X/PRR
D. & U. Crossing	158.5	"	X/BO
Greenville	159.3	"	
Penn	161.2	"	X/PRR
Ft. Jefferson	164.6	"	
Gravel Pit	166.2	"	
Savona	167.5	"	X/CC–R 52.0
Castine	171.8	"	
W. Manchester	173.9	Preble OH	X/PRR
Lewisburg	179.8	"	
W. Alexandria	187.0	"	
Ingomar	189.6	"	
Backus	193.0	Montgomery OH	
Farmersville	194.2	"	
Germantown	199.6	"	
Wiggins	201.2	"	
(Crossing)	203.2	Warren OH	X/BO
Carlisle	203.6	"	
Carlisle Jct.	203.9	"	J/CC
(Miami Riv. bridge)	205.0	"	
Franklin	205.1	"	

CONSTRUCTION/ABANDONMENT

DATE	ACT	END POINTS	MP	CHANGE	MI MAIN	SOURCE	NOTE
1888/11/23	B2	Addison Jct.–OH state line	18.8–41.1	+22.3	22.3	2	1
1896/4/25	B3	OD–Addison Jct.	1.2–18.8	+17.6	39.9	3	3
1976/4/1	X	MP 4.3–OH state line	4.3–41.1	−36.8			
1976/4/1	Y	OD–MP 4.3 (to CC-Y1N)	1.2–4.3	(3.1)	0		

OWNERSHIP (Michigan lines only)

1888	Cincinnati, Jackson & Mackinaw Railroad (B2)
1891/7/17	Cincinnati, Jackson & Mackinaw Railway, reorganize CJ&M Railroad
1896	Jackson & Cincinnati (B3), of segment
1897/1/15	Cincinnati Northern, purchase of Cincinnati, Jackson & Mackinaw Railroad
1898/6/1	Cincinnati Northern, purchase of Jackson & Cincinnati
1902/1/1	Cleveland, Cincinnati, Chicago & St. Louis, control of Cincinnati Northern
1930/2/1	New York Central, lease of Cleveland, Cincinnati, Chicago & St. Louis

1938/6/30   Cleveland, Cincinnati, Chicago & St. Louis, merged Cincinnati Northern
1968/2/1   Penn Central, assigned lease of Cleveland, Cincinnati, Chicago & St. Louis
1976/4/1   Conrail, purchase of Penn Central
1999/6/1   Norfolk Southern, purchase of Conrail

MICHIGAN DIVISION (CC-M)

	MILEAGE	COUNTY	CROSSINGS, JUNCTIONS, ETC.
(End)	1.6	Berrien	
Ben. Hbr.	0	"	C/PM-C 86.0
(Main St.)	0.3	"	X/BHCL-4 0.3
(Bridge)	1.6	"	B/PM-U 1.6
Napier	2.8	"	
(Bridge)	3.0	"	B/BHSJ-D 4.4
Sodus	7.1	"	
Hartman	10.1	"	
(Crossing)	12.5	"	X/BHSJ-D 15.4
Eau Claire	12.7	"	
Berrien Centre	15.0	"	
Fairland	19.0	"	
(Bridge)	22.6	"	B/SOM 12.3
(Bridge)	23.6	"	B/MC-W 192.4
Niles	23.8	"	
Niles Jct.	26.1	"	B-J/MC-N 2.2, B/SOM 9.2, f. M. C. Jct.
Beebe Siding	28.8	"	
Truitts	31.0	Cass	
(MI/IN state line)	33.4		
	———		
(MI/IN state line)	35.2		
Granger IN.	35.7	St. Joseph IN	X/GTW-C
Belleview	39.3	Elkhart IN	
Elkhart	44.8	"	
Dunlaps	50.2	"	
Goshen	55.3	"	
CX	55.5	"	X/NYC-T 122.8, J/LS-S 0
Yost	57.5	"	
Waterford	58.3	"	
New Paris Jct.	61.3	"	X/WB-D 161.4
New Paris	62.0	"	
Milford Jct.	66.3	Kosciusko IN	X/BO-B
Milford	67.5	"	
Leesburg	73.0	"	
Grandy	78.3	"	
Warsaw	79.7	"	X/PRR-F 358.7
Reeds	83.2	"	
Claypool	87.5	"	X/NKP
Silver Lk.	91.4	"	
Rose Hill	94.2	Wabash IN	
N. Manchester	99.0	"	X/PRR
Bolivar	101.6	"	X/ER
Urbana	106.1	"	
Speicher	109.1	"	
Wabash	113.4	"	X/WB-P 188.8
Treaty	119.1	"	
LaFontaine	123.6	"	
Fox	126.5	Grant IN	

Otes	"		
Marion IN	132.7	"	
3rd St.	133.0	"	X/NKP
Kent	133.4	"	X/PRR
Soldiers Home	135.5	"	
Jonesboro	138.3	"	
Fairmount	142.8	"	X/PRR
Summitville	148.1	Madison IN	
Alexandria	153.5	"	
(Crossing)	153.8	"	X/NKP
Alda	155.0	"	
Dow	162.6	"	X/PRR
(Crossing)	165.4	"	X/CC-I 247.4
Anderson	165.5	"	
Pearl St.	165.7	"	
C. I. Crossing	165.8	"	X/CI
P. R. R. Crossing	166.3	"	X/PRR
(Crossing)	166.6	"	X/CC-IS
S. Anderson Yard	166.7	"	
Alliance	171.0	"	
Emporia	172.7	"	
Markleville	174.8	"	
Shirley	181.0	Hancock IN	
(Crossing)	181.5	Henry IN	X/CC-R 107.3
Winkfield	183.5	"	
Knox	186.2	"	
Knightstown	188.2	"	X/PRR
Carthage	193.1	Rush IN	
Boyd	195.1	"	
Farmer	196.4	"	
Henderson	198.6	"	
Kern	203.5	"	
Rushville	204.5	"	
Bennetts Crossing	209.6	"	
Milroy	212.1	"	
Williamstown	215.2	Decatur IN	
Sandusky	217.6	"	
Greensburg	223.5	"	
GN	223.6	"	X/CC-C 62.8
Craig	225.0	"	X/CC-H 64.2
Horace	230.5	"	
Letts	232.4	"	f. Letts Corner
Westport	236.5	"	
Harper	238.9	"	f. Sardinia
Earl	240.4	"	f. Sherwood
Brewersville	243.4	Jennings IN.	
N. Vernon	248.9	"	J/BO

CONSTRUCTION/ABANDONMENT

DATE	ACT	END POINTS	MP	CHANGE	MI MAIN	SOURCE	NOTE
1882/7/3	B1	Goshen IN–Niles	33.4–23.8	+9.6		3	2
1882/11/13	B1	Niles–Ben. Hbr.	23.8–0	+23.8	33.4	3	2
1900 ca.	B4	In Ben. Hbr.					
		(to CC-YB)	0–1.6	(+1.6)	33.4		

| 1942 | X | Niles Jct.–Goshen | 26.4–33.4 | –7.0 | 26.4 | 1 |

1982	X	In Ben. Hbr. (CC-YB)	0–1.6	(–1.6)		
1982	X	Ben. Hbr.–Niles	0–25.9	–25.9		
1982	Y	In Niles (to CC-Y1M)	25.9–26.4	(0.5)	0	
1993	X	In Niles	25.9–26.4	(–0.5)	0	

OWNERSHIP (Michigan lines only)

1882	Cincinnati, Wabash & Michigan (B1)
1892/7/13	Cleveland, Cincinnati, Chicago & St. Louis (B4), control of CW&M
1913/12/17	Cleveland, Cincinnati, Chicago & St. Louis, merged CW&M
1930/2/1	New York Central, leased Cleveland, Cincinnati, Chicago & St. Louis
1968/2/1	Penn Central, assigned lease of Cleveland, Cincinnati, Chicago & St. Louis
1976/4/1	Conrail, purchase of Penn Central

ACQUISITION/DISPOSITION RECORD (Michigan mileage only)

DATE	ACT	CC–	END POINTS	CHANGE	MI MAIN	NOTE
1882/7/13	B1	M	Goshen–Niles	+9.6		2
11/13	B1	M	Niles–Ben. Hbr.	+23.8	33.4	2
1888/11/23	B2	N	Addison Jct.–OH state line	+22.3	55.7	1
1896/4/25	B3	N	OD–Addison Jct.	+17.6	73.3	3
1900 ca.	B4	YB	In Ben. Hbr.	(+1.6)	73.3	
1942	X	M	MP 26.4–IN state line	–7.0	66.3	

On 1 February 1968 this company was leased to Penn Central.

On 1 April 1976 part of this company was conveyed to Conrail and part retained by Penn Central.

1976	X	PC-[CC-N]	MP 4.3–OH state line	–36.8		
	Y	CNR-[CC-N]	OD-MP 4.3	(3.1)	26.4	
1976	CNR=26.4	PC=0	CC=26.4			
1982	X	CNR-[CC-M]	Ben. Hbr.–Niles	–25.9		
	Y	CNR-[CC-M]	In Niles (as CC-Y2M)	(0.5)		
	X	CNR-[CC-YB]	In Ben. Hbr.	(–1.6)	0	
1982	CNR=0	PC=0	CC=0			
1993	X	CNR-[CC-Y2M]	In Niles	(–0.5)	0	
1993	CNR=0	PC=0	CC=0			

Act Column Key

B1	Built by Cincinnati, Wabash & Michigan
B2	Built by Cincinnati, Jackson & Mackinaw
B3	Built by Jackson & Cincinnati
B4	Built by Cleveland, Cincinnati, Chicago & St. Louis
X	Abandoned
Y	Built/converted main track to yard track

Sources

1. ICC Finance Dockets.
2. Michigan, Commissioner of Railroads, *Annual Report,* 1889.
3. Michigan Railroad Commission, *Aids, Gifts, Grants.*

Notes

1. Source 2 states line was completed to Carlisle OH on 10 July 1889.
2. Construction was begun by the Elkhart, Niles & Lake Michigan, and the partially completed work was acquired by Cincinnati, Wabash & Lake Michigan at its merger with EN&LM on 23 May 1882.
3. The line had trackage rights over the Lake Shore & Michigan Southern line LS-W between Jackson and OD.

Coe Rail

For arrangement of stations, construction record, and prior ownerships, see Grand Trunk Western line GTW-A.

LINE (COE)

	MILEAGE	COUNTY	CROSSINGS, JUNCTIONS, ETC.
Wixom	0	Oakland	J/PM–T 70.4
Walled Lk.	3.1	"	
(End)	8.7	"	

CONSTRUCTION/ABANDONMENT

DATE	ACT	END POINTS	MP	CHANGE	MAIN	SOURCE	NOTE
1984/8	P	Line	0–8.7	+8.7	8.7		

OWNERSHIP

1984	Coe Rail	

This line formerly was Grand Trunk Western line GTW-A, MP 50.7 to MP 42.0.

ACQUISITION/DISPOSITION RECORD

See Mileage record above

Act Column Key

P   Purchased from Grand Trunk Western

Coldwater Train Railway

MAIN LINE (CTRY-A)

	MILEAGE	COUNTY	CROSSINGS, JUNCTIONS, ETC.
(Jct.)	0	Branch	J/LS-A 386.7
(End)	1.3	"	(sec 32 T6S R6W)

CONSTRUCTION/ABANDONMENT

DATE	ACT	END POINTS	MP	CHANGE	MAIN	SOURCE	NOTE
1905 ca.	B	Line	0–1.3	+1.3	1.3		
???	X	Line	0–1.3	–1.3	0		

OWNERSHIP

1905	Coldwater Train Railway	

Act Column Key

B   Built by Coldwater Train Railway
X   Abandoned

Note

1. The date of abandonment could not be determined and the mileage of this company is not included in the mileage table.

Colfax & Big Rapids

LINE (C&BR)

	MILEAGE	COUNTY	CROSSINGS, JUNCTIONS, ETC.
(Musk. Riv.)	0	Mecosta	(NE 1/4 sec 14 T15N R10W)
(Crossing)	0.1	"	X/GR&I-N 289.5
(Crossing)	0.9	"	X/PM-J 92.2
(Hillview Lk.)	5.5	"	(sec 3 T15N R9W)

CONSTRUCTION/ABANDONMENT

DATE	ACT	END POINTS	MP	CHANGE	MAIN	SOURCE	NOTE
1887/3/1	B	Line	0–5.5	+5.5	5.5	1	
1889	X	Line	0–5.5	–5.5	0	1	

OWNERSHIP

1887   Colfax & Big Rapids

ACQUISITION/DISPOSITION RECORD

See Mileage record above

Act Column Key

B   Built by Colfax & Big Rapids
X   Abandoned

Sources

1.   Michigan, Commissioner of Railroads, *Annual Reports,* 1887, 1890.

CONRAIL (Consolidated Rail Corporation)

On 1 April 1976 this company acquired part of Penn Central. For arrangement of stations, construction record, and prior ownerships, see Chicago, Kalamazoo & Saginaw (CK&S); Cleveland, Cincinnati, Chicago & St. Louis (CC); Detroit, Toledo & Milwaukee (DTM); Grand Rapids & Indiana (GR&I); Lake Shore & Michigan Southern (LS); Michigan Central (MC); and Pennsylvania (PRR). The lines acquired were:

LINE DES.	END POINTS	MP	MI MAIN	SOURCE	NOTE
CNR-					
[CC-M]	Ben. Hbr.–Niles	0–26.4	26.4		
[CC-YB]	In Ben. Hbr.	0–1.6	(1.6)		
[CC-N]	In Jackson	1.2–4.3	3.1		
[CK&S-A]	In Kal.	0.3–1.9	1.6		
[CK&S-YK]	In Kal.	1.3–2.6	(1.3)		
[CK&S-YS]	In Kal.	0–1.3	(1.3)		
[DTM-Y1D]	In Battle Creek	90.9–93.9	(3.0)		
[DTM-Y2D]	In Marshall	77.0–77.5	(0.5)		
[DTM-Y3D]	In Battle Creek	89.9–90.4	(0.5)		
[GR&I-S]	In Sturgis	146.4–150.6	4.2		
[GR&I-S]	Vicksburg–Gr. Rpds.	173.0–234.0	61.0		
[GR&I-N]	Gr. Rpds.–Comstock Park	234.0–239.5	5.5		
[GR&I-Y1M]	In Gr. Rpds.	2.6–7.4	(4.8)		
[GR&I-YG]	In Gr. Rpds.	Line	(3.9)		
[LS-A1]	OH state line–Riga	307.9–315.5	7.6		
[LS-A5]	Quincy–IN state line	376.6–424.1	47.5		
[LS-Y1M]	In Monroe	0–1.5	(1.5)		

[LS-YM]	In Monroe	0–1.1	(1.1)
[LS-D]	D&M Jct.–OH state line	3.3–54.5	51.2
[LS-J]	Lenawee Jct.–Clinton	0–13.6	13.6
[LS-Y1J]	In Jackson	40.1–42.1	(2.0)
[LS-Y4L]	In Albion	21.9–23.6	(1.7)
[LS-Y2L]	In Lans.	57.5–58.8	(1.3)
[LS-Y1L]	In Lans.	60.4–61.2	(0.8)
[LS-W]	OD–Haires	1.1–5.1	4.0
[LS-Y1W]	In Jackson	0.4–1.1	(0.7)
[LS-G]	White Pigeon Jct.–N. Yard	0–36.8	37.1
[LS-G]	Lamar–Gr. Rpds.	91.6–95.0	3.4
[LS-Y1G]	In Kal.	36.8–39.5	(2.7)
[LS-G2]	Plainwell–Otsego	46.8–52.7	5.9
[LS-GA]	Three Rivers bypass	Line	1.7
[LS-Y1S]	In Sturgis	27.4–29.5	(2.1)
[MC-E]	Det.–Jackson	1.2–75.4	74.2
[MC-Y1E]	In Det.	0.3–1.2	(0.9)
[MC-YP]	Ypsi. Belt	Line	(1.1)
[MC-YJ]	Jackson Belt	Line	(1.3)
[MC-YDE]	Exposition Spur	Line	(1.2)
[MC-YDF]	Exp. Spur extension	Line	(0.6)
[MC-YDD]	Delta Spur	Line	(1.0)
[MC-YDB]	Det. Belt Line	Line	(4.4)
[MC-YDC]	Det. Belt Extension	Line	(1.9)
[MC-YDM]	Det. Manufacturers	Line	(1.3)
[MC-DZ]	Junction Yard Br.	Line	4.2
[MC-T]	W. Det.–Toledo	2.7–49.5	46.8
[MC-B]	Bay Cty. Jct.–Rays Pit	2.2–28.2	26.0
[MC-A]	Jackson Jct.–OD	0–0.8	0.8
[MC-A]	Haires–Three Rivers	4.8–68.8	64.0
[MC-Y1A]	In Niles	102.8–104.0	(1.2)
[MC-Y2A]	In Three Rivers	69.5–70.9	(1.4)
[MC-N]	Niles–S. Bend IN	0–5.8	5.8
[MC-C]	Jackson–Kal.	75.4–145.0	69.6
[MC-YF]	Fort Custer Spur	Line	(1.7)
[MC-Y1K]	In Battle Creek	0.8–1.3	(0.5)
[MC-Y1H]	In Kal.	0.2–1.9	(1.7)
[MC-G]	Rives Jct.–Eaton Rapids	10.6–24.8	14.2
[MC-G]	Bowen–Gr. Rpds.	88.0–94.4	6.4
[MC-YLT]	Lans. Transit	Line	(0.8)
[MC-YLM]	Lans. Manufacturers	Line	(5.2)
[MC-S]	Jackson–N. Lans.	0.2–39.7	39.5
[MC-Z]	Det. Riv. Tunnel	226.3–227.7	1.4
[MC-Y1DD]	Part of Jct. Yd. Br.	2.0–3.3	(1.3)
[PRR-A]	Carleton–Ecorse Jct.	116.4–137.1	20.7
[PRR-YF]	Foreman Wye	0–0.2	(0.2)
[PRR-YU]	Union Belt	0–5.8	(5.8)

1976/4/1   CK&S=1.6   CC=29.5   DTM=0   GR&I=70.7   LS=172.0   MC=352.9   PRR=20.7   CNR=647.4

ACQUISITION/DISPOSITION RECORD

DATE	ACT	CNR–	END POINTS	MP	MI MAIN	SOURCE	NOTE
1976	Y	[CC-N]	In Jackson	1.2–4.3	(3.1) to CNR-[CC-Y1N]		
	Y	[GR&I-S]	In Sturgis	46.4–150.6	(4.2) to CNR-[GR&I-Y1S]		
	A	[LS-D]	D&M Jct.–OH state line	3.3–54.5	–51.2		1

	Y	[LS-G]	Lamar–Gr. Rpds.	91.6–95.0	(3.4)	to CNR-[LS-Y2G]
	Y	[MC-G]	Bowen–Gr. Rpds.	88.0–94.4	(6.4)	to CNR-[MC-Y1G]
	Y	[MC-S]	In N. Lans.	37.8–39.7	(1.9)	to CNR-[MC-Y1S]
1976		TOTAL	CK&S=1.6 CC=26.4 GR&I=66.5 LS=117.4 MC=344.6P PRR=20.7 CNR=577.2			
1978	Y	[CK&S-A]	In Kal. (to CK&S-YA)	0.3–1.9	(1.6)	to CNR-[CK&S-YA]
1978		TOTAL	CK&S=0 CC=26.4 GR&I=66.5 LS=117.4 MC=344.6 PRR=20.7 CNR=575.6			
1980 ca.	X	[DTM-Y2D]	In Marshall	77.0–77.5	(–0.5)	
	X	[DTM-Y3D]	In Battle Creek	89.9–90.4	(–0.5)	
	X	[LS-Y1S]	In Sturgis	27.4–29.5	(–2.1)	
1980		TOTAL	CC=26.4 GR&I=66.5 LS=117.4 MC=344.6 PRR=20.7 CNR=575.6			
1981	X	[LS-Y1M]	In Monroe	0–1.5	(1.5)	
	X	[MC-YDM]	Det. Manufacturers	Line	(–1.3)	
11/18	X	[MC-C]	In Battle Creek	119.8–121.4	–1.6	2
1981		TOTAL	CC=26.4 GR&I=66.5 LS=117.4 MC=343.0 PRR=20.7 CNR=574.0			
1982	X	[CC-YB]	In Ben. Hbr.	0–1.6	(–1.6)	
	X	[CC-M]	Ben. Hbr.–Niles	0–25.9	–25.9	
	Y	[CC-M]	In Niles	25.9–26.4	(0.5)	to CNR-[CC-Y2M]
	X	[CK&S-YH]	In Hastings	Line	(–0.9)	
	X	[GR&I-S]	Vicksburg–Upjohn	173.0–178.5	–5.5	
	Y	[GR&I-S]	Upjohn–Kal.	178.5–185.1	(6.6)	to CNR-[GR&I-Y2S]
	X	[GR&I-Y1M]	In Gr. Rpds.	2.6–7.4	(–4.8)	
	S1	[LS-J]	Lenawee Jct.–Clinton	0–13.6	–13.6	
	X	[LS-GA]	Three Rivers bypass	Line	–1.7	
	X	[LS-W3]	OD–Haires	1.1–5.1	–4.0	
8/15	X	[MC-G]	Rives Jct.–Eaton Rapids	10.6–24.8	–14.2	
	X	[MC-YDE]	Exposition Spur	Line	(–1.2)	
	X	[MC-YDF]	Exp. Spur Extension	Line	(–0.6)	
	X	[MC-YDB]	Det. Belt Line	2.8–4.4	(–1.6)	
	X	[MC-Y1DD]	Jct. Yard Branch	2.5–3.3	(–0.8)	
	X	[MC-A]	Haires–Three Rivers	4.8–68.8	–64.0	
	Y	[MC-A]	Jackson Jct.–OD	0–0.8	(0.8)	to CNR-[MC-Y3A]
1982		TOTAL	CC=0 GR&I=54.4 LS=98.1 MC=264.0 PRR=20.7 CNR=437.2			
1983	X	[LS-A1]	Ottawa Lk.–Riga	312.1–315.5	–3.4	
1983		TOTAL	GR&I=54.4 LS=94.7 MC=264.0 PRR=20.7 CNR=433.8			
1984	Z	[LS-A5]	Quincy–Sturgis	376.6–406.8	—	
	X	[CK&S-YS]	In Kal.	0–1.3	(–1.3)	
	X	[CK&S-YK]	In Kal.	1.3–2.6	(–1.3)	
	X	[MC-Y1H]	In Kal.	0.2–1.9	(–1.7)	
	X	[MC-Y1K]	In Battle Creek	0.7–1.3	(–0.6)	
/5/31	P2	[DT]	In Det.	Lines	16.8	
1984		TOTAL	DT=16.8 GR&I=54.4 LS=94.7 MC=264.0 PRR=20.7 CNR=450.6			
1985	X	[GR&I-YG]	Line	(–3.9)		
	X	[GR&I-S]	Pleasant Ave.–Gd. Rpds	233.2–234.0	–0.8	
	X	[GR&I-N]	Gr. Rpds.–MP 234.7	234.0–234.7	–0.7	
ca.	X	[MC-YJ]	Line	0–1.3	(–1.3)	
/5/1	S3	[MC-Z]	Det. Riv. Tunnel	226.3–227.7	–1.4	
1985		TOTAL	DT=16.8 GR&I=52.9 LS=94.7 MC=262.6 PRR=20.7 CNR=447.7			

1989 ca.	S4	[LS-A5]	Quincy–Sturgis	376.6–406.8	–30.2	
1989		TOTAL	DT=16.8 GR&I=52.9	LS=64.5 MC=262.6 PRR=20.7 CNR=417.5		
1993	X	[CC-Y2M]	In Niles	25.9–26.4	(–0.5)	
/12	S3	[GR&I-Y1S]	In Sturgis	146.4–150.6	(–4.2)	
/12	S3	[LS-A5]	Sturgis–White Pigeon Jct.	406.8–421.3	–14.5	
ca.	X	[MC-N]	Niles–St Marys IN	0.3–6.8	–5.5	
	Y	[MC-N]	In Niles (to Y1N)	0–0.3	(0.3)	
	X	[MCY2A]	In Three Rivers	69.5–70.1	(–0.6)	
1993		TOTAL	DT=16.8 GR&I=52.9	LS=50.0 MC=256.8 PRR=20.7 CNR=397.2		
1995/7	S2	[MC-C]	W. of Kal.	143.2–145.0	–1.8	
ca.	X	[CK&S-YA]	In Kal.	0.3–0.8	(–0.5)	
1995		TOTAL	DT=16.8 GR&I=52.9	LS=50.0 MC=255.0 PRR=20.7 CNR=395.4		
1996	L	[MC-S]	Lans.–N. Lans.	36.9–37.8	–0.9	3
1996		TOTAL	DT=16.8 GR&I=52.9	LS=50.0 MC=254.1 PRR=20.7 CNR=394.5		
1997/2	S2	[PRR-YF]	Foreman Wye	0–0.2	(–0.2)	
1997		TOTAL	DT=16.8 GR&I=52.9	LS=50.0 MC=254.1 PRR=20.7 CNR=394.5		

On 1 June 1999 most of Conrail in Michigan was conveyed to Norfolk Southern and part retained by Conrail (which became a company jointly owned by CSX Transportation and Norfolk Southern). The lines retained under Conrail were:

LINE DESIG.	END POINTS	MP	MI MAIN	SOURCE	NOTE
CNR-					
[MC-E]	15th St.–Town Line	1.2–7.4	6.2		
[MC-Y1E]	Original main line	0.3–1.2	(0.9)		
[MC-YDD]	Delta Spur	0–1.0	(1.0)		
[MC-YDB]	Det. Belt Line	0–2.8	(2.8)		
[MC-YDC]	Det. Belt Extension	Line	(1.9)		
[MC-DZ]	Jct. Yard Br.	0–4.2	4.2		
[MC-Y1DD]	Part of Jct. Yd. Br.	2.0–2.5	(0.5)		
[MC-T]	W. Det.–MP 20	2.7–20.0	17.3		
[MC-B]	Bay Cty. Jct.–Rays Pit	2.2–28.2	26.0		
[PRR-A]	Carleton–Ecorse Jct.	116.4–137.1	20.7		
[PRR-YU]	Union Belt	0–5.8	(5.8)		
[DT]	In Det.	Lines	16.8		

The lines conveyed to Norfolk Southern

LINE DESIG.	END POINTS	MP	MI MAIN	SOURCE	NOTE
NS-					
[CC-Y1N]	In Jackson	1.2–4.3	(3.1)		
[CK&S-YA]	In Kal.	0.8–1.9	(1.1)		
[DTM-Y1D]	In Battle Creek	90.9–93.9	(3.0)		
[GR&I-Y2S]	Upjohn–Kal.	178.5–185.1	(6.6)		
[GR&I-S]	Gibson St.–Pleasant Ave.	185.1–233.2	48.1		
[GR&I-N]	Winter St.–Comstock Park	234.7–239.5	4.8		
[LS-A1]	OH state line–Ottawa Lk.	307.9–312.1	4.2		
[LS-A5]	Wh. Pi. Jct.–IN state line	421.3–424.1	2.8		
[LS-YM]	In Monroe	0–1.1	(1.1)		
[LS-Y1J]	In Jackson	40.1–42.1	(2.0)		
[LS-Y4L]	In Albion	21.9–23.6	(1.7)		
[LS-Y2L]	In Lans.	57.5–58.8	(1.3)		

[LS-Y1L]	In Lans.	60.4–61.2	(0.8)
[LS-Y3W]	At OD	1.0–1.1	(0.1)
[LS-Y1W]	In Jackson	0.4–1.1	(0.7)
[LS-G]	Wh. Pi. Jct.–N. Yard	0–36.8	37.1
[LS-Y1G]	In Kal.	36.8–39.5	(2.7)
[LS-G2]	Plainwell–Otsego	46.8–52.7	5.9
[LS-Y2G]	In Gr. Rpds.	91.6–95.0	(3.4)
[MC-E]	Town Line–Jackson	7.4–75.4	68.0
[MC-YP]	Ypsi. Belt	Line	(1.1)
[MC-T]	MP 20–Toledo	20.0–49.5	29.5
[MC-Y1A]	In Niles	102.8–104.0	(1.2)
[MC-Y2A]	In Three Rivers	70.1–70.9	(0.8)
[MC-Y3A]	In Jackson	0–0.8	(0.8)
[MC-Y1N]	In Niles	0–0.3	(0.3)
[MC-C]	Jackson–Baron	75.4–119.8	44.4
[MC-C]	Gord–Kal.	121.4–143.2	21.8
[MC-Y1G]	Dutton–Gr. Rpds.	88.0–94.4	(6.4)
[MC-YLT]	Lans. Transit	Line	(0.8)
[MC-YLM]	Lans. Manufacturers	Line	(5.2)
[MC-S]	Jackson–Lans.	0.2–36.9	36.7
[MC-Y1S]	In N. Lans.	37.8–39.7	(1.9)

1999/6/1   TOTAL to CNR=91.2   to NS=303.3   TOTAL=394.5

OWNERSHIP

1976   Conrail (Consolidated Rail Corporation)
1999/6/1   Conrail, owned jointly by CSX Transportation and Norfolk Southern.

Act Column Key

L   Leased to CSX
P   Purchased from Penn Central
P2   Purchased from Detroit Terminal
S1   Sold to Southern Michigan Railroad Society
S2   Sold to Norfolk Southern
S3   Sold to Canadian National–Canadian Pacific joint ownership
S4   Sold to Branch & St. Joseph Counties Rail Users Association, line subsequently bought by Michigan Southern Railway
X   Abandoned
Y   Converted main track to yard track
Z   Service ended; rails left in place

Notes

1.   Lines LS-D and MC-T were parallel lines between Detroit and Toledo. With the end of separate ownerships at the inception of Conrail, this adjustment is made to treat the two lines as one double track line rather than two single track lines. Parts of line LS-D at West Detroit and between D&M Jct. and Beaubien Street were abandoned and part between Vinewood Avenue and Beaubien Street is considered double track with line MC-B. A segment of line MC-T in Toledo was abandoned.

2.   This segment was replaced by trackage rights over Grand Trunk Western line GTW-C effective at the same time. Amtrak moved its operations to the new station at Depot.

3.   Trackage rights were retained on this segment.

Coopersville & Marne

MAIN LINE (C&M-A)

For arrangement of stations, construction record, and prior ownerships, see Grand Trunk Western line GTW-D

ACQUISITION/DISPOSITION RECORD

DATE	ACT	END POINTS	MP	CHANGE	MAIN	SOURCE	NOTE
1989/12/14	P	Marne–Coopersville	166.6–173.0	6.4	6.4		
1996	P	Fuller–Marne	159.7–166.6	6.9	13.3		

OWNERSHIP

1989   Coopersville & Marne

Act Column Key

P   Purchased from Central Michigan

Corlies & Thunder Bay

MAIN LINE (CTB-A)

	MILEAGE	COUNTY	CROSSINGS, JUNCTIONS, ETC.
(Thunder Bay)	0	Alpena	(sec 24 T31M R8E)
(Jct.)	1.6	"	(W end grade later used by BCG&A)
(Thunder Riv.)	7.3	"	(sec 1 T31N R7E)

CONSTRUCTION/ABANDONMENT

DATE	ACT	END POINTS	MP	CHANGE	MAIN	SOURCE	NOTE
1864 ca.	B	Line	0–7.3	+7.3	7.3		
1868 ca.	X	Line	0–7.3	−7.3	0		

OWNERSHIP

1864   Corlies & Thunder Bay Train Railway

Act Column Key

B   Built by Corlies & Thunder Bay Train Railway
X   Abandoned

Notes

GENERAL   This road was largely a logging road of John Trowbridge & Brothers. That part of the grade between MP 0 and MP 1.6 was later used by the Boyne City, Gaylord & Alpena for its Alpena–Boyne City line. See that company for subsequent record.

Crawford & Manistee River

MAIN LINE (C&MR-A)

	MILEAGE	COUNTY	CROSSINGS, JUNCTIONS, ETC.
(Manistee Riv.)	0	Kalkaska	(SE 1/4 sec 25 T26N R6W)
(Jct.)	7.1	"	J/C&MR-B 0 (sec 10 T25N R5W)
(End)	10.0	"	(E line sec 36 T26N R5W)

BRANCH LINE (C&MR-B)

	MILEAGE	COUNTY	CROSSINGS, JUNCTIONS, ETC.
(Jct.)	0	Kalkaska	J/C&MR-A 7.1
(End)	3	"	(sec 13 T25N R5W)

CONSTRUCTION/ABANDONMENT

DATE	ACT	END POINTS	MP	CHANGE	MAIN	SOURCE	NOTE
1885/10/11	B	Manistee Riv.–End	0–10.0	+10.0	10.0	1	
1889	B	Branch	0–3.0	+3.0	13.0	1	
1904	X	All lines	0–10.0 & 0–3.0	–13.0	0	1	

OWNERSHIP

1885   Crawford & Manistee River

ACQUISITION/DISPOSITION RECORD

See Mileage Record above

Act Column Key

B   Built by Crawford & Manistee River
X   Abandoned

Sources

1.   Michigan, Commissioner of Railroads, *Annual Reports,* 1885, 1889, 1904.

CSX Transportation

On 2 September 1987 this company acquired Chesapeake & Ohio. For arrangement of stations, construction record, and prior ownerships, see individual Manistee & Northeastern (M&NE), Port Huron & Detroit (PHD) and Pere Marquette (PM) lines. Its Acquisition/Disposition Record is continued in two places: under the name of the former company and under the name of the new company. The lines acquired were:

LINE DESIG.	END POINTS	MP	MI MAIN	SOURCE	NOTE
CSX-					
[M&NE-YM1]	Manistee–Filer Cty.	0–3.5	(3.5)		
[M&NE-YM2]	In Manistee	0–1.5	(1.5)		
[PHD-A]	Pt. Hur.–Mar. Cty.	0–18.5	18.5		
[PM-T]	Sag.–Toledo OH	0–29.5 and 38.4–130.1	121.2		
[PM-Y1T]	In Flint	29.5–32.7	(3.2)		
[PM-Y2T]	In Flint	33.4–38.4	(5.0)		
[PM-FB]	Flint Belt	29.5–37.7	8.2		
[PM-B]	Sag.–Bay Cty.	0–17.0	17.0		
[PM-YBH]	Huron & Western	1.1–2.7	(1.4)		
[PM-YBS]	S. Bay Cty. Spur	0–1.9	(1.9)		
[PM-YBE]	Essexville Spur	0–2.4	(2.4)		
[PM-L]	Sag.–Lud.	0–137.6	137.6		
[PM-YL1]	4th Ward Branch, Lud.	0–2.2	(2.2)		
[PM-YL2]	Development Branch, Lud.	0–2.1	(2.1)		
[PM-M]	Walhalla–Manistee	0–26.8	26.8		
[PM-Y1LM]	In Mt. Pl.	12.4–14.7	(2.3)		
[PM-Y2LM]	In Coleman	0–0.8	(0.8)		
[PM-S]	Sag.–Bad Axe	0–62.6	62.6		
[PM-Y2SB]	part Bay Port Branch	0–0.9	(0.9)		
[PM-Q]	Sag.–Pt. Hur.	2.6–90.1	87.5		
[PM-YSB]	Sag. Belt Line	0.7–4.5	(3.8)		
[PM-YSL]	Loop Line, Sag.	0–1.3	(1.3)		

[PM-YSZ]	Zilwaukee Spur, Sag.	0–1.4	(1.4)
[PM-YSW]	W. Side Branch, Sag.	0–1.7 & 2.9–3.1	(1.9)
[PM-YSS]	S. Sag. Line, Sag.	0–4.2	(4.2)
[PM-V]	Paines–Edmore	7.7–59.7	52.0
[PM-Y1VT]	In Alma	0–0.4	(0.4)
[PM-D]	Delray–Wealthy St., G.R.	4.6–151.8	146.4
[PM-DW]	W. Det. Branch	0–7.9	7.9
[PM-YEL]	In E. Lans.	0–1.5	(1.5)
[PM-DZ]	Pleasant St.–Sunnyside	151.5–151.9	0.4
[PM-YDR]	Reeds Lk. Br., Gr.Rpds.	0–1.4	(1.4)
[PM-G]	Edmore–Elmdale	59.5–110.5	51.0
[PM-I]	Gr.Ledge–Eagle	0.8–4.3	3.5
[PM-C]	Gr. Rpds.–Porter IN	0–117.9	117.9
[PM-W]	New Buffalo–LaCrosse IN	34.2–0	1.2
[PM-H]	In Hartford	15.3–17.3	2.0
[PM-A]	Hamilton–Holland	12.9–23.0	
	And Cronje–Montague	24.5–72.3	57.9
[PM-A2]	Waverly–Cronje	23.6–24.5	0.9
[PM-Y1H]	In Holland	23.0–23.8	(0.8)
[PM-YH2]	In Holland	0–1.6	(1.6)
[PM-YM1]	S. Horn, Musk.	0–6.0	(6.0)
[PM-YM2]	In Musk.	31.3–35.6	(4.3)
[PM-YHG2]	In Gr. Hav.	0–1.3	(1.3)
[PM-R]	Berry–White Cloud	0–21.0	21.0
[PM-Y1R]	In White Cloud	30.2–31.0	(0.8)
[PM-P]	Sunnyside–Baldwin	0–73.8	73.8
		TOTAL	1015.3

ACQUISITION/DISPOSITION RECORD (continued)

DATE	ACT	LINE	END POINTS	CHANGE	MAIN	SOURCE	NOTE
		CSX-					
1987/11	X	[PM-L]	Evart–Clare	−23.7			
12/18	S6	[PM-G]	Elmdale–N. Greenville	−32.0			
12/18	S6	[PM-V]	Paines–Elwell	−36.8			
12/18	S6	[GTW-YMG]	In Greenville	(−0.6)	922.8		
1988/6	S7	[PM-L]	In Clare	−2.6			
ca.	X	[PM-L]	Clare–Baldwin	−31.6			
12/22	S4	[PM-S]	Sag.–Bad Axe	−58.5			
12/22	S4	[PM-YSB]	Bay Port Br.	(−0.9)			
	Y	[PM-S]	In Sag. (as PM-Y1S)	(4.1)			
	X	[PM-G]	N. Greenville–Edmore	−19.0			
	X	[PM-V]	Elwell–Edmore	−15.2			
	X	[PM-Q]	Avoca–W of Tappan	−9.8			
	X	[PM-W]	Alfred–Wellsboro IN	−1.2	780.8		
1989/4/3	X	[PM-L]	Midland–Clare	−28.4	752.4		
1990/2	S5	[PM-H]	In Hartford	−1.6			
2	Y	[PM-H]	In Hartford (as PMY1H)	(0.4)	750.4		
1996	S4	[PM-Y1S]	In Sag.	(−3.0)			
	T1	[PM-D]	Lans.–N. Lans.	+0.9	751.3		1
1997/10/1	X	[PM-A]	Berry–Montague	−10.2	741.1		
1998/4/28	S8	[PM-Q]	Hoyt–Brown Cty.	−51.7			2
	S9	[PM-Q]	Brown Cty.–Avoca	−19.2			3
	Y	[PM-Q]	W of Tappan–Port Huron (as PM-Y1Q)	(6.8)	663.4		
1999	P3	[PM-G]	Elmdale–Malta	+5.6	669.0		

Act Column Key

P3	Bought from Mid-Michigan
S4	Sold to Huron & Eastern
S5	Sold to Kalamazoo, Lake Shore & Chicago
S6	Sold to Mid-Michigan
S7	Sold to Tuscola & Saginaw Bay
S8	Sold to Saginaw Valley
S9	Sold to Detroit Edison Co.
T1	Leased from Conrail
X	Abandoned
Y	Converted to yard track

Notes

1. This lease replaced trackage rights.
2. Trackage rights over Grand Trunk Western between Tappan and Flint were substituted for this line upon its sale.
3. This segment was sold to Detroit Edison Company and railbanked by that company for future use.

Delray Connecting

OWNERSHIP

1905   Delray Connecting

Note

GENERAL   This company is a terminal switching road and not an intercity carrier. Its mileage is not included the Michigan mileage table in chapter 2. The line was built in 1904.

Delray Terminal

OWNERSHIP

1905   Delray Terminal

Note

GENERAL   This company is a terminal switching road and not an intercity carrier. Its mileage is not included the Michigan mileage table in chapter 2. The line was built in February 1905.

Detroit & Charlevoix

MAIN LINE (D&C-A)

	MILEAGE	COUNTY	CROSSINGS, JUNCTIONS, ETC.
Frederic	0.0	Crawford	J/MC-M 101.0
(Connection)	1.5	"	J/D&C-Z 0.1
Ausable Riv.	1.9	"	
Harvey Branch	2.8	"	J/D&C-A1 0, J/D&C-A2 0
Dale Branch	3	"	J/D&C-A3 0
Smith Siding	3.94	"	
(Jct.)	4.6	"	J/D&C-A4 0
Fayette	7.29	Otsego	J/D&C-A5 0
(Jct.)	7.9	"	J/D&C-A6 0, J/D&C-A7 0, J/D&C-A8 0
(E. wye switch)	11.5	Crawford	J/D&C-1 0
(W. wye switch)	11.8	"	J/D&C-1 0.2+0.1

New E. Branch	13.2	Otsego	J/D&C-A9 0
Edson Branch	13.7	"	J/D&C-A10 0
Water Tank	13.8	"	
(Jct.)	14.1	"	
Manistee Riv.	14.4	"	
Blue Lk. Jct.	14.56	Antrim	J/D&C-2 0
Mancelona Road	15.87	"	
Buckley & Douglas Spur	16	"	
Elmira Branch Switch	18.6	"	J/D&C-A12 0
(Crossing)	18.7	"	
Lk. Harold	20.34	"	J/D&C-A13 0
Morrison	21.3?	"	
Kelley	23.7?	"	
Alba	24.70	"	X/GR&I-N 391.3
(Jct.)	25.5	"	J/D&C-A14 0
Brennan	26-1/2	"	
Blanchards New Spur	27	"	
Shepards	28.78	"	J/D&C-A15 0
Green Riv.	29.88	"	
Valley Switch	31.5	"	J/D&C-A16, J/EJ&S-3A 1.1
(Crossing)	33.6	"	X/EJ&S-3 1.4
Graves Camp	33.21	"	
Jordan Riv.	35.02	"	
Webster	35.3	"	
Marble	36.35	"	X/EJ&S-A 6.4
E. Jordan	42.66	Charlevoix	
S. Arm	43.5	"	

CONSTRUCTION/ABANDONMENT

DATE	ACT	END POINTS	MP	CHANGE	MAIN	SOURCE	NOTE
1901/9/2	P1	Frederic–Alba	0–24.7	+24.7		2	1
1901/9/16	B1	Alba–S. Arm	24.7–43.5	+16.8	43.5	2	1
1931/6/30	X	S. Arm–Marble	43.5–36.4	–7.1	36.4	1	3
1932	X	Marble–Frederic	36.4–0	–36.4	0	1	

OWNERSHIP

1901	Detroit & Charlevoix
1907/5/2	Michigan Central, control of Detroit & Charlevoix
1916/9/20	Michigan Central, merger of Detroit & Charlevoix
1930/2/1	Michigan Central, leased to New York Central

M.C. CONNECTION (D&C-Z)

	MILEAGE	COUNTY	CROSSINGS, JUNCTIONS, ETC.
(Jct.)	0	Crawford	J/MC-M 102.5
(Jct.)	0.1	"	J/D&C-A 1.5

CONSTRUCTION/ABANDONMENT

DATE	ACT	END POINTS	MP	CHANGE	MAIN	SOURCE	NOTE
??		Line					2

DEWARD SPUR (D&C-1)

	MILEAGE	COUNTY	CROSSINGS, JUNCTIONS, ETC.
	[Frederic]		
(E. wye switch)	11.5	Crawford	J/D&C-A 11.5
(S. wye switch)	11.7	"	J/wye to D&C-A 11.8, 0.2 mi.
Deward	11.89	"	J/D&C-1A 0, J/D&C-1B 0

CONSTRUCTION/ABANDONMENT

DATE	ACT	END POINTS	MP	CHANGE	MAIN	SOURCE	NOTE
1901/9/2	P1	Line	11.5–11.9	+0.4	0.4		
1932	X	Line	11.5–11.9	−0.4	0	1	

OWNERSHIP

1901	Detroit & Charlevoix
1907/5/2	Control by Michigan Central
1916/9/20	Michigan Central, merger of Detroit & Charlevoix
1930/2/1	Michigan Central, leased to New York Central

BRANCH (D&C-1A)

	MILEAGE	COUNTY	CROSSINGS, JUNCTIONS, ETC.
Deward	0	Crawford	J/D&C-1 11.89
(End)	1.5	"	(sec17 T28N R4W)

CONSTRUCTION/ABANDONMENT

DATE	ACT	END POINTS	MP	CHANGE	MAIN	SOURCE	NOTE
??		Line					2

BRANCH (D&C1B)

	MILEAGE	COUNTY	CROSSINGS, JUNCTIONS, ETC.
Deward	0	Crawford	J/D&C-1 11.89
(CRA/KKA line)	1.3		
(Jct.)	1.9	Kalkaska	J/D&C-1BA
(End)	2.2	"	(sec12 T28N R5W)

CONSTRUCTION/ABANDONMENT

DATE	ACT	END POINTS	MP	CHANGE	MAIN	SOURCE	NOTE
??		Line					2

BRANCH (D&C-1BA)

	MILEAGE	COUNTY	CROSSINGS, JUNCTIONS, ETC.
(Jct.)	1.9	Kalkaska	J/D&C-1B 1.9
(End)	2.6	"	(sec12 T28N R5W)

CONSTRUCTION/ABANDONMENT

DATE	ACT	END POINTS	MP	CHANGE	MAIN	SOURCE	NOTE
??		Line					2

HARVEY BRANCH (D&C-A1)

	MILEAGE	COUNTY	CROSSINGS, JUNCTIONS, ETC.
Harvey Branch	0	Crawford	J/D&C-A 2.8
(End)	0.9	"	(sec22 T28N R4W)

CONSTRUCTION/ABANDONMENT

DATE	ACT	END POINTS	MP	CHANGE	MAIN	SOURCE	NOTE
??		Line					2

WARD BRANCH (D&C-A2)

	MILEAGE	COUNTY	CROSSINGS, JUNCTIONS, ETC.
Harvey Branch	0	Crawford	J/D&C-A 2.8
(End)	1.3	"	(sec16 T28N R4W)

CONSTRUCTION/ABANDONMENT

DATE	ACT	END POINTS		MP	CHANGE	MAIN	SOURCE	NOTE
??		Line						2

DALE BRANCH (D&C-A3) (LINE NOT LOCATED)

CONSTRUCTION/ABANDONMENT

DATE	ACT	END POINTS		MP	CHANGE	MAIN	SOURCE	NOTE
??		Line						2

ROSS BRANCH (D&C-A4)

	MILEAGE	COUNTY	CROSSINGS, JUNCTIONS, ETC.
(Jct.)	0	Crawford	J/D&C-A 4.6
(End)	0.8	"	(sec9 T28N R4W)

CONSTRUCTION/ABANDONMENT

DATE	ACT	END POINTS		MP	CHANGE	MAIN	SOURCE	NOTE
??		Line						2

FAYETTE BRANCH (D&C-A5)

	MILEAGE	COUNTY	CROSSINGS, JUNCTIONS, ETC.
Fayette	0	Otsego	J/D&C-A 7.29
(End)	0.6	"	(sec. 27? T29N R4W)

CONSTRUCTION/ABANDONMENT

DATE	ACT	END POINTS		MP	CHANGE	MAIN	SOURCE	NOTE
??		Line						2

CAMP 12 BRANCH (D&C-A6) (LINE NOT LOCATED PRECISELY)

	MILEAGE	COUNTY	CROSSINGS, JUNCTIONS, ETC.
(Jct.)	0	Otsego	J/D&C-A 7.9
(End)	"	(sec. 27 T29N R4W)	

CONSTRUCTION/ABANDONMENT

DATE	ACT	END POINTS		MP	CHANGE	MAIN	SOURCE	NOTE
??		Line						2

CAMP 28 BRANCH (D&C-A7) (LINE NOT LOCATED PRECISELY)

	MILEAGE	COUNTY	CROSSINGS, JUNCTIONS, ETC.
(Jct.)	0	Otsego	J/D&C-A 7.9
(End)	?	"	(sec. 28 T29N R4W)

DATE	ACT	END POINTS		MP	CHANGE	MAIN	SOURCE	NOTE
??		Line						2

ENSIGN BRANCH (D&C-A8) (LINE NOT LOCATED PRECISELY)

	MILEAGE	COUNTY	CROSSINGS, JUNCTIONS, ETC.
(Jct.)	0	Otsego	J/D&C-A 7.9
(End)	1/4	"	(sec. 28 T29N R4W)

DATE	ACT	END POINTS		MP	CHANGE	MAIN	SOURCE	NOTE
??		Line						2

EAST BRANCH (D&C-A9)

	MILEAGE	COUNTY	CROSSINGS, JUNCTIONS, ETC.
(Jct.)	0	Otsego	J/D&C-A 13.3

DATE	ACT	END POINTS		MP	CHANGE	MAIN	SOURCE	NOTE
??		Line						2

EDSON BRANCH (D&C-A10)

	MILEAGE	COUNTY	CROSSINGS, JUNCTIONS, ETC.
Edson Branch	0	Otsego	J/D&C-A 13.7
(End)	2.7	"	(sec. 20 T29N R4W)

DATE	ACT	END POINTS		MP	CHANGE	MAIN	SOURCE	NOTE
??		Line						2

RIVER BRANCH (D&C-A11) *(LINE NOT LOCATED PRECISELY)*

	MILEAGE	COUNTY	CROSSINGS, JUNCTIONS, ETC.
Blue Lk. Jct.	0	Antrim	J/D&C-A 14.56
(End)	1-1/2	"	(sec. 36 T29N R5W)

DATE	ACT	END POINTS		MP	CHANGE	MAIN	SOURCE	NOTE
??		Line						2

ELMIRA BRANCH (D&C-A12)

	MILEAGE	COUNTY	CROSSINGS, JUNCTIONS, ETC.
Elmira Branch Switch	0	Antrim	J/D&C-A 18.6
(Jct.)	0.1	"	J/logging road?
(Jct.)	0.7	"	J/D&C-A12A 0.7
(Jct.)	1.4	"	J/D&C-A12B 1.4
(Jct.)	1.5	"	J/D&C-A12C 1.5
(Jct.)	2.5	Otsego	
(Jct.)	5.4	"	
(Jct.)	5.9	"	
(Jct.)	6.3	"	
(Jct.)	8.7	"	(sec. 32 T31N R4W)

CONSTRUCTION/ABANDONMENT

DATE	ACT	END POINTS		MP	CHANGE	MAIN	SOURCE	NOTE
??		Line						2

CAMP 11 BRANCH (D&C-A12A) *(LINE NOT LOCATED PRECISELY)*

	MILEAGE	COUNTY	CROSSINGS, JUNCTIONS, ETC.
(Jct.)	0.7	Antrim	J/D&C-12A 0.7
(End)	2-1/2	"	(sec. 35 T30N R5W)

CONSTRUCTION/ABANDONMENT

DATE	ACT	END POINTS		MP	CHANGE	MAIN	SOURCE	NOTE
??		Line						2

PENCIL LAKE BRANCH (D&CA12B)

	MILEAGE	COUNTY	CROSSINGS, JUNCTIONS, ETC.
(Jct.)	1.4	Antrim	J/D&C-A12 1.4
(Jct.)	2.1	Otsego	J/D&C-A12B1, 2.1 mi. to 32 30N 4W
(Jct.)	2.1	"	J/D&C-A12B2, 1.0 mi. to 8 29N 4W
(Jct.)	3.1	"	J/D&C-A12B3, 2.3 mi. to 27 30N 4W, plus spurs
(End)	5.3	"	(sec. 10 T29N R4W)

CONSTRUCTION/ABANDONMENT

DATE	ACT	END POINTS	MP	CHANGE	MAIN	SOURCE	NOTE
??		Line					2

GOPHER BRANCH (D&C-A12C) (LINE NOT LOCATED PRECISELY)

	MILEAGE	COUNTY	CROSSINGS, JUNCTIONS, ETC.
(Jct.)	1.5	Antrim	J/D&C-A12 1.5
(End)	3-1/5	"	(sec. 25 T30N R5W)

CONSTRUCTION/ABANDONMENT

DATE	ACT	END POINTS	MP	CHANGE	MAIN	SOURCE	NOTE
??		Line					2

LAKE HAROLD BRANCH (D&C-A13)

	MILEAGE	COUNTY	CROSSINGS, JUNCTIONS, ETC.
Lk. Harold	0	Antrim	J/D&C-A 20.34
(End)	0.5	"	(sec. 34 T30N R5W)

CONSTRUCTION/ABANDONMENT

DATE	ACT	END POINTS	MP	CHANGE	MAIN	SOURCE	NOTE
??		ine					2

BRANCH (D&C-A14)

	MILEAGE	COUNTY	CROSSINGS, JUNCTIONS, ETC.
(Jct.)	0	Antrim	J/D&C-A 25.5
(End)	2.7	"	(sec. 18 T30N R5W)

CONSTRUCTION/ABANDONMENT

DATE	ACT	END POINTS	MP	CHANGE	MAIN	SOURCE	NOTE
??		Line					2

BRANCH (D&C-A15)

	MILEAGE	COUNTY	CROSSINGS, JUNCTIONS, ETC.
Shephards	0	Antrim	J/D&C-A 28.78
(End)	0.7	"	(sec. 34 T30N R6W)

CONSTRUCTION/ABANDONMENT

DATE	ACT	END POINTS	MP	CHANGE	MAIN	SOURCE	NOTE
??		Line					2

VALLEY BRANCH (D&C-A16)

	MILEAGE	COUNTY	CROSSINGS, JUNCTIONS, ETC.
Valley Switch	0	Antrim	J/D&C-A 31.5

(Branch extended east along Jordan River about 6 miles and included a number of spurs. No lines have been separately identified.)

CONSTRUCTION/ABANDONMENT

DATE	ACT	END POINTS	MP	CHANGE	MAIN	SOURCE	NOTE
??		Line					2

BLUE LAKE BRANCH (D&C-2)

	MILEAGE	COUNTY	CROSSINGS, JUNCTIONS, ETC.
Blue Lk. Jct.	0.0	Antrim	J/D&C-A 15.2
(Jct.)	1.2	"	J/D&C-2A 0
(Jct.)	1.4	"	J/D&C-2B 0
(Jct.)	3.2	"	J/D&C-2C 0

(ANT/KKA co line)	5.1		
(Jct.)	8.1	Kalkaska	J/D&C-2D 0

CONSTRUCTION/ABANDONMENT

DATE	ACT	END POINTS	MP	CHANGE	MAIN	SOURCE	NOTE
1901/9/2	P1	Blue Lk. Jct.–MP 8	0–8.0	+8.0	8.0	1	
1932	X	Blue Lk. Jct.–MP 8	0–8.0	–8.0	0	1	

OWNERSHIP

1901	Detroit & Charlevoix
1907/5/2	Control by Michigan Central
1916/9/20	Michigan Central, merger of Detroit & Charlevoix
1930/2/1	Michigan Central, leased to New York Central

SOUTH BRANCH (D&C-2A)

	MILEAGE	COUNTY	CROSSINGS, JUNCTIONS, ETC.
(Jct.)	0.0	Antrim	J/D&C-2 1.2
(End of track)	2.1	"	(sec35 T29N R5W)

DATE	ACT	END POINTS	MP	CHANGE	MAIN	SOURCE	NOTE
??		Line					2

HARDWOOD BRANCH (D&C-2B)

	MILEAGE	COUNTY	CROSSINGS, JUNCTIONS, ETC.
(Jct.)	0.0	Antrim	J/D&C-2 1.4
(Crossing)	2.1	"	X/logging road
(Jct.)	2.8	"	J/D&C-2B1 2.8
(End)	4.2	"	(sec. 5 T29N R5W)

DATE	ACT	END POINTS	MP	CHANGE	MAIN	SOURCE	NOTE
??		Line					2

BRANCH (D&C-2B1)

	MILEAGE	COUNTY	CROSSINGS, JUNCTIONS, ETC.
(Jct.)	2.8	Antrim	J/D&C-2B 2.8
(End)	3.9	"	(sec. 4 T29N R5W)

DATE	ACT	END POINTS	MP	CHANGE	MAIN	SOURCE	NOTE
??		Line					2

SAND LAKE BRANCH (D&C-2C)

	MILEAGE	COUNTY	CROSSINGS, JUNCTIONS, ETC.
(Jct.)	0	Antrim	J/D&C-2 3.2
(Jct.)	0.6	"	J/D&C-2C1 0.6
(Jct.)	1.2	"	J/D&C-2C2 1.2
(End)	4.0	Kalkaska	(sec. 4 T28N R5W)

DATE	ACT	END POINTS	MP	CHANGE	MAIN	SOURCE	NOTE
??		Line					2

SHOAR BRANCH (D&C-2C1) (LINE NOT LOCATED PRECISELY)

	MILEAGE	COUNTY	CROSSINGS, JUNCTIONS, ETC.
(Jct.)	0.6	Antrim	J/D&C-2C 0.6
(End)	2	"	(sec. 35 T29N R5W)

DATE	ACT	END POINTS	MP	CHANGE	MAIN	SOURCE	NOTE
??		Line					2

BRANCH (D&C-2C2) (LINE NOT LOCATED)

	MILEAGE	COUNTY	CROSSINGS, JUNCTIONS, ETC.
(Jct.)	1.2	Antrim	J/D&C-2C 1.2
(End)	?	"	(?)

DATE	ACT	END POINTS	MP	CHANGE	MAIN	SOURCE	NOTE
??		Line					2

BLUE LAKE SPUR (D&C-2D)

	MILEAGE	COUNTY	CROSSINGS, JUNCTIONS, ETC.
(Jct.)	0	Kalkaska	J/D&C-2 8.1
(End)	1/4	"	(sec. 15 T28N R5W)

CONSTRUCTION/ABANDONMENT

DATE	ACT	END POINTS	MP	CHANGE	MAIN	SOURCE	NOTE
??		Line					2

ACQUISITION/DISPOSITION RECORD

DATE	ACT	D&C–	END POINTS	CHANGE	MAIN	NOTE
1901/9/2	P1	A	Frederic–Alba	+24.7		1
9/2	P1	1	MP 11.5–Deward	+0.4		
9/2	P1	2	Blue Lk. Jct.–MP 8	+8.0		
1901/9/16	B1	A	Alba–S. Arm	+16.8	49.9	

On 20 September 1916 this company was acquired by Michigan Central.

DATE	ACT	D&C–	END POINTS	CHANGE	MAIN	NOTE
1931/6/30	X	A	S. Arm–Marble	−7.1	42.8	
1932	X	A	Marble–Frederic	−36.4		
	X	1	MP 11.5–Deward	−0.4		
	X	2	Blue Lk. Jct.–MP 8	−8.0	0	

Act Column Key

- B1 Built by Detroit & Charlevoix
- B2 Built by Michigan Central
- P1 Purchased from D. Ward—owned predecessor company
- S Sold to East Jordan & Southern
- X Abandonment

Sources

1. ICC, Finance Dockets.
2. Michigan Railroad Commission, *Aids, Gifts, Grants.*

Notes

GENERAL The construction and abandonment records for this property are incomplete. Prior to 1901 the property was operated as a private enterprise for the lumbering interests of David Ward, and later of his estate. This practice continued after its public carrier incorporation as the Detroit & Charlevoix on 2 January 1901.

The Michigan Central purchased 100% of the D&C common stock on 2 May 1907 and operated the carrier as a separate entity until 20 September 1916 when the D&C was merged into the MC.

1. Part of this property may have been in operation as early as 1886 on behalf of the lumbering operations of David Ward.
2. The date of construction and/or abandonment of this line could not be determined, and it is not included in the Acquisition/Disposition Record.
3. It appears that the East Jordan–South Arm segment may have been removed as early as 1918–1919.
4. The final train service over any part of the road appears to have been 30 June 1931. Abandonment of the entire line was approved by the ICC on 26 August 1932.

Detroit & Mackinac

MAIN LINE (D&M-S)

	MILEAGE	COUNTY	CROSSINGS, JUNCTIONS, ETC.
	[Bay Cty.]		
Foss	1.9	Bay	J/MC-YBN 1.8, J/PM-B 15.0, f. Bridge Jct.
(Crossing)	2.9	"	X/MC-YBH 2.4
N. Bay Cty.	3.0	"	J/GTW-S 56.4, J/PM-YBH 0
(Crossing)	3.7	"	X/BYCL-2 3.05
Water Works Spur	5.7	"	
Tobico	6.7	"	
Linwood Park	10.2	"	
Oakwood	10.8	"	
Linwood	12.0	"	J/D&M-Z1 0
Lengsville	13.6	"	
Brundage Spur	15.0	"	
Michie	16.5	"	
(Jct.)	19.2	"	J/D&M-Z2 0.5
Pinconning	19.9	"	X/MC-P2 0.6, f. Lk.
Lapan Spur	22.5	"	
Saganing	25.7	Arenac	
Pine Riv.	29.4	"	
Omer	34.2	"	J/D&M-G 0
Twining	39.3	"	
Turner	41.5	"	
Gypsum	42.3	"	
Farmer		Iosco	
Turtle	45.5	"	
National Cty. Spur	47.3	"	J/quarry spur, 2.1 miles
National Cty.	48.6	"	J/D&M-A 0
McIvor	50.5	"	f. Arn
White Rock	51.9	"	
Marks	54.2	"	
Alabaster Jct.	57.0	"	J/D&M-E 0

Tawas Cty. (old)	59.6	"	
Tawas Cty.E. Tawas	60.2	"	
E. Tawas (old)	61.0	"	
Tawas Beach Jct.	61.6	"	J/D&M-T 0
Bristol	64.7	"	
Kunze Siding	67.4	"	
Au Sable (old)	73.3	"	
AuSable Riv. Jct.	73.6	"	X/ASNW-A 0.8
Oscoda	74.2	"	
Au Sable Jct.	75.2	"	J/D&M-SA 0
Skeel	75.4	"	
Lincoln Jct.	79.3	"	J/D&M-O 79.3
Greenbush	86.3	Alcona	
Harrisville	91.8	"	
Sturgeon Point	95.5	"	
Alcona	98.4	"	
Black Riv.	102.7	"	J/D&M-O 108.4
Ossineke	112.5	Alpena	
Beebe Spur	117.8	"	
Hillman Jct.	123.3	"	J/D&M-H 0.7
Alpena (new)	124.0	"	
(Jct.)	124.4	"	J/D&M-YA 124.4
(Jct.)	124.7	"	J/D&M-N 124.7

CONSTRUCTION/ABANDONMENT

DATE	ACT	END POINTS	MP	CHANGE	MAIN	SOURCE	NOTE
1878/8/13	B1	Tawas Cty.–National Cty.	48.6–59.6	+11.0	11.0	3,4	
1881	B2	Tawas Cty.–E. Tawas	59.6–61.0	+1.4	12.4	3	
1883/12/3	B3	E. Tawas–Au Sable	61.0–73.3	+12.3	24.7	3	
1885/12/27	B3	Au Sable–Lincoln Jct.	73.3–79.3	+6.0	30.7	3	
1886/9/20	B3	Black Riv.–Alpena	102.7–124.4	+21.7	52.4	3	
1895 ca.	B4	In Alpena	124.4–124.7	+0.3	52.7		
1896/9/20	B4	Foss–National Cty.	1.9–48.6	+46.7	99.4	3	
1901/12/15	B4	Lincoln Jct.–Black Riv.	79.3–102.7	+23.4	122.8	3	
1987	Y	Foss–MP 4.9 (as D&M-Y1S)	1.9–4.9	(3.0)			
1987	X	MP 4.9–MP 17.8	4.9–17.8	−12.9	106.9		

OWNERSHIP

1878	Lake Huron & Southwestern (B1)
1880/2/12	Tawas & Bay County (B2), purchase of Lake Huron & Southwestern
1882/7/11	Bay City & Alpena, purchase of Tawas & Bay County
1883/3/31	Detroit, Bay City & Alpena (B3), renaming of Bay City & Alpena
1894/12/17	Detroit & Mackinac (B4), reorganization of Detroit, Bay City & Alpena
1992/2	Lake States Rail Corporation, buy Detroit & Mackinac

LINWOOD CROSSOVER (D&M-Z1)

	MILEAGE	COUNTY	CROSSINGS, JUNCTIONS, ETC.
Linwood	0	Bay	J/D&M-S 12.0
(Jct.)	0.6	"	J/MC-M 10.8

CONSTRUCTION/ABANDONMENT

DATE	ACT	END POINTS	MP	CHANGE	MAIN	SOURCE	NOTE
1976	B4	Line	0–0.6	+0.6	0.6		
1987	X	Line	0.0–6	−0.6	0		

OWNERSHIP

1976   Detroit & Mackinac (B4)

CROSSOVER (D&M-Z2)

	MILEAGE	COUNTY	CROSSINGS, JUNCTIONS, ETC.
(Jct.)	0	Bay	J/MC-M 17.9
(Jct.)	0.5	"	J/D&M-S 19.2

CONSTRUCTION/ABANDONMENT

DATE	ACT	END POINTS	MP	CHANGE	MAIN	SOURCE	NOTE
1987	B4	Line	0–0.5	+0.5	0.5		

OWNERSHIP

1987   Detroit & Mackinac (B4)

1992/2 Lake States Rail Corporation, buy Detroit & Mackinac

ALPENA OLD MAIN TRACK (D&M-YA)

	MILEAGE	COUNTY	CROSSINGS, JUNCTIONS, ETC.
[Bay Cty.]			
(Jct.)	124.4	Alpena	J/D&M-S 124.4
(E. wye switch)	124.8	"	J/D&M-N 124.7–0.5
Alpena (old)	125.2	"	

CONSTRUCTION/ABANDONMENT

DATE	ACT	END POINTS	MP	CHANGE	MAIN	SOURCE	NOTE
1886/9/20	B3	Line	124.4–125.2	+0.8	0.8	3	
1912	Y	Line	124.4–125.2	(0.8)	0	3	
??	X	Part	124.4–124.8	(–0.4)	0		

OWNERSHIP

1886   Detroit, Bay City & Alpena (B3)

1894/12/17 Detroit & Mackinac, reorganization of Detroit, Bay City & Alpena

1992/2   Lake States Rail Corporation, buy Detroit & Mackinac

AU SABLE SPUR (D&M-SA)

	MILEAGE	COUNTY	CROSSINGS, JUNCTIONS, ETC.
Au Sable Jct.	0	Iosco	J/D&M-S 75.2
(Jct.)	1.3	"	J/ASNW-A 2.9

CONSTRUCTION/ABANDONMENT

DATE	ACT	END POINTS	MP	CHANGE	MAIN	SOURCE	NOTE
1915/6/30	B4	Au Sable Jct.–MP 1.3	0–1.3	+1.3	1.3	3	
1927	X	Au Sable Jct.–MP 1.3	0–1.3	–1.3	0		

OWNERSHIP

1915   Detroit & Mackinac (B4)

AU GRES BRANCH (D&M-G)

	MILEAGE	COUNTY	CROSSINGS, JUNCTIONS, ETC.
Omer	0	Arenac	J/D&M-S 34.2
Umstead	4.4	"	
Wheeler Spur	4.7	"	
Souveigny	6.4	"	
Au Gres	8.1	"	
(End)	8.3	"	

CONSTRUCTION/ABANDONMENT

DATE	ACT	END POINTS	MP	CHANGE	MAIN	SOURCE	NOTE
1904/7/3	B4	Omer–Au Gres	0–8.3	+8.3	8.3	3	
1965	X	Omer–Au Gres	0–8.3	−8.3	0	2	

OWNERSHIP

1904	Detroit & Mackinac (B4)

ERIE & MICHIGAN RAILWAY & NAVIGATION (D&M-E)

	MILEAGE	COUNTY	CROSSINGS, JUNCTIONS, ETC.
Alabaster Jct.	0	Iosco	J/D&M-S 57.0
(Jct.)	0.6	"	J/D&M-EP 0.6
Grise	0.9	"	
Slingerland	2.9	"	
Robinson	3.7	"	
Alabaster	4.0	"	

CONSTRUCTION/ABANDONMENT

DATE	ACT	END POINTS	MP	CHANGE	MAIN	SOURCE	NOTE
1897	B4	Line	0–4.0	+4.0	4.0	4	

OWNERSHIP

1897	Detroit & Mackinac (B4)
1907/6/29	Leased to Erie & Michigan Railway & Navigation
uncertain	Lease canceled
1992/2	Lake States Rail Corporation, buy Detroit & Mackinac

PORT GYPSUM SPUR (D&M-EP)

	MILEAGE	COUNTY	CROSSINGS, JUNCTIONS, ETC.
(Jct.)	0.6	Iosco	J/D&M-E 0.6
Port Gypsum	1.3	"	

CONSTRUCTION/ABANDONMENT

DATE	ACT	END POINTS	MP	CHANGE	MAIN	SOURCE	NOTE
1897 ca.	B4	Line	0.6–1.3	+0.7	0.7		

OWNERSHIP

1897	Detroit & Mackinac (B4)
1907/6/29	Leased to Erie & Michigan Railway & Navigation
uncertain	Lease canceled
1992/2	Lake States Rail Corporation, buy Detroit & Mackinac

ORIGINAL MAIN LINE (PRESCOTT BR.)(D&M-A)

	MILEAGE	COUNTY	CROSSINGS, JUNCTIONS, ETC.
National Cty.	0	Iosco	J/D&M-S 48.6
Emery Jct.	0.3	"	J/D&M-B 0.3
Whittemore	4.1	"	
Mills	7.2	"	
Prescott	11.8	Ogemaw	
Shearer	16.1	Arenac	J/D&M-A2 0
Moffat	18.7	"	
Alger	23.0	"	J/MC-M 39.8, f. Wells

CONSTRUCTION/ABANDONMENT

DATE	ACT	END POINTS	MP	CHANGE	MAIN	SOURCE	NOTE
1878/8/13	B1	National Cty.–MP 2.2	0–2.2	+2.2	2.2	4	
1878	B1	MP 2.2–Prescott	2.2–11.8	+9.6	11.8	3	
1881	B2	Prescott–Shearer	11.8–16.1	+4.3	16.1	3	
1883/12/3	B3	Shearer–Alger	16.1–23.0	+6.9	23.0	3	
1896/9/20	X	Alger–Prescott	23.0–11.8	–11.2	11.8	3	
1943	X	National Cty.–Prescott	0–11.8	–11.8	0	4	

OWNERSHIP

1878	Lake Huron & Southwestern (B1)
1880/2/12	Tawas & Bay County (B2), purchase of Lake Huron & Southwestern
1882/7/11	Bay City & Alpena, purchase of Tawas & Bay County
1883/3/31	Detroit, Bay City & Alpena (B3), renaming of Bay City & Alpena
1894/12/17	Detroit & Mackinac, reorganization of Detroit, Bay City & Alpena

BUSH LAKE SPUR (D&M-A2)

	MILEAGE	COUNTY	CROSSINGS, JUNCTIONS, ETC.
Shearer	0	Arenac	J/D&M-A 16.1
Bush Lake	2.6	"	

CONSTRUCTION/ABANDONMENT

DATE	ACT	END POINTS	MP	CHANGE	MAIN	SOURCE	NOTE
1884	B3	Line	0–2.6	+2.6	2.6	3	
1886	B3	Extend	2.6–4.7	+2.1	4.7	3	
1888	X	Line	0–4.7	–4.7	0	3	

OWNERSHIP

1884	Detroit, Bay City & Alpena (B3)

TAWAS BEACH BRANCH (D&M-T)

	MILEAGE	COUNTY	CROSSINGS, JUNCTIONS, ETC.
Tawas Beach Jct.	0	Iosco	J/D&M-S 61.6
Tawas Beach	1.4	"	

CONSTRUCTION/ABANDONMENT

DATE	ACT	END POINTS	MP	CHANGE	MAIN	SOURCE	NOTE
1897/8/18	B4	Line	0–1.4	+1.4	1.4	4	
1925 ca.	X	Line	0–1.4	–1.4	0		

OWNERSHIP

1897	Detroit & Mackinac (B4)

BRANCH (D&M-AX3) LINE NOT LOCATED

CONSTRUCTION/ABANDONMENT

DATE	ACT	END POINTS	MP	CHANGE	MAIN	SOURCE	NOTE
1881	B2	Line	0–3.6	+3.6	3.6	3	
1886	X	Line	0–3.6	–3.6	0	3	

OWNERSHIP

1881	Bay City & Alpena (B2)
1883/3/31	Detroit, Bay City & Alpena, rename of Bay City & Alpena

WHITNEY BRANCH (D&M-SX2) *LINE NOT LOCATED*

CONSTRUCTION/ABANDONMENT

DATE	ACT	END POINTS	MP	CHANGE	MAIN	SOURCE	NOTE
1883	B3	Line	0–2.3	+2.3	2.3	3	
1889	B3	Extend	2.3–6.4	+4.1	6.4	3	
1895	X	Line	0–6.4	–6.4	0	3	

OWNERSHIP

1883	Detroit, Bay City & Alpena (B3)
1894/12/17	Detroit & Mackinac, reorganization of Detroit, Bay City & Alpena

EMERY BRANCH (D&M-SX3) *LINE NOT LOCATED*

CONSTRUCTION/ABANDONMENT

DATE	ACT	END POINTS	MP	CHANGE	MAIN	SOURCE	NOTE
1883	B3	Line	0–1.0	+1.0	1.0	3	
1889	X	Line	0–1.0	–1.0	0	3	

OWNERSHIP

1883	Detroit, Bay City & Alpena (B3)

CARPENTER BRANCH (D&M-SX4) *LINE NOT LOCATED*

CONSTRUCTION/ABANDONMENT

DATE	ACT	END POINTS	MP	CHANGE	MAIN	SOURCE	NOTE
1883	B3	Line	0–2.2	+2.2	2.2	3	
1886	X	Line	0–2.2	–2.2	0	3	

OWNERSHIP

1883	Detroit, Bay City & Alpena (B3)

ARNS BRANCH (D&M-SX5) *LINE NOT LOCATED*

CONSTRUCTION/ABANDONMENT

DATE	ACT	END POINTS	MP	CHANGE	MAIN	SOURCE	NOTE
1885	B3	Line	0–1.2	+1.2	1.2	3	
1895	X	Line	0–1.2	–1.2	0	3	

OWNERSHIP

1885	Detroit, Bay City & Alpena (B3)
1894/12/27	Detroit & Mackinac, reorganization of Detroit, Bay City & Alpena

CAMP 2 BRANCH (D&M-SX6) *LINE NOT LOCATED*

CONSTRUCTION/ABANDONMENT

DATE	ACT	END POINTS	MP	CHANGE	MAIN	SOURCE	NOTE
1886	B3	Line	0–5.0	+5.0	5.0	3	
1889	X	Line	0–5.0	–5.0	0	3	

OWNERSHIP

1886	Detroit, Bay City & Alpena (B3)

COMSTOCK'S BRANCH (D&M-SX7) LINE NOT LOCATED

CONSTRUCTION/ABANDONMENT

DATE	ACT	END POINTS	MP	CHANGE	MAIN	SOURCE	NOTE
1888	B3	Line	0–2.3	+2.3	2.3	3	
1889	B3	Extend	2.3–7.3	+5.0	7.3	3	
1895	X	Line	0–7.3	–7.3	0	3	

OWNERSHIP

1888	Detroit, Bay City & Alpena (B3)
1894/12/27	Detroit & Mackinac, reorganization of Detroit, Bay City & Alpena

SANBORN'S BRANCH (D&M-SX8) LINE NOT LOCATED

CONSTRUCTION/ABANDONMENT

DATE	ACT	END POINTS	MP	CHANGE	MAIN	SOURCE	NOTE
1889	B3	Line	0–2.0	+2.0	2.0	3	
1895	X	Line	0–2.0	–2.0	0	3	

OWNERSHIP

1888	Detroit, Bay City & Alpena (B3)
1894/12/27	Detroit & Mackinac, reorganization of Detroit, Bay City & Alpena

GRAHAM'S BRANCH (D&M-SX9) LINE NOT LOCATED

CONSTRUCTION/ABANDONMENT

DATE	ACT	END POINTS	MP	CHANGE	MAIN	SOURCE	NOTE
1889	B3	Line	0–2.1	+2.1	2.1	3	
1895	X	Line	0–2.1	–2.1	0	3	

OWNERSHIP

1888	Detroit, Bay City & Alpena (B3)
1894/12/27	Detroit & Mackinac, reorganization of Detroit, Bay City & Alpena

ROSE CITY BRANCH (D&M-B)

	MILEAGE [National Cty.]	COUNTY	CROSSINGS, JUNCTIONS, ETC.
Emery Jct.	0.3	Iosco	J/D&M-A 0.3
Hemlock Road	3.8	"	
Coopers Corners	5.0	"	
Taft	6.7	"	
Hale (Lk.)	11.5	"	
Loon Lk.	13.1	"	
Long Lk.	16.5	"	
Smith Jct.	19.2	Ogemaw	J/D&M-B2 19.2, f. Omaha Jct.?
Maltbys	22.2	"	f. Lane
Lupton	27.0	"	
Rose Cty.	31.8	"	

CONSTRUCTION/ABANDONMENT

DATE	ACT	END POINTS	MP	CHANGE	MAIN	SOURCE	NOTE
1886	B3	Emery Jct.–Maltbys	0.3–22.2	+21.9	21.9	3	
1893/1/1	B3	Maltbys–Rose Cty.	22.2–31.8	+9.6	31.5	3	
1930	X	Line	0.3–31.8	–31.5	0	4	

OWNERSHIP

1888	Detroit, Bay City & Alpena (B3)
1894/12/27	Detroit & Mackinac, reorganization of Detroit, Bay City & Alpena

THOMPSON SPUR (D&M-B2)

	MILEAGE	COUNTY	CROSSINGS, JUNCTIONS, ETC.
	[National Cty.]		
Smith Jct.	19.2	Ogemaw	J/D&M-B 19.2
S. Branch	20.0	"	
Thompson	22	Iosco	
(End)	26.5	Alcona	

CONSTRUCTION/ABANDONMENT

DATE	ACT	END POINTS	MP	CHANGE	MAIN	SOURCE	NOTE
1887/11/20	B3	Smith Jct.–MP 24.1	19.2–24.1	+4.9	4.9	3	
1888/11/18	B3	MP 24.1–MP 26.5	24.1–26.5	+2.4	7.3	3	
1891/1/7	X	MP 26.5–MP 22.7	26.5–22.7	–3.8	3.5		
1915 ca.	X	S. Branch–MP 22.7	20.0–22.7	–2.7	0.8		
1930	X	Line	19.2–20.0	–0.8	0	4	

OWNERSHIP

1888	Detroit, Bay City & Alpena (B3)
1894/12/27	Detroit & Mackinac, reorganization of Detroit, Bay City & Alpena

OLD MAIN LINE (LINCOLN BRANCH) (D&M-O)

	MILEAGE	COUNTY	CROSSINGS, JUNCTIONS, ETC.
	[Bay Cty.]		
Lincoln Jct.	79.3	Iosco	J/D&M-S 79.3
Gravel Pit Siding	81.8	Alcona	
Handy	84.9	"	
Mikado	87.4	"	f. W. Greenbush
Gustin	89.9	"	
Lincoln	93.9	"	f. W. Harrisville
Hawes	97.2	"	J/D&M-M 0, f. Mud Lk. Jct.
Henry	99.8	"	
Roe Lk.	101.9	"	
Black Riv.	108.4	"	J/D&M-S 102.7

CONSTRUCTION/ABANDONMENT

DATE	ACT	END POINTS	MP	CHANGE	MAIN	SOURCE	NOTE
1885/12/27	B3	Lincoln Jct.–MP 92.7	79.3–92.7	+13.4	13.4	3	
1886/5/17	P1	Black Riv.–MP 92.7	108.4–92.7	+15.7	29.1	3	1
1901/12/15	X	MP 94.7–Black Riv.	108.4–94.7	–13.7	15.4	3	
1928	X	Lincoln Jct.–MP 94.7	79.3–94.7	–15.4	0	4	

OWNERSHIP

1885	Detroit, Bay City & Alpena (B3)
1886/5/17	Detroit, Bay City & Alpena, purchase of Black River (P1) segment
1894/12/27	Detroit & Mackinac, reorganization of Detroit, Bay City & Alpena

MUD LAKE BRANCH (D&M-M)

	MILEAGE	COUNTY	CROSSINGS, JUNCTIONS, ETC.
Hawes	0	Alcona	J/D&M-O 97.2, f. Mud Lk. Jct.
Pritchards	5.9	"	
Mud Lk.	10.2	"	
Louds Jct.	10.9	"	

CONSTRUCTION/ABANDONMENT

DATE	ACT	END POINTS	MP	CHANGE	MAIN	SOURCE	NOTE
1886/5/17	P1	Hawes–Louds Jct.	0–10.9	+10.9	10.9	3	1
1888	B3	Extend	10.9–12.3	+1.4	12.3	3	
1896	X	Louds Jct.–Pritchards	12.3–5.9	–6.4	5.9	3	
1897	X	Pritchards–Hawes	5.9–0	–5.9	0	3	

OWNERSHIP

1886	Detroit, Bay City & Alpena (B3)	
1894/12/27	Detroit & Mackinac, reorganization of Detroit, Bay City & Alpena	

LOUDS BRANCH (D&M-MX2) LINE NOT LOCATED

CONSTRUCTION/ABANDONMENT

DATE	ACT	END POINTS	MP	CHANGE	MAIN	SOURCE	NOTE
1886	B3	Line	0–4.5	+4.5	4.5	3	
1887	B3	Extend line	4.5–7.0	+2.5	7.0	3	
1889	B3	Extend line	7.0–9.4	+2.4	9.4	3	
1896	X	Line	0–9.4	–9.4	0	3	

OWNERSHIP

1886	Detroit, Bay City & Alpena (B3)	
1894/12/27	Detroit & Mackinac, reorganization of Detroit, Bay City & Alpena	

MILLEN BRANCH (D&M-MX3) LINE NOT LOCATED

CONSTRUCTION/ABANDONMENT

DATE	ACT	END POINTS	MP	CHANGE	MAIN	SOURCE	NOTE
1886	B3	Line	0–4.0	+4.0	4.0	3	
1888	X	Part of line	1.3–4.0	–2.7	1.3	3	
1896	X	Line	0–1.3	–1.3	0	3	

OWNERSHIP

1886	Detroit, Bay City & Alpena (B3)	
1894/12/27	Detroit & Mackinac, reorganization of Detroit, Bay City & Alpena	

GUSTIN BRANCH (D&M-MX4) LINE NOT LOCATED

CONSTRUCTION/ABANDONMENT

DATE	ACT	END POINTS	MP	CHANGE	MAIN	SOURCE	NOTE
1886	B3	Line	0–2.5	+2.5	2.5	3	
1896	X	Line	0–2.5	–2.5	0	3	

OWNERSHIP

1886	Detroit, Bay City & Alpena (B3)	
1894/12/27	Detroit & Mackinac, reorganization of Detroit, Bay City & Alpena	

GUILFORDS BRANCH (D&M-MX5) LINE NOT LOCATED

CONSTRUCTION/ABANDONMENT

DATE	ACT	END POINTS	MP	CHANGE	MAIN	SOURCE	NOTE
1887	B3	Line	0–1.8	+1.8	1.8	3	
1896	X	Line	0–1.8	–1.8	0	3	

OWNERSHIP
    1887   Detroit, Bay City & Alpena (B3)
1894/12/27   Detroit & Mackinac, reorganization of Detroit, Bay City & Alpena

B. MILLS BRANCH (D&M-MX6) LINE NOT LOCATED

CONSTRUCTION/ABANDONMENT

DATE	ACT	END POINTS	MP	CHANGE	MAIN	SOURCE	NOTE
1887	B3	Line	0–4.2	+4.2	4.2	3	
1896	X	Line	0–4.2	–4.2	0	3	

OWNERSHIP
    1887   Detroit, Bay City & Alpena (B3)
1894/12/27   Detroit & Mackinac, reorganization of Detroit, Bay City & Alpena

PACK & WOODS SPUR (D&M-MX7) LINE NOT LOCATED

CONSTRUCTION/ABANDONMENT

DATE	ACT	END POINTS	MP	CHANGE	MAIN	SOURCE	NOTE
1887	B3	Line	0–2.1	+2.1	2.1	3	
1889	X	Line	0–2.1	–2.1	0	3	

OWNERSHIP
    1887   Detroit, Bay City & Alpena (B3)

MCDONALDS SPUR (D&M-MX8) LINE NOT LOCATED

CONSTRUCTION/ABANDONMENT

DATE	ACT	END POINTS	MP	CHANGE	MAIN	SOURCE	NOTE
1887	B3	Line	0–1.4	+1.7	1.7	3	
1896	X	Line	0–1.4	–1.7	0	3	

OWNERSHIP
    1887   Detroit, Bay City & Alpena (B3)
1894/12/27   Detroit & Mackinac, reorganization of Detroit, Bay City & Alpena

HAMILTON BRANCH (D&M-MX9) LINE NOT LOCATED

CONSTRUCTION/ABANDONMENT

DATE	ACT	END POINTS	MP	CHANGE	MAIN	SOURCE	NOTE
1887	B3	Line	0–2.3	+2.3	2.3	3	
1896	X	Line	0–2.3	–2.3	0	3	

OWNERSHIP
    1887   Detroit, Bay City & Alpena (B3)
1894/12/27   Detroit & Mackinac, reorganization of Detroit, Bay City & Alpena

LINDSEYS SPUR (D&M-MX10) LINE NOT LOCATED

CONSTRUCTION/ABANDONMENT

DATE	ACT	END POINTS	MP	CHANGE	MAIN	SOURCE	NOTE
1887	B3	Line	0–1.1	+1.7	1.7	3	
1889	X	Line	0–1.1	–1.7	0	3	

OWNERSHIP

1887	Detroit, Bay City & Alpena (B3)
1894/12/27	Detroit & Mackinac, reorganization of Detroit, Bay City & Alpena

WARD BRANCH (D&M-MX11) *LINE NOT LOCATED*

CONSTRUCTION/ABANDONMENT

DATE	ACT	END POINTS	MP	CHANGE	MAIN	SOURCE	NOTE
1887	B3	Line	0–2.0	+2.0	2.0	3	
1896	X	Line	0–2.0	–2.0	0	3	

OWNERSHIP

1887	Detroit, Bay City & Alpena (B3)
1894/12/27	Detroit & Mackinac, reorganization of Detroit, Bay City & Alpena

BONEY BRANCH (D&M-MX12) *LINE NOT LOCATED*

CONSTRUCTION/ABANDONMENT

DATE	ACT	END POINTS	MP	CHANGE	MAIN	SOURCE	NOTE
1887	B3	Line	0–1.2	+1.2	1.2	3	
1896	X	Line	0–1.2	–1.2	0	3	

OWNERSHIP

1887	Detroit, Bay City & Alpena (B3)
1894/12/27	Detroit & Mackinac, reorganization of Detroit, Bay City & Alpena

TURNER BRANCH (D&M-MX13) *LINE NOT LOCATED*

CONSTRUCTION/ABANDONMENT

DATE	ACT	END POINTS	MP	CHANGE	MAIN	SOURCE	NOTE
1887	B3	Line	0–1.1	+1.1	1.1	3	
1888	B3	Extend	1–1–5.3	+4.2	5.3	3	
1889	X	Line	0–5.3	–5.3	0	3	

OWNERSHIP

1887	Detroit, Bay City & Alpena (B3)

POTTERS BRANCH (D&M-MX14) *LINE NOT LOCATED*

CONSTRUCTION/ABANDONMENT

DATE	ACT	END POINTS	MP	CHANGE	MAIN	SOURCE	NOTE
1888	B3	Line	0–1.7	+1.7	1.7	3	
189	X	Line	0–1.7	–1.7	0	3	

OWNERSHIP

1888	Detroit, Bay City & Alpena (B3)
1894/12/27	Detroit & Mackinac, reorganization of Detroit, Bay City & Alpena

PARK & WOODS MILL BRANCH (D&M-MX15) *LINE NOT LOCATED*

CONSTRUCTION/ABANDONMENT

DATE	ACT	END POINTS	MP	CHANGE	MAIN	SOURCE	NOTE
1888	B3	Line	0–2.0	+2.0	2.0	3	
1896	X	Line	0–2.0	–2.0	0	3	

OWNERSHIP

1888	Detroit, Bay City & Alpena (B3)	
1894/12/27	Detroit & Mackinac, reorganization of Detroit, Bay City & Alpena	

HILLMAN BRANCH (D&M-H)

	MILEAGE	COUNTY	CROSSINGS, JUNCTIONS, ETC.
Hillman Jct	0.7	Alpena	J/D&M-S 123.3
Hillman Crossing	5.3	"	X/BC-A 85.5
Kerston	7.6	"	
Paxton	10.1	"	
King	11.1	"	
Emerson	12.5	"	
Lachine	15.8	"	
Selina	17.6	"	
Flanders		"	
Hillman	24.6	Montmorency	

CONSTRUCTION/ABANDONMENT

DATE	ACT	END POINTS	MP	CHANGE	MAIN	SOURCE	NOTE
1908	B4	Hillman Jct.–MP 8.7	0.7–8.7	+8.0	8.0	3	
1909/12/20	B4	MP 8.7–Hillman	8.7–24.6	+15.9	23.9	3	
1929	X	Hillman–Emerson	24.6–12.5	−12.1	11.8	4	
1967	X	Emerson–Paxton	12.5–10.1	−2.4	9.4	2	
1998	X	Hillman Jct.–Paxton	0.7–10.1	−9.4	0		

OWNERSHIP

1908	Detroit & Mackinac (B4)	
1992/2	Lake States Rail Corporation, buy Detroit & Mackinac	

ALPENA CEMENT QUARRY SPUR (AVERY BRANCH) (D&M-Q)

	MILEAGE	COUNTY	CROSSINGS, JUNCTIONS, ETC.
(Jct.)	0	Alpena	J/D&M-N 125.0
(Wye switch)	0.2	"	J/conn. to D&M-N 125.2, 0.2 mi.
(Crossing)	0.7	"	X/BC-A 91.5
(Huron Portland Cement Co.)	1.7	"	
(Jct.)	2.2	"	J/D&M-Q2 0
Alpena Cement Quarry	8.9	"	

CONSTRUCTION/ABANDONMENT

DATE	ACT	END POINTS	MP	CHANGE	MAIN	SOURCE	NOTE
1900 ca.	B4	Line	0–8.9	+8.9	8.9		
1930 ca.	X	MP 2.2–Quarry	2.2–8.9	−6.7			
1930 ca.	Y	MP 0–MP 2.2 (as D&M-YQ)	0–2.2	(2.2)	0		

OWNERSHIP

1908	Detroit & Mackinac (B4)	
1992/2	Lake States Rail Corporation, buy Detroit & Mackinac	

ROCKPORT QUARRY BRANCH (D&M-Q2)

	MILEAGE	COUNTY	CROSSINGS, JUNCTIONS, ETC.
(Jct.)	0	Alpena	J/D&M-Q 2.2
Rockport	11.4	"	
Rockport Quarry	11.6	"	
Bell	15.4	Presque Isle	
Kelly Island Quarry	18.2	"	

CONSTRUCTION/ABANDONMENT

DATE	ACT	END POINTS	MP	CHANGE	MAIN	SOURCE	NOTE
1924	B4	Line	0–11.6	+11.6	11.6	1	
1929	X	Line	0–11.6	−11.6	0	1	

OWNERSHIP

1924   Detroit & Mackinac (B4)

NORTHERN DIVISION (D&M-N)

	MILEAGE	COUNTY	CROSSINGS, JUNCTIONS, ETC.
	[Bay Cty.]		
(Jct.)	(0.5)	Alpena	J/D&M-YA 124.8
(Jct.)	124.7	"	J/D&M-S 124.7
Alpena Jct.	124.8	"	
(Jct.)	125.0	"	J/D&M-Q 0
(Jct., crossing)	125.2	"	X/BC-A 90.0, J/wye to D&M-Q 0.2, 0.2 mi.
Fletcher Jct.	127.7	"	J/D&M-NF 0
Cathro	133.2	"	
Bolton	135.5	"	
Polaski	140.4	Presque Isle	
Posen	143.5	"	f. Vincent
Rogers Cty. Jct.	144.7	"	J/D&M-R 1.2
Nowicki	147.0	"	
Metz	148.5	"	f. Hoffman
S. Rogers Cty.	149.7	"	
LaRocque	152.7	"	J/D&M-V 0
Bunton	155.9	"	
Big Cut	158.6	"	
Millersburg	161.6	"	
Providence	162.5	"	
Austins Siding	163.7	"	
Case	166.1	"	
Onaway	170.4	"	
(Jct.)	170.8	"	J/D&M-K 0
Tower	174.3	Cheboygan	J/D&M-L 0, J/D&M-W 0
Waveland	178.8	"	
Grant	184.9	"	
Aloha	188.4	"	
Randall Spur	190.7	"	
Inverness	193.1	"	
Cheboygan	196.5	"	J/MC-M 166.3
Cheboygan Dock	197.7	"	

CONSTRUCTION/ABANDONMENT

DATE	ACT	END POINTS	MP	CHANGE	MAIN	SOURCE	NOTE
1893/11/18	B5	Alpena–LaRocque	124.7–152.6	+27.9		3	
1893	B5	In Alpena	124.7+ 0.5	+0.5	28.4		
1898/9/11	B4	LaRocque–Onaway	152.6–170.4	+17.8	46.2	3	
1900/5/13	B4	Onaway–Tower	170.4–174.3	+3.9	50.1	3	
1904/5/22	B4	Tower–Inverness	174.3–193.1	+18.8	68.9	3	
1904/7/3	B4	Inverness–Cheboygan	193.1–196.5	+3.4	72.3	3	
1907/6/23	B4	Cheboygan–Cheboygan Dock	196.5–197.7	+1.2	73.5	3	
1912	Y	In Alpena (to D&M-Y1N)	124.7+0.5	(0.5)	73.0		
1960 ca.	X	In Cheboygan	197.1–197.7	−0.6	72.4		
1989/9	X	Hawks–Cheboygan	151.5–192.0	−40.5			

1989/9	Y	In Cheboygan (to D&M-Y2N)	192.0–197.1	(5.1)	26.8	
1993 ca.	X	In Cheboygan	192.0–197.1	(–5.1)	26.8	

OWNERSHIP
1893	Alpena & Northern (B5)
1895/4/16	Detroit & Mackinac (B4), purchase of Alpena & Northern
1992/2	Lake States Rail Corporation, buy Detroit & Mackinac

FLETCHER DAM SPUR (D&M-NF)

	MILEAGE	COUNTY	CROSSINGS, JUNCTIONS, ETC.
Fletcher Jct.	0	Alpena	J/D&M-N 127.7
Fletcher Dam	2.7	"	

CONSTRUCTION/ABANDONMENT

DATE	ACT	END POINTS	MP	CHANGE	MAIN	SOURCE	NOTE
??		Line					1

OWNERSHIP
??	Detroit & Mackinac (B4)

ROGERS CITY BRANCH (D&M-R)

	MILEAGE	COUNTY	CROSSINGS, JUNCTIONS, ETC.
	[Posen]		
Rogers Cty. Jct.	1.2	Presque Isle	J/D&M-N 144.7
Orchard	3.0	"	
Liske	6.2	"	
Calcite	12.0	"	f. Crawford Quarry
Rogers Cty.	14.8	"	

CONSTRUCTION/ABANDONMENT

DATE	ACT	END POINTS	MP	CHANGE	MAIN	SOURCE	NOTE
1911/6/18	B4	Rogers Cty. Jct.–Calcite	1.2–12.0	+10.8		3	
1911	B4	Calcite–Rogers Cty.	12.0–14.8	+2.8	13.6	3	

OWNERSHIP
1911	Detroit & Mackinac (B4)
1992/2	Lake States Rail Corporation, buy Detroit & Mackinac

JACKSON LAKE BRANCH (D&M-V)

	MILEAGE	COUNTY	CROSSINGS, JUNCTIONS, ETC.
LaRocque	0	Presque Isle	J/D&M-N 152.6
May Lk. Jct.	4.0	"	
Hurst	5.1	"	
Blond	8	"	
Pack Siding	11	"	
Rainy Lk.	13.3	"	
McPhee	20.5	Montmorency	
Valentine Lk.	23.9	"	
Jackson Lk.	25.7	"	
Conners Camp No. 2	28.6	"	

CONSTRUCTION/ABANDONMENT

DATE	ACT	END POINTS	MP	CHANGE	MAIN	SOURCE	NOTE
1894/9/23	B5	LaRocque–Jackson Lk.	0–25.7	+25.7	25.7	3	
1903/8/6	X	Jackson Lk.–Hurst	25.7–5.1	–20.6	5.1	3	
1923	X	Hurst–LaRocque	5.1–0	–5.1	0	1	

OWNERSHIP

1894	Alpena & Northern (B5)
1895/4/16	Detroit & Mackinac, purchase of Alpena & Northern

LEGRAND BRANCH (D&M-L)

	MILEAGE	COUNTY	CROSSINGS, JUNCTIONS, ETC.
Tower	0	Cheboygan	J/D&M-N 174.3
Churchill	2.3	"	
Millers	5.9	"	
LeGrand	8.1	"	
(End)	9.1	"	

CONSTRUCTION/ABANDONMENT

DATE	ACT	END POINTS	MP	CHANG	MAIN	SOURCE	NOTE
1900 ca.	B4	Line	0–9.1	+9.1	9.1		
1924	X	Line	0–9.1	–9.1	0	1	2

OWNERSHIP

1900	Detroit & Mackinac (B4)

DOG LAKE (WOLVERINE) BRANCH (D&M-W)

	MILEAGE	COUNTY	CROSSINGS, JUNCTIONS, ETC.
Tower	0	Cheboygan	J/D&M-N 174.3
(Jct.)	1.9	"	J/D&M-W3 0
Wolverine Switch	6.4	"	J/D&M-W2 0
(Jct.)	7.4	"	J/D&M-W4 0
(Jct.)	8.8	"	J/D&M-W5 0
(End)	10.9	"	

CONSTRUCTION/ABANDONMENT

DATE	ACT	END POINTS	MP	CHANGE	MAIN	SOURCE	NOTE
1900 ca.	B4	Line	0–10.9	+11.7	11.7		
1915/10/22	X	Line	0–10.9	–11.7	0		

OWNERSHIP

1900	Detroit & Mackinac (B4)

CLEVELAND BRANCH (D&M-W2)

	MILEAGE	COUNTY	CROSSINGS, JUNCTIONS, ETC.
Wolverine Switch	0	Cheboygan	J/D&M-W 6.4
(Jct.)	1.0	"	J/D&M-W2A 0
(Jct.)	4.6	"	J/MC
(Jct.)	5.2	"	(Sec 29 T33N R1E)

CONSTRUCTION/ABANDONMENT

DATE	ACT	END POINTS	MP	CHANGE	MAIN	SOURCE	NOTE
1900 ca.	B4	Line	0–5.2	+5.2	5.2		
1915 ca.	X	Line	0–5.2	–5.2	0		

OWNERSHIP

1900   Detroit & Mackinac (B4)

WOLVERINE BRANCH SPUR (D&M-W2A)

	MILEAGE	COUNTY	CROSSINGS, JUNCTIONS, ETC.
(Jct.)	0	Cheboygan	J/D&M-W2 1.0
(End)	2.9	"	

CONSTRUCTION/ABANDONMENT

DATE	ACT	END POINTS	MP	CHANGE	MAIN	SOURCE	NOTE
1900 ca.	B4	Line	0–2.9	+2.9	2.9		
1915 ca.	X	Line	0–2.9	–2.9	0		

OWNERSHIP

1900   Detroit & Mackinac (B4)

GILCHRIST SPUR (D&M-W3)

	MILEAGE	COUNTY	CROSSINGS, JUNCTIONS, ETC.
(Jct.)	0	Cheboygan	J/D&M-W 1.9
(Jct.)	2.0	"	J/D&M-W3A 2.0
(End)	6.7	"	(sec 10 T33N R1E)

DATE	ACT	END POINTS	MP	CHANGE	MAIN	SOURCE	NOTE
1900 ca.	B4	Line	0–6.7	+6.7	6.7		
1915 ca.	X	Line	0–6.7	–6.7	0		

OWNERSHIP

1900   Detroit & Mackinac (B4)

LAU SPUR (D&M-W3A)

	MILEAGE	COUNTY	CROSSINGS, JUNCTIONS, ETC.
(Jct.)	2.0	Cheboygan	J/D&M-W3 2.0
(End)	2.9	"	

DATE	ACT	END POINTS	MP	CHANGE	MAIN	SOURCE	NOTE
1900 ca.	B4	Line	2.0–2.9	+0.9	0.9		
1915 ca.	X	Line	2.0–2.9	–0.9	0		

OWNERSHIP

1900   Detroit & Mackinac (B4)

DOG LAKE SPUR (D&M-W4)

	MILEAGE	COUNTY	CROSSINGS, JUNCTIONS, ETC.
(Jct.)	0	Cheboygan	J/D&M-W 7.4
(End)	2.2	"	(Sec 13 T33N R1W)

DATE	ACT	END POINTS	MP	CHANGE	MAIN	SOURCE	NOTE
1900 ca.	B4	Line	0–2.2	+2.2	2.2		
1915 ca.	X	Line	0–2.2	–2.2	0		

OWNERSHIP

1900   Detroit & Mackinac (B4)

KICK BACK (D&M-W5)

	MILEAGE	COUNTY	CROSSINGS, JUNCTIONS, ETC.
(Jct.)	0	Cheboygan	J/D&M-W 8.8
(End)	4.2	"	(Sec 28 T34N R1W)

DATE	ACT	END POINTS	MP	CHANGE	MAIN	SOURCE	NOTE
1900 ca.	B4	Line	0–4.2	+4.2	4.2		
1915 ca.	X	Line	0–4.2	–4.2	0		

OWNERSHIP

1900   Detroit & Mackinac (B4)

BLACK RIVER QUARRY SPUR (D&M-K)

	MILEAGE	COUNTY	CROSSINGS, JUNCTIONS, ETC.
(Jct.)	0	Presque Isle	J/D&M-N 170.8
Black Riv. Quarry	5.2	"	

CONSTRUCTION/ABANDONMENT

DATE	ACT	END POINTS	MP	CHANGE	MAIN	SOURCE	NOTE
1905 ca.	B4	Line	0–5.2	+5.2	5.2		
1917/9/24	X	Line	0–5.2	–5.2	0		

OWNERSHIP

1905   Detroit & Mackinac (B4)

MICHIGAN CENTRAL LINES

The following lines were acquired from Penn Central Corporation:

DATE	D&M–	ACT	END POINTS	MP	CHANGE	MAIN	NOTE
1976/4/1	[MC-M1]	P2	Kawkawlin–Linwood	5.0–10.8	+5.8	5.8	
1976/4/1	[MC-M3]	P2	Salling–Mack. Cty.	115.8–182.6	+66.8	66.8	
1989/9		X	Cheboygan–Mack. Cty.	168.0–182.6	–14.6	52.2	

The following lines were operated as Designated Operator for State of Michigan:

DATE	D&M–	ACT	END POINTS	MP	CHANGE	DES.OPR. MAIN	NOTE
1976/4/1	[MC-M2]	C	Linwood–Salling	10.8–115.8	+105.0	105.0	
1976/4/1	[MC-Y1P]	C	In Pinconning	0–0.6	(+0.6)		
—	[MC-MR]	–	Grayling–Rasmus	0–5.6			3

Station list for each line is shown under Michigan Central lines MC-M, MC-MR, and MC-Y1P.

ACQUISITION/DISPOSITION RECORD

DATE	ACT	D&M–	END POINTS	CHANGE	MI MAIN	NOTE
1878/8/13	B1	S,A	Tawas Cty.–near Whittemore	+13.2		
	B1	A	Whittemore–Prescott	+9.6	22.8	
1881	B2	A	Prescott–Shearer	+4.3		
	B2	S	Tawas Cty.–E. Tawas	+1.4		
	B2	AX3	Branch	+3.6	32.1	
1883/12/3	B3	S	E. Tawas–Au Sable	+12.3		
	B3	A	Shearer–Alger	+6.9		
	B3	SX2	Whitney Branch	+2.3		
	B3	SX3	Emery Branch	+1.0		
	B3	SX4	Carpenter Branch	+2.2	56.8	
1884	B3	A2	Bush Lk. Spur	+2.6	59.4	

1885/12/27	B3	S	Au Sable–Lincoln Jct.	+6.0	
	B3	O	Lincoln Jct.–MP 92.7	+13.4	
	B3	SX5	Arns Branch	+1.2	80.0
1886/5/17	P1	O	Black Riv.–MP 92.7	+15.7	1
5/17	P1	M	Hawes–Loud Jct.	+10.9	
9/20	B3	S,YA	Black Riv.–Alpena(old)	+22.5	
	B3	A2	Bush Lk. Spur	+2.1	
	X	AX3	Branch	−3.6	
	X	SX4	Carpenter Branch	−2.2	
	B3	SX6	Camp 2 Branch	+5.0	
	B3	B	Emery Jct.–Maltbys	+21.9	
	B3	MX2	Louds Branch	+4.5	
	B3	MX3	Millen Branch	+4.0	
	B3	MX4	Gustin Branch	+2.5	163.3
1887/11/20	B3	B2	Thompson Spur	+4.9	
	B3	MX2	Louds Branch	+2.5	
	B3	MX5	Guilfords Branch	+1.8	
	B3	MX6	B. Mills Branch	+4.2	
	B3	MX7	Pack & Woods Spur	+2.1	
	B3	MX8	McDonalds Spur	+1.7	
	B3	MX9	Hamilton Branch	+2.3	
	B3	MX10	Lindseys Spur	+1.7	
	B3	MX11	Ward Branch	+2.0	
	B3	MX12	Boney Branch	+1.2	
	B3	MX13	Turner Branch	+1.1	188.8
1888	X	A2	Bush Lk. Spur	−4.7	
	B3	SX7	Comstocks Branch	+2.3	
/11/18	B3	B2	Thompson Spur	+2.4	
	B3	M	Mud Lk. Branch	+1.4	
	X	MX3	Millen Branch	−2.7	
	B3	MX13	Turner Branch	+4.2	
	B3	MX14	Potters Branch	+1.7	
	B3	MX15	Pack & Woods Mill Branch	+2.0	195.4
1889	B3	SX2	Whitney Branch	+4.1	
	X	SX3	Emery Branch	−1.0	
	X	SX6	Camp 2 Branch	−5.0	
	B3	SX7	Comstocks Branch	+5.0	
	B3	SX8	Sanborns Branch	+2.0	
	B3	SX9	Grahams Branch	+2.1	
	B3	MX2	Louds Branch	+2.4	
	X	MX7	Pack & Woods Spur	−2.1	
	X	MX10	Lindseys Spur	−1.7	
	X	MX13	Turner Branch	−5.3	195.9
1891/1/17	X	B2	Thompson Spur	−3.8	192.1
1893/1/1	B3	B	Maltbys–Rose Cty.	+9.6	
/11/18	B5	N	Alpena–LaRocque	+28.4	230.1
1894/9/23	B5	V	LaRocque–Jackson Lk.	+25.7	255.8
1895	X	SX2	Whitney Branch	−6.4	
	X	SX5	Arns Branch	−1.2	
	X	SX7	Comstocks Branch	−7.3	
	X	SX8	Sanborns Branch	−2.0	
	X	SX9	Grahams Branch	−2.1	
ca.	B4	S	In Alpena	+0.3	237.1
1896	X	M	Louds Jct.–Pritchards	−6.4	
	X	MX2	Louds Branch	−9.4	

	X	MX3	Millen Branch	−1.3	
	X	MX4	Gustin Branch	−2.5	
	X	MX5	Guilfords Branch	−1.8	
	X	MX6	B. Mills Branch	−4.2	
	X	MX8	McDonalds Spur	−1.7	
	X	MX9	Hamilton Branch	−2.3	
	X	MX11	Ward Branch	−2.0	
	X	MX12	Boney Branch	−1.2	
	X	MX14	Potters Mill Branch	−1.7	
	X	MX15	Pack & Woods Mill Branch	−2.0	
9/20	B4	S	Foss–National Cty.	+46.7	
9/20	X	A	Alger–Prescott	−11.2	236.1
1897/8/18	B4	T	Tawas Beach Branch	+1.4	
	B4	E	Alabaster Jct.–Alabaster	+4.0	
	B4	EP	Port Gypsum Spur	+0.7	
	X	M	Hawes–Pritchards	−5.9	236.3
1898/9/11	B4	N	LaRocque–Onaway	+17.8	254.1
1900/5/13	B4	N	Onaway–Tower	+3.9	
ca.	B4	L	Tower–LeGrand	+9.1	
ca.	B4	Q	Alpena Quarry Br.	+8.9	
ca.	B4	W	Dog Lk. Br.	+11.7	
ca.	B4	W2	Cleve. Br.	+5.2	
ca.	B4	W2A	Wolverine Br. Spur	+2.9	
ca.	B4	W3	Gilchrist Spur	+6.7	
ca.	B4	W3A	Lau Spur	+0.9	
ca.	B4	W4	Dog Lk. Spur	+2.2	
ca.	B4	W5	Kick Back	+4.2	309.8
1901/12/15	B4	S	Lincoln Jct.–Black Riv.	+23.4	
12/15	X	O	Black Riv.–Lincoln	−13.7	319.5
1903/8/6	X	V	Hurst–Jackson Lk.	−20.6	298.9
1904/5/22	B4	N	Tower–Inverness	+18.8	
7/3	B4	G	Omer–Au Gres	+8.3	
7/3	B4	N	Inverness–Cheboygan	+3.4	329.4
1905 ca.	B4	K	Black Riv. Quarry Br.	+5.2	334.6
1907/6/23	B4	N	Cheboygan–Cheboygan Dock	+1.2	335.8
1908	B4	H	Hillman Jct.–MP 8.7	+8.0	343.8
1909/12/20	B4	H	MP 8.7–Hillman	+15.9	359.7
1911/6/18	B4	R	Rogers Cty. Jct.–Calcite	+10.8	
	B4	R	Calcite–Rogers Cty.	+2.8	373.3

On 1 June 1912 this company leased and on 1 June 1914 purchased AuSable & Northwestern. The lines acquired were:

LINE DESIG.	END POINTS	MP	MAIN	SOURCE	NOTE
ASNW-A	AuSable–Comins	0–51.1	51.1		
ASNW-B	Hardy–Byers	0–6.5	6.5		
ASNW-5	Comins–Bonard	0–6	6.0		
		TOTAL	63.6		

DATE	ACT	D&M–	END POINTS	CHANGE	MAIN	NOTE
1912/12/11	B4	[ASNW-B]	Byers–Beevers	+4.3		
	B4	[ASNW-A2]	Five Ch. Br.	+4.6		
	X	[ASNW-5]	Comins–Bonard	−6.0		
ca.	Y	YA	In Alpena	(0.8)		
ca.	Y	N	In Alpena	(0.5)	438.5	
1914	B4	[ASNW-A2]	Extend Five Ch.. Br.	+2.6	441.1	

DATE	ACT	D&M–	END POINTS	CHANGE	MAIN	DESOPR	NOTE
1915/6/30	B4	SA	Au Sable Spur	+1.3			
	X	[ASNW-A]	AuSable–MP 2.9	–2.9			
ca.	X	B2	part Thompsons Spur	–2.7			
10/12	X	W	Dog Lk. Br.	–11.7			
ca.	X	W2	Cleve. Br.	–5.2			
ca.	X	W2A	Wolverine Br. Spur	–2.9			
ca.	X	W3	Gilchrist Spur	–6.7			
ca.	X	W3A	Lau Spur	–0.9			
ca.	X	W4	Dog Lk. Spur	–2.2			
ca.	X	W5	Kick Back	–4.2	403.0		
1917/9/24	X	K	Black Riv. Quarry Br.	–5.2			
ca.	X	[ASNW-B]	Curran–Beevers	–6.4	391.4		
1923 ca.	X	V	LaRocque–Hurst	–5.1	386.3		
1924	B4	Q2	Rockport Quarry Br.	+11.6			
	X	L	Tower–LeGrand	–9.1	388.8		2
1925 ca.	X	T	Tawas Beach Branch	–1.4	387.4		
1927	X	SA	Au Sable Spur	–1.3			
	X	[ASNW-A]	AuSable–Comins	–48.2			
	X	[ASNW-A2]	Five Channels Br.	–7.2			
	X	[ASNW-B]	Hardy–Curran	–4.4	326.3		
1928	X	O	Lincoln Jct.–Lincoln	–15.4	310.9		
1929	X	H	Hillman–Emerson	–12.1			
	X	Q2	Rockport Quarry Br.	–11.6	287.2		
1930	X	B	Emery Jct.–Rose Cty.	–31.5			
	X	B2	Thompson Spur	–0.8			
ca.	X	Q	Alpena Quarry Br.	–6.7			
ca.	Y	Q	Alpena Quarry Br.	–2.2	246.0.2		
1943	X	A	National Cty.–Prescott	–11.8	234.2		
1960 ca.	X	N	In Cheboygan	–0.6	233.6		
1965	X	G	Omer–AuGres	–8.3	225.3		
1967	X	H	Emerson–Paxton	–2.4	222.9		
DATE	**ACT**	**D&M–**	**END POINTS**	**CHANGE**	**MAIN**	**DESOPR**	**NOTE**
1976/4/1	P2	[MC-M1]	Kawkawlin–Linwood	+5.8			
4/1	P2	[MC-M3]	Salling–Mack. Cty.	+66.8			
4/1	C	[MC-M3]	Linwood–Salling	+105.0			
4/1	C	[MC-MR]	Grayling–Rasmus				3
4/1	C	[MC-Y1P]	In Pinconning	(+0.6)			
	B4	Z1	At Linwood	+0.6	296.1	105.0	
1987	X	Z1	At Linwood	–0.6			
	B4	Z2	At Pinconning	+0.5			
	X	S	MP 4.9–MP 17.8	–12.9			
	Y	S	Foss–MP 4.9 (as D&M-Y1S)	(3.0)	280.1	105.0	
1989/9	X	[MC-M3]	Cheboygan–Mack. Cty.	–14.6			
9	X	N	Hawks–Cheboygan	–40.5			
9	Y	N	In Cheboygan (as D&M-Y2N)	(5.1)	219.9	105.0	

In February 1992 this company was conveyed to Lake States Rail Corporation and in 1997 to Lake State Railway Co.

1993 ca.	X	[MC-M3]	Gaylord–Cheboygan	–47.5			4
	X	[D&M-Y2N]	In Cheboygan	(–5.1)	152.4	105.0	
1998	X	[D&M-H]	Hillman Jct.–Paxton	–9.4	143.0	105.0	5

Act Column Key

B1	Built by Lake Huron & Southwestern
B2	Built by Tawas & Bay County
B3	Built by Detroit, Bay City & Alpena
B4	Built by Detroit & Mackinac
B5	Built by Alpena & Northern
C	Operated as Designated Operator contract
L	Leased from AuSable & Northwestern, later purchased
P1	Purchased from Alger, Smith & Co.
P2	Purchased from Penn Central
X	Abandoned
Y	Converted to yard/industrial track

Sources

1. ICC, Finance Dockets.
2. MDOT office records.
3. Michigan Railroad Commission, *Aids, Gifts, Grants.*
4. Thornton, *High Iron.*

Notes

1. The date of construction of this line could not be determined.
2. ICC Finance Docket 3547 (1 December 1924) ordered the D&M to leave the section from Tower to MP 7.6 in place for rental by Lobdell-Emery Lumber Company. The final abandonment date has not been found.
3. There is no record of a transfer of this property by the Penn Central trustees to the State of Michigan or subsequently to the Detroit & Mackinac. It is assumed that the line was abandoned between 1976 and 1980 and not transferred from Penn Central.
4. Last train was run on this line 29 September 1990.
5. Service ended on this line about 1995.

Detroit & Toledo Shore Line

MAIN LINE (DTSL)

	MILEAGE	COUNTY	CROSSINGS, JUNCTIONS, ETC.
New York Ave.	0.0	Lucas OH	
Boulevard	0.60	"	X/TT
Lang	2.01	"	
(Line OH/MI)	3.2		
Mileage 3.4	3.5	Monroe	
Whiting	6.6	"	
Vienna (new)	7.72	"	
Vienna (old)	8.03	"	
Cousino	10.85	"	
La Salle	12.71	"	
Mortar Creek	13.9	"	
Greenings	16.19	"	
Plum Creek	16.8	"	X/MC spur
Monroe	17.40	"	X/LS-M 0+0.2
(Crossing)	17.8	"	X/MOCL-1 0.92
Warner (new)	18.6	"	
Ford Crossing	18.7	"	X/MC spur
Shore Line Quarry	19	"	
Warner (old)	19.43	"	
Stoney Creek	22.07	"	

Southport	23.34	"	
Newport	25.13	"	
Chapman	28.47	"	
S. Rockwood	29.97	"	
Rockwood (old)	30.69	Wayne	
Rockwood (new)	31.2	"	
Denby	34.1	"	X/MC spur
Edison	34.71	"	X/MC spur
Slocum Jct.	35.77	"	X/MC-TG 0.1
Trenton	36.82	"	
FN	37.31	"	X/DTI-M 11.0, X/LS-D 20.8, X/MC-T 15.5
Sibley	38.86	"	f. Trenton Jct.
Wyandotte	41.08	"	
Ecorse	43.44	"	
(Crossing)	43.5	"	X/MC spur
Dearoad	46.05	"	
Victoria Ave.	46.82	"	X/MC-DZ 0.6
Riv. Rouge	46.98	"	J/WAB-A 5.2
————via WAB-A and WAB-W			
(Delray)	47.63		
(W. Det.)	50.24		J/GTW-H 0.0

CONSTRUCTION/ABANDONMENT

DATE	ACT	END POINTS	MP	CHANGE	MI MAIN	SOURCE	NOTE
1903/9/8	B	New York Ave.–Riv. Rouge	0.0–47.0	+47.0	43.8	1	

OWNERSHIP

1903	Detroit & Toledo Shore Line
1981/6/26	Grand Trunk Western, buy D&TSL

Act Column Key

B   Built by Detroit & Toledo Shore Line

Sources

1. Michigan Railroad Commission, *Aids, Gifts, Grants.*

Detroit, Caro & Sandusky ————————————

MAIN LINE (DCS)

	MILEAGE	COUNTY	CROSSINGS, JUNCTIONS, ETC.
Bay Cty.	0	Bay	C/MC-B 108.9
Center Ave.	1.6	"	
(Crossing)	1.9	"	X/PM-B 13.2
(Crossing)	2.5	"	X/MC-YBL 2.2
Raby	3.8	"	
Farleigh	6.9	"	f. Cranage
Quanicassee	11.4	Tuscola	
Bradleyville	13.4	"	f. Bradley Farm, th. Bradley
Sharpville	15.4	"	
Downing	16.5	"	
Akron Coal Mine	18	"	
Akron	19.3	"	X/PM-S 24.4

Bloomfield	20.7	"	
Mitchell's	21.7	"	
Montei	22.8	"	
Gravel Pit	24	"	
Pleasant Hill	25	"	
Caro	28.2	"	
(Crossing)	28.8	"	X/MC-BC 13.24
Seeley	33	"	
Dayton	34.4	"	
Wellsford	37	"	f. Wells
Wilmot	39.3	"	X/GTW-P 64.9
Hemans	44.5	Sanilac	f. Brocton
Decker	46.5	"	
Douglas Siding	48.6	"	
Snover	50.6	"	
Elmer	52.6	"	
Hazelwood	56	"	
Herrick	57.6	"	J/PM-NS 7.4
Sandusky	58.4	"	
Walkers	60.9	"	
Watertown	63.6	"	
Cooks	65.1	"	
Stillson	66.0	"	
Peck	69.4	"	
Kerrwood	73.5	"	
Roseburg	76.1	"	
Erb	79	"	
Fargo	83.6	St.Clair	
Baird	86	"	
Ruby	87.6	"	
Wadham	94.6	"	
Westover	97.3	"	J/PM-Q 85.6
Tappan	97.9	"	J/GTW-C 332.1

CONSTRUCTION/ABANDONMENT

DATE	ACT	END POINTS	MP	CHANGE	MAIN	SOURCE	NOTE
1910/10/10	B	Bay Cty.–MP 29	0–29.0	+29.0	29.0	3	
1912/8/15	B	MP 29–Wilmot	29.0–39.3	+10.3	39.3	3	
1913/8/10	B	Wilmot–Snover	39.3–50.6	+11.3	50.6	3	
1914/6/10	B	Snover–Sandusky	50.6–59.4	+8.8	59.4	3	
1915/7/1	B	Sandusky–Peck	59.4–69.4	+10.0	69.4	3	
1916/10/27	B	Peck–Westover	69.4–97.9	+28.5	97.9	3	
1925 ca.	X	Bay Cty.–Caro	0–27.6	−27.6		2	
1925 ca.	X	Roseburg–Westover	76.1–97.9	−21.8	48.5	2	
1937	X	Roseburg–Peck	76.1–69.7	−6.4	42.1	2	
1948	X	Peck–Sandusky	69.7–58.7	−11.0	31.1	2	
1953	X	Caro–Sandusky	27.6–58.7	−31.1	0	1	

OWNERSHIP

1910	Detroit, Bay City & Western
1925/5/1	Detroit, Caro & Sandusky, bought Detroit, Bay City & Western

ACQUISITION/DISPOSITION RECORD
See Main Line record above

Act Column Key
    B   Built by Detroit, Bay City & Western
    X   Abandoned

Sources
    1. ICC, *Annual Report,* 1953.
    2. ICC, *Finance Dockets.*
    3. Michigan Railroad Commission, *Aids, Gifts, Grants.*

Detroit Connecting

For arrangement of stations, construction record, and prior ownerships, see Grand Trunk Western line GTW-D.

ACQUISITION/DISPOSITION RECORD

DATE	ACT	END POINTS	MP	CHANGE	MAIN	SOURCE	NOTE
1999/1	P	[GTW-D] Gratiot Ave.–Milw. Jct.	0.6–4.1	(+2.5)			

OWNERSHIP
    1999   Detroit Connecting

Act Column Key
    P   Purchased from Grand Trunk Western.

Notes
    GENERAL   This company is a terminal switching road and not an intercity carrier. Its mileage is not included the Michigan mileage table in chapter 2.

Detroit Terminal

MAIN LINE (DT-A)

	MILEAGE	COUNTY	CROSSINGS, JUNCTIONS, ETC.
Fordson	0.0	Wayne	J/MC-E 5.7
Michigan Ave.	0.6	"	X/PM-D 8.1, B/DUR-J 0.78, B/DSR-M 6.16
(Kingsley Ave.)	1.6	"	C/PRR-O 1.0
(Warren Ave.)	2.4	"	X/DSR-X 9.90
Warren Yards	2.5	"	
(Crossing)	3.6	"	X/DUR-L 2.23
W. Chi. Boulevard	4.1	"	X/PM-WD 3.2
(Grand Riv. Ave.)	4.4	"	X/DSR-R 5.93
(Oakman Boulevard)	4.7	"	X/DSR-OM 3.81
(Livernois Ave.)	6.1	"	J/PRR-UB 5.8, X/DSR-Q 8.65
(12th St.)	7.3	"	X/DSR-T 6.43
(Hamilton Ave.)	7.9	"	X/DSR-H 6.88
(Woodward Ave.)	8.5	"	B/DSR-W 6.65
Ford Jct.	9.3	"	X/GTW-D 7.1
(W end Davison Yard)	10.6	"	
(Mound Road)	11.6	"	X/DSR-A 1.21
N. Yard	12.2	"	X/MC-B 9.5
Forest Lawn	12.7	"	X/GTW-H 7.2

(Lynch Road)	13.0	"	X/DSR-ME 0.55
(VanDyke Ave.)	13.7	"	X/DSR-P 6.11, (X/DUR-C 1.40)
(Gratiot Ave.)	14.9	"	X/DUR-R 0.63, (X/DUR-R 0.62)
(Warren Ave.)	16.2	"	X/DSR-X 3.28
(Mack Ave.)	16.6	"	X/DSR-K 3.63
(Charlevoix Ave.)	17.3	"	X/DSR-C 1.33
(Jefferson Ave.)	17.8	"	X/DSR-J 6.00
(End)	18.0	"	

CONSTRUCTION/ABANDONMENT

DATE	ACT	END POINTS	MP	CHANGE	MAIN	SOURCE	NOTE
1912	B1	?	?	+13.7	13.7	2	1,2
1913	B1	?	?	+0.4	14.1	2	2
1914	B1	?	?	+3.8	17.9	2	2
1915	B1	?	?	+0.1	18.0	2	2
1962	X	?	?	−1.2	16.8	2	
1984/5/31	S1	Line	?	−16.8	0	1	

ACQUISITION/DISPOSITION RECORD

See above record

Act Column Key

B1   Built by DT
S1   Sold to Conrail (now CNR[DT])
X   Abandoned/adjustment

Sources

1. MDOT office records.
2. Michigan Railroad Commission, *Aids, Gifts, Grants.*

Notes

1. From 1912 incorporation until 1984 the company was owned 50% by Grand Trunk Western, 25% by Michigan Central, and 25% by New York Central; the latter two interests became 50% by Penn Central in 1968.
2. The specific location of the work has not been identified.

Detroit, Toledo & Ironton _____

MAIN LINE (DTI-M)

	MILEAGE	COUNTY	CROSSINGS, JUNCTIONS, ETC.
Det. (W. End Ave.)	0.0	Wayne	
(Dearborn Road)	0.4	"	X/DSR-DR 0.13
Delray	0.5	"	
(Crossing)	0.6	"	X/MC-YDE 0.8
Jefferson Ave.	0.7	"	X/DSR-WJ 2.25
(Jct.)	1.4	"	J/DELC
Short Cut	1.6	"	
(Crossing)	1.9	"	X/MC-YDR 1.1
Riv. Rouge	2.8	"	X/DUR-WR 0.81
S. Yard	3.2	"	
(Crossing)	3.7	"	X/DUR-W 2.65
Ecorse	3.8	"	
Mill	4.8	"	

Wyandotte	7.4	"	
Ford	8.5	"	
Firestone Yard	9.1	"	
Sibley	10.3	"	
FN	11.1	"	X/DTSL 37.3, X/LS-D 20.8, X/MC-T 15.5
Trenton Valley	11.4	"	
Trenton	12.1	"	
(Jct.)	12.9	"	J/CCS 17.6, aka Chandler on CCS
(Crossing)	13.0	"	X/DUR-T 13.2
D & I Jct.	15.2	"	J/DTI-D 0
Flat Rock Yard	17.2	"	
Flat Rock	18.2	"	
Huron	19.2	"	
Briar Hill	22.0	Monroe	
Karl	22.8	"	
Carleton	23.5	"	X/PM-T 105.2
Field	29.1	"	
Maybee Siding	29.1	"	
Scofield	29.5	"	
Doty	31.5	"	
Maybee	31.6	"	
Raisinville	34.6	"	J/DTI-Z 0, aka Durban
Mex	38.1	"	
Diann	39.8	"	X/AA-A 20.5
(Crossing)	42.5	"	X/LS-M 15.1
Petersburg	43.4	"	
Petersburg Jct.	44.4	"	J/DTI-T 0
(Crossing)	44.7	"	X/DTI-T2 6.9
Riga	51.8	Lenawee	X/LS-A 315.5, X/T&W-A 22.8
(MI/OH state line)	60.4		
Metamora OH	60.7	Fulton OH	f. Champion, X/T&W-B 24.3
Fulton	67.9	"	
Delta	74.3	"	X/NYC, X/WAB
Liberty Center	82.6	Henry OH	
Maumee	84.5	"	
Malinta	90.3	"	X/NKP
Stickney	92.1	"	
Hamler (old)	96.8	"	
Hamler (new) OH	97.6	"	X/B&O
Gallup		"	
Prentiss	102.5	Putnam OH	
Leipsic	106.0	"	X/NKP
XN	107.3	"	X/B&O
Kleman	111.0	"	
Ottawa	112.1	"	X/PRR
S. Ottawa	114.9	"	
Putnam	115.4	"	
Columbus Grove	119.7	"	
CG	120.7	"	X/ACY
Cairo	125.7	Allen OH	
DT&I Jct.	128.3	"	
Sugar Creek	129.3	"	
Ford Park	130.5	"	
Morris	131.0	"	X/NKP
Sugar Street	132.0	"	X/PRR

Lima	132.7	"	
SJ	133.6	"	X/EL
Midway	133.9	"	
Rousculp		"	
Uniopolis	142.5	Auglaize OH	
St. Johns	145.0	"	
Slater	147.3	"	X/NYC, f. Columbus Jct., J/DTI-OC
Geyer		"	
Jackson Center	153.5	Shelby OH	
Maplewood	158.0	"	
Quincy	164.4	Logan OH	X/CCC
Rosewood	169.9	Champaign OH	
St. Paris	176.7	"	X/PRR
Darnell		"	
Thackery	182.4	"	
Bryar	186.5	Clark OH	
Tremont Cty.	188.2	"	
Eagle Cty.	190.8	"	
Maitland	193.2	"	X/EL
Bechtel Ave.	194.0	"	
Abattoir	195.1	"	
Springfield	195.5	"	
Lagonda	197.7	"	
Jct.	200.5	"	X/CCC, X/PRR
Thorps	204.3	"	
Royal	205.4	"	
S. Charleston	210.1	"	X/PRR
S. Solon	216.0	Madison OH	
Blessings		Fayette OH	
Jeff.	222.4	"	X/DTI-OK 7
Parrott		"	
Heglers	227.7	"	
Fayne	229.7	"	X/B&O
Washington C. H.	234.3	"	X/B&O, X/PRR
Gleason		"	
Boyds		"	
Good Hope	241.1	"	
Ghormley		"	
Blue Rock	245.4	"	
Island Grove Mill	247.1	Highland OH	
Greenfield	247.8	Ross OH	
Thrifton	248.8	"	X/B&O
New Salem	250.2	"	
Fruitdale	252.3	"	
Humboldt	255	"	
Bainbridge	259.1	"	
Dills	259.5	"	
Storms	264.2	"	
Spargursville	265.4*	"	
*original line between Spargursville and Harris		"	
Summit	271.1*	"	
Summit 0.2 miles longer than present line			
Denver		"	
Peck	278.1	Pike OH	
Waverly	282.0	"	

Glen Jean	282.7	"	X/N&W
Greggs	286.0	"	X/C&O
Givens	287.8	"	
Robbins		"	P.O. Dever
Beaver	293.9	"	
Glade		Jackson OH	
Cove	298.7	"	
Simpsons		"	
Sharon	304.0	"	
Jackson	306.3	"	X/C&O, J/DTI-OW 0
B&O Jct.	308.6	"	J/B&O—via B&O
Bloom Jct.	330.0	Scioto OH	J/B&O
Andre	334.6	"	f. Hayward (P.O. Lyra)
Crawford		"	
Bondclay	337.5	"	
Superior	340.4	Lawrence OH	
Wagner		"	
Goldcamp	344.1	"	
Lawco	347.3	"	
Lisman (Jct.)	348.6	"	P.O. Culbertson, J/DTI-OD 0
Cannons Creek	349.1	"	
Pedro	349.7	"	
Royersville	351.4	"	
Vesuvius	352.4	"	
LaGrange	354.4	"	
Ironton OH	357.8	"	
(End)	359.0	"	J/N&W

CONSTRUCTION/ABANDONMENT

DATE	ACT	END POINTS	MP	CHANGE	MI MAIN	SOURCE	NOTE
1877/7/18	B1	Springfield–Dills	195.5–259.5	+64.0		1	
1893/12/28	B2	Springfield–Lima	195.5–132.7	+62.8			
1894/Spr.	B2	Dills–Jackson	259.5–306.3	+46.8		3	
1895 ca.	B3	Lima–Malinta	132.7–90.3	+42.4			
1897/11/15	P1	MP 12.9–Raisinville	12.9–34.6	+21.7	21.7	3	5
1898/8/18	B4	Det.–MP 12.9	0.0–12.9	+12.9	34.6	3	6
1902/9/25	P2	Ironton–Lisman	359.0–348.6	+10.4	34.6		10
1903/6/13	B5	Bloom Jct.–Lisman	330.0–348.6	+18.6			11
1903 ca.	B5	Jackson–B&O Jct.	306.3–308.6	+2.3	34.6		11
1929/11/6	B8	Durban–Malinta	34.6–90.3	+55.7	60.4		12
1966/2/14	X	S. Ottawa–DT&I Jct.	114.9–128.3	−13.4			16
1966/2/14	X	XN–Kleman	107.3–111.0	−3.7	60.4		16
1971	X	Det.–MP 1.7	0–1.7	−1.7	58.7	2	

OWNERSHIP

1877	Springfield, Jackson & Pomeroy (B1)
1879/10/11	Springfield Southern, reorganization of Springfield, Jackson & Pomeroy
1881/5/23	Ohio Southern (B2), possibly renaming of Springfield Southern
1895/3/25	Lima Northern (B3), reorganization of Ohio Southern
1896/7/6	Detroit & Lima Northern (B4), bought Lima Northern
1901/5/25	Detroit Southern (B5), reorganization of Detroit & Lima Northern
1905/5/2	Detroit, Toledo & Ironton Railway, reorganization of Detroit Southern
1914/2/20	Detroit, Toledo & Ironton Railroad (B8), reorganization of DT&I Railway
1983/6/14	Grand Trunk Western, purchase of Detroit, Toledo & Ironton Railroad

DEARBORN BRANCH (DTI-D)

	MILEAGE	COUNTY	CROSSINGS, JUNCTIONS, ETC.
D & I Jct.	0.0	Wayne	J/DTI-M 14.9
Fordhaven	2.3	"	
Woodhaven	2.5	"	
Penn	4.4	"	f. Curtis Siding
Penford	6.0	"	X/PRR-A 129.4
Allen Park	9.1	"	
Park	9.2	"	
Oakwood Jct.	10.3	"	X/WAB-A 8.7
Melvindale	12.4	"	X/MC-DD 3.2
Schaefer	13.5	"	X/MC-DZ 3.1
(Schaefer Highway)	13.6	"	X/DSR-M 7.88
Rouge Yard	13.6	"	
Fordson Yard	15.3	"	J/PM-D 6.9

CONSTRUCTION/ABANDONMENT

DATE	ACT	END POINTS	MP	CHANGE	MAIN	SOURCE	NOTE
1923/10/1	B7	D&I Jct.–Rouge Yard	0–13.6	+13.6	13.6	4	
1925 ca.	B7	Rouge Yard–Fordson Yard	13.6–15.3	+1.7	15.3		

OWNERSHIP

1923	Detroit & Ironton (B7)
1931/12/29	Detroit, Toledo & Ironton Railroad, purchase of Detroit & Ironton

OLD MAIN LINE (DTI-Z)

	MILEAGE	COUNTY	CROSSINGS, JUNCTIONS, ETC.
Raisinville	0.0	Monroe	J/DTI-M 34.6
Dundee	4.9	"	J/DTI-T2 0, J/DTM 0

CONSTRUCTION/ABANDONMENT

DATE	ACT	END POINTS	MP	CHANGE	MAIN	SOURCE	NOTE
1898 ca.	B4	Raisinville–Dundee	0–4.9	+4.9	4.9		7
1930/5	X	Raisinville–Dundee	0–4.9	−4.9	0	1	

OWNERSHIP

1898	Detroit & Lima Northern (B4)
1901/5/25	Detroit Southern (B5), reorganization of Detroit & Lima Northern
1905/5/2	Detroit, Toledo & Ironton Railway, reorganization of Detroit Southern
1914/2/20	Detroit, Toledo & Ironton Railroad (B8), reorganization of DT&I Railway

OLD TOLEDO CONNECTION (DTI-T2)

	MILEAGE	COUNTY	CROSSINGS, JUNCTIONS, ETC.
Dundee	0.0	Monroe	J/DTI-Z 4.9, J/DTM 0
Petersburg	5.5	"	X/LS-M 16.6
(Crossing)	6.9	"	X/DTI-M 44.7
(Jct.)	7.1	"	J/DTI-T 0.2

CONSTRUCTION/ABANDONMENT

DATE	ACT	END POINTS	MP	CHANGE	MAIN	SOURCE	NOTE
1913/3/4	B6	Petersburg–MP 7.1	5.5–7.1	+1.8	1.8	3	
1915/12/15	B6	Dundee–Petersburg	0–5.5	+5.5	7.1	3	
1930/5	X	Dundee–MP 7.1	0–7.1	−7.1	0		

OWNERSHIP

1913	Toledo, Ann Arbor & Jackson (B6)
1915/4/28	Toledo–Detroit, renaming of Toledo, Ann Arbor & Jackson

TOLEDO BRANCH (DTI-T)

	MILEAGE	COUNTY	CROSSINGS, JUNCTIONS, ETC.
Petersburg Jct.	0.0	Monroe	J/DTI-M 44.4
(Jct.)	0.2	"	J/DTI-T2 7.1
St. Anthony(s)	6.3	"	
Lambertville	9.5	"	
(MI/OH state line)	12.8		
Toledo	14.6	Lucas OH	
(Sylvania Ave.)	15.6	"	

CONSTRUCTION/ABANDONMENT

DATE	ACT	END POINTS	MP	CHANGE	MI MAIN	SOURCE	NOTE
1913/3/4	B6	MP 15.6–MP 0.2	15.6–0.2	+15.4	12.6	3	
1930/5	B8	Petersburg Jct.–MP 0.2	0–0.2	+0.2	12.8		
1950 ca.	X	In Toledo	14.6–15.6	–1.0			
1965/12/23	X	Petersburg Jct.–MP 11.5	0–11.5	–11.5	1.3	2	15
1967	X	MP 11.5–MP 14.0	11.5–14.0	–2.5	0	2	

OWNERSHIP

1913	Toledo, Ann Arbor & Jackson (B6)
1915/4/28	Toledo–Detroit, renaming of Toledo, Ann Arbor & Jackson
1916/5/1	Toledo–Detroit leased to Detroit, Toledo & Ironton
1931/12/29	Detroit, Toledo & Ironton Railroad (B8), purchase of Toledo–Detroit
1983/6/14	Grand Trunk Western, purchase of Detroit, Toledo & Ironton Railroad

TECUMSEH BRANCH (DTI-A)

	MILEAGE	COUNTY	CROSSINGS, JUNCTIONS, ETC.
Malinta OH	0.0	Henry OH	J/DTI-M 90.3
Napoleon	7.1	"	X/WAB
Gerald	11.7	"	
Naomi	13.4	Fulton OH	
Wauseon	17.9	"	X/NYC
Ottokee	21.5	"	
Oak Shade	26.1	"	
Denson OH	28.9	"	X/T&W-B 35.5
(OH/MI state line)	30.1		
Bimo	32.0	Lenawee	X/LS-F 22.0
Packard	35.1	"	
Lenawee		"	
Leaf	35.7	"	J/WAB-A 68.4, f. Lima Jct.
Sand Creek	38.8	"	
Madison	42.2	"	
Page	44.3	"	J/WAB-A 59.8, aka S. Adrian
(Crossing)	45.9	"	X/LS-A 329.2
Adrian	46.6	"	
(Crossing)	47.1	"	X/ADCL-1 1.05
Industrial Home	48.0	"	
Woodward	48	"	
Birdsall	50.0	"	
Prairie Siding	53	"	

Burmo	53.3	"
Tecumseh Pit	54.1	"
Tecumseh	55.4	"

J/DTM 16.1

CONSTRUCTION/ABANDONMENT

DATE	ACT	END POINTS	MP	MI CHANGE	MI MAIN	SOURCE	NOTE
1895 ca.	B3	Malinta OH–Leaf	0–35.7	+5.6	5.6		4
1897/5/25	B4	Page–Tecumseh	44.3–55.4	+11.1	16.7	3	
1901/6/30	B5	Leaf–Page	35.7–44.3	+8.6	25.3	3	9
1958/3/3	X	Leaf–Page	35.7–44.3	–8.6	16.7		14
1979/2/6	S2	Page–Tecumseh (to N&W-[DTI-A])	44.3–55.4	[11.1]			17
1979/2/8	S3	Bimo-Leaf (to LCRC-[DTI-A])	32.0–35.7	[3.7]			18
1979/4/1	X	Napoleon OH–Bimo	8.2–32.0	–1.9	0		
1985 ca.	S3	Page–MP 47.0	44.3–47.0	[2.7]			20
1985 ca.	X	MP 47.0–Tecumseh	47.0–55.4	[–8.4]			
1990/9/30	X	Bimo–Leaf	32.0–35.7	[–3.7]			
1990 ca.	X	Page–MP 46.0	44.3–46.0	[–1.7]			
1990 ca.	S4	MP 46.0–MP 47.0	46.0–47.0	[1.0]			20

OWNERSHIP

1895	Lima Northern (B3)
1896/7/6	Detroit & Lima Northern (B4), bought Lima Northern
1901/5/25	Detroit Southern (B5), reorganization of Detroit & Lima Northern
1905/5/2	Detroit, Toledo & Ironton Railway, reorganization of Detroit Southern
1914/2/20	Detroit, Toledo & Ironton Railroad (B8), reorganization of DT&I Railway
1979/2/6	Norfolk & Western, bought part of line
1979/2/8	Lenawee County Railroad, bought part of line
1980/7/23	Norfolk Southern, bought Norfolk & Western
1990	Adrian & Blissfield, bought part of line

DEAN BRANCH (DTI-OD)

	MILEAGE	COUNTY	CROSSINGS, JUNCTIONS, ETC.
Lisman OH	0	Lawrence OH	J/DTI-M 348.6
Lawrence	1	"	
Bartles	2.2	"	
Dean OH	4	"	

DATE	ACT	END POINTS	MP	CHANGE	MI MAIN	SOURCE	NOTE
??	?	Line	0–4	+4.0	0		19
1919	X	Bartles–Dean	2.2–4	–1.8	0		19
1942 ca.	X	Line	0–2.2	–2.2	0		19

ST. MARYS BRANCH (DTI-OC)

	MILEAGE	COUNTY	CROSSINGS, JUNCTIONS, ETC.
St. Mary's OH	0.0		
Slater	17.7		
Peoria OH	58.8		

DATE	ACT	END POINTS	MP	CHANGE	MI MAIN	SOURCE	NOTE
1898/8	B4	Slater–Peoria	17.7–58.8	+41.1	0		8
1898/11/1	B4	St. Mary's–Slater	0–17.7	+17.7	0		8
1900/12/1	S1	Line	0–58.8	–58.8	0		

WELLSTON BRANCH (DTI-OW)

	MILEAGE	COUNTY	CROSSINGS, JUNCTIONS, ETC.
Jackson OH	0	Jackson OH	J/DTI-M 306.3
Chapmans	3	"	
Coalton	5	"	X/B&O
Glen Roy	7	"	
Wellston	10	"	X/B&O, X/C&O
Ratchford	13	"	
Lincoln	16	"	
Cornelia OH	20	Vinton OH	

DATE	ACT	END POINTS	MP	CHANGE	MI MAIN	SOURCE	NOTE
1894/Spr.	B2	Jackson–Wellston	0–10	+10.0	0		
1894 ca.	B?	Wellston–Cornelia	10–20	+10.0	0		
1930	X	Jackson–Cornelia	0–20	−20.0	0		

KINGMAN BRANCH (DTI-OK)

	MILEAGE	COUNTY	CROSSINGS, JUNCTIONS, ETC.
Sedalia OH	0	Madison OH	
Buchwalter	4	Fayette OH	
Jeff.	7	"	X/DTI-M 222.4
Octa	12	"	X/B&O
Pearson	15	"	
Bowersville	17	Greene OH	
Port William	22	Clinton OH	
Ogles	25	"	
McKays	27	"	
Clare	"		

DATE	ACT	END POINTS	MP	CHANGE	MAIN	SOURCE	NOTE
1885 ca.	B2	Sedalia–Kingman	0–31	+31.0	0		2
1930 ca.	X	Kingman–Port William	31–22	−9.0	0		
1936 ca.	X	Port William–Jeff.	22–7	−15.0	0		
1941	X	Sedalia–Jeff.	0–7	−7.0	0		

ACQUISITION/DISPOSITION RECORD

DATE	ACT	DT&I–	END POINTS	CHANGE	MI MAIN	NOTE
1877/7/18	B1	M	Springfield–Dills	+64.0	0	1
1885	B2	OK	Sedalia–Kingman	+31.0	0	2
1893/12/28	B2	M	Springfield–Lima	+62.8	0	
1894/Spr.	B2	M	Dills–Jackson	+46.8		3
Spr.	B2	OW	Jackson–Wellston	+10.0		
?	B2	OW	Wellston–Cornelia	+10.0	0	
1895?	B3	M	Lima–Malinta	+42.4		
?	B3	A	Malinta–Leaf	+35.7	5.6	4
1897/5/25	B4	A	Page–Tecumseh	+11.1		
11/15	P1	M	MP 12.9–Raisinville	+21.7	38.4	5
1898/8/18	B4	M	Det.–MP 12.9	+12.9		6
?	B4	Z	Raisinville–Dundee	+4.9		7
8	B4	OC	Slater–Peoria	+41.1		8
11/1	B4	OC	St. Mary's–Slater	+17.7	56.2	8
1900/12/1	S1	OC	St. Mary's–Peoria	−58.8	56.2	
1901/6/30	B5	A	Leaf–Page	+8.6	64.8	9

1902	P2	M	Ironton–Lisman	+10.4	64.8	10
1903/6/13	B5	M	Bloom Jct.–Lisman	+18.6		11
?	B5	M	Jackson–B&O Jct.	+2.3	64.8	11
1913/3/4	B6	T	MP 0.2–Sylvania Ave.	+15.4		
3/4	B6	T2	Petersburg–MP 7.1	+1.6	79.0	
1915/12/15	B6	T2	Dundee–Petersburg	+5.5	84.5	
1919	X	OD	Bartles–Dean	−1.8	84.5	
1923/10/1	B7	D	D&I Jct.–Rouge Yard	+13.6	98.1	
1925?	B7	D	Rouge Yard–Fordson	+1.7	99.8	
1929/11/6	B8	M	Durban–Malinta	+55.7	125.6	12
1930/5	X	Z	Raisinville–Dundee	−4.9		13
	B8	T	Petersburg Jct.–MP 0.2	+0.2		
?	X	T2	Dundee–MP 7.1	−7.1		
?	X	OW	Jackson–Cornelia	−20.0	113.8	
1930?	X	OK	Kingman–Port William	−9.0	113.8	
?	X	T	In Toledo	−1.0	113.8	
1936?	X	OK	Port William–Jeff.	−15.0	113.8	
1941	X	OK	Sedalia–Jeff.	−7.0	113.8	
1942?	X	OD	Lisman–Bartles	−2.2	113.8	
1958/3/3	X	A	Leaf–Page	−8.6	105.2	14
1965/12/23	X	T	Petersburg Jct.–MP 11.5	−11.5	93.7	15
1966/2/14	X	M	S. Ottawa–DT&I Jct.	−13.4		16
2/14	X	M	XN–Kleman	−3.7	93.7	16
1967	X	T	MP 11.5–MP 14.0	−2.5	92.4	
1971	X	M	Det.–MP 1.7	−1.7	90.7	
1979/2/6	S2	A	Page–Tecumseh	−11.1		17
2/8	S3	A	Leaf–Bimo	−3.7		18
4/1	X	A	MP 8.2–Bimo	−23.8	74.0	

On 1983/6/14 this road was sold to Grand Trunk Western. The property conveyed was:

DTI-M MP 1.7-MP 60.4 (58.7 miles) to GTW-[DTI-M]

DTI-D MP 0-MP 15.3 (15.3 miles) to GTW-[DTI-D]

1985 ca.	S3	Page–MP 47.0	[2.7]	20
1985 ca.	X	MP 47.0–Tecumseh	[−8.4]	
1990/9/30	X	Bimo–Leaf	[−3.7]	
1990 ca.	X	Page–MP 46.0	[−1.7]	
1990 ca.	S4	MP 46.0–MP 47.0	[1.0]	20

On 15 February 1997 the Grand Trunk Western sold part of the property to Indiana & Ohio and retained part.

Act Column Key

B1	Built by Springfield, Jackson & Pomeroy
B2	Built by Ohio Southern
B3	Built by Lima Northern
B4	Built by Detroit & Lima Northern
B5	Built by Detroit Southern
B6	Built by Toledo–Detroit
B7	Built by Detroit & Ironton
B8	Built by Detroit, Toledo & Ironton
P1	Purchased from Detroit & Chicago
P2	Purchased from Iron Railway
S1	Sold to Toledo & Ohio Central
S2	Sold to Norfolk & Western
S3	Sold to Lenawee County Railroad

S4   Sold to Adrian & Blissfield
X   Abandoned
Y   Converted from main to yard track

Sources

1. ICC Finance Dockets.
2. MDOT office records.
3. Michigan Railroad Commission, *Aids, Gifts, Grants.*
4. Trostel, *Detroit, Toledo, and Ironton.*

Notes

1. Construction on this segment began at Springfield on 26 March 1877.
2. This line was constructed partially on a grade bought in March 1884 from the Columbus, Washington & Cincinnati. The Ohio Southern had operated a narrow gauge predecessor line between Jeffersonville and Roxanna which apparently was abandoned before this construction.
3. Construction on this segment began at Jackson on 7 December 1876, by the Springfield, Jackson & Pomeroy. That company and the Ohio Southern constructed a number of short branches to coal mines from this line. The earliest of these was the Eureka Mine Branch opened in June 1879. These mining branches have not been documented and are not included here.
4. This construction also included trackage rights on the Wabash into Adrian.
5. This property extended from Chandler to Dundee, 26.5 miles, and was completed on 13 November 1873, by the Chicago & Canada Southern, and passed by foreclosure sale in 1888 to the Detroit & Chicago. The purchaser abandoned the 4.8 miles west of Raisinville for lack of need and built line segment DTI-Z between Raisinville and Dundee on the north side of the River Raisin. See also Note 7.
6. This assumes the line was built to West End Avenue although Source 3 says it was built only to Delray.
7. This completion is assumed although the line may have been built in 1897 upon purchase of the Chandler–Dundee route. See also Note 5. In 1898 the D&LN arranged for trackage rights over 16.1 miles of the Detroit, Toledo & Milwaukee between Dundee and Tecumseh to connect this line to line segment DTI-A.
8. Station detail is not given because of the short length of management.
9. This construction replaced trackage rights over the Wabash.
10. A part of this line was completed between Ironton and the Vesuvius Tunnel Mine in 1849–1850 by the Iron Railroad, and extensions and branches to mines were made subsequently. The Iron Railroad owned 18.35 miles of line at the time of sale to the Detroit Southern.
11. These two segments were connected by 21.4 miles of trackage rights over the Baltimore & Ohio.
12. Construction on this segment began in 1924.
13. The trackage rights over the DT&M between Dundee and Tecumseh also were canceled, although when the DT&M line was abandoned in 1932 a short segment in Tecumseh was acquired.
14. Trackage rights over 8.6 miles of the Wabash were obtained in replacement.
15. With this abandonment the DT&I obtained trackage rights over the Ann Arbor between Diann and Toledo and also was able to retain a connection to its trackage in Toledo.
16. Trackage rights over 21.0 miles of the Baltimore & Ohio were obtained. This allowed access to the Kleman–South Ottawa segment which was retained as industrial track.
17. Operations under agreement began 5 May 1978.
18. Sale included trackage rights on N&W between Leaf and Adrian.
19. The date of construction and/or abandonment could not be determined, and this line is not included in the Acquisition/Disposition record.
20. The details of this transfer are not clear, but apparently this segment was bought by Lenawee County and subsequently part of it conveyed to Adrian & Blissfield.

Detroit, Toledo & Milwaukee

	MILEAGE	COUNTY	CROSSINGS, JUNCTIONS, ETC.
Dundee	0	Monroe	J/DTI-Z 4.9, J/AA-A 22.8
Rea	3.8	"	
Britton	9.4	Lenawee	X/WAB-A 46.7
Stevens	10.2	"	
Ridgeway	11.3	"	
Tecumseh	15.8	"	
Tecumseh Jct.	16.1	"	X/LS-J 8.5, J/DTI-A 55.4
Gravel Pit	16.9	"	
Russell Siding	17.9	"	
Tipton	21.8	"	
Pentecost	24.9	"	f. Sand Lk.
Onsted	28.3	"	
Lk. Rest	33.1	"	
Devils Lk.	33.8	"	
Addison Jct.	35.9	"	X/CC-N 18.8
Addison	36.8	"	
Knorr Lk.	38.3	Hillsdale	f. Knorr
Baker(s)	42.2	"	
Jerome	43.9	"	B/LS-Y 48.9
Moscow	46.8	"	
Hanover	51.2	Jackson	X/LS-W 14.0
Wheelerton	55.8	"	f. Pulaski
Grover	60.8	Calhoun	
Homer	65.1	"	X/LS-L 13.4, X/MC-A 24.3
Eckford	70.2	"	
Wilders	73.3	"	
(Connection)	77.1	"	J/to conn. MC-C 107.5, 0.2 miles
Marshall	77.4	"	
Ceresco	82.6	"	
Beadle Lk.	87.0	"	
Morgan Park	88.8	"	C/MC-K 3.3
(Crossing)	90.4	"	X/MC-K 1.4
(Crossing)	90.8	"	X/BCCL-5 0.3
Battle Creek	90.9	"	
(McCamley St.)	91.2	"	X/GTW-C 175.6
(Jct.)	91.6	"	J/MUR-WB 0.7
(Bridge)	97.8	Kal.	B/MC-C 128.4
Augusta	99.8	"	
Camp St. Louis	102.5	"	
Yorkville	103.4	"	
Richland	106.1	"	
Richland Jct.	108.8	"	X/CK&S-A 8.9, f. Flagg, th. Kal. Jct.
Doster	114.1	Allegan	
Neely	117.3	"	f. Pine Lk., th. Gun Marsh
Hooper	118.2	"	
Montieth	121.7	"	X/GR&I-S 202.1
Montieth Jct.	122.0	"	
Fisk	125.5	"	
Kellogg	128.1	"	
Allegan	132.9	"	X/LS-G 61.8, J/PM-A 1.0–0.8

CONSTRUCTION/ABANDONMENT

DATE	ACT	END POINTS	MP	CHANGE	MAIN	SOURCE	NOTE
1871/9	B1	Allegan–Montieth	132.9–121.7	+11.2	11.2	3	1
1883/11/29	B2	Montieth–Dundee	121.7–0	+121.7	132.9	3	2
1913/9/1	S	W. of Battle Creek–Allegan	93.9–132.9	–39.0		3	3
1913	Y	Battle Creek–west(DTM-Y1D)	90.9–93.9	(3.0)			
1913 ca.	X	Battle Creek–MP 90.4	90.9–90.4	–0.5	90.4		4
1918	Z	Marshall–Morgan Park	—		90.4	1	
1932/7/4	X	Dundee–Tecumseh	0–15.6	–15.6		1	5
1932/7/4	S	In Tecumseh	15.6–16.5	–0.9		1	5,6
1932/7/4	X	Tecumseh–Marshall	16.5–77.0	–60.5		1	
1932/7/4	Y	In Marshall (to DTM-Y2D)	77.0–77.5	(0.5)		1	
1932/7/4	X	Marshall–Morgan Park	77.5–88.8	–11.3	1.6	1	
1937/5/19	X	MP 89.9–Morgan Park	89.9–88.8	–1.1		1	
1937/5/19	Y	MP 89.9–MP 90.4(to DTM-Y3D)	89.9–90.4	(0.5)	0		
1980 ca.	X	In Marshall (DTM-Y2D)	77.0–77.5	(–0.5)			
1980 ca.	X	In Battle Creek (DTM-Y3D)	89.9–90.4	(–0.5)	0		

OWNERSHIP

1871	Mansfield, Coldwater & Lake Michigan (B1)
1877/12/13	Allegan & South Eastern, bought Mansfield, Coldwater & Lake Michigan
1883/3/13	Michigan & Ohio (B2), bought Allegan & South Eastern
1887/3/25	Cincinnati, Jackson & Mackinaw Railroad, bought Michigan & Ohio
1891/7/17	Cincinnati, Jackson & Mackinaw Railway, reorganization of CJ&M Railroad
1897/6/18	Toledo & Milwaukee, reorganization of CJ&M Railway
1897/7/22	Detroit, Toledo & Milwaukee, renaming of Toledo & Milwaukee
1899/1/1	Leased to Cincinnati Northern
1905/1/1	Leased to Michigan Central and Lake Shore & Michigan Southern jointly
1968/2/1	Leases assigned to Penn Central
1976/4/1	Conrail, purchase of leases and of Penn Central
1999/6/1	Norfolk Southern, purchase of Conrail

On 1 February 1968 this company was leased to Penn Central.
On 1 April 1976 this company was conveyed to Conrail.

DATE	ACT	CNR– END POINTS	CHANGE	MAIN	NOTE
1980 ca.	X	[DTM-Y2D] In Marshall	(–0.5)		
1980 ca.	X	[DTM-Y3D] In Battle Creek	(–0.5)	0	

On 1 June 1999 this company was conveyed to Norfolk Southern.

Act Column Key

B1	Built by Mansfield, Coldwater & Lake Michigan
B2	Built by Michigan & Ohio
S	Sold
X	Abandoned
Y	Converted to yard track
Z	Operations ended, tracks remained in place

Sources

1. ICC, Finance Dockets.
2. Michigan, Commissioner of Railroads, *Annual Report*, 1873.
3. Michigan Railroad Commission, *Aids, Gifts, Grants*.

Notes

1. This segment was completed as shown, conveyed to the Allegan & South Eastern on 28 August 1877, and operated by the Grand Rapids & Indiana for it, apparently under lease, from 1 January 1874, to 31 December 1882, and conveyed 13 March 1883, to the Toledo & Milwaukee which subsequently conveyed it to the Michigan & Ohio. Source 2 states that the line was completed 15.0 miles, apparently as far east as a point named Gun Marsh.

2. The Michigan & Ohio also obtained trackage rights over the now Ann Arbor Railroad from Dundee to Toledo, which were in effect from November 1883, to 31 December 1901.

3. This segment was sold to the Michigan & Chicago Railway, which converted it to electric operations. It was subsequently conveyed to the Michigan Railway. With the demise of that company the segment from Richland to Hooper, 13.2 miles, was conveyed to the Chicago, Kalamazoo & Saginaw (which see) on 25 July 1930, which operated it until abandonment.

4. At about this time the use of the DT&M depot in Battle Creek was discontinued and the Michigan Central depot substituted for it. It appears that Battle Creek Sturgis trains of the Michigan Central began operating over the DT&M between MP 90.4 and Morgan Park.

5. The Detroit, Toledo & Ironton, and its predecessors, held trackage rights over the segment Dundee to Tecumseh Jct. from about 1898 until 3 February 1930, and provided all service after 8 June 1925.

6. At abandonment shown this segment was conveyed to the DT&I.

Detroit Union Railroad Depot & Station _____

LINE (DURS)

	MILEAGE	COUNTY	CROSSINGS, JUNCTIONS, ETC.
18th St.	1.37	Wayne	J/FSUD 1.37
(21st St.)	1.4	"	
(Clark St.)	2.25	"	X/DSR-WJ 0.20
Solvay Ave.	3.85	"	
W. End Ave.	4.0	"	C/DTI-M 0

CONSTRUCTION/ABANDONMENT

DATE	ACT	END POINTS		MP	CHANGE	MAIN	SOURCE	NOTE
1882	B	Line		1.4–4.6	+3.2	3.2	1	
1972 ca.	Y	Line		1.4–4.6	(3.2)	0		

OWNERSHIP

1882	Detroit Union Railroad Depot & Station Co.
**1889/7/1	DURS leased to Detroit, Lansing & Northern; Flint & Pere Marquette; and Wabash jointly

ACQUISITION/DISPOSITION RECORD

See Mileage record above

Act Column Key

B   Built by Detroit Union Railroad Depot & Station
X   Abandoned
Y   Converted to yard track.

Sources

1.   Michigan Railroad Commission, *Aids, Gifts, Grants.*

East Jordan & Southern

MAIN LINE (EJ&S-A)

	MILEAGE	COUNTY	CROSSINGS, JUNCTIONS, ETC.
(End)	0	Charlevoix	
E. Jordan	0.3	"	
Mt. Bliss	4.0	Antrim	
Marble	6.4	"	X/D&C-A 37.2, f. Wards
Chestonia	7.7	"	
Pine Ridge	9.2	"	J/EJ&S-3 0
Hitchcock	11.4	"	J/EJ&S-2 0
Section 10	12.4	"	
Farmdale	13.0	"	
Staffords	14	"	
Wolcott	14.9	"	
Bellaire	18.6	"	J/PM-P 183.6

CONSTRUCTION/ABANDONMENT

DATE	ACT	END POINTS	MP	CHANGE	MAIN	SOURCE	NOTE
1901/10/1	B	E. Jordan–Bellaire	0–18.6	+18.6	18.6	2	1
1961	X	E. Jordan–Bellaire	0–18.6	–18.6	0	1	

OWNERSHIP
1901 East Jordan & Southern

BRANCH LINE (EJ&S-2)

	MILEAGE	COUNTY	CROSSINGS, JUNCTIONS, ETC.
Hitchcock	0	Antrim	J/EJ&S 11.4
Fountain	3.5	"	
Dingmans	6.4	"	

CONSTRUCTION/ABANDONMENT

DATE	ACT	END POINTS	MP	CHANGE	MAIN	SOURCE	NOTE
??		Line					2

OWNERSHIP
?? East Jordan & Southern

BRANCH LINE (EJ&S-3)

	MILEAGE	COUNTY	CROSSINGS, JUNCTIONS, ETC.
Pine Ridge	0	Antrim	J/EJ&S 9.2
(Crossing)	1.4	"	X/D&C 33.6
(Jct.)	1.9	"	J/EJ&S-3A 0
(Jct.)	2.5	"	J/EJ&S-3B, 2.6 mile spur
(Jct.)	2.6	"	J/EJ&S-3C, 0.4 mile spur
(Jct.)	3.5	"	J/EJ&S-3D, 1.4 mile spur; J/EJ&S-3E, 1.6 mile
(Jct.)	4.3	"	J/EJ&S-3F, 0.4 mile spur
(End)	6.9	"	

CONSTRUCTION/ABANDONMENT

DATE	ACT	END POINTS	MP	CHANGE	MAIN	SOURCE	NOTE
??		Line					2

OWNERSHIP

    ??   East Jordan & Southern

BRANCH LINE (EJ&S-3A)

	MILEAGE	COUNTY	CROSSINGS, JUNCTIONS, ETC.
(Jct.)	0	Antrim	J/EJ&S-3 1.9
(Jct.)	0.6	"	J/EJ&S-3A1, 0.5 mile spur
Valley Switch	. 1.1	"	J/D&C-A 32.2

CONSTRUCTION/ABANDONMENT

DATE	ACT	END POINTS	MP	CHANGE	MAIN	SOURCE	NOTE
??		Line					2

OWNERSHIP

    ??   East Jordan & Southern

ACQUSITION/DISPOSITION RECORD

DATE	ACT	EJ&S–	END POINTS	CHANGE	MI MAIN	NOTE
1901/10/1	B	A	E. Jordan–Bellaire	+18.6	18.6	1
1961	X	A	E. Jordan–Bellaire	−18.6	0	

Act Column Key

    B   Built by East Jordan & Southern

    P   Purchased from East Jordan Lumber Co.

    X   Abandoned

Sources

1. ICC, Finance Dockets.
2. Michigan Railroad Commission, *Aids, Gifts, Grants.*

Notes

1. This line was constructed by the East Jordan Lumber Co. between 1899 and 1901 and conveyed by that company on 1 October 1901 to the carrier.
2. The date of construction and/or abandonment of this line could not be determined accurately and this line is not included in the Acquisition/Disposition Record.

Empire & South Eastern

MAIN LINE (E&SE-A)

	MILEAGE	COUNTY	CROSSINGS, JUNCTIONS, ETC.
Empire Jct.	0	Benzie	J/M&NE-E 16.8
Petersville	2	"	
Lk. Jct.	4.6	Leelanau	J/E&SE-2 0
Main Top	7	"	
E. Empire	9	"	
Empire	11.2	"	

CONSTRUCTION/ABANDONMENT

DATE	ACT	END POINTS	MP	CHANGE	MAIN	SOURCE	NOTE
1900	B	Line	0–11.2	+11.	11.2	1	
1923	X	Line	0–11.2	−11.2	0		

OWNERSHIP

1900   Empire & South Eastern Railroad

BRANCH (E&SE-2)

	MILEAGE	COUNTY	CROSSINGS, JUNCTIONS, ETC.
Lk. Jct.	0	Leelanau	J/E&SE-A 4.6
Pearl Lk.	3.1	Benzie	

CONSTRUCTION/ABANDONMENT

DATE	ACT	END POINTS	MP	CHANGE	MAIN	SOURCE	NOTE
1905 ca.	B	Line	0–3.1	+3.1	3.1	1	
1916/12	X	Line	0–3.1	−3.1	0	1	

OWNERSHIP

1905   Empire & South Eastern

ACQUSITION/DISPOSITION RECORD

DATE	ACT	E&SE–	END POINTS	CHANGE	MI MAIN	NOTE
1900	B	A	Empire–Empire Jct.	+11.2	11.2	
1905 ca.	B	2	Lk. Jct.–Pearl Lk.	+3.1	14.3	
1916/12	X	2	Lk. Jct.–Pearl Lk.	−3.1	11.2	
1923	X	A	Empire–Empire Jct.	−11.2	0	

Act Column Key

B   Built by Empire & South Eastern
X   Abandoned

Sources

1.   Michigan Railroad Commission, *Aids, Gifts, Grants.*

Notes

GENERAL   Although this company was not an incorporated railroad company under Michigan law, it conducted its affairs in such a way that it appeared to be a common carrier. The railroad was a wholly-owned operation of the T. Wilce Company.

Fort Street Union Depot

LINE (FSUD)

	MILEAGE	COUNTY	CROSSINGS, JUNCTIONS, ETC.
Det.	0	Wayne	
6th St.	0.1	"	
(Bridge)	0.6	"	B/MC-E 0.9
18th St.	1.37	"	J/DURS 1.37

CONSTRUCTION/ABANDONMENT

DATE	ACT	END POINTS	MP	CHANGE	MAIN	SOURCE	NOTE
1893/1	B	Line	0–1.4	+1.4	1.4	1	
1972 ca.	X	E. end of line	0–1.0	−1.0			
1972 ca.	Y	W. end of line	1.0–1.4	(0.4)	0		

OWNERSHIP

    1893   Fort Street Union Depot
    **1889/12/10   Leased to Detroit, Lansing & Northern; Flint & Pere Marquette; Wabash; and Canadian Pacific, jointly

ACQUISITION/DISPOSITION RECORD

See Mileage record above

Act Column Key

        B   Built by Union Depot Company
        X   Abandoned
        Y   Converted to yard track.

Glencoe, Pinconning & Lake Shore and Pinconning ⎯⎯

MAIN LINE (GPLS-A)

	MILEAGE	COUNTY	CROSSINGS, JUNCTIONS, ETC.
Glencoe	0	Bay	
Pinconning	10.5	"	X/MC-M 19.0
Lake Huron	12.8	"	

CONSTRUCTION

DATE	ACT	END POINTS	MP	CHANGE	MAIN	SOURCE	NOTE
1876/3/17	P	Glencoe–Pinconning	0–10.5	+10.5		1	1
	B1	Pinconning–MP 12.8	10.5–12.8	+2.3	13.1	1	
1878	X	Glencoe–Pinconning	0–10.5	−10.5	2.3	1	

OWNERSHIP

    1876   Glencoe, Pinconning & Lake Shore (B1)
    1879/4/30   Pinconning, renamed Glencoe, Pinconning & Lake Shore

BRANCH (GPLS-B1)

	MILEAGE	COUNTY	CROSSINGS, JUNCTIONS, ETC.
Pinconning	2.3	Bay	J/GPLS-A 10.5
St. Johns	7.4	"	
Nine Mile (old)	9.0	"	J/GPLS-B2 0
Mt. Forest	10.3	"	J/GPLS-B3 0
Rhodes	13.5	Gladwin	
(Ttb. Riv.)	20.0	"	(sec 12 T17N R1E)

CONSTRUCTION

DATE	ACT	END POINTS	MP	CHANGE	MAIN	SOURCE
1878/9	B1	Pinconning–St. Johns	2.3–7.4	+5.1		1
12	B1	St. Johns–Mt. Forest	7.4–10.3	+2.9	7.0	1
1880	B2	Mt. Forest–Ttb. Riv.	10.3–20.0	+9.7	16.7	1

OWNERSHIP

    1878   Glencoe, Pinconning & Lake Shore (B1)
    1879/4/30   Pinconning (B2), renamed Glencoe, Pinconning & Lake Shore

BRANCH (GPLS-B2)

	MILEAGE	COUNTY	CROSSINGS, JUNCTIONS, ETC.
Nine Mile	0	Bay	J/GPLS–B1 9.0
Merick	5	"	(sec 6? T16N R4E)

CONSTRUCTION

DATE	ACT	END POINTS	MP	CHANGE	MAIN	SOURCE
1878/9	B1	Line	0–5.0	+5.0	5.0	1
1879	X	Line	0–5.0	−5.0	0	1

OWNERSHIP

1878	Glencoe, Pinconning & Lake Shore (B1)
1879/4/30	Pinconning, renamed Glencoe, Pinconning & Lake Shore

BRANCH (GPLS-B3)

	MILEAGE	COUNTY	CROSSINGS, JUNCTIONS, ETC.
Mt. Forest	0	Bay	J/GPLS-B1 10.3
Freeman	4.2	"	(now Bentley)

CONSTRUCTION

DATE	ACT	END POINTS	MP	CHANGE	MAIN	SOURCE
1879/5	B2	Line	0–4.2	+4.2	4.2	1

OWNERSHIP

1879	Pinconning (B2)

ACQUISITION/DISPOSITION RECORD

DATE	ACT	GPLS–	END POINTS	CHANGE	MI MAIN	NOTE
1876/3/17	P	A	Pinconning–Glencoe	+10.5	10.5	1
1876	B1	A	Pinconning–Lk. Huron	+2.3	12.8	
1878	X	A	Pinconning–Glencoe	−10.5		
/9	B1	B1	Pinconning–St. Johns	+5.1		
/9	B1	B2	Nine Mile–Merick	+5.0		
/12	B1	B1	St. Johns–Mt. Forest	+2.9	15.3	
1879	X	B2	Nine Mile–Merick	−5.0		
/5	B2	B3	Mt. Forest–Freeman	+4.2	14.5	
1880	B2	B1	Mt. Forest–Ttb. Riv.	+9.7		
/11/18	S		Entire property	−24.2	0	

Act Column Key

B1	Built by Glencoe, Pinconning & Lake Shore
B2	Built by Pinconning
P	Purchased from George Campbell & Co.
S	Sold to Saginaw Bay & Northwestern
X	Abandoned

Sources

1. Michigan, Commissioner of Railroads, *Annual Report,* 1878, 1880.

Notes

1. The segment between Glencoe and Pinconning apparently was constructed in 1874 by George Campbell & Co. It was conveyed by that company to the Glencoe, Pinconning & Lake Shore on 17 March 1876. The GP&LS was owned by George Campbell & Co.

Grand Rapids & Indiana

SOUTHERN DIV. (GR&I-S)

	MILEAGES [Richmond]	COUNTY	CROSSINGS, JUNCTIONS, ETC.
(Fort Wayne IN	91.9)	Allen IN	
—via PRR—			
Jct.	93.3	"	J/PRR
Spy Run	94.6	"	
Wallen	99.6	"	
Huntertown	104.1	"	
LaOtto	108.7	Noble IN	X/PRR
Swans	110.4	"	
Avilla	113.6	"	X/B&O
Conlog	117.3	"	
Kendallville	120.2	"	X/NYC
Hoffman	121.5	"	
Rome Cty.	127.3	"	
Kneipp Sanitarium	127.9	"	
Wolcottville	129.4	LaGrange IN	X/WAB
Valentine	134.4	"	
LaGrange	138.4	"	
Howe	143.7	"	
Crooked Creek	145.5	"	
(Line IN/MI)	146.4		
Sturgis	149.1	St. Joseph	
RK	149.4	"	X/LS-A 408.6, X/LS-S 29.0
North Sturgis	150.6	"	
Perrin	154.7	"	
Sunbrite	155.6	"	
Nottawa	157.9	"	
Wasepi	159.5	"	X/MC-A 61.2
Mendon	164.1	"	
Portage Lk.	168.1	"	
Vicksburg	173.0	Kal.	X/GTW-C 152.5, f. Brady
Baker		"	

Austin Lk.	178.0	"	J/GR&I-8, f. Austin
Upjohn	179.0	"	(relocated by Conrail)
Indianfield	180.4	"	
Scotts Siding	182	"	
Shelldrake	182.1	"	
UP	183.1	"	
PJ	183.5	"	
Pavilion Jct.	183.6	"	J/GTW-K 9.1
(Bridge)	183.9	"	B/CK&S-YK 1.5, B/GTW-YK 1.1
(Bridge)	184.1	"	B/MUR-S 66.75
Vine	184.6	"	
Gibson St.	185.1	"	X/LS-G 36.3
Kal.	185.4	"	
(Crossing)	185.4	"	X/KACL-1 0.24
Kal. Jct.	185.7	"	X/MC-C 143.2 (aka Tower 1)
Fox	185.8	"	J/wye to MC-C 143.3, 0.3 miles
Dock	187.1	"	
Coop	188.3	"	
Cooper	191.3	"	
County Spur	191.8	"	
Travis	193.1	"	
RC	195.8	Allegan	
JN	196.7	"	X/LS-G 48.3, X/MUR-W 12.75
Plainwell	196.8	"	
Mill	197.5	"	
Bowens	201	"	
Montieth	202.1	"	X/DTM 121.7 (also MUR-WB 31.27)
Martin	203.2	"	
Shelbyville	207.2	"	
(Bridge)	208.8	"	B/MUR-W 24.3
Bradley	210.0	"	
Wayland	213.0	"	
Moline	217.6	"	
Tolands	220	Kent	
Ross	221.0	"	
Stewart	222.7	"	
Karl	223.5	"	
Carlisle	224.5	"	
Fisher	227.5	"	
Solvay	229.0	"	
(Bridge)	231.0	"	B/MUR-W 45.9
Plaster Creek Jct.	231.2	"	J/GR&I-YG 0
S. Gr. Rpds.	231.6	"	
Burton	231.6	"	
Hughart	232.1	"	
S. Yard	232.7	"	
Graham St.	233.1	"	
Second Ave.	233.2	"	X/PM-D 151.5
Bartlett St.	233.6	"	J/GR&I-YG 3.1, J/MC-G 94.1
Williams St.	233.7	"	J/PM-C 0.3
Gr. Rpds.	234.0	"	J/GR&I-N 234.0

CONSTRUCTION

DATE	ACT	END POINTS	MP	CHANGE	MI MAIN	SOURCE	NOTE
1868	B1	Gr. Rpds.–S. Yard	232.7–234.0	+1.3	1.3	5	1
1870/6/22	B1	Ft. Wyn.–Sturgis	93.3–149.1	+55.8	4.0	5	2
1870/8	B1	Sturgis–Kal.	149.1–185.4	+36.3		5	
1870/9/13	B1	Kal.–S. Yard	185.4–232.7	+47.3	87.6		1
1976	X	Nottawa–Wasepi	157.9–159.4	−1.5			
1976	Y	At Sturgis (GR&I-Y1S)	146.4–150.6	(4.2)	81.9		
1977	S1	At Vicksburg (GR&I-Y2S)	171.9–173.0	−1.1			
1977	X	Mendon–Vicksburg	164.1–171.9	−7.8	73.0		
1982	X	N. Sturgis–Nottawa	150.6–157.9	−7.3			
1982	X	Wasepi–Mendon	159.4–164.1	−4.7			
1982	X	Vicksburg–Upjohn	173.0–178.5	−5.5			
1982	Y	Upjohn–Kal.(GR&I-Y2S)	178.5–185.1	(6.6)	48.9		
1985	X	Second Ave.–Gr. Rpds.	233.2–234.0	−0.8	48.1		
1993/12	S2	At Sturgis (GR&I-Y1S)	146.4–150.6	(−4.2)	48.1		

OWNERSHIP

1868	Grand Rapids & Indiana Railroad (B1)
1874	Pennsylvania Railroad, control of Grand Rapids & Indiana
1896/7/7	Grand Rapids & Indiana Railway, reorganized GR&I Railroad (controlled by Pennsylvania)
1953/12/1	Penndel Co. (Pennsylvania Railroad holding co.), merged GR&I
1968/2/1	Penn Central, bought Penndel
1976/4/1	Conrail, bought Penn Central
1999/6/1	Norfolk Southern, bought Conrail

PLASTER CREEK BRANCH (GR&I-YG)

	MILEAGE	COUNTY	CROSSINGS, JUNCTIONS, ETC.
Plaster Creek Jct.	0.0	Kent	J/GR&I-S 231.2
(Crossing)	0.9	"	X/GRHC 0.1
(S. wye switch)	1.0	"	J/spur to Plaster Creek (C/PM-C 2.2), 0.8 mi
(N. wye switch)	1.2	"	
Godfrey Ave.	2.2	"	J/PM-C 0.8
Bartlett St. Jct.	3.1	"	J/GR&I-S 233.6

CONSTRUCTION

DATE	ACT	END POINTS	MP	CHANGE	MAIN	SOURCE	NOTE
1890	B1	Line + spur	3.1 + 0.8	(+3.9)	0	5	
1985	X	Line + spur	3.1 + 0.8	(−3.9)	0		

OWNERSHIP

1890	Grand Rapids & Indiana (B1), controlled by Pennsylvania Railroad
1896/7/7	Grand Rapids & Indiana Railway, reorganized GR&I Railroad (controlled by Pennsylvania)
1953/12/1	Penndel Co. (Pennsylvania Railroad holding company), merged GR&I
1968/2/1	Penn Central, bought Penndel
1976/4/1	Conrail, bought Penn Central

MUSKEGON BRANCH (GR&I-M)

	MILEAGE	COUNTY	CROSSINGS, JUNCTIONS, ETC.
	[Grand Rapids]		
Musk. Jct.	2.6	Kent	J/GR&I-N 182.5
Bristol	4.4	"	

Kinney	7.4	"	
Penn Jct.	9.0	Ottawa	B/GTW-D 165.3
Walker	10.0	"	J/GTW-DM 0.8
Herrington	11.6	"	
Reno	12.9	"	
Conklin	17.2	"	f. W. Chester
Ravenna	22.4	Musk.	J/GR&I-M2 0
Sullivan	27.8	"	
Opdyke	30.5	"	
Eggleston	32.7	"	f. Cloverville
Kanitz	36.0	"	X/PM-AO 32.6, f. Fruitport Jct.
Shaw	36.5	"	X/GTW-YM 0.4
(Crossing)	37.9	"	X/MUCL-3 1.56
Musk. Heights	38.0	"	J/GR&I-YM 38.0
(Crossing)(11th & Henry)	39.1	"	X/PM-A 56.1
(Crossing)	39.2	"	X/MUCL-1 2.42
Western Ave. Jct.	39.3	"	X/PM-YM 0.1
Musk. (Docks)	39.5	"	

CONSTRUCTION

DATE	ACT	END POINTS	MP	CHANGE	MAIN	SOURCE	NOTE
1886/12/1	B4	Musk. Jct.–Musk.	2.6–39.5	+36.9	36.9	5	
1930	X	West end of line	39.5–39.3	−0.2	36.7	7	9
1961	X	Kinney–Walker	7.4–10.0	−2.6		5	
1961	Y	Musk. Jct.–Kinney(to Y1M)	2.6–7.4	(4.8)	29.3		
1983 ca.	X	Musk. Jct.–Kinney (Y1M)	2.6–7.4	[(−4.8)]	29.3		
1989	X	Walker–Musk.	10.0–39.3	[−29.3]	0		

OWNERSHIP

1886	Muskegon, Grand Rapids & Indiana (B4), controlled by GR&I
1886/6/9	Leased to Grand Rapids & Indiana Railroad, controlled by Pennsylvania Railroad
1896/7/7	Grand Rapids & Indiana Railway, reorganized GR&I Railroad (controlled by Pennsylvania)
1917/5/1	Grand Rapids & Indiana, bought Muskegon, Grand Rapids & Indiana
1953/12/1	Penndel Co. (Pennsylvania Railroad holding co.), merged GR&I
1968/2/1	Penn Central, bought Penndel
1976/4/1	Grand Trunk Western, bought line
1987/9/4	Central Michigan, bought line

MUSKEGON HEIGHTS BRANCH (GR&I-YM)

	MILEAGE	COUNTY	CROSSINGS, JUNCTIONS, ETC.
	[Grand Rapids]		
(Jct.)	38.0	Musk.	J/GR&I-M 38.0
(Crossing)(Waalkes St.)	38.5	"	X/PM-A 54.9
(Jct.)	39.3	"	J/GTW-YM 2.6

CONSTRUCTION

DATE	ACT	END POINTS	MP	CHANGE	MAIN	SOURCE	NOTE
1929	B10	Line	0–1.3	(+1.3)	0	7	
1989	X	Line	0–1.3	[(−1.3)]	0		

OWNERSHIP

1929	Grand Rapids & Indiana (B10), controlled by Pennsylvania Railroad
1953/12/1	Penndel Co. (Pennsylvania Railroad holding co.), merged GR&I

1968/2/1   Penn Central, bought Penndel
1976/4/1   Grand Trunk Western, bought line
1987/9/4   Central Michigan, bought line

SLOCUMS GROVE BRANCH (GR&I-M2)

	MILEAGE	COUNTY	CROSSINGS, JUNCTIONS, ETC.
Ravenna	0	Musk.	J/GR&I-M 22.4
Slocums Grove	3.8	"	

CONSTRUCTION

DATE	ACT	END POINTS	MP	CHANGE	MAIN	SOURCE	NOTE
1900	B10	Ravenna–Slocums Grove	0–3.8	+3.8	3.8	7	
1906	X	Entire line	3.8–0	−3.8	0	7	

OWNERSHIP

1900   Grand Rapids & Indiana Railway (B10), controlled by Pennsylvania Railroad

NORTHERN DIV. (GR&I-N)

	MILEAGE	COUNTY	CROSSINGS, JUNCTIONS, ETC.
	[Richmond]		
Gr. Rpds.	234.0	Kent	J/GR&I-S 234.0
(Fulton St.)	234.2	"	X/GRCL-7 0.17
(Grand River bridge)	234.3	"	
(Crossing)	234.5	"	X/MUR-W 94.4
Winter St.	234.7	"	X/PM-P 0.8
Lk. Michigan Drive	234.8	"	J/LS-G 95.0
Bridge St.	235.3	"	X/GRCL-15 0.55
(Leonard St.)	236.1	"	X/GRCL-18 0.38
Musk. Jct.	236.6	"	J/GR&I-M 2.6
Fuller	236.9	"	X/GTW-D 158.9
(Crossing)	239.2	"	X/PM-P 5.5
Comstock Park	239.4	"	f. Norths Mill, th. Mill Creek
Belmont	243.7	"	
Pantlind City	245	"	
Bushs	246	"	
S. Rockford	246.3	"	f. Childs Mill, th. Childsdale
Rockford	247.8	"	
Burchs Mill	253.0	"	
(Crossing)	254.7	"	X/GTW-M 56.4
Cedar Springs	255.2	"	
Lockwood	257.8	"	
Sand Lk.	260.3	"	
Pierson	262.3	Montcalm	
Hiram	264.2	"	f. Wood Lk. (old 263.9)
Maple Hill	265.9	"	
Dickinsons	267	"	
Howard City	268.0	"	J/PM-I 64.3, J/PM-V 82.5
Reynolds	269.0	"	(old 271.4)
Conger	271.6	"	
Morley	274.4	Mecosta	
Morley Siding	275.1	"	
Borland	278.1	"	f. Bell Siding (old 277.9)
Stanwood Siding	280.8	"	
Stanwood	281.0	"	
Rust	282.4	"	

Byers	285.9	"	B/MEC-A 0.2
Bigelows	288	"	
(Crossing)	289.5	"	X/C&BR 0.1
Big Rapids	289.9	"	aka Lower Big Rapids
Upper Big Rapids	290.4	"	X/PM-J 93.3
Stimson Jct.	292.2	"	J/GR&I-4 0
Paris	295.4	"	
Upper Paris	296.6	"	X/PPMR 0.1
Jacksons		"	
Crapo	298.3	Osceola	
Potters	299	"	
Mitchells	301.0	"	
Reed City	302.7	"	X/PM-L 89.2
Keegan	303.9	"	
Leyburns	304	"	
Orono	307.2	"	J/GR&I-3 0, f. Milton Jct.
Ashton	309.6	"	
Carlsons		"	
Dewings	311.6	"	
Hayes		"	
LeRoy	315.2	"	
S. Allens	318	"	
Newbergers	319	"	
(Crossing)	319.2	"	X/M&GR-A 54.6
Tustin	319.8	"	
Allens	322	"	
Richs	322	"	
Hoods	323	"	
Osceola Jct.	323.4	"	J/GR&I-2 0
Hobart	326.0	Wexford	f. Summit
Gerbers		"	
CN	331.5	"	X/AA-B 227.0
Cadillac	331.8	"	f. Clam Lk.
(Crossing)	332.8	"	X/C&NE 1.1
N. Yard	333.1	"	
Haskins	334	"	
Haring	335.4	"	f. Linden
Missaukee Jct.	335.9	"	J/GR&I-K 0
Bonds	337.8	"	f. Wexford
Bonds Mill (old)	339.9	"	
Gilbert	341.1	"	
Manton	344.0	"	
Metheany	345.8	"	
Clarks	347	"	
Haire	347.5	"	
(Manistee River bridge)	350.7	"	
Walton Jct.	352.8	Gr.Trav.	B/M&NE-R 38.8
(Jct.)	353.1	"	J/GR&I-T 0
Fife Lk.	357.8	"	
Houseman	360.9	Kalkaska	
Harts	361	"	
Farrens	363	"	
S. Boardman	363.3	"	
Stimson	364.8	"	
Mitchell Jct.		"	

Crofton	366.6	"	
Quimbys	367	"	
Thompson	368	"	
Kalkaska	371.5	"	X/PM-K 11.1
Herrings	373	"	
Darbys		"	
Leetsville	376.1	"	
Wilkins	379.6	"	
Westwood	381.1	"	f. Havana
Antrim	383.8	Antrim	J/GR&I-9 0, f. Furnace
Mancelona	384.9	"	
Wetzell	387.4	"	
Barnards	390	"	
(Crossing)	391.3	"	X/D&C-A 25.6
Alba	391.7	"	
Thelma	393.9	"	J/GR&I-10 0
Simons	395.6	"	
Elmira	400.1	Otsego	
Huntworth	400.5	"	
N. Elmira	401.5	"	B/BC-A 13.2
Spring Water	404.4	Antrim	
Robbins	406.6	Charlevoix	
Boyne Falls	409.0	"	J/BC-AB 7.2
Easton	410.3	"	X/BC-2 1.4
Hammers	413	"	
McManus	414.9	"	
Charltons	415	"	
Lk. Jct.	415.9	"	J/GR&I-5 0, f. Bear Lk. Jct.
Walloon Lk.	416.2	"	
Campbell	417.3	"	f. Clarion
Wabmeme	421	Emmet	
Formans	423.0	"	
(Jct.)	423.4	"	J/GR&I-11 0
Emmet St.	424.2	"	
Petoskey	424.8	"	
Rosedale	425.5	"	
(Jct.)	425.7	"	J/PM-P 226.2
Bay View	425.8	"	
Reed Ave.	426.2	"	
Edgewater	426.5	"	
Stevens	426	"	
Kegomic	427.0	"	J/GR&I-H 0, f. Harbor Springs Jct.
Round Lk.	428.1	"	
Wa-ya-ga-mung	428.7	"	
Conway	430.0	"	
Sunny Brook	430.9	"	
Oden	432.2	"	f. Oden–Oden
Indiana Point	432.9	"	
Ponshewaing	433.3	"	
Alanson	434.9	"	
Cases		"	
Brutus	438.5	"	
Pellston	442.6	"	
(Jct.)	443.0	"	J/GR&I-12 0
(Jct.)	443.3	"	J/GR&I-7 0

Van	445.6	"	
Lakewood	446.8	"	
Levering	448.6	"	f. Leverington
Walker		"	
Carp Lk.	452.7	"	
Wheeling	453.5	"	
Mack. Cty.	459.7	Cheboygan	
(Jct.)	459.8	"	J/MC-M 182.5

CONSTRUCTION

DATE	ACT	END POINTS	MP	CHANGE	MAIN	SOURCE	NOTE
1867/12/23	B1	Bridge St.–Cedar Springs	235.1–255.2	+20.1	20.1	5	5
1868	B1	Bridge St.–Gr. Rpds.	234.0–235.1	+1.1	21.2	5	
1869/6/21	B1	Cedar Springs–Morley	255.2–274.4	+19.2	40.4	3	
1870/8/12	B1	Morley–Paris	274.4–295.4	+21.0	61.4	5	
1871/12	B1	Paris–Cadillac	295.4–331.8	+36.4	97.8	5	
1872/9	B1	Cadillac–Fife Lk.	331.8–357.8	+26.0	123.8	5	
1874/5	B1	Fife Lk.–Petoskey	357.8–424.8	+67.0	190.8	5	6
1876/8	B1	Petoskey–Bay View	424.8–425.8	+1.0	191.8	3	
1882/2/1	B2	Bay View–Kegomic	425.8–427.0	+1.2	193.0	5	
1882/7/3	B3	Kegomic–N of Mack. Cty.	427.0–459.8	+32.8	225.8	5	7
1984/2/15	S3	Comstock Park–Petoskey	239.5–426.0	[186.5]	39.3		
1985	X	Gr. Rpds.–MP 234.7	234.0–234.7	−0.7	38.6		
1988 ca.	X	Alanson–Mac. Cty.	434.9–459.8	[−24.9]	13.7		
1992 ca.	X	Petoskey–Mac. Cty.	426.0–434.9	[−8.9]	4.8		

OWNERSHIP

1867	Grand Rapids & Indiana Railroad (B1)
1874	Pennsylvania Railroad, control of Grand Rapids & Indiana Railroad
1882	Bay View, Little Traverse & Mackinac (B2)
1882	Grand Rapids, Indiana & Mackinaw (B3)
1884/7/2	Grand Rapids & Indiana, bought Grand Rapids, Indiana & Mackinaw
1888/1/17	Grand Rapids & Indiana, bought Bay View, Little Traverse & Mackinac
1896/7/7	Grand Rapids & Indiana Railway, reorganized GR&I Railroad (controlled by Pennsylvania)
1953/12/1	Penndel Co. (Pennsylvania Railroad holding co.), merged GR&I
1968/2/1	Penn Central, bought Penndel
1976/4/1	Conrail, bought part of Penn Central line
1984	State of Michigan, bought part of Penn Central line
1988	Alanson & Petoskey, leased part of Penn Central line
1992	Alanson & Petoskey, lease canceled
1999/6/1	Norfolk Southern, bought Conrail

HARBOR SPRINGS BRANCH (GR&I-H)

	MILEAGE	COUNTY	CROSSINGS, JUNCTIONS, ETC.
Kegomic	0.0	Emmet	J/GR&I-N 427.0
Page	2.1	"	
Menonaqua (Beach)	2.1	"	
Ramona Park	3.2	"	
Roaring Brook	3.6	"	
E. Wequetonsing	4	"	
Wequetonsing	4.4	"	
W. Wequetonsing	5	"	
Harbor Springs	5.6	"	
(End of track)	6.3	"	

CONSTRUCTION

DATE	ACT	END POINTS	MP	CHANGE	MAIN	SOURCE	NOTE
1882/2/1	B2	Kegomic–Harbor Springs	0–5.8	+5.8	5.8	5	
1901	B10	Harbor Springs–north	5.8–6.3	+0.5	6.3	5	
1904	X	North end of line	6.3–5.9	−0.4	5.9	5	
1913	X	North end of line	5.9–5.8	−0.1	5.8	7	
1962	X	Kegomic–Harbor Springs	0–5.8	−5.8	0	4	

OWNERSHIP

1882	Bay View, Little Traverse & Mackinac (B2)
1888/1/17	Grand Rapids & Indiana Railroad, bought Bay View, Little Traverse & Mackinac
1896/7/7	Grand Rapids & Indiana Railway, reorganized Grand Rapids & Indiana Railroad
1953/12/1	Penndel Company (Pennsylvania Railroad holding company), merged GR&I

TRAVERSE CITY BRANCH (GR&I-T)

	MILEAGE	COUNTY	CROSSINGS, JUNCTIONS, ETC.
Walton Jct.	0.0	Gr. Trav.	J/GR&I-N 352.8
Holmes	2.8	"	
Leavells		"	
Summit City	6.2	"	
Westminster	8.0	"	
Kingsley	9.3	"	
Mayfield	12.6	"	f. Spring City
Cobb Jct.	13.1	"	
Slights	17.2	"	
Keystone	19.6	"	
Kerry	25.6	"	X/PM-P 147.8
Trav. Cty.	26.0	"	J/M&NE-NT 0

CONSTRUCTION

DATE	ACT	END POINTS	MP	CHANGE	MAIN	SOURCE	NOTE
1872/11/15	B5	Walton Jct.–Trav. Cty.	0–26.0	+26.0	26.0	6	8
1976	X	North end of line	26.0–25.2	−0.8	25.2	4	
1984/2/15	S3	Walton Jct.–Trav. Cty.	0–25.2	[25.2]	0		

OWNERSHIP

1872	Traverse City (B5), controlled by Pennsylvania Railroad
1883/1/1	Leased to Grand Rapids & Indiana Railroad, controlled by Pennsylvania Railroad
1896/7/7	Grand Rapids & Indiana Railway, reorganized GR&I Railroad (controlled by Pennsylvania)
1917/5/1	Grand Rapids & Indiana Railway, bought Traverse City
1953/12/1	Penndel Company (Pennsylvania Railroad holding co.), merged GR&I
1968/2/1	Penn Central, bought Penndel
1984/2/15	State of Michigan, bought line

MISSAUKEE BRANCH (GR&I-K)

	MILEAGE	COUNTY	CROSSINGS, JUNCTIONS, ETC.
Missaukee Jct.	0.0	Wexford	J/GR&I-N 335.9
Round Lk.		"	
Long Lk. Jct.	3.3	"	J/GR&I-K1 0
Round Lk. Jct.	4.7	Missaukee	J/GR&I-K2 0
(Crossing)	5.6	"	X/C&NE 7.5
Wagner	6.1	"	
Missaukee Park	8.5	"	
Sandstown	10.6	"	J/GR&I-K3 10.6

Cranmer	14	"	
Veneer Jct.	15.3	"	J/GR&I-K4 15.3
Mynnings	18.3	"	
Ardis Jct.	19.1	"	J/GR&I-K5 0
Ardis	22.5	"	
Cummer	24.0	"	
Merritt	25.3	"	
Wardville	28	"	f. Ward
Reedsburg	30	"	
Michelson	31.6	Roscommon	
(End of track)	31.9	"	

CONSTRUCTION

DATE	ACT	END POINTS	MP	CHANGE	MAIN	SOURCE	NOTE
1882	B1	Missaukee Jct.–Round Lk. Jct.	0–4.1	+4.1	4.1	5	
1890	B1	Round Lk. Jct.–Sandstown	4.1–10.6	+6.5	10.6	3	10
1894	B9	Sandstown–MP 16	10.6–16.0	+5.4	16.0	5	11
1906	B10	MP 16–Ardis Jct.	16.0–19.1	+3.1	19.1	5	12
1909	B10	Ardis Jct.–Michelson	19.1–31.9	+12.8	31.9	5	
1918	X	In Michelson	31.9–31.6	–0.3	31.6	7	
1930	X	Michelson–Merritt	31.6–25.3	–6.0	25.6	7	
1938	X	Merritt–Veneer Jct.	25.3–15.3	–10.3	15.3	7	
1964	S4	Missaukee Jct.–Veneer Jct.	0–15.3	[15.3]	0	4	25
1972	X	Sandstown–Veneer Jct.	10.6–15.3	[–4.7]			
1975	X	MP 4.5–Sandstown	4.5–10.6	[–6.1]			
1984	X	Missaukee Jct.–MP 4.5	0–4.5	[–4.5]			

OWNERSHIP

1882	Grand Rapids & Indiana Railroad (B1), controlled by Pennsylvania Railroad
1896/7/7	Grand Rapids & Indiana Railway (B10), reorganized GR&I Railroad (controlled by PRR)
1953/12/1	Penndel Co. (Pennsylvania Railroad holding co.), merged GR&I
1964	Cadillac & Lake City, bought line

LONG LAKE BRANCH (GR&I-K1)

	MILEAGE	COUNTY	CROSSINGS, JUNCTIONS, ETC.
Long Lk. Jct.	0.0	Wexford	J/GR&I-K 3.3
Long Lk.	0.8	"	

CONSTRUCTION

DATE	ACT	END POINTS	MP	CHANGE	MAIN	SOURCE	NOTE
1883	B1	Long Lk. Jct.–Long Lk.	0–0.8	+0.8	0.8	5	15
1889	X	Entire line	0.8–0	–0.8	0	5	

OWNERSHIP

1883	Grand Rapids & Indiana Railroad (B1), controlled by Pennsylvania Railroad

JENNINGS SPUR (GR&I-K2)

	MILEAGE	COUNTY	CROSSINGS, JUNCTIONS, ETC.
Round Lk. Jct.	0.0	Missaukee	J/GR&I-K 4.7
Jennings	3.5	"	f. Mitchell

CONSTRUCTION

DATE	ACT	END POINTS	MP	CHANGE	MAIN	SOURCE	NOTE
1882	B1	Round Lk. Jct.–Jennings	0–3.5	+3.5	3.5	5	
1890	X	North end of line	3.5–3.0	–0.5	3.0	3	
1927	X	Round Lk. Jct.–Jennings	3.0–0	–3.0	0	7	

OWNERSHIP

1882	Grand Rapids & Indiana Railroad (B1), controlled by Pennsylvania Railroad
1896/7/7	Grand Rapids & Indiana Railway, reorganized GR&I Railroad (controlled by PRR)

LAKE CITY BRANCH (GR&I-K3)

	MILEAGE	COUNTY	CROSSINGS, JUNCTIONS, ETC.
	[Missaukee Jct.]		
Sandstown	10.6	Missaukee	J/GR&I-K 10.6
Lk. City	11.6	"	

CONSTRUCTION

DATE	ACT	END POINTS	MP	CHANGE	MAIN	SOURCE	NOTE
1890	B1	Sandstown–Lk. City	10.6–11.6	+1.0	1.0	3	10
1918	B10	North end of line	11.6–11.8	+0.2	1.2	7	
1964	S4	Sandstown–Lk. City	10.6–11.8	[1.2]	0	4	25
1975	X	Sandstown–Lk. City	10.6–11.8	[–1.2]			

OWNERSHIP

1882	Grand Rapids & Indiana Railroad (B1), controlled by Pennsylvania Railroad
1896/7/7	Grand Rapids & Indiana Railway (B10), reorganized GR&I Railroad (controlled by PRR)
1953/12/1	Penndel Co. (Pennsylvania Railroad holding co.), merged GR&I
1964	Cadillac & Lake City, bought line

FALMOUTH (VENEER) BRANCH (GR&I-K4)

	MILEAGE	COUNTY	CROSSINGS, JUNCTIONS, ETC.
	[Missaukee Jct.]		
Veneer Jct.	15.3	Missaukee	J/GR&I-K 15.3
Herrick	16.9	"	J/GR&I-K4A
Koopman	17	"	
Falmouth	19.9	"	

CONSTRUCTION

DATE	ACT	END POINTS	MP	CHANGE	MAIN	SOURCE	NOTE
1894	B1	Veneer Jct.–Herrick	15.3–16.9	+1.6	1.6	5	
1908	B10	Herrick–Falmouth	16.9–19.9	+3.0	4.6	5	
1964	S4	Falmouth–Veneer Jct.	19.9–15.3	[4.6]	0	4	25
1972	X	Falmouth–Veener Jct.	19.9–15.3	[–4.6]			

OWNERSHIP

1882	Grand Rapids & Indiana Railroad (B1), controlled by Pennsylvania Railroad
1896/7/7	Grand Rapids & Indiana Railway (B10), reorganized GR&I Railroad (controlled by PRR)
1953/12/1	Penndel Co. (Pennsylvania Railroad holding co.), merged GR&I
1964	Cadillac & Lake City, bought line

WIDDICOMB SPUR (GR&I-K4A)

	MILEAGE	COUNTY	CROSSINGS, JUNCTIONS, ETC.
Herrick	0.0	Missaukee	J/GR&I-K4 16.9
(End of track)	6.6	"	

CONSTRUCTION

DATE	ACT	END POINTS	MP	CHANGE	MAIN	SOURCE	NOTE
1898	B7	Herrick–east	0–3.4	+3.4	3.4	5	13
1900	B10	Extend east	3.4–6.6	+3.2	6.6	5	
1908	X	Entire line	0–6.6	–6.6	0	7	

OWNERSHIP

1898   Widdicomb Furniture Co.(B7)
1898   Grand Rapids & Indiana Railway (B10), controlled by Pennsylvania Railroad, bought line

MISSAUKEE CITY BRANCH (GR&I-K5)

	MILEAGE	COUNTY	CROSSINGS, JUNCTIONS, ETC.
Ardis Jct.	0.0	Missaukee	J/GR&I-K 19.1
Missaukee City	2.8	"	
(End of track)	3.9	"	

CONSTRUCTION

DATE	ACT	END POINTS	MP	CHANGE	MAIN	SOURCE	NOTE
1906	B10	Ardis Jct.–Missaukee City	0–2.8	+2.8	2.8	5	
1909	B10	Extend north	2.8–3.9	+1.1	3.9	5	
1913	X	Entire line	3.9–0	–3.9	0	5	14

OWNERSHIP

1906   Grand Rapids & Indiana Railway (B10), controlled by Pennsylvania Railroad

OSCEOLA BRANCH (GR&I-2)

	MILEAGE	COUNTY	CROSSINGS, JUNCTIONS, ETC.
Osceola Jct.	0.0	Osceola	J/GR&I-N 323.4
Sutliffs	3.9	"	
Olga	?	Lk.	
Alyn	7.0	"	
Hoxeyville	?	Wexford	

CONSTRUCTION

DATE	ACT	END POINTS	MP	CHANGE	MAIN	SOURCE	NOTE
1885	B1	Osceola Jct.–Olga	0–7.0	+7.0	7.0	5	
1892	B1	Extend west	7.0–9.8	+2.8	9.8	5	
1897	X	W. end of line	9.8–7.0	–2.8	7.0	5	
1904	X	Olga–Sutliff	7.0–3.9	–3.1	3.9	5	
1906	X	Sutliff–MP 0.4	3.9–0.4	–3.5	0.4	5	
1907	X	Osceola Jct.–MP 0.4	0.4–0	–0.4	0	5	

OWNERSHIP

1882   Grand Rapids & Indiana Railroad (B1), controlled by Pennsylvania Railroad
1896/7/7   Grand Rapids & Indiana Railway, reorganized GR&I Railroad (controlled by PRR)

MANISTEE BRANCH (GR&I-3)

	MILEAGE	COUNTY	CROSSINGS, JUNCTIONS, ETC.
Milton Jct.	0.0	Osceola	J/GR&I-N 307.6
Deer Lk.	5.1	Lk.	
Lk. Jct.	5.3	"	J/GR&I-3A 0
Totten	8.8	"	
Luther	11.7	"	J/GR&I-3C 0
(Crossing)	13.1	"	X/M&GR-A 41.2
Carey	14.5	"	

CONSTRUCTION

DATE	ACT	END POINTS	MP	CHANGE	MAIN	SOURCE	NOTE
1882	B1	Milton Jct.–Carey	0–14.5	+14.5	14.5	5	
1900	X	Carey–M&GR Crossing.	14.5–13.1	–1.4	13.1	5	
1904	X	Entire line 13.1–0	–13.1	0		5	

OWNERSHIP

1882	Grand Rapids & Indiana Railroad (B1), controlled by Pennsylvania Railroad
1896/7/7	Grand Rapids & Indiana Railway, reorganized GR&I Railroad (controlled by PRR)

DEER LAKE SPUR (GR&I-3A)

	MILEAGE	COUNTY	CROSSINGS, JUNCTIONS, ETC.
Lk. Jct.	0.0	Lk.	J/GR&I-3 5.3
Raijuels	7.0	"	f. Pelton

CONSTRUCTION

DATE	ACT	END POINTS	MP	CHANGE	MAIN	SOURCE	NOTE
1883	B1	Lk. Jct.–Pelton	0–7.0	+7.0	7.0	5	
1894	X	Entire line 7.0–0	–7.0	0		5	16

OWNERSHIP

1882	Grand Rapids & Indiana Railroad (B1), controlled by Pennsylvania Railroad
1896/7/7	Grand Rapids & Indiana Railway, reorganized GR&I Railroad (controlled by PRR)

HAAKS SPUR (GR&I-3B)

	MILEAGE	COUNTY	CROSSINGS, JUNCTIONS, ETC.
Haaks Spur Jct.	0.0	Lk.	J/GR&I-3 ?
Haaks Mill	4.1	"	

CONSTRUCTION

DATE	ACT	END POINTS	MP	CHANGE	MAIN	SOURCE	NOTE
1891	B1	Haaks Spur Jct.–Haaks Mill	0–4.1	+4.1	4.1	5	
1900	X	Entire line	4.1–0	–4.1	0	5	

OWNERSHIP

1882	Grand Rapids & Indiana Railroad (B1), controlled by Pennsylvania Railroad
1896/7/7	Grand Rapids & Indiana Railway, reorganized GR&I Railroad (controlled by PRR)

NASONS BRANCH (GR&I-3C)

	MILEAGE	COUNTY	CROSSINGS, JUNCTIONS, ETC.
Luther	0.0	Lk.	J/GR&I-3 11.7
Nasons	5.0	"	

CONSTRUCTION

DATE	ACT	END POINTS	MP	CHANGE	MAIN	SOURCE	NOTE
1882 ca.	B1	Luther–Nasons	0–5.0	+5.0	5.0	7	
1889	X	Entire line 5.0–0	–5.0	0		7	

OWNERSHIP

1882   Grand Rapids & Indiana Railroad (B1), controlled by Pennsylvania Railroad

LUDINGTON BRANCH (GR&I-4)

	MILEAGE	COUNTY	CROSSINGS, JUNCTIONS, ETC.
Stimson Jct.	0.0	Mecosta	J/GR&I-N 292.2
Doyle City	?		
Merrits	5.8	Newaygo	
Park	6.3?	"	
Vincent	8.9	"	aka Hardys

CONSTRUCTION

DATE	ACT	END POINTS	MP	CHANGE	MAIN	SOURCE	NOTE
1890	B6	Stimson Jct.–Vincent	0–8.9	+8.9	8.9	5	17
1896	X	Vincent–Merrits	8.9–5.8	–3.1	5.8	5	
1899	X	Entire line 5.8–0	–5.8	0		5	

OWNERSHIP

1890   Big Rapids & Western (B6), owned by Grand Rapids & Indiana Railroad, controlled by Pennsylvania Railroad
1896/7/7   Grand Rapids & Indiana Railway (B10), reorganized GR&I Railroad (controlled by PRR)

BEAR LAKE (LATER WALLOON LAKE) BRANCH (GR&I-5)

	MILEAGE	COUNTY	CROSSINGS, JUNCTIONS, ETC.
Lk. Jct.	0.0	Charlevoix	J/GR&I-N 415.9, f. Bear Lk. Jct.
Walloon Lk. (old)	1.1	"	f. Bear Lk.

CONSTRUCTION

DATE	ACT	END POINTS	MP	CHANGE	MAIN	SOURCE	NOTE
1892/6	B1	Walloon Lk.(new)–Bear Lk.	0–1.1	+1.1	1.1	5	
1910	X	In Walloon Lk.(old)	1.1–1.0	–0.1	1.0	7	
1928	X	Entire line	1.0–0	–1.0	0	7	

OWNERSHIP

1892   Grand Rapids & Indiana Railroad (B1), controlled by Pennsylvania Railroad
1896/7/7   Grand Rapids & Indiana Railway (B10), reorganized GR&I Railroad (controlled by PRR)

BOGARDUS BRANCH (GR&I-7)

	MILEAGE	COUNTY	CROSSINGS, JUNCTIONS, ETC.
(Jct.)	0.0	Emmet	J/GR&I-N 443.3
Bogardus	4.9	"	

CONSTRUCTION

DATE	ACT	END POINTS	MP	CHANGE	MAIN	SOURCE	NOTE
1901	B10	Pellston–Bogardus	0–4.9	+4.0	4.0	5	18
1910	X	Entire line 4.9–0	–4.0	0		5	19

OWNERSHIP

1901   Grand Rapids & Indiana Railway (B10), controlled by Pennsylvania Railroad

LONG LAKE BRANCH (GR&I-8)

	MILEAGE	COUNTY	CROSSINGS, JUNCTIONS, ETC.
Austin Lk.	0.0	Kal.	J/GR&I-S 178.0
Long Lk.	0.8	"	

CONSTRUCTION

DATE	ACT	END POINTS	MP	CHANGE	MAIN	SOURCE	NOTE
1886/2	B1	Austin Lk.–Long Lk.	0–0.8	+0.8	0.8		20
1914	X	Entire line	0.8–0	–0.8	0	5	

OWNERSHIP

1886   Grand Rapids & Indiana Railroad (B1), controlled by Pennsylvania Railroad

1896/7/7   Grand Rapids & Indiana Railway, reorganized GR&I Railroad (controlled by PRR)

WILKINS BRANCH (GR&I-9)

	MILEAGE	COUNTY	CROSSINGS, JUNCTIONS, ETC.
Antrim	0.0	Antrim	J/GR&I-N 383.8
(End of Track)	1.8	"	

CONSTRUCTION

DATE	ACT	END POINTS	MP	CHANGE	MAIN	SOURCE	NOTE
1905	B10	Antrim–east	0–1.8	+1.8	1.8	5	
1909	X	Entire line	1.8–0	–1.8	0	5	21

OWNERSHIP

1905   Grand Rapids & Indiana Railway (B10), controlled by Pennsylvania Railroad

THELMA BRANCH (GR&I-10)

	MILEAGE	COUNTY	CROSSINGS, JUNCTIONS, ETC.
Thelma	0.0	Antrim	J/GR&I-N 393.9
(End of track)	5.8	"	

CONSTRUCTION

DATE	ACT	END POINTS	MP	CHANGE	MAIN	SOURCE	NOTE
1905	B10	Thelma–east	0–4.5	+4.5	4.5	5	
1909	B10	Extend east	4.5–5.8	+1.3	5.8	5	21
1913	X	Entire line	5.8–0	–5.8	0	5	22

OWNERSHIP

1905   Grand Rapids & Indiana Railway (B10), controlled by Pennsylvania Railroad

BEAR RIVER BRANCH (GR&I-11)

	MILEAGE	COUNTY	CROSSINGS, JUNCTIONS, ETC.
(Jct.)	0.0	Emmet	J/GR&I-N 423.4
(End of track)	1.4	"	

CONSTRUCTION

DATE	ACT	END POINTS	MP	CHANGE	MAIN	SOURCE	NOTE
1905	B10	Formans–north	0–1.3	+1.3	1.3	5	
1908	B10	Extend north	1.3–1.4	+0.1	1.4	7	
1917	X	Entire line	1.4–0	–1.4	0	7	

OWNERSHIP

1905   Grand Rapids & Indiana Railway (B10), controlled by Pennsylvania Railroad

BELDING HALL BRANCH (GR&I-12)

	MILEAGE	COUNTY	CROSSINGS, JUNCTIONS, ETC.
(Jct.)	0.0	Emmet	J/GR&I-N 443.0
(End of track)	1.8	"	

CONSTRUCTION

DATE	ACT	END POINTS	MP	CHANGE	MAIN	SOURCE	NOTE
1906	B10	Pellston–east	0–1.8	+1.8	1.8	5	
1914	X	Entire line	1.8–0	−1.8	0	5	23

OWNERSHIP

1906   Grand Rapids & Indiana Railway (B10), controlled by Pennsylvania Railroad

SOUTHERN DIV. (GR&I-R)

	MILEAGE	COUNTY	CROSSINGS, JUNCTIONS, ETC.
Richmond IN (via PRR)	0.0	Wayne IN	
Newman	0.3	"	J/PRR
Parry		"	
Chester	4.3	"	
Woodford		"	
Fountain City	8.9	"	
Lynn	15.3	Randolph IN	X/CCCSL
Snow Hill	18.6	"	
Woods	19.6	"	
Winchester	24.5	"	X/CCCSL
Stone	28.9	"	
Ridgeville	33.0	"	X/PRR
Collett	38.9	Jay IN	
Portland IN	43.2	"	X/NKP
Briant	50.3	"	
Geneva	54.2	Adams IN	
Berne	58.8	"	
Monroe	64.8	"	
(Crossing)	70.4	"	X/ER
Decatur	70.7	"	X/NKP
Williams	77.2	"	
Hoagland	79.6	Allen IN	
Adams	86.6	"	J/PRR
—via PRR—			
(Ft. Wyn. IN	91.9)	"	

CONSTRUCTION

DATE	ACT	END POINTS	MP	CHANGE	MI MAIN	SOURCE	NOTE
1870/7	B8	Richmond Jct.–Winchester	0.8–24.5	+23.7	0	2	3
1871/12/25	B8	Winchester–Adams	24.5–86.6	+62.1	0	2	2
1875 ca.	B8	Newman–Richmond Jct.	0.3–0.8	+0.5	0	4	

IN abandonments not shown

OWNERSHIP

1870	Cincinnati, Richmond & Fort Wayne (B8)
1871/6/1	Grand Rapids & Indiana Railroad, leased Cincinnati, Richmond & Fort Wayne
1874	Pennsylvania Railroad, control of Grand Rapids & Indiana
1896/7/7	Grand Rapids & Indiana Railway, reorganized GR&I Railroad (controlled by Pennsylvania)
1953/12/1	Penndel Co. (Pennsylvania Railroad holding co.), merged GR&I

ACQUISITION/DISPOSITION RECORD

DATE	ACT	GR&I–	END POINTS	CHANGE	MI MAIN	NOTE
1867/12/23	B1	N	Bridge St.–Cedar Springs	+20.1	20.1	5
1868	B1	N,S	Bridge St.–S. Yard	+2.4	22.5	1
1869/6/21	B1	N	Cedar Springs–Morley	+19.2	41.7	
1870/6/22	B1	S	Jct.–Sturgis (MI=2.7 miles)	+55.8		2
8	B1	S	Sturgis–Kal.	+36.3		
8/12	B1	N	Morley–Paris	+21.0		
9/13	B1	S	Kal.–S. Yard	+47.3	149.0	
1871	L	R	Richmond Jct.–Adams	+85.8		2,3,24
/12	B1	N	Paris–Cadillac	+36.4	185.4	
1872/9	B1	N	Cadillac–Fife Lk.	+26.0		
11/15	B5	T	Walton Jct.–Trav. Cty.	+26.0	237.4	8
1874/5	B1	N	Fife Lk.–Petoskey	+67.0	304.4	6
1876/8	B1	N	Petoskey–Bay View	+1.0	305.4	
1882/2/1	B2	N,H	Bay View–Harbor Springs	+7.0		
7/3	B3	N	Kegomic–Mackinaw City	+32.9		7
	B1	K,K2	Missaukee Jct.–Jennings	+7.6		
	B1	3	Milton Jct.–Carey	+14.5		
	B1	3C	Luther–Nasons	+5.0	372.4	
1883	B1	K1	Long Lk. Jct.–Long Lk.	+0.8		15
	B1	3A	Lk. Jct.–Pelton	+7.0	380.2	
1885	B1	2	Osceola Jct.–Olga	+7.0	387.2	
1886/2	B1	8	Austin Lk.–Long Lk.	+0.8		20
12/1	B4	M	Musk. Jct.–Musk. (Dock)	+36.9	424.9	
1889	X	K1	Long Lk. Jct.–Long Lk.	−0.8		
	X	3C	Luther–Nasons	−5.0	419.1	
1890	B1	K,K3	Round Lk. Jct.–Lk. City	+7.5		10
	B1	YG	Plaster Creek Jct.–Bartlett St.	(+3.9)		
	B6	4	Stimson Jct.–Vincent	+8.9		17
	X	K2	Jennings–east	−0.5	435.0	
1891	B1	3B	Haaks Spur Jct.–Haaks Mill	+4.1	439.1	
1892/6	B1	5	Walloon Lk.–Bear Lk.	+1.1		
	B1	2	Osceola Br. Extension	+2.8	443.0	
1894	B1	K	Sandstown–MP 16	+5.4		11
	B1	K4	Veneer Jct.–Herrick	+1.6		
	X	3A	Lk. Jct.–Pelton	−7.0	443.0	16
1896	X	4	Vincent–Merrits	−3.1	439.9	
1897	X	2	Osceola Br. Extension	−2.8	437.1	
1898	B7	K4A	Herrick–east	+3.4	440.5	13
1899	X	4	Stimson Jct.–Merrits	−5.8	434.7	
1900	B10	M2	Ravenna–Slocums Grove	+3.8		
	B10	K4A	Herrick–east extension	+3.2		
	X	3	Carey–M&GR Crossing	−1.4		
	X	3B	Haaks Spur Jct.–Haaks Mill	−4.1	436.2	
1901	B10	7	Pellston–Bogardus	+4.0		
	B10	H	Harbor Springs–north	+0.5	440.7	
1904	X	2	Olga–Sutliff	−3.1		
	X	3	Milton Jct.–west	−13.1		
	X	H	Harbor Springs–north	−0.4	424.1	
1905	B10	9	Antrim–east	+1.8		
	B10	10	Thelma–east	+4.5		
	B10	11	Formans–north	+1.3	431.7	
1906	B10	K,K5	MP 16–Missaukee City	+5.9		12

	X	2	Sutliff–MP 0.4	–3.5		
	B10	12	Pellston–east	+1.8		
	X	M2	Ravenna–Slocums Grove	–3.8	432.1	
1907	X	2	Osceola Jct.–MP 0.4	–0.4	431.7	
1908	B10	K4	Herrick–Falmouth	+3.0		
	X	K4A	Herrick–east	–6.6		
	B10	11	Formans–north	+0.1	428.2	
1909	B10	K	Ardis Jct.–Michelson	+12.8		
	B10	K5	Missaukee City–north	+1.1		
	X	T	N end of line	–0.1		
	X	9	Antrim–east	–1.8		21
	B10	10	Thelma–east extension	+1.3	441.5	21
1910	X	7	Pellston–Bogardus	–4.0		19
	X	5	In Walloon Lk. (old)	–0.1	437.4	
1913	X	K5	Ardis Jct.–Missaukee City	–3.9		14
	X	H	North of Harbor Springs	–0.1		
	X	10	Thelma–east	–5.8	427.6	22
1914	X	8	Austin Lk.–Long Lk.	–0.8		
	X	12	Pellston–east	–1.8	425.0	23
1917	X	11	Formans–north	–1.4	423.6	
1918	B10	K3	In Lk. City	+0.2		
	X	K	In Michelson	–0.3	423.5	
1927	X	K2	Round Lk. Jct.–Jennings	–3.0	420.5	
1928	X	5	Walloon Lk.–Bear Lk.	–1.0	419.5	
1929	B10	YM	Musk. Heights Branch	(+1.3)	419.5	
1930	X	K	Michelson–Merritt	–6.0		
	X	M	In Musk.	–0.2	413.3	
1938	X	K	Veneer Jct.–Merritt	–10.3	403.0	
1961	X	M	Kinney–Walker	–2.6		
	Y	M	Musk. Jct.–Kinney (to Y1M)	(4.8)	395.6	
1962	X	H	Kegomic–Harbor Springs	–5.8	389.8	
1964	S4	K	Missaukee Jct.–Veneer Jct.	[15.3]		25
	S4	K3	Sandstown–Lk. City	[1.2]		25
	S4	K4	Veneer Jct.–Falmouth	[4.6]	368.7	25

On 1 February 1968 this company was conveyed to Penn Central.

1976	X	[GR&I-T]	In Trav. Cty. 25.2–26.0	–0.8	367.9

On 1 April 1976 part of this company was conveyed to Grand Trunk Western, part to Conrail, and part retained by the trustees of Penn Central. The lines were:

LINE DESIG.	END POINTS	MP	MI MAIN	SOURCE	NOTE
CNR-[GR&I-S]	In Sturgis	146.4–150.6	4.2		
PC-[GR&I-S]	N. Sturgis–Vicksburg	150.6–173.0	22.4		
CNR-[GR&I-S]	Vicksburg–Gr. Rpds.	173.0–234.0	61.0		
CNR-[GR&I-YG]	Plaster Creek Branch	3.1+0.8	(3.9)		
CNR-[GR&I-Y1M]	Musk. Jct.–Kinney	2.6–7.4	(4.8)		
GTW-[GR&I-M]	Walker–Musk.	10.0–39.3	29.3		
GTW-[GR&I-YM]	Musk. Heights Branch	38.0–39.3	(1.3)		
CNR-[GR&I-N]	Gr. Rpds.–Comstock Park	234.0–239.5	5.5		
PC-[GR&I-N]	Comstock Park–Mack. Cty.	239.5–459.8	220.3		
PC-[GR&I-T]	Walton Jct.–Trav. Cty.	0–25.2	25.2		
1976/4/1	TOTAL CNR=70.7 GTW=267.9 PC=297.2 GR&I=367.9				

DATE	ACT	XXX– END POINTS	MP	CHANGE	NOTE
1976	Y	CNR-[GR&I-S] In Sturgis (to GR&I-Y1S)	146.4–150.6	(4.2)	
	X	PC-[GR&I-S] Nottawa–Wasepi	157.9–159.4	–1.5	
1976	TOTAL	CNR=66.5 GTW=29.3 MICH=0 PC=266.4 GR&I=362.2			
1977	S1	PC-[GR&I-S]In Vicksburg	171.9–173.0	[1.1]	
	Y	GTW-[GR&I-S] In Vicksburg	171.9–173.0	[(1.1)]	
	X	PC-[GR&I-S] Mendon–Vicksburg	164.1–171.9	–7.8	
1977	TOTAL	CNR=66.5 GTW=29.3 MICH=0 PC=257.5 GR&I=353.3			
1982	X	CNR-[GR&I-S] Vicksburg–Upjohn	173.0–178.5	–5.5	
	Y	CNR-[GR&I-S](to Y2S) Upjohn–Kal.	178.5–185.1	(6.6)	
	X	CNR-[GR&I-Y1M] In Gr. Rpds.	2.6–7.4	(–4.8)	
	X	PC-[GR&I-S] N. Sturgis–Nottawa	150.6–157.9	–7.3	
	X	PC-[GR&I-S] Wasepi–Mendon	159.4–164.1	–4.7	
1982	TOTAL	CNR=54.4 GTW=29.3 MICH=0 PC=245.5 GR&I=329.2			
1984/2/15	S3	PC-[GR&I-N] Comstock Park–Bay View	239.5–426.0	[186.5]	
2/15	S3	PC-[GR&I-T] Walton Jct.–Trav. Cty.	0–25.2	[25.2]	
1984	TOTAL	CNR=54.4 GTW=29.3 MICH=211. PC=33.8 GR&I=329.2			
1985	X	CNR-[GR&I-S] Second Ave.–Gr. Rpds.	233.2–234.0	–0.8	
	X	CNR-[GR&I-N] Gr. Rpds.–Winter St.	234.0–234.7	–0.7	
1985	TOTAL	CNR=52.9 GTW=29. MICH=211.7 PC=33.8 GR&I=327.7			
1987/9/4	S5	GTW-[GR&I-M] Walker–Musk.	10.0–39.3	[29.3]	
9/4	S5	GTW-[GR&I-YM] In Musk.	38.0–39.3	[(1.3)]	
ca.	X	MICH-[GR&I-N] In Cadillac	331.5–332.5	[–1.0]	
ca.	Y	MICH-[GR&I-N] N. Yard south	332.5–333.1	[(0.6)]	
		CMGN=29.3 CNR=52.9 MICH=210.1 PC=33.8 GR&I=326.1			
1988 ca.	X	PC-[GR&I-N] Mack. City–Alanson	434.9–459.8	–24.9	9
	L	PC-[GR&I-N] Petoskey–Alanson	426.0–434.9	–8.9	9
1988	TOTAL	CMGN=29.3 CNR=52.9 MICH=210.1 PC=8.9 GR&I=301.2			
1989	X	CMGN-[GR&I-M] Walker–Musk.	10.0–39.3	[–29.3]	
	X	CMGN-[GR&I-YM] In Musk.	38.0–39.3	[(–1.3)]	
1988	TOTAL	CMGN=0 CNR=52.9 MICH=210.1 PC=8.9 GR&I=271.9			
1991	X	MICH-[GR&I-N] Comstock Park–Cadillac	239.5–331.5	[–92.0]	
1991	TOTAL	CMGN=0 CNR=52.9 MICH=118.1 PC=8.9 GR&I=179.9			
1992 ca.	XL	PC-[GR&I-N] Petoskey–Alanson	426.0–434.9	+8.9	
	X	PC-[GR&I-N] Petoskey–Alanson	426.0–434.9	–8.9	
1992	TOTAL	CNR=52.9 MICH=118.1 PC=0 GR&I=171.0			
1993/12	S3	CNR-[GR&I-Y1S] In Sturgis	146.4–150.6	[(4.2)]	
1993	TOTAL	CNR=52.9 MICH=118.1 PC=0 GR&I=171.0			

On 1 June 1999 52.9 miles of Conrail main line was conveyed to Norfolk Southern.

Act Column Key

A   Adjust mileage

B   Built by Grand Rapids & Indiana

B2   Built by Bay View, Little Traverse & Mackinaw

B3   Built by Grand Rapids, Indiana & Mackinaw
B4   Built by Muskegon, Grand Rapids & Indiana
B5   Built by Traverse City
B6   Built by Big Rapids & Western
B7   Built by Widdicomb Furniture
B8   Built by Cincinnati, Richmond & Fort Wayne
B9   Built by D A Blodgett & Co
 L   Leased from Cincinnati, Richmond & Fort Wayne
 P   Purchase
S1   Sold to Grand Trunk Western
S2   Sold to Michigan Southern
S3   Sold to State of Michigan
S4   Sold to Cadillac & Lake City
S5   Sold to Central Michigan
 X   Abandoned
 Y   Yard track

Sources

1. Baxter, *Grand Rapids.*
2. ICC, *Valuation Docket 351.*
3. Michigan, Commissioner of Railroads, *Annual Reports,* 1873, 1876, 1890.
4. MDOT office records.
5. Michigan Railroad Commission, *Aids, Gifts, Grants.*
6. Page, *The Traverse Region.*
7. Pennsylvania Railroad, letter to Michigan Tax Commissioner, 15 March 1943.

Notes

1. The southern terminus is given as South Grand Rapids. The location named here is based on mileage shown constructed.
2. Mileage does not include trackage rights mileage to reach Fort Wayne.
3. Mileage does not include trackage rights mileage to reach Richmond.
4. This construction is not separately identified but appears necessary to derive total line mileage. Date of construction is not known.
5. Source 7 gives southern terminus as Bridge Street and completion date as 25 December 1867; mileage shown is to that point. Source 5 gives 20.9 miles built; Source 7 gives 21.1 miles built.
6. Sources 1 and 7 give completion date as 25 November 1873.
7. Mileage is to connection with Michigan Central Railroad, 0.1 mile north of Mackinaw City.
8. Source 5 gives date as December 1872.
9. In about 1930 trackage rights were arranged over Grand Trunk Western west of Shaw and passenger trains began using the GTW station at Peck Street; the use of the Pere Marquette station was discontinued at the same time.
10. Source 7 gives date as 1880.
11. Records are unclear in locating the construction received from D. A. Blodgett & Co. but no records show if constructed before the date shown.
12. This construction is assumed, given the construction shown for the Missaukee City Branch (GR&I-K5).
13. This section was obtained from Widdicomb Furniture Co. in 1898 but no records show if construction was before that year.
14. Source 7 gives date as 1912.
15. There is some uncertainty about this construction. Sources 5 and 3 are the source of this data. It may be that this line is confused with the nearly contemporaneous construction of line GR&I-8.
16. Source 7 gives date as 1895.
17. Line owned by Big Rapids & Western, wholly-owned by GR&I after 1888. Source 7 gives construction date as 1889.
18. Source 7 gives date as 1900.

19. Source 7 gives date as 1909.
20. See Note 15 applying to line GR&I-K1. Sources 5 and 7 give date as 1905.
21. Source 7 gives date as 1908.
22. Source 7 gives data as –1.1 miles in 1911 and –4.7 miles in 1912.
23. Source 7 gives date as 1913.
24. Mileage is not included in cumulative totals.
25. Sold to Cadillac & Lake City.
26. Sold to Grand Trunk Western.

Grand Rapids Eastern

In July 1993 this company acquired part of Central Michigan. The lines acquired were:

LINE DESIG.	END POINTS	MP	MI MAIN	SOURCE
GRE-				
GTW-D	Ionia–Fuller	123.5–159.7	36.2	
GTW-YGR	In Gr. Rpds.	0–1.4	(1.4)	
GTW-[PM-Y1]	In Ionia	0–1.2	(1.2)	
		TOTAL	36.2	

OWNERSHIP
1993   Grand Rapids Eastern

Grand Trunk Western

	INDEX	PAGE
GTW-		
A	M. A. L. (Richmond–Jackson)	215–16
B	Cass City–Bad Axe	210–11
C	Chicago Div. (Chicago–Port Huron)	198–203
C+	Original main lines, Chicago Div.	203–5
D	Detroit Div. (Detroit–Grand Haven)	206–8
D+	Original main lines, Detroit Div.	208–9
D+	Spurs off Detroit Div. main line	209–10, 218
H	West Detroit–Port Huron	214–15
K	Kalamazoo Branch	219
M	Ashley–Muskegon, plus spur	216–17
MR	Muskegon Railway & Navigation Co	218
P	Pontiac–Caseville	211–12
S	Saginaw Branch, also spurs	212–13
Z	St. Clair Tunnel	203
YF	Old main line–Flint	205
YK	Kalamazoo yard	219

CHICAGO DIV. (GTW-C)

	MILEAGE	COUNTY	CROSSINGS, JUNCTIONS, ETC.
Chi. (via C&WI)	0.0	Cook IL	
Archer Ave. (via C&WI)		"	
39th St. (via C&WI)		"	
41st St. (via C&WI)		"	
47th St. (via C&WI)	4.60	"	
C&WI Jct.	4.85	"	J/C&WI 4.9
Halsted St.	5.12	"	(old 5.17)

Racine Ave.	5.62	"	f. Centre Ave.
Ashland Ave.	6.12	"	
Oakley Ave.	7.0	"	
Western Ave.	7.06	"	
Morrell Park	8.15	"	
Elsdon Jct.	8.6	"	J/GTW-CA 3.9
Elsdon	8.79	"	
Glendale	9.27	"	
59th St.	9.78	"	
Chi. Lawn	10.31	"	
67th St.		"	
Marq. Park	11.28	"	
McCaffrey	11.30	"	
Hayford	11.79	"	X/BRC
Clarkdale		"	
Ashburn	12.80	"	X/Wabash
Ste. Maria	13.68	"	(old 13.43)
Evergreen Park	14.47	"	
Tracy Ave.	15.52	"	
Mt. Greenwood	16.52	"	
Mt. Hope	17.05	"	(old 17.28)
Clifton		"	
Oak Hill	17.55	"	
Brick Yard		"	
Lincoln Cemetery	18.05	"	
Wireton	18.55	"	
York St.	19.00	"	
Blue Island (2nd)	19.51	"	X/CRI&P
Blue Island (1st)	19.66	"	
Blue Island (3rd)	20.2	"	
Posen	20.81	"	
W. Harvey	22.19	"	
(Crossing)	23.1	"	X/B&OCT
Harvey	23.17	"	B/IC
Thornton Jct.	25.20	"	X/C&EI
Oak Glen IL	28.63	"	
(Line IL/IN)	30.6		
(Crossing) IN	31.3	Lk. IN	X/CI&L
Munster	31.4	"	
Maynard	31.56	"	X/PRR
Hays	33.97	"	X/CI&S
Griffith	36.08	"	X/EJ&E, X/MC-J,X/C&O,X/ER
Bothwells	38.76	"	
Lottaville	39.62	"	
Turkey Creek	41.24	"	
Atkins	41.97	"	
Adams	43.29	"	
Pierces	44.35	"	
Ainsworth	45.20	"	
Smalls	48.29	Porter IN	
Springmans Crossing	48.93	"	
Sedley	50.34	"	
Sommers	52.24	"	
(Crossing)	52.6	"	X/NKP
Ft. Wyn. Crossing	52.69	"	X/PRR

Valparaiso	55.80	"	J/GTW-CO4 0
Haskells	63.89	LaPorte IN	X/CI&L
Union Mills	70.14	"	
Wellsboro	71.08	"	X/B&O, X/PM
Kingsbury	74.82	"	B/WAB (old 75.05)
Stillwell	80.17	"	X/NKP
Swifts	83.31	"	
Mill Creek	84.51	"	
Crumstown	91.57	St.Joseph IN	f.Crums Point
Vandalia Jct.	97.5	"	X/NYC, J/NJI&I, J/PRR
I.I.& I.Jct.	99.0	"	J/NYC
Olivers	99.16	"	
Arnold St.	99.52	"	X/NYC, J/GTW-CO2 99.5
(S. Bend (via NYC)	100.19	"	
High St.	101.09	"	J/NYC
(Greenlawn Ave.)	102.4	"	J/GTW-CO2 102.1
——————————(Mileage east is via GTW-CO2)			
(Greenlawn Ave.)	102.1	"	
Mishawaka	104.03	"	
(Jct.)	104.1	"	J/NYC-E&WBr
Granger IN	110.88	"	
(Line IN/MI)	111.1		
Edwardsburg	113.97	Cass	
Jefferson	117.1	"	
(Crossing)	122.66	"	X/MC-A 90.3
Cassopolis	122.90	"	
Penn	127.25	"	f. Jamestown
Wakelee	131.46	"	f. Volinia
Cross Bank	134.2	"	
Marcellus	135.77	"	
Chamberlains	140.29	Kal.	f. Leesburg
Schoolcraft	146.77	"	X/LS-G 23.0
Harborlite	150.2	"	
Ice Siding	151	"	
Vicksburg	152.23	"	X/GR&I-S 173.0, f. Brady
Indian Lk.	154.79	"	
Pavilion	157.20	"	J/GTW-K 0
Scotts	160.14	"	
Climax	164.98	"	
Renton	169.34	Calhoun	(old 169.13)
(Jct.)	169.4	"	J/GTW-CO3 169.4
Airport	172.0	"	
(Jct.)	174.8	"	J/GTW-CO3 174.4
(Kendall St.)	175.1	"	B/BCCL-8 0.81
Gord	175.5	"	J/MC-C 121.4
(Crossing)	175.6	"	X/DTM 91.2
Depot (Amtrak sta.)	175.8	"	
Battle Creek (old sta.)	175.8	"	
(Capital Ave.)	175.8	"	X/BCCL-5 0.27
Rose	175.9	"	
(Jct.)	176.5	"	J/MC-K 1.1
(Main St.)	176.6	"	X/BCCL-4 0.45
Battle Creek	176.64	"	
(Elm St.)	176.7	"	J/MC-K 0.9
Baron	176.7	"	J/MC-C 119.6+0.2

Nichols	176.87	"	X/MC-C 119.7
(Michigan Ave.)	176.9	"	X/BCCL-1 0.88
Nichols Yard	177.30	"	
Emmett St.	178.6	"	
Battle Creek Yard	179.2	"	
McAllister Rd.	181.2	"	
Penfield	182.50	"	
Madisons	185	"	
Lime Siding	188.2	Eaton	
Bellevue	189.20	"	
State Rd.	191.8	"	
Olivet	194.34	"	
Alperos	?	"	
Shepards	196.6	"	f. Moores
Wallis	200	"	
Charlotte	202.41	"	X/MC-G 35.0
Potterville	208.70	"	
Sevastapol	210.4	"	
Mill	214.8	"	
Millett	216.20	"	
Lans. (2nd)	216.8	"	
Hope	217.6	"	
(Waverly Rd.)	218.0	Ingham	X/LACL-4 2.47
(Jct.)	219.5	"	J/MC-YLM 5.4
Washington St.	220.8	"	X/LACL-1 1.01
Lans.	220.94	"	
(Crossing)	221.2	"	X/LS-L 58.7
(Crossing)	221.4	"	X/MC-S 35.9
Cedar	221.5	"	
(Pennsylvania Ave.)	221.5	"	B/LACL-8 1.16
Trowbridge	223.51	"	X/PM-D 84.8,f.Chi. Jct.
E. Lans.	223.9	"	
Meridian	226-1/2	"	
Haslett	229.04	"	f. Haslett Park
Woodhull	?	Shiawassee	
Shaftsburg	235.70	"	
Perry	240.02	"	
Morrice	242.19	"	
Bancroft	248.47	"	
Durand	253.29	"	X/GTW-D 67.0, J/GTW-S 0, X/AA-A 95.5
E. Durand	255.4	"	
Duffield	257.23	Genesee	
Crapo	258.2	"	
Crapo Farm	259.79	"	
Swartz Creek	261.46	"	
Mundy	262.65	"	J/GTW-YF 262.7
W. Flint	263.8	"	
Torrey	267.2	"	(old 267.01)
(Bridge)	269.3	"	B/PM-T 34.6
(Sag. St.)	270.05	"	B/FLCL-1 1.61
Flint	270.10	"	f. S. Flint
(Crossing)	271.8	"	X/PM-FB 33.6
Jct.	273.2	"	J/GTW-YF 273.7

————————————(Mileage east is via GTW-YF)

(Jct.)	273.7	"	
Belsay Yard	274.23	"	
Belsay	275.3	"	
E. Flint	276.7	"	
Davison	279.24	"	
Potters Lk.	282.64	Lapeer	
Elba	283.23	"	
Oaklet	286.8	"	f. Nepessing
W. Lapeer	287.0	"	
Mich. Home Siding	287.97	"	
E. Lapeer	289.2	"	
Lapeer	290.02	"	X/MC-B 59.8
Attica	297.28	"	
Stanley Pit	300	"	
(Bridge)	301.8	"	B/GTW-P 44.2
Imlay City	301.96	"	
W. Imlay City	302.1	"	
E. Imlay City	304.5	"	
Capac Peat Siding	306.48	St.Clair	f. Paper Plant
Capac	309.34	"	
W. Emmett	316.4	"	
Emmett	317.88	"	
E. Emmett	319.2	"	
Goodells	322.93	"	
Sanborn	323-3/4	"	
Sunnyside	325.52	"	f. Thornton
Cornell	327-3/4	"	
W. Tappan	329.0	"	
(Crossing)	331.8	"	X/PM-Q 85.8
Tappan	332.11	"	X/GTW-H 55.6, J/DCS 97.9
Tunnel Yard	333.42	"	J/PHD 0.6
Pt. Hur.	333.92	"	
Pt. Hur. (Amtrak sta.)	334.2	"	
16th St.	334.3	"	J/GTW-Z
(Military St.)	335.1	"	X/PHCL-1 0.69
(Griswold St.)	335.5	"	J/conn. to PM-Q 89.6, .01 mi.
Court St.	335.8	"	

CONSTRUCTION

DATE	ACT	END POINTS	MP	CHANGE	MI MAIN	SOURCE	NOTE
1869/11	B4	Court St.–Emmett	335.5–317.9	+17.6	17.6	5	
1870/1/1	B6	Battle Creek–Bellevue	175.8–189.2	+13.4		5	7
2/14	B6	Bellevue–Charlotte	189.2–202.4	+13.2		5	
6/8	B4	Emmett–Capac	317.9–309.3	+8.6		5	
6/13	B6	Charlotte–Lans.	202.4–220.9	+18.5		5	
7/28	B4	Capac–Imlay City	309.3–302.0	+7.3		5	
10/15	B6	Battle Creek–MP 174.8	175.8–174.8	+1.0		5	7
10/15	B6	MP 169.4–Climax	169.4–165.0	+4.4		5	
12	B4	Imlay City–Attica	302.0–297.3	+4.7	88.7	5	
1871/5/25	B4	Attica–Davison	297.3–279.2	+18.1		5	
6	B6	Climax–Cassopolis	165.0–122.9	+42.1			
12/13	B4	Davison–MP 273.7	279.2–273.7	+5.5	154.4	5	
1872/Aut.	B6	Cassopolis–MP 102.1	122.9–102.1	+20.8	166.2	5	
1873/10/13	B6	MP 99.5–Valparaiso	99.5–55.8	+43.7	166.2	2	

1876	B8	Elsdon Jct.–Thornton Jct.	8.6–25.2	+16.6	166.2	3	
1877/1/1	B7	Lans.–Mundy	220.9–262.7	+41.8	208.0	2	
1879/12	B9	Thornton Jct.–Valparaiso	25.2–55.8	+30.6	208.0	3	
1881	B11	Elsdon Jct.–C&WI Jct.	4.9–8.6	+3.7	208.0	3	11
1892	Y	In Pt. Hur. (to GTW-YCP)	335.5–334.3	(1.2)	206.8		13
1904	B16	West of Battle Creek	169.4–174.8	+5.4	212.2	2	
1927	B16	Mundy–S. Flint–Belsay	262.7–273.2	+10.5	222.7		
1929	B22	High St.–MP 102	101.1–102.4	+1.3	222.7		21

OWNERSHIP

1869	Port Huron & Lake Michigan (B4)
1870	Peninsular (B6)
1876	Chicago & Southern (B8)
1877	Chicago & Northeastern (B7)
1878/7/30	Chicago & Lake Huron, merger of Port Huron & Lake Michigan and Peninsular
1878/8/5	Chicago & State Line, bought Chicago & Southern
1879	North Western Grand Trunk (B9)
1880/4/6	Chicago & Grand Trunk, merger of Chicago & Huron, Chicago & State Line, Chicago & Northeastern, and North Western Grand Trunk; control by Grand Trunk Railway of Canada
1881	Grand Trunk Junction (B11)
1900/11/20	Grand Trunk Western Railway (B16), reorganization of Chicago & Grand Trunk
1928/11/1	Grand Trunk Western Railroad (B22), merger of Grand Trunk Western Railway
1930/11/30	Grand Trunk Western Railroad, merger of Grand Trunk Junction

ST. CLAIR TUNNEL (GTW-Z)

	MILEAGE [Chicago]	COUNTY	CROSSINGS, JUNCTIONS, ETC.
16th St.	334.3	St.Clair	J/GTW-C 334.3
(Bridge)	335.0	"	B/PHCL-1 0.52
(Intern'l boundary)	335.4		

CONSTRUCTION

DATE	ACT	END POINTS	MP	CHANGE	MI MAIN	SOURCE	NOTE
1891/10/24	B15	16th St.–Can. boundary	334.3–335.4	+1.1	1.1	5	12

1998 a new St. Clair tunnel was completed and replaced the previous tunnel without a change in mileage

OWNERSHIP

| 1891 | St. Clair Tunnel Co. (B15), controlled by Grand Trunk Railway of Canada |
| 1958/3/31 | Canadian National Railway, merger of St. Clair Tunnel Co. |

OLD MAIN LINE IN CHICAGO (GTW-CA)

	MILEAGE	COUNTY	CROSSINGS, JUNCTIONS, ETC.
26th St. IL	0	Cook IL	
Elsdon Jct.	3.9	"	J/GTW-C 8.6

CONSTRUCTION

DATE	ACT	END POINTS	MP	CHANGE	MI MAIN	SOURCE	NOTE
1876	B8	Line	0–3.9	+3.9	0	3	
1887/7/20	S1	Line	0–3.9	–3.9	0	3	

OWNERSHIP

1876	Chicago & Southern (B8)
1878/8/5	Chicago & State Line, bought Chicago & Southern
1880/4/6	Chicago & Grand Trunk, merger of Chicago & State Line

OLD MAIN LINE IN SOUTH BEND (GTW-CO2)

	MILEAGE [Chi.]	COUNTY	CROSSINGS, JUNCTIONS, ETC.
Arnold St. IN	99.52	St.Joseph IN	J/GTW-C 99.5
S. Bend (orig. depot)	100.46	"	
(Greenlawn Ave.)	102.1	"	J/GTW-C 102.4

CONSTRUCTION

DATE	ACT	END POINTS	MP	CHANGE	MI MAIN	SOURCE	NOTE
1872/Fall	B6	Greenlawn Ave.–S. Bend	102.1–100.5	+1.6	0	5	9
1873/10/13	B6	S. Bend–Arnold St.	100.5–99.5	+1.0	0		9
1929	X	Line	99.5–102.1	–2.6	0		20

OWNERSHIP

1872	Peninsular (B6)
1878/7/30	Chicago & Lake Huron, merger of Peninsular
1880/4/6	Chicago & Grand Trunk, merger of Chicago & Lake Huron
1900/11/20	Grand Trunk Western Railway, reorganization of Chicago & Grand Trunk
1928/11/1	Grand Trunk Western Railroad, merger of Grand Trunk Western Railway

OLD MAIN LINE IN BATTLE CREEK (GTW-CO3)

	MILEAGE [Chicago]	COUNTY	CROSSINGS, JUNCTIONS, ETC.
(Jct.)	169.4	Calhoun	J/GTW-C 169.4
Helmers	171.5	"	
(Jct.)	174.4	"	J/GTW-C 174.8

CONSTRUCTION

DATE	ACT	END POINTS	MP	CHANGE	MAIN	SOURCE	NOTE
1870/10/15	B6	Line	169.4–174.4	+5.0	5.0	5	
1904	X	West end of line	169.4–173.9	–4.5		2	14
1904	Y	East end of line(to GTW-YB)	173.9–174.4	(0.5)	0		14
1998	X	Line (GTW-YB)	173.9–174.4	(–0.5)	0		

OWNERSHIP

1872	Peninsular (B6)
1878/7/30	Chicago & Lake Huron, merger of Peninsular
1880/4/6	Chicago & Grand Trunk, merger of Chicago & Lake Huron
1900/11/20	Grand Trunk Western Railway, reorganization of Chicago & Grand Trunk
1928/11/1	Grand Trunk Western Railroad, merger of Grand Trunk Western Railway

OLD MAIN LINE IN VALPARAISO (GTW-CO4)

	MILEAGE	COUNTY	CROSSINGS, JUNCTIONS, ETC.
Valparaiso IN	0	Porter IN	J/GTW-C 55.8
(Jct.)	1.1	"	J/PRR

CONSTRUCTION

DATE	ACT	END POINTS	MP	CHANGE	MI MAIN	SOURCE	NOTE
1873/10/13	B6	Line	0–1.1	+1.1	0		
1879	X	Line	0–1.1	–1.1	0		

OWNERSHIP

1872	Peninsular (B6)
1878/7/30	Chicago & Lake Huron, merger of Peninsular

OLD MAIN LINE IN FLINT (GTW-CF)(LATER GTW-YF)

	MILEAGE	COUNTY	CROSSINGS, JUNCTIONS, ETC.
	[Chicago]		
Mundy	262.65	Genesee	J/GTW-C 262.7
Otterburn	264.04	"	
(Crossing)	270.0	"	X/PM-T 33.3
(Sag. St.)	270.1	"	X/FLCL-1 2.81
N. Flint	270.19	"	(orig. Flint sta.)
Crapo St.	270.7	"	X/FLCL-4 0.99
Kearsley	272.5	"	X/PM-FB 32.9
(Jct.)	273.7	"	J/GTW-C 273.2

CONSTRUCTION

DATE	ACT	END POINTS	MP	CHANGE	MAIN	SOURCE	NOTE
1871/12/13	B4	MP 273.7–N. Flint	273.7–270.2	+3.5	3.5	5	8
1877/1/1	B7	N. Flint–Mundy	270.2–262.7	+7.5	11.0	2	8
1927	Y	Mundy–Belsay (to GTW-YF)	262.7–273.7	(11.0)	0		17
1980 ca.	X	In Flint	270.7–169.9	(–0.8)	0		

OWNERSHIP

1871	Port Huron & Lake Michigan (B4)
1877	Chicago & Northeastern (B7)
1878/7/30	Chicago & Lake Huron, merger of Port Huron & Lake Michigan
1880/4/6	Chicago & Grand Trunk, merger of Chicago & Lake Huron and Chicago Grand Trunk, controlled by Grand Trunk Railway of Canada
1900/11/20	Grand Trunk Western Railway, reorganization of Chicago & Grand Trunk
1928/11/1	Grand Trunk Western Railroad, merger of Grand Trunk Western Railway

DETROIT DIV. (GTW-D)

	MILEAGE	COUNTY	CROSSINGS, JUNCTIONS, ETC.
Det. (Brush St.)	0.0	Wayne	
Det. (new)	0.3	"	
(Connection)	0.7	"	C/MC-YDM 1.3
Jefferson Ave.	0.9	"	B/DSR-J 1.96
(Congress St.)	0.92	"	X/DSR-FC 1.01
(Fort St.)	0.98	"	X/DSR-FC 3.21
(Lafayette St.)	1.05	"	X/DSR-MLA 0.83
(Monroe St.)	1.12	"	B/DSR-ML 0.83
(Madison (Macomb) St.)	1.18	"	B/DSR-F 6.68
(Sherman St.)	1.55	"	B/DSR-F3 0.50
Gratiot Ave.	1.73	"	J/GTW-DD 0, B/DSR-G 1.41
(Mack Ave.)	2.2	"	B/DSR-C 5.55
(Forest Ave.)	2.9	"	X/DSR-X 4.14
Lk. Shore Jct.	3.31	"	J/LS-D 3.2
(Milw. Ave.)	3.9	"	X/DSR-CM 6.16

Boulevard Switch	4.06	"	
Milw. Jct.	4.13	"	X/GTW-H 4.6, X/MC-B 6.7
Clay Ave.	4.25	"	
Kenwood	5.5	"	
Chrysler Center	6.1	"	
Highland Park	6.58	"	f. Jerome Park
(Davison Ave.)	6.6	"	X/DSR-DE 1.12
Ford Jct.	7.21	"	X/DT-A 9.3
(Crossing)	7.9	"	X/DUR-Q 1.0
Masson	8.0	"	f. 8-Mile Siding
Statefair	9.25	"	
Ferndale	10.89	Oakland	f. Urbanrest
Pleasant Ridge	11.97	"	
(Crossing)	13.13	"	X/DUR-F 0.10
Royal Oak	13.18	"	J/GTW-DO 13.2
Oakwood Blvd.	14.32	"	
Birmingham	17.75	"	
Charing Cross	19.90	"	
Bloomfield Hills	21.24	"	
A	21.24	"	J/GTW-DO 21.5
Belt Line	22.64	"	J/GTW-YP 8.9
S. Blvd.	24.27	"	X/POCL-4 0.19
Foote St.	24.62	"	
(Sag. St.)	24.7	"	X/POCL-1 0.29
M.A.L. Cross	25.23	"	X/GTW-A 35.3
(Huron St.)	26.0	"	X/POCL-3 0.25
Pontiac	26.06	"	

────────────(Mileage west is via GTW-DO)

Pontiac	26.34	Oakland	
(Jct.)	26.5	"	J/GTW-P 0.2
(Johnson St.)	26.85	"	X/POCL-2 0.79
(Jct.)	27.8	"	J/GTW-YDP 0
Pontiac Yard	27.9	"	J/GTW-YP 0
W. Pontiac	30.26	"	
Drayton Plains	31.14	"	
Waterford	33.29	"	
Windiate	34.37	"	
Clarkston	35.23	"	
Andersonville	38.54	"	f. Springfield
Davisburg	41.45	"	
(Crossing)	46.3	"	X/PM-T 85.1
Holly	46.49	"	
Fenton	50.74	"	
Paxton	53.63	Genesee	
Linden	55.29	"	
Gaines	62.63	"	
Pitt	65.5	Shiawassee	C/AA-A 93.9
(Crossing)	66.8	"	X/AA-A 95.2
Durand	66.97	"	X/GTW-C 253.3, J/GTW-S 0
Vernon	70.15	"	
(Jct.)	75.3	"	J/GTW-YDC 0
Corunna	75.52	"	
San	76.5	"	C/AA-A 104.8
(Washington St.)	78.5	"	X/MUR-NO 32.9
Owosso	78.52	"	

Owosso Jct.	79.17	"	X/MC-S 63.6, C/AA-B 107.8
Burton	84.33	"	f. Mungerville
Ovid	88.78	Clinton	
Shepardsville	91.49	"	
St. Johns	98.13	"	
Dallas	106.7	"	
Fowler	107.43	"	
Pewamo	112.79	Ionia	
Muir	117.73	"	
(Crossing)	123.8	"	X/PM-I 25.4
Ionia	124.16	"	
State Prison	125.48	"	
Gravel Pit	128.33	"	
Saranac	132.47	"	
Malta	138.95	Kent	X/PM-G 104.9
Lowell	139.38	"	f. Segwun (Segwan)
Ada	148.01	"	
Dewey	152.55	"	f. Saddleback Siding
Lafayette	157.00	"	
Gr. Rpds. (1st & 3rd.)	157.52	"	
Plainfield Ave.	157.6	"	X/GRCL-11 1.57
(Taylor St.)	158.0	"	X/GRCL-12 0.35
Terminal Jct.	158.21	"	J/GTW-DG 158.2
Fuller	158.85	"	X/GR&I-N 236.9, X/PM-P 3.0
Indian Creek	163.1	"	
Penn Jct.	165.29	Ottawa	B/GR&I-M 9.0, J/GTW-DM 0
Marne	166.57	"	
(Bridge)	168.2	"	B/GRGHM-A 9.0
Coopersville	172.58	"	
Dennison	175.6	"	
Nunica	179.45	"	X/PM-AO 19.9
Cemetery Crossing	184.8	"	
Spring Lk.	186.35	"	
(Drawbridge)	186.8	"	
(Jct.)	186.95	"	J/GTW-YGH 186.9
Ferrysburg	187.10	"	J/PM-A 44.8
(Drawbridge)	187.2	"	
(Jct.)	187.7	"	J/PM-A 44.2
Gr. Hav.	188.30	"	

CONSTRUCTION

DATE	ACT	END POINTS	MP	CHANGE	MAIN	SOURCE	NOTE
1838/7/21	B1	Jefferson Ave.–Royal Oak	0.9–13.2	+12.3	12.3	1	1
1843/7/4	B1	A–Pontiac	21.2–26.0	+4.8	17.1	1	4
1852	B1	Det.–Jefferson Ave.	0–0.9	+0.9	18.0	1	
1855/10/2	B2	Pontiac–Fenton	26.3–50.7	+24.4	42.4	5	
1856/7/1	B2	Fenton–Owosso	50.7–78.5	+27.8	70.2	5	
1857/1/14	B2	Owosso–St. Johns	78.5–98.1	+19.6		1	
8/12	B2	St. Johns–Ionia	98.1–124.2	+26.1	115.9	1	
1858/7/4	B2	Ionia–Gr. Rpds.	124.2–157.5	+33.3		1	5
8/30	B2	Gr. Rpds.–Spring Lk.	157.5–186.4	+28.9		1	
11/22	B2	Spring Lk.–MP 187.0	186.4–187.02	+0.6	178.7	5	6
1870/1/1	B2	MP 187.0–Gr. Hav.(new)	187.0–188.3	+1.3	180.0	7	
1931	B22	Royal Oak–Bloomfield Hills	13.2–21.2	+8.0	188.0	2	
1973	X	In Det.	0–0.2	–0.2	187.8	6	

DATE	ACT	END POINTS	MP	CHANGE	MAIN	SOURCE	NOTE
1977/7/6	X	Coopersville–Grand Haven	173.0–188.3	−15.3	172.5	6	28
1983	X	In Det.	0.2–0.6	−0.4	172.1		
1987/9/4	S6	Durand–Coopersville	67.0–173.0	[106.0]	66.1		
1989/12/14	S13	Marne–Coopersville	166.6–173.0	[6.4]	66.1		
1991	X	Owosso–Ionia	82.2–123.5	[−41.3]	66.1		
1993/7	S14	Ionia–Fuller	123.5–159.7	[36.2]	66.1		
1996	S13	Fuller–Marne	159.7–166.6	[6.9]	66.1		
1998	X	MP 0.6–Gratiot Ave.	0.6–1.7	−1.1			
1998/12/23	S9	Gratiot Ave.–Milw. Jct.	1.7–4.0	[2.3]	62.7		

OWNERSHIP

1838	Detroit & Pontiac (B1)
1855/4/19	Detroit & Milwaukee Railway (B2), merger of Detroit & Pontiac
1860/10/22	Detroit & Milwaukee Railroad, reorganization of Detroit & Milwaukee Railway
1878/10/28	Detroit, Grand Haven & Milwaukee, reorganization of Detroit & Milw. Railroad
1882/8/12	DGH&M controlled by Grand Trunk Railway of Canada
1928/11/1	Grand Trunk Western Railroad (B22), merger of DGH&M
1987/9/4	Central Michigan (S6), bought part of line
1989/12/14	Coopersville & Marne (S13), bought part of line from Central Michigan
1993/7	Grand Rapids Eastern (S14), bought part of line from Central Michigan
1998/12/13	Detroit Connecting Railroad (S9), bought part of line

OLD MAIN LINE (GTW-DO)

	MILEAGE [Det.]	COUNTY	CROSSINGS, JUNCTIONS, ETC.
Royal Oak	13.2	Oakland	J/GTW-D 13.2
Birmingham	18.4	"	
A	21.5	"	J/GTW-D 21.2

CONSTRUCTION

DATE	ACT	END POINTS	MP	CHANGE	MAIN	SOURCE	NOTE
1839/8/16	B1	Royal Oak–Birmingham	13.2–18.5	+5.3	5.3	1	2
1843/7/4	B1	Birmingham–A	18.5–21.5	+3.0	8.3	1	4
1931	X	Royal Oak–A	13.2–21.5	−8.3	0		22

OWNERSHIP

1839	Detroit & Pontiac (B1)
1855/4/19	Detroit & Milwaukee Railway, merger of Detroit & Pontiac
1860/10/22	Detroit & Milwaukee Railroad, reorganization of Detroit & Milwaukee Railway
1878/10/28	Detroit, Grand Haven & Milwaukee, reorganization of Detroit & Milw. Railroad
1882/8/12	DGH&M controlled by Grand Trunk Railway of Canada
1928/11/1	Grand Trunk Western Railroad, merger of DGH&M

IONIA SPUR (GTW-[PM-YI])

Purchased industrial line in Ionia: Pere Marquette line PM-I, 1.2 miles in length, which see.

DATE	ACT	END POINTS	MP	CHANGE	MAIN	SOURCE	NOTE
1983	P4	In Ionia	24.9–26.1	(+1.2)			
1987/9/4	S6	In Ionia	24.9–26.1	(−1.2)			
1993/7	S14	In Ionia	24.9–26.1	[(1.2)]			

ORIGINAL LINE TO DETROIT (GTW-DD)

	MILEAGE	COUNTY	CROSSINGS, JUNCTIONS, ETC.
Gratiot Ave.	0	Wayne	J/GTW-D 1.8
Det. (first station)	1.2	"	(Gratiot & Farmer)

CONSTRUCTION

DATE	ACT	END POINTS	MP	CHANGE	MAIN	SOURCE	NOTE
1842	B1	Line	0–1.2	+1.2	1.2	1	3
1852	X	Line	0–1.2	–1.2	0	1	

OWNERSHIP

1842   Detroit & Pontiac (B1)

GRAND RAPIDS TERMINAL (GTW-DG)(LATER GTW-YGR)

	MILEAGE [Detroit]	COUNTY	CROSSINGS, JUNCTIONS, ETC.
Terminal Jct.	158.21	Kent	J/GTW-D 158.2
Gr. Rpds. (2nd sta.)	159.72	"	

CONSTRUCTION

DATE	ACT	END POINTS	MP	CHANGE	MAIN	SOURCE	NOTE
1906/1	B18	Terminal Jct.–Gr. Rpds.	0–1.5	+1.5	1.5	2	15
1948	Y	Entire line (to GTW-YGR)	0–1.5	(1.4)	0	2	
1987/9/4	S6	Entire line	0–1.5	[(1.5)]	0		23
1993/7	S14	Entire line	0–1.5	[(1.5)]	0		

OWNERSHIP

1906	Grand Rapids Terminal Co (B18), controlled by Detroit, Grand Haven & Milwaukee
1928/11/1	Grand Trunk Western, merger of Grand Rapids Terminal
1987/9/4	Central Michigan (S6), bought line
1993/7	Grand Rapids Eastern (S14), bought line

ORIGINAL GRAND HAVEN LINE (GTW-DA)(LATER GTW-YGH)

	MILEAGE [Detroit]	COUNTY	CROSSINGS, JUNCTIONS, ETC.
(Jct.)	186.95	Ottawa	J/GTW-D 186.95
(Crossing)	187.1	"	X/PM-A 44.9
Grand Haven (original sta.)	188.77	"	

CONSTRUCTION

DATE	ACT	END POINTS	MP	CHANGE	MAIN	SOURCE	NOTE
1858/11/22	B2	MP 187.0–Gr. Hav.	187.0–188.8	+1.8	1.8	5	6
1870/8/15	Y	Line (To GTW-YGH)	187.0–188.8	(1.8)	0	7	
1935 ca.	X	W. end line	188.8–187.6	(–1.2)	0		
1940 ca.	X	Line	187.0–187.6	(–0.6)	0		

OWNERSHIP

1858	Detroit & Milwaukee Railroad (B2)
1878/10/28	Detroit, Grand Haven & Milwaukee, reorganization of Detroit & Milwaukee Railroad
1882/8/12	DGH&M controlled by Grand Trunk Railway of Canada
1928/11/1	Grand Trunk Western Railroad (B22), merger of DGH&M

PONTIAC BELT (GTW-YP)

	MILEAGE	COUNTY	CROSSINGS, JUNCTIONS, ETC.
(Jct.)	0.0	Oakland	J/GTW-D 26.9
P.O.N. Jct.	2.5	"	X/GTW-P 2.6
MAL Jct.	7.5	"	X/GTW-A 33.6
Belt Line	8.9	"	J/GTW-D 22.6

CONSTRUCTION

DATE	ACT	END POINTS	MP	CHANGE	MAIN	SOURCE	NOTE
1931/5/18	B22	Line	0–8.9	(+8.9)	0	2	

OWNERSHIP

1931   Grand Trunk Western Railroad (B22)

CORUNNA (KERBY) MINE SPUR (GTW-YDC)

	MILEAGE	COUNTY	CROSSINGS, JUNCTIONS, ETC.
(Jct.)	0	Shiawassee	J/GTW-D 75.3
(Crossing)	0.1	"	X/AA-A 103.5
Corunna (Kerby) Mine	2.0	"	

CONSTRUCTION

DATE	ACT	END POINTS	MP	CHANGE	MAIN	SOURCE	NOTE
1873	B2	Line	0–2.0	(+2.0)	0	4	
1945 ca.	X	Line	0–2.0	(–2.0)	0		

OWNERSHIP

1873	Detroit & Milwaukee Railroad (B2)
1878/10/28	Detroit, Grand Haven & Milwaukee, reorganization of Detroit & Milwaukee Railroad
1882/8/12	DGH&M controlled by Grand Trunk Railway of Canada
1928/11/1	Grand Trunk Western Railroad (B22), merger of DGH&M

PONTIAC STATE HOSPITAL SPUR (GTW-YDP)

	MILEAGE	COUNTY	CROSSINGS, JUNCTIONS, ETC.
(Jct.)	0	Oakland	J/GTW-D 27.8
(End of track)	0.7	"	

CONSTRUCTION

DATE	ACT	END POINTS	MP	CHANGE	MAIN	SOURCE	NOTE
Line	B2	Line	0–0.7	(+0.7)	0	4	

OWNERSHIP

1875	Detroit & Milwaukee Railroad (B2)
1878/10/28	Detroit, Grand Haven & Milwaukee, reorganization of Detroit & Milwaukee Railroad
1882/8/12	DGH&M controlled by Grand Trunk Railway of Canada
1928/11/1	Grand Trunk Western Railroad (B22), merger of DGH&M

BAD AXE BRANCH (GTW-B)

	MILEAGE	COUNTY	CROSSINGS, JUNCTIONS, ETC.
Cass City	0.0	Tuscola	
(Jct.)	0.25	"	J/GTW-P 74.1
Polmantier	4.8	"	
Greenleaf	7.49	Sanilac	
Atwater	11.02	Huron	
McIntyre	14.02	"	
(Jct.)	18.1	"	J/spur to PM-N 69.6, 0.4 mi.
Bad Axe	18.58	"	

CONSTRUCTION

DATE	ACT	END POINTS	MP	CHANGE	MAIN	SOURCE	NOTE
1913/9/28	B21	Cass City–Bad Axe	0.3–18.6	+18.3	18.3	5	
1951/5/1	X	Entire line	0.3–18.6	–18.3	0	2	27

OWNERSHIP

1913	Detroit & Huron (B21), controlled by Grand Trunk Western Railway
1928/11/1	Grand Trunk Western Railroad, merger of Detroit & Huron

P. O. & N. SUBDIV. (GTW-P)

	MILEAGE	COUNTY	CROSSINGS, ETC.
Pontiac (via GTW-D)	0.0	Oakland	
(Jct.)	0.2	"	J/GTW-D 26.5
(Oakland Ave.)	0.5	"	X/POCL-2 0.34
P.O.N. Jct.	2.5	"	X/GTW-YP 2.5
Eames	6.21	"	
Scripps Wildwood Siding	8.26	"	
Randall Beach	9.20	"	f. Cole
Indianwood Siding	10.79	"	
(Bridge)	13.8	"	B/DUR-F 28.18
Oxford (old)	13.92	"	X/MC-B 43.6
Oxford (new)	15.22	"	
Shoup	18.30	"	
Leonard	21.26	"	
Dryden	27.28	Lapeer	
Imlay Jct.	32.9	"	
(Bridge)	33.1	"	B/GTW-C 301.8
Lum	39.30	"	
Kings Mills	42.49	"	
N. Branch	48.62	"	
Clifford	54.74	"	X/PM-Q 39.9
Kingston	61.65	Tuscola	
Wilmot (new)	64.85	"	X/DCS 39.6
Wilmot (old)	65.5	"	
Massey Siding	66.84	"	
Deford	68.56	"	f. Bruce
Quick Siding	70.73	"	
(Jct.)	74.1	"	J/GTW-B 0.0
Cass City	74.35	"	
Gagetown	80.01	"	
Watrous	84	Huron	
(Jct.)	84.4	"	J/MC-BC 33.9
Owendale	84.84	"	
Linkville	86.90	"	f. Winsor
Niebauers Siding	88.73	"	
Pigeon	91.75	"	X/PM-S 50.0, f. Berne Jct.
Berne	93.1	"	
Stewart Siding	95.83	"	
Caseville	99.39	"	
(End)	99.9	"	

CONSTRUCTION

DATE	ACT	END POINTS	MP	CHANGE	MAIN	SOURCE	NOTE
1883/10/8	B12	Pontiac–Caseville	0.2–99.9	+99.7	99.7	5	
1930	X	In Caseville	99.9–99.6	−0.3	99.4	2	
1983/7/6	X	Caseville–Pigeon	99.6–92.8	−6.8	92.6	6	
1986/1/13	X	Kings Mill–Pigeon	42.6–92.8	−50.2	42.4	6	
1986 ca.	X	Randall Beach–Kings Mill	9.1–42.6	−33.5	8.9		

OWNERSHIP

1883	Pontiac, Oxford & Port Austin (B12)
1889/9/24	Pontiac, Oxford & Northern, bought Pontiac, Oxford & Port Austin
1909/11/2	PO&N, control obtained by Grand Trunk Western Railway
1928/11/1	Grand Trunk Western Railroad, merger of Pontiac, Oxford & Northern

BAY CITY TERMINAL (GTW-SB)

	MILEAGE	COUNTY	CROSSINGS, JUNCTIONS, ETC.
	[Durand]		
(S wye switch)	51.93	Bay	J/GTW-S 51.9
(Jct.)	52.1	"	J/wye to J/GTW-S 52.2, .2 miles
(Crossing)	52.5	"	X/MC-YBS 1.1
Bay City (7th St. station)	53.19	"	

CONSTRUCTION

DATE	ACT	END POINTS	MP	CHANGE	MAIN	SOURCE	NOTE
1913/9/28	B20	MP 51.7–Bay City (7th St.)	51.7–52.9	+1.2	1.2	2	
1941	X	Entire line	51.7–52.9	−1.2	0		

OWNERSHIP

1913	Bay City Terminal Co (B20), controlled by Grand Trunk Western Railway
1928/11/1	Grand Trunk Western Railway, merger of Bay City Terminal

ALICIA FARM (VERNE MINE) BRANCH (GTW-YSA)

	MILEAGE	COUNTY	CROSSINGS, JUNCTIONS, ETC.
Prairie Farm Jct.	0	Sag.	J/GTW-S 28.0
(End of track)	8.8	"	

CONSTRUCTION

DATE	ACT	END POINTS	MP	CHANGE	MAIN	SOURCE	NOTE
1905 ca.	B16	Entire line	0–6.8	(+6.8)	0		
1946	X	Entire line	0–6.8	(−6.8)	0		

OWNERSHIP

1905	Grand Trunk Western Railway (B16)
1928/11/1	Grand Trunk Western Railroad, merger of Grand Trunk Western Railway

SAGINAW SUBDIV (GTW-S)

	MILEAGE	COUNTY	CROSSINGS, JUNCTIONS, ETC.
Durand (joint w/AA-A)	0	Shiawassee	J/GTW-D 67.0
(Jct.)	0.1	"	J/AA-A 95.6
Lennon	6.28	"	
Flushing	12.87	Genesee	
Clay Track	14.1	"	
Brent Creek	17.11	"	
Montrose	21.15	"	
Burt	25.44	Sag.	f. Taymouth
Moiles Siding	26.3	"	
Verne	27.39	"	
Prairie Farm Jct.	27.95	"	J/GTW-SA 0, f. Verne Mine Jct.
Fosters	29.68	"	
Orville	32.94	"	
Robys Spur	34.38	"	
Sag. Freight Yard	37.48	"	
(Crossing)	37.8	"	X/PM-YSS 1.5 (Sheridan Ave.)

(Holland Ave.)	38.55	"	X/SACL-10 0.65
Brewster Siding	38.61	"	
Meredith St. Jct.	39.07	"	
MX	39.16	"	J/MC-BS 20.2
Sag. (old)	39.21	"	
(Washington Ave.)	39.7	"	X/SACL-2 0.37
(Water St.)	39.8	"	X/PM-YSW 1.0
Genesee Ave.	40.02	"	adjacent Sag. on MC-S
(Genesee Ave.)	40.05	"	X/SACL-4 0.43
Mershon	40.68	"	C/MC-S 102.2, X/PM-L 0.7
(Crossing)	40.71	"	X/MUR-EW 11.75
Carrollton	41.89	"	
(Crossing)	42.27	"	X/MUR-EW 10.15
Zilwaukee	43.63	"	
McClures	44.74	"	
Melbourne	46.60	"	
Interurban Crossing	47.98	Bay	X/MUR-EW 4.98
Greens Sdg.	49.7	"	
Brooks	50.53	"	
Mac	50.9	"	
Salzburg	51.55	"	
(Switch S. wye)	51.93	"	J/GTW-SB 51.9
(Switch N. wye)	52.16	"	J/GTW-SB
(Crossing)	52.2	"	X/MC-S 113.3
(Midland St.)	53.0	"	X/BYCL-1 0.81
Bay City	53.09	"	f. W. Bay City
(Jct.)	53.1	"	J/spur to MC-L 3.07, 0.5 mi.
(Crossing)	54.22	"	X/MC-M 1.1
(Marq. St.)	54.6	"	X/BYCL-2 1.27
Banks	55.2	"	
N. Bay City	56.21	"	X/D&M-S 3.0, X/MC-YBH 2.2
Wenona Beach	58.89	"	
Oa-at-ka Beach	58.9	"	

CONSTRUCTION

DATE	ACT	END POINTS	MP	CHANGE	MAIN	SOURCE	NOTE
1888/10/23	B14	Durand–Flushing	0–12.9	+12.9		5	
12/17	B14	Flushing–E. Sag.	12.9–39.2	+26.3	39.2	5	
1890/1/11	B1	E. Sag.–Oa-at-ka Beach	39.2–58.9	+19.7	58.9	5	
1928 ca.	X	Meredith St. Jct.–Mershon	39.0–40.6	−1.6	57.3		18
1930 ca.	X	N. Bay City–Oa-at-ka Beach	58.9–56.6	−2.3	55.0		
1983	X	Mac–Carrollton	51.0–44.4	−6.6	48.4		
1987/9/4	S6	Entire line		[48.4]	0		
1996	X	Mac–MP 54.2	51.0–54.2	[−3.2]			
1996	Y	MP 54.2–N. Bay City	54.2–56.6	[(2.4)]			

OWNERSHIP

1888	Toledo, Saginaw & Mackinaw (B14)
1890/10/31	Cincinnati, Saginaw & Mackinaw, bought TS&M; leased by G T Railway of Canada
1943/1/1	Grand Trunk Western Railroad, merger of Cincinnati, Saginaw & Mackinaw
1987/9/4	Central Michigan (S6), bought line

SELFRIDGE A.F.B. SPUR (GTW-YMC)

	MILEAGE	COUNTY	CROSSINGS, JUNCTIONS, ETC.
Sugar Spur	0	Macomb	J/GTW-H 23.0
(Crossing)	0.9	"	X/DUR-R 16.70
Selfridge A. F. B.	2.3	"	

CONSTRUCTION

DATE	ACT	END POINTS	MP	CHANGE	MAIN	SOURCE	NOTE
1917	B16	Line	0–2.3	(+2.3)	0	5	
1996 ca.	S8	Line	0–2.3	(−2.3)	0		29

OWNERSHIP

1917	Grand Trunk Western Railway (B16)
1928/11/1	Grand Trunk Western Railroad, merger of Grand Trunk Western Railway
1996 ca.	Michigan Transit Museum, bought line

MT. CLEMENS SUBDIV. (GTW-H)

	MILEAGE	COUNTY	CROSSINGS, JUNCTIONS, ETC.
W. Det.	0.0	Wayne	J/WAB-W 0, X/MC-E 2.9
Mich. Ave.	0.45	"	B/DSR-M 3.17
Vinewood Ave.	0.7	"	
24th St.	1.1	"	
(Buchanan Ave.)	1.2	"	B/DSR-C 9.06
(Warren Ave.)	1.6	"	B/DSR-X 6.82
Grand River Ave.	1.9	"	B/DSR-R 2.48
(14th St.)	2.1	"	B/DSR-Q 3.17
Avery Ave.	2.33	"	
12th St.	2.4	"	
Trumbull Ave.	2.7	"	B/DSR-T 2.16
Holden Rd.	3.0	"	
(Hamilton Ave.)	3.0	"	B/DSR-H 3.51
Woodward Ave.	3.6	"	B/DSR-W 3.25
Beaubien St.	3.8	"	X/LS-D 4.4, X/MC-B 5.9, B/DSR-OK 3,28
Brush St.	4.0	"	
(Milw. Ave.)	4.2	"	B/DSR-GB 5.14
Russell St.	4.4	"	B/DSR-CM 6.50
Milw. Jct.	4.57	"	X/GTW-D 4.1
(Crossing)	5.11	"	X/MC-YDB 0 (on MC: Belt Line)
(Chene St.)	5.2	"	B/DSR-A 4.69
E. Yard	6.64	"	
Forest Lawn	7.19	"	X/DT 12.7, X/MC-YDC 1.7
Mount Olivet (VanDyke Ave.)	8.34	"	X/DSR-P 7.63, (X/DUR-C 2.92)
Nolan Yard	9.14	"	
Gillen Yard	10.10	"	(aka Eight Mile Rd.)
Double Track Switch	11.35	Macomb	
E. Det.	12.09	"	
Fraser	16.48	"	f. Utica Plank
(Crossing)	21.9	"	X/MCCL-1 1.03
Mt. Clem.	21.97	"	
Sugar Spur	22.98	"	J/GTW-YMC 0
Chesterfield	26.61	"	J/DUR-RZ 0
Milton	28.9	"	
New Haven	32.21	"	f. New Baltimore
Richmond	37.92	"	J/GTW-A 0, f. Ridgeway, th. Lenox

(Jct.)	38.6	"	J/MC-DM 14.0
Columbus	44.88	St.Clair	
Smith Creek	48.61	"	
Tappan	55.60	"	X/GTW-C 332.1, X/PM-Q 86.1
(Pt. Hur., via GTW-C	57.4)		
(Crossing)	58.7	"	X/PM-N 1.7
(Pine Grove Ave.)	58.8	"	X/PHCL-1 2.91
Fort Gratiot	59.5	"	

CONSTRUCTION

DATE	ACT	END POINTS	MP	CHANGE	MAIN	SOURCE	NOTE
1859/11/21	B3	W. Det.–Ft. Gratiot	0–59.5	+59.5	59.5	2,4	
1892 ca.	Y	Tappan–Ft. Gratiot(to GTW-YPH)	55.6–59.5	(3.9)	55.6		13

OWNERSHIP

1859   Chicago, Det. & Canada Grand Trunk Junction (B3); controlled by Grand Trunk Railway of Canada
1928/11/1   Grand Trunk Western Railroad, merger of CD&CGTJ

JACKSON SUBDIV. (GTW-A)

	MILEAGE	COUNTY	CROSSINGS, JUNCTIONS, ETC.
Richmond	0.0	Macomb	J/GTW-H 37.9, f. Ridgeway, th. Lenox
Main St.	0.55	"	f. Richmond
Armada	7.28	"	
Romeo	14.17	"	
Washington	19.88	"	
Gravel Pit	22.1	"	
Shelby	22.3	"	
Rochester Jct.	25.23	Oakland	X/MC-B 30.0
Rochester	26.31	"	X/DUR-F 14.25
Auburn Heights	31.68	"	f. Amy, th. Auburn
MAL Jct.	33.60	"	X/GTW-YP 7.5
(Sanford St.)	34.56	"	X/POCL-5 0.51
(Sag. St..)	35.21	"	X/POCL-1 0.75
MAL Crossing	35.29	"	X/GTW-D 25.2
Sylvan Lk.	37.6	"	
(Bridge)	39.8	"	B/DUR-L 23.75
Orchard Lk.	39.96	"	
Walled Lk.	47.59	"	
Wixom	50.71	"	X/PM-T 70.4
Slaters Pit	53.76	"	
New Hudson	55.14	"	
South Lyon	59.00	"	X/PM-D 36.1, (J/AA-S 60.4)
Rushton	61.74	Livingston	
Whitmore Lk.	64.48	"	
(Jct.)	67.2	"	J/AA-O1 61.1
Hamburg	67.42	"	
(Crossing)	69.8	"	X/AA-A 61.8
Lakeland	69.87	"	
Hamburg Jct.	70.3	Washtenaw	J/AA-A 62.3
Pettysville	71.5	"	
Pinckney	74.95	"	
Anderson	78.62	"	
Gregory	82.48	"	
Stockbridge	87.64	Ingham	
Munith	92.92	Jackson	

Henrietta	95.26	"	
Roots	98.08	"	
New Prison Siding	102.16	"	
(Crossing)	104.38	"	X/MC-G 2.1, J/J&N 0
Jackson	105.92	"	

CONSTRUCTION

DATE	ACT	END POINTS	MP	CHANGE	MAIN	SOURCE	NOTE
1869/12/9	B5	Richmond–Romeo	0–14.2	+14.2	14.2	5	10
1879/3	B10	Romeo–Rochester	14.2–26.3	+12.1	26.3	5	
1880/10	B10	Rochester–MAL Crossing	26.3–35.3	+9.0	35.3	5	
1883/10	B10	MAL Crossing–S. Lyon	35.3–59.0	+23.7	59.0	5	
1884/9/1	B10	S. Lyon–Jackson	59.0–105.9	+46.9	105.9	5	
1946 ca.	X	In Pontiac	33.6–35.3	−1.7	104.2		
1975	X	Jackson–Lakeland	105.9–70.3	−35.6	68.6	6	
1983	X	Lakeland–S. Lyon	70.3–60.3	−10.0	58.6	6	
1984/3/21	X	S. Lyon–Wixom	60.3–50.7	−9.6		6	
1984/8	S2	Wixom–Walled Lk.	50.7–42.0	−8.7			
1984 ca.	Y	MAL Crossing–Sylvan Lk.	35.3–38.3	(3.0)			
1984 ca.	X	Sylvan Lk.–Walled Lk.	38.3–42.0	−3.7	33.6		
1998	X	Richmond–MAL Jct.	0–33.6	−33.6			
1998	X	MAL Crossing–Sylvan Lk.	35.3–38.3	(−3.0)	0		

OWNERSHIP

1869	Michigan Air Line Railroad (B5)
1872/4/13	St. Clair River, Pontiac & Jackson, leased Michigan Air Line Railroad
1872/7/20	St. Clair & Chicago Air Line, renaming of St. Clair River, Pontiac & Jackson
1875/11/23	Michigan Air Line Railway, bought rights of St. Clair & Chicago Air Line
1877/10/15	Grand Trunk Railway of Canada, control of Michigan Air Railway
1928/11/1	Grand Trunk Western Railroad, merger of Michigan Air Line Railway
1984/8	Coe Rail (S2), bought part of line

MUSKEGON, *LATER* GREENVILLE SUBDIVISION (GTW-M)

	MILEAGE	COUNTY	CROSSINGS, JUNCTIONS, ETC.
(Owosso)	(20.5 via AA-B)		
Ashley	0.0	Gratiot	J/AA-B 128.3
Ola	4.48	"	
Pompeii	6.44	"	
Perrinton	10.48	"	
Middleton	12.02	"	
Carson City	18.93	Montcalm	
Butternut	22.43	"	
Vickeryville	24.93	"	
Bushnell		"	
Sheridan	30.72	"	
Virgil	31.10	"	X/PM-J 44.4
Millers	35.14	"	
Eureka Place	37.78	"	
Greenville	40.38	"	X/PM-G 80.7
Lincoln Lk.	45.55	Kent	
Harvard	48.97	"	
Evans	50.88	"	
Sheffield	52.73	"	
Cedar Springs	56.38	"	
(Crossing)	56.8	"	X/GR&I-N 254.7

Reeds	61.71	"	
Camp Lk.	63.3	"	
Saxon	65.32	"	X/PM-P 15.2
Sparta	65.49	"	
Gooding	69.71	"	f. Lisbon
Harrisburg	74.58	Ottawa	
Slocums	77.33	Musk.	f. Slocums Grove
Hines Crossing	79.3	"	
Moorland	81.57	"	
Halls	84.2	"	
Simpson	93.37	"	X/PM-AO 33.4, J/GTW-YM 0
Musk. (new)	94.7	"	(Peck St. sta.)
(Sanford St.)	94.7	"	X/MUCL-3 1.30
Jefferson St.	94.74	"	
(Jct.)	95.8	"	J/GTW-YMA 95.8
Musk. (old)	95.97	"	

CONSTRUCTION

DATE	ACT	END POINTS	MP	CHANGE	MAIN	SOURCE	NOTE
1887/9/24	B13	Ashley–Carson City	0–18.9	+18.9		5	
1888/8/1	B13	Carson City–Musk.	18.9–96.0	+77.1	96.0	5	
1928 ca.	X	In Musk.	95.8–96.0	–0.2	95.8		
1946	X	Greenville–Simpson	90.1–41.0	–49.1		2	
1946	Y	In Musk. (to GTW-Y1M)	90.1–93.4	(3.3)			
1946	Y	In Greenville (to GTW-Y2M)	41.0–40.4	(0.6)	42.8		
1976/4/1	P1	Owosso Jct.–Ashley	—	+20.6	63.4		26
1983/1/26	S5	In Greenville (GTW-Y2M)	40.4–41.0	[(0.6)]			
1983/2/27	X	Carson City–Greenville	19.3–40.4	–21.1	42.3		
1984 ca.	X	Middleton–Carson City	12.0–19.3	–7.3			31
1984/8?	S3	Ashley–Middleton	0–12.0	[12.0]	23.0		
1987/8	S4	Owosso Jct.–Ashley	—	[20.6]	2.4		
1987/9/4	S6	In Musk.	93.4–95.8	[2.4]			
1987/9/4	S6	In Musk. (GTW-Y1M)	90.1–93.4	[(3.3)]	0		
1989	X	In Musk. (GTW-Y1M)	90.1–91.1	[(–1.0)]			
1990/12/12	S15	In Musk. (GTW-M)	93.4–95.8	[–2.4]			
1990/12/12	S15	In Musk. (GTW-Y1M)	91.1–95.8	[(–4.7)]			

OWNERSHIP

1887	Toledo, Saginaw & Muskegon (B13), controlled by G T Railway of Canada
1928/11/1	Grand Trunk Western Railroad, merger of Toledo, Saginaw & Muskegon
1984	private owners (S3), bought part of line
1987/8	State of Michigan (S4), bought part of line
1987/9/4	Central Michigan (S6), bought remnant of line
1990/12/12	Michigan Shore (S15), bought line

SPUR TO MUSKEGON DOCKS (GTW-YMA)

	MILEAGE [Ashley]	COUNTY	CROSSINGS, JUNCTIONS, ETC.
(Jct.)	95.8	Musk.	J/GTW-M 95.8
(Crossing, Western & 9th)	95.9	"	X/PM-A 56.2, X/MUCL-1 2.42
(Crossing, Western Ave.)	96.0	"	X/PM-YM1-01
(Docks)	96.2	"	

CONSTRUCTION

DATE	ACT	END POINTS	MP	CHANGE	MAIN	SOURCE	NOTE
1888 ca.	B13	Line	95.8–96.2	(0.4)	0		
1987/9/4	S6	Line	95.8–96.2	[0.4]	0		
1989	X	Line	95.8–96.2	[(–0.4)]			

OWNERSHIP

1888	Toledo, Saginaw & Muskegon (B13), controlled by G T Railway of Canada
1928/11/1	Grand Trunk Western Railroad, merger of Toledo, Saginaw & Muskegon
1987/9/4	Central Michigan (S6), bought line

MUSKEGON RY & NAVIGATION (GTW-MR)

	MILEAGE	COUNTY	CROSSINGS, JUNCTIONS, ETC.
Simpson	0.0	Musk.	J/GTW-M 93.4
Shaw	0.4	"	X/GR&I-M 36.5
(Sanford St.)	2.2	"	X/MUCL-3 2.44
(Crossing)	2.3	"	X/PM-A 54.3
(Jct.)	2.6	"	J/GR&I-YM 1.3
Henry St.	3.0	"	
(Jct.)	4.0	"	J/indl. spur, 1.5 miles
(Lk. Shore Dr.)	5.2	"	X/MUCL-1 4.58
(Crossing)	5.2	"	X/PM-YM 2.2
Docks	5.5	"	

CONSTRUCTION

DATE	ACT	END POINTS	MP	CHANGE	MAIN	SOURCE	NOTE
1923	B23	Simpson–Docks	0–5.5	+5.5	5.5	2	
1987/9/4	S6	Simpson–Docks	0–5.5	[5.5]	0		
1990/12/12	S15	Simpson–MP 4	0–4.0	[(–4.0)]			
1990	X	MP 4.0–Docks	4.0–5.5	[(–1.5)]			

OWNERSHIP

1923	Muskegon Railway & Navigation Co (B23)
1926/10/20	MR&N, control obtained by Grand Trunk Western Railway
1955/8/28	Grand Trunk Western Railroad, merger of MR&N
1987/9/4	Central Michigan, bought line
1990/12/12	Michigan Shore, bought line

MUSKEGON BRANCH CONNECTION (GTW-DM)

	MILEAGE	COUNTY	CROSSINGS, JUNCTIONS, ETC.
Penn Jct.	0.0	Ottawa	J/GTW-D 165.3
Walker	0.84	"	J/GR&I-M 10.0

CONSTRUCTION

DATE	ACT	END POINTS	MP	CHANGE	MAIN	SOURCE	NOTE
1929	B22	Penn Jct.–Walker	0–0.8	+0.8	0.8	2	19
1987/9/4	S6	Entire line	0–0.8	[0.8]	0		
1989	X	Entire line	0–0.8	[–0.8]	0		

OWNERSHIP

1929	Grand Trunk Western Railroad (B22)
1987/9/4	Central Michigan (S6), bought line

KALAMAZOO BRANCH (GTW-K)

	MILEAGE	COUNTY	CROSSINGS, JUNCTIONS, ETC.
Pavilion	0.0	Kal.	J/GTW-C 157.2
Pomeroy	2.51	"	
Kealey	4.32	"	
Beckwith Siding	6.55	"	
Kilgore Yard	6.5	"	
Pavilion Jct. (new)	9.0	"	J/GR&I-S 183.6
(Bridge)	9.49	"	B/MUR-S 66.6
—PJ	9.5	"	J/GR&I-S 183.1
Pavilion Jct. (old)	9.58	"	J/CK&S-S 1.3, J/GTW-YK 1.3
(Jct.)	10.5	"	J/CK&S-S 0.3
(Crossing)	11.00	"	X/LS-G 36.3
(Mich. Ave.)	11.31	"	X/KACL-1 0.28
Kal.	11.32	"	J/GTW-YK 3.1

CONSTRUCTION

DATE	ACT	END POINTS	MP	CHANGE	MAIN	SOURCE	NOTE
1910/8/1	L1	Pavilion–Pavilion Jct.	0–9.5	+9.5		5	16
1910/8/8	B19	Pavilion Jct.–Kal.	9.5–11.3	+1.8	11.3	5	
1984	X	Kal.–Pavilion Jct.	11.3–9.5	–1.8	9.5		30
1990	X	Pavilion Jct.–south	9.5–9.0	–0.5	9.0		30

OWNERSHIP

1910   Chicago & Kalamazoo Terminal (B19) (controlled by Grand Trunk Western; leased segment from Chicago, Kalamazoo & Saginaw (L1)

1928/11/1   Grand Trunk Western Railroad, merger of Chicago & Kalamazoo Terminal

KALAMAZOO YARD (GTW-YK)

	MILEAGE	COUNTY	CROSSINGS, JUNCTIONS, ETC.
(Portage St.)	0.0	Kal.	
(Bridge)	1.1	"	B/GR&I-S 183.9
Pavilion Jct.	1.3	"	J/GTW-K 9.5
—via GTW-K			
Kal.	3.1	"	J/GTW-K 11.3
BO	3.3	"	MC-C 143.1
(Mosel Ave.)	4.8	"	
(End of track)	8.8	"	

CONSTRUCTION

DATE	ACT	END POINTS	MP	CHANGE	MAIN	SOURCE	NOTE
1908	B19	Pavilion Jct.–Portage St.	0–1.3	(+1.3)	0	5	
1910	B19	Kal.–Mosel Ave.	3.1–4.8	(+1.7)	0		
1935 ca.	B22	Mosel Ave.–north	4.8–8.8	(+4.0)	0		
1966 ca.	X	North end of line	5.3–8.8	(–3.5)	0		
1966	X	Kal.–north	3.1–4.1	(–1.0)	0		24
1984 ca.	X	Portage St.–Pavilion Jct.	0–1.3	(–1.3)	0		

OWNERSHIP

See line GTW-K above

ACQUISITION/DISPOSITION RECORD

DATE	ACT	GTW–	END POINTS	CHANGE	MI MAIN	NOTE
1838/7/21	B1	D	Jefferson Ave.–Royal Oak	+12.3	12.3	1
1839/8/16	B1	DO	Royal Oak–Birmingham	+5.3	17.6	2

1842	B1	DD	Gratiot Ave.,Dequindre–Farmer	+1.2	18.8	3
1843/7/4	B1	D,DO	Birmingham–Pontiac	+7.8	26.6	4
1852	B1	D	Det.–Jefferson Ave.	+0.9		
	X	DD	Gratiot Ave., Dequindre–Farmer	−1.2	26.3	
1855/10/2	B2	D	Pontiac–Fenton	+24.4	50.7	
1856/7/1	B2	D	Fenton–Owosso	+27.8	78.5	
1857/1/14	B2	D	Owosso–St. Johns	+19.6		
8/12	B2	D	St. Johns–Ionia	+26.1	124.2	
1858/7/4	B2	D	Ionia–Gr. Rpds.	+33.3		5
8/30	B2	D	Gr. Rpds.–Spring Lk.	+28.9		
11/22	B2	D,DA	Spring Lk.–Grand Haven(old)	+2.4	188.8	6
1859/11/21	B3	H	W. Det.–Fort Gratiot	+59.5	248.3	
1869/11	B4	C	Pt. Hur.(Court St.)–Emmett	+17.6		
12/9	B5	A	Ridgeway–Romeo	+14.2	280.1	10
1870/1/1	B6	C	Battle Creek(old)–Bellevue	+13.4		7
2/14	B6	C	Bellevue–Charlotte	+13.2		
6/8	B4	C	Emmett–Capac	+8.6		
6/13	B6	C	Charlotte–Lans.	+18.5		
7/28	B4	C	Capac–Imlay City	+7.3		
10/15	B6	C,CO3	Battle Creek(old)–Climax	+10.4		7
12	B4	C	Imlay City–Attica	+4.7		
	B2	D	Ferrysburg–Gr. Hav.	+1.3		
	Y	D	Ferrysburg–Gr. Hav.(old)	(1.8)	355.7	
1871/5/25	B4	C	Attica–Davison	+18.1		
6	B6	C	Climax–Cassopolis	+42.1		
12/13	B4	C,YF	Davison–(N.) Flint	+9.0	424.9	8
1872/Fall	B6	C,CO2	Cassopolis–S. Bend (MI=11.8)	+22.4	436.7	9
1873	B2	DC	Corunna Coal Mine Spur	(+2.0)		
/10/13	B6	C,CO4	S. Bend–Valparaiso (MI=0)	+45.8	436.7	9
1875/	B2	DP	Pontiac Hospital Br.	(+0.7)	436.7	
1876/	B8	C,CA	Chi.(26thSt)–Thornton Jct. IL (=0)	+20.5	436.7	
1877/1/1	B7	C,YF	Lans.–(N.) Flint	+49.3	486.0	8
1879/3	B10	A	Romeo–Rochester	+12.1		10
12	B9	C	Thornton Jct IL–Valparaiso IN (MI=0)	+30.6		
	X	CO4	In Valparaiso IN (MI=0)	−1.1	498.1	
1880/10	B10	A	Rochester–MAL Crossing	+9.0	507.1	
1881	B11	CA	Elsdon Jct.–C&WI Jct.IL (MI=0)	+3.7	507.1	11
1883/10	B10	A	MAL Crossing–S. Lyon	+23.7		
10/8	B12	P	(Pontiac)–Caseville	+99.7	630.5	
1884/9/1	B10	A	S. Lyon–Jackson	+46.9	677.4	
1887/7/20	S1	CA	Elsdon–26th St.IL (MI=0)	−3.9		
9/24	B13	M	Ashley–Carson City	+18.9	696.3	
1888/8/1	B13	M	Carson City–Musk.	+77.1		
	B13	YMA	In Musk.	(+0.4)		
10/23	B14	S	Durand–Flushing	+12.9		
12/17	B14	S	Flushing–E. Sag.	+26.3	812.6	
1890/1/11	B14	S	E. Sag.–Oa-at-ka Beach	+19.7	832.3	
1891/10/24	B15	Z	16th St.–Can. boundary	+1.1	833.4	12
1892	Y	C	16th St.–Court St.(to YCP)	(1.2)		13
	Y	H	Tappan–Ft. Gratiot(to YPH)	(3.9)	828.3	13
1904	B16	C	W. of Battle Creek	+5.4		
	Y	CO3	W. of Battle Creek (to YB)	(0.5)		
	X	CO3	W. of Battle Creek	−4.5	828.7	14
1905?	B17	SA	Verne Mine Branch	(+6.8)	828.7	
1906/1	B18	DG	Terminal Jct.–Gr. Rpds.	+1.5	830.2	15

1908	B19	YK	Portage St.–Pavilion Jct.	(+1.3)	830.2	
1910/8/1	L1	K	Pavilion–Pavilion Jct.	+9.5		
	B19	K	Pavilion Jct.–Kal.	+1.8		16
	B19	YK	Kal.–Mosel Ave.	(+1.7)	841.5	
1913/9/28	B20	SB	Branch to Bay City(7th St.)	+1.2		
	B21	B	Cass City–Bad Axe	+18.3	861.0	
1917	B16	YMC	Selfridge A. F. B. Spur	(+2.3)	861.0	
1923	B23	MR	Simpson–Docks	+5.5	866.5	
1927	B16	C	Mundy–S.Flint–Belsay	+10.5		
	Y	YF	Mundy–N.Flint–Belsay	(11.0)	866.0	17
1928?	X	S	Sag. River bridge	−1.6		18
	X	M	In Musk.	−0.2	864.2	
1929	B22	DM	Penn Jct.–Walker	+0.8		19
	X	CO2	Arnold St.–Greenlawn Ave. (MI=0)	−2.5		20
	B22	C	High St.–Greenlawn Ave. (MI=0)	+1.2	865.0	21
1930	X	P	In Caseville	−0.3		
?	X	S	No. Bay City–Oa-at-ka Beach	2.3	862.4	
1931/5/18	B22	YP	Pontiac Belt Line	(+8.9)		
	B22	D	Royal Oak–Bloomfield Hills	+8.0		
	X	D	Royal Oak–Bloomfield Hills	−8.3	862.1	22
1935?	X	YGH	Ferrysburg–Gr. Hav. (old)	(−1.2)		
	B22	YK	In Kal.	(+4.0)	862.1	
1940?	X	YGH	Near Ferrysburg	(−0.6)	862.1	
1941	X	SB	To Bay City (7th St.)	−1.2	860.9	
1945 ca	X	YDC	Corunna Coal Mine Br.	(−2.0)	860.9	
1946	X	M	Greenville–Simpson	−49.1		
	Y	M	In Greenville (to GTW-Y2M)	(0.6)		
	Y	M	In Musk. (to GTW-Y1M)	(3.3)		
	X	A	In Pontiac	−1.7		
	X	YSA	Verne Mine Branch	(−6.8)	806.2	
1948	Y	DG	Terminal Jct.–Gr. Rpds.(to YGR)	(1.5)		23
	Y	YGR	At Gr. Rpds.	(−0.1)	804.7	
1951/5/1	X	B	Cass City–Bad Axe	−18.3	786.4	27
1966	X	YK	In Kal.	(−4.5)	786.4	24
1973	X	D	In Det.	−0.2	786.2	25
1975	X	A	Lakeland–Jackson	−35.6	750.6	

On 1 April 1976 this company acquired various lines from Penn Central and Ann Arbor. For arrangement of stations, construction record, and prior ownerships, see Ann Arbor (AA), Grand Rapids & Indiana (GRI), and Michigan Central (MC) lines as identified. The property acquired was:

LINE DESIG.		END POINTS	MP	MAIN	SOURCE	NOTE
GTW-						
	[AA-A]	Pitt–Owosso	93.9–107.1	+13.2		
	[AA-B]	Owosso–Ashley	107.1–128.3	+21.2		26
	[GR&I-M]	Walker–Musk.	10.0–39.3	+29.3		
	[GR&I-YM]	In Musk.	38.0–39.3	(+1.3)		
	[MC-YG]	In Charlotte	32.0–35.4	(+3.4)		
	[MC-Y3B]	In Lapeer (from MC-B)	58.4–60.3	(+1.9)		
	[MC-Y2B]	In Oxford (from MC-B)	42.2–45.0	(+2.8)		
	[MC-BS]	S.B. Jct.–Denmark Jct.	6.0–20.7	+14.7		
	[MC-Y1S]	In Owosso (from MC-S)	61.1–64.2	(+3.1)		
	[MC-Y2S]	Swan Creek–S.B. Jct. (MS-S)	91.8–101.2	(+9.4)		
	[MC-S]	S.B. Jct.–Bay City W.S.	101.2–104.6	+13.4		
	[MC-Y2M]	Bay City E.S.–Bay City WS	0–0.7	(+0.7)		
	[MC-M]	Bay City W.S.–Kawkawlin	0.7–5.0	+4.3		

[MC-YBN]	N. Water St. Spur	0–2.5		(+2.5)		
[MC-Y1B]	Bay City ES–Water St.Jct.	108.9–106.1		(+2.8)		
[MC-YBL]	Water St.Jct.–26th St.	3.0–6.1		(+3.1)		
[MC-YBS]	S. Water St. Spur	0.8–2.4		(+1.6)		
[MC-L]	BC&BCJct–Midland	1.7–19.7		+18.0		
[MC-YM1]	In Midland	0–3.0		(+3.0)		
[MC-YM2]	In Midland	0–0.6		(+0.6)		

(AA = 34.4; GR&I = 29.3; MC = 50.4; TOTAL = 114.1)

DATE	ACT	GTW–	END POINTS	CHANGE	MAIN	NOTE
1976	X	[AA-A]	Pitt–Owosso	−13.2		27
	Y	[AA-B]	Owosso–Owosso Jct.(to AA-YB)	(0.6)	850.9	
1977	P2	[GR&I-Y2S]	In Vicksburg	(+1.1)		
7/6	X	D	Coopersville–Gr. Hav.	−15.3	835.6	28
1980?	X	[MC-Y3B]	In Lapeer	(−0.5)		
	X	[MC-YG]	In Charlotte	(−0.4)		
	X	YF	In Flint	(−0.8)	835.6	
1981/5/1	S7	[MC-BS]	Denmark Jct.–Harger	[9.5]		
5/1	Y	[MC-BS]	MX–Harger (to [MC-Y4S]	(4.7)		
10/1	P5	[DTSL]	Line	+43.8	865.2	
1983/6/14	P6	[DTI-M]	Det.–OH state line	+58.7		
	P6	[DTI-D]	Dearborn–D&I Jct.	+15.3		
	X	D	In Det.	−0.4		
	P4	[PM-YI]	In Ionia	(+1.2)		
	S5	Y2M	In Greenville	[(−0.6)]		
	X	M	Carson City–Greenville	−21.1		
	X	S	Mac–Carrollton	−6.6		
/7/6	X	P	Pigeon–Caseville	−6.8		
/10/19	X	A	Lakeland–S. Lyon	−10.0		
	X	[MC-Y2S]	In Swan Creek	(−0.7)	894.3	
1984	X	[MC-L]	In Midland	−0.8		
/3/21	X	A	Wixom–S. Lyon	−9.6		
/8	S2	A	S. Lyon–Walled Lk.	[8.7]		
?	S3	M	Middleton–Carson City	[7.3]		
/8	S7	M	Ashley–Middleton	[12.0]		
	X	K	Pavilion Jct.–Kal.	−1.8		
	X	YK	Portage St.–Pavilion Jct.	(−1.3)		
?	Y	A	MAL Crossing–Sylvan Lk. (as YAP)	(3.0)		
?	X	A	Sylvan Lk.–Walled Lk.	−3.7	847.4	
1986/1/13	X	P	Kings Mill–Pigeon	−50.2		
ca.	X	P	Randall Beach–Kings Mill	−33.5		
	X	[MC-Y2B]	In Oxford	(−2.8)	763.7	
1987/8	S4	[AA-B]	Owosso Jct.–Ashley	[20.6]		
9/4	S6	D	Durand–Coopersville	[106.0]		
9/4	S6	YGR	Grand Rapids Terminal	[(1.5)]		
9/4	S6	DM	Penn Jct.–Walker	[0.8]		
9/4	S6	S	Durand–Bay City	[48.4]		
9/4	S6	M	In Musk.	[2.4]		
9/4	S6	YMA	To Musk. Docks	[(0.4)]		
9/4	S6	Y1M	In Musk.	[(3.3)]		
9/4	S6	MR	Musk. RW & Navigation	[5.5]		
9/4	S6	[GR&I-M]	Walker–Musk.	[29.3]		
9/4	S6	[GR&I-YM]	In Musk.	[(1.3)]		
9/4	S6	[MC-Y1S]	In Owosso	[(3.1)]		
9/4	S6	[MC-S]	S.B. Jct.–Bay City W.S.	[13.4]		

9/4	S6	[MC-Y2S]	Swan Creek–S.B. Jct.	[(8.7)]		
9/4	S6	[MC-Y2M]	Bay City E.S.–Bay City W.S.	[(0.7)]		
9/4	S6	[MC-M]	Bay City W.S.–Kawkawlin	[4.3]		
9/4	S6	[MC-L]	BC&BC Jct–Midland	[17.2]		
9/4	S6	[MC-YBN]	Woodside–end	[(2.5)]		
9/4	S6	[MC-Y1B]	Bay City E.S.–Water St. Jct.	[(2.8)]		
9/4	S6	[MC-YBL]	Water St. Jct.–26th St.	[(3.1)]		
9/4	S6	[MC-YBS]	S. Water St. Spur	[(1.6)]		
9/4	S6	[MC-BS]	S.B.Jct.–MX	[0.5]		
9/4	S6	[MC-Y4S]	MX–Harger	[(4.7)]		
9/4	S6	[MC-YM1]	In Midland	[(3.0)]		
9/4	S6	[MC-YM2]	In Midland	[(0.6)]		
9/4	S6	[PM-YI]	In Ionia	[(1.2)]		
9/4	S6	[AA-YB]	In Owosso	[(0.6)]	515.3	
1990	X	K	Pavilion Jct.–south	–0.5	514.8	
1996 ca.	S8	YMC	Line	[(2.3)]	514.8	29
1997/2/15	S12	[DTI-M]	Diann–OH state line	[20.6]	494.2	
1998	X	YB		(–0.5)		
	X	D	MP 0.6–Gratiot Ave.	–1.1		
12/23	S9	D	Gratiot Ave.–Milw. Jct.	–2.3		
	X	A	Richmond–MAL Jct.	–33.6		
	X	A	MAL Crossing–Sylvan Lk.	(–3.0)	457.2	
1999	S10	[MC-YG]	In Charlotte	[(–3.0)]		
	S11	[MC-Y3B]	In Lapeer	[(–1.4)]	457.2	

Act Column Key

A	Adjust mileage
B1	Built by Detroit & Pontiac
B2	Built by Detroit & Milwaukee
B3	Built by Chicago, Detroit & Canada Grand Trunk Jct.
B4	Built by Port Huron & Lake Michigan
B5	Built by Michigan Air Line Railroad
B6	Built by Peninsular
B7	Built by Chicago & Northeastern
B8	Built by Chicago & Southern
B9	Built by North Western Grand Trunk
B10	Built by Michigan Air Line Railway
B11	Built by Grand Trunk Jct.
B12	Built by Pontiac, Oxford & Port Austin
B13	Built by Toledo, Saginaw & Muskegon
B14	Built by Toledo, Saginaw & Mackinaw
B15	Built by St. Clair Tunnel
B16	Built by Grand Trunk Western Railway
B17	Built by Cincinnati, Saginaw & Mackinaw
B18	Built by Grand Rapids Terminal
B19	Built by Chicago & Kalamazoo Terminal
B20	Built by Bay City Terminal
B21	Built by Detroit & Huron
B22	Built by Grand Trunk Western Railroad
B23	built by Muskegon Railway & Navigation
L1	Leased from Chicago, Kalamazoo & Saginaw
P1	Purchased from Ann Arbor
P2	Purchased from Penn Central (formerly MC)
P3	Purchased from Penn Central (formerly GR&I)
P4	Purchased from Chesapeake & Ohio/CSX

P5   Purchased Detroit & Toledo Shore Line
P6   Purchased Detroit, Toledo & Ironton
S1   Sold to Atchison, Topeka & Santa Fe
S2   Sold to Coe Rail
S3   Sold to private owners
S4   Sold to State of Michigan
S5   Sold to Chesapeake & Ohio
S6   Sold to Central Michigan
S7   Sold to Tuscola & Saginaw Bay
S8   Sold to Michigan Transit Museum
S9   Sold to Detroit Connecting Railroad
S10 Sold to Charlotte Southern
S11 Sold to Lapeer Industrial
S12 Sold to Indiana & Ohio
S13 Sold to Coopersville & Marne
S14 Sold to Grand Rapids Eastern
S15 Sold to Michigan Shore
X   Abandoned
Y   Converted to yard/industrial track
Z   Operations ended

Sources

1. Farmer, *Detroit and Wayne County.*
2. Hopper, *Canadian National Railways.*
3. ICC, *Valuation Docket 445.*
4. Michigan, Commissioner of Railroads, *Annual Report,* 1873.
5. Michigan Railroad Commission, *Aids, Gifts, Grants.*
6. MDOT office records.
7. Percival, "Railroads in Ottawa County."

Notes

1. Sources 4 and 5 give Autumn 1838 as opening date. This may be the date that steam locomotives replaced the use of horses.
2. Sources 4 and 5 give Spring 1841 as opening date.
3. This line was located in Gratiot Avenue
4. Sources 4 and 5 give Autumn 1844 as opening date.
5. The original Grand Rapids station was at MP 157.5 at Plainfield Avenue
6. The original Grand Haven station was on the north side of the Grand River opposite the 1870 station which was on the south side of the river in downtown Grand Haven.
7. The original Battle Creek station was at MP 175.8 on the west side of Capital Avenue.
8. The original Flint station was at MP 270.2 at Harrison Street in downtown Flint and later known as North Flint.
9. The original South Bend station was at MP 100.5 at Division (now Western Avenue) and Michigan Avenue The track was in the center of Western Avenue.
10. Sources 4 and 5 state the line was completed a total of 20.8 miles to Shelby but was operated only to Romeo. The segment between Romeo and Shelby was put in service in 1879 when the line was opened to Rochester.
11. Also acquired were 4.9 miles of trackage rights on the Chicago & Western Indiana to Dearborn Station. Source 2 gives the completion date as 1880.
12. The mileage shown is that in the United States. The tunnel was completed 30 August, the first train passed through on 18 September.
13. This trackage remained in place as yard trackage coincident with the opening of the St. Clair River Tunnel as GTW-YCP and GTW-YPH.
14. This segment was located through the present site of Kellogg Air Base and was replaced by the present main line GTW-C 169.4 to 174.8.

15. The station shown was at Michigan Avenue.
16. This line was built by the Chicago, Kalamazoo & Saginaw and opened to service on 1 December 1901.
17. This segment was replaced by present main line GTW-C 262.7 to 273.2.
18. With this abandonment approximately 1.0 mile of track south of Mershon was retained as yard track. Also trackage rights were obtained over the Michigan Central, 1.6 miles, between Meredith Street Junction and Mershon.
19. This construction also included obtaining trackage rights on 26.5 miles of the Grand Rapids & Indiana to Shaw on line GTW-YM.
20. This segment was replaced by present main line GTW-C 99.5 to 102.4.
21. This construction also included obtaining trackage rights on 1.6 miles of the New York Central between Arnold Street and High Street and the use of the NYC South Bend station.
22. The line abandoned was along the east side of Woodward Avenue through Birmingham and was replaced by present main line GTW-D 13.2 to 21.2.
23. With the closing of the Michigan Street station, the south 0.2 miles of trackage was abandoned and the remaining 1.3 miles retained as yard track.
24. The abandonment also included obtaining trackage rights on Conrail to reach the remnant of the line on the north side of Kalamazoo.
25. Abandonment was to the north side of Riopelle Street.
26. Trackage rights over the Ann Arbor from Owosso Junction to Ashley were in effect from 1887 until this purchase.
27. Parts of this segment were retained to reach local industries.
28. MP 187.1 to MP 187.7 was sold to Chessie System for use as part of line PM-A, and MP 186.8 to MP 187.1 sold to State of Michigan to be conveyed to a private owner for use as an industrial track.
29. The disposition of this branch is unclear, but it appears that part of it may have been abandoned and part of it sold to the Michigan Transit Museum.
30. Trackage rights over Conrail were obtained to allow connection to line GTW-YK.
31. A portion of this segment was sold to private industrial owners and service provided by Tuscola & Saginaw Bay.

Grass Lake & Manistee River *(line not located exactly)*

MAIN LINE (GL&MR-A)

	MILEAGE	COUNTY	CROSSINGS, JUNCTIONS, ETC.
(Manistee Riv.)	0	Kalkaska	(sec 35 T26N R6W)
(Jct.)	8.0	"	J/GL&MR-B 0
(End)	12.0	Crawford	(sec 30 T25N R4W)

BRANCH (GL&MR-B)

	MILEAGE	COUNTY	CROSSINGS, JUNCTIONS, ETC.
(Jct.)	0	Kalkaska	J/GLMR-A 8.0
(End)	1.5	"	(sec 35 T25N R5W)

OWNERSHIP

1886	Grass Lake & Manistee River

ACQUSITION/DISPOSITION RECORD

DATE	ACT	GL&MR–	END POINTS	CHANGE	MI MAIN	SOURCE
1886/9/3	B	A	Line	+8.0		1
9/3	B	B	Line	+1.5	9.5	1
1888	B	A	Extend line	+4.0	13.5	1
1892	X	A	Line	−12.0		1
	X	B	Line	−1.5	0	1

Act Column Key

B   Built by Grass Lake & Manistee River

X   Abandoned

Sources

1.   Michigan, Commissioner of Railroads, *Annual Reports,* 1888, 1892.

Harbor Springs

MAIN LINE (HS-A)

	MILEAGE	COUNTY	CROSSINGS, JUNCTIONS, ETC.
Harbor Springs	0	Emmet	
Stutsmanville	7.2	"	

CONSTRUCTION

DATE	ACT	END POINTS	MP	CHANGE	MAIN	SOURCE
1902/7/1	B	Line	0–7.2	+7.2	7.2	1
1911	Z	Line				1
1912	X	Line	0–7.2	–7.2	0	1

OWNERSHIP

1902   Harbor Springs Railway.

Act Column Key

B   Build by Harbor Springs Railway

X   Abandoned

Z   Operations suspended

Sources

1.   Koch, *Shay Locomotive*

Notes

GENERAL   The Harbor Springs Railway was locally and colloquially known as "The Hemlock Central." It was built by Ephraim Shay primarily as a logging railroad with only limited common carrier use. The company built and abandoned a number of branch lines which have not been documented here, most of which were in service for only a year or two.

Hillsdale County

The Hillsdale County operated the following lines under contract with the State of Michigan which had acquired ownership of the lines or had leased them from the owner. See page for Michigan, State of.

For arrangement of stations, construction record, and prior ownerships, see Lake Shore lines LS-A, LS-Y, LS-L, and LS-W.

ACQUISITION/DISPOSITION RECORD

DATE	ACT	HCRC–	END POINTS	MP	CHANGE	MICH.DES.OPR. MAIN	YARD	NOTE
1976/4/1	C	[LS-A4]	Hillsdale–Quincy	361.0–376.6	+15.6			
4/1	C	[LS-Y1Y]	In Hillsdale	60.4–61.1	(+0.7)			
4/1	C	[LS-Y]	Hillsdale–Bankers	61.1–65.6	+4.5			
4/1	C	[LS-L]	Jonesville–Litchfield	0.6–6.9	+6.3			

4/1	C	[LS-W2]	In Jonesville	24.1–25.3	(+1.2)			
4/1	C	[LS-W]	Bankers–Steubenville	31.1–44.7	+13.6	40.0	1.9	1
1993	XC		All lines		0	0		2

Act Column Key

C   Operated under Designated Operator contract with State of Michigan

Source

MDOT records

Notes

1.   HCRC also operated a line from the MI/IN state line to Steubenville IN under contract with State of Indiana.
2.   Operation of all lines was transferred to Indiana Northeastern.

Hobart & Manistee River *(line not located exactly)*

MAIN LINE (H&MR)

	MILEAGE	COUNTY	CROSSINGS, JUNCTIONS, ETC.
(Manistee Riv.)	0	Manistee	(sec3? T21N R13W)
(County line)	3.9		
(End)	9.2	Wexford	?

CONSTRUCTION

DATE	ACT	END POINTS	MP	CHANGE	MAIN	SOURCE	NOTE
1879/9/1	B	Line	0–9.2	+9.2	9.2	1	
1890/5/1	X	Line	0–9.2	–9.2	0	1	

OWNERSHIP

1879   Hobart & Manistee River

Act Column Key

B   Built by Hobart & Manistee River
X   Abandoned

Sources

1.   Michigan, Commissioner of Railroads, *Annual Reports,* 1879–1890.

Huron & Eastern

For arrangement of stations, construction record, and prior ownerships, see Pere Marquette lines PM-N, PM-NS, PM-NH, and PM-S.

ACQUISITION/DISPOSITION RECORD

						MICHIGAN		
						OWNED	DES.OPR.	
DATE	ACT	HERC–	END POINTS	MP	CHANGE	MAIN	MAIN	NOTE
1986/3/27	P1	[PM-N]	Croswell–Bad Axe	24.7–70.1	+45.4			
	P1	[PM-N]	Bad Axe–Kinde	70.1–79.5	+9.4			
	P1	[PM-NS]	Poland–Sandusky	0–7.1	+7.1			
	P1	[PM-NH]	Palms–Harbor Beach	0–18.3	+18.3			
	P1	[PM-S]	In Bad Axe	62.6–63.9	+1.3	81.5		
1988/12/22	P1	[PM-S]	Sag.–Bad Axe	4.1–62.6	+58.5	140.0		

1991/1/22	C	[MC-B]	Millington–Munger	79.3–101.1	+21.8			1
1/22	C	[MC-BS]	Denmark Jct.–Richville	4.8–6.0	+1.2			1
1/22	C	[MC-BC]	Caro Jct.–Colling	0.4–22.4	+22.0			1
1/22	P2	[MC-BS]	Richville–Harger	6.0–15.5	+9.5	149.5	45.0	
1996/6	X	[PM-NH]	Harbor Beach–Ruth	18.3–7.8	−10.5			2
	P1	[PM-S]	In Sag.	1.1–4.1	+3.0	142.0	45.0	

OWNERSHIP

1986   Huron & Eastern, wholly owned subsidiary of RailAmerica Corp.

Act Column Key

C   Operated under Designated Operator contract with State of Michigan

P1   Purchased from CSX.

P2   Purchased from Tuscola & Saginaw Bay

Notes

1.   This line was formerly operated by Tuscola & Saginaw Bay.

2.   Operations ended September 1997.

Indiana & Ohio

MAIN LINE (IORY)

For arrangement of stations, construction record, and prior ownerships, see Detroit, Toledo & Ironton line DTI-M.

CONSTRUCTION

DATE	ACT	IORY–	END POINTS	MP	CHANGE	MI MAIN	NOTE
1997/2/15	P	[DTI-M]	Diann–OH state line	39.8–60.4	+20.6	20.6	

OWNERSHIP

1997   Indiana & Ohio Railway.

Act Column Key

P   Purchased from Grand Trunk Western

Notes

GENERAL   Indiana & Ohio is a wholly owned subsidiary of RailTex Corp.

Indiana Northeastern

The Indiana Northeastern operated the following lines under contract with the State of Michigan which had acquired ownership of the lines or had leased them from the owner. See page for Michigan, State of.

For arrangement of stations, construction record, and prior ownerships, see Lake Shore lines LS-A, LS-Y, LS-L, and LS-W.

ACQUISITION/DISPOSITION RECORD

DATE	ACT	INNE–	END POINTS	MP	CHANGE	MICH.DES.OPR. MAIN	SOURCE
1993	C	[LS-A4]	Hillsdale–Quincy	361.0–376.6	+15.6		
	C	[LS-Y1Y]	In Hillsdale	60.4–61.1	(+0.7)		

C	[LS-Y]	Hillsdale–Bankers	61.1–65.6	+4.5		
C	[LS-L]	Jonesville–Litchfield	0.6–6.9	+6.3		
C	[LS-W2]	In Jonesville	24.1–25.3	(+1.2)		
C	[LS-W]	Bankers–Steubenville	31.1–44.7	+13.6	40.0	1

Act Column Key

C   Operated under Designated Operator contract with State of Michigan

Notes

1.   Also operated a line from the MI/IN state line to Steubenville IN under contract with State of Indiana.

Jackson & Northern

MAIN LINE (J&N-A)

	MILEAGE	COUNTY	CROSSINGS, JUNCTIONS, ETC.
(M.A.L. Crossing)	0	Jackson	C/GTW-A 104.4
(End)	2.9	"	(sec 11 T2S R1W)

CONSTRUCTION

DATE	ACT	END POINTS	MP	CHANGE	MAIN	NOTE
1912 ca.	B	Line	0–2.9	+2.9	2.9	1
???	X	Line	0–2.9	–2.9	0	1

OWNERSHIP

1912   Jackson & Northern Railroad

Act Column Key

B   Built by Jackson & Northern
X   Abandoned

Notes

1.   The date of abandonment could not be determined accurately and this company is not included in the mileage table in Chapter 2.

Kalamazoo, Lake Shore & Chicago Railway

MAIN LINE (KLSC-A)

	MILEAGE	COUNTY	CROSSINGS, JUNCTIONS, ETC.
Kal.	0	Kal.	Adjacent to MC-C 144.1
Oshtemo	5.1	"	
Brighton	6.8	"	
Rix	8.1	"	
Walker	8.8	"	
Eassom	10	"	
Mattawan	11.6	Van Buren	
(Connection)	11.7	"	C/MC-C 156.4
Newbre	13.8	"	
(Jct.)	15.3	"	J/KLSC-C 4.2
Lawton	16.0	"	J/MC-C 160.6, J/PM-H 34.0
Paw Paw	20.0	"	
—via Pere Marq. line PM-H			
S. Haven	50.0		

CONSTRUCTION

DATE	ACT	END POINTS	MP	CHANGE	MAIN	SOURCE	NOTE
1907	B1	Kal.–Paw Paw	0–15.3	+15.3			1
1907/4/15	L	Lawton–S. Haven	16.0–50.0	+33.4		2	2
1907	X	Lawton–Paw Paw	16.0–20.0	–4.0	49.4	1	
1916/5/31	XL	Lawton–S. Haven	16.0–50.0	–33.4	16.0	2	
1924	X	Kal.–Lawton	0–16.0	–16.0	0	1	

OWNERSHIP

1907   Kalamazoo, Lake Shore & Chicago

See Pere Marquette line PM-H for construction record and prior and subsequent ownership of Lawton–South Haven line.

"CALICO GRADE" (KLSC-C)

	MILEAGE	COUNTY	CROSSINGS, JUNCTIONS, ETC.
(Paw Paw)	0	Van Buren	J/KLSC-A 20.0, PM-H 30.0
(Jct.)	4.2	"	J/KLSC-A 15.3

CONSTRUCTION

DATE	ACT	END POINTS	MP	CHANGE	MAIN	SOURCE	NOTE
1905	B1	Line	0–4.2	+4.2	4.2		2
1907	X	Line	0–4.2	–4.2	0		2

OWNERSHIP

1907   Kalamazoo, Lake Shore & Chicago

PAW PAW LAKE BRANCH (KLSC-P)

	MILEAGE	COUNTY	CROSSINGS, JUNCTIONS, ETC.
Toquin	0	Van Buren	J/PM-H 11.2
Emanuel Station	0	"	
Elmwood	3.5	Berrien	
Windermere	4	"	
Blakes	4-1/2	"	
Paw Paw Lk.	5	"	

CONSTRUCTION

DATE	ACT	END POINTS	MP	CHANGE	MAIN	SOURCE	NOTE
1911 ca.	B1	Line	0–5	+5.0	5.0		3
1914/6	X	Line	0–5	–5.0	0	2	4

OWNERSHIP

1911   Kalamazoo, Lake Shore & Chicago

ACQUSITION/DISPOSITION RECORD

DATE	ACT	KLSC–	END POINTS	CHANGE	MI MAIN	NOTE
1905	B1	C	(Paw Paw–Lawton)	+4.2	4.2	
1907	B1	A	Kal.–Paw Paw	+20.0		1
/4/15	L	A	Lawton–S. Haven	+33.4		2
	X	C	Lawton–Paw Paw	–4.2	49.4	
1911 ca.	B1	P	Paw Paw Lk. Branch	+5.0	54.4	3
1914/6	X	P	Paw Paw Lk. Branch	–5.0	49.4	4
1916/5/31	XL	A	Lawton–S. Haven	–33.4	16.0	
1924	X	A	Kal.–Lawton	–16.0	0	

Act Column Key

B1 Built by Kalamazoo, Lake Shore & Chicago
L   Leased from Pere Marquette
X   Abandoned
XL Lease from Pere Marquette canceled

Sources

1. ICC, *Finance Docket 3367.*
2. Michigan Railroad Commission, *Aids, Gifts, Grants.*

Notes

1. This construction involved two segments: between Kalamazoo and the State Hospital grounds and between Mattawan and west of Newbre, approximately 1.6 and 2.4 miles respectively, on the right of way of the Michigan Central; construction between Newbre and Lawton of approximately 2.0 miles on right of way adjoining the Michigan Central; construction between Lawton and Paw Paw on the "Calico grade;" and acquisition of an abandoned route of the Michigan Central between the State Hospital grounds and Mattawan of approximately 10.0 miles.
2. In about 1905, prior to the lease of the Pere Marquette line between Lawton and Paw Paw, the KLS&C built a line on a unused grade extending from Paw Paw to 0.7 miles east of Lawton. The line was abandoned when the lease of the Pere Marquette line was made.
3. Source 2 gives the length of this line as 4.4 miles.
4. Source 2 says service ended this date; subsequent actual abandonment date not found.
5. See record for Pere Marquette line PM-H for prior ownership record.

Kalamazoo, Lake Shore & Chicago Railroad

For arrangement of stations, construction record, and prior ownerships, see Pere Marquette line PM-H.

ACQUISITION/DISPOSITION RECORD

DATE	ACT	LINE	END POINTS	MP	CHANGE	MI MAIN	SOURCE	NOTE
KLSC-								
1986/8/14	P1	[PM-H]	Paw Paw–Hartford	30.4–17.3	+13.1	13.1		
1990/2	P1	[PM-H]	In Hartford	17.3–15.7	+1.6	14.7		
1995/9/11	S	[PM-H]	Hartford–Paw Paw	15.7–30.4	–14.7	0		

OWNERSHIP

1986 Kalamazoo, Lake Shore & Chicago Railroad Division, Southwestern Michigan Railroad.

Act Column Key

P1 Purchased from CSX Transportation
S   Sold to West Michigan Railroad

Kent–Barry–Eaton Connecting

The Kent–Barry–Eaton Connecting operated the lines shown below under contract with the State of Michigan which had acquired ownership of the lines or had contractual arrangements with Penn Central. See page for Michigan, State of.

For arrangement of stations, construction record, and prior ownerships, see Michigan Central line MC-G and Chicago, Kalamazoo & Saginaw CK&S-YH.

ACQUISITION/DISPOSITION RECORD

DATE	ACT	KBEC–	END POINTS	MP	CHANGE	MICH.DES.OPR. MAIN
1979/7/15	C	[MC-G]	Vermontville–Bowen	46.1–88.0	41.9	
	C	[CKS-YH]	In Hastings	30.0–30.9	(+0.9)	41.9
1982/3/31	XC	[MC-G]	Vermontville–Caledonia	46.1–79.0	–32.9	
	XC	[CKS-YH]	In Hastings	30.0–30.9	(–0.9)	9.0
1983	XC	[MC-G]	Caledonia–Bowen	79.0–88.0	–9.0	0

OWNERSHIP

1979   Title to all lines operated by this company remained with the State of Michigan or with Penn Central, the prior owner.

Act Column Key

C   Operated under Designated Operator contract
XC   Contract ended

Lake County

MAIN LINE (LAC)

	MILEAGE	COUNTY	CROSSINGS, JUNCTIONS, ETC.
(Pere Marq. River)	0	Lk.	(sec29 T18N R14W)
(Crossing)	0.2	"	X/PM-L 115.5
(Crossing–Danaher & Melendy)		"	(sec27 T19N R14W)
(Crossing)		"	X/M&GR
(End)	11.0	"	(sec5 T19N R14W)

CONSTRUCTION

DATE	ACT	END POINTS	MP	CHANGE	MAIN	SOURCE
1880/8/20	B	South end of line	0–3.8	+3.8	3.8	1
1881	B	Extend line	3.8–6.0	+2.2	6.0	1
1882	B	Extend line	6.0–8.0	+2.0	8.0	1
1887	B	Extend line	8.0–11.0	+3.0	11.0	1
1892	X	South end of line	0–0.2	–0.2	10.8	1
1894	X	Line	0.2–11.0	–10.8	0	1

OWNERSHIP

1880   Lake County

Act Column Key

B   Built by Lake County
X   Abandoned

Sources

1.   Michigan, Commissioner of Railroads, *Annual Reports,* 1882, 1887, 1893, 1894.

Lake George & Muskegon River

MAIN LINE (LGMR-A)

	MILEAGE	COUNTY	CROSSINGS, JUNCTIONS, ETC.
(Musk. River)	0	Clare	(sec21 T19N R6W)
(Jct.)	1.5	"	J/AA-B 200.2 (SE q sec22 T19N R6W)
(Jct.)	3.0	"	J/LGMR-D 0 (sec25 T19N R6W)
(Crossing)	5.7	"	X/AA-B 195.1
(Jct.)	6.6	"	J/LGMR-B 0 (sec8 T18N R5W)
(Adjacent AA-B 193.1)	7.6	"	
(Jct.)	8.3	"	J/AA-B 192.1 (sec16 T18N R5W)
(End)	11.2	"	(sec26? T18N R5W)

CONSTRUCTION

DATE	ACT	END POINTS	MP	CHANGE	MAIN	SOURCE	NOTE
1877/1/28	B	Line	0–7.6	+7.6	7.6	1	
1878	B	Extend line	7.6–11.2	+3.6	11.2	1	
1882	S	Line	0–11.2	−11.2	0	1	

OWNERSHIP

1877   Lake George & Muskegon River

BRANCH (LGMR-B)

	MILEAGE	COUNTY	CROSSINGS, JUNCTIONS, ETC.
(Jct.)	0	Clare	J/LGMR-A 6.6
(End)	1.8	"	(sec9 T18N R5W)

CONSTRUCTION

DATE	ACT	END POINTS	MP	CHANGE	MAIN	SOURCE	NOTE
1877	B	Line	0–1.8	+1.8	1.8	1	
1882	S	Line	0–1.8	−1.8	0		

OWNERSHIP

1877   Lake George & Muskegon River

BRANCH (LGMR-XC)

	MILEAGE	COUNTY	CROSSINGS, JUNCTIONS, ETC.
(W. end)	0	Clare	
Stafford	0.25	"	X/LGMR-A ?
(E. end)	1.25	"	

CONSTRUCTION

DATE	ACT	END POINTS	MP	CHANGE	MAIN	SOURCE	NOTE
1878	B	Line	0–1.3	+1.3	1.3	1	
1880	X	Line	0–1.3	−1.3	0	1	

OWNERSHIP

1878   Lake George & Muskegon River

BRANCH (LGMR-D)

	MILEAGE	COUNTY	CROSSINGS, JUNCTIONS, ETC.
(Jct.)	0	Clare	J/LGMR-A 3.0
(Crossing, present line)	0.3	"	X/AA-B 197.5
(Jct., line E)	1.8	"	(sec29 T19N R5W)

	MILEAGE		CROSSINGS, JUNCTIONS, ETC.
(Lily Lk.)	4.2	"	(sec34 T19N R5W)
(End)	ca.7.0	"	(sec36 T19N R5W)

CONSTRUCTION

DATE	ACT	END POINTS	MP	CHANGE	MAIN	SOURCE	NOTE
1879	B	Line	0–7.0	+7.0	7.0	1	
1882	X	Line	0–7.0	–7.0	0		

OWNERSHIP

1879   Lake George & Muskegon River

BRANCH (LGMR-E)

	MILEAGE	COUNTY	CROSSINGS, JUNCTIONS, ETC.
(Jct.)	0	Clare	J/LGMR-D 1.8
(End)	1.8	"	(sec17 T19N R5W)

CONSTRUCTION

DATE	ACT	END POINTS	MP	CHANGE	MAIN	SOURCE	NOTE
1881	B	Line	0–1.8	+1.8	1.8	1	
1882	X	Line	0–1.8	–1.8	0	1	

OWNERSHIP

1881   Lake George & Muskegon River

ACQUISITION/DISPOSITION RECORD

DATE	ACT	LGMR–	END POINTS	CHANGE	MI MAIN	NOTE
1877/1/28	B	A	Main line	+7.6		
	B	B	Branch	+1.8	9.4	
1878	B	A	Main line	+3.6		
	B	XC	Branch	+1.3	14.3	
1879	B	D	Branch	+7.0	21.3	
1880	X	XC	Branch	–1.3	20.0	
1881	B	E	Branch	+1.8	21.8	
1882	S	A	Main line	–11.2		
	S	B	Branch	–1.8		
	X	D	Branch	–7.0		
	X	E	Branch	–1.8	0	

Act Column Key

B   Built by Lake George & Muskegon River
S   Sold to private owners
X   Abandoned

Sources

1.   Michigan Railroad Commission, *Aids, Gifts, Grants.*

Lake Shore & Michigan Southern _____

OLD ROAD (LS-A)

	MILEAGE [Buffalo]	COUNTY	CROSSINGS, JUNCTIONS, ETC.
Toledo OH	296.43	Lucas OH	
Swan Creek	297.63	"	
Air Line Jct. Yard	298.43	"	
Vulcan	300.23	"	
(E. end E&K)	300.31	"	J/LS-A2 3.9
Richards	302.06	"	
Sylvania OH	306.59	"	
(Line OH/MI)	307.92		
Michigan Elevator	309.0	Monroe	
Ottawa Lk.	311.28	"	
Wood	313.43	Lenawee	
(Crossing)	315.43	"	X/DT&I-M 52.7
Riga	316.49	"	f. Knights
Blissfield	318.58	"	
Grosvenor	321.23	"	J/LS-F 7.6, f. Blissfield Jct.
(W. end E&K)	322.13	"	J/LS-A2 25.7
Palmyra	322.85	"	
Lenawee Jct.	324.67	"	J/LS-J 0, J/LS-M 29.3
(Crossing)	327.9	"	X/LS-A2 31.2
WB	328.26	"	X/WAB-A 59.0
Adrian	328.78	"	
(Crossing)	329.18	"	X/DT&I-A 45.9
Cadmus	335.95	"	f. Dover
Clayton	339.80	"	
(Bridge)	346.07	"	B/CC-N 29.8
Hudson	346.24	"	
Pittsford	352.55	Hillsdale	
Osseo	356.31	"	
Wagners Track	359	"	
Bawbeese	360	"	
(Bridge)	361.5	"	B/LS-YO 60.5
(Jct.)	361.92	"	J/LS-Y 60.9
Hillsdale	362.11	"	
Ft. Wyn. Jct.	366.01	"	X/LS-W 25.3
Jonesville	366.61	"	
(Jct.)	367.36	"	J/LS-L 0.6
Allen	371.71	"	
Quincy	378.22	"	
Wilson Siding	378.9	Branch	
Coldwater	384.61	"	
Cement Work Siding	386.5	"	
(Jct.)	386.75	"	J/CTRY-A 0
Batavia	389.81	"	

Bronson	395.37	"		
Wood	398.4	"		
Burr Oak	402.10	St. Joseph	f. Locks	
Sturgis	408.33	"		
RK	408.61	"	X/LS-S 29.0, X/GRI-S 149.4	
Douglass	413.0	"		
Klinger Lk.	413.97	"	f. Klingers	
Oakwood	414.9	"		
Fawn Riv.	416.8	"		
Wh. Pi.	420.07	"	J/LS-G 0	
(Sw. W wye G R Br)	420.5	"		
White Pigeon Jct.	421.31	"	J/LS-G 0.4-0.7	
CP 10	422.55	"	aka Vistula East	
(Line MI/IN)	424.09			
CP 11 IN	425.41	Elkhart IN	aka Vistula IN	
Bristol	430.49	"		
Morehous	434.64	"		
(S.W. E&W Br.)	438.33	"		
B	438.71	"	aka CP 421	
Elkhart IN	438.86	"		
(S. Bend IN	(453.9)			

CONSTRUCTION

DATE	ACT	END POINTS	MP	CHANGE	MI MAIN	SOURCE	NOTE
1836/11/2	B1	Vulcan–Palmyra	300.3–322.1	+14.2	14.2	2	1
1838/8/9	B4	Palmyra–Lenawee Jct.	322.1–324.7	+2.6	16.8	2,6	2
1840/11/23	B3	Lenawee Jct.–Adrian	324.7–328.8	+4.1	20.9	4,6	4
1842/Sum.	B3	Adrian–Clayton	328.8–339.8	+11.0	31.9	6	
1843/5/27	B3	Clayton–Hudson	339.8–346.3	+6.5		6	
1843/9/25	B3	Hudson–Hillsdale	346.3–362.1	+15.8	54.2	6	
1850/9	B5	Hillsdale–Jonesville	362.1–366.6	+4.5		4,6	
1850/12/10	B5	Jonesville–Coldwater	366.6–384.6	+18.0	76.7	4,6	
1851/3	B5	Coldwater–Sturgis	384.6–408.3	+23.7		4,6	
1851/7	B5	Sturgis–Wh. Pi.	408.3–420.1	+11.8		4,6	
1851/10/4	B5	Wh. Pi.–S. Bend IN	420.1–438.8	+4.0	116.2	4,6	6
1855 ca.	B5	Toledo–MP 300.3	296.4–300.3	116.2			8
1962	X	Osseo–Hudson	346.2–356.3	−10.1	106.1	5	
1967	X	Clayton–Hudson	339.7–346.2	−6.5	99.6	5	
1972/5	X	Hillsdale–Osseo	356.3–360.6	−4.3	95.3	5	
1973/3	X	Adrian–Clayton	333.6–339.7	−6.1	89.2	5	
1978	X	In Hillsdale	360.6–361.0	−0.4	88.8	5	
1979	X	In Adrian	332.9–333.6	−0.7	88.1	5	
1982/11	S1	Riga–Lenawee Jct.	315.5–325.5	[10.0]	78.1		
1983	X	Ottawa Lk.–Riga	312.1–315.5	−3.4	74.7	5	
1984/2/15	S1	Lenawee Jct.–Adrian	325.5–332.9	[7.4]			
1984/2/15	S1	Hillsdale–Quincy	361.0–376.6	[15.6]	51.7		
1989/8	S2	Quincy–Sturgis	376.6–406.8	[30.2]	21.5		27
1993/12	S3	Sturgis–Wh. Pi. Jct.	406.8–421.3	[14.5]	7.0		

OWNERSHIP

1836	Erie & Kalamazoo (B1)	
1838	Palmyra & Jacksonburgh (B4)	
1840	State of Michigan (B3), of segment	

1844	State of Michigan, bought Palmyra & Jacksonburgh
1846/12/28	Michigan Southern, bought of State of Michigan
1849/8/1	Erie & Kalamazoo, leased to Michigan Southern; assigned to successors
1855/4/25	Michigan Southern & Northern Indiana, merger of Michigan Southern
1869/4/6	Lake Shore & Michigan Southern, merger of Michigan Southern & Northern Indiana
1915/1/1	New York Central, merger of Lake Shore & Michigan Southern
1968/2/1	Penn Central, merger of New York Central
1976/4/1	Conrail, bought parts of Penn Central
1984/2/15	State of Michigan, bought parts of line of Penn Central
1999/6/1	Norfolk Southern, bought parts of Conrail

E & K LINE (LS-A2)

	MILEAGE	COUNTY	CROSSINGS, JUNCTIONS, ETC.
Port Lawrence OH	0	Lucas OH	
(Jct.)	3.9	"	J/LS-A 300.3
(Jct.)	25.7	Lenawee	J/LS-A 322.1
(Crossing)	31.2	"	X/LS-A 327.9
(Bridge)	31.6	"	B/WAB-A 58.7
Adrian (old)	32.8	"	

CONSTRUCTION

DATE	ACT	END POINTS	MP	CHANGE	MI MAIN	SOURCE	NOTE
1836/11/2	B1	Port Lawrence–MP 300.3	0–3.9	+3.9		2	1
1836/11/2	B1	MP 322.1–Adrian (old)	25.7–32.8	+7.1	7.1	2	1
1854 ca.	X	Port Lawrence–MP 300.3	0–3.9	–3.9	7.1		8
1875 ca.	X	In Adrian (old)	31.2–32.8	–1.6	5.5		
1887	X	MP 322.1–Adrian (old)	25.7–31.2	–5.5	0		

OWNERSHIP

1836	Erie & Kalamazoo (B1)
1849/8/1	Leased to Michigan Southern, and assigned to successors

JACKSON BRANCH (LS-J)

	MILEAGE	COUNTY	CROSSINGS, JUNCTIONS, ETC.
Lenawee Jct.	0.0	Lenawee	J/LS-A 324.7, J/LS-M 29.3
Raisin Center	2.15	"	X/WAB-A 54.8
Chases	3.3	"	
Sutton	4.83	"	
Tecumseh Jct.	8.50	"	J/DT&I-A 55.4, X/DTM 16.1, f. Tecumseh Jct.
Tecumseh	9.01	"	
Clinton	13.48	"	
Hogan	16.59	Washtenaw	
River Raisin	17.21	"	
Manchester	21.34	"	
Manchester Jct.	21.98	"	X/LS-Y 25.4
Norvell	28.69	Jackson	
Napoleon	32.03	"	
Eldred	36.47	"	
(Sw. MC wye)	41.27	"	
OD	41.33	"	J/CC-N 1.2, X/LS-W 1.2, X/MC-A 0.8
Jackson	42.10	"	

CONSTRUCTION

DATE	ACT	END POINTS	MP	CHANGE	MAIN	SOURCE	NOTE
1838/8/9	B4	Lenawee Jct.–Tecumseh	0–9.0	+9.0	9.0	2,6	2
1855	B5	Tecumseh–Manchester	9.0–21.3	+12.3	21.3	4,6	
1857/7	B6	Manchester–Jackson	21.3–42.1	+20.8	42.1	4,6	10
1960	X	Manchester–Jackson	22.0–40.1	−18.1		5	
1960	Y	In Jackson (to LS-Y1J)	40.1–42.1	(2.0)	22.0		
1964	X	Manchester–Clinton	13.6–22.0	−8.4	13.6	5	
1982	S4	Lenawee Jct.–Clinton	0–13.6	[13.6]	0		

OWNERSHIP

1838	Palmyra & Jacksonburgh (B4)
1844	State of Michigan, bought Palmyra & Jacksonburgh
1846/12/28	Michigan Southern (B5), bought State of Michigan
1855/4/25	Michigan Southern & Northern Indiana (B6), merger of Michigan Southern
1869/4/6	Lake Shore & Michigan Southern, merger of Mich. South. & No. Indiana
1915/1/1	New York Central, merger of Lake Shore & Michigan Southern
1968/2/1	Penn Central, merger of New York Central
1976/4/1	Conrail, bought Penn Central
1999/6/1	Norfolk Southern, bought Conrail

MONROE BRANCH (LS-M)

	MILEAGE	COUNTY	CROSSINGS, JUNCTIONS, ETC.
Monroe	0.0	Monroe	X/LS-D 40.5, J/LS-YM 0
Washington St.	0.78	"	
(Monroe St.)	0.86	"	X/DUR-T 30.92
Monroe (orig. sta.)	1.0	"	
(Crossing)	1.54	"	X/PM-T 115.1
Strasburg	6.19	"	
Ida	9.90	"	
(Crossing)	12.4	"	X/AA-A 18.6, f. Monroe Jct.
Federman	12.45	"	
(Crossing)	15.1	"	X/DTI-M 42.8
(Crossing)	16.6	"	X/DTI-T2 5.6
Petersburg	17.06	"	
Deerfield	20.54	Lenawee	
(Crossing)	22.2	"	X/CCS 53.5, f. Corbus
Sisson	23.66	"	
Wellsville	26.08	"	
Lenawee Jct.	29.29	"	J/LS-A 324.7, J/LS-J 0

CONSTRUCTION

DATE	ACT	END POINTS	MP	CHANGE	MAIN	SOURCE	NOTE
1838 ca.	B2	Monroe–LaPlaisance Bay	0.4–0	+0.4	0.4	6	3
1840/11/23	B3	Monroe–Lenawee Jct.	0.8–29.3	+28.5		4,6	4
1840	B3	In Monroe	0.4–0.8	+0.4	29.3	4,6	
1953	X	Monroe–Ida	2.1–9.5	−7.4	21.9	5	
1953	Y	In Monroe (to LS-Y1M)	0–2.1	(2.1)	19.8		
1970 ca.	X	In Monroe (LS-Y1M)	1.5–2.1	(−0.6)	19.8	5	
1976	X	Ida–Lenawee Jct.	9.5–29.1	−19.6		5	
1976	Y	At Lenawee Jct. (as LS-Y2M)	29.1–29.3	(0.2)	0		
1981	X	In Monroe (LS-Y1M)	1.5–2.1	(−1.5)	0		
1984/2/15	S1	At Lenawee Jct. (LS-Y2M)	29.1–29.3	[(−0.2)]	0		

OWNERSHIP

1838	River Raisin & Lake Erie (B2)
1840	State of Michigan (B3)
1846/12/28	Michigan Southern, purchase of State of Michigan
1855/4/25	Michigan Southern & Northern Indiana, merger of Mich. Southern
1869/4/6	Lake Shore & Michigan Southern, merger of Mich. South. & No. Indiana
1915/1/1	New York Central, merger of Lake Shore & Mich. Southern
1968/2/1	Penn Central, merger of New York Central
1974/2/15	State of Michigan, bought part of line of Penn Central
1976/4/1	Conrail, bought part of Penn Central

MONROE YARD (LS-YM)

	MILEAGE	COUNTY	CROSSINGS, JUNCTIONS, ETC.
Monroe	0.0	Monroe	J/LS-M 0, X/LS-D 40.5
(Crossing)	0.1	"	X/MC-T 35.4
(Crossing)	0.2	"	X/DTSL 17.4
(End of track)	2.5	"	(LaPlaisance Bay)

CONSTRUCTION

DATE	ACT	END POINTS	MP	CHANGE	MAIN	SOURCE	NOTE
1827 ca.	–	At LaPlaisance Bay	at 2.5	0	?	8	
1838 ca.	B2	Monroe–LaPlaisance Bay	0–2.5	+2.5	2.5	6	3
1846 ca.	X	East end of line	1.1–2.5	–1.4	1.1		5
1846 ca.	Y	In Monroe	0–1.1	(1.1)	0		

OWNERSHIP

1827	LaPlaisance Harbor Bay Co. (disposition uncertain)
1838	State of Michigan (B2), of segment
1846/12/28	Michigan Southern, bought of State of Michigan
1855/4/25	Michigan Southern & Northern Indiana, merger of Mich. Southern
1869/4/6	Lake Shore & Michigan Southern, merger of Mich. South. & No. Indiana
1915/1/1	New York Central, merger of Lake Shore & Mich. Southern
1968/2/1	Penn Central, merger of New York Central
1976/4/1	Conrail, bought Penn Central
1999/6/1	Norfolk Southern, bought Conrail

FAYETTE BRANCH (LS-F)

	MILEAGE	COUNTY	CROSSINGS, JUNCTIONS, ETC.
Grosvenor	0.0	Lenawee	J/LS-A 321.2
Harrison's	0.64	"	X/T&W-A 12.8
Baldwin's Crossing	2.15	"	
Ogden	4.59	"	
Jasper	7.98	"	
Weston	11.64	"	
Bimo	14.53	"	X/DT&I-A 32.0
Morenci	18.22	"	
(Line MI/OH)	20.50		
Ritters	21.43	Fulton OH	
Fayette	24.96	"	
(End)	25.21	"	

CONSTRUCTION

DATE	ACT	END POINTS	MP	CHANGE	MI MAIN	SOURCE	NOTE
(For full detail of entire line, see Canada Southern)							
1872/7/4	B15	Grosvenor–Fayette OH	0–25.2	+25.2	20.5	8	
1873/11/13	B15	Slocum Jct.–Grosvenor	—	+41.9	62.4	6,8	8
1893	X	Grosvenor–Corbus	—	–5.5	56.9	6	17
1897	X	Slocum Jct.–Chandler	—	–0.4			
1897/11/15	S	Chandler–Dundee	—	[25.5]			18
1897 ca.	X	Dundee–Corbus	—	–10.5	20.5	6	19
1941	X	Morenci–Fayette OH	18.6–25.2	–6.6	18.6	3	
1982	X	W of Grosvenor–Weston	1.7–11.4	–9.7	8.9	5	
1984/2/15	S1	Grosvenor–west	0–1.7	[1.7]			
1984/2/15	S1	Weston–Morenci	11.4–18.6	[7.2]	0		
1991 ca.	X	Weston–Morenci	11.4–18.6	[–7.2]	0		

OWNERSHIP

1872	Chicago & Canada Southern (B15), of segment
1879/11	Chicago & Canada Southern, leased to Lake Shore & Michigan Southern
1888/11/11	Detroit & Chicago, reorganize of Chicago & Canada Southern, owned by LS&MS
1915/1/1	New York Central, merger of Detroit & Chicago
1968/2/1	Penn Central, merger of New York Central
1984/2/15	State of Michigan, bought line of Penn Central

DETROIT BRANCH (LS-D)

	MILEAGE	COUNTY	CROSSINGS, JUNCTIONS, ETC.
(Det., via GTW-D)	0.0		
(Gratiot Ave., via GTW-D)	1.73		
D. & M. Jct.	3.34	Wayne	J/GTW-D 3.2
Beaubien St.	4.4	"	J/MC-B 5.9, X/GTW-H 3.8B/DSR-OK 3.28
Woodward Ave.	4.70	"	B/DSR-W 3.25
(Hamilton Ave.)	5.2	"	B/DSR-H 3.51
(Trumbull Ave.)	5.5	"	B/DSR-T 2.16
(14th St.)	6.1	"	B/DSR-Q 3.17
(Grand River Ave.)	6.35	"	B/DSR-R 2.48
(Warren Ave.)	6.6	"	X/DSR-X 6.82
Vinewood Ave.	7.2	"	J/MC-B 3.1
(Michigan Ave.)	7.74	"	B/DSR-M 3.17
W. Det.	8.19	"	X/MC-E 2.9
(Jct. Ave.)	8.2	"	B/DSR-GB 10.83
(Vernor Highway)	9.2	"	X/DSR-A 12.69
(Fort St.)	9.8	"	B/DSR-F 0.63
(Dearborn Rd.)	10.6	"	X/DSR-DR 0.62
Delray	10.7	"	X/PM-D 4.5, X/WAB-A 4.4
D. T. Switch	10.85	"	
River Rouge	11.41	"	
YD	11.8	"	J/MC-DZ 0, f. Pleasant St.
Ecorse	14.30	"	
Wyandotte	16.97	"	
Sibley	19.89	"	
FN	20.8	"	X/DT&I-M 11.0, X/DTSL 37.3
Trenton	21.34	"	
Chandler	22.4	"	X/CCS 17.5
Rockwood	27.50	"	f. Huron

Strongs Siding	28.5	"	
Newport	33.11	Monroe	f. Swan Creek
Stony Creek	37.5	"	
SC	37.8	"	
(Jct.)	39.1	"	J/PM-TZ 2.5
Warner	39.23	"	
(Elm St.)	40.2	"	X/MOCL-1 0.94
Monroe	40.50	"	X/LS-M 0, X/LS-YM 0
LaSalle	45.36	"	
Vienna	50.28	"	
Vienna Jct.	53.01	"	
(Line MI/OH)	54.52		
N (Cross. AA)	55.45	Lucas OH	
K (Cross. TT)	56.55	"	
Alexis	56.56	"	
W. Toledo	57.95	"	
Wagon Works Jct.	59.28	"	
Wagon Works	59.84	"	
Z	62.05	"	
(Toledo via NYC)	64.11	"	

CONSTRUCTION

DATE	ACT	END POINTS	MP	CHANGE	MI MAIN	SOURCE	NOTE
1855/12/25	B7	D&M Jct.–Monroe	3.3–40.5	+37.2	37.2	6,8	9
1856/7	B7	Monroe–Z	40.5–64.0	+21.5	51.2	8	
1976/4/1	A	D&M Jct.–OH state line	3.3–54.5	−51.2	0		28

OWNERSHIP

1855	Detroit, Monroe & Toledo
1856/7/1	Detroit, Monroe & Toledo, leased to Michigan Southern & Northern Indiana; lease assigned to successors
1915/1/1	New York Central, merger of Detroit, Monroe & Toledo
1968/2/1	Penn Central, merger of New York Central
1976/4/1	Conrail, bought Penn Central
1999/6/1	Norfolk Southern, bought Conrail

YPSILANTI BRANCH, OLD LINE IN HILLSDALE (LS-YO)

	MILEAGE [Ypsi.]	COUNTY	CROSSINGS, JUNCTIONS, ETC.
(Jct.)	59.6	Hillsdale	J/LS-Y 59.6
(Bridge)	61.5	"	B/LS-A 361.5
Hillsdale (old)	62	"	
(Jct.)	62.7	"	J/LS-Y 63.5

CONSTRUCTION

DATE	ACT	END POINTS	MP	CHANGE	MAIN	SOURCE	NOTE
1872/1	B12	MP 59.6–Hillsdale	59.6–62	+2.4		4,6	
1872/11	B12	Hillsdale–MP 62.7	62–62.7	+0.7	3.1	4,6	
1881 ca.	X	Line	59.6–62.7	−3.1	0		15

OWNERSHIP

1872	Detroit, Hillsdale & Indiana (B12), of segment
1875/1/30	Detroit, Hillsdale & Southwestern, reorganize Detroit, Hillsdale & Ind.
1881	Detroit, Hillsdale & Southwestern, leased to Lake Shore & Mich. Southern

YPSILANTI BRANCH (LS-Y)

	MILEAGE	COUNTY	CROSSINGS, JUNCTIONS, ETC.
(Ypsi., via MC-E)	0.0	Washtenaw	
(Jct.)	0.36	"	J/MC-E 29.9
(Crossing)	2.6	"	X/DUR-J 2.77
Pittsfield Jct.	7.06	"	X/AA-A 40.4
Saline	11.08	"	
Bridgewater	17.32	"	
Manchester	24.43	"	
Manchester Jct.	25.43	"	X/LS-J 22.0
Watkins	29.75	Jackson	
Brooklyn	35.68	"	
Cement City	40.69	"	f. Woodstock
(Bridge CN)	40.8	"	B/CC-N 14.0
Somerset	43.45	Hillsdale	
Somerset Centre	45.26	"	
Jerome	48.88	"	
(Bridge)	49.0	"	B/DTM 44.0
N. Adams	53.62	"	
(Jct.)	59.6	"	J/LS-YO 59.6
(Connection)	60.9	"	J/LS-A 361.9
Hillsdale	61.12	"	
(Connection)	61.2	"	J/LS-A 362.2
(Sw. W wye)	61.5	"	
(Jct.)	63.5	"	J/LS-YO 62.7
Bankers	65.6	"	J/LS-W 31.1

CONSTRUCTION

DATE	ACT	END POINTS	MP	CHANGE	MAIN	SOURCE	NOTE
1871/7	B12	Ypsi.–Saline	0.4–11.1	+10.7	10.7	6	13
1871/9/23	B12	Saline–Manchester	11.1–24.4	+13.3	24.0	6	
1872/1	B12	Manchester–Hillsdale	24.4–59.6	+35.2	59.2	4,6	
1872/11	B12	Hillsdale–Bankers	63.5–65.6	+2.1	61.3	4,6	
1881 ca.	B13	In Hillsdale	59.6–63.5	+3.9	65.2		15
1961	X	Bridgewater–Brooklyn	17.5–34.2	−16.7		5	
1961	X	Cement City–N. Adams	40.2–53.3	−13.1	35.4	5	
1967	X	Saline–Bridgewater	11.2–17.5	−6.3	29.1	5	
1969	X	Ypsi.–Pittsfield Jct.	0.4–4.8	−4.4		5	
1969	S5	Pittsfield Jct.–Saline	4.8–11.2	[6.4]	18.3	5	21
1970	X	Brooklyn–Cement City	34.2–40.2	−6.0	12.3	5	
1972	X	Hillsdale–N. Adams	53.3–60.4	−7.1	5.2	5	
1972	Y	In Hillsdale (to LS-Y1Y)	60.4–61.1	(0.7)	4.5		
1984/2/15	S1	Hillsdale–Bankers	61.1–65.6	[4.5]			
1984/2/15	S1	In Hillsdale (LS-Y1Y)	60.4–61.1	[(0.7)]	0		

OWNERSHIP

1872	Detroit, Hillsdale & Indiana (B12), of segment
1875/1/30	Detroit, Hillsdale & Southwestern (B13), reorganize Detroit, Hillsdale & Indiana
1881/9/5	Detroit, Hillsdale & Southwestern, leased to Lake Shore & Mich. Southern
1915/1/1	Lease assigned to New York Central
1968/2/1	Penn Central, bought DH&SW
1969	Ann Arbor Railroad, bought part of line
1984/2/15	State of Michigan, bought line of Penn Central

LANSING BRANCH (LS-L)

	MILEAGE	COUNTY	CROSSINGS, JUNCTIONS, ETC.
(Jonesville via LS-A)	0.0		
(Jct.)	0.6	Hillsdale	J/LS-A 367.6
Litchfield	6.68	"	
(Crossing)	13.50	Calhoun	X/MC-A 24.1, X/DTM 65.1
Homer	13.96	"	
Condit	17.31	"	
A	21.9	"	X/MC-C 96.0, B/MUR-S 19.95
Albion	22.33	"	
Hayes Wheel Co.	22.9	Jackson	
Coalville	26.3	"	J/spur to coal mine, 1.0 mi.
Devereaux	28.72	"	
Springport	32.79	Eaton	
Charlesworth	37.70	"	
(Crossing)	41.8	"	X/MC-G 24.6
Eaton Rapids	42.47	"	
Kingsland	47.77	"	
Dimondale	51.98	"	
Packard	54.97	Ingham	
(Forest St.)	58.2	"	X/LACL-1 1.46
Reo Jct.	58.76	"	
(Crossing)	58.93	"	X/GTW-C 221.2
South St.	58.93	"	
(Mich. Ave.)	60.0	"	B/LACL-6 0.39
Lans.	60.06	"	
(Crossing)	60.5	"	X/MC-YLT 0.4
(Grand River Ave.)	61.0	"	X/LACL-5 2.35
N. Lans.	61.16	"	J/MC-YLM 0, J/PM-D 88.8

CONSTRUCTION

DATE	ACT	END POINTS	MP	CHANGE	MAIN	SOURCE	NOTE
1872/1/7	B14	Jonesville–Albion	0.6–22.3	+21.7	21.7	4,6	14
1872/9/30	B14	Albion–Eaton Rapids	22.3–42.4	+20.1	41.8	4,6	
1873/1/13	B14	Eaton Rapids–N. Lans.	42.4–61.3	+18.9	60.6	6	
1941	X	Springport–Eaton Rapids	33.1–41.8	−8.7		3	
1941	X	Eaton Rapids–Lans.	42.4–57.5	−15.1		3	
1941	Y	In Eaton Rapids (to LS-Y3L)	41.8–42.4	(0.6)			
1941	Y	In Lans. (to LS-Y2L)	57.5–61.2	(3.7)	32.5		
1943	X	Litchfield–Homer	6.9–13.5	−6.6		3	
1943	X	Homer–Albion	14.0–21.7	−7.7		3	
1943	Y	In Homer (to LS-Y6L)	13.5–14.0	(0.5)			
1943	Y	In Albion (to LS-Y5L)	21.7–21.9	(0.2)	17.5		
1956 ca.	X	In Lans. (LS-Y1L)	58.8–59.7	(−0.9)			
1956 ca.	–	In Lans. (Y1L renamed Y2L)	57.5–58.8	(1.3)	17.5		
1967	X	In Albion (LS-Y5L)	21.7–21.9	(−0.2)	17.5		
1968/9/1	Y	In Albion (to LS-Y4L)	21.9–23.8	(1.9)			
1968/9/1	X	Albion–Springport	23.8–33.1	−9.3	6.3	5	
1975	X	In Lans. (LS-Y1L)	59.7–60.4	(−0.7)			
1975	X	In Eaton Rapids (LS-Y3L)	41.8–42.4	(−0.6)			
1975	X	In Albion (LS-Y4L)	23.6–23.8	(−0.2)			
1975	X	In Homer (LS-Y6L)	13.4–13.9	(−0.5)	6.3		
1984/2/15	S1	Jonesville–Litchfield	0.6–6.9	[6.3]	0		

OWNERSHIP

1872	Northern Central Michigan; wholly owned by Lake Shore & Mich. Southern
1897/5/1	Leased to Lake Shore & Michigan Southern
1915/1/1	New York Central, merger of Lake Shore & Michigan Southern
1968/2/1	Penn Central, merger of New York Central
1976/4/1	Conrail, bought part of lines of Penn Central
1984/2/15	State of Michigan, bought part of lines of Penn Central
1999/6/1	Norfolk Southern, bought Conrail

G & M BRANCH (LS-S)

	MILEAGE	COUNTY	CROSSINGS, JUNCTIONS, ETC.
Goshen IN	0.0	Elkhart IN	
Williams	4.18	"	
Burns	6.48	"	
Middlebury	9.26	"	
Oak	12.73	LaGrange IN	
Pashan	14.25	"	
Shipshewana	16.43	"	
Seyberts	20.42	"	
Twin Lk.	23.24	"	
(Line IN/MI)	25.60		
Sturgis	28.9	St. Joseph	
(Prop.line LS/MC)	29.0	"	
RK	29.0	"	X/GR&I-S 149.4, X/LS-A 408.6
Findley	36.15	"	J/MC-K 35.1

CONSTRUCTION

DATE	ACT	END POINTS	MP	CHANGE	MI MAIN	SOURCE	NOTE
1888 ca.	B16	Sturgis–Goshen IN (MI=3.4)	0–29.0	+29.0	3.4	6	
1890/2/1	L1	Sturgis–Findley	29.0–36.2	+7.2	10.6	6	16
1935	X	Sturgis–Findley	29.5–36.2	−6.7	3.9	5	
1960	X	Shipshewana–Sturgis (MI=1.8)	16.9–27.4	−10.5			
1960	Y	In Sturgis (to LS-Y1S)	27.4–29.5	(2.1)	0		
1980 ca.	X	In Sturgis (as LS-Y1S)	27.4–29.5	(−2.1)	0		

OWNERSHIP

1888	Canada & St. Louis
1889/10/29	Sturgis, Goshen & St. Louis, reorganization of Canada & St. Louis
1889/12/1	Sturgis, Goshen & St. Louis, leased by Lake Shore & Mich. Southern
1890	Lake Shore & Michigan Southern, leased part of Battle Creek & Sturgis
1915/6/11	New York Central, merger of Sturgis, Goshen & St. Louis
1968/2/1	Penn Central, merger of New York Central
1976/4/1	Conrail, bought Penn Central

GRAND RAPIDS BRANCH (LS-G)

	MILEAGES	COUNTY	CROSSINGS, JUNCTIONS, ETC.
Wh. Pi.	0.0	St.Joseph	J/LS-A 420.1
Wh. Pi. Jct.	(0.7)	"	
(Jct.)	0.4	"	J/line to White Pigeon Jct., 0.7 mi.
CP 18	0.6	"	
Constantine	3.92	"	J/spur to orig. end, 0.4 mi.
Florence	7.35	"	

Three Rivers Jct.	9.6	"	J/LS-GA 69.9; CR named CP River
VE	10.78	"	X/MC-A 70.1
Fourth St.	10.8	"	
Three Rivers (new)	11.0	"	
Three Rivers (old)	11.39	"	
CP Cowling	13.3	"	
CP Park	15.2	"	
Moorepark	16.40	"	f. Parkville
Flowerfield	19.89	"	
Schoolcraft (new)	23.05	Kal.	X/GTW-C 146.8, f. CF
Schoolcraft (old)	23.40	"	
Portage	29.86	"	
Kal	32.9	"	
Comfort Siding	33.8	"	
Cork	34.0	"	
S. Yard	34.13	"	
(Portage St.)	36.0	"	X/KACL-6 0.66
(Crossing)	36.3	"	X/GR&I-S 185.1; CR named Gib
(Crossing)	36.3	"	X/GTW-K 11.0
(Property line)	36.5	"	
(Michigan Ave.)	36.56	"	X/KACL-1 0.30
Kal.	36.58	"	
BO	36.76	"	X/MC-C 143.1
N. Yard	36.88	"	
(Crossing)	37.0	"	X/CK&S yard spur
Cooper	42.32	"	
Argenta	45.54	"	f. Silver Creek
Plainwell	48.08	Allegan	
JN	48.26	"	X/GR&I-S 196.6
Otsego (old)	52.06	"	
Otsego (new)	52.7	"	
Abronia	56.07	"	f. W. Watson
Allegan	61.85	"	J/DTM 132.9, J/PM-A 1.0–0.8, X/MUR-WA 10.68
Miner Lk.	65.46	"	
Hopkins	69.12	"	
Hilliards	73.04	"	
Dorr	76.71	"	
Herps	79.62	"	
Byron Center	82.64	Kent	f. Byron
Wentworth	88.66	"	
Kellys	89.8	"	
(Bridge)	90.1	"	B/GRHC-A 2.5
Lamar	91.12	"	X/PM-C 3.5
Eagle Mills	92.82	"	
Gr. Rpds.	94.53	"	
(Fulton St.)	94.6	"	X/GRCL-7 0.71
(Crossing)	94.9	"	X/GR&I-N 234.8
(End)	94.99	"	J/PM-P 0.9

CONSTRUCTION

DATE	ACT	END POINTS	MP	CHANGE	MAIN	SOURCE	NOTE
1852	B5	White Pigeon–Constantine	0–3.9	+3.9	3.9	4,6	7
1855	B8	Constantine–Three Rivers	3.9–11.4	+7.5	11.4	4,6	
1867/5/3	B9	Kal.–Three Rivers	36.5–11.4	+25.1	36.5	4,6	
1868/11/23	B10	Kal.–Allegan	36.5–61.8	+25.3	61.8	4	
1869/3/1	B10	Allegan–Gr. Rpds.(end)	61.8–95.0	+33.2	95.0	1,6	11
1958	X	In White Pigeon	0–0.4	–0.4		7	
1958	B17	Wh. Pi. Jct.–MP 0.4	0.4+0.7	+0.7	95.3	7	20
1972	X	N. Yard–Plainwell	39.5–46.8	–7.3		5	
1972	Y	In Kal. (to LS-Y1G)	36.8–39.5	(2.7)	85.3	5	
1976	X	Otsego–Lamar	52.7–91.6	–38.9			
1976	Y	In Gr. Rpds.(to LS-Y2G)	91.6–95.0	(3.4)	43.0		

OWNERSHIP

1852	Michigan Southern (B5), leased 1864/11/21 to St. Joseph Valley
1855	St. Joseph Valley (B8)
1867	Kalamazoo & Schoolcraft and Schoolcraft & Three Rivers (both B9)
1868	Kalamazoo, Allegan & Grand Rapids (B10)
1869/8/14	Kalamazoo & White Pigeon, merger of St. Joseph Valley, Kalamazoo & Schoolcraft, and Schoolcraft & Three Rivers; 100% owned by Lake Shore & Mich. Southern
1869/9/21	Kalamazoo, Allegan & Grand Rapids, leased to Lake Shore & Mich. Southern
1915/1/1	New York Central (B17), merger of Kalamazoo & White Pigeon; lease of KA&GR
1968/2/1	Penn Central, merger of New York Central; lease assigned of KA&GR
1976/4/1	Conrail, bought Penn Central
1999/6/1	Norfolk Southern, bought Conrail

AIR LINE CONNECTION (LS-GA)

	MILEAGE	COUNTY	CROSSINGS, JUNCTIONS, ETC.
	[Jackson Jct.]		
(Jct.)	68.2	St.Joseph	J/MC-A 68.8
Three Rivers Jct.	69.9	"	J/LS-G 9.6

CONSTRUCTION

DATE	ACT	END POINTS	MP	CHANGE	MAIN	SOURCE	NOTE
1958	B17	Line	68.2–69.9	+1.7	1.7	7	
1982	X	Line	68.2–69.9	–1.7	0	5	

OWNERSHIP

1958	New York Central (B17)
1968/2/1	Penn Central, merger of New York Central
1976/4/1	Conrail, bought Penn Central

FORT WAYNE BRANCH (LS-W)

	MILEAGE	COUNTY	CROSSINGS, JUNCTIONS, ETC.
(Jackson, via MC-E)	0.0		
(Jct.)	0.49	Jackson	J/MC-E 75.1
Fort Wayne Switch	1.0	"	J/MC-A 0.7
OD	1.12	"	X/LS-J 41.3
(Francis St.)	1.75	"	X/JACL-3 1.06
Aspinwall	2.11	"	
Haires	5.13	"	J/MC-A 4.8
Wilsons	6.55	"	

Horton	10.43	"	f. Baldwin Mills
Hanover	14.04	"	X/DTM 51.2
Stony Point	16.22	"	
Mosherville	18.83	Hillsdale	f. E. Mosherville, th. Scipio
Jonesville	24.58	"	
Ft. Wyn. Jct.	25.29	"	X/LS-A 366.0
Hillsdale	x		
Bankers	31.09	"	J/LS-Y 65.6
Reading	35.79	"	
Montgomery	41.16	"	
(Line MI/IN)	44.68		
Ray	44.79	Steuben IN	
Fremont	48.86	"	
Angola	56.21	"	
Pleasant Lk.	60.46	"	
Steubenville	63.45	"	X/WB
Summit	64.67	DeKalb IN	
WX	70.38	"	X/NY
Waterloo	70.43	"	
Auburn	75.44	"	
Auburn Jct.	76.58	"	
(Cross. B&O-PRR)	76.58	"	X/BO, X/PV
St. Johns	80.11	"	
New Era	81.63	"	
Stoners	84.68	Allen IN	
Hunterville	86.39	"	
Carrolls Crossing	88.39	"	
Academie	90.74	"	
N. Ft. Wyn.	94.81	"	
Ft. Wyn.	96.24	"	
(Cross. NKP)	97.4	"	X/NK
(Cross. GR&I)	97.7	"	X/GR
(Cross. PRR)	97.9	"	X/PF
(End)	97.99	"	

CONSTRUCTION

DATE	ACT	END POINTS	MP	CHANGE	MI MAIN	SOURCE	NOTE
1869/11/22	B11	East Ave.–Reading	0.4–35.8	+35.4	35.4	4,6	12
1870/1/17	B11	Reading–Angola IN	35.8–56.2	+20.4	44.3	4,6	
1870/12/5	B11	Angola IN–Ft. Wyn.	56.2–98.0	+41.8	44.3	6	8
1940	Y	In Jackson (to LS-Y1W)	0.4–1.1	(0.7)	43.6		
1973/1	X	Waterloo IN–Pleasant Lk.	60.5–70.4	−9.9			8
1973/6/15	X	Ft. Wyn. Jct.–Bankers	25.3–31.1	−5.8		5	
1973/6/15	X	Haires–Horton	5.1–10.5	−5.4	32.4	5	
1976	X	Horton–Jonesville	10.5–24.1	−13.6	18.8	5	
1982	X	OD–Haires	1.1–5.1	−4.0	14.8	5	
1984/2/15	S1	In Jonesville	24.1–25.3	[1.2]			
1984/2/15	S1	Bankers–IN state line	31.1–44.7	[13.6]	0		

OWNERSHIP

1869	Fort Wayne, Jackson & Saginaw (B11)
1879/12/31	Fort Wayne & Jackson, reorganization of Ft. Wayne, Jackson & Saginaw
1882/8/24	Leased to Lake Shore & Michigan Southern

1915/1/1   Lease assigned to New York Central
1968/2/1   Lease assigned to Penn Central
1976/4/1   Conrail, bought part of line of Penn Central
1984/2/15 State of Michigan, bought part of line of Penn Central

AQUISITION/DISPOSITION RECORD

DATE	ACT	LS–	END POINTS	CHANGE	MI MAIN	NOTE
1836/11/2	B1	A,A2	Port Lawrence OH–Adrian	+21.3	21.3	1
1838/8/9	B4	A,J	Palmyra Jct.–Tecumseh	+11.6		2
	B2	M,YM	In Monroe	+2.9	35.8	3
1840/11/23	B3	A,M	Monroe–Adrian	+32.6		4
	B3	M	In Monroe	+0.4	68.8	
1842/Sum.	B3	A	Adrian–Clayton	+11.0	79.8	
1843/5/27	B3	A	Clayton–Hudson	+6.5		
9/25	B3	A	Hudson–Hillsdale	+15.8	102.1	
1846 ca.	X	YM	In Monroe	–1.4		5
	Y	YM	In Monroe	(1.1)	99.6	
1850/9	B5	A	Hillsdale–Jonesville	+4.5		
12/10	B5	A	Jonesville–Coldwater	+18.0	122.1	
1851/3	B5	A	Coldwater–Sturgis	+23.7		
7	B5	A	Sturgis–Wh. Pi.	+11.8		
10/4	B5	A	Wh. Pi.–S. Bend IN	+4.0	161.6	6
1852	B5	G	Wh. Pi.–Constantine	+3.9	165.5	7
c1854	B5	A	Toledo–MP 300.3	+3.9		8
	X	A2	Port Lawrence–MP 300.3	–3.9	165.5	8
1855	B5	J	Tecumseh–Manchester	+12.3		
	B8	G	Constantine–Three Rivers	+7.5		
/12/25	B7	D	Det.–Monroe	+37.2	222.5	9
1856/7	B7	D	Monroe–Toledo	+14.0	236.5	
1857/7	B6	J	Manchester–Jackson	+20.8	257.3	10
1867/5/3	B9	G	Kal.–Three Rivers	+25.1	282.4	
1868/11/23	B10	G	Kal.–Allegan	+25.3	307.7	
1869/3/1	B10	G	Allegan–Gr. Rpds.	+33.2		11
11/22	B11	W	Jackson–Reading	+35.4	376.3	12
1870/1/17	B11	W	Reading–Angola IN	+8.9		
12/5	B11	W	Angola IN–Ft. Wyn. IN	+41.8	385.2	18
1871/7	B12	Y	Ypsi.–Saline	+10.7		13
9/23	B12	Y	Saline–Manchester	+13.3	409.2	
1872/1	B12	Y,YO	Manchester–Hillsdale	+37.6		
1/7	B14	L	Jonesville–Albion	+21.7		14
7/4	B15	F	Grosvenor–Fayette OH	+20.5		
9/30	B14	L	Albion–Eaton Rapids	+20.1		
11	B12	Y,YO	Hillsdale–Bankers	+2.8	511.9	
1873/1/13	B14	L	Eaton Rapids–N. Lans.	+18.8		
11/13	B15	F	Slocum Jct.–Grosvenor	+41.9	572.6	8
1875 ca.	X	A2	In Adrian	–1.6	571.0	
1881 ca.	B13	Y	In Hillsdale	+3.9		15
	X	Y	In Hillsdale	–3.1	571.8	15
1887	X	A2	Palmyra–Adrian	–5.5	566.3	
1888	B16	S	Sturgis–Goshen IN	+4.4	569.8	
1890/2/1	L1	S	Sturgis–Findley	+7.2	576.9	16
1893	X	F	Grosvenor–Corbus	–5.5	571.4	17
1897	X	F	Slocum Jct.–Chandler	–0.4		
/11/15	S	F	Chandler–Dundee	–25.5		18

	X	F	Dundee–Corbus	−10.5	535.0	19
1935	X	S	Sturgis–Findley	−6.7	528.3	
1940	Y	W	In Jackson (to Y1W)	(0.7)	527.6	
1941	X	F	Morenci–Fayette OH	−1.9		
	X	L	Springport–Eaton Rapids	−8.7		
	X	L	Eaton Rapids–Lans.	−15.1		
	Y	L	In Eaton Rapids (to Y3L)	(0.6)		
	Y	L	In Lans. (to Y2L)	(3.7)	497.6	
1943	X	L	Litchfield–Homer	−6.6		
	X	L	Homer–Albion	−7.7		
	Y	L	In Homer (to Y6L)	(0.5)		
	Y	L	In Albion (to Y5L)	(0.2)	482.6	
1953	X	M	Monroe–Ida	−7.4		
	Y	M	In Monroe (to Y1M)	(2.1)	473.1	
1956 ca.	X	Y1L	In Lans.	(−0.9)	473.1	
1958	X	G	In White Pigeon	−0.4		
	B17	G	In White Pigeon	+0.7		20
	B17	GA	In Three Rivers	+1.7	475.1	
1960	X	J	Manchester–Jackson	−18.1		
	Y	J	In Jackson (to Y1J)	(2.0)		
	X	S	Sturgis–Shipshewana IN	−1.8		
	Y	S	In Sturgis (to Y1S)	(2.1)	451.1	
1961	X	Y	Bridgewater–Brooklyn	−16.7		
	X	Y	Cement City–N. Adams	−13.1	421.3	
1962	X	A	Osseo–Hudson	−10.1	411.2	
1964	X	J	Manchester–Clinton	−8.4	402.8	
1967	X	A	Clayton–Hudson	−6.5		
	X	Y5L	In Albion	(−0.2)		
	X	Y	Saline–Bridgewater	−6.3	390.0	

On 1 February 1968 this company was merged into Penn Central.

DATE	ACT	PC–	END POINTS	MP	CHANGE	MI MAIN	NOTE
1968/9/1	X	[LS-L]	Albion–Springport	23.8–33.1	−9.3		
9/1	Y	[LS-L]	In Albion (to Y4L)	21.9–23.8	(1.9)	378.8	
1969	X	[LS-Y]	Ypsi.–Pittsfield Jct.	0.4–4.8	−4.4		
	S5	[LS-Y]	Pittsfield Jct.–Saline	4.8–11.2	[6.4]	368.0	21
1970	X	[LS-Y]	Brooklyn–Cement City	34.2–40.2	−6.0		
	X	[LS-Y1M]	In Monroe	1.5–2.1	(−0.6)	362.0	
1972/5	X	[LS-A]	Hillsdale–Osseo	356.3–360.6	−4.3		
	X	[LS-G]	N. Yard–Plainwell	39.5–46.8	−7.3		
	Y	[LS-G]	In Kal. (to Y1G)	36.8–39.5	(2.7)		
	X	[LS-Y]	Hillsdale–N. Adams	60.4–53.3	−7.1		
	Y	[LS-Y]	In Hillsdale (to Y1Y)	60.4–61.1	(0.7)	339.9	
1973/1	X	[LS-W]	Waterloo IN–Pleasant Lk. IN	60.5–70.4	—		8
3	X	[LS-A]	Adrian–Clayton	333.6–339.7	−6.1		
6/15	X	[LS-W]	Ft. Wyn. Jct.–Bankers	25.3–31.1	−5.8		
6/15	X	[LS-W]	Haires–Horton	5.1–10.5	−5.4	322.6	
1975	X	[LS-Y1L]	In Lans.	59.7–60.4	(−0.7)		
	X	[LS-Y3L]	In Eaton Rapids	41.8–42.4	(−0.6)		
	X	[LS-Y4L]	In Albion	23.6–23.8	(−0.2)		
	X	[LS-Y6L]	In Homer	13.4–13.9	(−0.5)	322.6	

On 1 April 1976 part of Penn Central was conveyed to Conrail and part retained by Penn Central. The lines were:

LINE DESIG.	END POINTS	MP	MAIN	MI SOURCE	NOTE
CNR-[LS-A1]	OH state line–Riga	307.9–315.5	7.6		
PC-[LS-A]	Riga–West of Adrian	315.5–333.6	18.1		
PC-[LS-A]	Hillsdale–Quincy	360.6–376.6	16.0		
CNR-[LS-A5]	Quincy–IN state line	376.6–424.1	47.5		
PC-[LS-M]	Ida–Lenawee Jct.	9.5–29.3	19.8		
CNR-[LS-Y1M]	In Monroe	0–1.5	(1.5)		
CNR-[LS-YM]	In Monroe	0–1.1	(1.1)		
PC-[LS-F]	Grosvenor–Morenci	0–18.6	18.6		
CNR-[LS-D]	D&M Jct–OH state line	3.3–54.5	51.2		
CNR-[LS-J]	Lenawee Jct.–Clinton	0–13.6	13.6		
CNR-[LS-Y1J]	In Jackson	40.1–42.1	(2.0)		
PC-[LS-Y]	Hillsdale–Bankers	61.1–65.6	4.5		
PC-[LS-Y1Y]	In Hillsdale	60.4–61.1	(0.7)		
PC-[LS-L]	Jonesville–Litchfield	0.6–6.9	6.3		
CNR-[LS-Y4L]	In Albion	21.9–23.6	(1.7)		
CNR-[LS-Y2L]	In Lans.	57.5–58.8	(1.3)		
CNR-[LS-Y1L]	In Lans.	60.4–61.2	(0.8)		
CNR-[LS-Y1W]	In Jackson	0.4–1.1	(0.7)		
CNR-[LS-W]	OD–Haires	1.1–5.1	4.0		
PC-[LS-W]	Horton–Ft. Wyn. Jct.	10.5–25.3	14.8		
PC-[LS-W]	Bankers–IN state line	31.1–44.7	13.6		
CNR-[LS-G]	Wh. Pi. Jct.–N. Yard	0–36.8	37.1		
PC-[LS-G]	Otsego–Lamar	52.7–91.6	38.9		
CNR-[LS-G]	Lamar–Gr. Rpds.	91.6–95.0	3.4		
CNR-[LS-Y1G]	In Kal.	36.8–39.5	(2.7)		
CNR-[LS-G2]	Plainwell–Otsego	46.8–52.7	5.9		
CNR-[LS-GA]	Three Rivers bypass	Line	1.7		
CNR-[LS-Y1S]	In Sturgis	27.4–29.5	(2.1)		

1976/4/1   CNR=172.0   PC=150.6   LS=322.6

DATE	ACT	XXX–	END POINTS	MP	CHANGE	NOTE
1976	X	PC-[LS-M]	Ida–Lenawee Jct.	9.5–29.1	–19.6	
	Y	PC-[LS-M]	At Lenawee Jct.(to Y2M)	29.1–29.3	(0.2)	
	X	PC-[LS-W]	Horton–Jonesville	10.5–24.1	–13.6	
	Y	CNR-[LS-G]	Lamar–Gr. Rpds.(to Y2G)	91.6–95.0	(3.4)	
	A	CNR-[LS-D]	D&M Jct.–OH state line	3.3–54.5	–51.2	
	X	PC-[LS-G]	Otsego–Lamar	52.7–91.6	–38.9	

1976 YEAR   CNR=117.4   PC=78.3   LS=195.7

DATE	ACT	XXX–	END POINTS	MP	CHANGE	NOTE
1978	X	PC-[LS-A]	In Hillsdale	360.6–361.0	–0.4	

1978 YEAR   CNR=117.4   PC=77.9   LS=195.3

DATE	ACT	XXX–	END POINTS	MP	CHANGE	NOTE
1979	X	PC-[LS-A]	In Adrian	332.9–333.6	–0.7	

1979 YEAR   CNR=117.4   PC=77.2   LS=194.6

DATE	ACT	XXX–	END POINTS	MP	CHANGE	NOTE
1980 ca.	X	CNR-[LS-Y1S]	In Sturgis	27.4–29.5	(–2.1)	

1980 YEAR   CNR=117.4   PC=77.2   LS=194.6

DATE	ACT	XXX–	END POINTS	MP	CHANGE	NOTE
1981	X	CNR-[LS-Y1M]	In Monroe	0–1.5	(–1.5)	

1981 YEAR   CNR=117.4   PC=77.2   LS=194.6

1982	S4	CNR-[LS-J] Lenawee Jct.–Clinton	0–13.6	[13.6]
	X	CNR-[LS-GA] Three Rivers bypass	Line	–1.7
	X	CNR-[LS-W]OD–Haires	1.1–5.1	–4.0
	S1	PC-[LS-A] Riga–Lenawee Jct.	315.5–325.5	[10.0]
	X	PC-[LS-F] W of Grosvenor–Weston	1.7–11.4	–9.7
	X	PC-[LS-Y1Y] In Hillsdale	60.4–61.1	(–0.7)

1982 YEAR   CNR=98.1   MICH=10.0   PC=57.5   SMRS=13.6   LS=179.2

| 1983 | X | CNR-[LS-A] Ottawa Lk.–Riga | 312.1–315.5 | –3.4 |

1983 YEAR   CNR=94.7   MICH=10.0   PC=57.5   SMRS=13.6   LS=175.8

1984	Z	CNR-[LS-A] Quincy–Sturgis	376.6–406.8	—
/2/15	S1	PC-[LS-A] Lenawee Jct.–Adrian	325.5–332.9	–7.4
2/15	S1	PC-[LS-A] Hillsdale–Quincy	361.0–376.6	–15.6
2/15	S1	PC-[LS-M] At Lenawee Jct.	29.1–29.3	(–0.2)
2/15	S1	PC-[LS-F] At Grosvenor	0–1.7	–1.7
2/15	S1	PC-[LS-F] Weston–Morenci	11.4–18.8	–7.2
2/15	S1	PC-[LS-Y] Hillsdale–Bankers	61.1–65.6	–4.5
2/15	S1	PC-[LS-Y1Y] In Hillsdale	60.4–61.1	(–0.7)
2/15	S1	PC-[LS-L] Jonesville–Litchfield	0.6–6.9	–6.3
2/15	S1	PC-[LS-W] In Jonesville	24.1–25.3	–1.2
2/15	S1	PC-[LS-W] Bankers–IN state line	31.1–44.7	–13.6

1984 YEAR   CNR=94.7   MICH=67.5   PC=0   SMRS=13.6   LS=175.8

| 1989 ca. | S3 | CNR-[LS-A] Quincy–Sturgis | 376.6–406.8 | –30.2 | 64.5 |

1989 YEAR   CNR=64.5   MICH=67.5   MSRR=30.2   PC=0   SMRS=13.6   LS=175.8

| 1991 ca. | X | MICH-[LS-F] Weston–Morenci | 11.4–18.6 | [–7.2] |

1991 YEAR   CNR=64.5   MICH=60.3   MSRR=30.2   PC=0   SMRS=13.6   LS=168.6

| 1993/12 | S3 | CNR-[LS-A] Sturgis–Wh. Pi. Jct. | 406.8–421.3 | [14.5] |

1993 YEAR   CNR=50.0   MICH=60.3   MSRR=44.7   PC=0   SMRS=13.6   LS=168.6

On 1 June 1999 Conrail was conveyed to Norfolk Southern.

[LS-A1]	OH state line–Ottawa Lk.	307.9–312.1	4.2
[LS-A5]	Wh. Pi. Jct.–IN line	421.3–424.1	2.8
[LS-YM]	In Monroe	0–1.1	(1.1)
[LS-Y1W]	In Jackson	0.4–1.1	(0.7)
[LS-G]	Wh. Pi. Jct.–BO	0–36.8	37.1
[LS-Y1G]	In Kal.	36.8–39.5	(2.7)
[LS-G2]	Plainwell–Otsego	46.8–52.7	5.9
[LS-Y2G]	In Gr. Rpds.	91.6–95.0	(3.4)
[LS-Y2L]	In Lans.	57.5–58.8	(1.3)
[LS-Y1L]	In Lans.	60.4–61.2	(0.8)

1999 YEAR   MICH=60.3   MSRR=44.7   NS=50.0   PC=0   SMRS=13.6   LS=168.6

Act Column Key

A	Adjust mileage
B1	Built by Erie & Kalamazoo, leased to MS 1 August 1849
B2	Built by River Raisin & Lake Erie, sold to State of Michigan 14 September 1840
B3	Built by State of Michigan, sold to MS 28 December 1846
B4	Built by Palmyra & Jacksonburgh, sold to State of Michigan 1844
B5	Built by Michigan Southern, merged into MS&NI 5 April 1855
B6	Built by Michigan South & Northern Indiana, merged into LS&MS 16 April 1869

B7	Built by Detroit Monroe & Toledo, leased to MS&NI 1 July 1856
B8	Built by St Joseph Valley, merged into K&WP 14 August 1869
B9	Built by Kalamazoo & White Pigeon, owned at organization by LS&MS
B10	Built by Kalamazoo Allegan & Grand Rapids, leased to LS&MS 21 September 1869
B11	Built by Fort Wayne Jackson & Saginaw, successor leased to LS&MS 5 January 1880
B12	Built by Detroit Hillsdale & Indiana, reorganized as DH&SW
B13	Built by Detroit Hillsdale & SouthWestern, leased to LS&MS 5 September 1881
B14	Built by Northern Central Michigan, owned at organization by LS&MS
B15	Built by Chicago & Canada Southern, control obtained in June 1876 when property reorganized as Detroit & Chicago
B16	Built by Canada & St Louis, purchased 17 August 1889
B17	Built by New York Central
L1	Leased from Battle Creek & Sturgis, 1 February 1890
S1	Sold to State of Michigan
S2	Sold to Branch & St. Joseph Counties Rail Users Association
S3	Sold to Michigan Southern
S4	Sold to Southern Michigan Railroad Society.
S5	Sold to Ann Arbor Railroad
X	Abandonment
Y	Converted main track to yard/industrial track

Sources

1. Baxter, *Grand Rapids.*
2. Bonner, *Memoirs of Lenawee.*
3. ICC *Finance Dockets.*
4. Michigan, Commissioner of Railroads, *Annual Report,* 1873.
5. MDOT office records.
6. Michigan Railroad Commission, *Aids, Gifts, Grants.*
7. New York Central engineering records.
8. Wing, *History of Monroe County.*

Notes

GENERAL The record of construction and abandonment follows each line. Act Column entries beginning with "B" are of lines which may or may not have been under the control of the Lake Shore & Michigan Southern. Most of the properties were controlled under lease and subsequently purchased. The Ownership record has the affiliation with the LS&MS.

1. The date shown is supported by the majority of sources. Source 6 gives completion as 20 June 1837, which appears to be the date that steam locomotives replaced the use of horses as motive power.

2. The 1845 Annual Report of the Internal Improvement Board indicates that the P&J completed its line as far as Clinton in 1838. It appears that wooden rails were installed and horses were used as motive power. The use of the part north of Tecumseh was discontinued after a year or two. The mileage north of Tecumseh is not included at this time.

3. A short segment was opened by the LaPlaisance Harbor Bay Company at its docks in about 1827. This trackage, no more than 0.1 miles in length, appears to have been the first railroad trackage laid in Michigan.

4. This segment had some use between Monroe and Petersburg by late 1839 (Source 6), but was not opened formally to public use. The Monroe depot was located at Harrison Street.

5. The actual date of abandonment is not determinable, but this segment was not conveyed by the state to the Michigan Southern in 1846.

6. The segment mileage given is to the Elkhart depot. Timothy E. Howard's *A History of St. Joseph County, Indiana* (Chicago, 1907), page 237, states that the section between White Pigeon and the Michigan–Indiana state line was built by Judge Thomas S. Stanfield on behalf of the Michigan Southern. This section, called the Portage Railroad, was owned by Stanfield for ten years and leased to the Michigan Southern. No dates are given. No documentation of this action is on file with the State of Michigan.

7. This segment extended 0.4 miles beyond the present Constantine depot to the bank of the St. Joseph River, running parallel to Depot Street. This segment was superseded in 1855 by the extension of the line to Three

Rivers and discontinued and removed at an unknown later date. The original charter of the Michigan Sourthern required that it reach the St. Joseph River and this extension fulfilled the provision. This line was leased to the St. Joseph Valley Railroad on 21 November 1864, which held the property until 14 August 1869.

8. This work is shown for information only.

9. This segment also held trackage rights on 3.3 miles of the Detroit, Grand Haven & Milwaukee (later Grand Trunk Western) to reach and use the Detroit depot of that company.

10. The mileage shown is to the station for Jackson at Milwaukee Street.

11. This end of this segment is at Lake Michigan Drive, Grand Rapids, at a connection with the Grand Rapids, Newaygo & Lake Shore (later Pere Marquette). Source 1 states a train was run on the date shown to fulfill an obligation for municipal assistance; regular service began May 22.

12. This segment also held trackage rights on 0.4 miles of the Michigan Central to reach and use the Jackson depot of that road. Between MP 1.0 and Haires this line and the Michigan Central's Air Line (MC-A) were operated jointly as a double track line. Mileage between Fort Wayne Jct. and Bankers is via the direct line and not via Hillsdale.

13. This segment also held trackage rights on 0.4 miles of the Michigan Central to reach and use the Ypsilanti depot of that road.

14. This segment also used 0.6 miles of the Old Road (LS-A) to reach Jonesville.

15. This construction and abandonment is assumed to have occurred at about the time the Lake Shore acquired the lease of the property.

16. This segment was opened in Jan. 1889, leased from the Battle Creek & Sturgis as shown, which company was controlled by the Michigan Central.

17. The actual date of abandonment is not determinable. Source 6 states it was not used after 1888 and abandoned not later than 1893.

18. This segment was sold to the Detroit & Lima Northern (later, Detroit, Toledo & Ironton).

19. This abandonment is inferred given the sale of the line east of Dundee in 1897 and the earlier abandonment of the line west of Corbus.

20. This alteration took place as part of the rehabilitation of the Jackson–Elkhart line. The original east wye remained in place to some extent as an industrial track. There was no alteration in Mile Post numbers on LS-G.

21. This segment was sold to the Ann Arbor Railroad and is shown under that road as AA-G.

22. This segment was provided service under state subsidy agreement beginning 1 April 1976. Conrail was the designated operator until 30 September 1977, Lenawee County Railroad until 1990, Adrian & Blissfield thereafter.

23. This segment was provided service under state subsidy agreement beginning 1 April 1976. Conrail was the designated operator until 30 September 1977, Lenawee County Railroad until 1990, Adrian & Blissfield thereafter.

24. This segment was provided service under state subsidy agreement beginning 1 April 1976. Conrail was the designated operator until 31 March 1978, Lenawee County Railroad until 1990, Adrian & Blissfield thereafter.

25. Service ended Aug. 1981, on this segment due to flood damage to the River Raisin bridge. The segment was embargoed to traffic on 30 September 1981.

26. This segment was provided service under state subsidy agreement beginning 1 April 1976. The Hillsdale County Railroad was the designated operator.

27. Service ended between Quincy and Sturgis in 1984 and service resumed by purchaser in 1989.

28. This line paralleled Michigan Central line MC-T. This removes the duplicate mileage and converts the line to a double track.

Lake States Transportation and Lake State Railway

For arrangement of stations, construction record, and prior ownerships, see Detroit & Mackinac (D&M) and Michigan Central (MC) lines as shown.

ACQUISITION/DISPOSITION RECORD

DATE	ACT	LSRC–	END POINTS	MP	MICH. OWNED MAIN	MICHIGAN. DESIG.OPR. MAIN	NOTE
1992/2	P	[D&M-S]	Pinconning–Alpena	17.8–124.4	106.9		
	L	[D&M-Y1S]	In Bay City	1.9–4.9	(3.0)		
	L	[D&M-Z2]	Crossover, Pinconning	0–0.5	0.5		
	L	[D&M-YA]	At Alpena	124.4–124.8	(0.4)		
	L	[D&M-E]	Alabaster Jct.–Alabaster	0–4.0	4.0		
	L	[D&M-EP]	Port Gypsum Spur	0.6–1.3	0.7		
	L	[D&M-H]	Hillman Jct–Paxton	0.7–10.1	9.4		
	L	[D&M-YQ]	In Alpena	0–2.2	(2.2)		
	L	[D&M-Y1N]	In Alpena	0–0.5	(0.5)		
	L	[D&M-N]	Alpena–Hawks	124.7–151.5	26.8		
	L	[D&M-Y2N]	In Cheboygan	192.0–197.1	(5.1)		
	L	[D&M-R]	Rogers City Jct–Rogers City	1.2–14.8	13.6		
	L	[MC-1M]	Kawkawlin–Linwood	5.0–10.8	5.8		
	C	[MC-M2]	Linwood–Salling	10.8–115.8		105.0	
	L	[MC-M3]	Salling–Cheboygan	115.8–168.0	52.2		
	C	[MC-Y1P]	In Pinconning	0–0.6		(0.6)	
				TOTAL	219.9	105.0	
1993 ca.	X	[MC-M3]	Gaylord–Cheboygan	120.5–168.0	−47.5		1
	X	[D&M-Y2N]	In Cheboygan	192.0–197.1	(−5.1)		
				TOTAL	152.4	105.0	
1998	X	[D&M-H]	Hillman Jct–Paxton	0.7–10.1	−9.4		2
				TOTAL	143.0	105.0	

OWNERSHIP
1992 Lake States Transportation Co., leased from Detroit & Mackinac
1997 Lake State Railway, purchased from Detroit & Mackinac all lines leased to Lake States Transp.

Act Column Key
C Operated under Designated Operator contract with State of Michigan
L Leased from Detroit & Mackinac
X Abandoned

Notes
1. Last train was run on this line 29 September 1990.
2. Service ended on this line about 1995.

Lapeer Industrial

For arrangement of stations, construction record, and prior ownerships, see Michigan Central line MC-B.

ACQUISITION/DISPOSITION RECORD

DATE	ACT	LAPI–	END POINTS	MP	CHANGE	MAIN	SOURCE	NOTE
1999/6	P	[MC-Y3B]	Lapeer–south	59.8–58.4	(+1.4)			

OWNERSHIP

1999   Lapeer Industrial Railroad, wholly owned subsidiary of Adrian & Blissfield.

Act Column Key

P   Purchased from Grand Trunk Western

Notes

GENERAL   This company is a terminal switching road and not an intercity carrier. Its mileage is not included the Michigan mileage table in chapter 2.

Leelanau Transit and Traverse City, Leelanau & Manistique

CONSTRUCTION

DATE	ACT	TCLM–	END POINTS	CHANGE	MAIN	NOTE
1903/6/28	B	[M&NE-N]	Hatchs–Northport	+23.8		1
	B	[M&NE-NT]	In Trav. Cty.	+1.0	24.8	2
1919/5/23	S	All	All lines			
6/6	L1	All	All lines	−24.8	0	3

OWNERSHIP

1903	Traverse City, Leelanau & Manistique Railroad
1908/9/14	Traverse City, Leelanau & Manistique Railway, reorganize TCL&M Railroad
1919/5/23	Leelanau Transit, purchased TCL&M Railway
1919/6/6	Manistee & Northeastern, lease of Leelanau Transit

Between 1919 and 1982 see Manistee & Northeastern record of lines M&NE-N and M&NE-NT.

LEELANAU TRANSIT CO.

CONSTRUCTION

DATE	ACT	LTR–	END POINTS	CHANGE	MAIN	NOTE
1982 ca.	L2	[M&NE-A]	Hatchs–MP 68.5	+3.9		4
	XL	[M&NE-N]	Hatchs–MP 29.3	+23.8	27.7	
1990 ca.	X,XL	[M&NE-N]	Hatchs–MP 68.5	−3.9	23.8	4
1995 ca.	X	[M&NE-N]	MP 29.3–MP 18.0	−11.3	12.5	5
1996 ca.	X	[M&NE-N]	MP 5.5–MP 18.0	−12.5	0	5

OWNERSHIP

The Leelanau Transit was leased to the Manistee & Northeastern in 1919, subsequently leased to the Pere Marquette and then to Chesapeake & Ohio which surrendered the lease in ca.1982. Leelanau Transit subsequently operated under its own name and beginning in 1992 as "Leelanau Scenic."

Act Column Key

- B Built by Traverse City, Leelanau & Manistique Railroad
- L1 Leased to Manistee & Northeastern
- L2 Purchased from CSX Transportation
- S1 Sold to Leelanau Transit
- X Abandoned to Chesapeake & Ohio
- XL Lease cancelled

Notes

1. This date is from Robert E. Burton's "Car Ferry from Northport", *Michigan History* 51:1 (Spring 1967), pp. 1–17. Michigan Railroad Commission, *Aids, Gifts, Grants* gives 1906 for Hatchs–Northport section and does not report the Traverse City construction separately. The operation also included 5.6 miles of trackage rights on Manistee & Northeastern line M&NE-A between Hatchs and Traverse City. The line was not operated for parts of 1918 and 1919.

2. This completion date is assumed from the fact that the Grand Rapids & Indiana performed the construction work on the line and operated it for its owners under contract.

3. For the years from 1919 to 1982, see the record of Manistee & Northeastern.

4. It is assumed that this segment was leased from CSX since it was abandoned after line PM-P was sold to the State of Michigan.

5. The actual dates of abandonment could not be found. Operations apparently ended after summer 1994. A short segment of track was retained at Hatchs for equipment storage.

Lenawee County

The Lenawee County operated the following lines under contract with the State of Michigan which had acquired ownership of the lines or had contractual arrangements with Penn Central. See page for Michigan, State of.

For arrangement of stations, construction record, and prior ownerships, see Lake Shore & Michigan Southern lines LS-A, LS-F, and LS-J, and Detroit, Toledo & Ironton line DTI-A.

ACQUISITION/DISPOSITION RECORD

DATE	ACT	LCRC–	END POINTS	MP	CHANGE	MICHIGAN DESIG.OPR. MAIN	MICH. OWNED MAIN	NOTE
1977/10/1	C	[LS-A3]	Lenawee Jct.–Adrian	325.5–333.6	+8.1	8.1		
1978/4/1	C	[LS-F]	Grosvenor–Morenci	0–18.6	+18.6	26.7		
1979/2/8	P1	[DTI-A]	Leaf–Bimo	32.0–35.7				
			plus new wye P		+3.8	26.7	3.8	
1982/10/1	C	[LS-A2]	Lenawee Jct.–Riga	315.5–325.5	+10.0			
10/1	C	[LS-Y2J]	At Lenawee Jct.	0–0.3	+0.3			
	X	[LS-F]	MP 1.7–MP 11.4	1.7–11.4	–9.7	27.3	3.8	1
1985 ca.	P2	[DTI-A]	Page–MP 47	44.3–47.0	(+2.7)	27.3	3.8	2
1990/9/30	XC	[LS-all]	All designated operator lines		–27.3			
	S	[DTI-A]	MP 46–MP 47	46.0–47.0	[(–1.0)]			2
	X	[DTI-A]	Page–MP 46	44.3–46.0	(–1.7)			
9/30	X	[DTI-A]	Leaf–Bimo	32.0–35.7	–3.8	0	0	

OWNERSHIP

1976 All lines, except [DTI-A], by the State of Michigan or by prior owner Penn Central.

Act Column Key

C	Operated under Designated Operator contract
P1	Purchased from Detroit, Toledo & Ironton
P2	Purchased from Norfolk Southern
S	Apparently sold to Adrian & Blissfield
X	Abandoned
XC	Designated Operator contract cancelled

Notes

1. Service ended on this section due to embargo dated 30 September 1981, caused by damage to River Raisin bridge.
2. This section apparently was bought at the same time as the Leaf–Bimo segment. It was operated only as an industrial track. Apparently it passed to the Adrian & Blissfield as successor owners.

Lewiston & Southeastern

MAIN LINE (L&SE-A)

	MILEAGE	COUNTY	CROSSINGS, JUNCTIONS, ETC.
Lewiston	0	Montmorency	J/MC-MT 27.7
(County line)	2.4	"	
(Jct.)	5.5	Oscoda	J/L&SE-B 5.5 (sec15 T28N R1E)
(Jct.)	8.0	"	J/L&SE-C 8.0 (sec18 T28N R2E)
(Crossing)	8.7	"	X/ASNW-2 24.7 (sec17 T28N R2E)
(End)	14.5	"	(sec9 T27N R2E)

CONSTRUCTION

DATE	ACT	END POINTS	MP	CHANGE	MAIN	SOURCE	NOTE
1896/5/26	B	Lewiston–MP 10	0–10.0	+10.0	10.0	1	
1899	B	MP 10–MP 14.5	10.0–14.5	+4.5	14.5	2	
1901	X	MP 8–MP 14.5	8.0–14.5	−6.5	8.0	2	
1910	X	Lewiston–MP 8	0–8.0	−8.0	0	2	

OWNERSHIP

1896   Lewiston & Southeastern

BRANCH (L&SE-B)

	MILEAGE	COUNTY	CROSSINGS, JUNCTIONS, ETC.
(Jct.)	5.5	Oscoda	J/L&SE-A 5.5
(End)	8.5	"	(sec35 T28N R2E)

CONSTRUCTION

DATE	ACT	END POINTS	MP	CHANGE	MAIN	SOURCE	NOTE
1896	B	Line	5.5–8.5	+3.0	3.0	1	
1901	X	Line	5.5–8.5	−3.0	0	2	

OWNERSHIP

1896   Lewiston & Southeastern

BRANCH (L&SE-C)

	MILEAGE	COUNTY	CROSSINGS, JUNCTIONS, ETC.
(Jct.)	8.0	Oscoda	J/L&SE-A 8.0
(End)	11.0	"	(sec15 T28N R2E)

CONSTRUCTION

DATE	ACT	END POINTS	MP	CHANGE	MAIN	SOURCE	NOTE
1909	B	Line	8.0–10.0	+2.0	2.0	2	
1910	X	Line	8.0–10.0	−2.0	0	2	

OWNERSHIP

1909   Lewiston & Southeastern

ACQUISITION/DISPOSITION RECORD

DATE	ACT	LS&E–	END POINTS	CHANGE	MI MAIN	NOTE
1896/5/26	B	A	Lewiston–MP 10.0	+10.0		
	B	B	MP 5.5–MP 8.5	+3.0	13.0	
1899	B	A	MP–10.0–MP 14.5	+4.5	17.5	
1901	X	A	MP 8.0–MP 14.5	−6.5		
	X	B	MP 5.5–MP 8.5	−3.0	8.0	
1903	B	?	?–?	+7.0	15.0	
1909	B	C	MP 8.0–MP 11.0	+3.0	18.0	
1910	X	all	All lines	−18.0	0	

Act column

B   Built by Lewiston & Southeastern
X   Abandoned

Sources

1.   Michigan Commissioner of Railroads *Annual Report,* 1896.
2.   Michigan Railroad Commission, *Aids, Gifts, Grants.*

Notes

GENERAL   This property was used principally as a logging road and not as a common carrier although it was incorporated under the General Railway Act. The record of construction and abandonment is incomplete.

Ludington & Northern

MAIN LINE (LUN-A)

	MILEAGE	COUNTY	CROSSINGS, JUNCTIONS, ETC.
Dowland St.	0.0	Mason	
—in Rath St.			
Ludington Ave	0.4	"	
(Jct.)	1.4	"	J/PM-YL1 2.2, Spur 0.2 miles
Cemetery	1.5	"	
Epworth Heights	2.5	"	
(Jct.)	2.6	"	J/LUN-B 2.6
(End)	4.4	"	

CONSTRUCTION

DATE	ACT	END POINTS	MP	CHANGE	MAIN	SOURCE	NOTE
1895	B1	Epworth Heights–south	0–2.5+0.2	+2.7		1	
1901	B2	Epworth Heights–MP 2.6	2.5–2.6	+0.1	2.8	1	
1910/5/1	B2	MP 2.6–MP 4.4	2.6–4.4	+1.8	4.6	1	
1919 ca.	X	MP 0–1.4		−1.4	3.2		
1997 ca.	X	Line	1.4–4.4+0.2	−3.2	0		1

OWNERSHIP

1895	Epworth League Railway (B1)
1901/7/13	Ludington & Northern (B2), renaming of Epworth League Railway

BRANCH (LUN-B)

	MILEAGE	COUNTY	CROSSINGS, JUNCTIONS, ETC.
(Jct.)	2.6	Mason	J/LUN-A 2.6
Lincoln Fields	3.0	"	
Weimer	5.3	"	
Hamlin Lk.	6.3	"	
North Bayou	7.3	"	

CONSTRUCTION

DATE	ACT	END POINTS	MP	CHANGE	MAIN	SOURCE	NOTE
1901	B2	MP 2.6–Hamlin Lk.	2.6–6.3	+3.7	3.7	1	
1906	B2	Hamlin Lk.–N. Bayou	6.3–7.3	+1.0	4.7	1	
1919 ca.	X	Line	2.6–7.3	–4.7	0		

OWNERSHIP

1901	Ludington & Northern (B2)

ACQUISITION/DISPOSITION RECORD

DATE	ACT	LUN–	END POINTS	CHANGE	MI MAIN	NOTE
1895	B1	A	0–2.5+0.2	+2.7	2.7	
1901	B2	A,B	2.5–6.3	+3.8	6.5	
1906	B2	B	6.3–7.3	+1.0	7.5	
1910/5/1	B2	A	2.6–4.4	+1.8	9.3	
1919 ca.	X	A	0–1.4	–1.4		
	X	B	2.6–7.3	–4.7	3.2	
1997 ca.	X	A	1.4–4.4+0.2	–3.2	0	1

Act Column Key

B1	Built by Epworth League Railway
B2	Built by Ludington & Northern
X	Abandoned

Sources

1. Michigan Railroad Commission, *Aids, Gifts, Grants.*

Notes

1. This date is the Surface Transportation Board abandonment authorization. The line had been operated only occasionally for some years before this date.

Mancelona & North Western

MAIN LINE (M&NW-A)

	MILEAGE	COUNTY	CROSSINGS, JUNCTIONS, ETC.
Line not located			

CONSTRUCTION/ABANDONMENT

1892 ca.	B	Line
???	X	Line

OWNERSHIP

1892   Mancelona & North Western Railway

Act Column Key

B   Built by Mancelona & North Western

X   Abandoned

Manistee & Grand Rapids

MAIN LINE (M&GR-A)

	MILEAGE	COUNTY	CROSSINGS, JUNCTIONS, ETC.
Manistee	0	Manistee	
(Jct.)	3.3	"	J/M&GR-YM 0.7
Oakhill	4	"	
Filer Cty.	5.2	"	
(Jct.)	6.0	"	J/M&NE-YM1 3.9
Marsh	7.8	"	B/PM-M 19.3
Hoags (Siding)	11.9	Mason	
Tomlin	14	"	
Sauble	14.6	"	f. Au Sable River
Elmton	16.0	"	f. Howells Siding, th. Howells
Millerton	22.3	"	J/M&GR-X5 0, f. Canfield Camp
Sheepdale	25	Lake	f. Lions Crossing?
Sauble (old)	25.3	"	
Peacock	31.2	"	X/PM-P 84.9, f. Canfields
Pines	34.2	"	
(Jct.)	36.9	"	J/M&L-?
States Switch	38.4	"	may be sited at Carey
Carey	39.7	"	J/M&GR-X4 0, f. Careyville
(Crossing)	41.2	"	X/GR&I-3 13.1
Luther	41.8	"	
Keenan	43.9	"	J/M&GR-X4 0
Canfields Wye	44.7	"	
Hoist	46.4	"	
Perrys	47	"	
Edgetts	47.0	"	
(Crossing)	48.5	"	X/M&L-?
Riverbank	48.7	Osceola	
Larsen	49.9	"	
Hewitts Lk.	52.0	"	f. Hewitts
Tustin	54.6	"	B/GR&I-N 319.2
Anderson	57.8	"	J/M&GR-X3 0, maybe f. Rolfe
Dighton	60.9	"	J/M&GR-X2 0, f. Flanners
Hartwick Switch	62.9	"	X/M&GR-7 0
Dennis	64.4	"	
Crocker	67.4	"	
Marion	72.0	"	J/AA-B 208.6

CONSTRUCTION/ABANDONMENT

DATE	ACT	END POINTS	MP	CHANGE	MAIN	SOURCE	NOTE
1892/12/20	B	MP 3.3–Peacock	3.3–31.2	+27.9	27.9	1	
1895	B	Manistee–MP 3.3	0–3.3	+3.3	31.2	1	
1896/7/1	B	Peacock–Canfields Wye	31.2–44.7	+13.5	44.7	1	

1900/12/1	B	Canfields Wye–Dighton	44.7–60.9	+16.2	60.9	1
1906/1/1	B	Dighton–Marion	60.9–72.0	+11.1	72.0	1
1921 ca.	X	Manistee–Marion	0–72.0	−72.0	0	

OWNERSHIP

| 1892 | Manistee & Grand Rapids |
| 1913/11/25 | Michigan East & West, reorganization of Manistee & Grand Rapids |

BRANCH (M&GR-1) *(LINE NOT LOCATED)*

	MILEAGE	COUNTY	CROSSINGS, JUNCTIONS, ETC.
Hartwick Switch	0	Osceola	J/M&GR-A 62.9
(End)	5.0	"	

CONSTRUCTION/ABANDONMENT

DATE	ACT	END POINTS	MP	CHANGE	MAIN	SOURCE	NOTE
1902/4/1	B	Hartwick Switch–MP 2.2	0–2.2	+2.2	2.2	1	
1906	B	MP 2.2–MP 5.0	2.2–5.0	+2.8	5.0	1	
1915	X	Line	0–5.0	−5.0	0	1	

OWNERSHIP

| 1902 | Manistee & Grand Rapids |
| 1913/11/25 | Michigan East & West, reorganization of Manistee & Grand Rapids |

BRANCH (M&GR-X2) *(LINE NOT LOCATED)*

	MILEAGE	COUNTY	CROSSINGS, JUNCTIONS, ETC.
Dighton	0	Osceola	J/M&GR-A 60.9
Camp 32	3.1	"	

CONSTRUCTION/ABANDONMENT

DATE	ACT	END POINTS	MP	CHANGE	MAIN	SOURCE	NOTE
1901/12/1	B	Line	0–3.1	+3.1	3.1	1	
1902	X	Line	0–3.1	−3.1	0	1	

OWNERSHIP

| 1901 | Manistee & Grand Rapids |

BRANCH (M&GR-X3) *(LINE NOT LOCATED)*

	MILEAGE	COUNTY	CROSSINGS, JUNCTIONS, ETC.
Anderson	0	Osceola	J/M&GR-A 57.8
Rose Lk.	2	"	

CONSTRUCTION/ABANDONMENT

DATE	ACT	END POINTS	MP	CHANGE	MAIN	SOURCE	NOTE
	??	Line					2

OWNERSHIP

| ?? | Manistee & Grand Rapids |

BRANCH (M&GR-X4) *(LINE NOT LOCATED)*

	MILEAGE	COUNTY	CROSSINGS, JUNCTIONS, ETC.
Keenan	0	Lake	J/M&GR-A 43.9
Haaks	8	"	

CONSTRUCTION/ABANDONMENT

DATE	ACT	END POINTS	MP	CHANGE	MAIN	SOURCE	NOTE
1900	B	Line	0–8	+8.0	8.0	1	
1901	X	Line	0–8	−8.0	0	1	

OWNERSHIP

1900	Manistee & Grand Rapids

BRANCH (M&GR-X5) *(LINE NOT LOCATED)*

	MILEAGE	COUNTY	CROSSINGS, JUNCTIONS, ETC.
Millerton	0	Mason	J/M&GR-A 22.3
Barretts	8	"	

CONSTRUCTION/ABANDONMENT

DATE	ACT	END POINTS	MP	CHANGE	MAIN	SOURCE	NOTE
1901	B	Line	0–8	+8.0	8.0	1	
1902	X	Line	0–8	−8.0	0	1	

OWNERSHIP

1901	Manistee & Grand Rapids

BRANCH (M&GR-YM)

	MILEAGE	COUNTY	CROSSINGS, JUNCTIONS, ETC.
(Jct.)	0	Manistee	J/M&NE-YM1 0.7
(Jct.)	0.7	"	J/M&GR-A 3.3

CONSTRUCTION/ABANDONMENT

DATE	ACT	END POINTS	MP	CHANGE	MAIN	SOURCE	NOTE
1892/12/20	B	Line	0–0.7	+0.7	0.7	1	
1895	Y	Line	0–0.7	(0.7)	0		1
1921 ca.	X	Line	0–0.7	(−0.7)	0		

OWNERSHIP

1892	Manistee & Grand Rapids
1913/11/25	Michigan East & West, reorganization of Manistee & Grand Rapids

ACQUISITION/DISPOSITION RECORD

DATE	ACT	M&GR–	END POINTS	CHANGE	MI MAIN	NOTE
1892/12/20	B	A,YM	Manistee–Peacock	+31.2	28.6	
1895	B	A	Manistee–MP 3.3	+3.3		
	Y	YM	In Manistee	(+0.7)	31.2	1
1896/7/1	B	A	Peacock–Canfields Wye	+13.5	44.7	
1900/12/1	B	A	Canfields Wye–Dighton	+16.2		
	B	X4	Keenan–Haaks	+8.0	68.9	
1901	X	X4	Keenan–Haaks	−8.0		
	B	X5	Millerton–Barretts	+8.0		
/12/1	B	X2	Dighton–Camp 32	+3.1	72.0	
1902	X	X2	Dighton–Camp 32	−3.1		
	X	X5	Millerton–Barretts	−8.0		
/4/1	B		Hartwick Switch–MP 2.2	+2.2	63.1	
1906/1/1	B	A	Dighton–Marion	+11.1		
	B		Hartwick Switch–MP 5	+2.8	77.0	
1915	X		Hartwick Switch–MP 5	−5.0	72.0	
c.1921	X	A,YM	Manistee–Marion	−72.7	0	

Act Column Key

B Built by Manistee & Grand Rapids

X Abandoned

Y Converted from main track to yard track

Sources

1. Michigan Railroad Commission, *Aids, Gifts, Grants.*

Notes

1. This change is assumed since the line remained in place after the completion of the new main line to the riverfront in Manistee. At the time of abandonment of the company it appears a part of the line was retained for industrial use by the Manistee & North Eastern.

2. The date of construction and/or abandonment of this line could not be determined accurately and therefore it is not included in the Acquisition/Disposition Record.

Manistee & Luther

OWNERSHIP

1886 Manistee & Luther

The construction and abandonment record of the Manistee & Luther is incomplete and not always accurate. The road was used as a logging road of the R. G. Peters Salt & Lumber Co.

In about 1886 the M&L built its line from Eastlake to the vicinity of Luther. During the next 10 years it constructed and abandoned a number of branches in this area.

About 1895 it appears to have abandoned most of its trackage around Luther and constructed entirely new lines from Eastlake to the vicinity of Hoxeyville in southwestern Wexford County. It continued operations in that area until 1913 at which time service was discontinued. The tracks were removed in 1914 and 1915.

Manistee & Northeastern

MAIN LINE (M&NE-A)

	MILEAGE	COUNTY	CROSSINGS, JUNCTIONS, ETC.
Manistee	0	Manistee	J/M&NE-YM1 0
(Bridge, Manistee River)	0.2	"	
(Arthur St.)	0.4	"	X/MACL-B 0.81
(Jct.)	0.4	"	J/PM-M 26.2
(Jct.)	0.9	"	J/M&NE-YM2 0
(Jct.)	1.0	"	J/PM-M 25.6
(Lk. Sh. Rd.)	1.2	"	X/MACL-C 0.12

Polock Hill	4.8	"	
Camp 1 Switch	6.1	"	f. B. & D. Camp No. 1
Newland	6.3	"	
Wealthy	6.6	"	
Arundal	8	"	
Douglas	8.3	"	f. B. & D. Camp No. 2, th. Lk. View Farm
Onekama Jct.	9.8	"	J/M&NE-O 9.8
Norwalk	11.8	"	f. Goodrich
Chief Lk.	15.1	"	
Bear Creek	18.3	"	J/M&NE-1 0
Kaleva	19.9	"	X/PM-P 110.1, f. Manistee Crossing
River Branch Jct.	21.3	"	J/M&NE-R 1.4
(Jct.)	21.4	"	J/M&NE-4 0
Maple Grove	23	"	
Wards	24	"	
Lemon Lk.	25.2	"	
(Jct.)	28.4	"	J/M&NE-6 0
Copemish	29.4	"	X/AA-C 267.6
Nelsons Switch	30.8	"	
Nessen Cty.	32.9	Benzie	
Twin Lk. Branch	37.6	Gr.Trav.	J/M&NE-2 0
Twin Mountain	38	"	
Karlin	39.2	"	f. Horicon
Grant Center	41.0	"	f. Green Lk.
Pine Park	43.6	"	f. Wylies
Interlochen	44.6	"	X/PM-P 134.2
Long Lk. Branch	45.7	"	J/M&NE-5 0
Filers Switch	47.3	"	J/M&NE-3 0
Platte River Jct.	49.3	Benzie	J/M&NE-E 0, f. Shermans Mill, a.k.a. Melva
Lk. Ann	51.7	"	
Cedar Run	55.3	Gr.Trav.	
Ruthardts	56.2	Leelanau	
Solon	59.7	"	J/M&NE-P 0
Bahles Switch	61	"	
Fouch	62.6	"	f. Carp Lk.
Hatchs (Crossing)	64.6	"	J/M&NE-N 5.5
Trav. Resort	67.6	"	
Rennies	68.1	"	f. Greilickville
Trav. Cty. (Bay St.)	69.8	Gr.Trav.	J/M&NE-NT 1.0, J/PM-YTC 148.5

CONSTRUCTION/ABANDONMENT

DATE	ACT	END POINTS	MP	CHANGE	MAIN	SOURCE	NOTE
1888/11/20	B	Manistee–Nessen Cty.	0–32.9	+32.9	32.9	4	1
1890/10/13	B	Nessen Cty.–Lk. Ann	32.9–51.7	+18.8	51.7	4	
1892/7/1	B	Lk. Ann–Trav. Cty.	51.7–69.8	+18.1	69.8	4	
1934	X	MP 20.2–Solon	20.2–59.7	−39.5	29.3	2	4
1954	X	Kaleva–MP 20.2	19.9–20.2	−0.3			
1954	X	Solon–Hatchs	59.7–64.6	−4.9	25.1		
1982	X	Manistee–Kaleva	0–19.9	−19.9			
1982	X	Hatchs–Trav. Cty.	64.6–69.8	−5.2	0		

OWNERSHIP

1888	Manistee & Northeastern Railroad
1926/9/4	Manistee & Northeastern Railway, reorganized Manistee & Northeastern Railroad
1931/12	Pere Marquette, control of Manistee & Northeastern
1947/4/1	Chesapeake & Ohio, merger of Pere Marquette, and control of M&NE
1955/11/30	Chesapeake & Ohio, merger of Manistee & Northeastern

FILER CITY BRANCH (M&NE-YM1)

	MILEAGE	COUNTY	CROSSINGS, JUNCTIONS, ETC.
Manistee	0	Manistee	J/M&NE-A 0
Manistee (1st sta.)	0.5	"	
(Jct.)	0.7	"	J/M&GR-YM 0
Filer Cty.	2.9	"	
(Jct.)	3.9	"	J/M&GR-A 6.0

CONSTRUCTION/ABANDONMENT

DATE	ACT	END POINTS	MP	CHANGE	MAIN	SOURCE	NOTE
1888 ca.	B	MP 0–MP 0.5	0–0.5	+0.5	0.5		
1890 ca.	Y	MP 0–MP 0.5 (to YM1)	0–0.5	(0.5)			
1890 ca.	B	MP 0.5–MP 3.9	0.5–3.9	(+3.4)	0		
1921 ca.	X	MP 3.5–MP 3.9	3.5–3.9	(–0.4)	0		

OWNERSHIP

1888	Manistee & Northeastern (B), of segment Railroad
1926/9/4	Manistee & Northeastern Railway, reorganized Manistee & Northeastern Railroad
1931/12	Pere Marquette, control of Manistee & Northeastern
1947/4/1	Chesapeake & Ohio, merger of Pere Marquette, and control of M&NE
1955/11/30	Chesapeake & Ohio, merger of Manistee & Northeastern

LAKE SHORE BRANCH (M&NE-YM2)

	MILEAGE	COUNTY	CROSSINGS, JUNCTIONS, ETC.
(Jct.)	0	Manistee	J/M&NE-A 0.9
Manistee Harbor	1.5	"	
Novelty Works	2.2	"	

CONSTRUCTION/ABANDONMENT

DATE	ACT	END POINTS	MP	CHANGE	MAIN	SOURCE	NOTE
1892	B	MP 0–Manistee Harbor	0–1.5	(+1.5)	0	4	
1901	B	Man. Harbor–Novelty Works	1.5–2.2	(+0.7)	0	4	
1954 ca.	X	South end of branch	2.2–1.5	(–0.7)	0		

OWNERSHIP

1892	Manistee & Northeastern Railroad
1926/9/4	Manistee & Northeastern Railway, reorganized Manistee & Northeastern Railroad
1931/12	Pere Marquette, control of Manistee & Northeastern
1947/4/1	Chesapeake & Ohio, merger of Pere Marquette, and control of M&NE
1955/11/30	Chesapeake & Ohio, merger of Manistee & Northeastern

ONEKAMA BRANCH (M&NE-O)

	MILEAGE	COUNTY	CROSSINGS, JUNCTIONS, ETC.
	[Manistee]		
Onekama Jct.	9.8	Manistee	J/M&NE-A 9.8
Brookfield	11.9	"	
Onekama	12.6	"	

CONSTRUCTION/ABANDONMENT

DATE	ACT	END POINTS	MP	CHANGE	MAIN	SOURCE	NOTE
1889/1/14	B	Onekama Jct.–Onekama	9.8–12.6	+2.8	2.8	4	
1972	X	Onekama Jct.–Onekama	9.8–12.6	–2.8	0	3	

OWNERSHIP

1889	Manistee & Northeastern Railroad
1926/9/4	Manistee & Northeastern Railway, reorganized Manistee & Northeastern Railroad
1931/12	Pere Marquette, control of Manistee & Northeastern
1947/4/1	Chesapeake & Ohio, merger of Pere Marquette, and control of M&NE
1955/11/30	Chesapeake & Ohio, merger of Manistee & Northeastern

RIVER BRANCH (M&NE-R)

	MILEAGE [Kaleva]	COUNTY	CROSSINGS, JUNCTIONS, ETC.
River Branch Jct.	1.4	Manistee	J/M&NE-A 21.3
Marilla	6.8	"	
Sands Siding	9	"	
Miners Rollway	12	Wexford	
Harmons Mill	13	"	
Claggetts	15.1	"	B/AA-C 256.3
Glengarry	16.8	"	
Walls	18	"	
Buckley	23.8	"	f. Wexford
Baxter	31.4	"	
Walton	38.8	Gr. Trav.	B/GR&I-N 352.8
Springfield	43.6	Kalkaska	
Deiberts	48.5	"	
Rowley	50.1	"	
McGee	52.2	"	
(Crossing)	56.1	"	X/PM-K 19.5
O'Neil	58.0	"	
Sigma	61.0	"	
Angling	62.8	"	
Riverview	70.6	"	
Resort	74	Crawford	
Portage Jct.	76.1	"	J/MC-MR 2.3
(Jct.)	78.4	"	J/MC-M 92.6
(Grayling, via MC-M)	78.7)	"	

CONSTRUCTION/ABANDONMENT

DATE	ACT	END POINTS	MP	CHANGE	MAIN	SOURCE	NOTE
1895	B	River Branch Jct.–MP 5.4	1.4–5.4	+4.0	4.0	4	
1903	B	MP 5.4–Glengarry	5.4–16.8	+11.4	15.4	4	
1904/11/21	B	Glengarry–Wexford	16.8–23.8	+7.0	22.4	4	
1909	B	Wexford–Sigma	23.8–61.0	+37.2	59.6	4	
1910	B	Sigma–Grayling	61.0–78.4	+17.4	77.0	4	
1925	X	River Branch Jct.–MP 76.1	1.4–76.1	–74.7	2.3	2	3
1955 ca.	S	Near Grayling	76.1–78.4	–2.3	0		

OWNERSHIP

1895	Manistee & Northeastern Railroad
1926/9/4	Manistee & Northeastern Railway, reorganized Manistee & Northeastern Railroad
1931/12	Pere Marquette, control of Manistee & Northeastern

BEAR CREEK BRANCH (M&NE-1)

	MILEAGE	COUNTY	CROSSINGS, JUNCTIONS, ETC.
Bear Creek	0	Manistee	J/M&NE-A 18.3
Conger	1.7	"	X/PM-P 108.2
Peters Camp	5.0	"	
Canfields Camp	6.0	"	
(End)	8.0	"	

CONSTRUCTION/ABANDONMENT

DATE	ACT	END POINTS	MP	CHANGE	MAIN	SOURCE	NOTE
1890/5/1	B	Bear Creek–Peters Camp	0–5.0	+5.0	5.0	4	
1892	B	Peters Camp–Canfields Camp	5.0–6.0	+1.0	6.0	4	
1895	B	Canfields Camp–east	6.0–8.0	+2.0	8.0	4	
1898	X	MP 3.0–MP 8.0	3.0–8.0	−5.0	3.0	4	
1899	X	Bear Creek–MP 3.0	0–3.0	−3.0	0	4	

OWNERSHIP

1890   Manistee & Northeastern Railroad

TWIN LAKE BRANCH (M&NE-2)

	MILEAGE	COUNTY	CROSSINGS, JUNCTIONS, ETC.
Twin Lk. Branch	0	Gr.Trav.	J/M&NE-A 37.6
Twin Lk.	1.6	Benzie	
Bendon	6.5	"	(no connection with PM-P at Bendon)

CONSTRUCTION/ABANDONMENT

DATE	ACT	END POINTS	MP	CHANGE	MAIN	SOURCE	NOTE
1892	B	MP 0–MP 2.0	0–2.0	+2.0	2.0	4	
1893	B	MP 2.0–Bendon	2.0–6.5	+4.5	6.5	4	
1895	X	Line	0–6.5	−6.5	0	4	

OWNERSHIP

1892   Manistee & Northeastern Railroad

FILERS BRANCH (M&NE-3)

	MILEAGE	COUNTY	CROSSINGS, JUNCTIONS, ETC.
Filers Switch	0	Gr.Trav.	J/M&NE-A 47.3
B. & D. Camps	4.0	"	
(End)	6.0	"	

CONSTRUCTION/ABANDONMENT

DATE	ACT	END POINTS	MP	CHANGE	MAIN	SOURCE	NOTE
1897	B	Filers Switch–B. & D. Camps	0–4.0	+4.0	4.0	4	
1898	B	B. & D. Camps–MP 6	4.0–6.0	+2.0	6.0	4	
1900	X	MP 6–MP 1	6.0–1.0	−5.0	1.0	4	
1901	X	Filers Switch–MP 1	1.0–0	−1.0	0	4	

OWNERSHIP

1897   Manistee & Northeastern Railroad

BRANCH (M&NE-4)

	MILEAGE	COUNTY	CROSSINGS, JUNCTIONS, ETC.
(Jct.)	0	Manistee	J/M&NE-A 21.4
(End)	3	"	

CONSTRUCTION/ABANDONMENT

DATE	ACT	END POINTS	MP	CHANGE	MAIN	SOURCE	NOTE
1898	B	Line	0–3.0	+3.0	3.0	4	
1901	X	Line	0–3.0	–3.0	0	4	

OWNERSHIP

1898   Manistee & Northeastern Railroad

LONG LAKE BRANCH (M&NE-5)

	MILEAGE	COUNTY	CROSSINGS, JUNCTIONS, ETC.
Long Lk. Branch	0	Gr. Trav.	J/M&NE-A 45.7
(End)	3.0	"	

CONSTRUCTION/ABANDONMENT

DATE	ACT	END POINTS	MP	CHANGE	MAIN	SOURCE	NOTE
1899	B	Long Lk. Branch–MP 2	0–2.0	+2.0	2.0	4	
1900	B	MP 2–MP 3	2.0–3.0	+1.0	3.0	4	
1901	X	Line	0–3.0	–3.0	0	4	

OWNERSHIP

1899   Manistee & Northeastern Railroad

BETSEY RIVER BRANCH (M&NE-6)

	MILEAGE	COUNTY	CROSSINGS, JUNCTIONS, ETC.
(Jct.)	0	Manistee	J/M&NE-A 28.4
Henry	2.8	"	X/A&BR 17.8, X/PM-P 117.0
(End)	8.0	Benzie	

CONSTRUCTION/ABANDONMENT

DATE	ACT	END POINTS	MP	CHANGE	MAIN	SOURCE	NOTE
1900	B	MP 0–MP 5	0–5.0	+5.0	5.0	4	
1901	B	MP 5–MP 8	5.0–8.0	+3.0	8.0	4	
1904	X	MP 8–MP 0	8.0–0	–8.0	0	4	

OWNERSHIP

1900   Manistee & Northeastern Railroad

PLATTE RIVER BRANCH (M&NE-E)

	MILEAGE	COUNTY	CROSSINGS, JUNCTIONS, ETC.
Platte River Jct.	0	Benzie	J/M&NE-A 49.3
Allyn	4.1	"	
Hayes	6.8	"	
Cruse	8.6	"	f. State Rd.
Honor	10.6	"	
(Jct.)	11.1	"	J/PM-P6 9.6
Achas	14	"	
Stormer	15.4	"	
Empire Jct.	16.8	"	J/E&SE-A 0

CONSTRUCTION/ABANDONMENT

DATE	ACT	END POINTS	MP	CHANGE	MAIN	SOURCE	NOTE
1898/12/21	B	Platte River Jct.–MP 13.4	0–13.4	+13.4	13.4	4	
1900	B	MP 13.4–MP 16.4	13.4–16.4	+3.0	16.4	4	
1901	B	MP 16.4–Empire Jct.	16.4–16.8	+0.4	16.8	4	
1924	X	Line	0–16.8	–16.8	0	2	

OWNERSHIP

1898   Manistee & Northeastern Railroad

NORTHPORT BRANCH (M&NE-N)

	MILEAGE [Trav. Cty.]	COUNTY	CROSSINGS, JUNCTIONS, ETC.
Hatchs (Crossing)	5.5	Leelanau	J/M&NE-A 64.6
Heimforth	7.5	"	
Bingham	9.4	"	
N. Bingham		"	
Keswick	11.5	"	
Leelanau	13.1	"	
Suttons Bay	16.7	"	
Manseau	20	"	
Omena	23.7	"	
Clovers		"	
Northport	29.0	"	
(End)	29.3	"	

CONSTRUCTION/ABANDONMENT

DATE	ACT	END POINTS	MP	CHANGE	MAIN	SOURCE	NOTE
1903/6/28	B2	Hatchs–MP 29.3	5.5–29.3	+24.8	24.8	1	2
1982 ca.	XL	Hatchs–MP 29.3	5.5–29.3	−24.8	0		

OWNERSHIP

1903	Traverse City, Leelanau & Manistique
1919/5/23	Leelanau Transit Co., bought Traverse City, Leelanau & Manistique
1919/6/6	Manistee & Northeastern Railroad, leased Leelanau Transit
1926/9/4	Manistee & Northeastern Railway, reorganized Manistee & Northeastern Railroad
1931/21	Pere Marquette, control of Manistee & Northeastern
1947/4/1	Chesapeake & Ohio, merger of Pere Marquette, and control of M&NE (and lease of Leelanau Transit)
1955/11/30	Chesapeake & Ohio, merged Manistee & Northeastern, leased Leelanau Transit
1982 ca.	Leelanau Transit lease to C&O canceled

TRAVERSE CITY MAIN TRACK (M&NE-NT)

	MILEAGE	COUNTY	CROSSINGS, JUNCTIONS, ETC.
(End)	0	Gr.Trav.	J/GR&I-T 26.0
Trav. Cty. (Bay St.)	1.0	Gr.Trav.	J/M&NE-A 69.8, J/PM-YTC 148.5

CONSTRUCTION/ABANDONMENT

DATE	ACT	END POINTS	MP	CHANGE	MAIN	SOURCE	NOTE
1903/6/28	B2	Line	0–1.0	+1.0	1.0	1	5
1919	Y	Line	0–1.0	(1.0)	0		
1954 ca.	X	Line	0–1.0	(−1.0)	0		

OWNERSHIP

1903	Traverse City, Leelanau & Manistique (B2)
1919/5/23	Leelanau Transit Co., bought Traverse City, Leelanau & Manistique
1919/6/6	Manistee & Northeastern Railroad, leased Leelanau Transit
1926/9/4	Manistee & Northeastern Railway, reorganized Manistee & Northeastern Railroad
1931/21	Pere Marquette, control of Manistee & Northeastern
1947/4/1	Chesapeake & Ohio, merger of Pere Marquette, and control of M&NE (and lease of Leelanau Transit)

PROVEMONT (GLEN ARBOR) BRANCH (M&NE-P)

	MILEAGE	COUNTY	CROSSINGS, JUNCTIONS, ETC.
Solon	0	Leelanau	J/M&NE-A 59.7
Cedar Cty.	3.2	"	f. Cedar
Isadore	5.3	"	
Bodus	7.4	"	
Schomberg	8.7	"	
Elton	11	"	
Provemont	14.5	"	

CONSTRUCTION/ABANDONMENT

DATE	ACT	END POINTS	MP	CHANGE	MAIN	SOURCE	NOTE
1894/12/1	B	Solon–MP 3.0	0–3.0	+3.0	3.0	4	
1895	B	MP 3.0–MP 3.5	3.0–3.5	+0.5	3.5	4	
1899	B	MP 3.5–MP 3.8	3.5–3.8	+0.3	3.8	4	
1902/12/17	B	MP 3.8–Provemont	3.8–14.5	+10.7	14.5	4	
1944	X	Provemont–Cedar Cty.	14.5–3.8	−10.7	3.8	2	
1954	X	Cedar Cty.–Solon	3.8–0	−3.8	0		

OWNERSHIP

1894	Manistee & Northeastern Railroad
1926/9/4	Manistee & Northeastern Railway, reorganized Manistee & Northeastern Railroad
1931/12	Pere Marquette, control of Manistee & Northeastern
1947/4/1	Chesapeake & Ohio, merger of Pere Marquette, and control of M&NE

ACQUISITION/DISPOSITION RECORD

DATE	ACT	M&NE–	END POINTS	CHANGE	MI MAIN	NOTE
1888/11/20	B	A,YM1	Manistee–Nessen Cty.	+33.4	33.4	1
1889/1/14	B	O	Onekama Jct.–Onekama	+2.8	36.2	
1890/5/1	B	1	Bear Creek Br.	+5.0		
10/13	B	A	Nessen Cty.–Lk. Ann	+18.8		
	Y	YM1	In Manistee	(0.5)		
	B	YM1	Manistee–Filer Cty.	(+3.4)	59.5	
1892/7/1	B	A	Lk. Ann–Trav. Cty.	+18.1		
	B	YM2	Lk. Sh. Br.	(+1.5)		
	B	2	Twin Lk. Br.	+2.0		
	B	1	Bear Creek Br.	+1.0	80.6	
1893	B	2	Twin Lk. Br.	+4.5	85.1	
1894/12/1	B	P	Solon–Cedar Cty.	+3.0	88.1	
1895	B	P	In Cedar Cty.	+0.5		
	B	1	Bear Creek Br.	+2.0		
	X	2	Twin Lk. Br.	−6.5		
	B	R	River Branch Jct.–east	+4.0	88.1	
1897	B	3	Filers Br.	+4.0	92.1	
1898	B	1	Bear Creek Br.	−5.0		
	B	3	Filers Br.	+2.0		
	B	4	Branch	+3.0		
/12/21	B	E	Platte River Jct.–Honor	+13.4	105.5	
1899	X	1	Bear Creek Br.	−3.0		
	B	5	Long Lk. Br.	+2.0		
	B	P	In Cedar Cty.	+0.3	104.8	
1900	X	3	Filers Br.	−5.0		
	B	5	Long Lk. Br.	+1.0		
	B	E	Platte River Br.	+3.0		

	B	6	Betsey River Br.	+5.0	108.8	
1901	B	YM2	Lk. Sh. Br.	(+0.7)		
	X	3	Filers Br.	−1.0		
	X	4	Branch	−3.0		
	X	5	Long Lk. Br.	−3.0		
	B	6	Betsey River Br.	+3.0		
	B	E	Platte River Br.	+0.4	105.2	
1902/12/17	B	P	Cedar Cty.–Provemont	+10.7	115.9	
1903	B	R	MP 5.4–Glengarry	+11.4	127.3	
1904/11/21	B	R	Glengarry–Wexford	+7.0		
	X	6	Betsey River Br.	−8.0	126.3	
1909	B	R	Wexford–Sigma	+37.2	163.5	
1910	B	R	Sigma–Grayling	+17.4	180.9	
1919/6/6	L	N	Hatchs–Northport	+23.8		2
	L	NT	In Trav. Cty.	(+1.0)	204.7	5
1921 ca.	X	YM1	At Filer Cty.	(−0.4)	204.7	
1924	X	E	Platte River Br.	−16.8	187.9	
1925	X	R	River Branch Jct.–Portage Jct.	−74.7	113.2	3
1934	X	A	Kaleva–Solon	−39.5	73.7	4
1944	X	P	Provemont–Cedar Cty.	−10.7	63.0	
1954	X	A	In Kaleva	−0.3		
	X	A	In Trav. Cty.	(−1.0)		
	X	A	Solon–Hatchs	−4.9		
	X	P	Solon–Cedar Cty.	−3.8		
	X	YM2	Lk. Sh. Br.	(−0.7)	54.0	
1955 ca.	S	R	Near Grayling	−2.3	51.7	

On 30 November 1955 this company was conveyed to Chesapeake & Ohio. Its Acquisition/Disposition Record is continued in two places: under the name of the former company and under the name of the new company. The lines conveyed were:

LINE DESIG.			END POINTS	MP	MAIN
[M&NE-A]			Manistee–Kaleva and	0–19.9	
			Hatchs–Trav. Cty.	64.6–69.8	25.1
[M&NE-YM1]			Manistee–Filer Cty.	0–3.5	(3.5)
[M&NE-YM2]			In Manistee	0–1.5	(1.5)
[M&NE-N]			Hatchs–Northport	5.5–29.3	23.8
[M&NE-O]			Onekama Jct–Onekama	9.8–12.6	2.8
			TOTAL		51.7
1972	X	O	Onekama Jct.–Onekama	−2.8	48.9
1982	X	A	Manistee–Kaleva	−19.9	
	X	A	Hatchs–Trav. Cty.	−5.2	
Ca.	XL	N	Hatchs–Northport	−23.8	0

Act Column Key

B	Built by Manistee & Northeastern
B2	Built by Traverse City, Leelanau & Manistique
L	Leased from Leelanau Transit
S	Sold to Michigan Central
X	Abandoned
XL	Lease canceled
Y	Converted from main to yard track

Sources

1. Burton, "Car Ferry from Northport."
2. ICC, *Finance Dockets*.
3. MDOT records.
4. Michigan Railroad Commission, *Aids, Gifts, Grants*.

Notes

1. Regular service began between Manistee and Bear Creek on 14 January 1889.
2. Mileage for this line before 1919 is shown under Traverse City, Leelanau & Manistique and after ca.1982 is given under Leelanau Transit, which see. Source 4 gives the opening date as 1906.
3. The segment between Grayling and Portage Jct. was retained and operated by the Michigan Central line MC-MR, under lease, until its subsequent sale. This mileage is not included in MC mileage.
4. After 11 September 1932, until abandonment, freight traffic moved via Pere Marquette line PM-P between Kaleva and Interlochen.
5. This construction is assumed given that the Grand Rapids & Indiana both constructed and then operated the Traverse City, Leelanau & Manistique in its early years.

Mason & Oceana

MAIN LINE (M&O-A)

	MILEAGE	COUNTY	CROSSINGS, JUNCTIONS, ETC.
Buttersville	0	Mason	
Riverton	8.1	"	f. Harleys
Wileys	11.1	"	
Fern	14.4	"	f. Adamsville
Camp	19	Oceana	f. New South Branch Camp
Water Tank	22	"	
Peachville	21.9	"	f. South Branch Camp
Lake	25	"	J/spur, f. Fisher Camp
Walkerville	27.2	"	f. Stetson
Goodrich	31.0	"	
Gale	33.9	"	
Maple	37	"	

CONSTRUCTION/ABANDONMENT

DATE	ACT	END POINTS	MP	CHANGE	MAIN	SOURCE	NOTE
1887/1/6	B	Buttersville–MP 21.3	0–21.3	+21.3	21.3	1	
1888/1/20	B	MP 21.3–Walkerville	21.3–27.2	+5.9	27.2	1	
1902/6/10	B	Walkerville–Goodrich	27.2–31.0	+3.8	31.0	1	
1904/6/1	B	Goodrich–Maple	31.0–37.0	+6.0	37.0	1	
1906	X	Maple–Goodrich	37.0–31.0	−6.0	31.0	1	
1908	X	Goodrich–Walkerville	31.0–27.2	−3.8	27.2	1	
1909/12/1	X	Walkerville–Buttersville	27.2–0	−27.2	0	1	

OWNERSHIP

1887 Mason & Oceana

ACQUISITION/DISPOSITION RECORD

See Mileage record above.

Act column

B Built by Mason & Oceana
X Abandoned

Sources

1. Michigan Railroad Commission, *Aids, Gifts, Grants*.

Notes

GENERAL   The Mason & Oceana was a wholly owned property of the Butters Lumber Co. and was used principally as an industrial property of that company. It constructed numerous spurs for lumbering purposes, which have not been documented, most of which were used for only a short time.

Mecosta

MAIN LINE (MEC-A)

	MILEAGE	COUNTY	CROSSINGS, JUNCTIONS, ETC.
(Musk. River)	0	Mecosta	(sec36 T15N R10W)
Byers	0.2	"	B/GR&I-N 285.9
(Jct., line B)	1.0	"	(sec32 T15N R9W)
Rodney	6.2	"	X/PM-J 85.2
Horseshoe Lk.	9.5	"	(sec22 T15N R8W)

CONSTRUCTION/ABANDONMENT

DATE	ACT	END POINTS	MP	CHANGE	MAIN	SOURCE	NOTE
1883/3/1	B	MP 0–Horseshoe Lk.	0–9.5	+9.5	9.5	1	
1885	X	MP 1–Horseshoe Lk.	1.0–9.5	−8.5	1.0	1	
1888	X	MP 0–MP 1	0–1.0	−1.0	0	1	

OWNERSHIP

1883   Mecosta

BRANCH (MEC-B)

	MILEAGE	COUNTY	CROSSINGS, JUNCTIONS, ETC.
(Jct.)	1.0	Mecosta	J/line A 1.0
(End)	4.0	"	sec 3 T14N R9W

CONSTRUCTION/ABANDONMENT

DATE	ACT	END POINTS	MP	CHANGE	MAIN	SOURCE	NOTE
1885/10/11	B	Line	1.0–4.0	+3.0	3.0	1	
1888	X	Line	1.0–4.0	−3.0	0	1	

OWNERSHIP

1885   Mecosta

BRANCH (MEC-XC) (BRANCH NOT LOCATED)

CONSTRUCTION/ABANDONMENT

DATE	ACT	END POINTS	MP	CHANGE	MAIN	SOURCE	NOTE
1886	B	Not located	11.0 miles	+11.0	11.0	1	
1887	X	Not located	5.0 miles	−5.0	6.0	1	
1888	X	Not located	6.0 miles	−6.0	0	1	

OWNERSHIP

1886   Mecosta

ACQUSIITION/DISPOSITION RECORD

DATE	ACT	MEC–	END POINTS	CHANGE	MI MAIN	NOTE
1883/3/1	B	A	Musk. River–Horseshoe Lk.	+9.5	9.5	
1885	X	A	Jct.–Horseshoe Lk.	–8.5		
1885/10/11	B	B	Jct.–End	+3.0	4.0	
1886	B	XC	Unlocated branches	+11.0	15.0	
1887	X	XC	Unlocated branches	–5.0	10.0	
1888	X	A,B,XC	Entire line	–10.0	0	

Act Column Key

B Built by Mecosta
X Abandoned

>Sources

1. Michigan, Commissioner of Railroads, *Annual Reports,* 1883, 1885, 1888.

Michigan, State of

Between 1838 and 1846 the State of Michigan built, acquired, and operated the following Lines as shown in the records of Lake Shore (LS) and Michigan Central (MC):

ACQUSIITION/DISPOSITION RECORD

DATE	ACT	LINE	END POINTS	CHANGE	MI MAIN	NOTE
1838/2/3	B1	MC-E,EO1	Det.–Ypsi.	+29.6		
Spr.	B1	MC-EO2	In Det.	(+0.7)	29.6	
1839/10/17	B1	MC-E,EO3	Ypsi.–A.A.	+7.5	37.1	
1840/11/23	B1	LS-M,A	Monroe–Adrian	+32.6		
	P1	LS-M,YM	In Monroe	+2.9		
	B1	LS-M	In Monroe	+0.4	73.0	
1841/6/30	B1	MC-E,EO4	A.A.–Dexter	+10.8		
12/31	B1	MC-E	Dexter–Jackson	+28.6	112.4	
1842/Sum.	B1	LS-A	Adrian–Clayton	+11.0	123.4	
1843/5/27	B1	LS-A	Clayton–Hudson	+6.5		
	B1	LS-A	Hudson–Hillsdale	+15.8	145.7	
1844/3	X	MC-EO2	In Det.	(–0.7)		
6/15	B1	MC-C	Jackson–Albion	+20.4		
8/12	B1	MC-C,CO1	Albion–Marshall	+11.7		
	P2	LS-J	Palmyra Jct.–Tecumseh	+11.6	189.4	
1845/11/25	B1	MC-C,CO1	Marshall–Battle Creek	+13.0	202.4	
1846/2/2	B1	MC-C	Battle Creek–Kal.	+23.0		
9/24	S1	all MC	Det.–Kal.	–144.6		
12/28	S2	all LS	Monroe–Hillsdale & branch	–80.8	0	

For station list see Lake Shore lines and Michigan Central lines. The mileage record shown above is for information only and is duplicated in the record of the respective successor owners.

On 1 April 1976 the State of Michigan began purchasing and leasing lines and issuing designated operator contracts to preserve service. For the arrangement of stations, construction record, and prior ownership, see the record for each individual line as shown herein under its earlier ownership: Ann Arbor (AA); Chicago, Milwaukee, St. Paul & Pacific (MILW); Duluth, South Shore & Atlantic (DSSA); Grand Rapids & Indiana (GR&I); Lake Shore (LS); Michigan Central (MC); Mineral Range (MR); and Pere Marquette (PM). The Acquisition/Disposition Record during State of Michigan ownership is continued for each line after 1 April 1976.

ACQUSIITION/DISPOSITION RECORD

DATE	ACT	LINE	END POINTS	MP	MI MAIN	NOTE
		MICH-				
1976/4/1	P1	[AA-A]	Toledo OH–A.A.	5.7–47.5	+41.8	1,2
4/1	P1	[AA-A]	A.A.–Pitt	47.5–93.9	+46.4	3
4/1	P1	[AA-B]	Ashley–Alma	128.3–145.4	+17.1	3
4/1	P1	[AA-B]	Alma–Cadillac	145.4–227.1	+81.7	4
4/1	P1	[AA-G]	Pittsfield–Saline	0–MP 6.4	+6.4	2
1976 TOTAL		AA=193.4	MICH=193.4			
1980/7	P1	[AA-C]	Cadillac–Frankfort	227.1–292.2	+65.1	4,18
7	P1	[AA-F]	To Boat Landing	290.3–291.8	+1.5	4,18
9	P5	[MC-M]	Linwood–Sallings	10.8–115.8	+105.0	5
9	P5	[MC-Y1P]	At Pinconning	0–0.6	(+0.6)	5
1980 TOTAL		AA=260.0	MC=105.0	MICH=365.0		
1982/2	P2	[PM-P]	Grawn–Williamsburg	158.1(136.4)–180.8(159.1)	+22.7	6
2	P2	[PM-P]	Charlevoix–Bay View	231.4(209.7)–248.0(226.2)	+16.5	6,17
2	P2	[PM-YTC]	At Trav. Cty.	0–1.3	(+1.3)	
9	P4	[MILW-O]	Channing–Ont.	315.3–408.3	+93.0	7
11	P5	[LS-A2]	Riga–Lenawee Jct.	315.5–325.5	+10.0	8
1982 TOTAL		AA=260.0 LS=10.0 MC=105.0 MILW=93.0 PM=39.2 MICH=507.2				
1983/7	P4	[MILW-A]	Iron. Mtn.–Channing	290.6–315.8	+25.2	9
1983 TOTAL		AA=260.0 LS=10.0 MC=105.0 MILW=118.2 PM=39.2 MICH=532.4				
1984/2/15	P5	[MC-B]	Millington–Munger	79.3–101.1	+21.8	10
2/15	P5	[MC-BC]	Caro Jct.–Colling	0.4–22.4	+22.0	10
2/15	P5	[MC-BS]	Denmark Jct.–Richville	4.8–6.0	+1.2	10
2/15	P5	[MC-S]	Owosso–Swan Creek	64.2–91.3	+27.1	3
2/15	P5	[LS-A4]	Hillsdale–Quincy	361.0–376.6	+15.6	11
2/15	P5	[LS-A3]	Lenawee Jct.–Adrian	325.5–332.9	+7.4	12
2/15	P5	[LS-Y2M]	At Lenawee Jct.	29.1–29.3	(+0.2)	
2/15	P5	[LS-F1]	Grosvenor–west	0–1.7	+1.7	12,13
2/15	P5	[LS-F2]	Weston–Morenci	11.4–18.6	+7.2	12,13
2/15	P5	[LS-Y1Y]	At Hillsdale	60.4–61.1	(+0.7)	11
2/15	P5	[LS-Y]	Hillsdale–Bankers	61.1–65.6	+4.5	11
2/15	P5	[LS-L]	Jonesville–Litchfield	0.6–6.9	+6.3	11
2/15	P5	[LS-W]	IN state line–Bankers	44.7–31.1	+13.6	11
2/15	P5	[LS-W2]	At Jonesville	25.3–24.1	(+1.2)	11
2/15	P5	[GR&I-N]	Comstock Park–Petoskey	239.5–426.0	+186.5	14,15
2/15	P5	[GR&I-T]	Walton Jct.–Trav. Cty.	0–25.2	+25.2	14
1984 TOTAL		AA=260.0 GR&I=211.7 LS=66.3 MC=177.1 MILW=118.2 PM=39.2 MICH=872.5				
1987/8/6	P3	[AA-B]	Owosso–Ashley	109.4–129.0	+19.6	16
9/21	P6	[DSSA-H]	Arnheim–Hough.	33.8–48.2	+14.4	
9/21	P6	[MR-M]	Hough.–Shore Line Jct.	–0.5–0.5	+1.0	
9/21	P6	[MR-H]	Shore Line Jct.–Lk. Linden	0.4–9.9	+9.4	
ca.	X	[GR&I-N]	In Cadillac	331.5–332.5	–1.0	15
ca.	Y	[GR&I-N]	At N. Yard	332.5–333.1	(0.6)	15
1987 TOTAL		AA=279.6 DSSA=14.4 GR&I=210.1 LS=66.3 MC=177.1 MILW=118.2 MR=10.4 PM=39.2 MICH=915.3				

1991	X	[GRI-N]	Comstock Park–Cadillac	239.5–331.5	–92.0	15
	X	[PM-P]	Charlevoix–Bay View	231.4(209.7)–248.0(226.2)	–16.5	6
ca.	X	[LS-F]	Weston–Morenci	11.4–18.6	–7.2	

1991 TOTAL AA=279.6 DSSA=14.4 GR&I=118.1 LS=59.1 MC=177.1 MILW=118.2 MR=10.4 PM=22.7
MICH=799.6

	X	[AA-C]	Thom.–Frankfort	271.2–292.2	–21.0	
	X	[AA-F]	to Boat Landing	290.3–291.8	–1.5	

1994 TOTAL AA=257.1 DSSA=14.4 GR&I=118.1 LS=59.1 MC=177.1 MILW=118.2 MR=10.4 PM=22.7
MICH=777.1

1995	X	[DSSA-H]	Arnheim–Hough.	33.8–48.2	–14.4	
	X	[MR-M]	Hough.–Shore Line Jct.	–0.5–0.5	–1.0	
	X	[MR-H]	Shore Line Jct.–Lk. Linden	0.7–10.1	–9.4	

1995 TOTAL AA=257.1 GR&I=118.1 LS=59.1 MC=177.1 MILW=118.2 PM=22.7 MICH=752.3

Act Column Key

P1   Purchased from Ann Arbor
P2   Purchased from Chesapeake & Ohio
P3   Purchased from Grand Trunk Western
P4   Purchased from Chicago, Milwaukee, St. Paul & Pacific
P5   Purchased from Penn Central
P6   Purchased from Soo Line
S1   Sold to Michigan Central
S2   Sold to Michigan Southern
X   Abandoned
Y   Converted from main track to yard track

Notes

GENERAL   The service provided, as shown below between 1 April 1976 and its purchase by the state, was by contract between the state, the owner of the property, and a designated operator.

1.   Mileage owned in Ohio is not included.

2.   This segment was provided service by designated operator beginning 1 April 1976 with Conrail, and succeeded 1 October 1977 by Michigan Interstate.

3.   This segment was provided service by designated operator beginning 1 April 1976 with Conrail, succeeded 1 October 1977 by Michigan Interstate, and 1 October 1982 by Tuscola & Saginaw Bay.

4.   This segment was provided service by designated operator beginning 1 April 1976 with Conrail, succeeded 1 October 1977 by Michigan Interstate, 1 October 1982 by Michigan Northern, and 6 May 1984 by Tuscola & Saginaw Bay.

5.   This segment was provided service by designated operator beginning 1 April 1976 with Detroit & Mackinac.

6.   This segment was provided service by designated operator beginning 19 February 1982 with Michigan Northern, and succeeded 1 October 1984 by Tuscola & Saginaw Bay. The Mile Posts shown are the C&O's renumbered locations and are 21.7 miles higher than those shown in the station list for line PM-P.

7.   This segment was provided service by designated operator beginning September 1982 with Escanaba & Lake Superior.

8.   This segment was provided service by designated operator beginning 1 April 1976 with Conrail, and succeeded 1 October 1982 by Lenawee County Railroad.

9.   This segment was provided service by designated operator beginning July 1983 with Escanaba & Lake Superior.

10. This segment was provided service by designated operator beginning 1 April 1976 with Conrail, and succeeded 1 October 1977 by Tuscola & Saginaw Bay.

11. This segment was provided service by designated operator beginning 1 April 1976 with Hillsdale County Railroad.

12. This segment was provided service by designated operator beginning 1 April 1976 with Conrail and succeeded 1 October 1977 by Lenawee County Railroad.

13. The connection between lines LS-F1 and LS-F2 (9.7 miles) was also operated between 1 April 1976 and 1982, at which time the connecting segment was abandoned by Penn Central.

14. This segment was provided service by designated operator beginning 1 April 1976 with Michigan Northern, and succeeded 1 October 1984 by Tuscola & Saginaw Bay.

15. The segment between Comstock Park (MP 239.5) and Reed City (MP 302.0) was rail-banked on 1 October 1984, the segment between Reed City (MP 302.0) and Cadillac (MP 331.5) was rail-banked in about 1987, and the rails subsequently removed the entire distance in 1991. The segment in Cadillac between MP 331.5 and MP 332.5 is herein shown abandoned in 1987 and that part between MP 332.5 and North Yard (MP 331.1) is shown as converted to yard track.

16. This segment was provided service by designated operator beginning 6 August 1987 with Tuscola & Saginaw Bay.

17. This segment was rail-banked about 1988.

18. The segment between Thompsonville (MP 271.2) and Frankfort (MP 292.4) and the branch to Boat Landing (1.5 miles) were rail-banked about 1988. It appears that the segment between Yuma (MP 250.0) and Thompsonville (MP 271.2) was not used after this date, but appears not to have been formally rail-banked.

Michigan Central

DETROIT DIV. (MC-E)

	MILEAGE	COUNTY	CROSSINGS, JUNCTIONS, ETC.
Detroit (Third St.)	0	Wayne	(2nd station)
(Bridge)	0.52	"	B/FSUD 0.6
(Fort St.)	0.65	"	B/DSR-F 4.17
(Howard St.)	0.85	"	B/DSR-U2 0.98
(Porter St.)	1.0	"	B/DSR-U 0.58
(Bagley St.)	1.2	"	B/DSR-A 10.77
15th St.	1.2	"	J/MC-Z 227.3
Detroit	1.39	"	(3rd station)
20th St.	1.61	"	
(21st St.)	1.7	"	J/MC-EO1 1.9
(Jct.)	2.02	"	J/
(E wye switch)	2.15	"	
Bay Cty. Jct.	2.23	"	J/MC-B 2.2
(Scotten Ave.)	2.4	"	B/DSR-SC 0.37
CP Scotten	2.4	"	
(W wye switch)	2.43	"	
Springwells	2.5	"	
(Jct.)	2.72	"	J/MC-T 2.7
(Crossing)	2.87	"	X/LS-D 8.2
(Crossing)	2.89	"	X/GTW-H 0-WAB-W 0
W. Detroit	2.91	"	J/PM-DW 0
(Jct. Ave.)	2.93	"	B/DSR-GB 10.79
Military	3.2	"	
Livernois Ave.	3.32	"	
Jct. Yard	4.0	"	
Lonyo	4.5	"	
J (Tower)	5.21	"	
Wyoming	5.4	"	
Mulkey Ave.	5.52	"	B/DSR-MR 0.70
(Bridge)	5.65	"	B/PM-D 7.1
Miller	5.68	"	J/DT 0, f. Fordson
(Schaefer Ave.)	6.4	"	B/DSR-M 7.19
Town Line	7.37	"	J/MC-DZ 4.2
CP Mort	9.2	"	
(Jct.)	9.55	"	J/MC-DD 6.0
Dearborn	10.18	"	
Inkster	13.56	"	
Eloise	15.22	"	f. County House
Wayne	17.69	"	(old 17.50)
Wayne Jct.	18.13	"	X/PM-T 90.2
Cog	19.3	"	
Hannan Rd.	19.6	"	
Haggerty	20.6	"	
Sheldon	22.20	"	
Secords	22.8	"	
Denton(s)	24.77	"	
Raw	25.7	"	

Willow Run	26.56	Washtenaw	
Wiard	26.73	"	
CP Ypsi	28.1	"	
(Crossing)	29.3	"	X/DUR-J 24.07
Ypsi.	29.40	"	J/MC-YP 0
Forest	29.7	"	
(Jct.)	29.78	"	J/LS-Y 0.5
(Jct.)	30.0	"	J/MC-E03 30.0
Shanghai Pit	31.76	"	
(Jct.)	33.2	"	J/MC-E03 32.9
Geddes	33.38	"	
A.A. (first)	37.24	"	
A.A. (second)	37.4	"	
(Bridge)	37.61	"	B/AA-A 46.2
W. A.A.	37.8	"	
(Jct.)	38.0	"	J/MC-E04 38.0
Fosters	40.39	"	
Osborn Pit	41.38	"	
Delhi	42.54	"	
Scio	44.18	"	
Kinnear	45.12	"	
(Jct.)	45.4	"	J/MC-E04 46.6
Dexter	46.75	"	
Four Mile Lk.	51.27	"	
CP Lk.	51.9	"	
Davidson	52	"	
Chelsea	54.04	"	
CP Chelsea	56.0	"	
Sylvan	58.1	"	
Francisco	61.05	Jackson	f. Franciscoville
Grass	65.0	"	
Grass Lk.	65.15	"	
Leoni	68.19	"	
(Bridge)	70.67	"	B/DUR-J 64.1, B/MUR-SG 5.3
Ballard Rd.	70.8	"	
Michigan Center	71.51	"	
Falahee Rd.	72.7	"	(now E. Jackson)
East Yard	73.12	"	
(Jct.)	74.36	"	J/MC-YJ 0
Jackson Jct.	74.38	"	J/MC-A 0
East Ave.	75.02	"	J/LS-W 0.4
Jackson	75.43	"	C/MC-C 75.4

CONSTRUCTION/ABANDONMENT

DATE	ACT	END POINTS	MP	CHANGE	MAIN	SOURCE	NOTE
1838/2/3	B1	21st St.–Ypsi.	1.7–29.4	+27.7	27.7	3	1
1839/10/17	B1	Ypsi.–MP 30.0	29.4–30.0	+0.6		7	
1839/10/17	B1	MP 33.2–A.A.	33.2–37.2	+4.0	32.3	7	
1841/6/30	B1	A.A.–MP 38.0	37.2–38.0	+0.8		7	
1841/6/30	B1	MP 45.4–Dexter	45.4–46.8	+1.4	34.5	7	
1841/12/29	B1	Dexter–Jackson	46.8–75.4	+28.6	63.1	7	3
1848/5/30	B2	Det.–21st St.	0–1.7	+1.7			
1848 ca.	B2	MP 30.0–MP 33.2	30.0–33.2	+3.2			
1848 ca.	B2	MP 38.0–MP 45.4	38.0–45.4	+7.4	75.4		

1911	Y	Det.–MP 1.2 (to MC-Y1E)	0–1.2	(1.2)	74.2	

1972	X	Detroit–MP 0.3 (MC-Y1E)	0–0.3	(–0.3)	74.2	

OWNERSHIP

1838	State of Michigan (B1)
1846/9/24	Michigan Central (B2), bought State of Michigan "Central" line
1930/2/1	New York Central, lease of Michigan Central
1968/2/1	Penn Central, merger of New York Central (with lease of Michigan Central)
1976/4/1	Conrail, purchase of Penn Central
1999/6/1	Norfolk Southern, purchase of part of Conrail line

ORIGINAL LINE TO DETROIT (MC-EO1)

	MILEAGE	COUNTY	CROSSINGS, JUNCTIONS, ETC.
Detroit (1st station)	0	Wayne	J/MC-EO2 0 (NE corner Griswold & Fort)
(21st St.)	1.9	"	J/MC-E 1.7

CONSTRUCTION/ABANDONMENT

DATE	ACT	END POINTS	MP	CHANGE	MAIN	SOURCE	NOTE
1838/2/5	B1	Det.–21st St.	0–1.9	+1.9	1.9	7	1
1848	X	Det.–21st St.	0–1.9	–1.9	0		

OWNERSHIP

1838	State of Michigan (B1)
1846/9/24	Michigan Central, bought State of Michigan "Central" line

RIVERFRONT SPUR (MC-EO2)

	MILEAGE	COUNTY	CROSSINGS, JUNCTIONS, ETC.
Detroit (1st station)	0	Wayne	J/MC-EO1 0
(Woodward and Atwater)	0.3	"	

CONSTRUCTION/ABANDONMENT

DATE	ACT	END POINTS	MP	CHANGE	MAIN	SOURCE	NOTE
1838/Spr.	B1	Line	0–0.3	(+0.3)		3	2
1838/Spr.	B1	Spurs	0.4 miles	(+0.4)	0	3	2
1844/3	X	Line & spurs	0.7 miles	(–0.7)	0		

OWNERSHIP

1840	State of Michigan (B1)

OLD LINE, YPSILANTI–ANN ARBOR (MC-EO3)

	MILEAGE	COUNTY	CROSSINGS, JUNCTIONS, ETC.
	[Third St.]		
(Jct.)	30.0	Washtenaw	J/MC–E 30.0
(Jct.)	32.9	"	J/MC–E 33.2

CONSTRUCTION/ABANDONMENT

DATE	ACT	END POINTS	MP	CHANGE	MAIN	SOURCE	NOTE
1839/10/17	B1	Line	30.0–32.9	+2.9	2.9	7	
1848 ca.	X	Line	30.0–32.9	–2.9	0		5

OWNERSHIP

1839	State of Michigan (B1)
1846/9/24	Michigan Central, bought State of Michigan "Central" line

OLD LINE, ANN ARBOR–DEXTER (MC-EO4)

	MILEAGE	COUNTY	CROSSINGS, JUNCTIONS, ETC.
	[Third St.]		
(Jct.)	38.0	Washtenaw	J/MC-E 38.0
(Jct.)	46.6	"	J/MC-E 45.4

CONSTRUCTION/ABANDONMENT

DATE	ACT	END POINTS	MP	CHANGE	MAIN	SOURCE	NOTE
1841/6/30	B1	Line	38.0–46.6	+8.6	8.6	7	
1848 ca.	X	Line	38.0–46.6	–8.6	0		6

OWNERSHIP

1841	State of Michigan (B1)
1846/9/24	Michigan Central, bought State of Michigan "Central" line

YPSILANTI BELT (MC-YP)

	MILEAGE	COUNTY	CROSSINGS, JUNCTIONS, ETC.
Ypsi.	0.0	Washtenaw	J/MC-E 29.4
(End)	1.05	"	

CONSTRUCTION/ABANDONMENT

DATE	ACT	END POINTS	MP	CHANGE	MAIN	SOURCE	NOTE
1865 ca.	B2	Line	0–1.1	(+1.1)	0		

OWNERSHIP

1865	Michigan Central (B2)
1930/2/1	New York Central, lease of Michigan Central
1968/2/1	Penn Central, merger of New York Central (with lease of Michigan Central)
1976/4/1	Conrail, purchase of Penn Central
1999/6/1	Norfolk Southern, purchase of Conrail

JACKSON BELT (MC-YJ)

	MILEAGE	COUNTY	CROSSINGS, JUNCTIONS, ETC.
(Jct.)	0.0	Jackson	J/MC-E 74.36
(End)	1.28	"	

CONSTRUCTION/ABANDONMENT

DATE	ACT	END POINTS	MP	CHANGE	MAIN	SOURCE	NOTE
1865 ca.	B2	Line	0–1.3	(+1.3)	0		
1985 ca.	X	Line	0–1.3	(–1.3)	0		

OWNERSHIP

1865	Michigan Central (B2)
1930/2/1	New York Central, lease of Michigan Central
1968/2/1	Penn Central, merger of New York Central (with lease of Michigan Central)
1976/4/1	Conrail, purchase of Penn Central

EXPOSITION SPUR (MC-YDE)

	MILEAGE	COUNTY	CROSSINGS, JUNCTIONS, ETC.
(Jct.)	0	Wayne	J/MC-T 5.58
(Connection)	0.32	"	J/MC-YDD 0.14
(Crossing)	0.78	"	X/DT&I-M 0.6
(Jct.)	1.09	"	J/MC-YDF 0
Delray Freight House	1.20	"	

CONSTRUCTION/ABANDONMENT

DATE	ACT	END POINTS	MP	CHANGE	MAIN	SOURCE	NOTE
1892 ca.	B11	Line	0–1.2	(+1.2)	0		
1982	X	Line	0–1.2	(−1.2)	0		

OWNERSHIP

1873	Toledo, Canada Southern & Detroit (B11), owned by Canada Southern
1906/1/2	Michigan Central, leased Toledo, Canada Southern & Detroit
1916/9/27	Michigan Central, merger of Toledo, Canada Southern & Detroit
1930/2/1	New York Central, leased Michigan Central
1968/2/1	Penn Central, merger of New York Central (with lease of Michigan Central)
1976/4/1	Conrail, purchase of Penn Central

EXPOSITION SPUR EXTENSION (MC-YDF)

	MILEAGE	COUNTY	CROSSINGS, JUNCTIONS, ETC.
(Jct.)	0	Wayne	J/MC-YDE 1.09
(Crossing)	0.28	"	X/WAB-??
(End)	0.59	"	

CONSTRUCTION/ABANDONMENT

DATE	ACT	END POINTS	MP	CHANGE	MAIN	SOURCE	NOTE
1892 ca.	B11	Line	0–0.6	(+0.6)	0		
1982	X	Line	0–0.6	(−0.6)	0		

OWNERSHIP

1873	Toledo, Canada Southern & Detroit (B11), owned by Canada Southern
1906/1/2	Michigan Central, leased Toledo, Canada Southern & Detroit
1916/9/27	Michigan Central, merger of Toledo, Canada Southern & Detroit
1930/2/1	New York Central, leased Michigan Central
1968/2/1	Penn Central, merger of New York Central (with lease of Michigan Central)
1976/4/1	Conrail, purchase of Penn Central

DELTA SPUR (MC-YDD)

	MILEAGE	COUNTY	CROSSINGS, JUNCTIONS, ETC.
(Jct.)	0	Wayne	J/MC-T 5.84
(Connection)	0.14	"	J/MC-YDE 0.32
(End)	1.02	"	

CONSTRUCTION/ABANDONMENT

DATE	ACT	END POINTS	MP	CHANGE	MAIN	SOURCE	NOTE
1892 ca,	B11	Line	0–1.0	(+1.0)	0		

OWNERSHIP

1873	Toledo, Canada Southern & Detroit (B11), owned by Canada Southern
1906/1/2	Michigan Central, leased Toledo, Canada Southern & Detroit
1916/9/27	Michigan Central, merger of Toledo, Canada Southern & Detroit
1930/2/1	New York Central, leased Michigan Central
1968/2/1	Penn Central, merger of New York Central (with lease of Michigan Central)

DETROIT BELT LINE (MC-YDB)

	MILEAGE	COUNTY	CROSSINGS, JUNCTIONS, ETC.
Belt Line Jct.	0.0	Wayne	J/MC-B 7.2
(Crossing)	0.06	"	X/GTW-H 5.1

Chene St.	0.15	"	
Harper Ave.	0.96	"	X/DSR-ME 2.24
Harper Yard	1.23	"	J/MC-YDC 0
(Palmer Ave.)	1.33	"	X/DSR-CM 4.67
Boulevard	1.70	"	
Palmer Ave. Yard	1.90	"	X/DSR-PE 0.16
Gratiot Ave.	2.47	"	X/DSR-G 2.86
Mack Rd.	2.89	"	X/DSR-K 0.52
(Charlevoix Ave.)	3.0	"	X/DSR-C 4.01
Waterloo St.	3.36	"	
Kercheval Ave.	3.56	"	X/DSR-F 8.52
Champlain St.	3.98	"	(aka Lafayette St.), X/DSR-ML 2.14
Beaufait Station	4.18	"	(aka Jefferson Ave.), X/DSR-J 3.22
Wight St.	4.36	"	
Transit Jct.	4.40	"	J/MC-YDM 0, (Meldrum Ave.)

CONSTRUCTION/ABANDONMENT

DATE	ACT	END POINTS	MP	CHANGE	MAIN	SOURCE	NOTE
1909	B26	Line	0–4.4	(+4.4)	0	7	
1982	X	MP 2.8–MP 4.4	2.8–4.4	(–1.6)	0		

OWNERSHIP

1909	Detroit Belt Line (B26), leased by Michigan Central
1916/12/26	Michigan Central, bought Detroit Belt Line
1930/2/1	New York Central, leased Michigan Central
1968/2/1	Penn Central, merger of New York Central (with lease of Michigan Central)
1976/4/1	Conrail, purchase of Penn Central

DETROIT BELT LINE EXTENSION (MC-YDC)

	MILEAGE	COUNTY	CROSSINGS, JUNCTIONS, ETC.
Harper Yard	0.0	Wayne	J/MC-YDB 1.23
(Lynch Rd.)	1.5	"	X/DSR-ME 0.58
(Crossing)	1.82	"	X/GTW-H 7.2
North Yard	1.91	"	J/MC-B 8.6

CONSTRUCTION/ABANDONMENT

DATE	ACT	END POINTS	MP	CHANGE	MAIN	SOURCE	NOTE
1915 ca.	B2	Line	0–1.9	(+1.9)	0		29

OWNERSHIP

1915	Michigan Central (B2)
1930/2/1	New York Central, leased Michigan Central
1968/2/1	Penn Central, merger of New York Central (with lease of Michigan Central)
1976/4/1	Conrail, purchase of Penn Central

DETROIT MANUFACTURERS (MC-YDM)

	MILEAGE	COUNTY	CROSSINGS, JUNCTIONS, ETC.
Transit Jct.	0.0	Wayne	J/MC-YDC 4.40 (Meldrum Ave.)
(Joseph Campau St.)	0.7	"	X/DSR-ME 7.02
(Chene St.)	0.9	"	X/DSR-ME 6.76
Dequindre St.	1.26	"	J/GTW-D 0.7

CONSTRUCTION/ABANDONMENT

DATE	ACT	END POINTS	MP	CHANGE	MAIN	SOURCE	NOTE
1902 ca.	B23	Line	0–1.3	(+1.3)	0		
1985	X	Line	0–1.3	(–1.3)	0		

OWNERSHIP

1902	Detroit Manufacturers (B23), of segment
1902/4/1	Michigan Central, leased Detroit Manufacturers
1930/2/1	New York Central, leased Michigan Central
1968/2/1	Penn Central, merger of New York Central (with lease of Michigan Central)
1976/4/1	Conrail, purchase of Penn Central

RIVER ROUGE SPUR (MC-YDR)

	MILEAGE	COUNTY	CROSSINGS, JUNCTIONS, ETC.
YD	0.0	Wayne	J/MC-T 6.5
(Crossing)	1.1	"	X/DTI-M 1.9
(Great Lakes Ave.)	2.1	"	X/DUR-WR 0.95
(End)	2.8	"	

CONSTRUCTION/ABANDONMENT

DATE	ACT	END POINTS	MP	CHANGE	MAIN	SOURCE	NOTE
	??	Line					24

OWNERSHIP

??	Michigan Central
1930/2/1	New York Central, leased Michigan Central
1968/2/1	Penn Central, merger of New York Central (with lease of Michigan Central)

DETROIT, DELRAY & DEARBORN (MC-DD)

	MILEAGE	COUNTY	CROSSINGS, JUNCTIONS, ETC.
Delray	0	Wayne	J/MC-T 5.3
(Crossing)	0.1	"	X/LS-D 10.2
(Oakwood, Fort St.)	1.20	"	J/MC-DZ 0.9
—via MC-DZ			
(Dearborn Rd.)	1.97	"	J/MC-DZ 1.7
Allen Rd.	3.0	"	
(Crossing)	3.2	"	X/DT&I-D 12.4
(End of track)	3.33	"	
Thomas Rd.	4.2	"	
Dearborn Jct.	6.02	"	J/MC-E 9.55

CONSTRUCTION/ABANDONMENT

DATE	ACT	END POINTS	MP	CHANGE	MAIN	SOURCE	NOTE
1895/10/5	B21	Dearborn Jct.–Fort St.	1.2–6.0	+4.8	4.8	7	
		Delray–Fort St.	0–1.2 via Wabash RR				
1912 ca.	X	MP 3.3–Dearborn Jct.	3.3–6.0	–2.7			
1912 ca.	T	Fort St.–Dearborn Rd.	1.2–2.0	–0.8			35
1912 ca.	Y	Dearborn Rd.–MP 3.3 (to Y1DD)	2.0–3.3	(1.3)	0		
1982	X	MP 2.5–MP 3.3	2.5–3.3	(–0.8)	0		

OWNERSHIP

1895	Detroit, Delray & Dearborn (B21), owned by Michigan Central
1916/9/29	Michigan Central, merger of Detroit, Delray & Dearborn

1930/2/1 New York Central, leased Michigan Central
1968/2/1 Penn Central, merger of New York Central (with lease of Michigan Central)
1976/4/1 Conrail, purchase of Penn Central

JUNCTION YARD BRANCH (MC-DZ)

	MILEAGE	COUNTY	CROSSINGS, JUNCTIONS, ETC.
YD	0	Wayne	J/MC-T 6.51
(Crossing)	0.08	"	X/LS-D 11.8
(Crossing)	0.62	"	X/DTSL 46.8 (Victoria St.)
Oakwood	0.74	"	X/WAB 5.6, B/DUR-T 0.82
(Fort St.)	0.93	"	J/MC-DD 1.20
Oakwood Jct.	1.68	"	X/WAB-YD 0.6
(Dearborn Rd)	1.70	"	J/MC-DD 2.0
Schaefer	3.05	"	X/DT&I-D 13.5
(Switch)	3.47	"	J/wye to Jct. Yard
Town Line	4.21	"	J/MC-E 7.37

CONSTRUCTION/ABANDONMENT

DATE	ACT	END POINTS	MP	CHANGE	MAIN	SOURCE	NOTE
1906	B21	YD–Fort St.	0–0.9	+0.9	0.9		
1912 ca.	T	Fort St.–Dearborn Rd.	0.9–1.7	+0.8			35
1912 ca.	B21	Dearborn Rd.–Town Line	1.7–4.2	+2.5	4.2		

OWNERSHIP

1906	Detroit, Delray & Dearborn (B21), owned by Michigan Central
1916/9/29	Michigan Central, merger of Detroit, Delray & Dearborn
1930/2/1	New York Central, leased Michigan Central
1968/2/1	Penn Central, merger of New York Central (with lease of Michigan Central)
1976/4/1	Conrail, purchase of Penn Central

TOLEDO BRANCH (MC-T)

	MILEAGE [Third St.]	COUNTY	CROSSINGS, JUNCTIONS, ETC.
(Jct.)	2.72	Wayne	J/MC-E 2.7
W. Detroit	2.89	"	
CP Waterman	3.7	"	
S. Yards	3.78	"	
(Vernor Highway)	4.0	"	X/DSR-A 12.69
(Fort St.)	4.9	"	B/DSR-F 0.63
Woodmere	4.95	"	
Delray	5.28	"	X/PM-D 4.5, X/WAB-A 4.4, J/MC-DD 0
(Dearborn Rd.)	5.3	"	X/DSR-DR 0.62
Exposition Spur	5.58	"	J/MC-YDE 0
Delta Switch	5.84	"	J/MC-YDD 0
(River Rouge Drawbridge)	6.10	"	
Double Track Switch	6.12	"	
(Jct.)	6.39	"	J/MC-DZ 0.1
YD	6.51	"	J/MC-DD 0, J/MC-YDR 0, f. Pleasant St.
River Rouge	6.75	"	
Visger	7.8	"	
Ecorse	9.01	"	
CP Mill	9.3	"	f. Mill St.?
Fords	10.70	"	
Wyandotte	11.68	"	
Sibley	14.60	"	

(Crossing)	15.45	"	X/DT&I-M 11.0
FN	15.48	"	
(Crossing)	15.50	"	X/DTSL 37.3
Trenton	16.05	"	
Seymours Track	16.45	"	
(Switch to MC-TG)	16.95	"	
Slocum Jct.	17.00	"	J/CCS 17.1, J/MC-TG 0, f. Trenton Crossing
Gibraltar	19.81	"	
Rockwood	22.2	"	
S. Rockwood	22.84	Monroe	
Newport	27.69	"	
Stony Creek	30.77	"	
Sandy	32.72	"	f. Fix Brothers Siding
Frenchtown	33.50	"	
Warner	34.02	"	
(Elm St.)	35.04	"	X/MOCL-1 0.90
(Bridge River Raisin)	35.07	"	
(Crossing)	35.33	"	X/LS-YM 0.1
Monroe	35.40	"	
Greening Bros.Sdg.	36.51	"	
CP Dunbar	36.6	"	
LaSalle	40.12	"	
CP LaSalle	40.2	"	
Vienna	45.02	"	
Vienna Jct.	47.91	"	J/MC-TV 0
(N end New yard)	47.9	"	
(S end New yard)	48.36	"	
(MI/OH state line)	49.52		
N	50.35	Lucas OH	X/AA-A 4.9
Alexis	50.35	"	
K	51.45	"	X/TT
Alexis(frt. hse.)	51.47	"	
Toledo Belt	52.17	"	J/MC-YTB 0
W. Toledo	52.85	"	
(Central Ave.)	53.84	"	
(Connection)	54.08	"	
J/conn. to L(Nebraska Ave.)	56.16	"	
(Bridge)	56.60	"	B/NYC
(Colburn St.)	57.17	"	
C. S. Jct. Ofc	57.33	"	
(Jct.)	57.33	"	J/MC-YTW 57.33
(Crossing)	57.49	"	X/NKP
C. S. Jct.	57.52	"	
(Jct.)	57.54	"	J/NKP
(Jct.)	57.79	"	J/WAB

CONSTRUCTION/ABANDONMENT

DATE	ACT	END POINTS	MP	CHANGE	MI MAIN	SOURCE	NOTE
1873/9/1	B11	MP 2.72–C. S. Jct.	2.7–57.8	+55.1	46.8	7	
1945 ca.	X	Nebraska Ave–Colburn St.	56.2–57.2	−1.0			
1945 ca.	Y	Alexis–Nebraska Ave.(to MC-Y1T)	50.4–56.2	(5.8)			
1945 ca.	Y	Colburn St.–End (to MC-Y2T)	57.2–57.8	(0.6)	46.8		
1961	X	Alexis OH–Toledo Belt	50.4–52.2	−1.8	46.8		

OWNERSHIP

1873	Toledo, Canada Southern & Detroit (B11), owned by Canada Southern
1882/12/12	Michigan Central, operating agreement of Canada Southern
1906/1/2	Michigan Central, leased Toledo, Canada Southern & Detroit
1916/9/27	Michigan Central, merger of Toledo, Canada Southern & Detroit
1930/2/1	New York Central, leased Michigan Central
1968/2/1	Penn Central, merger of New York Central (with lease of Michigan Central)
1976/4/1	Conrail, purchase of Penn Central
1999/6/1	Norfolk Southern, purchase of part of Conrail line

C. S. JCT. SPUR TRACK (MC-YTW)

	MILEAGE [Third St.]	COUNTY	CROSSINGS, JUNCTIONS, ETC.
(Jct.)	57.33	Lucas OH	J/MC-T 57.33
MC/Wabash ownership	58.40	"	
(Jct.)	58.42	"	J/WAB

CONSTRUCTION/ABANDONMENT

DATE	ACT	END POINTS	MP	CHANGE	MI MAIN	SOURCE	NOTE
1873/9/1	B11	Line	57.3–58.4	(+1.1)	0		

OWNERSHIP

1873	Toledo, Canada Southern & Detroit (B11), owned by Canada Southern
1882/12/12	Michigan Central, operating agreement of Canada Southern
1906/1/2	Michigan Central, leased Toledo, Canada Southern & Detroit
1916/9/27	Michigan Central, merger of Toledo, Canada Southern & Detroit
1930/2/1	New York Central, leased Michigan Central
1968/2/1	Penn Central, merger of New York Central (with lease of Michigan Central)

TOLEDO BELT (MC-YTB)

	MILEAGE	COUNTY	CROSSINGS, JUNCTIONS, ETC.
Toledo Belt OH	0.0	Lucas, OH	J/MC-T 52.17
(S wye switch)	0.44	"	
W. Toledo Stock Yds	0.74	"	
(Crossing)	1.49	"	X/interurban
North Toledo yard office	1.70	"	
(Crossing)	2.55	"	X/AA
(Crossing)	2.65	"	X/TT
(Jct.)	2.67	"	J/AA
(Jct.)	3.17	"	J/PRR
(Jct.)	3.48	"	J/W&LE

CONSTRUCTION/ABANDONMENT

DATE	ACT	END POINTS	MP	CHANGE	MI MAIN	SOURCE	NOTE
1891	P2	Line	0–3.5	(+3.5)	0		30

OWNERSHIP

1891	Toledo, Canada Southern & Detroit, owned by Canada Southern
1906/1/2	Michigan Central, leased Toledo, Canada Southern & Detroit
1916/9/27	Michigan Central, merger of Toledo, Canada Southern & Detroit
1930/2/1	New York Central, leased Michigan Central
1968/2/1	Penn Central, merger of New York Central (with lease of Michigan Central)

GROSSE ILE BRANCH (MC-TG)

	MILEAGE	COUNTY	CROSSINGS, JUNCTIONS, ETC.
Slocum Jct.	0	Wayne	J/MC-T 17.1, J/CCS 17.1
(Crossing)	0.1	"	X/DTSL 35.8
Sunnyside	0.9	"	
Stock Yards	1.4	"	
Grosse Ile Shops	1.8	"	
Grosse Ile	2.4	"	
Stony Island	3.1	"	

CONSTRUCTION/ABANDONMENT

DATE	ACT	END POINTS	MP	CHANGE	MAIN	SOURCE	NOTE
1873/9	B12	Line	0–3.1	+3.1	3.1	7	
1929	X	Line	0–3.1	–3.1	0	4	43

OWNERSHIP

1873	Canada Southern Bridge Co.(B12), controlled by Canada Southern Railway
1882/12/12	Michigan Central, operating agreement of CSB

VIENNA JCT.–HALLETT LINE (MC-TV)

	MILEAGE	COUNTY	CROSSINGS, JUNCTIONS, ETC.
Vienna Jct.	0	Monroe	J/MC-T 47.91
(MI/OH state line)	1.43		
Hallett OH	3.22	Lucas OH	J/TT

CONSTRUCTION/ABANDONMENT

DATE	ACT	END POINTS	MP	CHANGE	MI MAIN	SOURCE	NOTE
1925 ca.	B2	Line	0–3.2	+3.2	1.4		
1958	X	Line	0–3.2	–3.2	0		

OWNERSHIP

1925	Michigan Central (B2), of segment
1930/2/1	New York Central, leased Michigan Central

BAY CTY. BRANCH (MC-B)

	MILEAGE [Third St.]	COUNTY	CROSSINGS, JUNCTIONS, ETC.
Bay Cty. Jct.	2.23	Wayne	J/MC-E 2.23
CP Spring Words	2.4	"	
Michigan Ave.	2.63	"	B/DSR-M 3.02
Vinewood Ave.	3.07	"	J/LS-D 7.2
26th St. team track	3.11	"	
Buchanan St.	3.36	"	B/DSR-C 9.06
(Warren Ave.)	3.75	"	B/DSR-X 6.82
Grand Riv. Ave.	4.00	"	B/DSR-R 2.48
(14th St.)	4.25	"	B/DSR-Q 3.17
12th St. Stock Yard	4.41	"	
12th St.	4.49	"	
(Trumbull Ave.)	4.85	"	B/DSR-T 2.16
(Hamilton Ave.)	5.15	"	B/DSR-H 2.51
Woodward Ave.	5.65	"	B/DSR-W 3.25
(Crossing)	5.86	"	X/LS-D 4.4
Beaubien St.	5.92	"	X/GTW-H 3.8, B/DSR-OK 3.28
(Milw. St.)	6.3	"	B/DSR-GB 5.14

Milw. Jct.	6.72	"	X/GTW-D 4.1
Russell St.	6.82	"	B/DSR-CM 6.50
Belt Line Jct.	7.24	"	J/MC-YDB 0
N. Yard	8.63	"	J/MC-YDC 1.91
(Crossing)	9.57	"	X/DT 12.2
N. Detroit (new)	9.58	"	
CP N. Yard	9.6	"	
(Nevada Ave.)	10.2	"	X/DSR-A 0.62
N. Detroit (old)	10.28	"	
Norris	10.5	"	
Mound Rd. Yard	12.5	Macomb	
Centre Line (old)	13.77	"	
TM	13.8	"	
Center Line (new)	15.77	"	
Warren (old)	17.04	"	f. Glenwood
Hoffs Siding	17.68	"	
Spinning(s)	18.0	"	
Sterling Yard	20.10	"	
Warren (new)	20.70	"	
Utica	23.81	"	
Utica Bend Switch	26.1	"	
Packard Switch	26.23	"	
Depews Siding	27.38	"	
Rays Pit	28.49	"	
Yates	28.64	Oakland	
Rochester Jct.	29.97	"	
(Crossing)	30.00	"	X/GTW-A 25.2
Rochester	30.89	"	
(Crossing)	30.91	"	X/DUR-F 14.79
Goodisons	34.89	"	
Rudds Mill	38.67	"	
(Bridge)	39.6	"	B/DUR-F 23.85
Lk. Orion	40.27	"	f. Orion
Baileys Wye	41.80	"	f. Baileys Pit
Oxford Freight House	43.22	"	(1st Oxford sta.)
Oxford	43.56	"	
(Crossing)	43.58	"	X/GTW-P 13.9
Thomas	47.54	"	
Metamora	52.04	Lapeer	
Hunters Creek	55.27	"	
Lapeer Jct.	59.81	"	X/GTW-C 290.0
Lapeer	60.34	"	(old 59.99)
Carpenter	65.50	"	
Columbiaville	69.01	"	
Otter Lk.	73.59	"	
(Crossing)	73.68	"	
Millington	79.52	Tuscola	
Gooden Creek	83.93	"	
V	85.95	"	X/PM-Q 19.4
Vassar	86.18	"	
Caro Jct.	86.54	"	J/MC-BC 0.36
Sneels Siding	90.31	"	
(Jct.)	91.01	"	J/MC-BS 4.83
Denmark Jct.	91.15	"	

Berlin	91.82	"	
Reese	94.44	"	
(Crossing)	94.45	"	X/PM-S 12.5
Arn	98.23	Bay	
Munger	100.91	"	
Byer Siding	102.75	"	
Water St. Jct.	106.06	"	X/MC-YBL 2.8
Centre Ave.	107.07	"	X/PM-B 13.2
(Sherman St.)	108.7	"	X/BYCL-7 0.86
Bay Cty. E. S.	108.94	"	J/MC-M 0

CONSTRUCTION/ABANDONMENT

DATE	ACT	END POINTS	MP	CHANGE	MAIN	SOURCE	NOTE
1872/10/31	B13	Bay Cty. Jct.–Oxford	2.2–43.2	+41.0		7	
1872/11/30	B13	Oxford–Lapeer	43.2–60.4	+17.2		7	
1872/12/31	B13	Lapeer–Otter Lk.	60.4–73.6	+13.2	71.4	7	
1873/3/31	B13	Otter Lk.–Vassar	73.6–86.2	+12.6		7	
1873/7/31	B13	Vassar–Bay Cty. E. S.	86.2–108.9	+22.7	106.7	7	
1962	X	Munger–Water St. Jct.	101.1–106.1	–5.0	101.7	6	
1962	Y	In Bay Cty. (as MC-Y1B)	106.1–108.9	(2.8)	98.9		
1976/4/1	S2	In Bay Cty. (MC-Y1B)	106.1–108.9	[(–2.8)]			
1976/4/1	S2	In Lapeer	58.4–60.3	[1.9]			
1976/4/1	S2	In Oxford	42.2–45.0	[2.8]			
1976	X	Rays Pit-Oxford	28.2–42.2	–14.0			
1976	X	Oxford–Lapeer	45.0–58.4	–13.4			
1976	X	Lapeer–Millington	60.3–79.3	–19.0	47.8		
1984/2/15	S1	Millington–Munger	79.3–101.1	[21.8]	26.0		46

OWNERSHIP

1872	Detroit & Bay City (B13)
1881/3/10	Michigan Central leased Detroit & Bay City
1916/9/27	Michigan Central, merger of Detroit & Bay City
1930/2/1	Penn Central, merger of New York Central (with lease of Michigan Central)
1976/4/1	Conrail and Grand Trunk Western bought parts of line of Penn Central
1984/2/15	State of Michigan, bought part of line of Penn Central

BAY CITY BELT LINE (MC-YBL)

	MILEAGE	COUNTY	CROSSINGS, JUNCTIONS, ETC.
(End)	0	Bay	
Essexville	0.3	"	X/PM-YBE 0.7
(Crossing)(Main St.)	1.4	"	X/MC-YBN 2.4
(Crossing)	2.2	"	X/DCS 2.5
Water St. Jct.	2.80	"	X/MC-B 106.06
Lincoln Ave.	4.80	"	
(Farragut St.)	5.1	"	X/BYCL-5 1.39
(Crossing)	5.36	"	X/PM-B 10.9
(Broadway St.)	5.8	"	X/BYCL-4 1.71
(27th St.)	5.94	"	J/MC-YBS 2.1

CONSTRUCTION/ABANDONMENT

DATE	ACT	END POINTS	MP	CHANGE	MAIN	SOURCE	NOTE
1889	B15	Water St. Jct.–27th St.	2.8–5.9	(+3.1)	0		
1895 ca.	B15	MP 0–Water St. Jct.	0–2.8	(+2.8)	0		

1930 ca.	X	MP 0–Water St. Jct.	0–2.8	(–2.8)	0		29
1976/4/1	S2	Line	2.8–5.9	[(3.1)]	0		

OWNERSHIP

1889	Bay City Belt Line (B15), of segment
1889 ca.	Detroit & Bay City (B13), purchased from Bay City Belt Line
1916/9/24	Michigan Central, merger of Detroit & Bay City
1930/2/1	New York Central leased Michigan Central
1968/2/1	Penn Central, merger of New York Central (with lease of Michigan Central)
1976/4/1	Grand Trunk Western, bought line
1987/9/4	Central Michigan, bought line

SOUTH WATER STREET SPUR (MC-YBS)

	MILEAGE	COUNTY	CROSSINGS, JUNCTIONS, ETC.
(Jct.)	0	Bay	J/MC-M 0.29
(Enter Water St.)	0.1	"	
(9th St.)	0.8	"	
(Crossing)	1.1	"	X/GTW-SB 52.5
(LaFayette St.)	1.9	"	
(26th St.)	2.0	"	
(27th St.)	2.1	"	J/MC-YBL 5.94
Harrison St. Spur	2.52	"	
(Jct.)(33rd St.)	2.70	"	J/PM-YBS 0.6
(35th St., Cass Ave.)	2.9	"	
(End)	3.52	"	

CONSTRUCTION/ABANDONMENT

DATE	ACT	END POINTS	MP	CHANGE	MAIN	SOURCE	NOTE
1879	L	MP 0–MP 2.9	0–2.9	(+2.9)	0		20
1885 ca.	B15	MP 2.9–MP 3.5	2.9–3.5	(+0.6)	0		29
1900 ca.	X	MP 0–MP 0.8	0–0.8	(–0.8)	0		29
1950 ca.	X	MP 2.9–MP 3.5	2.9–3.5	(–0.6)	0		29
1960 ca.	X	MP 2.4–MP 2.9	2.4–2.9	(–0.5)	0		29
1976/4/1	S2	Line	0.8–2.4	(–1.6)	0		

OWNERSHIP

1879	Bay City Street Railway, leased to Detroit & Bay City
1882/2/212	Michigan Central leased Detroit & Bay City
1886/1/1	Detroit & Bay City (B15), purchased from Bay City Street Railway
1916/9/24	Michigan Central, merger of Detroit & Bay City
1930/2/1	New York Central leased Michigan Central
1968/2/1	Penn Central, merger of New York Central (with lease of Michigan Central)
1976/4/1	Grand Trunk Western, bought line
1987/9/4	Central Michigan, bought line

NORTH WATER STREET SPUR (MC-YBN)

	MILEAGE	COUNTY	CROSSINGS, JUNCTIONS, ETC.
(Crossing)	0	Bay	J/MC-M 0.29
N. Water St. Jct.	0.3	"	X/PM-B 16.5
Foss	1.57	"	J/D&M-S 1.9
(W wye switch)	1.7	"	
(Jct.)	1.9	"	J/PM-B 15.0
(Crossing)(Main St.)	2.1	"	X/MC-YBL 1.4
(End)	2.5	"	

CONSTRUCTION/ABANDONMENT

DATE	ACT	END POINTS	MP	CHANGE	MAIN	SOURCE	NOTE
1879	L	Line	0–2.2	(+2.2)	0		21
1885 ca.	B15	Extend line	2.2–2.5	(+0.3)	0		
1976/4/1	S2	Line	0–2.5	(–2.5)	0		

OWNERSHIP

1879	Bay City Street Railway, leased to Detroit & Bay City
1882/2/212	Michigan Central leased Detroit & Bay City
1886/1/1	Detroit & Bay City (B15), purchased from Bay City Street Railway
1916/9/24	Michigan Central, merger of Detroit & Bay City
1930/2/1	New York Central leased Michigan Central
1968/2/1	Penn Central, merger of New York Central (with lease of Michigan Central)
1976/4/1	Grand Trunk Western, bought line
1987/9/4	Central Michigan, bought line

HECLA BELT (MC-YBH)

	MILEAGE	COUNTY	CROSSINGS, JUNCTIONS, ETC.
(Jct.)	0	Bay	J/MC-M 2.04
(Patterson St.)	1.65	"	X/BYCL-2 2.37
(Crossing)	2.2	"	X/GTW-S 56.2
(Crossing)	2.3	"	X/D&M-S 2.9
(End)	3.5	"	

CONSTRUCTION/ABANDONMENT

DATE	ACT	END POINTS	MP	CHANGE	MAIN	SOURCE	NOTE
1902 ca.	B24	Line	0–3.5	(+3.5)	0	7	
1974 ca.	X	Line	0–3.5	(–3.5)	0		

OWNERSHIP

1902	Hecla Belt Line (B24), of segment
1912/12/30	Michigan Central, bought Hecla Belt Line
1930/2/1	New York Central leased Michigan Central
1968/2/1	Penn Central, merger of New York Central (with lease of Michigan Central)

SAGINAW BRANCH (MC-BS)

	MILEAGE [Vassar]	COUNTY	CROSSINGS, JUNCTIONS, ETC.
(Jct.)	4.83	Tuscola	J/MC-B 91.01
Denmark Jct.	4.97	"	
Richville	6.46	"	
Veenfliets	8.34	Sag.	
Frankentrost	12.04	"	
Buena Vista	14.44	"	
Harger Track	17.25	"	
Hoyt	18.08	"	X/PM-T 2.2
(Genesee Ave.)	18.89	"	X/SACL-1 1.30
(Warren Ave.)	19.3	"	X/SACL-10 1.57
(Jct.)	19.9	"	J/PM-YSV 0
(Jct.)	20.07	"	J/spur to E. Sag. (1st sta), 0.4 mi.
MX	20.16	"	X/GTW-S 39.1
E. Sag.	20.22	"	X/SACL-2 0.53 (Washington Ave.)
(Crossing)	20.3	"	X/PM-YSG 1.2

(Drawbridge)	20.38	"		
W. Shore Interlocking	20.50	"	X/PM-YSW 1.2	
(Switch, S wye)	20.6	"		
S. B. Jct.	20.74	"	J/MC-S 101.0	

CONSTRUCTION/ABANDONMENT

DATE	ACT	END POINTS	MP	CHANGE	MAIN	SOURCE	NOTE
1879/1/25	B13	Denmark Jct.–Sag. E. S.	4.8–20.3	+15.5	15.5	7	
1879 ca.	B13	Sag. E.S.–S. B. Jct.	20.3–20.7	+0.4	15.9		19
1976/4/1	S2	Richville–S. B. Jct.	6.0–20.7	−14.7	1.2		
1984/2/15	S1	Denmark Jct.–Richville	4.8–6.0	−1.2	0		46

OWNERSHIP

1879	Detroit & Bay City (B13)
1881/2/21	Michigan Central leased Detroit & Bay City
1916/9/27	Michigan Central, merger of Detroit & Bay City
1930/2/1	New York Central leased Michigan Central
1968/2/1	Penn Central, merger of New York Central (with lease of Michigan Central)
1976/4/1	Grand Trunk Western, bought part of line
1984/2/15	State of Michigan, bought part of line
1987/9/4	Central Michigan, bought line from Grand Trunk Western

MICHIGAN MIDLAND BRANCH (MC-DM)

	MILEAGE	COUNTY	CROSSINGS, JUNCTIONS, ETC.
St. Clair Springs	0.0	St. Clair	
(Riverside Ave.)	0.2	"	X/DUR-R 55.27
Carltons Crossing	2.32	"	
Butlins	4.72	"	
Adair	8.00	"	
Gravel Pit	13.77	"	
(Jct.)	14.03	Macomb	J/GTW-H 38.6
(Lenox, via GTW-H)	14.72	"	

CONSTRUCTION/ABANDONMENT

DATE	ACT	END POINTS	MP	CHANGE	MAIN	SOURCE	NOTE
1873/12/7	B10	St. Clair Springs–Lenox	0–14.0	+14.0	14.0	7	
1932/9/23	X	Entire line	0–14.0	−14.0	0	4	37

OWNERSHIP

1873	Michigan Midland & Canada (B10)
1882	Canada Southern, control of Michigan Midland & Canada
1882/12/12	Michigan Central, operating agreement of Canada Southern
1906/9/24	St. Clair & Western, reorganize Michigan Midland & Canada, owned by CS

CARO BRANCH (MC-BC)

	MILEAGE	COUNTY	CROSSINGS, JUNCTIONS, ETC.
	[Vassar]		
Caro Jct.	0.36	Tuscola	J/MC-B 86.54
Bank Sand	2.61	"	
Perkins	3.11	"	
Watrousville	5.44	"	
Ross Crossing	7.15	"	
Wahjamega	9.37	"	
Peninsular St.	12.71	"	

Caro (1st sta.)	13.03	"	
(Crossing)	13.24	"	X/DCS 28.8
Caro (2nd sta.)	13.67	"	
Atwood	16.07	"	
Gravel Pit	17.11	"	
Purdy	19.04	"	
Patterson	19.90	"	
Hutchinson	20.96	"	
Colling	22.07	"	
Duro	24.10	"	
Ashmore	25.30	"	
Karr	25.36	"	f. State Rd.
Robinson	26.61	"	f. County Line
Bach (2nd sta.)	28.06	Huron	
Bach (1st sta.)	29.09	"	
Patton	31.56	"	
Owendale	33.85	"	J/GTW-P 84.8

CONSTRUCTION/ABANDONMENT

DATE	ACT	END POINTS	MP	CHANGE	MAIN	SOURCE	NOTE
1878/7/22	B13	Caro Jct.–Caro	0.4–13.0	+12.6	12.6	7	
1901	B22	Caro–Owendale	13.0–33.9	+20.9	33.5	7	
1942	X	Owendale–Bach	33.9–28.3	−5.6	27.9	8	
1973/7/1	X	Bach–Colling	28.3–22.4	−5.9	22.0	6	
1984/2/15	S1	Caro Jct.–Colling	0.4–22.4	−22.0	0		46

OWNERSHIP

1878	Detroit & Bay City (B13)
1881/3/10	Detroit & Bay City leased to Michigan Central
1901	Caro & Lake Huron (B22)
1908/5/8	Caro & Lake Huron sold to Detroit & Bay City
1916/9/24	Michigan Central, merger of Detroit & Bay City
1930/2/1	New York Central leased Michigan Central
1968/2/1	Penn Central, merger of New York Central (with lease of Michigan Central)
1984/2/15	State of Michigan, bought line

LAPEER & NORTHERN BRANCH (MC-BL)

	MILEAGE	COUNTY	CROSSINGS, JUNCTIONS, ETC.
	[Lapeer]		
(Jct.)	0.3	Lapeer	J/MC-B 60.7
Fish Lk.		"	
Stephens	6.0	"	
Five Lakes	8.0	"	

CONSTRUCTION/ABANDONMENT

DATE	ACT	END POINTS	MP	CHANGE	MAIN	SOURCE	NOTE
1872	B14	Lapeer–north	0.3–4.0	+3.7	3.7	7	
1873	B14	Extend line	4.0–4.5	+0.5	4.2	7	
1874	B14	Extend line	4.5–5.0	+0.5	4.7	7	
1876	B14	Extend to Five Lakes	5.0–8.0	+3.0	7.7	7	
1888	X	Line	0.3–8.0	−7.7	0	7	

OWNERSHIP

1872	Lapeer & Northern (B14), owned by Detroit & Bay City

AIR LINE (MC-A)

	MILEAGE	COUNTY	CROSSINGS, JUNCTIONS, ETC.
Jackson Jct.	0.0	Jackson	J/MC-E 74.38
Ft. Wyn. Switch	0.54	"	J/LS-W 1.0
OD	0.83	"	X/LS-J 41.3
(Francis St.)	1.45	"	X/JACL-3 1.06
Aspinwall Mfg.	1.75	"	
Haires	4.80	"	J/LS-W 5.1
Snyders	8.21	"	
Spring Arbor	10.27	"	
CP2	11.00	"	
Reynolds	12.73	"	
CP3	13.00	"	
Concord	14.54	"	
(Jct.)	17.0	"	J/MC-AO 17.0
(Jct.)	21.3	Calhoun	J/MC-AO 20.8
Homer (2nd station)	24.08	"	X/DTM 65.1
(Crossing)	24.10	"	X/LS-L 13.4
Homer (1st station)	24.28	"	
Clarendon Coal Station	26.34	"	
Clarendon	27.38	"	
CP4	27.5	"	
Track Tank Siding	29.15	"	
CP5	29.5	"	
Tekonsha	33.98	"	
Osborns	35.90	"	
Burlington	37.96	"	
Union Cty.	42.15	Branch	
CP6	45.20	"	
CP7	47.20	"	
Sherwood	49.00	"	
Colon Gravel Pit Siding	53.47	St.Joseph	
Colon	54.28	"	
Fairfax	56.23	"	X/MC-K 30.8, f. Colon Jct.
Wasepi Track Pan	57.72	"	
Wasepi	61.20	"	X/GR&I-S 159.5, f. Nottawa
CP8	61.21	"	
CP9	63.30	"	
Centerville	64.88	"	P. O. Centreville
(Jct.)	68.8	"	J/LS-GA 68.2
Three Rivers	70.07	"	
VE	70.14	"	X/LS-G 10.8
(End of track)	70.90	"	
Fabius	74.83	"	
Corey	77.37	Cass	
Jones	79.41	"	
Newburg	80.85	"	
Vandalia	85.34	"	
Sandy Beach	87.91	"	
Shore Acres	88.7	"	
Forest Hall	89.45	"	f. Diamond Lk.
AP	90.34	"	X/GTW-C 122.6
Cassopolis	90.51	"	
Dailey	94.73	"	
Air Line Jct.	97.58	"	J/MC-A2 97.58

Barron Lk.	99.87	"	
Kennedy	100.70	"	
Hill	103.57	Berrien	
(Jct.)	103.70	"	J/MC-N 0.3
Niles	104.01	"	J/MC-C 191.90, J/MC-W 191.90

CONSTRUCTION/ABANDONMENT

DATE	ACT	END POINTS	MP	CHANGE	MAIN	SOURCE	NOTE
1870/Sum.	B8	Jackson Jct.–MP 17.0	0–17.0	+17.0		7	
1870/Sum.	B8	MP 21.3–Homer	21.3–24.3	+3.0		7	
1870/Fall	B8	Homer–Three Rivers	24.3–70.1	+45.8	65.8	7	
1871/2	B8	Three Rivers–Niles	70.1–104.0	+33.9	99.7	7	
1901 ca.	B2	MP 17.0–MP 21.3	17.0–21.3	+4.3	104.0		32
1933	X	Air Line Jct.–E of Niles	97.6–102.8	−5.2		4	45
1933	Y	In Niles (to MC-Y1A)	102.8–104.0	(1.2	97.6		
1940	X	OD–Haires	0.8–4.8	−4.0	93.6		39
1943	X	In Three Rivers–A. L. Jct.	70.9–97.6	−26.7		8	
1943	Y	In Three Rivers (to MC-Y2A)	70.1–70.9	(0.8)	66.1		
1958	Y	In Three Rivers (to MC-Y2A)	68.8–70.1	(1.3)	64.8		41
1968 ca.	X	In Three Rivers (MC-Y2A)	68.8–69.5	(−0.7)	64.8		
1982	X	Haires–Three Rivers	4.8–68.8	−64.0		6	
1982	Y	Jackson Jct.–OD	0–0.8	(0.8)	0		

OWNERSHIP

1870	Michigan Air Line Railroad (B8)
1871/2	Michigan Central (B2), leased Michigan Air Line Railroad
1916/9/27	Michigan Central, merged Michigan Air Line Railroad
1930/2/1	New York Central, leased Michigan Central
1968/2/1	Penn Central, merged New York Central (with lease of Michigan Central)
1976/4/1	Conrail, purchase of Penn Central
1999/6/1	Norfolk Southern, purchase of Conrail

OLD MAIN LINE, VIA PULASKI (MC-AO)

	MILEAGE [Jackson Jct.]	COUNTY	CROSSINGS, JUNCTIONS, ETC.
(Jct.)	17.0	Jackson	J/MC-A 17.0
Pulaski	18.73	"	
(Jct.)	20.8	Calhoun	J/MC-A 21.3

CONSTRUCTION/ABANDONMENT

DATE	ACT	END POINTS	MP	CHANGE	MAIN	SOURCE	NOTE
1870/Sum.	B8	Line	17.0–20.8	+3.8	3.8	7	
1901 ca.	X	Line	17.0–20.8	−3.8	0		33

OWNERSHIP

1870	Michigan Air Line Railroad (B8)
1871/2	Michigan Central, leased Michigan Air Line Railroad

AIR LINE JUNCTION BRANCH (MC-A2)

	MILEAGE [Jackson Jct.]	COUNTY	CROSSINGS, JUNCTIONS, ETC.
Air Line Jct.	97.58	Cass	J/MC-A 97.58
East End	101.22	"	J/MC-C 107.92

CONSTRUCTION/ABANDONMENT

DATE	ACT	END POINTS	MP	CHANGE	MAIN	SOURCE	NOTE
1920 ca.	B2	Line	97.6–101.2	+4.6	4.6		36
1943	X	Line	97.6–101.2	–4.6	0		

OWNERSHIP

1920	Michigan Central (B2)
1930/2/1	New York Central, leased Michigan Central

SOUTH BEND BRANCH (MC-N)

	MILEAGE	COUNTY	CROSSINGS, JUNCTIONS, ETC.
Lake St.	0.0	Berrien	J/MC-C 191.78
(Jct.)	0.30	"	J/MC-A 103.70
Main St.	1.05	"	
Niles Jct.	2.17	"	B/CC-M 26.1, B/SOM 9.2, f. M.C.Jct.
Bertrand	4.80	"	
(MI/IN state line)	5.75		
Websters IN	6.86	St.Joseph IN	
St. Marys Sdg.	9.40	"	
Notre Dame	9.56	"	
(Jct.)	9.61	"	J/MC-N2 0
S. Bend IN	11.66	"	
(End of track)	11.72	"	

CONSTRUCTION/ABANDONMENT

DATE	ACT	END POINTS	MP	CHANGE	MI MAIN	SOURCE	NOTE
1872	B8	MP 0.3–S. Bend	0.3–11.7	+11.4	5.5	7	17
1920	B2	Lake St.–MP 0.3	0–0.3	+0.3	5.8		36
1975 ca.	X	In S. Bend (MI=0)	9.6–11.7	–2.1	5.8		
1993 ca.	X	Niles–St Marys IN(MI=5.5)	0.3–9.4	–9.1			
1993 ca.	Y	In Niles (to MC–Y1N)	0–0.3	(0.3)	0		

OWNERSHIP

1872	Michigan Air Line Railroad (B8), leased by Michigan Central
1916/9/27	Michigan Central (B2), merger of Michigan Air Line Railroad
1930/2/1	New York Central, lease of Michigan Central
1968/2/1	Penn Central, merger of New York Central (with lease of Michigan Central)
1976/4/1	Conrail, purchase of Penn Central
1999/6/1	Norfolk Southern, purchase of Conrail

M. C. CONNECTING BRANCH (MC-N2)

	MILEAGE	COUNTY	CROSSINGS, JUNCTIONS, ETC.
(Jct.) IN	0.0	St.Joseph IN	J/MC-N 9.61
(Bridge, St.Joseph River)	1.03	"	
(Prop line MC/II&I)	1.31	"	
(Bridge, Portage Ave.)	1.32	"	
(Switch, NYC wye)	2.66	"	
NX	2.84	"	X/NYC
Olivers IN	3.23	"	
(S. Bend via NYC)	(4.31)	"	

CONSTRUCTION/ABANDONMENT

DATE	ACT	END POINTS	MP	CHANGE	MI MAIN	SOURCE	NOTE
1905 ca.	B8	MP 0–MP 1.3	0–1.3	+1.3	0		
1905 ca.	B27	MP 1.3–MP 3.2	1.3–3.2	+1.9	0		

OWNERSHIP

1905	Michigan Air Line Railroad (B8), leased to Michigan Central
1905	Indiana, Illinois & Iowa (B27)
1906/4/6	Chicago, Indiana & Southern (controlled by Lake Shore & Michigan Southern), merged Indiana, Illinois & Iowa
1915/1/1	New York Central, merger of Chicago, Indiana & Southern
1916/9/27	Michigan Central, merger of Michigan Air Line Railroad
1930/2/1	New York Central leased Michigan Central
1968/2/1	Penn Central, merger of New York Central (with lease of Michigan Central)
1976/4/1	Conrail, purchase of Penn Central
1999/6/1	Norfolk Southern, purchase of Conrail

MIDDLE DIV. (MC-C)

	MILEAGE [Third St.]	COUNTY	CROSSINGS, JUNCTIONS, ETC.
Jackson	75.43	Jackson	J/MC-E 75.43
(Main St.)	75.53	"	(now CP Jackson) X/JACL-2 0.20
Pearl St.	75.64	"	J/MC-G 0.21
(Jackson St.)	76.1	"	B/JACL-5 0.19
Wildwood Ave.	77.7	"	
West Hill	78.39	"	(now CP Hill)
Trumbulls	80.77	"	
Sandstone	81.62	"	f. Barry
Parma	86.23	"	f. Gidleys
N. Concord	89.05	"	f. Concord
Bloomerville Pit	90.71	"	
Bath Mills	92.19	"	
Newburg Mills	94.03	Calhoun	
Albion (freight house)	95.70	"	
Albion	95.74	"	
A	95.95	"	X/LS-L 21.9, B/MUR-S 19.95
CP Albion	96.2	"	
Hartung	97.6	"	
CP 99	98.8	"	
Marengo	101.04	"	
Marshall Track Pan	106.44	"	
(Jct.)	106.9	"	J/MC-CO1 106.9
Marshall	107.47	"	C/DTM 77.1
(Jct.)	107.9	"	J/MC-CO1 108.0
Ceresco	112.73	"	
Wheatfield	114.38	"	f. Whites Crossing
Levittown	115.2	"	
CP Levitt	116.3	"	
Ray	117.8	"	
Hinman Yard	118.9	"	
Post	119.3	"	
Nichols	119.66	"	X/GTW-C 176.9
(Baron)	119.8	"	J/GTW-C 176.7
(Jct.)	119.85	"	J/MC-K 0.6

(Michigan Ave.)	119.93	"	X/BCCL-1 0.61
Main Yard	120.3	"	
(Battle Creek, 1st station)	120.4	"	
(Capital Ave.)	120.48	"	X/BCCL-6 0.11
Battle Creek	120.56	"	
(Main St.)	120.89	"	X/BCCL-2 0.34
(Gord)	121.4	"	J/GTW-C 175.5
Rumley Yard	121.7	"	
Rumley	122.0	"	
Clark	122.7	"	
CP Custer	124.4	"	
Ft. Custer Crossover	124.9	"	J/MC-YF 0
Bedford	126.2	"	
(Bridge)	128.00	Kal.	B/DTM 97.8
Augusta	130.17	"	
Augusta Coal Chutes	131.41	"	
(Bridge)	134.16	"	B/MUR-S 58.2
Galesburg	134.58	"	
Consumers Power	138.5	"	
Comstock	139.49	"	
CP Comstock	139.9	"	
(Rex Paper Co.)	140.2	"	
Thorn	141.2	"	
Botsford	141.97	"	
East Ave.	142.50	"	(now W. Botsford) B/KACL-1 0.75
View	142.6	"	
Harris	142.9	"	
(Crossing)	142.95	"	X/MUR-W 0.70
(Crossing)	142.99	"	X/CK&S-A 0.2
BO	143.09	"	
(Crossing)	143.10	"	X/LS-K 36.8
(Crossing)	143.11	"	X/GTW-YK 3.3
Tower 1	143.16	"	X/GR&I-S 185.7, f.-Kal. Jct.
(Burdick St.)	143.36	"	X/KACL-7 0.28
Kal.	143.37	"	
(Jct.)	143.58	"	J/MC-H 0.21
(W. Main St.)	144.04	"	Adjoins KLSC 0, X/KACL-2 0.61
Asylum	144.9	"	
Asylum Switch	145.5	"	J/MC-CO2 145.5
CP Oshtemo	147.1	"	(now CP 147)
CP 150	150.5	"	
Miller	150.45	"	
Mattawan	156.41	Van Buren	J/MC-CO2 155.63
CP 160	160.2	"	
Lawton	160.60	"	
CP 161 (first)	161.0	"	
CP 161 (second)	161.5	"	
CP 162	162.7	"	
White Oak	163.0	"	
Lawton Track Pan	163.3	"	
Decatur	168.30	"	
Glenwood	173.22	Cass	
CP 176	176.4	"	
CP 178	178.1	"	
Dowagiac	179.51	"	

CP W. Dowagiac	180.1	"	(now CP 180)
Pokagon	185.36	"	
E. End	187.92	"	J/MC-A2 101.2
Hump Office	189.10	"	
CP Hump	189.3	"	
CP 190	190.5	"	
(Jct.)	191.78	Berrien	J/MC-N 0
Lake St.	191.81	"	
Niles	191.90	"	J/MC-W 191.90

CONSTRUCTION/ABANDONMENT

DATE	ACT	END POINTS	MP	CHANGE	MAIN	SOURCE	NOTE
1844/6/25	B1	Jackson–Albion	75.4–95.8	+20.4		7	
1844/8/12	B1	Albion–MP 106.9	95.8–106.9	+11.1	31.5	7	
1845/11/25	B1	MP 107.9–Battle Creek	107.9–120.4	+12.5	44.0	7	4
1846/2/2	B1	Battle Creek–Kal.	120.4–143.4	+23.0	67.0	7	
1848/6/28	B2	Kal.–MP 145.5	143.4–145.5	+2.1		3	
1848/6/28	B2	Mattawan–Lawton	156.4–160.6	+4.2		3	
1848/10/1	B2	Lawton–Niles	160.6–191.9	+31.3	104.6	3	
1865 ca.	B2	In Marshall	106.9–107.9	+1.0	105.6		
1901 ca.	B2	MP 145.5–Mattawan	145.5–156.4	+10.9	116.5		
1976/4/1	S3	Kal.–Niles	145.0–191.9	−46.9	69.6		
1981/11/18	X	In Battle Creek	119.8–121.4	−1.6	68.0		
1995/7	S3	At Kal.	143.2–145.0	−1.8	66.2		

OWNERSHIP

1844	State of Michigan (B1)
1846/9/24	Michigan Central (B2), bought State of Michigan "Central" line
1930/2/1	Michigan Central, leased to New York Central
1968/2/1	Penn Central, merger of New York Central (with lease of Michigan Central)
1976/4/1	Amtrak, purchase of Penn Central line, Kalamazoo–west
1976/4/1	Conrail, purchase of Penn Central line, Kalamazoo–east
1999/6/1	Norfolk Southern, purchase of Conrail

OLD MAIN LINE, MARSHALL (MC-CO1)

	MILEAGE	COUNTY	CROSSINGS, JUNCTIONS, ETC.
	[Third St.]		
(Jct.)	106.9	Calhoun	J/MC-C 106.9
Marshall (1st station)	107.45	"	
(Jct.)	108.0	"	J/MC-C 107.9

CONSTRUCTION/ABANDONMENT

DATE	ACT	END POINTS	MP	CHANGE	MAIN	SOURCE	NOTE
1844/8/12	B1	MP 106.9–Marshall	106.9–107.5	+0.6	0.6	7	
1845/11/25	B1	Marshall–MP 108	107.5–108.0	+0.5	1.1	7	
1865 ca.	X	Line	106.9–108.0	−1.1	0		13

OWNERSHIP

1844	State of Michigan (B1)
1846/9/24	Michigan Central, bought State of Michigan "Central" line

OLD MAIN LINE, KALAMAZOO–MATTAWAN (MC-CO2)

	MILEAGE	COUNTY	CROSSINGS, JUNCTIONS, ETC.
	[Third St.]		
Asylum Switch	145.5	Kal.	J/MC-C 145.5
Oshtemo	149.14	"	f. Ostemo
Mattawan	155.63	Van Buren	J/MC-C 156.41

CONSTRUCTION/ABANDONMENT

DATE	ACT	END POINTS	MP	CHANGE	MAIN	SOURCE	NOTE
1848/6/28	B2	Asylum Switch–Mattawan	145.5–155.6	+10.1	10.1	3	
1901 ca.	X	Line	145.5–155.6	−10.1	0		31

OWNERSHIP

1848	Michigan Central (B2)	

FORT CUSTER SPUR (MC-YF)

	MILEAGE	COUNTY	CROSSINGS, JUNCTIONS, ETC.
Fort Custer Crossover	0	Calhoun	J/MC-C 124.9
Fort Custer	1.7	"	

CONSTRUCTION/ABANDONMENT

DATE	ACT	END POINTS	MP	CHANGE	MAIN	SOURCE	NOTE
1916 ca.	B2	Line	0–1.7	(+1.7)	0		

OWNERSHIP

1916	Michigan Central (B2)
1930/2/1	New York Central, leased Michigan Central
1968/2/1	Penn Central, merger of New York Central (with lease of Michigan Central)
1976/4/1	Conrail, purchase of Penn Central
1999/6/1	Norfolk Southern, purchase of Conrail

SOUTH HAVEN BRANCH (MC-H)

	MILEAGE	COUNTY	CROSSINGS, JUNCTIONS, ETC.
	[Kal.]		
(Jct.)	0.21	Kal.	J/MC-C 143.58
(N. St.)	0.58	"	X/KACL-8 0.56
Brownells	4.01	"	
Doubling Track	5.52	"	f. Brickyard Siding
Balch	5.93	"	f. Hopkins
Alamo	9.09	"	
Williams	11.28	"	
Harrison	12.33	VanBuren	
Mentha	12.76	"	
Severns	13.39	"	
Kendall	14.84	"	
Pine Grove	17.53	"	f. Pine Grove Mills
Gobles	18.50	"	f. Gobleville
Bloomingdale	22.99	"	
Berlamont	24.97	"	f. Bear Lk. Mills
Columbia	27.72	"	
Grand Jct.	29.20	"	X/PM-C 53.8
Maple Forest	30.27	"	f. Browns Mills
Lacota	31.97	"	
Kibbie	35.05	"	
S. Haven	39.59	"	

(Jct.)	39.7	"	J/PM-H 0
(Crossing)	39.8	"	X/PM-H 0.1
(End of yard track)	40.2	"	

CONSTRUCTION/ABANDONMENT

DATE	ACT	END POINTS	MP	CHANGE	MAIN	SOURCE	NOTE
1870/3/1	B7	Kal.–Kendall	0.2–14.8	+14.6		1	
1870/7/4	B7	Kendall–Bloomingdale	14.8–23.0	+8.2	22.8	1	
1871/1/2	B7	Bloomingdale–S. Haven	23.0–39.6	+16.6	39.4	7	
1973/9/1	X	MP 1.9–S. Haven	1.9–39.6	–37.7		8	
1973/9/1	Y	MP 0.2–MP 1.9 (to MC-Y1H)	0.2–1.9	(1.7)	0		
1984	X	MP 0.2–MP 1.9 (MC-Y1H)	0.2–1.9	(–1.7)	0		

OWNERSHIP

1870	Kalamazoo & South Haven (B7)
1870/7/1	Michigan Central, leased Kalamazoo & South Haven
1916/9/27	Michigan Central, merger of Kalamazoo & South Haven
1930/2/1	New York Central, leased Michigan Central
1968/2/1	Penn Central, merger of New York Central (with lease of Michigan Central)
1976/4/1	Conrail, bought Penn Central

BATTLE CREEK BRANCH (MC-K)

	MILEAGE	COUNTY	CROSSINGS, JUNCTIONS, ETC.
(Battle Creek	0)	Calhoun	
(Jct.)	0.71	"	J/MC-C 119.85
(Jct.)	0.88	"	J/GTW-C 176.7
(Main St.)	1.09	"	J/GTW-C 176.5, X/BCCL-4 0.45
(Crossing)	1.50	"	X/DTM 90.4
Morgan Park	3.25	"	C/DTM 88.7
Adams	5.67	"	f. Brick Yard Siding
Sonoma	8.09	"	
Chamberlain Crossing	9.12	"	
Joppa	11.25	"	
East Leroy	12.85	"	
Browns Siding	17.03	"	
Athens	18.64	"	
Gravel Pit	21.6	Branch	
Factoryville	23.13	St. Joseph	
Leonidas	25.89	"	
Fairfax	30.77	"	X/MC-A 56.2, f. Colon Jct.
Findley	35.09	"	J/LS-S 36.5
(Sturgis)	42.3)	"	(via LS-S)

CONSTRUCTION/ABANDONMENT

DATE	ACT	END POINTS	MP	CHANGE	MAIN	SOURCE	NOTE
1889/1	B18	Battle Creek–Sturgis	0.7–42.3	+41.6	41.6	7	
1890/2/1	L	Sturgis–Findley	42.3–35.1	–7.2	34.4	7	28
1935	X	Findley–near Battle Creek	35.1–1.3	–33.8		8	
1935	Y	In Battle Creek (to MC-Y1K)	0.7–1.3	(0.6)	0		
1984	X	In Battle Creek (MC-Y1K)	0.7–1.3	(–0.6)	0		

OWNERSHIP

1889	St. Louis, Sturgis & Battle Creek (B18)
1889/11/13	Battle Creek & Sturgis, reorganization of St. Louis, Sturgis & Battle Creek

1890/2/1   Michigan Central, lease of Battle Creek & Sturgis
1930/2/1   New York Central, lease of Michigan Central (and of BC&S)
1968/2/1   Penn Central, merger of New York Central (with lease of Michigan Central)
1976/4/1   Conrail, bought Penn Central

LEE & PORTER TRACK (MC-WB)

	MILEAGE	COUNTY	CROSSINGS, JUNCTIONS, ETC.
(Jct.)	0	Berrien	J/MC-W 198.46
(End)	1.88	"	

CONSTRUCTION/ABANDONMENT

DATE	ACT	END POINTS	MP	CHANGE	MAIN	SOURCE	NOTE
1895	B29	Line	0–1.9	(+1.9)	0	7	
1976 ca.	X	Line	0–1.9	(–1.9)	0		

OWNERSHIP

1895	Buchanan & St. Joseph River (B29), controlled to Michigan Central
1919/6/12	Michigan Central, merger of Buchanan & St. Joseph River
1930/2/1	New York Central, leased Michigan Central
1968/2/1	Penn Central, merger of New York Central (with lease of Michigan Central)

ST. JOSEPH BRANCH (MC-J)

	MILEAGE	COUNTY	CROSSINGS, JUNCTIONS, ETC.
(Jct.) IN	2.57	St.Joseph IN	J/PRR
Prairie Ave.	1.95	"	
SS&S Jct.	0.0	"	
(Crossing)	0.08	"	X/GTW-C 99.0
Lydick	5.89	"	X/NYC, f. Rugby
Shimps Siding	9.06	"	
Warwick IN	10.92	"	
(IN/MI state line)	11.70		
(Bridge)	14.87	Berrien	B/MC-W 205.32
Galien (old)	15.46	"	J/spur to MC-W 206.01, 0.5 miles
Glendora	20.76	"	
Snow	23.41	"	
Baroda	25.67	"	
Derby	29.74	"	
Vineland	32.89	"	
II&I Sand Pit	33.40	"	
(Bridge)	33.9	"	B/SOM 31.9
St. Joseph Jct.	35.68	"	J/MC-JB 0
(Wayne St.)	36.1	"	B/BHCL-1 1.1
St. Joseph	36.86	"	
(Jct.)	36.97	"	J/PM-C 87.7
(St. Joseph, via PM)	37.14)	"	

CONSTRUCTION/ABANDONMENT

DATE	ACT	END POINTS	MP	CHANGE	MAIN	SOURCE	NOTE
1890/8/4	B19	St. Joseph–S.Bend IN (MI=25.3)	0–37.0	+39.6	25.3	7	
1942/12/23	X	SS&S Jct.–Baroda (MI=13.3)	0–25.0	–25.0	12.0	4	40
1958	X	Baroda–St. Joseph Jct.	25.0–35.1	–10.1	1.9	8	
1973/3/1	X	St. Joseph Jct.–MP 37.0	35.1–37.0	–1.9	0	8	

OWNERSHIP

1890	Indiana & Lake Michigan (B19)
1890/8/4	Terre Haute & Indianapolis leased Indiana & Lake Michigan
1899/1/20	St. Joseph, South Bend & Southern, reorganization of Indiana & Lake Michigan
1900/2/23	SJSB&S leased to Indiana, Illinois & Iowa
1905/3/15	II&I lease of SJSB&S assigned to Michigan Central
1906/4/6	Chicago, Indiana & Southern, merger of Indiana, Illinois & Iowa
1916/1/1	New York Central, merger of Chicago, Indiana & Southern
1930/2/1	New York Central, leased Michigan Central
1949 ca.	Michigan Central, bought SJSB&S
1968/2/1	Penn Central, merger of New York Central (with lease of Michigan Central)

BENTON HARBOR EXTENSION (MC-JB)

	MILEAGE	COUNTY	CROSSINGS, JUNCTIONS, ETC.
St. Joseph Jct.	0	Berrien	J/MC-N 35.68
(Morrison Channel Drawbridge)	0.12	"	
(St. Joseph Riv. Drawbridge)	0.84	"	
Ben. Hbr.	1.61	"	
(End of track)	1.63	"	

CONSTRUCTION/ABANDONMENT

DATE	ACT	END POINTS	MP	CHANGE	MAIN	SOURCE	NOTE
1901	B27	Line	0–1.6	+1.6	1.6	7	
1973/3/1	X	Line	0–1.6	–1.6	0	8	44

OWNERSHIP

1901	Indiana, Illinois & Iowa (B27)
1905/3/15	Michigan Central, lease of Indiana, Illinois & Iowa
1906/4/6	Chicago, Indiana & Southern, merger of Indiana, Illinois & Iowa
1916/1/1	New York Central, merger of Chicago, Indiana & Southern
1930/2/1	New York Central, leased Michigan Central
1968/2/1	Penn Central, merger of New York Central (with lease of Michigan Central)

WEST DIVISION (MC-W)

	MILEAGE	COUNTY	CROSSINGS, JUNCTIONS, ETC.
	[Third St.]		
Niles	191.90	Berrien	J/MC-A 104.01, J/MC-C 191.90
CP 192	192.0	"	
(Bridge)	192.20	"	B/SOM 11.3
(Bridge)	192.28	"	B/CC-M 23.6
(Bridge, St. Joseph Riv.)	192.32	"	
(Jct.)	194.9	"	J/MC-WO 194.9
(Jct.)	198.2	"	J/MC-WO 197.9
(Jct.)	198.46	"	J/MC-WB 0
Buchanan	198.50	"	
CP 200	200.1	"	
Dayton	203.00	"	
(Bridge)	205.32	"	B/MC-J 14.87
Galien	206.01	"	
Barnetts	209.19	"	
Avery	210.04	"	
Three Oaks	211.74	"	
CP Three Oaks	211.8	"	(now CP 211)
CP 213	213.7	"	

(Bridge)	217.11	"	B/PM-C 113.1
New Buffalo	218.94	"	C/PM-CO 115.4
(Bridge)	220.05	"	B/PM-W 34.9
Grand Beach	222.09	"	
Vetterlys Crossing	222.44	"	
(MI/IN state line)	222.72		
Corymbo IN	223.58	LaPorte IN	
CP 226	226.2	"	
(Yard office)	227.30	"	
(Jct.)	228.38	"	J/NKP
Drawbridge	228.47	"	
(Jct.)	228.57	"	J/MON
Mich. Cty.(old)	228.82	"	
Mich. Cty.(new)	228.88	"	
Tenth St.	229.67	"	X/CSSSB
Prison Track	229.78	"	
Furnessville	236.60	Porter IN	
CP 238	238.9	"	
Porter	240.62	"	
PO	240.70	"	X/NYC (now CP482)
Kilverys Sand Pit	245.63	"	
Crisman	246.05	"	
Willow Creek	246.59	"	
(Crossing)	246.61	"	X/B&O
(Crossing)	246.64	"	X/WAB
E. Gary	249.78	Lake IN	J/MC-WJ 0, f. Lake
Gary	255.09	"	
(Crossing)	256.26	"	X/PRR
Tolleston	256.28	"	
Ivanhoe	259.58	"	
(Crossing)	259.58	"	X/EJ&E
Gibson Transfer	260.28	"	
Gibson	261.73	"	
(Crossing)	261.73	"	X/IHB
Columbia Ave.	263.71	"	
Calumet Ave.	264.23	"	
(Switch, E Chi. Belt)	264.49	"	
Hammond IN	264.68	"	
(Crossing)	264.87	"	X/NKP
(Crossing)	264.88	"	X/street ry
(Crossing)	264.89	"	X/ERIE
(Crossing)	264.90	"	X/MON
Hammond (old station) IN	265.02	"	
(IN/IL state line)	265.17		
Calumet Cty. IL	265.26	Cook IL	
Hammond Yard (E end)	265.92	"	
Burnham Ave.	266.00	"	
Hammond Yard (W end)	266.47	"	
(Crossing)	266.49	"	X/CJ
(Crossing)	266.51	"	X/Term RR
(Crossing)	266.52	"	X/PRR
Calumet Park	266.53	"	
Calumet River Drawbridge	267.59	"	
(City limit–Chi.)	268.50	"	
KD	270.49	"	

(Sw. Kensington Yd)	271.58	"	
(Connection)	271.64	"	J/IC
Kensington	271.66	"	
(End MC)	272.02	"	
(Jct.) IL	272.05	"	J/IC—begin via IC—
(Burnside	274.31)	"	
(Grand Crossing	276.81)	"	
(Sixty–third St.	278.30)	"	
(Woodlawn	278.37)	"	
(Hyde Park	279.67)	"	
(43rd St.	280.94)	"	
(39th St.	281.64)	"	
(31st St.	282.63)	"	
(22nd St.	283.70)	"	
(Chi.–12th St.	284.74)	"	
(Jct.)	285.27	"	J/IC—end via IC—
Van Buren St.	285.36	"	
Chi.–Randolph St	285.98	"	
S. Water St.	286.12	"	
(End of track) IL	286.22	"	

CONSTRUCTION/ABANDONMENT

DATE	ACT	END POINTS	MP	CHANGE	MAIN	MI SOURCE	NOTE
1849/4/23	B2	Niles–MP 194.8	191.9–194.9	+3.0		3	
1849/4/23	B2	MP 198.2–New Buffalo	198.2–218.9	+20.7	23.7	3	7
1850/10/29	B2	New Buffalo–Mich. Cty.	218.9–228.9	+10.0	27.5	3	
1852/5/1	B2	Mich. Cty.–Kensington	228.9–272.0	+43.1	27.5		8
1855 ca.	B2	In Chi.	285.3–286.2	+0.9	27.5		9
1903 ca.	B2	East of Buchanan	194.8–198.2	+3.3	30.8		34
??	X	In Chi.	286.2–285.3	−0.9	30.8		
1976/4/1	S3	Niles–Porter	191.9–240.6	−48.7	0		

OWNERSHIP

1849	Michigan Central (B2)
1930/2/1	New York Central, leased Michigan Central
1968/2/1	Penn Central, merger of New York Central (with lease of Michigan Central)
1976/4/1	Amtrak, bought line, Niles–Porter
1976/4/1	Conrail, bought line, Porter west
1999/6/1	Norfolk Southern, bought Penn Central

JOLIET BRANCH (MC-WJ)

	MILEAGE	COUNTY	CROSSINGS, JUNCTIONS, ETC.
E. Gary IN	0.0	Lake IN	J/MC-W 249.78 f. Lake
New Chi.	1.82	"	
Liverpool	2.93	"	X/PRR
S. Gary	5.38	"	X/NKP, f. Glen Park
Ross	7.78	"	
Griffith (freight)	10.15	"	
(Crossing)	10.21	"	X/EJ&E
(Crossing)	10.33	"	X/ERIE
(Crossing)	10.34	"	X/GTW-C
Griffith	10.34	"	
Hartsdale (freight)	12.18	"	

	MILEAGE	COUNTY	CROSSINGS, JUNCTIONS, ETC.
Hartsdale	12.75	"	X/PRR
(Crossing)	15.25	"	X/MON
Dyer IN	15.44	"	
(IN/IL state line)	15.66		
(Bridge) IL	20.85	Cook IL	B/CHTT
Chi. Heights	21.36	"	X/C&EI
Matteson	24.80	"	X/IC
Beverly Farm Siding	30.50	Will IL	
Frankfort	32.47	"	
Summit Sw.	35.10	"	
Spencer	37.14	"	
(Bridge)	38.43	"	B/WAB
Steele	38.56	"	
Thompsons Siding	41.41	"	
(Crossing)	43.54	"	X/EJ&E
(Crossing)	44.0	"	X/CRIP
(Switch, Joliet Yd)	44.14	"	
Joliet (freight)	44.37	"	
Joliet	44.46	"	
Eastern Ave.	44.63	"	
(Crossing)	44.80	"	X/ATSF
(Jct.) IL	44.81	"	J/ALT

DATE	ACT	END POINTS	MP	CHANGE	MI MAIN	SOURCE	NOTE
1854	B3	Line	0–44.8	+44.8	0		
1976	X	E. Gary–Hartsdale IN	0–12.8	–12.8	0		

OWNERSHIP
- 1854/9/7 Joliet & Northern Indiana (B3), leased by Michigan Central
- 1930/2/1 New York Central, leased Michigan Central
- 1968/2/1 Penn Central, merger of New York Central (with lease of Michigan Central)
- 1976/4/1 Conrail, purchase of Penn Central
- 1999/6/1 Norfolk Southern, purchase of Conrail

OLD MAIN LINE, BUCHANAN (MC-WO)

	MILEAGE [Third St.]	COUNTY	CROSSINGS, JUNCTIONS, ETC.
(Jct.)	194.9	Berrien	J/MC-W 194.9
(Jct.)	197.9	"	J/MC-W 198.2

CONSTRUCTION/ABANDONMENT

DATE	ACT	END POINTS	MP	CHANGE	MAIN	SOURCE	NOTE
1849/4/23	B2	Line	194.9–197.9	+3.0	3.0	3	
1903 ca.	X	Line	194.9–197.9	–3.0	0		34

OWNERSHIP
- 1849 Michigan Central (B2)

GRAND RAPIDS BRANCH (MC-G)

	MILEAGE	COUNTY	CROSSINGS, JUNCTIONS, ETC.
(Jackson)	0.0	Jackson	—via MC-C—
Pearl St.	0.21	"	J/MC-C 75.64
Prison Side Track	0.87	"	

Station A	1.47	"	
MAL Crossing	2.13	"	X/GTW-A 104.4
Lans. Ave.	2.71	"	
Clay Pit	4.17	"	
Van Horns	6.09	"	
Henrys Crossing	7.75	"	
Rives Jct. (new)	10.41	"	J/MC-S 10.41
Rives Jct. (old)	10.62	"	J/MC-S 10.62
(Bridge)	10.7	"	B/MUR-N 10.8
Arland	14.71	"	
Onondaga	17.55	Ingham	
Smiths	22.46	Eaton	
Eaton Rapids	24.21	"	
(Crossing)	24.66	"	X/LS-L 41.8
Charlotte	34.93	"	
(Crossing)	35.05	"	X/GTW-C 202.4
Chester	40.21	"	
"Deep Cut"	41.59	"	
Vermontville	46.17	"	
Nashville	49.82	Barry	
Morgan	54.87	"	
Thorn Apple	55.52	"	
Quimby	57.70	"	
Hastings Freight House	61.42	"	
(Crossing)	61.78	"	X/CK&S-A 30.6
Hastings	62.05	"	
Gravel Pit	64.94	"	
Irving	69.50	"	
Middleville	73.25	"	
Parmelee	76.15	"	
Caledonia	79.32	Kent	
Dutton	84.04	"	
Bowen	87.90	"	
Fair Grounds	90.0	"	
S. Gr. Rpds.	92.18	"	
Hughart	92.64	"	
Franklin St.	93.5	"	
Second Ave.	93.82	"	X/PM-D 151.5
Bartlett St.	94.1	"	J/GR&I-S 233.6 (site of first station)
(End MC track)	94.37	"	—via GR&I-S—
(Gr. Rpds.(psgr)	94.47)	"	

CONSTRUCTION/ABANDONMENT

DATE	ACT	END POINTS	MP	CHANGE	MAIN	SOURCE	NOTE
1865/12	B5	Pearl St.–Rives Jct.	0.2–10.6	+10.4	10.4	7	
1868/7/4	B6	Rives Jct.–Eaton Rapids	10.6–24.2	+13.6		7	
8/15	B6	Eaton Rapids–Charlotte	24.2–34.9	+10.7	34.7	7	15
1869/1/26	B6	Charlotte–Nashville	34.9–49.8	+14.9		2	
2/22	B6	Nashville–Hastings F. H.	49.8–61.4	+11.6	61.2	2	
1870/1/1	B6	Hast. F. H.–Gr. Rpds.	61.4–94.4	+33.0	94.2	7	16
1976/4/1	T	Pearl St.–Rives Jct. transferred to line MC-S	0.2–10.6	−10.4			
1976	Y	Gr. Rapids–Bowen(to MC-Y1G)	88.0–94.4	(6.4)			
1976	X	Eaton Rapids–Charlotte	24.8–32.0	−7.2		6	

1976/4/1	S2	At Charlotte	32.0–35.4	–3.4			
1976	X	Charlotte–Vermontville	35.4–46.1	–10.7	56.1	6	
1982/4/1	X	Vermontville–Caledonia	46.1–79.0	–32.9	23.2		47
1982/8/15	X	Rives Jct.–Eaton Rapids	10.6–24.8	–14.2	9.0	6	
1983	X	Caledonia–Bowen	79.0–88.0	–9.0	0	6	

OWNERSHIP

1865	Jackson, Lansing & Saginaw (B5)
1868	Grand River Valley (B6)
1870/8/15	Grand River Valley leased to Michigan Central
1871/9/1	Jackson, Lansing & Saginaw leased to Michigan Central
1916/9/15	Michigan Central, merger of Grand River Valley
1916/9/27	Michigan Central, merger of Jackson, Lansing & Saginaw
1930/2/1	New York Central, lease of Michigan Central
1968/2/1	Penn Central, merger of New York Central (with lease of Michigan Central)
1976/4/1	Conrail, bought Penn Central
1999/6/1	Norfolk Southern, bought Conrail

INTERURBAN TRACK (MC-YG)

	MILEAGE	COUNTY	CROSSINGS, JUNCTIONS, ETC.
(End)	0.0	Kent	
(Jct.)	0.3	"	J/LS-G 94.4
(Bridge)	0.8	"	B/PM-C 1.0
(Crossing)	1.8	"	X/GR&I-YG 1.0+0.1
(Jct.)	2.7	"	J/GR&I-YG 0.4

CONSTRUCTION/ABANDONMENT

DATE	ACT	END POINTS	MP	CHANGE	MAIN	SOURCE	NOTE
1929/6	P4	Line	0–2.7	(+2.7)	0	8	
1970 ca.	X	Line	0–2.7	(–2.7)	0		

OWNERSHIP

1926	Michigan Central, bought from Michigan Railway
1930/2/1	New York Central, leased Michigan Central
1968/2/1	Penn Central, merger of New York Central (with lease of Michigan Central)

LANSING TRANSIT (MC-YLT)

	MILEAGE	COUNTY	CROSSINGS, JUNCTIONS, ETC.
(Jct.)	0	Ingham	J/MC-S 37.2
(Cedar St.)	0.3	"	X/LACL-8 0.46
(Crossing)	0.4	"	X/LS-L 60.5
(End)	0.77	"	

CONSTRUCTION/ABANDONMENT

DATE	ACT	END POINTS	MP	CHANGE	MAIN	SOURCE	NOTE
1888	B17	Line	0–0.8	(+0.8)	0	7	

OWNERSHIP

1888	Lansing Transit (B17), owned 50%–Mich. Central, 50%–Lake Shore & M. S.
1888/2/18	Michigan Central, leased Lansing Transit
1930/2/1	New York Central, leased Michigan Central
1968/2/1	Penn Central, merger of New York Central (with lease of Michigan Central)
1976/4/1	Conrail, bought Penn Central

LANSING MANUFACTURERS (MC-YLM)

	MILEAGE	COUNTY	CROSSINGS, JUNCTIONS, ETC.
Turner St.	0	Ingham	J/LS-L 61.3
Sag. Rd. Yard	2.7	"	
(St. Joseph St.)	3.0	"	X/LACL-4 0.62
(W. St.)	4.4	"	
(Jct.)	5.22	"	J/GTW-C 219.5

CONSTRUCTION/ABANDONMENT

DATE	ACT	END POINTS	MP	CHANGE	MAIN	SOURCE	NOTE
1905/6	B25	Line	0–5.2	(+5.2)	0	7	

OWNERSHIP

1905	Lansing Manufacturers (B25)
1905/6	Michigan Central and Lake Shore & Michigan Southern, jointly leased Lansing Manufacturers
1915/1/1	New York Central, merger of Lake Shore & Michigan Southern
1930/2/1	New York Central, leased Michigan Central
1968/2/1	Penn Central, merger of New York Central (with lease of Michigan Central)
1976/4/1	Conrail, bought Penn Central
1999/6/1	Norfolk Southern, bought Conrail

SAGINAW BRANCH (MC-S)

	MILEAGE	COUNTY	CROSSINGS, JUNCTIONS, ETC.
	[Jackson]		
Rives Jct.	10.41	Jackson	J/MC-G 10.41, old 10.62
Leslie	15.51	Ingham	
Underwood	19.00	"	
Eden	20.54	"	
Wickes	22.5	"	
Kilwinning	23.05	"	
Mason	25.03	"	old 24.82
Holt	30.32	"	
LA	32.5	"	
Lans. Yard	33.79	"	
(Crossing)	35.87	"	X/GTW-C 221.4, Cedar St. on GTW
MA	36.87	"	J/PM-D 87.4, X/LACL-6 0.64 (now CP MA)
Lans.	36.92	"	
(Jct.)	37.2	"	J/MC-YLT 0
(Grand Riv. Ave.)	37.82	"	X/LACL-5 2.62
N. Lans.	37.83	"	J/PM-D 88.3 (now CP N. Lans.)
Chandler	42.29	Clinton	
Bath	44.96	"	
Laingsburg	52.02	Shiawassee	
Bennington	58.54	"	
Maple River Pit	60.44	"	
Owosso (2nd station)	63.62	"	X/AA-B 107.8, X/GTW-D 79.2, f. Owosso Jct.
Owosso (1st station)	63.89	"	
Dewey	65.60	"	
Henderson	70.21	"	
Oakley	74.24	Sag.	
Chesaning	78.09	"	old 78.17
Groveton	81.59	"	
Fergus	82.91	"	
(Jct.)	84.75	"	J/MC-S1 0
St. Charles	85.67	"	

Garfield	89.70	"	
Swan Creek	92.63	"	
(Jct.)	92.77	"	J/MC-S6 0
(Jct.)	93.80	"	J/MC-S7 0
Mercers Sdg.	94.59	"	
Paines	95.60	"	J/PM-V 7.7
Fordney	98.84	"	
(Crossing)	98.87	"	X/PM-YSB 3.9
(Michigan Ave.)	99.1	"	X/SACL-6 2.40
(Hamilton Ave.)	99.2	"	X/SACL-6A 0.37
(Mack. St.)	99.75	"	X/SACL-8 0.91
Sag. Cty.	99.99	"	a.k.a Court St.
(Jct.)	100.6	"	J/PM-YSW 1.7
(Remington St.)	100.7	"	X/SACL-10 0.10
(S wye switch)	100.92	"	
S. B. Jct.	101.16	"	J/MC-BS 20.7
(N wye switch)	101.23	"	
Sag.	101.54	"	(Genesee Ave.), f. N. Sag.
(Genesee Ave.)	101.56	"	X/SACL-4 0.46
Mershon	102.22	"	X/PM-L 0.7, J/GTW-S 40.6
(Carrollton Rd.)	102.26	"	X/MUR-EW 11.75
Eastmans	102.39	"	
Shields	103.24	"	old 102.85
Carrolton	103.42	"	
(Zilwaukee Rd.)	103.88	"	X/MUR-EW 10.15
Zilwaukee	105.08	"	
(Zilwaukee Rd.)	105.42	"	X/MUR-EW 8.70
McClures	106.36	"	
(Jct.)	109.13	"	J/MC-S2 0
(Jct.)	110.85	"	J/MC-S3 0
Brooks	111.61	Bay	
(Jct.)	112.35	"	J/MC-S4 0
Salzburg	112.56	"	
(Jct.)	112.98	"	J/MC-S5 0
(W. Main St.)	113.31	"	X/GTW-S 52.1
(Midland St.)	114.2	"	X/BYCL-1 0.51
(S wye switch)	114.47	"	
Bay Cty. W. S.	114.64	"	J/MC-M 0.66, f. W. Bay Cty.

CONSTRUCTION/ABANDONMENT

DATE	ACT	END POINTS	MP	CHANGE	MAIN	SOURCE	NOTE
1858	B4	Owosso–Laingsburg	63.9–52.1	+11.8	11.8	5	10
1859	B4	Laingsburg–Bath	52.1–45.0	+7.1	18.9	5	11
1861/9/4	B4	Bath–N. Lans.	45.0–37.9	+7.1	26.0	5	12
1863/8/25	B4	N. Lans.–Lans.	37.9–36.9	+1.0	27.0	7	
1865/12	B5	Rives Jct.–Mason	10.6–24.8	+14.2	41.2	7	
1866/6/25	B5	Mason–Lans.	24.8–36.9	+12.1	53.3	7	
1867/10/11	B5	Owosso–St. Charles	63.9–85.7	+21.8		7	
1867/12/6	B5	St. Charles–Bay Cty.	85.7–113.3	+27.6	102.7	7	14
1871/1/31	B5	In Bay Cty.	113.3–114.6	+1.3	104.0	7	
1976/4/1	T	Pearl St.–Rives Jct. transferred from line MC-G	0.2–10.6	+10.4			
1976/4/1	Y	N.Lans.–N.(as MC-Y1S)	37.8–39.7	(1.9)			
1976	X	N. Lans.–Owosso	39.7–61.1	–21.4		6	

1976/4/1	S2	In Owosso	61.1–64.2	[3.1]	
1976	X	At Swan Creek	91.3–91.8	−0.5	
1976/4/1	S2	Swan Creek–Bay Cty. W.S.	91.8–114.6	[22.8]	64.7
1984/2/15	S1	Owosso–Swan Creek	64.2–91.3	[27.1]	37.6
1996	L4	MA–N. Lans.	36.9–37.8	−0.9	36.7

OWNERSHIP

1858	Amboy, Lansing & Traverse Bay (B4)
1865	Jackson, Lansing & Saginaw (B5)
1867/1/4	Jackson, Lansing & Saginaw bought Amboy, Lansing & Traverse Bay
1871/9/1	Michigan Central, leased Jackson, Lansing & Saginaw
1916/9/27	Michigan Central, merger of Jackson, Lansing & Saginaw
1930/2/1	New York Central leased Michigan Central
1968/2/1	Penn Central, merger of New York Central (with lease of Michigan Central)
1976/4/1	Grand Trunk Western, bought Penn Central line, Owosso–north
1976/4/1	Conrail, bought Penn Central line, Lansing–south
1984/2/15	State of Michigan, bought part of line of Penn Central
1987/9/4	Central Michigan, bought line from Grand Trunk Western
1999/6/1	Norfolk Southern, bought Conrail

ROBERT GAGE COAL CO. SPUR (MC-S1)

	MILEAGE	COUNTY	CROSSINGS, JUNCTIONS, ETC.
(Jct.)	0	Sag.	J/MC-S 84.75
(End)	1.89	"	

CONSTRUCTION/ABANDONMENT

DATE	ACT	END POINTS	MP	CHANGE	MAIN	SOURCE	NOTE
	??	Line	0–1.9				24

OWNERSHIP

?? Jackson, Lansing & Saginaw (B5), leased to Michigan Central

PITTSBURG COAL CO. SPUR (MC-S2)

	MILEAGE	COUNTY	CROSSINGS, JUNCTIONS, ETC.
(Jct.)	0	Sag.	J/MC-S 109.13
(End)	2.96	"	

CONSTRUCTION/ABANDONMENT

DATE	ACT	END POINTS	MP	CHANGE	MAIN	SOURCE	NOTE
	??	Line	0–3.0				24

OWNERSHIP

?? Jackson, Lansing & Saginaw (B5), leased to Michigan Central

VALLEY COAL CO. SPUR (MC-S3)

	MILEAGE	COUNTY	CROSSINGS, JUNCTIONS, ETC.
(Jct.)	0	Sag.	J/MC-S 110.85
(End)	0.87	"	

CONSTRUCTION/ABANDONMENT

DATE	ACT	END POINTS	MP	CHANGE	MAIN	SOURCE	NOTE
	??	Line	0–0.9				24

OWNERSHIP

?? Jackson, Lansing & Saginaw (B5), leased to Michigan Central

CENTRAL COAL CO. SPUR (MC-S4)

	MILEAGE	COUNTY	CROSSINGS, JUNCTIONS, ETC.
(Jct.)	0	Bay	J/MC-S 112.35
(End)	1.01	"	

CONSTRUCTION/ABANDONMENT

DATE	ACT	END POINTS	MP	CHANGE	MAIN	SOURCE	NOTE
	??	Line	0–1.0				24

OWNERSHIP

?? Jackson, Lansing & Saginaw (B5), leased to Michigan Central

SALZBURG COAL CO. SPUR (MC-S5)

	MILEAGE	COUNTY	CROSSINGS, JUNCTIONS, ETC.
(Jct.)	0	Bay	J/MC-S 112.98
(End)	0.50	"	

CONSTRUCTION/ABANDONMENT

DATE	ACT	END POINTS	MP	CHANGE	MAIN	SOURCE	NOTE
	??	Line	0–0.5				24

OWNERSHIP

?? Jackson, Lansing & Saginaw (B5), leased to Michigan Central

BLISS COAL MINE SPUR (MC-S6)

	MILEAGE	COUNTY	CROSSINGS, JUNCTIONS, ETC.
(Jct.)	0	Sag.	J/MC-S 92.77
(End)	1.2	"	

CONSTRUCTION/ABANDONMENT

DATE	ACT	END POINTS	MP	CHANGE	MAIN	SOURCE	NOTE
	??	Line	0–1.2				24

OWNERSHIP

?? Jackson, Lansing & Saginaw (B5), leased to Michigan Central

BANNER COAL MINE SPUR (MC-S7)

	MILEAGE	COUNTY	CROSSINGS, JUNCTIONS, ETC.
(Jct.)	0	Sag.	J/MC-S 93.80
(End)	1.64	"	

CONSTRUCTION/ABANDONMENT

DATE	ACT	END POINTS	MP	CHANGE	MAIN	SOURCE	NOTE
	??	Line	0–1.6				24

OWNERSHIP

?? Jackson, Lansing & Saginaw (B5), leased to Michigan Central

MIDLAND BRANCH (MC-L)

	MILEAGE	COUNTY	CROSSINGS, JUNCTIONS, ETC.
	[Bay Cty.]		
B.C.& B.C.Jct.	1.66	Bay	J/MC-M 1.66
(Jct.)	3.07	"	J/spur to GTW-S 53.0, 0.5 miles
Coal Jct.	4.27	"	J/MC-L2 0
Bay Jct.	6.75	"	J/MC-L3 0

Monitor	7.13	"	
Arrow	8.1	"	
Bangor	8.34	"	J/MC-L4 0
Coryells	9.68	"	
Auburn	11.02	"	
Rooneys	11.98	"	
Fisherville	12.99	"	
Flajoles	14.88	"	
Colden	15.98	Midland	f. County Line
(Jct.)	16.4	"	J/MC-YM1 16.4
(Jct.)	18.84	"	J/MC-YM2 0
(Crossing	18.9	"	X/M&HUB 3.0
Midland	19.58	"	
(End of track)	19.73	"	

CONSTRUCTION/ABANDONMENT

DATE	ACT	END POINTS	MP	CHANGE	MAIN	SOURCE	NOTE
1889/12	B28	B.C.&B.C.Jct–Midland	1.7–19.7	+18.0	18.0	7	
1976/4/1	S2	Line	1.7–19.7	−18.0	0		

OWNERSHIP

1889	Bay City & Battle Creek (B28)
1890/2/1	Michigan Central leased Bay City & Battle Creek
1916/9/27	Michigan Central, merger of Bay City & Battle Creek
1930/2/1	New York Central leased Michigan Central
1968/2/1	Penn Central, merger of New York Central (with lease of Michigan Central)
1976/4/1	Grand Trunk Western, purchase of Penn Central line
1987/9/4	Central Michigan, bought line

DOW CHEMICAL SPUR (MC-YM1)

	MILEAGE	COUNTY	CROSSINGS, JUNCTIONS, ETC.
(Jct.)	0	Midland	J/MC-L 16.4
(End)	3.0	"	J/PM-L 18.5

CONSTRUCTION/ABANDONMENT

DATE	ACT	END POINTS	MP	CHANGE	MAIN	SOURCE	NOTE
1899	P2	Line	0–3.0	(+3.0)	0		
1976/4/1	S2	Line	0–3.0	[(−3.0)]	0		

OWNERSHIP

1899	Bay City & Battle Creek, purchased from Midland & Hubbard
1916/9/27	Michigan Central, merger of Bay City & Battle Creek
1930/2/1	New York Central, leased Michigan Central
1968/2/1	Penn Central, merger of New York Central (with lease of Michigan Central)
1976/4/1	Grand Trunk Western, purchase of Penn Central line
1987/9/4	Central Michigan, bought line

MIDLAND YARD (MC-YM2)

	MILEAGE	COUNTY	CROSSINGS, JUNCTIONS, ETC.
(Jct.)	0	Midland	J/MC-L 18.9
(Jct.)	0.6	"	J/PM-L 18.9

CONSTRUCTION/ABANDONMENT

DATE	ACT	END POINTS	MP	CHANGE	MAIN	SOURCE	NOTE
1910 ca.	B28	Line	0–0.6	(+0.6)	0		
1976/4/1	S2	Line	0–0.6	[(–0.6)]	0		

OWNERSHIP

1910	Bay City & Battle Creek (B28), controlled by Mich. Central
1916/9/27	Michigan Central, merger of Bay City & Battle Creek
1930/2/1	New York Central, leased Michigan Central
1968/2/1	Penn Central, merger of New York Central (with lease of Michigan Central)
1976/4/1	Grand Trunk Western, purchase of Penn Central line
1987/9/4	Central Michigan, bought line

MICHIGAN COAL MINING CO. SPUR (MC-L2)

MILEAGE		COUNTY	CROSSINGS, JUNCTIONS, ETC.	
Coal Jct.	0	Bay	J/MC-L 4.27
Mich. Mine	1.44	"	
(End)	2.2	"	

CONSTRUCTION/ABANDONMENT

DATE	ACT	END POINTS	MP	CHANGE	MAIN	SOURCE	NOTE
1898 ca.	B28	Line	0–2.2	+2.2			24
1915 ca.	X	Line	0–2.2	–2.2			24

OWNERSHIP

1898	Bay City & Battle Creek (B28), leased to Michigan Central
1916/9/27	Michigan Central, merger of Bay City & Battle Creek

BAY COAL MINING CO. SPUR (MC-L3)

	MILEAGE	COUNTY	CROSSINGS, JUNCTIONS, ETC.
Bay Jct.	0	Bay	J/MC-L 6.75
Coalfax	2.40	"	
Hecla Jct.	3.50	"	J/spur to Hecla Coal Mine No. 2, 0.46 miles
Hecla Coal Mine	5.22	"	

CONSTRUCTION/ABANDONMENT

DATE	ACT	END POINTS	MP	CHANGE	MAIN	SOURCE	NOTE
1898 ca.	B28	Line	0–5.2	+5.2			24
1930/12	X	Line	0–5.2	–5.2			24

OWNERSHIP

1898	Bay City & Battle Creek (B28), leased to Michigan Central
1916/9/27	Michigan Central, merger of Bay City & Battle Creek

WOLVERINE COAL CO. SPUR (MC-L4)

	MILEAGE	COUNTY	CROSSINGS, JUNCTIONS, ETC.
Bangor	0	Bay	J/MC-L 8.34
Wolverine Mine	0.7	"	

CONSTRUCTION/ABANDONMENT

DATE	ACT	END POINTS	MP	CHANGE	MAIN	SOURCE	NOTE
1898 ca.	B28	Line	0–0.7	+0.7			24
1930 ca.	X	Line	0–0.7	–0.7			24

OWNERSHIP

1898	Bay City & Battle Creek (B28), leased to Michigan Central
1916/9/27	Michigan Central, merger of Bay City & Battle Creek

MACKINAW BRANCH (MC-M)

	MILEAGE	COUNTY	CROSSINGS, JUNCTIONS, ETC.
Bay Cty. E.S.	0	Bay	J/MC-B 108.94
Woodside	0.17	"	X/PM-B 16.7
(Jct.)	0.29	"	J/MC-YBN 0, J/MC-YBS 0
(Drawbridge)	0.42	"	
Bay Cty. W.S.	0.68	"	J/MC-S 114.64
(Marq. St.)	0.8	"	B/BYCL-2 0.71
Hart St.	1.04	"	X/GTW-S 54.1
B.C. & B.C. Jct.	1.66	"	J/MC-L 1.66
(Jct.)	2.04	"	J/MC-YBH 0
(Crossing)	2.05	"	X/PM-YBH 2.2
Wenona	2.67	"	
Kawkawlin	4.74	"	
Linwood	10.72	"	f. Terry
(Jct.)	10.8	"	J/D&M-Z1 0.6
Gilberts	11.81	"	
Lengsville	12.29	"	
Loyer	12.71	"	
State Rd.	15.11	"	f. Maxwell
(Jct.)	17.9	"	J/D&M-Z2 0
(S wye switch)	18.82	"	
Pinconning	18.85	"	old location 18.72
(Crossing)	19.05	"	J/MC-P 0, J/MC-P2 0
White Feather	21.56	"	
Worth	23.61	Arenac	
Eddys	25.40	"	
Standish	27.70	"	
Deep River	30.16	"	
Sterling	32.40	"	
Dunham	32.90	"	
Ortman	34	"	
Quinn	35.22	"	
Wells	39.76	"	J/D&M-A 23.0
Alger	40.71	"	
Culver	41.49	"	
Summit	43.9	Ogemaw	
Greenwood	44.64	"	f. Georgetown
Loranger	47.80	"	J/MC-ME 0, f. Welch
Hauptman (old)	49.96	"	
Hauptman (new)	50.31	"	J/MC-M7 0
West Branch	52.70	"	
Ogemaw	56.06	"	
Cranage	56.45	"	
Millers	58.33	"	a.k.a. Bohnet
Germains	60.75	"	
Beaver Lk.	60.86	"	J/MC-MS 0
(Jct.)	64.20	Roscommon	J/MC-M6 0
St. Helens	64.44	"	J/SHL&S-A 0
Tierney	66.05	"	J/MC-M8 0
Geels	69.40	"	

Moore	71.57	"	
Hodgmans	76.25	"	J/MC-M5 0
Roscommon	77.10	"	
Louds Spur	81	"	
Cheney	83.72	Crawford	P.O. Pere Cheney
Horrigan	87.48	"	
Manistee Switch	87.69	"	J/MC-M9 0
Grayling	92.34	"	
(Jct.)	92.60	"	J/MC-MT 0.26
(Jct.)	92.62	"	J/MC-MR 0.28, J/M&NE-R 78.4
Hanson	97.01	"	J/MC-M10 0
(Jct.)	100.68	"	J/MC-M15 0
Frederic	101.01	"	J/D&C-A 0, J/MC-M11 0, f. Forest
(Jct.)	104.5	"	J/MC-M12 0
Stephens Trestle	106.82	"	
Waters	108.97	Otsego	f. Wrights Lk.
Otsego Lk.	111.69	"	old 111.78, f. Otsego
Arbutus Beach	113.52	"	
Wah Wah Soo	114.66	"	
Oak Grove	115.12	"	
(Jct.)	115.27	"	J/MC-MB 0
Salling	115.44	"	f. Bagley
(Crossing)	119.0	"	X/BC-A 23.2
Gaylord	119.20	"	
Harold	124.79	"	f. Yuill
Logan	125.60	"	
Zickgraff	126.83	"	
Vanderbilt	127.70	"	
(Jct.)	128.65	"	J/MC-M4 0
(Jct.)	129.76	"	J/MC-M13 0
Maltbys	131.85	"	
Thorns	133.00	Cheboygan	
(Jct.)	134.81	"	J/MC-MP 0
Trowbridge	135.00	"	
(Jct.)	137.15	"	J/MC-M3 0
Wolverine	138.34	"	
Haakwood	140.47	"	
(Jct.)	140.59	"	J/MC-MH 0
Rondo	141.51	"	
Parks Mill	141.87	"	
Merritts	143	"	
Hamby	145.37	"	f. Diver, a.k.a. State Rd.
Indian River	148.41	"	
Grand View	151.75	"	
Topinabee	153.94	"	
Bushville	156.75	"	
Long Point	157.21	"	
Birchwood	158.60	"	f. Lakewood
Silver Beach	159.32	"	
Mullet Lk.	160.39	"	P. O. Mullett Lk.
(Jct.)	164.70	"	J/MC-M14 0
Cheboygan	166.24	"	J/D&M-N 196.5
Lakeside	170.45	"	
Point Nipigon	172.98	"	
Nelson	174.5	"	

(Jct.)	175.9	"	J/MC-M2 0	
Freedom	176.50	"		
Mack.	182.30	"	P. O. Mack. Cty.	
(Jct.)	182.5	"	J/GR&I-N 459.8	
(Ferry dock)	182.61	"		

CONSTRUCTION/ABANDONMENT

DATE	ACT	END POINTS	MP	CHANGE	MAIN	SOURCE	NOTE
1871/1/31	B5	Bay Cty. W.S.–Kawkawlin	0.7–4.7	+4.0		7	
1871/8/31	B5	Kawkawlin–Standish	4.7–27.7	+23.0		7	
1871/12/31	B5	Standish–Wells	27.7–39.8	+12.1	39.1	7	
1873/5	B5	Wells–Otsego Lk.	39.8–111.8	+72.0		7	
1873/7	B5	Otsego Lk.–Gaylord	111.8–119.2	+7.4	118.5	7	18
1881	B13	Bay Cty. E.S.–Bay Cty. W.S.	0–0.7	+0.7		7	25
1881/12/18	B5	Gaylord–Mack.	119.2–182.3	+63.1	182.3	7	
1882	B5	Mack.–ferry dock	182.3–182.6	+0.3	182.6	7	
1976/4/1	S2	Bay Cty. E.S.–Kawkawlin	0–5.0	[5.0]			
1976/4/1	S4	Kawkawlin–Linwood	5.0–10.8	[5.8]			
1976/4/1	S4	Sallings–Mack.	115.8–182.6	[66.8]			
1980/9	S1	Linwood–Sallings	10.8–115.8	[105.0]	0		48
1989/9	X	Cheboygan–Mack.	168.0–182.6	[–14.6]		6	
1993	X	Gaylord–Cheboygan	120.5–168.0	[–47.5]			

OWNERSHIP

1871	Jackson, Lansing & Saginaw (B5)
1871/9/1	Michigan Central, leased Jackson, Lansing & Saginaw
1881	Detroit & Bay City (B13), of segment, leased by Michigan Central
1916/9/27	Michigan Central, merger of Jackson, Lansing & Saginaw and Detroit & Bay City
1930/2/1	New York Central, leased Michigan Central
1968/2/1	Penn Central, merger of New York Central (with lease of Michigan Central)
1976/4/1	Detroit & Mackinac, bought part of Penn Central line
1976/4/1	Grand Trunk Western, bought part of line
1987/9/4	Central Michigan, bought line from Grand Trunk Western
1980/9	State of Michigan, bought part of Penn Central line

EDWARDS LAKE BRANCH (MC-ME)

	MILEAGE	COUNTY	CROSSINGS, JUNCTIONS, ETC.
Loranger	0	Ogemaw	J/MC-M 47.80
Chi. Siding	2.6	"	
Ice Tracks	2.9	"	
Georges Lk.	3.3	"	
Edwards Lk.	6.66	"	

CONSTRUCTION/ABANDONMENT

DATE	ACT	END POINTS	MP	CHANGE	MAIN	SOURCE	NOTE
1885 ca.	B5	Line	0–6.7	+6.7	6.7		
1924	X	Line	0–6.7	–6.7	0		

OWNERSHIP

1885	Jackson, Lansing & Saginaw (B5), leased to Michigan Central
1916/9/27	Michigan Central, merger of Jackson, Lansing & Saginaw

SAGES LAKE BRANCH (MC-MS)

	MILEAGE	COUNTY	CROSSINGS, JUNCTIONS, ETC.
Beaver Lk.	0	Ogemaw	J/MC-M 60.86
Slayton		"	
Piper	6.1	"	J/MC-MS1 6.1
Ambroses	7.1	"	
Sages Lk.	8.0	"	

CONSTRUCTION/ABANDONMENT

DATE	ACT	END POINTS	MP	CHANGE	MAIN	SOURCE	NOTE
1885 ca.	B5	Line	0–8.0	+8.0	8.0		
1892	X	Line	0–8.0	–8.0	0		

OWNERSHIP

1885   Jackson, Lansing & Saginaw (B5), leased to Michigan Central

SPUR OFF SAGES LAKE BRANCH (MC-MS1)

	MILEAGE	COUNTY	CROSSINGS, JUNCTIONS, ETC.
	[Beaver Lk.]		
Piper	6.1	Ogemaw	J/MC-MS 6.1
(End)	7.3	"	(sec13 T23N R1E)

CONSTRUCTION/ABANDONMENT

DATE	ACT	END POINTS	MP	CHANGE	MAIN	SOURCE	NOTE
1885 ca.	B5	Line	6.1–7.3	+1.2	1.2		
1892	X	Line	7.3–6.1	–1.2	0		

OWNERSHIP

1885   Jackson, Lansing & Saginaw (B5), leased to Michigan Central

PORTAGE LAKE BRANCH (MC-MR)

	MILEAGE	COUNTY	CROSSINGS, JUNCTIONS, ETC.
(Jct.)	0	Crawford	J/MC-M 92.62
Portage Lk. Jct.	2.3	"	J/M&NE-R 76.1 (spur to end, 0.66 miles)
(S wye switch)	2.6	"	
(Jct.)	3.8	"	
Rasmus	5.60	"	

CONSTRUCTION/ABANDONMENT

DATE	ACT	END POINTS	MP	CHANGE	MAIN	SOURCE	NOTE
1914	B5	Portage Lk. Jct.–Rasmus	2.3–5.6	+3.3	3.3		
1955 ca.	P5	Grayling–Portage Lk. Jct.	0–2.3	+2.3	5.6		
1980	X	Line	0–5.6	–5.6	0		49

OWNERSHIP

1904	Jackson, Lansing & Saginaw (B5), leased to Michigan Central
1916/9/27	Michigan Central, merger of Jackson, Lansing & Saginaw
1930/2/1	New York Central, leased Michigan Central
1968/2/1	Penn Central, merger of New York Central (with lease of Michigan Central)

TWIN LAKES BRANCH (MC-MT)

	MILEAGE	COUNTY	CROSSINGS, JUNCTIONS, ETC.
	[Grayling]		
(Jct.)	0.26	Crawford	J/MC-M 92.60
Tylers	4.40	"	J/MC-MT3 0
Alexander	5.10	"	J/MC-MT7 0
Mertz Branch Jct.	6.00	"	J/MC-MT4 0
Kneeland	7.56	"	
Bucks	10.77	"	
Judges	14.59	"	
(Doubling Track)	14.80	"	
Lovells	17.63	"	
Clear Lk. Jct.	19.00	"	J/MC-MT2, f. Putnams
Bills	22	"	
Dana	24.26	Montmorency	
Vienna Jct.	27.03	"	J/MC-MT5 0
Lewiston	27.73	"	J/L&SE-A 0

CONSTRUCTION/ABANDONMENT

DATE	ACT	END POINTS	MP	CHANGE	MAIN	SOURCE	NOTE
1892	B10	Line	0.3–27.7	+27.4	27.4	7	
1933/10/17	X	Line	0.8–27.7	−26.9		8	38
1933/10/17	Y	In Grayling	0.3–0.8	(0.5)	0	8	
1948/7/19	X	In Grayling	0.3–0.8	(−0.5)	0	8	

OWNERSHIP

1892	Grayling, Twin Lakes & Northeastern (B20), owned by Michigan Central
1901/7/13	Jackson, Lansing & Saginaw (leased to Michigan Central), merger of GTL&NE
1916/9/27	Michigan Central, merger of Jackson, Lansing & Saginaw
1930/2/1	New York Central, leased Michigan Central

CLEAR LAKE BRANCH (MC-MT2)

	MILEAGE	COUNTY	CROSSINGS, JUNCTIONS, ETC.
Clear Lk. Jct.	0	Crawford	J/MC-MT 19.00
Pratts	5.8	Otsego	
Chamberlain Br. Jct.	11.0	"	J/MC-MT2A 11.0
Chamberlin	11.4	"	J/MC-MB 12.5
Johannesburg	12.8	"	

CONSTRUCTION/ABANDONMENT

DATE	ACT	END POINTS	MP	CHANGE	MAIN	SOURCE	NOTE
1904 ca.	B5	Clear Lk. Jct.–Johannesburg	0–12.8	+12.8	12.8		29
1912 ca.	X	Clear Lk. Jct.–Chamberlin	0–11.4	−11.4	1.4		
1912 ca.	X	Chamberlin–Johannesburg	11.4–12.8	−1.4	0		42

OWNERSHIP

1904	Jackson, Lansing & Saginaw (B5), leased to Michigan Central
1916/9/27	Michigan Central, merger of Jackson, Lansing & Saginaw
1930/2/1	New York Central, leased Michigan Central

CHAMBERLAIN BRANCH (MC-MT2A)

	MILEAGE	COUNTY	CROSSINGS, JUNCTIONS, ETC.
	[Clear Lk. Jct.]		
Chamberlain Br. Jct.	11.0	Otsego	J/MC-MT2 11.0
(End)	11.87	"	

CONSTRUCTION/ABANDONMENT

DATE	ACT	END POINTS	MP	CHANGE	MAIN	SOURCE	NOTE
1904 ca.	B5	Line	11.0–11.9	(+0.9)	0		
1912 ca.	X	Line	11.0–11.9	(–0.9)	0		

OWNERSHIP

1904   Jackson, Lansing & Saginaw (B5), leased to Michigan Central

TYLER BRANCH (MC-MT3)

	MILEAGE	COUNTY	CROSSINGS, JUNCTIONS, ETC.
Tylers	0	Crawford	J/MC-MT 4.40
(Jct.)	1.7	"	J/MC-MT3A 1.7
(End)	3.7	"	(sec7 T27N R3W)

CONSTRUCTION/ABANDONMENT

DATE	ACT	END POINTS	MP	CHANGE	MAIN	SOURCE	NOTE
1904 ca.	B5	Line	0–3.7	+3.7	3.7		
1912 ca.	X	Line	0–3.7	–3.7	0		

OWNERSHIP

1904   Jackson, Lansing & Saginaw (B5), leased to Michigan Central

TYLER BRANCH, SPUR (MC-MT3A)

	MILEAGE	COUNTY	CROSSINGS, JUNCTIONS, ETC.
(Jct.)	1.7	Crawford	J/MC-MT3 1.7
(End)	2.9	"	(sec30 T27N R3W)

CONSTRUCTION/ABANDONMENT

DATE	ACT	END POINTS	MP	CHANGE	MAIN	SOURCE	NOTE
1904 ca.	B5	Line	1.7–2.9	+1.2	1.2		
1912 ca.	X	Line	1.7–2.9	–1.2	0		

OWNERSHIP

1904   Jackson, Lansing & Saginaw (B5), leased to Michigan Central

MERTZ BRANCH (MC-MT4)

	MILEAGE	COUNTY	CROSSINGS, JUNCTIONS, ETC.
Mertz Branch Jct.	0	Crawford	J/MC-MT 6.0
Robinson	3.2	"	J/MC-MT4A 3.2
Douglas Branch Switch	4.7	"	J/MC-MT4B 4.7, branch not located
Hardgrove	5.4	"	(sec25 T28N R3W)

CONSTRUCTION/ABANDONMENT

DATE	ACT	END POINTS	MP	CHANGE	MAIN	SOURCE	NOTE
1896	B20	Line	0 –5.4	+5.4	5.4	7	
1930 ca.	X	Line	0–5.4	–5.4	0		

OWNERSHIP

1892   Grayling, Twin Lakes & Northeastern (B20), owned by Michigan Central
1901/7/13   Jackson, Lansing & Saginaw (leased to Michigan Central), merger of GTL&NE
1916/9/27   Michigan Central, merger of Jackson, Lansing & Saginaw

ROBINSON BRANCH (MC-MT4A)

	MILEAGE	COUNTY	CROSSINGS, JUNCTIONS, ETC.
Robinson	3.2	Crawford	J/MC-MT4 3.2
(End)	7.4	"	(sec20 T28N R2W)

CONSTRUCTION/ABANDONMENT

DATE	ACT	END POINTS	MP	CHANGE	MAIN	SOURCE	NOTE
1896 ca.	B20	Line	3.2–7.4	+4.2	4.2		
1912 ca.	X	Line	3.2–7.4	–4.2	0		

OWNERSHIP

| 1892 | Grayling, Twin Lakes & Northeastern (B20), owned by Michigan Central |
| 1901/7/13 | Jackson, Lansing & Saginaw (leased to Michigan Central), merger of GTL&NE |

DAVIDSON BRANCH (MC-MT5)

	MILEAGE	COUNTY	CROSSINGS, JUNCTIONS, ETC.
Vienna Jct.	0	Montmorency	J/MC-MT 27.03
(Jct.)	0.4	"	J/MC-MT6 0
(Crossing)	1.4	"	X/ASNW-2 32.1
(Jct.)	2.9	"	J/spur
Vincent	5.3	"	
Wood Mill	5.6	"	
Bigelow	7.3	"	
Sarvey	7.8	"	
(Jct.)	8.2	"	J/spur
Donnelly Branch Jct.	9.0	"	J/MC-MT5A 9.0
Kneeland–Bigelow Camp 3	9.25	"	
Massneik	10.14	"	
Davidson Wye Switch	10.82	"	J/MC-MT5B 10.8
Lundeen	11.84	"	J/MC-MT5C 11.8

CONSTRUCTION/ABANDONMENT

DATE	ACT	END POINTS	MP	CHANGE	MAIN	SOURCE	NOTE
1900 ca.	B20	Vienna Jct.–Lundeen	0–11.8	+11.8	11.8	7	
1928/7/21	X	MP 11.0–Lundeen	11.0–11.8	–0.8	11.0	8	
1929/9/6	X	MP 0.3–MP 11.0	0.3–11.0	–10.7	0.3	8	
1933/10/17	X	Vienna Jct.–MP 0.3	0–0.3	–0.3	0	8	

OWNERSHIP

1892	Grayling, Twin Lakes & Northeastern (B20), owned by Michigan Central
1901/7/13	Jackson, Lansing & Saginaw (leased to Michigan Central), merger of GTL&NE
1916/9/27	Michigan Central, merger of Jackson, Lansing & Saginaw

DONNELLY BRANCH (MC-MT5A)

	MILEAGE	COUNTY	CROSSINGS, JUNCTIONS, ETC.
	[Vienna Jct.]		
Donnelly Branch Jct.	9.0	Montmorency	J/MC-MT5 9.0
Hennessey	10	"	
K-B Camp 8	10.4	"	
Ligney	11	"	
Whites Camp 28	12.3	"	
(End)	12.9	"	(sec2 T30N R1E)

CONSTRUCTION/ABANDONMENT

DATE	ACT	END POINTS	MP	CHANGE	MAIN	SOURCE	NOTE
1904 ca.	B5	Line	9.0–12.9	+3.9	3.9		
1925 ca.	X	Line	9.0–12.9	−3.9	0		

OWNERSHIP

1904	Jackson, Lansing & Saginaw (B5), leased to Michigan Central
1916/9/27	Michigan Central, merger of Jackson, Lansing & Saginaw

DAVIDSON WYE BRANCH (MC-MT5B)

	MILEAGE	COUNTY	CROSSINGS, JUNCTIONS, ETC.
	[Vienna Jct.]		
Davidson Wye Switch	10.8	Montmorency	J/MC-MT5 10.8
Woodrow	13	"	
Kevan	13.0	"	
Wallace	13.7	"	J/MC-MT5B1 13.7
Martin	14.4	"	J/MC-MT5B2 14.4
Barger Branch	15.2	"	J/MC-MT5B3 15.2
Big Rock	16.3	"	J/MC-MT5B4 16.3
Francis	16.6	"	J/MC-MT5B5 16.6
(End)	17.2	"	(sec5 T30N R2E)

CONSTRUCTION/ABANDONMENT

DATE	ACT	END POINTS	MP	CHANGE	MAIN	SOURCE	NOTE
1904 ca.	B20	Line	10.8–17.2	+6.4	6.4		
1925 ca.	X	Line	10.8–17.2	−6.4	0		

OWNERSHIP

1892	Grayling, Twin Lakes & Northeastern (B20), owned by Michigan Central
1901/7/13	Jackson, Lansing & Saginaw (leased to Michigan Central), merger of GTL&NE
1916/9/27	Michigan Central, merger of Jackson, Lansing & Saginaw

KEVAN BRANCH (MC-MT5B1)

	MILEAGE	COUNTY	CROSSINGS, JUNCTIONS, ETC.
	[Vienna Jct.]		
Wallace	13.7	Montmorency	J/MC-MT5B 13.7
(End)	15.0	"	(sec12 T30N R1E)

CONSTRUCTION/ABANDONMENT

DATE	ACT	END POINTS	MP	CHANGE	MAIN	SOURCE	NOTE
1904 ca.	B5	Line	13.7–15.0	+1.3	1.3		
1925 ca.	X	Line	13.7–15.0	−1.3	0		

OWNERSHIP

1904	Jackson, Lansing & Saginaw (B5), leased to Michigan Central
1916/9/27	Michigan Central, merger of Jackson, Lansing & Saginaw

MARTINS BRANCH (MC-MT5B2)

	MILEAGE	COUNTY	CROSSINGS, JUNCTIONS, ETC.
	[Vienna Jct.]		
Martin	14.4	Montmorency	J/MC-MT5B 14.4
(End)	14.9	"	(sec17 T30N R2E)

CONSTRUCTION/ABANDONMENT

DATE	ACT	END POINTS	MP	CHANGE	MAIN	SOURCE	NOTE
1904 ca.	B5	Line	14.4–14.9	(+0.5)	0		
1925 ca.	X	Line	14.4–14.9	(–0.5)	0		

OWNERSHIP

1904	Jackson, Lansing & Saginaw (B5), leased to Michigan Central
1916/9/27	Michigan Central, merger of Jackson, Lansing & Saginaw

BARGER BRANCH (MC-MT5B3)

	MILEAGE	COUNTY	CROSSINGS, JUNCTIONS, ETC.
	[Vienna Jct.]		
Barger Branch	15.2	Montmorency	J/MC-MT5B 15.2
(End)	16.3	"	(sec16 T30N R2E)

CONSTRUCTION/ABANDONMENT

DATE	ACT	END POINTS	MP	CHANGE	MAIN	SOURCE	NOTE
1904 ca.	B5	Line	15.2–16.3	+1.1	1.1		
1925 ca.	X	Line	15.2–16.3	–1.1	0		

OWNERSHIP

1904	Jackson, Lansing & Saginaw (B5), leased to Michigan Central
1916/9/27	Michigan Central, merger of Jackson, Lansing & Saginaw

BIG ROCK SPUR (MC-MT5B4)

	MILEAGE	COUNTY	CROSSINGS, JUNCTIONS, ETC.
	[Vienna Jct.]		
Big Rock	16.3	Montmorency	J/MC-MT5B 16.3
(End)	16.8	"	(sec8 T30N R2E)

CONSTRUCTION/ABANDONMENT

DATE	ACT	END POINTS	MP	CHANGE	MAIN	SOURCE	NOTE
1904 ca.	B5	Line	16.3–16.8	(+0.5)	0		
1925 ca.	X	Line	16.3–16.8	(–0.5)	0		

OWNERSHIP

1904	Jackson, Lansing & Saginaw (B5), leased to Michigan Central
1916/9/27	Michigan Central, merger of Jackson, Lansing & Saginaw

FRANCIS BRANCH (MC-MT5B5)

	MILEAGE	COUNTY	CROSSINGS, JUNCTIONS, ETC.
	[Vienna Jct.]		
Francis	16.6	Montmorency	J/MC-MT5B 16.6
(End)	17.9	"	(sec6 T30N R2E)

CONSTRUCTION/ABANDONMENT

DATE	ACT	END POINTS	MP	CHANGE	MAIN	SOURCE	NOTE
1904 ca.	B5	Line	16.6–17.9	+1.3	1.3		
1925 ca.	X	Line	16.6–17.9	–1.3	0		

OWNERSHIP

1904	Jackson, Lansing & Saginaw (B5), leased to Michigan Central
1916/9/27	Michigan Central, merger of Jackson, Lansing & Saginaw

MCCORMICK BRANCH (MC-MT5C)

	MILEAGE	COUNTY	CROSSINGS, JUNCTIONS, ETC.
	[Vienna Jct.]		
Lundeen	11.8	Montmorency	J/MC-MT5 11.8
(End)	14.3	"	(sec36 T30N R1E)

CONSTRUCTION/ABANDONMENT

DATE	ACT	END POINTS	MP	CHANGE	MAIN	SOURCE	NOTE
1910 ca.	B5	Line	11.8–14.3	+2.5	2.5		
1925 ca.	X	Line	11.8–14.3	−2.5	0		

OWNERSHIP

1904	Jackson, Lansing & Saginaw (B6), leased to Michigan Central
1916/9/27	Michigan Central, merger of Jackson, Lansing & Saginaw

BEAR LAKE BRANCH (MC-MT6)

	MILEAGE	COUNTY	CROSSINGS, JUNCTIONS, ETC.
(Jct.)	0	Montmorency	J/MC-MT5 0.4
(Jct.)	1.7	"	J/spur, 1.2 miles to Spectacle Lk.
(Jct.)	3.4	"	J/spur, 2.6 miles to Gee Lk.
(Jct.)	4.2	"	J/spur, 1.3 miles to sec31 T30N R1E
Bear Lk.	5.5	Otsego	

CONSTRUCTION/ABANDONMENT

DATE	ACT	END POINTS	MP	CHANGE	MAIN	SOURCE	NOTE
1895 ca.	B20	Line	0–5.5	+5.5	5.5		
1904 ca.	X	Line	0–5.5	−5.5	0		

OWNERSHIP

1892	Grayling, Twin Lakes & Northeastern (B20), owned by Michigan Central
1901/7/13	Jackson, Lansing & Saginaw (leased to Michigan Central), merger of GTL&NE

ALEXANDER BRANCH (MC-MT7)

	MILEAGE	COUNTY	CROSSINGS, JUNCTIONS, ETC.
Alexander	0	Crawford	J/MC-MT 5.1
(End)	5.5	"	

CONSTRUCTION/ABANDONMENT

DATE	ACT	END POINTS	MP	CHANGE	MAIN	SOURCE	NOTE
1895 ca.	B20	Line	0–5.5	+5.5	5.5		
1910 ca.	X	Line	0–5.5	−5.5	0		

OWNERSHIP

1892	Grayling, Twin Lakes & Northeastern (B20), owned by Michigan Central
1901/7/13	Jackson, Lansing & Saginaw (leased to Michigan Central), merger of GTL&NE

BAGLEY BRANCH (MC-MB)

	MILEAGE	COUNTY	CROSSINGS, JUNCTIONS, ETC.
Sallings	0	Otsego	J/MC-M 115.27
(Jct.)	2.1	"	J/spur, 0.8 miles
(Jct.)	3.2	"	J/spur, 1.4 miles
Trombley	4.21	"	
McGraw Branch Jct.	5.8	"	J/MC-MB2 5.8
Johannesburg Jct.	7.06	"	J/MC-MB3 7.1
Deming		"	

Crowley	9.81	"	
Chamberlin	12.47	"	J/MC-MT2 11.4
Nugent	12.69	"	J/MC-MB4 12.7
Johannesburg	13.83	"	

CONSTRUCTION/ABANDONMENT

DATE	ACT	END POINTS	MP	CHANGE	MAIN	SOURCE	NOTE
1887 ca.	B5	Sallings–McGraw Br. Jct.	0–5.8	+5.8	5.8		
1900 ca.	B5	McGraw Jct.–Johannesburg Jct.	5.8–7.1	+1.3	7.1		29
1912 ca.	B5	Johannesburg Jct.–Chamberlin	7.1–12.5	+5.4	12.5		29
1912 ca.	B5	Chamberlin–Johannesburg	12.5–13.8	+1.3	13.8		42
1931/1/15	X	Sallings–Johannesburg	0–13.8	–13.8	0	8	

OWNERSHIP

1887	Jackson, Lansing & Saginaw (B5), leased to Michigan Central
1916/9/27	Michigan Central, merger of Jackson, Lansing & Saginaw
1930/2/1	New York Central leased Michigan Central

BAGLEY BRANCH CONTINUATION (MC-MB2)

	MILEAGE	COUNTY	CROSSINGS, JUNCTIONS, ETC.
	[Sallings]		
McGraw Branch Jct.	5.8	Otsego	J/MC-MB 5.8
(Jct.)	8.1	"	J/spur, 0.8 miles
(Jct.)	9.3	"	J/spur, 0.4 miles
(End)	9.9	"	(sec36 T30N R2W)
(Jct.)	11.9	"	J/spur, 0.9 miles
(Ell Lk.)	13.5	"	(sec8 T29N R1W)

CONSTRUCTION/ABANDONMENT

DATE	ACT	END POINTS	MP	CHANGE	MAIN	SOURCE	NOTE
1887 ca.	B5	Line	5.8–13.5	+7.7	7.7		29
1900 ca.	X	Line	13.5–5.8	–7.7	0		29

OWNERSHIP

1887	Jackson, Lansing & Saginaw (B5), leased to Michigan Central

MCGRAW BRANCH (MC-MB3)

	MILEAGE	COUNTY	CROSSINGS, JUNCTIONS, ETC.
Johannesburg Jct.	0	Otsego	J/MC-MB 7.06
Mathews		"	
Davis	1.9	"	
Ritska		"	
Burns	2.6	"	
New Toledo		"	
Crowl(s)		"	
Ice Track	5.4	"	J/MC-MB3A 0
Fairbanks		"	
Jennings Branch Jct.	6.8	"	J/MC-MB3B 0
Victor	7.9	"	J/MC-MB3C 0
Franks		"	
Clark		"	
Roosevelt		"	
Martindale	10.0	"	J/MC-MB3D 0
Sweeney	11.0	"	

CONSTRUCTION/ABANDONMENT

DATE	ACT	END POINTS	MP	CHANGE	MAIN	SOURCE	NOTE
1900 ca.	B5	MP 0–MP 6.2	0–6.2	+6.2	6.2		29
1910 ca.	B5	MP 6.2–Sweeney	6.2–11.0	+4.8	11.0		29
1919	X	Martindale–Sweeney	10.0–11.0	–1.0	10.0	8	
1923/8	X	Jennings Br. Jct.–Martindale	6.8–10.0	–3.2	6.8	8	
1929/7	X	Johannesburg Jct.–Jennings Br.	0–6.8	–6.8	0	8	

OWNERSHIP

1900	Jackson, Lansing & Saginaw (B5), leased to Michigan Central
1916/9/27	Michigan Central, merger of Jackson, Lansing & Saginaw

ICE TRACK (MC-MB3A)

	MILEAGE	COUNTY	CROSSINGS, JUNCTIONS, ETC.
Ice Track	0	Otsego	J/MC-MB3 5.4
(End)	1.0	"	(sec36 T31N R2W)

CONSTRUCTION/ABANDONMENT

DATE	ACT	END POINTS	MP	CHANGE	MAIN	SOURCE	NOTE
1910 ca.	B5	Line	0–1.0	+1.0	1.0		29
1914 ca.	X	Line	0–1.0	–1.0	0		29

OWNERSHIP

1910	Jackson, Lansing & Saginaw (B5), leased to Michigan Central
1916/9/27	Michigan Central, merger of Jackson, Lansing & Saginaw

JENNINGS BRANCH (MC-MB3B)

	MILEAGE	COUNTY	CROSSINGS, JUNCTIONS, ETC.
Jennings Branch Jct.	0	Otsego	J/MC-MB3 6.8
Slade	1	"	
Lankey	2	"	
Leonard Branch Jct.	2.6	"	J/MC-MB3B1 0
Dupont	4	"	
S. H. Company	5	"	
(Jct.)	5.0	"	J/spur, 0.8 miles (to sec10 T31N R2W)
(Jct.)	6.6	"	J/MC-MB3B2 0
S. H. Company	7	"	
(End)	8.5	"	(sec28 T32N R2W)

CONSTRUCTION/ABANDONMENT

DATE	ACT	END POINTS	MP	CHANGE	MAIN	SOURCE	NOTE
1910 ca.	B5	Line	0–8.5	+8.5	8.5		29
1926	X	MP 6.9–MP 8.5	6.9–8.5	–1.6	6.9	8	
1929/7	X	MP 0–MP 6.9	0–6.9	–6.9	0	8	

OWNERSHIP

1910	Jackson, Lansing & Saginaw (B5), leased to Michigan Central
1916/9/27	Michigan Central, merger of Jackson, Lansing & Saginaw

LEONARD BRANCH (MC-MB3B1)

	MILEAGE	COUNTY	CROSSINGS, JUNCTIONS, ETC.
Leonard Branch Jct.	0	Otsego	J/MC–MB3B1 2.6
Koul	1/2	"	
(End)	1.7	"	(sec16 T31N R2W)

CONSTRUCTION/ABANDONMENT

DATE	ACT	END POINTS	MP	CHANGE	MAIN	SOURCE	NOTE
1913 ca.	B5	Line	0–1.7	+1.7	1.7		29
1921	X	Line	0–1.7	−1.7	0	8	

OWNERSHIP

1913	Jackson, Lansing & Saginaw (B5), leased to Michigan Central
1916/9/27	Michigan Central, merger of Jackson, Lansing & Saginaw

SPUR (MC-MB3B2)

	MILEAGE	COUNTY	CROSSINGS, JUNCTIONS, ETC.
(Jct.)	0	Otsego	J/MC-MB3B 6.6
(End)	1.2	"	(sec35 T32N R2W)

CONSTRUCTION/ABANDONMENT

DATE	ACT	END POINTS	MP	CHANGE	MAIN	SOURCE	NOTE
1915 ca.	B5	Line	0–1.2	+1.2	1.2		29
1923/1	X	West end of line	0.2–1.2	−1.0	0.2	8	
1929/7	X	Line	0–0.2	−0.2	0	8	

OWNERSHIP

1915	Jackson, Lansing & Saginaw (B5), leased to Michigan Central
1916/9/27	Michigan Central, merger of Jackson, Lansing & Saginaw

SARGEANT SPUR (MC-MB3C)

	MILEAGE	COUNTY	CROSSINGS, JUNCTIONS, ETC.
Victor	0	Otsego	J/MC-MB3 7.9
(Crossing)	0.1	"	X/BC-A 31.8
Gleason	1.7	"	(sec13 T31N R2W)

CONSTRUCTION/ABANDONMENT

DATE	ACT	END POINTS	MP	CHANGE	MAIN	SOURCE	NOTE
1910 ca.	B5	Line	0–1.7	+1.7	1.7		29
1923/9	X	East end of line	0.3–1.7	−1.4	0.3	8	
1924/10	X	Line	0–0.3	−0.3	0	8	

OWNERSHIP

1910	Jackson, Lansing & Saginaw (B5), leased to Michigan Central
1916/9/27	Michigan Central, merger of Jackson, Lansing & Saginaw

MCKINNONS SPUR (MC-MB3D)

	MILEAGE	COUNTY	CROSSINGS, JUNCTIONS, ETC.
Martindale	0	Otsego	J/MC-MB3 10.0
McKinnons	1.0	"	(sec32 T31N R1W)

CONSTRUCTION/ABANDONMENT

DATE	ACT	END POINTS	MP	CHANGE	MAIN	SOURCE	NOTE
1910 ca.	B5	Line	0–1.0	+1.0	1.0		29
1923/8	X	Line	0–1.0	−1.0	0	8	

OWNERSHIP

1910	Jackson, Lansing & Saginaw (B5), leased to Michigan Central
1916/9/27	Michigan Central, merger of Jackson, Lansing & Saginaw

TYRUS BRANCH (MC-MB4)

	MILEAGE	COUNTY	CROSSINGS, JUNCTIONS, ETC.
Nugent	12.7	Otsego	J/MC-MB 12.69
Dauss	16	"	
Wardrop	17.1	"	(sec26 T30N R1W)

CONSTRUCTION/ABANDONMENT

DATE	ACT	END POINTS	MP	CHANGE	MAIN	SOURCE	NOTE
1912 ca.	B5	Line	12.7–17.1	+4.4	4.4		29
1923/1	X	East end of line	16.1–17.1	–1.0	3.4	8	
1924/10	X	Line	12.7–16.1	–3.4	0	8	

OWNERSHIP

1912	Jackson, Lansing & Saginaw (B5), leased to Michigan Central
1916/9/27	Michigan Central, merger of Jackson, Lansing & Saginaw

PIGEON RIVER BRANCH (MC-MP)

	MILEAGE	COUNTY	CROSSINGS, JUNCTIONS, ETC.
(Jct.)	0	Cheboygan	J/MC-M 134.81
(Jct.)	1.1	"	J/Mitchell & Belcher Lumber Co. line
Smith Mill	1.4	"	
Sturgeon Branch	4.7	Otsego	J/MC-MP2 0
Bank 6	7.5	"	
Needham	8.0	"	J/MC-MP3 0
Cornwells Mills	9.2	"	

CONSTRUCTION/ABANDONMENT

DATE	ACT	END POINTS	MP	CHANGE	MAIN	SOURCE	NOTE
1896	B5	Trowbridge–Cornwells Mills	0–9.2	+9.2	9.2		29
1916 ca.	X	Needham–Cornwells Mills	8.3–9.2	–0.9	8.3		29
1927/6/18	X	Trowbridge–Needham	0–8.3	–8.3	0	8	

OWNERSHIP

1896	Jackson, Lansing & Saginaw (B5), leased to Michigan Central
1916/9/27	Michigan Central, merger of Jackson, Lansing & Saginaw

STURGEON BRANCH (MC-MP2)

	MILEAGE	COUNTY	CROSSINGS, JUNCTIONS, ETC.
Sturgeon Branch	0	Otsego	J/MC-MP 4.7
(End)	1.8	"	(sec11 T32N R2W)

CONSTRUCTION/ABANDONMENT

DATE	ACT	END POINTS	MP	CHANGE	MAIN	SOURCE	NOTE
	??	Line					24

OWNERSHIP

??	Jackson, Lansing & Saginaw (B5), leased to Michigan Central
1916/9/27	Michigan Central, merger of Jackson, Lansing & Saginaw

RICHARDSON BRANCH (MC-MP3)

	MILEAGE	COUNTY	CROSSINGS, JUNCTIONS, ETC.
Needham	0	Otsego	J/MC-MP 8.0
(Jct.)	1.9	Cheboygan	J/MC-MP3E (McDade Spur), 1.0 miles
Remick	2.7	"	
Page Branch Jct.	4.7	"	J/MC-MP3A 0

Steinhoff	5.3	"	
Caldwell	5.3	"	J/MC-MP3B 0
Hill	6.4	"	J/MC-MP3C 0
Hart	6.7	"	J/MC-MP3D 0

CONSTRUCTION/ABANDONMENT

DATE	ACT	END POINTS	MP	CHANGE	MAIN	SOURCE	NOTE
1907 ca.	B5	Line	0–6.7	+6.7	6.7	8	
1927/6/18	X	Line	0–6.7	–6.7	0	8	

OWNERSHIP

1907	Jackson, Lansing & Saginaw (B5), leased to Michigan Central
1916/9/27	Michigan Central, merger of Jackson, Lansing & Saginaw

PAGE BRANCH (MC-MP3A)

	MILEAGE	COUNTY	CROSSINGS, JUNCTIONS, ETC.
Page Branch Jct.	0	Cheboygan	J/MC-MP3 4.7
Page	0.4	"	
Cardinal Branch	2.6	"	
Forest Jct.	2.7	"	
(End)	6.2	"	(sec3 T33N R1W)

CONSTRUCTION/ABANDONMENT

DATE	ACT	END POINTS	MP	CHANGE	MAIN	SOURCE	NOTE
1907 ca.	B5	Line	0–6.2	+6.2	6.2	8	
1927/6/18	X	Line	0–6.2	–6.2	0	8	

OWNERSHIP

1907	Jackson, Lansing & Saginaw (B5), leased to Michigan Central
1916/9/27	Michigan Central, merger of Jackson, Lansing & Saginaw

BLACK RIVER BRANCH (MC-MP3B)

	MILEAGE	COUNTY	CROSSINGS, JUNCTIONS, ETC.
Caldwell	0	Cheboygan	J/MC-MP3 5.3
Herrick	1.7	Otsego	
Hardwood Lk.	2.8	"	
Keogh	5.6	"	(approx. sec10 T31N R1W)

CONSTRUCTION/ABANDONMENT

DATE	ACT	END POINTS	MP	CHANGE	MAIN	SOURCE	NOTE
1912 ca.	B5	Line	0–5.6	+5.6	5.6	8	
1926 ca.	X	South end of line	3.1–5.6	–2.5	3.1	8	
1927/6/18	X	Line	0–3.1	–3.1	0	8	

OWNERSHIP

1912	Jackson, Lansing & Saginaw (B5), leased to Michigan Central
1916/9/27	Michigan Central, merger of Jackson, Lansing & Saginaw

MARBLE BRANCH (MC-MP3C)

	MILEAGE	COUNTY	CROSSINGS, JUNCTIONS, ETC.
Hill	0	Cheboygan	J/MC-MP3 6.4
Farr Branch Jct.	1.6	Otsego	J/MC-MP3C1 0
Hendricks	3.1	"	
Lloyd	4.4	"	(approx. sec24 T32N R1W)

CONSTRUCTION/ABANDONMENT

DATE	ACT	END POINTS	MP	CHANGE	MAIN	SOURCE	NOTE
1910 ca.	B5	Line	0–4.4	+4.4	4.4	8	
1921/9	X	South end of line	2.1–4.4	−2.3	2.1	8	
1924/7	X	Line	0–2.1	−2.1	0	8	

OWNERSHIP

1910	Jackson, Lansing & Saginaw (B5), leased to Michigan Central
1916/9/27	Michigan Central, merger of Jackson, Lansing & Saginaw

FARR BRANCH (MC-MP3C1)

	MILEAGE	COUNTY	CROSSINGS, JUNCTIONS, ETC.
Farr Branch Jct.	0	Otsego	J/MC-MP3C 1.6
Berne	2.3	Montmorency	

CONSTRUCTION/ABANDONMENT

DATE	ACT	END POINTS	MP	CHANGE	MAIN	SOURCE	NOTE
1910 ca.	B5	Line	0–2.3	+2.3	2.3	8	
1921/9	X	Line	0–2.3	−2.3	0	8	

OWNERSHIP

1910	Jackson, Lansing & Saginaw (B5), leased to Michigan Central
1916/9/27	Michigan Central, merger of Jackson, Lansing & Saginaw

QUIGLEY BRANCH (MC-MP3D)

	MILEAGE	COUNTY	CROSSINGS, JUNCTIONS, ETC.
Hart	0	Cheboygan	J/MC-MP3 6.7
Whalen Jct.	0.7	"	
Lentz	1.3	"	

CONSTRUCTION/ABANDONMENT

DATE	ACT	END POINTS	MP	CHANGE	MAIN	SOURCE	NOTE
??		Line	24				

OWNERSHIP

??	Jackson, Lansing & Saginaw (B5), leased to Michigan Central
1916/9/27	Michigan Central, merger of Jackson, Lansing & Saginaw

HAAKWOOD BRANCH (MC-MH)

	MILEAGE	COUNTY	CROSSINGS, JUNCTIONS, ETC.
(Jct.)	0	Cheboygan	J/MC-M 140.59
S. Wye	0.7	"	
N. Branch Jct.	2.31	"	J/MC-MH3 0
(Jct.)	4.2	"	J/MC-M3
Hemlock	4.75	"	
(Jct.)	5.7	"	J/Hanson Spur, 0.9 miles
Hungerford		"	
Hursts	8.0	"	J/Hurst Spur, 0.3 miles
Wylies	8.09	"	J/Wylies Spur
Saddlers	8.2	"	J/Saddlers Spur
(Jct.)	9.3	"	J/Gilchrist Spur, 0.5 miles
Newell Branch Jct.	10.3	"	J/MC-MH2 0
Afton	11.13	"	f. Osborn
(End)	11.89	"	
(Jct.)	12.3	"	J/Quarry Spur, 0.2 miles

(Jct.)	12.5	"	J/MC-MH5 0
(Jct.)	14.3	"	J/MC-MH6 0
(Jct.)	15.8	"	J/spur, 1.8 miles
(Jct.)	16.2	"	J/spur, 0.3 miles
(Jct.)	16.9	"	J/spur, 2.4 miles
(Jct.)	17.9	"	J/Batchelors Branch, 1.3 miles
Mosherman	18.6	"	J/Mosherman Spur, 0.8 miles
Thorwald	20.5	"	(sec26 T35N R1W)

CONSTRUCTION/ABANDONMENT

DATE	ACT	END POINTS	MP	CHANGE	MAIN	SOURCE	NOTE
1900 ca.	B5	MP 0–MP 12	0–12.0	+12.0	12.0		29
1907 ca.	B5	MP 12–End	12.0–20.5	+8.5	20.5		29
1913 ca.	X	MP 14.8–End	14.8–20.5	–5.7	14.8		29
1919	X	MP 12.9–MP 14.8	12.9–14.8	–1.9	12.9	8	
1937/48/	X	MP 0–MP 12.9	0–12.9	–12.9	0	8	

OWNERSHIP

1900	Jackson, Lansing & Saginaw (B5), leased to Michigan Central
1916/9/27	Michigan Central, merger of Jackson, Lansing & Saginaw
1930/2/1	New York Central, leased Michigan Central

NEWELL BRANCH (MC-MH2)

	MILEAGE	COUNTY	CROSSINGS, JUNCTIONS, ETC.
Newell Branch Jct.	0	Cheboygan	J/MC-MH 10.3
(Jct.)	1.0	"	J/Marvins Spur, 0.3 miles
(Jct.)	1.9	"	J/Blanchards Spur, 0.2 miles
(Jct.)	3.1	"	J/MC-MH2A 0
(Jct.)	3.6	"	J/spur
(Jct.)	6.7	"	J/MC-MH2B 0
(End)	7.5	"	(sec19 T34N R1E)

CONSTRUCTION/ABANDONMENT

DATE	ACT	END POINTS	MP	CHANGE	MAIN	SOURCE	NOTE
1907 ca.	B5	Line	0–7.5	+7.5	7.5		29
1915 ca.	X	MP 6.7–MP 7.5	6.7–7.5	–0.8	6.7		29
1919/6	X	MP 3.1–MP 6.7	3.1–6.7	–3.6	3.1	8	
1925/12	X	MP 1.6–MP 3.1	1.6–3.1	–1.5	1.6	8	
1926/8	X	Newell Br. Jct.–MP 1.6	0–1.6	–1.6	0	8	

OWNERSHIP

1907	Jackson, Lansing & Saginaw (B5), leased to Michigan Central
1916/9/27	Michigan Central, merger of Jackson, Lansing & Saginaw

BRADY BRANCH (MC-MH2A)

	MILEAGE	COUNTY	CROSSINGS, JUNCTIONS, ETC.
(Jct.)	0	Cheboygan	J/MC-MH2 3.1
(End)	2.1	"	(sec21 T34N R1W)

CONSTRUCTION/ABANDONMENT

DATE	ACT	END POINTS	MP	CHANGE	MAIN	SOURCE	NOTE
1917 ca.	B2	Line	0–2.1	+2.1	2.1	8	
1925/12	X	Line	0–2.1	–2.1	0	8	

OWNERSHIP

1917   Michigan Central (B2), of segment

REDWOOD SPUR (MC-MH2B)

	MILEAGE	COUNTY	CROSSINGS, JUNCTIONS, ETC.
(Jct.)	0	Cheboygan	J/MC-MH2 6.7
(End)	1.7	"	(sec11 T34N R1W)

CONSTRUCTION/ABANDONMENT

DATE	ACT	END POINTS	MP	CHANGE	MAIN	SOURCE	NOTE
	??	Line					24

OWNERSHIP

??   Jackson, Lansing & Saginaw (B5), leased to Michigan Central
1916/9/27   Michigan Central, merger of Jackson, Lansing & Saginaw

NORTH BRANCH (MC-MH3)

	MILEAGE	COUNTY	CROSSINGS, JUNCTIONS, ETC.
N. Branch Jct.	0	Cheboygan	J/MC-MH 2.31
(End)	2.8	"	

CONSTRUCTION/ABANDONMENT

DATE	ACT	END POINTS	MP	CHANGE	MAIN	SOURCE	NOTE
	??	Line					24

OWNERSHIP

??   Jackson, Lansing & Saginaw (B5), leased to Michigan Central
1916/9/27   Michigan Central, merger of Jackson, Lansing & Saginaw

BRANCH (MC-MH5)

	MILEAGE	COUNTY	CROSSINGS, JUNCTIONS, ETC.
(Jct.)	0	Cheboygan	J/MC-MH 12.5
(End)	4.8	"	(sec35 T35N R1W)

CONSTRUCTION/ABANDONMENT

DATE	ACT	END POINTS	MP	CHANGE	MAIN	SOURCE	NOTE
	??	Line					24

OWNERSHIP

??   Jackson, Lansing & Saginaw (B5), leased to Michigan Central
1916/9/27   Michigan Central, merger of Jackson, Lansing & Saginaw

SILVER LAKE BRANCH (MC-MH6)

	MILEAGE	COUNTY	CROSSINGS, JUNCTIONS, ETC.
(Jct.)	0	Cheboygan	J/MC-MH 14.3
(Jct.)	1.1	"	J/MC-MH6B 0
(Jct.)	2.0	"	J/S wye switch to MC-MH6A, 0.4 miles
(Jct.)	2.6	"	J/MC-MH6A 0
(Jct.)	4.0	"	J/MC-MH6C 0
(End)	4.5	"	(sec5 T35N R1W)

CONSTRUCTION/ABANDONMENT

DATE	ACT	END POINTS	MP	CHANGE	MAIN	SOURCE	NOTE
1913 ca.	B5	Line	0–4.0	+4.0	4.0	8	
1917 ca.	B2	Extend line	4.0–4.5	+0.5	4.5	8	
1918	X	Line	0–4.5	–4.5	0	8	

OWNERSHIP

1913	Jackson, Lansing & Saginaw (B5), leased to Michigan Central
1916/9/27	Michigan Central (B2), merger of Jackson, Lansing & Saginaw

BELL BRANCH (MC-MH6A)

	MILEAGE	COUNTY	CROSSINGS, JUNCTIONS, ETC.
(Jct.)	0	Cheboygan	J/MC-MH6 2.6
(Wye switch)	0.5	"	J/S wye switch
(End)	1.1	"	(sec7 T35N R1W)

CONSTRUCTION/ABANDONMENT

DATE	ACT	END POINTS	MP	CHANGE	MAIN	SOURCE	NOTE
1913 ca.	B5	Line	0–1.1	+1.1	1.1	8	
1918	X	Line	0–1.1	–1.1	0	8	

OWNERSHIP

1913	Jackson, Lansing & Saginaw (B5), leased to Michigan Central
1916/9/27	Michigan Central, merger of Jackson, Lansing & Saginaw

WHITINGS SPUR (MC-MH6B)

	MILEAGE	COUNTY	CROSSINGS, JUNCTIONS, ETC.
(Jct.)	0	Cheboygan	J/MC-MH6 15.4
(End)	1.2	"	(sec13 T35N R2W)

CONSTRUCTION/ABANDONMENT

DATE	ACT	END POINTS	MP	CHANGE	MAIN	SOURCE	NOTE
1914 ca.	B5	Line	0–1.2	+1.2	1.2		29
1918	X	Line	0–1.2	–1.2	0		29

OWNERSHIP

1914	Jackson, Lansing & Saginaw (B5), leased to Michigan Central
1916/9/27	Michigan Central, merger of Jackson, Lansing & Saginaw

BRANCH (MC-MH6C)

	MILEAGE	COUNTY	CROSSINGS, JUNCTIONS, ETC.
(Jct.)	0	Cheboygan	J/MC-MH6 4.0
(End)	1.5	"	(sec5 T35N R1W)

CONSTRUCTION/ABANDONMENT

DATE	ACT	END POINTS	MP	CHANGE	MAIN	SOURCE	NOTE
1914 ca.	B5	Line	0–1.5	+1.5	1.5		29
1918	X	Line	0–1.5	–1.5	0		29

OWNERSHIP

1914	Jackson, Lansing & Saginaw (B5), leased to Michigan Central
1916/9/27	Michigan Central, merger of Jackson, Lansing & Saginaw

PATTERSON BRANCH (MC-M2)

	MILEAGE	COUNTY	CROSSINGS, JUNCTIONS, ETC.
(Jct.)	0	Cheboygan	J/MC-M 175.9
(End)	4.9	"	(sec23 T38N R3W)

CONSTRUCTION/ABANDONMENT

DATE	ACT	END POINTS	MP	CHANGE	MAIN	SOURCE	NOTE
1910 ca.	B5	Line	0–4.9	+4.9	4.9		29
1920	X	Line	0–4.9	–4.9	0	8	

OWNERSHIP

1910	Jackson, Lansing & Saginaw (B5), leased to Michigan Central
1916/9/27	Michigan Central, merger of Jackson, Lansing & Saginaw

NUNDA BRANCH (MC-M3)

	MILEAGE	COUNTY	CROSSINGS, JUNCTIONS, ETC.
(Jct.)	0	Cheboygan	J/MC-M 137.15
(Jct.)	2.2	"	J/Buell Banking Br., 0.4 miles
(Jct.)	5.7	"	J/Hayes Br., 0.3 miles
(Jct.)	7.2	"	J/MC-MH 4.2

CONSTRUCTION/ABANDONMENT

DATE	ACT	END POINTS	MP	CHANGE	MAIN	SOURCE	NOTE
1897 ca.	B5	Line	0–7.2	+7.2	7.2		29
1900 ca.	X	MP 0–MP 2.2	0–2.2	–2.2	5.0		29
1914 ca.	X	MP 2.2–MP 7.2	2.2–7.2	–5.0	0	8	

OWNERSHIP

1897	Jackson, Lansing & Saginaw (B5), leased to Michigan Central

BUELL BRANCH (MC-M4)

	MILEAGE	COUNTY	CROSSINGS, JUNCTIONS, ETC.
(Jct.)	0	Otsego	J/MC-M 128.65
Spiegel Branch Switch	3.1	"	J/MC-M4A 3.1
(End)	3.76	Cheboygan	(sec33 T33N R3W)

CONSTRUCTION/ABANDONMENT

DATE	ACT	END POINTS	MP	CHANGE	MAIN	SOURCE	NOTE
1900 ca.	B5	Line	0–3.7	+3.7	3.7		29
1925	X	Line	0–3.7	–3.7	0	8	

OWNERSHIP

1900	Jackson, Lansing & Saginaw (B5), leased to Michigan Central
1916/9/27	Michigan Central, merger of Jackson, Lansing & Saginaw

SPIEGEL BRANCH (MC-M4A)

	MILEAGE	COUNTY	CROSSINGS, JUNCTIONS, ETC.
Spiegel Branch Switch	3.1	Otsego	J/MC-M4 3.1
Spiegels Camp		"	
Sullivan		Cheboygan	
Banghart	7.3	"	

CONSTRUCTION/ABANDONMENT

DATE	ACT	END POINTS	MP	CHANGE	MAIN	SOURCE	NOTE
1900 ca.	B5	Line	3.1–7.3	+4.2	4.2		29
1925 ca.	X	Line	3.1–7.3	–4.2	0	8	

OWNERSHIP

1900	Jackson, Lansing & Saginaw (B5), leased to Michigan Central
1916/9/27	Michigan Central, merger of Jackson, Lansing & Saginaw

ROSCOMMON GRAVEL PIT BRANCH (MC-M5)

	MILEAGE	COUNTY	CROSSINGS, JUNCTIONS, ETC.
Hodgemans	0	Roscommon	J/MC-M 76.25
Roscommon Gravel Pit	4.0	Crawford	(sec27 T25N R2W)

CONSTRUCTION/ABANDONMENT

DATE	ACT	END POINTS	MP	CHANGE	MAIN	SOURCE	NOTE
1910 ca.	B5	Line	0–4.0	+4.0	4.0		29
1935/11/2	X	Line	0–4.0	–4.0	0	8	

OWNERSHIP

1910	Jackson, Lansing & Saginaw (B5), leased to Michigan Central
1916/9/27	Michigan Central, merger of Jackson, Lansing & Saginaw
1931/2/1	New York Central, leased Michigan Central

CAMERON BRANCH (MC-M6)

	MILEAGE	COUNTY	CROSSINGS, JUNCTIONS, ETC.
(Jct.)	0	Roscommon	J/MC-M 64.20
(End)	5.25	"	(sec6 T22N R1W)

CONSTRUCTION/ABANDONMENT

DATE	ACT	END POINTS	MP	CHANGE	MAIN	SOURCE	NOTE
??	B5	Line	0–5.3				24
1917	X	Line	0–5.3				24

OWNERSHIP

??	Jackson, Lansing & Saginaw (B5), leased to Michigan Central
1916/9/27	Michigan Central, merger of Jackson, Lansing & Saginaw

HAUPTMAN BRANCH (MC-M7)

	MILEAGE	COUNTY	CROSSINGS, JUNCTIONS, ETC.
Hauptman	0	Ogemaw	J/MC-M 50.31
Cooks	1.0	"	
Wilsons	3.90	"	
Gillis	6.71	"	
Ross	8.70	"	J/MC-M7B 8.7
Casey	9.70	Roscommon	
Bradleys Wye	10.10	"	
Jordan Br. Switch	15.00	"	J/MC-M7A 15.0
(End)	15.13	"	
Boyce	25.0	"	(sec9 T21N R3W)

CONSTRUCTION/ABANDONMENT

DATE	ACT	END POINTS	MP	CHANGE	MAIN	SOURCE	NOTE
1884 ca.	B5	Hauptman–Bradleys Wye	0–10.1	+10.1	10.1		29
1890 ca.	B5	Bradleys Wye–Boyce	10.1–25.0	+14.9	25.0		29
1900 ca.	X	Boyce–Hauptman	25.0–0	–25.0	0		29

OWNERSHIP

1884	Jackson, Lansing & Saginaw (B5), leased to Michigan Central

JORDAN BRANCH (MC-M7A)

	MILEAGE	COUNTY	CROSSINGS, JUNCTIONS, ETC.
Jordan Branch Switch	15.00	Roscommon	J/MC-M7 15.00
Nolan	17.90	"	(sec19 T21N R1W)

CONSTRUCTION/ABANDONMENT

DATE	ACT	END POINTS	MP	CHANGE	MAIN	SOURCE	NOTE
1890 ca.	B5	Line	15.0–17.9	+2.9	2.9		29
1900 ca.	X	Line	17.9–15.0	–2.9	0		29

OWNERSHIP

1890   Jackson, Lansing & Saginaw (B5), leased to Michigan Central

NORN BRANCH (MC-M7B)

	MILEAGE	COUNTY	CROSSINGS, JUNCTIONS, ETC.
Ross	8.70	Ogemaw	J/MC-M7 8.70
Norn	10.10	"	

CONSTRUCTION/ABANDONMENT

DATE	ACT	END POINTS	MP	CHANGE	MAIN	SOURCE	NOTE
1884 ca.	B5	Line	8.7–10.1	+1.4	1.4		
1900 ca.	X	Line	10.1–8.7	–1.4	0		

OWNERSHIP

1884   Jackson, Lansing & Saginaw (B5), leased to Michigan Central

TIERNEY BRANCH (MC-M8)

	MILEAGE	COUNTY	CROSSINGS, JUNCTIONS, ETC.
Tierney	0	Roscommon	J/MC-M 66.05
(End)	3.1	"	(sec35 T24N R1W)

CONSTRUCTION/ABANDONMENT

DATE	ACT	END POINTS	MP	CHANGE	MAIN	SOURCE	NOTE
	??	Line					24

OWNERSHIP

??   Jackson, Lansing & Saginaw (B5), leased to Michigan Central
1916/9/27   Michigan Central, merger of Jackson, Lansing & Saginaw

BRADLEY BRANCH (MC-M9)

	MILEAGE	COUNTY	CROSSINGS, JUNCTIONS, ETC.
(Jct.)	0	Crawford	J/MC-M 87.69
(End)	0.8	"	(sec31 T26N R4W)

CONSTRUCTION/ABANDONMENT

DATE	ACT	END POINTS	MP	CHANGE	MAIN	SOURCE	NOTE
	??	Line					24

OWNERSHIP

??   Jackson, Lansing & Saginaw (B5), leased to Michigan Central
1916/9/27   Michigan Central, merger of Jackson, Lansing & Saginaw

AU SABLE BRANCH (MC-M10)

	MILEAGE	COUNTY	CROSSINGS, JUNCTIONS, ETC.
Hanson	0	Crawford	J/MC-M 97.01
(End)	2.5	"	(sec35 T27N R4W)

CONSTRUCTION/ABANDONMENT

DATE	ACT	END POINTS	. MP	CHANGE	MAIN	SOURCE	NOTE
??		Line					24

OWNERSHIP

??	Jackson, Lansing & Saginaw (B5), leased to Michigan Central
1916/9/27	Michigan Central, merger of Jackson, Lansing & Saginaw

FREDERIC BRANCH (MC-M11)

	MILEAGE	COUNTY	CROSSINGS, JUNCTIONS, ETC.
Frederic	0	Crawford	J/MC-M 101.0
(Jct.)	1.9	"	J/MC-M11A 1.9
(Jct.)	3.0	"	J/MC-M11B 3.0
(End)	4.5	"	(sec29 T28N R3W)

CONSTRUCTION/ABANDONMENT

DATE	ACT	END POINTS	MP	CHANGE	MAIN	SOURCE	NOTE
1886 ca.	B5	Line	0–4.5	+4.5	4.5		29
1900 ca.	X	MP 1.9–MP 4.5	1.9–4.5	−2.6	1.9		29
1910 ca.	X	Frederic–MP 1.9	0–1.9	−1.9	0		29

OWNERSHIP

1886	Jackson, Lansing & Saginaw (B5), leased to Michigan Central

SPUR OFF FREDERIC BRANCH (MC-M11A)

	MILEAGE	COUNTY	CROSSINGS, JUNCTIONS, ETC.
(Jct.)	1.9	Crawford	J/MC-M11 1.9
(End)	3.5	"	(sec13 T28N R4W)

CONSTRUCTION/ABANDONMENT

DATE	ACT	END POINTS	MP	CHANGE	MAIN	SOURCE	NOTE
1886 ca.	B5	Line	1.9–3.5	+1.6	1.6		29
1910 ca.	X	Line	1.9–3.5	−1.6	0		29

OWNERSHIP

1886	Jackson, Lansing & Saginaw (B5), leased to Michigan Central

SPUR OFF FREDERIC BRANCH (MC-M11B)

	MILEAGE	COUNTY	CROSSINGS, JUNCTIONS, ETC.
(Jct.)	3.0	Crawford	J/MM-M11 3.0
(End)	4.7	"	(sec18 T28N R3W)

CONSTRUCTION/ABANDONMENT

DATE	ACT	END POINTS	MP	CHANGE	MAIN	SOURCE	NOTE
1886 ca.	B5	Line	3.0–4.7	+1.7	1.7	29	
1900 ca.	X	Line	3.0–4.7	−1.7	0	29	

OWNERSHIP

1886	Jackson, Lansing & Saginaw (B5), leased to Michigan Central

MICHELSON BRANCH (MC-M12)

	MILEAGE	COUNTY	CROSSINGS, JUNCTIONS, ETC.
(Jct.)	0	Crawford	J/MC-M 104.5
(End)	2.0	"	(sec2 T28N R4W)

CONSTRUCTION/ABANDONMENT

DATE	ACT	END POINTS	MP	CHANGE	MAIN	SOURCE	NOTE
??		Line					24

OWNERSHIP

??	Jackson, Lansing & Saginaw (B5), leased to Michigan Central
1916/9/27	Michigan Central, merger of Jackson, Lansing & Saginaw

VANDERBILT BRANCH (MC-M13)

	MILEAGE	COUNTY	CROSSINGS, JUNCTIONS, ETC.
(Jct.)	0	Otsego	J/MC-M 129.76
(End)	1.70	"	(sec13 T32N R3W)
(Pickerel Lk.)	6.4	"	(sec11 T32N R2W)

CONSTRUCTION/ABANDONMENT

DATE	ACT	END POINTS	MP	CHANGE	MAIN	SOURCE	NOTE
1886 ca.	B5	Line	0–6.4	+6.4	6.4		29
1891 ca.	X	MP 1.7–MP 6.4	6.4–1.7	–4.7	1.7		29
1907 ca.	X	MP 0–MP 1.7	1.7–0	–1.7	0		29

OWNERSHIP

1886	Jackson, Lansing & Saginaw (B5), leased to Michigan Central

WALSH BRANCH (MC-M15)

	MILEAGE	COUNTY	CROSSINGS, JUNCTIONS, ETC.
(Jct.)	0	Crawford	J/MC-M 100.68
(Jct.)	0.9	"	J/spur, 0.9 miles
(End)	2.1	"	(sec27 T28N R4W)

CONSTRUCTION/ABANDONMENT

DATE	ACT	END POINTS	MP	CHANGE	MAIN	SOURCE	NOTE
??		Line					24

OWNERSHIP

??	Jackson, Lansing & Saginaw (B5), leased to Michigan Central
1916/9/27	Michigan Central, merger of Jackson, Lansing & Saginaw

GLADWIN BRANCH (MC-P)

	MILEAGE	COUNTY	CROSSINGS, JUNCTIONS, ETC.
(Crossing)	0	Bay	X/MC-M 19.05, J/MC-P2 0
Beardsley	2.60	"	
Woodville	3.32	"	
St. John	5.05	"	
Nine Mile	5.42	"	
(Jct.)	6.6	"	J/MC-P4 0
(Jct.)	7.74	"	J/MC-PS 0
(Jct.)	7.86	"	J/MC-PN 0
Mount Forrest	8.01	"	
Rhodes	11.05	Gladwin	
(Jct.)	11.10	"	J/MC-P7 0
Smiths	14.80	"	
Hawes Bridge	17.7	"	
Highwood	17.80	"	
Winegars	21.55	"	
Howrys	23.50	"	

Bliss Branch	25.05	"	
Stephens Siding	26.00	"	
Gladwin	27.43	"	
(End)	27.82	"	

CONSTRUCTION/ABANDONMENT

DATE	ACT	END POINTS	MP	CHANGE	MAIN	SOURCE	NOTE
1880/11/18	P1	Pinconning–Mt. Forrest	0–8.0	+8.0	8.0	7	22
1881	B16	Mt. Forrest–Rhodes	8.0–11.1	+3.1	11.1	7	
1887	B16	Rhodes–Gladwin	11.1–27.8	+16.7	27.8	7	
1962/Sum.	X	Gladwin–near Pinconning	27.8–0.6	–27.2		8	
1962/Sum.	Y	In Pinconning (to MC-Y1P)	0.6–0	(0.6)	0		48

OWNERSHIP

1880	Saginaw Bay & Northwestern (B16)
1883/2/15	Michigan Central, leased Saginaw Bay & Northwestern
1901/7/13	Jackson, Lansing & Saginaw, merger of Saginaw Bay & Northwestern
1916/9/27	Michigan Central, merger of Jackson, Lansing & Saginaw
1930/2/1	New York Central, leased Michigan Central
1968/2/1	Penn Central, merger of New York Central (with lease of Michigan Central)
1980/9	State of Michigan, bought Penn Central line

SAGINAW BAY SPUR (MC-P2)

	MILEAGE	COUNTY	CROSSINGS, JUNCTIONS, ETC.
(Crossing)	0	Bay	X/MC-M 19.05, J/MC-P 0
(Crossing)	0.67	"	X/D&M-S 19.9
(Sag. Bay trestle)	2.61	"	

CONSTRUCTION/ABANDONMENT

DATE	ACT	END POINTS	MP	CHANGE	MAIN	SOURCE	NOTE
1880/11/18	P1	Line	0–2.6	+2.6	2.6	7	22
1901 ca.	X	MP 1.2–MP 2.6	1.2–2.6	–1.4			29
1901 ca.	Y	MP 0–MP 1.2 (to MC-Y2P)	0–1.2	(1.2)	0		
1935	X	MP 1.2–MP 0.8	1.2–0.8	(–0.4)	0	8	
1937	X	MP 0.6–MP 0.8	0.6–0.8	(–0.2)	0	8	
1945	X	MP 0.4–MP 0.6	0.4–0.6	(–0.2)	0	8	
1953	X	MP 0.2–MP 0.4	0.2–0.4	(–0.2)	0	8	
1963 ca.	X	MP 0–MP 0.2	0–0.2	(–0.2)	0		29

OWNERSHIP

1880	Saginaw Bay & Northwestern (B16)
1883/2/15	Michigan Central, leased Saginaw Bay & Northwestern
1901/7/13	Jackson, Lansing & Saginaw, merger of Saginaw Bay & Northwestern
1916/9/27	Michigan Central, merger of Jackson, Lansing & Saginaw
1930/2/1	New York Central, leased Michigan Central

SOUTH BRANCH (MC-PS)

	MILEAGE	COUNTY	CROSSINGS, JUNCTIONS, ETC.
(Jct.)	0	Bay	J/MC-P 7.74
Browns	0.85	"	J/MC-PS2 0.85
Fisher Jct.	1.57	"	
Hudson	1.69	"	
Campbell	2.75	"	

CONSTRUCTION/ABANDONMENT

DATE	ACT	END POINTS	MP	CHANGE	MAIN	SOURCE	NOTE
1880/11/18	P1	Line	0–2.8	+2.8	2.8		22,23
1910 ca.	X	Line	0–2.8	−2.8	0		

OWNERSHIP

1880	Saginaw Bay & Northwestern (B16)
1883/2/15	Michigan Central, leased Saginaw Bay & Northwestern
1901/7/13	Jackson, Lansing & Saginaw (leased to MC), merger of Saginaw Bay & Northwestern

SULLIVAN BRANCH (MC-PS2)

	MILEAGE	COUNTY	CROSSINGS, JUNCTIONS, ETC.
Browns	0.85	Bay	J/MC-PS 0.85
McRaes	3.00	"	f. Sullivans

CONSTRUCTION/ABANDONMENT

DATE	ACT	END POINTS	MP	CHANGE	MAIN	SOURCE	NOTE
1880/11/18	P1	Line	0.9–3.0	+2.1	2.1	7	22
1882	X	Line	0.9–3.0	−2.1	0	7	

OWNERSHIP

1880	Saginaw Bay & Northwestern (B16)

NORTH BRANCH (MC-PN)

	MILEAGE	COUNTY	CROSSINGS, JUNCTIONS, ETC.
(Jct.)	0	Bay	J/MC-P 7.86
Freeman	4.08	"	J/MC-PN2 4.08
Bentley	4.44	"	
Redy	5.30	"	
Glovers Jct.	7.30	"	
Moores Jct.	9.25	Arenac	J/MC-PN3 9.25
Ogden	10.73	"	
Babcocks Wye	14.05	"	J/MC-PN4 14.05
Hardluck	15.95	Gladwin	
Bricks	20.2	"	
Raymonds	22.45	"	

CONSTRUCTION/ABANDONMENT

DATE	ACT	END POINTS	MP	CHANGE	MAIN	SOURCE	NOTE
1880/11/18	P1	MP 0–Freeman	0–4.1	+4.1	4.1	7	22
1885 ca.	B16	Freeman–Raymonds	4.1–22.5	+18.4	22.5		29
1910 ca.	X	Raymond–Bentley	22.5–4.7	−17.8	4.7		29
1933/7/1	X	Bentley–MP 0	4.7–0	−4.7	0	8	

OWNERSHIP

1880	Saginaw Bay & Northwestern (B16)
1883/2/15	Michigan Central, leased Saginaw Bay & Northwestern
1901/7/13	Jackson, Lansing & Saginaw (leased to MC), merger of Saginaw Bay & Northwestern
1916/9/27	Michigan Central, merger of Jackson, Lansing & Saginaw
1930/2/1	New York Central, leased Michigan Central

FREEMAN BRANCH (MC-PN2)

	MILEAGE	COUNTY	CROSSINGS, JUNCTIONS, ETC.
Freeman	4.08	Bay	J/MC-PN 4.08
(End)	6.1	"	

CONSTRUCTION/ABANDONMENT

DATE	ACT	END POINTS	MP	CHANGE	MAIN	SOURCE	NOTE
1882 ca.	B16	Line	4.1–6.1	+2.0	2.0		29
1910 ca.	X	Line	4.1–6.1	–2.0	0		29

OWNERSHIP

1882	Saginaw Bay & Northwestern (B16)	
1883/2/15	Michigan Central, leased Saginaw Bay & Northwestern	
1901/7/13	Jackson, Lansing & Saginaw (leased to MC), merger of Saginaw Bay & Northwestern	

MOORES BRANCH (MC-PN3) (BRANCH NOT LOCATED)

	MILEAGE	COUNTY	CROSSINGS, JUNCTIONS, ETC.
Moores Jct.	9.25	Arenac	J/MC-PN 9.25
(End)	?	"	

CONSTRUCTION/ABANDONMENT

DATE	ACT	END POINTS	MP	CHANGE	MAIN	SOURCE	NOTE
??		Line					24

OWNERSHIP

??	Saginaw Bay & Northwestern (B16)	
1883/2/15	Michigan Central, leased Saginaw Bay & Northwestern	
1901/7/13	Jackson, Lansing & Saginaw (leased to MC), merger of Saginaw Bay & Northwestern	

SPUR (MC-PN4)

	MILEAGE	COUNTY	CROSSINGS, JUNCTIONS, ETC.
Babcocks Wye	14.05	Arenac	J/MC-PN 14.05
Davidson	15.9	"	

CONSTRUCTION/ABANDONMENT

DATE	ACT	END POINTS	MP	CHANGE	MAIN	SOURCE	NOTE
1885 ca.	B16	Line	14.1–15.9	+1.8	1.8		29
1910 ca.	X	Line	15.9–14.1	–1.8	0		29

OWNERSHIP

1885	Saginaw Bay & Northwestern (B16), of segment	
1883/2/15	Michigan Central, leased Saginaw Bay & Northwestern	
1901/7/13	Jackson, Lansing & Saginaw (leased to MC), merger of Saginaw Bay & Northwestern	

LINE, MT. FORREST–TITTABAWASSEE RIVER (MC-P3)

	MILEAGE	COUNTY	CROSSINGS, JUNCTIONS, ETC.
Mount Forrest	8.0	Bay	J/MC-P 8.01
(Ttb. Riv.)	17.7	Gladwin	

CONSTRUCTION/ABANDONMENT

DATE	ACT	END POINTS	MP	CHANGE	MAIN	SOURCE	NOTE
1880/11/18	P1	Line	8.0–17.7	+9.7	9.7		29
1887	X	Line	8.0–17.7	–9.7	0		29

OWNERSHIP

1880	Saginaw Bay & Northwestern (B16)	
1883/2/15	Michigan Central, leased Saginaw Bay & Northwestern	

MCGRAWS BRANCH (MC-P4)

	MILEAGE	COUNTY	CROSSINGS, JUNCTIONS, ETC.
(Jct.)	0	Bay	J/MC-P 6.6
Hitchcock	2.4	"	
Town Line	2.8	"	
Cogswell	3.8	"	J/MC-P4A 3.8 (sec 26 T18N R3E)
Stantons	6.7	"	(sec14 T18N R3E)

CONSTRUCTION/ABANDONMENT

DATE	ACT	END POINTS	MP	CHANGE	MAIN	SOURCE	NOTE
1885 ca.	B16	Line	0–6.7	+6.7	6.7		29
1901 ca.	X	Line	0–6.7	–6.7	0		29

OWNERSHIP

1885	Saginaw Bay & Northwestern (B16), leased to Michigan Central
1901/7/13	Jackson, Lansing & Saginaw (leased to MC), merger of Saginaw Bay & Northwestern

ROGERS BRANCH (MC-P4A)

	MILEAGE	COUNTY	CROSSINGS, JUNCTIONS, ETC.
Cogswell	3.8	Bay	J/MC-P4 3.8
(End)	5.7	Arenac	(sec19 T18N R4E)

CONSTRUCTION/ABANDONMENT

DATE	ACT	END POINTS	MP	CHANGE	MAIN	SOURCE	NOTE
1882	B16	Line	3.8–5.7	+1.9	1.9		29
1901 ca.	X	Line	3.8–5.7	–1.9	0		29

OWNERSHIP

1882	Saginaw Bay & Northwestern (B16)
1883/2/15	Michigan Central leased Saginaw Bay & Northwestern
1901/7/13	Jackson, Lansing & Saginaw (leased to MC), merger of Saginaw Bay & Northwestern

ESTEY BRANCH (MC-P7)

	MILEAGE	COUNTY	CROSSINGS, JUNCTIONS, ETC.
(Jct.)	0	Gladwin	J/MC-P 11.10
Estey	3.61	"	
(End)	3.83	"	

CONSTRUCTION/ABANDONMENT

DATE	ACT	END POINTS	MP	CHANGE	MAIN	SOURCE	NOTE
1901 ca.	B16	Line	0–3.8	+3.8	3.8		29
1908 ca.	X	Line	0–3.8	–3.8	0		29

OWNERSHIP

1901	Saginaw Bay & Northwestern (B16), leased by Mich. Central
1901/7/13	Jackson, Lansing & Saginaw (leased to MC), merger of Saginaw Bay & Northwestern
1916/9/27	Michigan Central, merger of Jackson, Lansing & Saginaw
1930/2/1	New York Central leased Michigan Central

NOTE

There appear to have been other branches built by the Saginaw Bay & Northwestern between 1882 and 1901. The changes in mileage, other than documented above, are reported in the annual mileage section under line designation MC-PXX. Source 7 states that all branches, except those documented above, were abandoned by about 1901.

CANADA SOUTHERN RAILWAY (DETROIT RIVER TUNNEL CO.) (MC-Z)

	MILEAGE	COUNTY	CROSSINGS, JUNCTIONS, ETC.
	[Susp.Br.]		
(Jct.) ON	224.4		J/MC-U 224.4
(Windsor–new)	224.69		
(Connection)	224.8		C/MC-U 224.8
(E portal	225.42		
(ON/MI boundary)	226.31		
(W portal)	226.99		
(15th St.)	227.3		
(Detroit)	227.5		
20th St.	227.7		J/MC-E 1.61

CONSTRUCTION/ABANDONMENT

DATE	ACT	END POINTS	MP	CHANGE	MI MAIN	SOURCE	NOTE
1910/10/16	B30	Line	224.4–227.7	+3.3	1.4	7	
1989 ca.	S5	Line	224.4–227.7	−3.3	0		

OWNERSHIP

1910	Detroit River Tunnel Co. (B30), owned by Michigan Central
1930/2/1	New York Central, leased Michigan Central
1968/2/1	Penn Central, merger of New York Central (with lease of Michigan Central)
1976/4/1	Conrail, bought Penn Central

CANADA SOUTHERN RAILWAY (CANADA DIV. MAIN LINE) (MC-U)

	MILEAGE	COUNTY	CROSSINGS, JUNCTIONS, ETC.
Suspension Bridge NY	0.19		
(E end property line)	0		
(E end bridge)	0.02		
(NY/ON int'l boundary)	0.14		
(W end bridge)	0.33		
Niagara Falls ON	0.43		
(Jct.)	0.52		J/MC-UN 16.85
Victoria Park	1.65		
Falls View	2.73		
Montrose Jct.	3.03		J/MC-UN 14.34
Montrose	4.09		
CP 6	6.2		
CP 10	10.8		
(N wye switch)	13.68		
WX	13.70		X/CN, J/MC-UB 16.84
Welland	14.17		
(Jct.)	14.55		J/TH&B
Hewitt	19.30		
Forks Creek Pump House	20.00		
Perry	23.52		
Montague	26.08		f. Wellandsport
E & O Crossing	30.5		
Attercliffe	31.73		
(Jct.)	38.98		J/CN
(Crossing)	39.06		X/CN
Canfield Jct.	39.06		
Edward	43.86		

Cayuga	45.53	
(Bridge, Grand River)	46.27	
Lythmore	48.33	
Dufferin	51.39	
Hagersville	55.45	
(Crossing)	55.48	X/CN
Ingles Quarry Spur	55.78	
Airport	59.5	
Townsend	61.02	
Villa Nova	63.27	
Waterford	68.20	
(Jct.)	68.51	J/TH&B
Windham ON	74.77	
LaSalette	78.90	J/CN, f/ Port Dover Jct.
Hawtrey	80.13	
Cornell	85.21	
Tillsonburg	90.65	
(Pump House)	90.91	
(Bridge)	90.94	B/CN
Brownsville	96.48	
Springfield	101.91	
Aylmer	104.38	
Kingsmill	107.15	
Yarmouth	111.45	X/CN
Ball	114.23	J/CP
St. Thomas	115.10	
BX	115.23	J/L&PS
(Crossing)	115.39	X/L&PS
St. Clair Jct.	119.33	J/MC-US 4.23
Shedden	124.16	
Iona	128.10	
Dutton	134.03	
W. Lorne	140.57	f. Bismarck
Rodney	144.97	
Taylor	148.44	
(Pump House)	148.76	
Muirkirk	150.93	
Highgate	153.10	
Ridgetown	158.74	
Mull	164.61	f. Harwich
Fargo	169.61	
(Crossing)	169.63	X/PM
Charing Cross	171.99	
Buxton	178.28	
Fletcher	182.28	
Tilbury	189.22	
Comber	195.82	
(Jct.)	196.36	J/MC-UL 0.54
Ruscomb	200.81	
Woodslee	204.75	
Essex	210.29	J/MC-UA 0
Maidstone Cross	214.82	
Pelton	219.13	X/PM
Tower #4	221.71	
Howard Ave.	221.83	

Tower #3	223.75		
(Jct.)	224.4		J/MC-Z 224.4
Windsor (new)	224.69		
(Jct.)	224.8		J/MC-Z 224.8
Round House	224.90		
Windsor (old) ON	226.09		
(Ferry slip)	226.22		

CANADA SOUTHERN RAILWAY (NIAGARA BRIDGE) (MC-UN)

	MILEAGE	COUNTY	CROSSINGS, JUNCTIONS, ETC.
Niagara Jct. ON	2.10		J/MC-UB 2.10
Canadian Ship Yard	3.59		
Black Creek	6.83		
Chippawa	12.62		
Montrose Jct.	14.34		J/MC-U 3.03
(Jct.)	16.85		J/MC-U 0.52
Clifton	16.93		(old Niagara Falls sta. on this line)
(Crossing)	17.58		X/CN
(Crossing)	18.27		X/CN
Stamford	19.58		
St. David	21.59		
Queenston	23.36		
Larkin	24.18		
(Jct.)	27.42		J/Paradise Grove Spur, 1.09 miles
(Jct.)	28.48		J/Chautauqua Spur, 0.06 miles
Queen St.	29.07		
Niagara-on-the-Lake ON	29.61		

CANADA SOUTHERN RAILWAY (FORT ERIE LINE) (MC-UB)

	MILEAGE	COUNTY	CROSSINGS, JUNCTIONS, ETC.
Fort Erie ON	0		J/CN, f. Bridgeburg
Victoria	1.15		
Niagara Jct.	2.10		J/MC-UF 2.84, J/MC-UN 2.10
CP 2	2.8		
Stevensville	7.15		
Netherby	10.68		
Brookfield	12.65		
CP 13	13.4		
(S Wye switch)	16.82		
WX ON	16.84		J/MC-U 13.70, X/CN

CANADA SOUTHERN RAILWAY (OLD FORT ERIE BRIDGE) (MC-UF)

	MILEAGE	COUNTY	CROSSINGS, JUNCTIONS, ETC.
Fort Erie ON	0		
(Crossing)	1.09		X/CN
Race Track Spur	2.02		
(Crossing)	2.81		X/CN
Niagara Jct. ON	2.84		J/MC-UB 2.10

CANADA SOUTHERN RAILWAY (ST. CLAIR BRIDGE) (MC-US)

	MILEAGE	COUNTY	CROSSINGS, JUNCTIONS, ETC.
	[St.Thomas]		
St. Clair Jct. ON	4.23		J/MC-U 119.33
Air Line Crossing	5.40		X/CN
Southwold	9.34		

Muncey	13.54		
Melbourne	19.27		
(Crossing)	22.29		X/CN, f. Appin
(Crossing)	24.50		X/CP
Appin Rd.	25.75		
Walkers	29.89		
Alvinston	35.28		
Fairbanks Spur	38.75		
Inwood	40.99		
Weidman	42.30		
Glen Rae	43.80		
Holmesdale	44.98		
Oil Cty. Jct.	48.17		J/MC-USO 0.02
Oil Cty.	48.19		
Petrolia Jct.	50.17		J/MC-USP 0
Brigden	56.56		
Kimballs	59.81		
Courtright Jct.	65.82		X/PM
Courtright ON	66.38		
(End)	66.58		

CANADA SOUTHERN RAILWAY (OIL SPRINGS BR.) (MC-USO)

	MILEAGE	COUNTY	CROSSINGS, JUNCTIONS, ETC.
Oil Cty. Jct. ON	0.02		J/MC-US 48.19
Oil Springs	2.37		
Dawn	4.04		
Eddy ON	5.14		
(End)	5.31		

CANADA SOUTHERN RAILWAY (PETROLIA BR. (MC-USP)

	MILEAGE	COUNTY	CROSSINGS, JUNCTIONS, ETC.
Petrolia Jct. ON	0		J/MC-US 50.17
Corey	1.23		
Petrolia ON	4.85		
(End)	6.62		

CANADA SOUTHERN RY (AMHERSTBURG BR.) (MC-UA)

	MILEAGE	COUNTY	CROSSINGS, JUNCTIONS, ETC.
Essex ON	0		J/MC-U 210.29
Decews Spur	2.73		
Misners	3.44		
Edgars	4.78		
Lovetts Siding	6.38		
(Crossing)	7.23		J/PM
McGregor	7.92		
Reaume Spur	8.80		
Southwick	12.67		
(Crossing)	14.17		X/EssexTerm
Quarries	14.21		
Gordon	15.74		
Amherstburg ON	16.88		
(End)	16.94		

CANADA SOUTHERN RAILWAY (LEAMINGTON BRIDGE) (MC-UL)

	MILEAGE	COUNTY	CROSSINGS, JUNCTIONS, ETC.
	[Comber]		
(Jct.)	0.54		J/MC-U 196.36
Roslyn	3.31		
Ainslies Spur	5.16		
Staples	5.41		f. Elenwood
Oakland	7.09		
Blythswood	8.78		
Wigle	10.60		f. Lewiston
(Crossing)	13.43		
Leamington	13.78		
Sea Cliff Park	15.91		
(End)	16.06		

ACQUISITION/DISPOSITION RECORD

DATE	ACT	MC–	END POINTS	CHANGE	MI MAIN	NOTE
1838/2/3	B1	E,EO1	Det.–Ypsi.	+29.6		1
Spr.	B1	EO2	In Det.	(+0.7)	29.6	2
1839/10/17	B1	E,EO3	Ypsi.–A.A.	+7.5	37.1	
1841/6/30	B1	E,EO4	A.A.–Dexter	+10.8		
12/31	B1	E	Dexter–Jackson	+28.6	76.5	3
1844/3	X	EO2	In Detroit	(−0.7)		
6/25	B1	C	Jackson–Albion	+20.4		
8/12	B1	C,CO1	Albion–Marshall	+11.7	108.6	
1845/11/25	B1	C,CO1	Marshall–Battle Creek	+13.0	121.6	4
1846/2/2	B1	C	Battle Creek–Kal.	+23.0	144.6	
1848 ca.	X	EO3	West of Ypsi.	−2.9		5
	B2	E	West of Ypsi.	+3.2		
	X	EO4	West of A.A.	−8.6		6
	B2	E	West of A.A.	+7.4		
5/30	X	EO1	In Detroit	−1.9		
5/30	B2	E	Det. (3rd St.)–21st St.	+1.7		
6/28	B2	C,CO2	Kal.–Lawton	+16.4		
10/1	B2	C	Lawton–Niles	+31.3	191.2	
1849/4/23	B2	W,WO	Niles–New Buffalo	+26.7	217.9	7
1850/10/29	B2	W	New Buffalo–Michigan Cty. IN	+10.0		
				(MI miles +3.8)	221.7	
1852/5/1	B2	W	Mich. Cty.–Kensington IL	+43.1	221.7	8
1854	B3	WJ	E. Gary–Joliet IL	+44.8	221.7	
ca.1855	B2	W	In Chi. IL	+0.9	221.7	9
1858	B4	S	Owosso–Laingsburg	+11.8	233.5	10
1859	B4	S	Laingsburg–Bath	+7.1	240.6	11
1861/9/4	B4	S	Bath–N. Lans.	+7.1	247.7	12
1863/8/25	B4	S	N. Lans.–Lans.	+1.0	248.7	
1865 ca.	X	CO1	In Marshall	−1.1		13
ca.	B2	C	In Marshall	+1.0		
ca.	B2	YP	In Ypsi.	(+1.1)		
ca.	B2	YJ	In Jackson	(+1.3)		
/12	B5	G,S	Jackson–Mason	+24.6	273.2	
1866/6/25	B5	S	Mason–Lans.	+12.1	285.3	
1867/10/11	B5	S	Owosso–St. Charles	+21.8		
12/6	B5	S	St. Charles–Bay Cty.	+27.6	334.7	14
1868/7/4	B6	G	Rives Jct.–Eaton Rapids	+13.6		

8/15	B6	G	Eaton Rapids–Charlotte	+10.7	359.0	15
1869/1/26	B6	G	Charlotte–Nashville	+14.9		
2/22	B6	G	Nashville–Hastings Ft. Hse.	+11.6	385.5	
1870/1/1	B6	G	Hastings F. H.–Gr. Rpds.	+33.0		16
3/10	B7	H	Kal.–Kendall	+14.6		
7/4	B7	H	Kendall–Bloomingdale	+8.2		
Sum.	B8	A,AO	Jackson Jct.–Homer	+23.8		
Fall	B8	A	Homer–Three Rivers	+45.8	510.9	
1871/1/2	B7	H	Bloomingdale–S. Haven	+16.6		
1/31	B5	S,M	Bay Cty.–Kawkawlin	+5.3		
2	B8	A	Three Rivers–Niles	+33.9		
8/31	B5	M	Kawkawlin–Standish	+23.0		
12/31	B5	M	Standish–Wells	+12.1	601.8	
1872	B8	N	Niles–S. Bend IN (MI miles +5.5)	+11.4		17
10/31	B13	B	Bay Cty. Jct–Oxford	+41.0		
11/30	B13	B	Oxford–Lapeer	+17.2		
	B14	BL	Lapeer & Northern	+3.7		
12/31	B13	B	Lapeer–Otter Lk.	+13.2	682.4	
1873/3/31	B13	B	Otter Lk.–Vassar	+12.6		
5	B5	M	Wells–Otsego Lk.	+72.0		
7	B5	M	Otsego Lk.–Gaylord	+7.4		18
7/31	B13	B	Vassar–Bay Cty. E.S.	+22.7		
	B14	BL	Lapeer & No. extension	+0.5		
9/1	B11	T	Det.–Toledo OH (MI miles +46.8)	+55.1		
9/1	B11	YTW	In Toledo OH	(+1.1)		
9	B12	TG	Slocum Jct.–Grosse Ile	+3.1		
12/7	B10	DM	St. Clair Springs–Lenox	+14.0	861.5	
1874	B14	BL	Lapeer & Northern extension	+0.5	862.0	
1876	B14	BL	Lapeer & Northern extension	+3.0	865.0	
1878/7/22	B13	BC	Caro Jct.–Caro	+12.6	877.6	
1879/1/25	B13	BS	Denmark Jct.–Sag.	+15.5		
ca.	B13	BS	In Sag.	+0.4		19
	L1	YBS	S. Water St. Spur	(+2.9)		20
	L1	YBN	N. Water St. Spur	(+2.2)	893.5	21
1880/11/18	P1	P	Pinconning–Mt. Forrest	+8.0		22
11/18	P1	P2	Pinconning–Sag. Bay	+2.6		22
11/18	P1	PN	Mt. Forrest–Freeman	+4.1		22
11/18	B16	PS	Mt. Forrest–Campbell	+2.8		22,23
11/18	B16	PS2	Sullivan Br.	+2.1		22
11/18	P1	P3	Mt. Forrest–Ttb. Riv.	+9.7	922.8	22
1881	B16	P	Mt. Forrest–Rhodes	+3.1		
	B13	M	Bay Cty. E.S.–Bay Cty. W.S.	+0.7		25
12/18	B5	M	Gaylord–Mack. Cty.	+63.1	989.7	
1882	B16	P4A	Rogers Br.	+1.9		
ca.	B16	PN2	Freeman Br.	+2.0		
	X	PS2	Sullivan Br.	−2.1		
	B16	PXX	SB&NW changes	+12.5		26
	B5	M	In Mack. Cty.	+0.3		
12/12	L2	U	Suspension Bridge–Essex	+210.3		27
12/12	L2	UA	Essex–Amherstburg	+16.9		27
12	L2	U	Essex–Windsor	+15.9		27
12	L2	UF	Old Fort Erie Br.	+2.8		27
12	L2	UB	Fort Erie–Welland	+16.8		27
12	L2	UN	Niagara Br.	+26.4		27
12	L2	US	St. Clair Br.	+66.6	1004.3	27

1884	B16	PXX	SB&NW	+11.8		26
ca.	B5	M7	Hauptman Br.	+10.1		
ca.	B5	M7B	Norn Br.	+1.4	1027.6	
1885 ca.	B16	PN	Freeman–Raymonds	+18.4		
ca.	B16	P4	McGraws Br.	+6.7		
ca.	B16	PN4	Br. to Davidson	+1.8		
	X	PXX	SB&NW	−10.2		26
ca.	B15	YBS	S. Water St. Spur	(+0.6)		29
ca.	B15	YBN	N. Water St. Spur	(+0.3)		
ca.	B5	ME	Loranger–Edwards Lk.	+6.7		
ca.	B5	MS	Beaver Lk.–Sages Lk.	+8.0		
ca.	B5	MS1	Spur off Sages Lk. Br.	+1.2	1060.2	
1886	B16	PXX	SB&NW	+1.6		26
ca.	B5	M11	Frederic Br.	+4.5		
ca.	B5	M11A	Frederic Br. spur	+1.6		29
ca.	B5	M11B	Frederic Br. spur	+1.7		29
ca.	B5	M13	Vanderbilt Br.	+6.4	1076.0	29
1887	X	P3	Mt. Forrest–Ttb. Riv.	−9.7		
	B16	P	Rhodes–Gladwin	+16.7		
	B16	PXX	SB&NW	+14.0		26
ca.	B5	MB,MB2	Bagley Br.	+13.5	1110.5	
1888	X	BL	Lapeer & Northern line	−7.7		
	B17	YLT	Lans. Transit	(+0.8)		
	B16	PXX	SB&NW	+1.7	1104.5	26
1889	B13	YBL	Bay Cty. Belt Line	(+3.1)		
/1	B18	K	Battle Creek–Sturgis	+41.6		
/12	B28	L	BC&BC Jct.–Midland	+18.0		
	B16	PXX	SB&NW	+2.1		26
	L2	UL	Leamington Br.	+13.8	1166.2	27
1890/2/1	L3	K	Findley–Sturgis	−7.2		28
8/4	B19	J	St. Joseph–S. Bend IN (MI miles +25.3)	+29.6		
ca.	B5	M7	Hauptman Br. extension	+14.9		
ca.	B5	M7A	Jordan Br.	+2.9	1202.1	
1891	X	PXX	SB&NW	−2.1		26
	P2	YTB	Toledo Belt OH	(+3.5)		30
ca.	X	M13	Vanderbilt Br.	−4.7	1195.3	29
1892	B20	MT	Grayling–Lewiston	+27.4		
	X	PXX	SB&NW	−2.1		26
ca.	B11	YDE	Exposition Spur	(+1.2)		
ca.	B11	YDF	Exposition Spur Extension	(+0.6)		
ca.	B11	YDD	Delta Spur	(+1.0)		
	X	MS	Beaver Lk.–Sages Lk.	−8.0		
	X	MS1	Spur off Sages Lk. Br.	−1.2	1211.4	
1893	X	PXX	SB&NW	−5.0	1206.4	26
1895/10/5	B21	DZ	Dearborn Jct.–Fort St.	+4.8		
ca.	B15	YBL	Bay Cty. Belt Line	(+2.8)		
	B29	WB	In Buchanan	(+1.9)		
ca.	B20	MT6	Bear Lk. Br.	+5.5		
ca.	B20	MT7	Alexander Br.	+5.5	1222.2	
1896	B20	MT4	Mertz Branch	+5.4		
	B16	PXX	SB&NW	+2.9		26
ca.	B20	MT4A	Robinson Br.	+4.2		
	B5	MP	Trowbridge–Cornwells Mills	+9.2	1243.9	
1897	X	PXX	SB&NW	−0.4		26
ca.	B5	M3	Nunda Br.	+7.2	1250.7	

1899	P3	YM1	In Midland	(+3.0)		
	B16	PXX	SB&NW	+0.2	1250.9	26
1900 ca.	X	YBS	Part of S. Water St. Spur	(−0.8)		
ca.	B20	MT5	Davidson Br.	+11.8		
ca.	B5	MB	McGraw Br.	+1.3		29
ca.	B5	MB3	McGraw Br.	+6.2		
ca.	X	MB1	Part of Bagley Br.	−7.7		29
ca.	B5	MH	Haakwood Br.	+12.0		29
ca.	X	M3	Nunda Br.	−2.2		
ca.	B5	M4	Buell Br.	+3.7		29
ca.	B5	M4A	Spiegel Br.	+4.2		
ca.	B5	M7	Hauptman Br.	−25.0		29
ca.	X	M7A	Jordan Br.	−2.9		29
ca.	X	M7B	Norn Br.	−1.4		29
ca.	X	M11	part of Frederic Br.	−2.6		29
ca.	X	M11B	Frederic Br. spur	−1.7		29
ca.	X	PXX	SB&NW	−27.0	1219.6	26
1901	B22	BC	Caro–Owendale	+20.9		
	B27	JB	Ben. Hbr. Extension	+1.6		
ca.	B2	C	Kal.–Mattawan	+10.9		
ca.	X	CO2	Kal.–Mattawan	−10.1		31
ca.	B8	A	Concord–Homer	+4.3		32
ca.	X	AO	Concord–Homer	−3.8		33
ca.	X	P2	East of Pinconning	−1.4		
ca.	Y	P2	East of Pinconning (to Y2P)	(1.2)		
ca.	X	P4	McGraws Br.	−6.7		
ca.	X	P4A	Rogers Br.	−1.9		
ca.	B16	P7	Rhodes–Estey	+3.8	1236.0	29
1902 ca.	B23	YDM	Det. Manufacturers	(+1.3)		
ca.	B24	YBG	Hecla Belt Line	(+3.5)	1236.0	
1903 ca.	B2	W	East of Buchanan	+3.3		
ca.	X	WO	East of Buchanan	−3.0	1236.3	34
1904 ca.	B5	MT2	Clear Lk. Br.	+12.8		29
ca.	B5	MT2A	Chamberlain Br.	(+0.9)		29
ca.	B5	MT3	Tyler Br.	+3.7		
ca.	B5	MT3A	Tyler Br. spur	+1.2		
ca.	B5	MT5A	Donnelly Br.	+3.9		
ca.	B5	MT5B	Davidson Wye Br.	+6.4		
ca.	B5	MT5B1	Kevan Br.	+1.3		
ca.	B5	MT5B2	Martins Br.	(+0.5)		
ca.	B5	MT5B3	Barger Br.	+1.1		
ca.	B5	MT5B4	Big Rock Spur	(+0.5)		
ca.	B5	MT5B5	Francis Br.	+1.3		
ca.	X	MT6	Bear Lk. Br.	−5.5	1262.5	
1905 ca.	B8	N2	In S. Bend IN	+1.3		
	B27	N2	In S. Bend IN (MI miles = 0)	+1.9		
/6	B25	YLM	Lans. Manufacturers	(+5.2)	1262.5	
1906	B21	DZ	Jct. Yard Br.	+0.9	1263.4	
1907 ca.	X	M13	Vanderbilt Br.	−1.7		29
ca.	B5	MH	Haakwood Br.	+8.5		
ca.	B5	MH2	Newell Br.	+7.5		
ca.	B5	MP3	Richardson Br.	+6.7		
ca.	B5	MP3A	Page Br.	+6.2	1290.6	
1908 ca.	X	P7	Rhodes–Estey	−3.8	1286.8	29
1909	B26	YDB	Detroit Belt Line	(+4.4)	1286.8	

1910/10/16	B30	Z	Detroit River Tunnel Co. (MI=1.4)	+3.3		
ca.	X	PN	Raymond–Bentley	−17.8		
ca.	X	PN2	Freeman Br.	−2.0		
ca.	X	PN4	Babcocks Wye–Davidson	−1.8		
ca.	X	PS	Mt. Forrest–Campbell	−2.8		
ca.	B5	MB3	McGraw Br.	+4.8		
ca.	B5	MB3A	Ice Track	+1.0		
ca.	B5	MB3B	Jennings Br.	+8.5		
ca.	B5	MB3C	Sargeant Spur	+1.7		
ca.	B5	MB3D	McKinnons Spur	+1.0		
ca.	B5	MP3C	Marble Br.	+4.4		
ca.	B5	MP3C1	Farr Br.	+2.3		
ca.	B5	MT5C	McCormick Br.	+2.5		
ca.	X	MT7	Alexander Br.	−5.5		
ca.	B5	M2	Patterson Br.	+4.9		
ca.	B5	M5	Roscommon Gravel Pit Br.	+4.0		29
ca.	X	M11	Frederic Br.	−1.9		
ca.	X	M11A	Frederic Br. spur	−1.6		
ca.	B28	YM2	In Midland	(+0.6)	1289.9	
1911	Y	E	In Det. (to MC-Y1E)	(1.2)	1288.7	
1912 ca.	X	DD	Part of DD&D	−2.7		35
ca.	Y	DD	Part of DD&D (to MC-Y1DD)	(1.3)		
ca.	B21	DZ	Part of Jct. Yard Br.	+2.5		
ca.	X	MT2	Clear Lk. Jct.–Chamberlin	−12.8		
ca.	X	MT2A	Chamberlain Br.	(−0.9)		
ca.	X	MT3	Tyler Br.	−3.7		
ca.	X	MT3A	Tyler Br. spur	−1.2		
ca.	X	MT4A	Robinson Br.	−4.2		
ca.	B5	MB	Johannesburg Jct.–Johannesburg		+6.7	29
ca.	B5	MB4	Tyrus Br.	+4.4		
ca.	B5	MP3B	Black Riv. Br.	+5.6	1282.0	
1913 ca.	B5	MB3B1	Koul Br.	+1.7		
ca.	X	MH	Haakwood Br.	−5.7		
ca.	B5	MH6	Silver Lk. Br.	+4.0		
ca.	B5	MH6A	Bell Br.	+1.1	1283.1	
1914	B5	MR	Portage Lk. Jct.–Rasmus	+3.3		
ca.	X	M3	Nunda Br.	−5.0		
ca.	X	MB3A	Ice Track	−1.0		
ca.	B5	MH6B	Whitings Spur	+1.2		
ca.	B5	MH6C	Silver Lk. Br. spur	+1.5	1283.1	
1915 ca.	B2	YDC	Belt Line Extension	(+1.9)		29
ca.	B5	MB3B2	Jennings Br. spur	+1.2		
ca.	X	MH2	Newell Br.	−0.8	1283.5	
1916 ca.	B2	YF	Fort Custer Spur	(+1.7)		
ca.	X	MP	Pigeon River Br.	−0.9	1282.6	
1917 ca.	B5	MH2A	Brady Br.	+2.1		
ca.	B5	MH6	Silver Lk. Br.	+0.5	1285.2	
1918	X	MH6	Silver Lk. Br.	−4.5		
	X	MH6A	Bell Br.	−1.1		
	X	MH6B	Whitings Spur	−1.2		
	X	MH6C	Silver Lk. Br. spur	−1.5	1276.9	
1919	X	MB3	McGraw Br.	−1.0		
	X	MH	Haakwood Br.	−1.9		
6	X	MH2	Newell Br.	−3.6	1270.4	
1920	X	M2	Patterson Br.	−4.9		

ca.	B2	A2	Air Line Jct.–East End	+4.6		36
ca.	B2	N	In Niles	+0.3	1270.4	36
1921 ca.	X	MB3B1	Koul Br.	−1.7		
9	X	MP3C	Marble Br.	−2.3		
9	X	MP3C1	Farr Br.	−2.3	1264.1	
1923/1	X	MB3B2	Jennings Br. spur	−1.0		
1	X	MB4	Tyrus Br.	−1.0		
8	X	MB3	McGraw Br.	−3.2		
8	X	MB3D	McKinnons Spur	−1.0		
8	X	MB3C	Sargeant Spur	−1.4	1256.5	
1924	X	ME	Loranger–Edwards Lk.	−6.7		
7	X	MP3C	Marble Br.	−2.1		
	X	MB3C	Sargeant Spur	−0.3		
10	X	MB4	Tyrus Br.	−3.4	1244.0	
1925 ca.	B2	TV	Vienna Jct.–Hallett (MI miles +1.4)	+3.2		
ca.	X	MT5A	Donnelly Br.	−3.9		
ca.	X	MT5B	Davidson Wye Br.	−6.4		
ca.	X	MT5B1	Kevan Br.	−1.3		
ca.	X	MT5B2	Martins Br.	(−0.5)		
ca.	X	MT5B3	Barger Br.	−1.1		
ca.	X	MT5B4	Big Rock Spur	(−0.5)		
ca.	X	MT5B5	Francis Br.	−1.3		
ca.	X	MT5C	McCormick Br.	−2.5		
	X	M4	Buell Br.	−3.7		
	X	M4A	Spiegel Br.	−4.2		
12	X	MH2	Newell Br.	−1.5		
12	X	MH2A	Brady Br.	−2.1	1217.4	
1926	X	MB3B	Jennings Br.	−1.6		
8	X	MH2	Newell Br.	−1.6		
ca.	X	MP3B	Black River Br.	−2.5	1211.7	
1927/6/18	X	MP	Trowbridge–Needham	−8.3		
6/18	X	MP3	Richardson Br.	−6.7		
6/18	X	MP3A	Page Br.	−6.2		
6/18	X	MP3B	Black River Br.	−3.1	1187.4	
1928/7/21	X	MT5	At Lundeen	−0.8	1186.6	
1929	X	TG	Slocum Jct.–Grosse Ile	−3.1		43
	P4	YG	In Gr. Rpds.	(+2.7)		
7	X	MB3	McGraw Br.	−6.8		
7	X	MB3B	Jennings Br.	−6.9		
7	X	MB3B2	Jennings Br. spur	−0.2		
9/6	X	MT5	Davidson Br.	−10.7	1158.9	
1930 ca.	X	YBL	Part of Bay Cty. Belt Line	(−2.8)		29
ca.	X	MT4A	Mertz Br.	−5.4	1153.5	
1931	X	MB	Sallings–Johannesburg	−13.8	1139.7	
1932/9/23	X	DM	St. Clair Springs–Lenox	−14.0	1125.7	37
1933/7/1	X	PN	Bentley–Mt. Forrest	−4.7		
	Y	A	In Niles (to MC-Y1A)	(1.2)		
	X	A	Air Line Jct.–Niles	−5.2		
10/17	X	MT	Grayling–Lewiston	−26.9		38
10/17	Y	MT	In Grayling	(0.5)		
10/17	X	MT5	At Vienna Jct.	−0.3	1086.9	
1935	X	K	Battle Creek–Findley	−33.8		
	Y	K	In Battle Creek (to MC-Y1H)	(0.6)		
11/2	X	M5	Roscommon Gravel Pit Br.	−4.0		
	X	Y2P	In Pinconning	(−0.4)	1048.5	

DATE	ACT	MC–	END POINTS	CHANGE	MI MAIN	NOTE
1937/4/8	X	MH	Haakwood Br.	−12.9		
	X	Y2P	In Pinconning	(−0.2)	1035.6	
1940	X	A	OD–Haires	−4.0	1031.6	39
1942	X	BC	Owendale–Bach	−5.6		
/12/23	X	J	SS&S Jct IN–Baroda (MI miles −13.9)	−25.6	1012.7	40
1943	X	A2	Air Line Jct.–East End	−4.6		
	X	A	Three Rivers–Air Line Jct.	−26.7		
	Y	A	In Three Rivers (to MC-Y2A)	(0.8)	980.6	
1945 ca.	X	T	In Toledo OH	−1.0		
	Y	T	In Toledo OH	(6.4)		
	X	Y2P	In Pinconning	(−0.2)	980.6	
1948/7/19	X	MT	In Grayling	(−0.5)	980.6	
1950 ca.	X	YBS	Part of S. Water St. Spur	(−0.6)	980.6	29
1953	X	Y2P	In Pinconning	(−0.2)	980.6	
1955	P5	MR	Grayling–Portage Lk. Jct.	+2.3	982.9	
1958	X	TV	Vienna Jct.–Hallett OH (MI miles −1.4)	−3.2		
	Y	A	East of Three Rivers (MC-Y2A)	(1.3)		41
	X	J	Baroda–St. Joseph Jct.	−10.0	970.1	
1960 ca.	X	YBS	Part of S. Water St. Spur	(−0.5)	970.1	29
1961	X	T	In Toledo OH	−1.8	970.1	
1962	X	B	Munger–Water St. Jct.	−5.0		
	Y	B	In Bay Cty. (to MC-Y1B)	(2.8)		
	X	P	Pinconning–Gladwin	−27.2		
	Y	P	In Pinconning (to MC-Y1P)	(0.6)	934.5	
1963 ca.	X	Y2P	In Pinconning	(−0.2)	934.5	29

On 1 February 1968 this company was conveyed to Penn Central.

DATE	ACT	MC–	END POINTS	CHANGE	MI MAIN	NOTE
1968 ca.	X	Y2A	In Three Rivers	(−0.7)	934.5	
1970 ca.	X	YG	In Gr. Rpds.	(−2.7)	934.5	
1972	X	Y1E	In Detroit	(−0.3)	934.5	
1973/3/1	X	J	In St. Joseph	−1.9		44
3/1	X	JB	Ben. Hbr. Extension	−1.6		
7/1	X	BC	Bach–Colling	−5.9		
9/1	X	H	Kal.–S. Haven	−37.7		
9/1	Y	H	In Kal. (to MC-Y1H)	(1.7)	885.7	
1974 ca.	X	YBH	Hecla Belt Line	(−3.5)	885.7	
1975 ca.	X	N	In S. Bend IN	−2.1	885.7	

On 1 April 1976 part of Penn Central was conveyed to Conrail and part retained by Penn Central. The lines were:

LINE DESIG.	END POINTS	MP	MI MAIN	SOURCE	NOTE
CNR-[MC-Z]	Det. River Tunnel	226.3–227.7	1.4		
CNR-[MC-E]	Det.–Jackson	1.2–75.4	74.2		
CNR-[MC-Y1E]	In Det.	0.3–1.2	(0.9)		
CNR-[MC-YP]	Ypsi. Belt	Line	(1.1)		
CNR-[MC-YJ]	Jackson Belt	Line	(1.3)		
CNR-[MC-YDE]	Exposition Spur	Line	(1.2)		
CNR-[MC-YDF]	Exp. Spur extension	Line	(0.6)		
CNR-[MC-YDD]	Delta Spur	Line	(1.0)		
CNR-[MC-YDB]	Det. Belt Line	Line	(4.4)		
CNR-[MC-YDC]	Det. Belt Extension	Line	(1.9)		
CNR-[MC-YDM]	Det. Manufacturers	Line	(1.3)		
CNR-[MC-DZ]	Jct. Yard Br.	Line	4.2		

CNR-[MC-Y1DD]	Part of Jct. Yd. Br.	2.0–3.3	(1.3)
CNR-[MC-T]	W. Det.–Toledo	2.7–49.5	46.8
CNR-[MC-B]	Bay Cty. Jct.–Rays Pit	2.2–28.2	26.0
PC-[MC-B]	Rays Pit–Munger	28.2–101.1	72.9
PC-[MC-Y1B]	Water St Jct.–Bay Cty. ES	106.1–108.9	(2.8)
PC-[MC-YBL]	Bay Cty. Belt Line	Line	(3.1)
PC-[MC-YBS]	S. Water St. Spur	Line	(1.6)
PC-[MC-YBN]	N. Water St. Spur	Line	(2.5)
PC-[MC-BC]	Caro Jct.–Bach	0.4–22.4	22.0
PC-[MC-BS]	Denmark Jct.–Sag.	4.8–20.7	15.9
CNR-[MC-A]	Jackson Jct.–OD	0–0.8	0.8
CNR-[MC-A]	Haires–Three Rivers	4.8–68.8	64.0
CNR-[MC-Y1A]	In Niles	102.8–104.0	(1.2)
CNR-[MC-Y2A]	In Three Rivers	69.5–70.9	(1.4)
CNR-[MC-N]	Niles–S. Bend IN	0–5.8	5.8
CNR-[MC-C]	Jackson–Kal.	75.4–145.0	69.6
PC-[MC-C]	Kal.–Niles	145.0–191.9	46.9
CNR-[MC-YF]	Fort Custer Spur	Line	(1.7)
CNR-[MC-Y1K]	In Battle Creek	0.8–1.3	(0.5)
CNR-[MC-Y1H]	In Kal.	0.2–1.9	(1.7)
PC-[MC-W]	Niles–Chi. IL	191.9–222.7	30.8
PC-[MC-WB]	Lee & Porter Track	Line	(1.9)
CNR-[MC-G]	Rives Jct.–Eaton Rapids	10.6–24.8	14.2
PC-[MC-G]	Eaton Rapids–Bowen	24.8–88.0	63.2
CNR-[MC-G]	Bowen–Gr. Rpds.	88.0–94.4	6.4
CNR-[MC-S]	Jackson–N. Lans.	0.2–39.7	39.5
PC-[MC-S]	N. Lans.–Bay Cty. WS	39.7–114.6	74.9
CNR-[MC-YLT]	Lans. Transit	Line	(0.8)
CNR-[MC-YLM]	Lans. Manufacturers	Line	(5.2)
PC-[MC-L]	BC&BC Jct.–Midland	1.7–19.7	18.0
PC-[MC-YM1]	Dow Chemical Spur	Line	(3.0)
PC-[MC-YM2]	Midland Yard	Line	(0.6)
PC-[MC-M]	Bay Cty. ES–Mack. Cty.	0–182.6	182.6
PC-[MC-MR]	Grayling–Rasmus	0–5.6	5.6
PC-[MC-Y1P]	In Pinconning	0–0.6	(0.6)
1976/4/1	CNR=352.9 PC=532.8 MC=885.7		

DATE	ACT	LINE	END POINTS	MP	MAIN	SOURCE NOTE
1976	X	[MC-B]	Rays Pit–Oxford	28.2–42.2	–14.0	
	S2	[MC-B]	At Oxford	42.2–45.0	[2.8]to GTW-[MC-Y2B]	
	X	[MC-B]	Oxford–Lapeer	45.0–58.4	–13.4	
	S2	[MC-B]	At Lapeer	58.4–60.3	[1.9]to GTW-[MC-Y3B]	
	X	[MC-B]	Lapeer–Millington	60.3–79.3	–19.0	
	S2	[MC-Y1B]	Water St Jct–Bay Cty. ES	106.1–108.9	[(2.8)] to GTW-[MC-Y1B]	
	S2	[MC-BS]	Richville–Sag.	6.0–20.7	[14.7]to GTW-[MC-BS]	
	S2	[MC-YBL]	Bay Cty. Belt Line	Line	[(3.1)] to GTW-[MC-YBL]	
	S2	[MC-YBS]	S. Water St. Spur	Line	[(1.6)] to GTW-[MC-YBS]	
	S2	[MC-YBN]	N. Water St. Spur	Line	[(2.5)] to GTW-[MC-YBN]	
	S3	[MC-C]	Kal.–Niles	145.0–191.9	[46.9]to AMK-[MC-C]	
	S3	[MC-W]	Niles–Porter IN	191.9–222.7	[30.8]to AMK-[MC-W]	
	X	[MC-WB]	Lee & Porter Track	Line	(–1.9)	
	X	[MC-G]	Eaton Rapids–Charlotte	24.8–32.0	–7.2	
	S2	[MC-G]	At Charlotte	32.0–35.4	[3.4]to GTW-[MC-Y2G]	
	X	[MC-G]	Charlotte–Vermontville	35.4–46.1	–10.7	
	Y	CNR-[MC-G]	Bowen–Gr. Rpds.	88.0–94.4	[(6.4)] to CNR-[MC-Y1G]	

	Y	CNR-[MC-S]	At N. Lans.	37.8–39.7		[(1.9)] to CNR-[MC-Y3S]
	X	[MC-S]	N. Lans.–Owosso	39.7–61.1	–21.4	
	S2	[MC-S]	At Owosso	61.1–64.2		[3.1]to GTW-[MC-Y1S]
	X	[MC-S]	At Swan Creek	91.3–91.8	–0.5	
	S2	[MC-S]	Swan Creek–Sag.	91.8–101.2		[9.4]to GTW-[MC-Y2S]
	S2	[MC-S]	Sag.–Bay Cty. WS	101.2–114.6		[13.4]to GTW-[MC-S]
	S2	[MC-L]	BC&BC Jct.–Midland	1.7–19.7		[18.0]to GTW-[MC-L]
	S2	[MC-YM1]	Dow Chemical Spur	Line		[(3.0)] to GTW-[MC-YM1]
	S2	[MC-YM2]	Midland Yard	Line		[(0.6)] to GTW-[MC-YM2]
	S2	[MC-M]	Bay Cty. ES–Bay Cty. WS	0–0.7		[0.7] to GTW-[MC-Y2M]
	S2	[MC-M]	Bay Cty. WS–Kawkawlin	0.7–5.0		[4.3]to GTW-[MC-M]
	S4	[MC-M]	Kawkawlin–Linwood	5.0–10.8		[5.8]to D&M-[MC-M1]
	S4	[MC-M]	Salling–Mack. Cty.	115.8–182.6		[66.8]to D&M-[MC-M2]
1976 TOTAL		AMK=77.7 CNR=344.6 D&M=72.6 GTW=50.4 PC=224.6 MC=769.9				
1980/9	S1	[MC-M]	Linwood–Sallings	10–8.115.8	[105.0]	
9	S1	[MC-Y1P]	In Pinconning	0–0.6	[(0.6)]	
9	X	[MC-MR]	Grayling–Rasmus	0–5.6	–5.6	49
ca.	X	GTW-[MC-Y3B]	In Lapeer	58.4–58.9	[(–0.5)]	
ca.	X	GTW-[MC-Y2G]	In Charlotte	35.0–35.4	[(–0.4)]	
1980 TOTAL		AMK=77.7 CNR=344.6 D&M=72.6 GTW=50. MICH=105.0 PC=114.0 MC=764.3				
1981/5/1	S6	GTW-[MC-BS]	Richville–Harger	6.0–15.5		[9.5]to TSBY-[MC-BS]
5/1	Y	GTW-[MC-BS]	Harger–MX	15.5–20.2		(4.7)to GTW-[MC-Y4S]
11/18	X	CNR-[MC-C]	In Battle Creek	119.8–121.4	[–1.6]	
1982 TOTAL		AMK=77.7 CNR=343.0 D&M=72.6 GTW=36.2 MICH=105.0 PC=114.0 TSBY=9.5 MC=758.0				
1982/4/1	X	[MC-G]	Vermontville–Caledonia	46.1–79.0	–32.9	
8/15	X	CNR-[MC-G]	Rives Jct–Eaton Rapids	10.6–24.8	[–14.2]	
	X	CNR-[MC-YDE]	Exposition Spur	Line	[(–1.2)]	
	X	CNR-[MC-YDF]	Exp. Spur Extension	Line	[(–0.6)]	
	X	CNR-[MC-YDB]	Detroit Belt Line	2.8–4.4	[(–1.6)]	
	X	CNR-[MC-Y1DD]	Jct. Yard Branch	2.5–3.3	[(–0.8)]	
	X	CNR-[MC-A]	Haires–Three Rivers	4.8–68.8	[–64.0]	
	Y	CNR-[MC-A]	Jackson Jct.–OD	0–0.8		[(0.8)] to CNR-[MC-Y3A]
1982 TOTAL		AMK=77.7 CNR=264.0 D&M=72.6 GTW=36.2 MICH=105.0 PC=81.1 TSBY=9.5 MC=646.1				
1983	X	[MC-G]	Caledonia–Bowen	79.0–88.0	–9.0	
	X	GTW-[MC-Y2S]	At Swan Creek	91.8–92.5	[(–0.7)]	
1983 TOTAL		AMK=77.7 CNR=264.0 D&M=72.6 GTW=36.2 MICH=105.0 PC=72.1 TSBY=9.5 MC=637.1				
1984/2/15	S1	[MC-B]	Millington–Munger	79.3–101.1	[21.8]	46
2/15	S1	[MC-BC]	Caro Jct.–Colling	0.4–22.4	[22.0]	
2/15	S1	[MC-BS]	At Denmark Jct.	4.8–6.0	[1.2]	
2/15	S1	[MC-S]	Owosso–Swan Creek	64.2–91.3	[27.1]	
	X	GTW-[MC-L]	At Midland	18.9–19.7	[–0.8]	
	X	CNR-[MC-Y1H]	In Kal.	0.2–1.9	[(–1.7)]	
	X	CNR-[MC-Y1K]	In Battle Creek	0.7–1.3	[(–0.6)]	
1984 TOTAL		AMK=77.7 CNR=264.0 D&M=72.6 GTW=35.4 MICH=177.1 PC=0 TSBY=9.5 MC=636.3				
1985/5/1	S5	CNR-[MC-Z]	Det. River Tunnel	226.3–227.7	[–1.4]	
ca.	X	CNR-[YJ]	Jackson Belt	0–1.3	[(–1.3)]	
	X	CNR-[YDM]	Det. Manufacturers	Line	[(–1.3)]	
1985 TOTAL		AMK=77.7 CNR=262.6 D&M=72.6 GTW=35.4 MICH=177.1 PC=0 TSBY=9.5 MC=634.9				

1986	X	GTW-[MC-Y2B] At Oxford	42.2–45.0	[(–2.8)]
1986 TOTAL		AMK=77.7 CNR=262.6 D&M=72.6 GTW=35.4 MICH=177.1 PC=0 TSBY=9.5 MC=634.9		

1987/9/4	S7	GTW-[MC-Y1S] In Owosso	61.1–64.2	(3.1)
9/4	S7	GTW-[MC-Y2S] Swan Creek–S.B.Jct.	92.5–101.2	(8.7)
9/4	S7	GTW-[MC-S] S.B.Jct–Bay Cty. WS	101.2–114.6	13.4
9/4	S7	GTW-[MC-Y1M] Bay Cty. ES–Bay Cty. WS	0–0.7	(0.7)
9/4	S7	GTW-[MC-M] Bay Cty. WS–Kawkawlin	0.7–5.0	4.3
9/4	S7	GTW-[MC-L] BC&BC Jct.–Midland	1.7–18.9	17.2
9/4	S7	GTW-[MC-YM1] In Midland	0–3.0	(3.0)
9/4	S7	GTW-[MC-YM2] In Midland	0–0.6	(0.6)
9/4	S7	GTW-[MC-YBN] Woodside–end	0.4–2.9	(2.5)
9/4	S7	GTW-[MC-Y3B] Bay Cty. ES–Water St. J.	106.1–108.9	(2.8)
9/4	S7	GTW-[MC-YBL] WaterSt.J.–26th St.	3.0–6.4	(3.1)
9/4	S7	GTW-[MC-YBS] S. Water St.	1.1–2.7	(1.6)
9/4	S7	GTW-[MC-BS] S.B.Jct.–MX	20.7–20.2	0.5
9/4	S7	GTW-[MC-Y4B] MX–Harger	20.2–15.5	(4.7)
1987 TOTAL		AMK=77.7 CMGN=35.4 CNR=262.6 D&M=72.6 GTW=0MICH=177.1 TSBY=9.5 MC=634.9		

1989/9	X	D&M-[MC-M] Cheboygan–Mack. Cty	168.0–182.6	[–14.6]
1989 TOTAL		AMK=77.7 CMGN=35.4 CNR=262.6 D&M=58.0 MICH=177.1 TSBY=9.5 MC=620.3		

1991	S10	TSBY-[MC-BS] Richville–Harger	6.0–15.5	[9.5]
1991 TOTAL		AMK=77.7 CMGN=35.4 CNR=262.6 D&M=58.0 H&E=9.5 MICH=177.1 TSBY=0 MC=620.3		

1993	X	D&M-[MC-M] Gaylord–Cheboygan	120.5–168.0	[–47.5]
	X	CNR-[MC-N] Niles–St Marys IN	0.3–5.8	[–5.5]
	Y	CNR-[MC-N] In Niles (to MC-Y1N)	0–0.3	[(0.3)]
1993 TOTAL		AMK=77.7 CMGN=35.4 CNR=256.8 D&M=10.5 H&E=9.5 MICH=177.1 MC=567.0		

1995/7	S3	CNR-[MC-C] In Kal.	143.2–145.0	[1.8]
1995 TOTAL		AMK=79.5 CMGN=35.4 CNR=255.0 D&M=10.5 H&E=9.5 MICH=177.1 MC=567.0		

1996	L4	CNR-[MC-S] Lans.–N. Lans.	36.9–37.8	[–0.9]
1996 TOTAL		AMK=79.5 CMGN=35.4 CNR=254.1 CSX=0.9 D&M=10.5 H&E=9.5 MICH=177.1 MC=555.0		

1999/1	S8	GTW-[MC-Y2G] In Charlotte	32.0–35.0	[(3.0)]
6	S9	GTW-[MC-Y3B] In Lapeer	58.9–60.3	[(1.4)]
1999 TOTAL		AMK=79.5 CMGN=35.4 CNR=254.1 CSX=0.9 D&M=10.5 H&E=9.5 MICH=177.1 MC=567.0		

On 1 June 1999 part of Conrail was conveyed to Norfolk Southern and part retained by Conrail. The lines conveyed were:

LINE DES.	END POINTS	MP	MI MAIN
CNR-[MC-E]	Det.–Town Line	1.2–7.4	6.2
NS-[MC-E]	Town Line–Jackson	7.4–75.4	68.0
CNR-[MC-Y1E]	In Det.	0.3–1.2	(0.9)
CNR-[MC-YDD]	Delta Spur	Line	(1.0)
CNR-[MC-YDB]	Det. Belt Line	Line	(2.8)
CNR-[MC-YDC]	Belt Line Extension	Line	(1.9)
CNR-[MC-YDM]	Det. Manufacturers	Line	(1.3)
CNR-[MC-DZ]	Jct. Yard Branch	Line	4.2
CNR-[MC-Y1DD]	Part of Jct. Yard Br.	Line	(0.5)
NS-[MC-YP]	Ypsi. Belt	Line	(1.1)
CNR-[MC-T]	W. Det.–MP 20	2.7–20.0	17.3

NS-[MC-T]	MP 20–Toledo OH	20.0–49.5	29.5
CNR-[MC-B]	Bay Cty. Jct.–Rays Pit	2.2–28.2	26.0
NS-[MC-Y1A]	In Niles	102.8–104.0	(1.2)
NS-[MC-Y2A]	In Three Rivers	70.1–70.9	(0.8)
NS-[MC-Y3A]	In Jackson	0–0.8	(0.8)
NS-[MC-Y1N]	In Niles	0–0.3	(0.3)
NS-[MC-C]	Jackson–Baron	75.4–119.8	44.4
NS-[MC-C]	Gord–Kal.	121.4–143.2	21.8
NS-[MC-YF]	Fort Custer Spur	Line	(1.7)
NS-[MC-Y1G]	Bowen–Gr. Rpds.	88.0–94.4	(6.4)
NS-[MC-YLT]	Lans. Transit	Line	(0.8)
NS-[MC-YLM]	Lans. Manufacturers	Line	(5.2)
NS-[MC-S]	Jackson–N. Lans.	0.2–36.9	36.7
NS-[MC-Y1S]	In N. Lans.	37.8–39.7	(1.9)
TOTAL	CNR=53.7 NS=200.4 TOTAL=254.1		
1999 TOTAL	AMK=79.5 CMGN=35.4 CNR=53.7 CSX=0.9 D&M=10.5 H&E=9.5 MICH=177.1 NS=200.4		
	MC=567.0		

Act Column Key

A	Adjust mileage
B1	Built by State of Michigan
B2	Built by Michigan Central
B3	Built by Joliet & Northern Indiana
B4	Built by Amboy, Lansing & Traverse Bay
B5	Built by Jackson, Lansing & Saginaw
B6	Built by Grand River Valley
B7	Built by Kalamazoo & South Haven
B8	Built by Michigan Air Line
B9	Built by Canada Southern Railway
B10	Built by Michigan, Midland & Canada
B11	Built by Toledo, Canada Southern & Toledo
B12	Built by Canada Southern Bridge Co.
B13	Built by Detroit & Bay City
B14	Built by Lapeer & Northern
B15	Built by Bay City Belt Line
B16	Built by Saginaw Bay & Northwestern
B17	Built by Lansing Transit
B18	Built by St. Louis, Sturgis & Battle Creek
B19	Built by Indiana & Lake Michigan
B20	Built by Grayling, Twin Lakes & Northeastern
B21	Built by Detroit, Delray & Dearborn
B22	Built by Caro & Lake Huron
B23	Built by Detroit Manufacturers
B24	Built by Hecla Belt Line
B25	Built by Lansing Manufacturers
B26	Built by Detroit Belt Line
B27	Built by Indiana, Illinois & Iowa
B28	Built by Bay City & Battle Creek
B29	Built by Buchanan & St. Joseph River
B30	Built by Detroit River Tunnel Co.
L1	Leased from Bay City St. Railway
L2	Operating agreement, later leased, from Canada Southern Railway
L3	Leased to Lake Shore & Michigan Southern
L4	Leased to CSX Transportation
P1	Purchased from Pinconning Railroad

P2   Purchased from Toledo & Michigan Belt Railway
P3   Purchased from Midland & Hubbard
P4   Purchased from Michigan Railway
P5   Purchased from Manistee & North Eastern
S1   Sold to State of Michigan
S2   Sold to Grand Trunk Western
S3   Sold to Amtrak
S4   Sold to Detroit & Mackinac
S5   Sold to Canadian National–Canadian Pacific joint ownership
S6   Sold to Tuscola & Saginaw Bay
S7   Sold by Grand Trunk Western to Central Michigan
S8   Sold by Grand Trunk Western to Charlotte Southern
S9   Sold by Grand Trunk Western to Lapeer Industrial
S10 Sold by Tuscola & Saginaw Bay to Huron & Eastern
T   Transfer between lines, see Note
X   Abandonment
Y   Converted main track to yard/industrial track

Sources

1. Durant, *History of Kalamazoo County.*
2. Ensign, *Allegan and Barry Counties.*
3. Farmer, *Detroit and Wayne County.*
4. ICC, *Finance Dockets.*
5. Michigan Commissioner of Railroads, *Annual Report,* 1873.
6. MDOT records.
7. Michigan Railroad Commission, *Aids, Gifts, Grants.*
8. Michigan Central Railroad records.

Notes

1. This line extended from the southeast corner of Michigan and Griswold, out Michigan Avenue, and connected with the present line in the vicinity of 21st St. Source 7 says the line was put in service on 5 February. Source 3 states that the road was in operation to Dearborn "as early as January, 1838."
2. This was an industrial spur that extended from the station on Michigan Avenue, down Woodward Avenue to Atwater Street, and for 1000 feet in each direction on Atwater.
3. The original Jackson station was on the south side of the right of way approximately 0.1 mile west of East Ave., near or on the site of the former freight house. The Board of Internal Improvement Annual Report for 1842 implies that the line was in place at that date but was not finished for regular operations until early 1842.
4. The original Battle Creek station was on the south side of the right of way just east of Monroe Street, near the site of the former freight house.
5. This segment was located entirely south of the Huron River and was replaced by the present main line MC-E 30.0 to 33.2.
6. This segment was located entirely south of the Huron River and was replaced by the present main line MC-E 38.0 to 45.4.
7. This line may have extended somewhat further to allow access to steamship docks. These were operated by the MC until the completion of the line into Chicago in 1852.
8. Trackage rights on the Illinois Central were used from Kensington into Chicago.
9. This segment was to the MC South Water Street station.
10. The north end of this segment appears to have been just north of West Main Street, near the site of the former freight house. Source 7 gives the completion date as November 1860.
11. Source 7 gives the completion date as 24 December 1860.
12. Source 7 gives the completion date as 19 November 1862.
13. This segment was located north of the present main line and was replaced by the present main line MC-C 106.9 to 107.9.

14. The end of the line was at a place named Wenonah and appears to have been in the vicinity of West. Main St. The site is not to be confused with the later Wenona Yards.

15. Source 7 gives the completion date as Autumn 1868.

16. The original station was at Bartlett St.

17. The station was at Niles and Washington Avenues.

18. There is some evidence that the line extended about 4 miles north of Gaylord.

19. There is some confusion in Source 5 as to the construction of the segment between East Saginaw and Saginaw Bay Junction. The annual report for the D&BC states the section was owned by the Michigan Central, yet all of the expense of construction was charged to the D&BC. The D&BC, however, also stated that it owned the entire mileage. It may be that the segment between Denmark Junction and the East Saginaw freight house (on an 0.4 mile spur north of MP 20.07) was completed in 1878, and the extension to Saginaw Bay Junction in 1879. The entire segment is considered herein as owned by the Detroit & Bay City and opened in 1879.

20. Some evidence exists that this segment was built as early as 1865 and operated with horses as a street railway. The date shown here is the date of the lease.

21. Some evidence exists that this segment was built as early as 1872 and operated with horses as a street railway. The date shown here is the date of the lease.

22. For the construction record prior to 1880, see the entry for Glencoe, Pinconning & Lake Shore. The date shown here is the date of acquisition by the Saginaw Bay & Northwestern.

23. The records of the South Branch are confusing and such as exist are incomplete. The record does not disclose if this South Branch was built before the transfer to the Saginaw Bay & Northwestern or after; it is assumed here to have completed after.

24. The date of construction and/or abandonment could not be determined and, therefore, this line is not included in the mileage shown in the Acquisition/Disposition Record.

25. The date of this construction is not given explicitly by Sources 5 and 7, but it is inferred from the company reports in Source 5.

26. The construction/abandonment record of the branches of the SB&NW is quite incomplete. After 1883 the company made no itemization of its branches to the Michigan Railroad Commissioner. It is assumed here that the company's total mileage is correct as reported to the Commissioner and annual adjustments that can not be identified specifically are reported as net changes under line MC-PXX.

27. Operating control of this segment was obtained on the date shown, but the construction was done at an earlier date.

28. This segment was leased to the Lake Shore & Michigan Southern.

29. This date has not been determined accurately, but the work appears to have been done at about this time.

30. This segment was acquired on the date shown, but was constructed at an earlier date.

31. This segment was located through Oshtemo and was replaced by the present Main Line MC-C MP 145.5 to MP 156.4. It was subsequently sold to the Kalamazoo, Lake Shore & Chicago in 1907, which see.

32. The mile posts on line MC-A west of Homer are confused by three events. First, the new segment between MP 17.0 and MP 21.3 was constructed to reduce the ruling grade west from Jackson. The relocated line was 0.54 miles longer than the original route. The west end of the original line was 20.8 miles west of Jackson Jct. and the same location via the new line was 21.3 miles. Second, the location of the Concord depot was changed from MP 14.54 to MP 14.72 about 1905. Third, the Homer depot was moved approximately 0.16 miles east from its original site to the Lansing Branch crossing. Company sources after 1901 vary between using the original mileage, the revised mileage via the new line, and a combination of the two. The mileages shown herein, from Homer west, are via the new line.

33. This segment was replaced by line MC-A 17.0 to 21.3.

34. This segment was replaced by line MC-W 194.9 to 198.2.

35. As part of this abandonment 0.8 miles of line MC-DD has been reassigned to line MC-DZ.

36. This work was done as part of the construction of the Niles yard.

37. About one mile of this line appears to have been sold to the Port Huron & Detroit to reach local industry in St. Clair.

38. A short segment in Grayling was retained as industrial track.

39. This track had been used jointly with the Lake Shore & Michigan Southern as one side of a double-track line between OD and Haires. The track appears to have been retained as a storage track for a period of time after its official abandonment.

40. The line between SS&S Junction IN and Galien had not been used for a number of years before its official abandonment.

41. This change was made as a result of the reconstruction of MC-A as part of the Jackson–Elkhart route.

42. This segment is a transfer from line MC-MT2 to line MC-MB incidental to the abandonment of line MC-MT2.

43. Source 8 states 2.5 miles abandoned at this time; source 4 authorized 2.3 miles. The date of abandonment of the segment east to Stony Island could not be found.

44. The easterly 0.2 miles of this segment may have been abandoned in 1931.

45. Source 4 states the last passenger service was run 28 June 1925, and the last freight service in August 1929.

46. This property was operated by Conrail beginning 1 April 1976, under State of Michigan contract, and by Tuscola & Saginaw Bay beginning 1 October 1977, until conveyed to the state.

47. This property was operated by Conrail beginning 1 April 1976, under State of Michigan contract, and beginning 15 July 1979, by Kent–Barry–Eaton Connecting, until abandonment.

48. This property was operated by Detroit & Mackinac beginning 1 April 1976, under State of Michigan contract.

49. The disposition of this line could not be determined accurately. Apparently it did not pass to the State of Michigan with the sale of line MC-M, nor did it pass to Detroit & Mackinac. It is assumed to have been abandoned.

Michigan Interstate

Michigan Interstate conducted its operations under the name "Ann Arbor Railroad System."

Michigan Interstate operated the following lines under contract with the State of Michigan which had acquired ownership of the lines or had contractual arrangements with Ann Arbor or Penn Central. See page for Michigan, State of.

For arrangement of stations, construction record, and prior ownerships, see Ann Arbor lines, AA-A, AA-B, AA-C, AA-F, and AA-G, and Michigan Central line MC-S.

ACQUISITION/DISPOSITION RECORD

DATE	ACT	MIST–	END POINTS	MP	CHANGE	MI MAIN	SOURCE	NOTE
1977/10/1	C	[AA-A]	Toledo OH–Pitt	5.7–93.9	+88.2			1,2
10/1	C	[AA-B]	Ashley–Cadillac	128.3–227.1	+98.8			1
10/1	C	[AA-C]	Cadillac–Frankfort	227.1–292.4	+65.3			
10/1	C	[AA-F]	Line to Boat Landing	290.3–291.8	+1.5			
10/1	C	[AA-G]	Pittsfield–Saline	0–6.4	+6.4			
10/1	C	[MC-S]	Owosso–Swan Creek	64.2–91.3	+27.1	287.3		1
1982/10/1	T	[AA-A]	A.A.–Pitt	93.9–47.5	–46.4			3,6
10/1	T	[AA-B]	Ashley–Cadillac	128.3–227.1	–98.8			4
10/1	T	[AA-C]	Cadillac–Frankfort	227.1–292.4	–65.3			5
10/1	T	[AA-F]	Line to Boat Landing	290.3–291.8	–1.5			5
10/1	T	[MC-S]	Owosso–Swan Creek	64.2–91.3	–27.1	48.2		3

OWNERSHIP

Ownership of all lines operated by this company remained with the State of Michigan or with the trustees of Ann Arbor or Penn Central, the prior owners.

Act Column Key

C   Operated under Designated Operator contract

T   Designated Operator contract ended and transferred to another operator

Notes

1. Lines AA-A and AA-B were connected by use of trackage rights on GTW-D and GTW-[AA-B] between Pitt and Ashley. Line MC-S was connected by trackage rights in Owosso on GTW-[MC-Y1S].
2. Mileage operated in Ohio are not included.
3. Operations on this segment were continued by Tuscola & Saginaw Bay.
4. Operations on this segment were continued from Alma south and on Owosso–Swan Creek by Tuscola & Saginaw Bay, and from Alma north by Michigan Northern. Michigan Northern, which see, was subsequently replaced by Tuscola & Saginaw Bay.
5. Operations on this segment were continued by Michigan Northern, which see, which was subsequently replaced by Tuscola & Saginaw Bay.
6. Operations from Ann Arbor south and on the Saline Branch were continued by Michigan Interstate as Designated Operator, but without subsidy.

Michigan Northern

The Michigan Northern operated the following lines under contract with the State of Michigan which had acquired ownership of the lines or had contractual arrangements with Penn Central. See also page Michigan, State of.

For arrangement of stations, construction record, and prior ownerships, see Ann Arbor lines AA-B, AA-C, and AA-F; Grand Rapids & Indiana lines GR&I-N and GR&I-T; and Pere Marquette line PM-P.

ACQUISITION/DISPOSITION RECORD

DATE	ACT	MIGN–	END POINTS	MP	CHANGE	MI MAIN	SOURCE	NOTE
1976/4/1	C	[GR&I-N]	Comstock Pk.–Mack.Cy	239.5–459.8	+220.3			
4/1	C	[GR&I-T]	Walton Jct.–Trav. Cy	0–25.3	+25.2	245.5		
1982/2/19	C	[PM-P]	Grawn–Williamsburg	158.1–180.8	+22.7			1
2/19	C	[PM-P]	Charlevoix–Bay View	231.4–248.0	+16.5			1
10/1	C	[AA-B]	Alma–Cadillac	145.4–227.1	+81.7			2
10/1	C	[AA-C]	Cadillac–Frankfort	227.1–292.4	+65.3			2
10/1	C	[AA-F]	Line to Boat Landing	290.3–291.8	+1.5	433.2		2
1984/10/1	E,T	[GR&I-N]	Comstock Park–Petoskey	239.5–426.0	−196.5			3
10/1	T	[GR&I-T]	Walton Jct.–Trav. Cy	0–25.2	−25.2			
5/6	T	[AA-B]	Alma–Cadillac	145.4–227.1	−81.7			
5/6	T	[AA-C]	Cadillac–Frankfort	227.1–292.4	−65.3			
5/6	T	[AA-F]	Line to Boat Landing	290.3–291.8	−1.5			
10/1	T	[PM-P]	Grawn–Williamsburg	158.1–180.8	−22.7			
10/1	T	[PM-P]	Charlevoix–Bay View	231.4–248.0	−16.5	33.8		
1988 ca.	F	[GR&I-N]	Petoskey–Mack. Cty	426.0–459.8	−33.8	0		4

OWNERSHIP

Ownership of lines operated by this company remained with the State of Michigan or with the trustees of Penn Central, the prior owner.

Act Column Key

C Operated under Designated Operator contract
E Designated Operator contract ended
F Operations under agreement ended
T Designated Operator contract ended and transferred to another operator

Notes

1. Mile posts shown are C&O renumbered locations and 21.7 miles higher than shown for line PM-P.
2. Michigan Northern succeeded Michigan Interstate as Designated Operator.

3. The Designated Operator contract ended for that part between Comstock Park and Cadillac, and was transferred to Tuscola & Saginaw Bay north of Cadillac.
4. The Michigan Northern continued to operate the segment between Petoskey and Mackinaw City under an agreement with the trustees of Penn Central. Operations were intermittent; the date of last service was about 1988.

Michigan Shore

For arrangement of stations, construction record, and prior ownership, see Grand Trunk Western lines GTW-MR and GTW-YMB.

ACQUISITION/DISPOSITION RECORD

DATE	ACT	MISH–	END POINTS	MP	CHANGE	MI MAIN	SOURCE	NOTE
1990/12/12	P	[GTW-MR] Shaw–MP 4.0		0–4.0	(+4.0)			
12/12	P	[GTW-Y1M] In Musk.		91.1–95.8	(+4.7)	0		
1992	X	[GTW-Y1M] In Musk.		94.8–95.8	(–1.0)	0		

OWNERSHIP

1990   Michigan Shore, wholly owned subsidiary of RailTex Inc.

Act Column Key

P   Purchased from Central Michigan
X   Abandoned

Notes

GENERAL   This company is a terminal switching road and not an intercity carrier. Its mileage is not included the Michigan mileage table in chapter 2.

Michigan Southern

For arrangement of stations, construction record, and prior ownership, see Lake Shore line LS-A and Grand Rapids & Indiana line GR&I-S.

ACQUISITION/DISPOSITION RECORD

DATE	ACT	MSRR–	END POINTS	MP	CHANGE	MI MAIN	SOURCE	NOTE
1989/8	C	LS-A5	Sturgis–Quincy	376.6–406.8	+30.2	30.2		1
1993/12	P	LS-A5	Wh. Pi. Jct–Sturgis	406.8–421.3	+14.5			
	P	GRI-Y1S	In Sturgis	146.4–150.6	(+4.2)	44.7		

OWNERSHIP

1989   Michigan Southern.

Act Column Key

C   Operated under contract for owner, Branch & St. Joseph Counties Rail Users Association.
P   Purchased from Conrail

Notes

1. It could not be determined if Michigan Southern eventually purchased this segment or continued to operate under contract.

Midland & Hubbard

MAIN LINE (M&HUB)

	MILEAGE	COUNTY	CROSSINGS, JUNCTIONS, ETC.
(Jct.)	0	Midland	J/PM-L 18.5
(Crossing)	3.0	"	X/MC-L 16.4
Hubbard	10.0	"	

CONSTRUCTION/ABANDONMENT

DATE	ACT	END POINTS	MP	CHANGE	MAIN	SOURCE	NOTE
1894/1/1	B	Line	0–10.0	+10.0	10.0	1	
1899	S	In Midland	0–3.0	–3.0			
1899	X	MP 3–Hubbard	3.0–10.0	–7.0	0		

OWNERSHIP

1894	Midland & Hubbard.
1894/6/20	Midland & Northern, leased Midland & Hubbard.

ACQUISITION/DISPOSITION RECORD
See Ownership record above.

Act column Key
B   Built by Midland & Hubbard
S   Sold to Bay City & Battle Creek (see Michigan Central record)
X   Abandoned

Sources
1.   Michigan, Commissioner of Railroads, *Annual Report,* 1894.

Midland Train Railway

MAIN LINE (MTRY) (LINE NOT LOCATED)

	MILEAGE	COUNTY	CROSSINGS, JUNCTIONS, ETC.
(Midland)	0	Midland	(sec 21 T14N R2E)
(End of line)	12	"	(sec 36 T13N R1E)

CONSTRUCTION/ABANDONMENT

DATE	ACT	END POINTS	MP	CHANGE	MAIN	SOURCE	NOTE
Ca.1886	B	Line	0–12	+12.0	12.0		
Ca.??	X	Line	0–12	–12.0	0		

OWNERSHIP
1886   Midland Train Railway (B1)

Act Column Key
B   Built by Midland Train Railway
X   Abandoned

Sources

Notes
GENERAL   No details could be found of the construction or abandonment of this company.

Mid-Michigan

For arrangement of stations, construction record, and prior ownership, see Pere Marquette lines PM-V and PM-G

ACQUISITION/DISPOSITION RECORD

DATE	ACT	MMRR–	END POINTS	MP	CHANGE	MI MAIN	SOURCE	NOTE
1987/12/18	P	PM-V	Paines–Elwell	7.7–44.5	+36.8			
12/18	P	PM-G	Elmdale–N. Greenville	110.5–78.5	+32.0			
12/18	P	PM-[GTW-YMG]	In Greenville	40.4–41.0	(+0.6)	68.8		
1990/7	X	PM-G	In Alma	39.9–40.9	−1.0	67.8		1
1999	S	PM-G	Elmdale–Ionia	110.5–104.9	−5.6	62.2		

OWNERSHIP

1987   Mid-Michigan

Act Column Key

P   Purchased from CSX Transportation
S   Sold to CSX Transportation
X   Abandoned

Notes

1.   This segment was replaced with trackage rights over parallel Ann Arbor line AA-B (owned by State of Michigan).

Muskegon River & Cat Creek

MAIN LINE (MRCC)

	MILEAGE	COUNTY	CROSSINGS, JUNCTIONS, ETC.
(Musk. Riv.)	0	Osceola	(sec16 T17N R9W)
(Crossing)	0.5	"	X/PM-L 82.6
(End)	4.0	"	(N line sec32 T18N R9W)

CONSTRUCTION/ABANDONMENT

DATE	ACT	END POINTS	MP	CHANGE	MAIN	SOURCE	NOTE
1878 ca.	B	Line	0–4.0	+4.0	4.0		1
1880 ca.	X	Line	0–4.0	−4.0	0		

OWNERSHIP

1878   Muskegon River & Cat Creek

ACQUISITION/DISPOSITION RECORD

See Ownership record above.

Act Column Key

B   Built by Muskegon River & Cat Creek
X   Abandoned

Sources

Notes

1.   The corporate reports of this company do not appear to have been filed with the Michigan Railroad Commissioner. The dates are estimates.

Muskegon River & Rose Lake

MAIN LINE (MRRL)

	MILEAGE	COUNTY	CROSSINGS, JUNCTIONS, ETC.
(Musk. River)	0	Osceola	(sec34 T18N R8W)
Wings Jct.	0.2	"	X/PM-L 79.8
(End)	7.5	"	(sec36 T19N R9W)

CONSTRUCTION/ABANDONMENT

DATE	ACT	END POINTS	MP	CHANGE	MAIN	SOURCE	NOTE
1878/12/28	B	Line	0–7.5	+7.5	7.5	1	
1881	X	Line	0–7.5	–7.5	0	1	

OWNERSHIP

1878   Muskegon River & Rose Lake

ACQUISITION/DISPOSITION RECORD

See Ownership record above.

Act Column Key

B   Built by Muskegon River & Rose Lake
X   Abandoned

Sources

1.   Michigan, Commissioner of Railroads, *Annual Reports,* 1878, 1881.

Muskrat Lake & Clam River

MAIN LINE (MLCR)

	MILEAGE	COUNTY	CROSSINGS, JUNCTIONS, ETC.
(Clam River)	0	Missaukee	(sec33 T22N R7W)
(End)	5.0	"	(sec19 T22N R7W)
(Lk. Missaukee)	8.0	"	(sec6 T22N R7W)

CONSTRUCTION/ABANDONMENT

DATE	ACT	END POINTS	MP	CHANGE	MAIN	SOURCE	NOTE
1882/1/1	B	Clam River–MP 5	0–5.0	+5.0		1	
1882/12/25	B	MP 5–Lk. Missaukee	5.0–8.0	+3.0	8.0	1	
1886	X	Line	0–8.0	–8.0	0	1	

OWNERSHIP

1882   Muskrat Lake & Clam River.

ACQUISITION/DISPOSITION RECORD

See Ownership record above.

Act Column Key

B   Built by Muskrat Lake & Clam River
X   Abandoned

Sources

1.   Michigan, Commissioner of Railroads, *Annual Report,* 1882,1886.

New York Central

On 11 June 1915 the New York Central was formed by the merger of a number of companies. In Michigan the company was Lake Shore & Michigan Southern (LS), which see for all NYC Michigan mileage.

On 1 February 1930 this company leased Chicago, Kalamazoo & Saginaw (CK&S); Cleveland, Cincinnati, Chicago & St. Louis (CC); Detroit, Toledo & Milwaukee (DTM); and Michigan Central (MC). The Acquisition/Disposition Record is continued under the name each former constituent company. The mileage totals given here are for information only.

	CK&S	CC	DTM	LS	MC	SYSTEM
1930 YEAR TOTAL	57.4	73.3	90.4	535.0	1153.5	1909.6
1931 YEAR TOTAL	57.4	73.3	90.4	535.0	1139.7	1895.8
1932 YEAR TOTAL	57.4	73.3	1.6	535.0	1125.7	1793.0
1933 YEAR TOTAL	57.4	73.3	1.6	535.0	1086.9	1754.2
1935 YEAR TOTAL	57.4	73.3	1.6	528.3	1048.5	1709.1
1937 YEAR TOTAL	30.9	73.3	0	528.3	1035.6	1668.1
1940 YEAR TOTAL	30.9	73.3	0	527.6	1031.6	1663.4
1941 YEAR TOTAL	30.9	73.3	0	497.6	1031.6	1633.4
1942 YEAR TOTAL	22.4	66.3	0	497.6	1012.7	1599.0
1943 YEAR TOTAL	22.4	66.3	0	482.6	980.6	1551.9
1953 YEAR TOTAL	22.4	66.3	0	473.1	980.6	1542.4
1955 YEAR TOTAL	22.4	66.3	0	473.1	982.9	1544.7
1958 YEAR TOTAL	22.4	66.3	0	475.1	970.1	1533.9
1960 YEAR TOTAL	22.4	66.3	0	451.1	970.1	1509.9
1961 YEAR TOTAL	17.9	66.3	0	421.3	970.1	1475.6
1962 YEAR TOTAL	17.9	66.3	0	411.2	934.5	1429.9
1964 YEAR TOTAL	17.9	66.3	0	402.8	934.5	1421.5
1967 YEAR TOTAL	17.9	66.3	0	390.0	934.5	1408.7
1968/2/1 TOTAL	17.9	66.3	0	390.0	934.5	1408.7

On 1 February 1968 this company was conveyed to Penn Central. Its Acquisition/Disposition Record is continued in two places: under the name of each original constituent company and under the name of the new company. The lines conveyed were:

LINE DESIG.	END POINTS	MP	MI MAIN	SOURCE	NOTE
[CK&S-A]	Kal.–Richland Jct.	0–9.2	9.2		
[CK&S-[DTM]]	Richland–Hooper	0–8.7	8.7		
[CK&S-YH]	In Hastings	30.0–30.9	(0.9)		
[CC-M]	Ben. Hbr.–Niles Jct.	0–26.4	26.4		
[CC-N]	OD–OH state line	1.2–41.1	39.9		
[CC-YB]	Ben. Hbr. yard line	0–1.6	(1.6)		
[DTM-Y1D]	In Battle Creek	90.9–93.9	(3.0)		
[DTM-Y2D]	In Marshall	77.0–77.5	(0.5)		
[DTM-Y3D]	In Battle Creek	89.9–90.4	(0.5)		
[LS-A]	Toledo OH–Clayton	307.9–339.7	31.8		
[LS-A]	Osseo–Elkhart IN	356.3–424.1	67.8		
[LS-J]	Lenawee Jct.–Clinton	0–13.6	13.6		
[LS-Y1J]	In Jackson	40.1–42.1	(2.0)		
[LS-M]	Ida–Lenawee Jct.	9.5–29.3	19.8		
[LS-Y1M]	In Monroe	0–2.1	(2.1)		
[LS-YM]	In Monroe	0–1.1	(1.1)		
[LS-F]	Grosvenor–Morenci	0–18.6	18.6		
[LS-D]	D&M Jct.–Toledo	3.3–54.5	51.2		
[LS-Y]	Ypsi.–Saline	0.4–11.2	10.8		
[LS-Y]	Brooklyn–Cement Cty.	34.2–40.2	6.0		

[LS-Y]	N. Adams–Bankers	53.3–65.6	12.3
[LS-S]	In Sturgis	27.4–29.5	(2.1)
[LS-L]	Jonesville–Hillsdale	0.6–6.9	6.3
[LS-L]	In Homer	13.4–13.9	(0.5)
[LS-Y6L]	Albion–Springport	21.9–33.1	11.2
[LS-Y3L]	In Eaton Rapids	41.8–42.4	(0.6)
[LS-Y2L]	In Lans.	57.5–58.8	(1.3)
[LS-Y1L]	In Lans.	59.7–61.2	(1.5)
[LS-G]	White Pigeon	0.7+0.4–95.0	95.3
[LS-GA]	Three Rivers bypass	68.2–69.9	1.7
[LS-W]	OD–Ft. Wyn. IN	1.1–44.7	43.6
[LS-Y1W]	In Jackson	0.4–1.1	(0.7)
[MC-Z]	Det. River Tunnel	226.3–227.7	1.4
[MC-E]	Det.–Jackson	1.2–75.4	74.2
[MC-Y1E]	In Det.	0–1.2	(1.2)
[MC-YP]	Ypsi. Belt	Line	(1.1)
[MC-YJ]	Jackson Belt	Line	(1.3)
[MC-YDE]	Exp. Spur	Line	(1.2)
[MC-YDF]	Exp. Spur extension	Line	(0.6)
[MC-YDD]	Delta Spur	Line	(1.0)
[MC-YDB]	Det. Belt Line	Line	(4.4)
[MC-YDC]	Det. Belt Extension	Line	(1.9)
[MC-YDM]	Det. Manufacturers	Line	(1.3)
[MC-Y1DD]	DD&D Line	Line	(1.3)
[MC-DZ]	Junction Yard Br.	0–4.2	4.2
[MC-T]	W. Det.–Toledo	2.7–49.5	46.8
[MC-B]	Bay Cty. Jct.–Munger	2.2–101.1	98.9
[MC-Y1B]	Water St.Jct.–Bay Cty. ES	106.1–108.9	(2.8)
[MC-YBL]	Bay Cty. Belt Line	Line	(3.1)
[MC-YBS]	S. Water St. Spur	Line	(1.6)
[MC-YBN]	N. Water St. Spur	Line	(2.5)
[MC-YBH]	Hecla Belt	Line	(3.5)
[MC-BS]	Denmark Jct.–Sag.	4.8–20.7	15.9
[MC-BC]	Caro Jct.–Bach	0.4–28.3	27.9
[MC-A]	Jackson Jct.–OD	0–0.8	0.8
[MC-A]	Haires–Three Rivers	4.8–68.8	64.0
[MC-Y1A]	In Niles	102.8–104.0	(1.2)
[MC-Y2A]	In Three Rivers	69.5–70.9	(1.4)
[MC-N]	Niles–S. Bend IN	0–5.8	5.8
[MC-C]	Jackson–Niles	75.4–191.9	116.5
[MC-YF]	Fort Custer Spur	Line	(1.7)
[MC-H]	Kal.–S. Haven	0.2–39.6	39.4
[MC-Y1K]	In Battle Creek	0.8–1.3	(0.6)
[MC-J]	In St. Joseph	35.1–37.0	1.9
[MC-JB]	Ben. Hbr. Spur	0–1.6	1.6
[MC-W]	Niles–Chi. IL	191.9–222.7	30.8
[MC-WB]	Lee & Porter Track	Line	(1.9)
[MC-G]	Pearl St.–Gr. Rpds.	0.2–94.4	94.2
[MC-YG]	In Gr. Rpds.	Line	(2.7)
[MC-YLT]	Lans. Transit	Line	(0.8)
[MC-YLM]	Lans. Manufacturers	Line	(5.2)
[MC-S]	Rives Jct.–Bay Cty. WS	10.6–114.6	104.0
[MC-L]	BC&BC Jct.–Midland	1.7–19.7	18.0
[MC-YM1]	Dow Chemical Spur	Line	(3.0)
[MC-YM2]	Midland Yard	Line	(0.6)

[MC-M]	Bay Cty. ES–Mack. Cty.	0–182.6	182.6
[MC-MR]	Portage Lk. Br.	0–5.6	5.6
[MC-Y1P]	In Pinconning	0–0.6	(0.6)
1968/2/1	TOTAL CK&S=17.9 CC=66.3 DTM=0 LS=390.0 MC=934.5 NYC=1408.7		

Norfolk & Western _____

ACQUISITION/DISPOSITION RECORD

On 16 October 1964 this company acquired Wabash Railroad. See Wabash lines for arrangement of stations, prior construction/abandonment record, and prior ownership. Its Acquisition/Disposition Record is continued in two places: under the name of the former company and under the name of the new company. The lines acquired were:

LINE DESIG.	END POINTS	MP	MI MAIN	SOURCE	NOTE
N&W-					
[WAB-A]	Delray–OH state line	4.4–80.2	75.8		
[WAB-WD]	W. Det.–Delray	0–2.5	2.5		
[WAB-YD]	Det. spur	0–1.1	(1.1)		
		TOTAL	78.3		

DATE	ACT	N&W-	END POINTS	CHANGE	MAIN	SOURCE	NOTE
1979/2/6	P	[DTI-A]	Page–Tecumseh	+11.1	89.4		

On 23 July 1980 this company was conveyed to Norfolk Southern. Its Acquisition/Disposition Record is continued in two places: under the name of the original company and under the name of the new company. The lines conveyed were:

LINE DESIG.	END POINTS	MP	MI MAIN
NS-			
[WAB-A]	Delray–OH state line	4.4–80.2	75.8
[WAB-WD]	W. Det.–Delray	0–2.5	2.5
[WAB-YD]	Det. spur	0–1.1	(1.1)
[DTI-A]	Page–Tecumseh	44.3–55.4	11.1
		TOTAL	89.4

Act Column Key

P   Purchased from Detroit, Toledo & Ironton

Norfolk Southern _____

ACQUISITION/DISPOSITION RECORD

On 23 July 1980 this company acquired Norfolk & Western. The lines conveyed were:

LINE DESIG.	END POINTS	MP	MI MAIN	SOURCE	NOTE
NS-					
[WAB-A]	Delray–OH state line	4.4–80.2	75.8		
[WAB-WD]	W. Det.–Delray	0–2.5	2.5		
[WAB-YD]	Det. spur	0–1.1	(1.1)		
[DTI-A]	Page–Tecumseh	44.3–55.4	11.1		
		TOTAL	89.4		

DATE	ACT	NS–	END POINTS	MP	CHANGE	MI MAIN	SOURCE	NOTE
ca.1985	X [DTI-A]		MP 47.0–Tecumseh	47.0–55.4	−8.4			
ca.1985	S [DTI-A]		Page–MP 47.0	44.3–47.0	−2.7	78.3		1
1997/2	P [PRR-YF]		Foreman Wye	0–0.2	(+0.2)	78.3		

On 1 June 1999 this company acquired most of Conrail. The lines acquired were:

LINE DESIG.	END POINTS	MP	MI MAIN	NOTE
NS–				
[CC-Y1N]	In Jackson	1.2–4.3	(3.1)	
[CK&S-YA]	In Kal.	0.8–1.9	(1.1)	
[DTM-Y1D]	In Battle Creek	90.9–93.9	(3.0)	
[GR&I-Y2S]	Upjohn–Kal.	178.5–185.1	(6.6)	
[GR&I-S]	Gibson St.–Pleasant Ave.	185.1–233.2	48.1	
[GR&I-N]	Winter St.–Comstock Park	234.7–239.5	4.8	
[LS-A1]	OH state line–Ottawa Lk.	307.9–312.1	4.2	
[LS-A5]	Wh. Pi. Jct.–IN state line	421.3–424.1	2.8	
[LS-YM]	In Monroe	0–1.1	(1.1)	
[LS-Y1J]	In Jackson	40.1–42.1	(2.0)	
[LS-Y4L]	In Albion	21.9–23.6	(1.7)	
[LS-Y2L]	In Lans.	57.5–58.8	(1.3)	
[LS-Y1L]	In Lans.	60.4–61.2	(0.8)	
[LS-Y1W]	In Jackson	0.4–1.1	(0.7)	
[LS-G]	Wh. Pi. Jct.–N. Yard	0–36.8	37.1	
[LS-Y1G]	In Kal.	36.8–39.5	(2.7)	
[LS-G2]	Plainwell–Otsego	46.8–52.7	5.9	
[LS-Y2G]	In Gr. Rpds.	91.6–95.0	(3.4)	
[MC-E]	Town Line–Jackson	7.4–75.4	68.0	
[MC-YP]	Ypsi. Belt	Line	(1.1)	
[MC-T]	MP 20–Toledo	20.0–49.5	29.5	
[MC-Y1A]	In Niles	102.8–104.0	(1.2)	
[MC-Y2A]	In Three Rivers	70.1–70.9	(0.8)	
[MC-Y3A]	In Jackson	0–0.8	(0.8)	
[MC-Y1N]	In Niles	0–0.3	(0.3)	
[MC-C]	Jackson–Baron	75.4–119.8	44.4	
[MC-C]	Gord–Kal.	121.4–143.2	21.8	
[MC-Y1G]	Bowen–Gr. Rpds.	88.0–94.4	(6.4)	
[MC-YLT]	Lans. Transit	Line	(0.8)	
[MC-YLM]	Lans. Manufacturers	Line	(5.2)	
[MC-S]	Jackson–N. Lans.	0.2–36.9	36.7	
[MC-Y1S]	In N. Lans.	37.8–39.7	(1.9)	
1999/6/1	TOTAL GR&I=52.9 LS=50.0 MC=200.4 WAB=78.3 NS=381.6			
1999/7	X [WAB-YD] In Det.	0.5–1.1	(−0.6)	
1999	TOTAL GR&I=52.9 LS=50.0 MC=200.4 WAB=78.3 NS=381.6			

OWNERSHIP

1999   Norfolk Southern

Act Column Key

P   Purchased from Conrail

S   Sold to Lenawee County Railroad

X   Abandoned

Notes

1. This segment in Adrian apparently was sold to the Lenawee County Railroad as an industrial track at the time the remainder of the branch north of Adrian was abandoned.

North Branch & Sauble River *(line not located exactly)*

MAIN LINE (NBSR) *(LINE NOT LOCATED)*

	MILEAGE	COUNTY	CROSSINGS, JUNCTIONS, ETC.
(Pere Marq. Riv.)	0	Mason	(sec21 T18N R15W)
(Crossing)	0.5	"	X/PM-L 120.2
(End)	ca.10	"	(sec4? T19N R15W)

CONSTRUCTION/ABANDONMENT

DATE	ACT	END POINTS	MP	CHANGE	MAIN	SOURCE	NOTE
1888/8	B	Line	0–10	+10.0	10.0	1	
1896 ca.	X	Line	0–10	–10.0	0	1	

OWNERSHIP

1888   North Branch & Sauble River

ACQUISITION/DISPOSITION RECORD

See Ownership record above.

Act Column Key

B   Built by North Branch & Sauble River
X   Abandoned

Sources

1. Michigan Commissioner of Railroads, *Annual Reports,* 1888, 1897.

Ohio & Morenci

MAIN LINE (O&M)

	MILEAGE	COUNTY	CROSSINGS, JUNCTIONS, ETC.
Allen Jct. OH	0	Lucas OH	
Berkey	3.1	"	
Metamora	6.6	Fulton OH	
Champion	8.4	"	X/DTI-M 60.7
Whiteville	10.4	"	
Lyons	15.6	"	
Denson OH	19.6	"	X/DTI-A 28.9
(OH/MI state line)	21.1		
Morenci	23.4	Lenawee	
(End)	23.7	"	

CONSTRUCTION/ABANDONMENT

DATE	ACT	END POINTS	MP	CHANGE	MAIN	SOURCE	NOTE
1933/7/1	P	Line	0–23.7	+23.7	2.4	2	
1938	X	Allen Jct.–Berkey	0–3.1	–3.1	2.4	2	
1950	X	Berkey–Morenci	3.1–23.7	–20.6	0	1	

OWNERSHIP

1933   Ohio & Morenci, purchased from Toledo & Western

Act Column Key

P   Purchased from Toledo & Western

X   Abandonment

Sources

1.   ICC, *Finance Dockets.*
2.   Sell and Findlay, *The Teeter & Wobble.*

Notes

GENERAL   The line was purchased from Toledo & Western, which see.

Osceola, Lake & Wexford

MAIN LINE (OL&W-A)

	MILEAGE	COUNTY	CROSSINGS, JUNCTIONS, ETC.

Line not located

OWNERSHIP

1892   Osceola, Lake & Wexford

Notes

GENERAL   It appears that this line, incorporated in 1892, was anticipated to be an extension of the Osceola Branch of the Grand Rapids & Indiana (line GR&I-2, which see). Whether this company conducted operations independently of the GR&I or was operated by the Grand Rapids & Indiana has not been determined.

Paris & Pere Marquette River

MAIN LINE (PPMR) (LINE NOT LOCATED PRECISELY)

	MILEAGE	COUNTY	CROSSINGS, JUNCTIONS, ETC.
(Musk. River)	0	Mecosta	(sec10 T16N R10W)
Upper Paris	0.1	"	X/GR&I-N 296.6
(County line)			
(Crossing)		Newaygo	
(County line)			
(End)	16	Lake	(sec31? T17N R11W)

CONSTRUCTION/ABANDONMENT

DATE	ACT	END POINTS	MP	CHANGE	MAIN	SOURCE
1884/7/19	B	Musk. River–end	0–16.0	+16.0	16.0	1
1889	X	Musk. River–end	0–16.0	–16.0	0	1

OWNERSHIP

1884   Paris & Pere Marquette River.

ACQUISITION/DISPOSITION RECORD

See Ownership record above.

Act Column Key
- B Built by Paris & Pere Marquette River
- X Abandoned

Sources
1. Michigan Commissioner of Railroads, *Annual Reports,* 1884, 1889.

Penn Central

On 1 February 1968 Penn Central acquired all of the property listed under these ownerships: Chicago, Kalamazoo & Saginaw (CK&S); Cleveland, Cincinnati, Chicago & St. Louis (CC); Detroit, Toledo & Milwaukee (DTM); Grand Rapids & Indiana (GR&I), Lake Shore & Michigan Southern (LS); Michigan Central (MC); and Pennsylvania (PRR). The lines acquired were:

LINE DESIG.	END POINTS	MP	MI MAIN	SOURCE	NOTE
PC-					
[CK&S-A]	Kal.–Richland Jct.	0–9.2	9.2		
[CK&S-[DTM]]	Richland–Doster	0–8.7	8.7		
[CK&S-YH]	In Hastings	30.3–30.9	(0.9)		
[CK&S-YS]	Kal.–Pavilion Jct.	0–1.3	(1.3)		
[CK&S-YK]	In Kal.	1.3–2.6	(1.3)		
[CC-M]	Ben. Hbr.–Niles Jct.	0–26.4	26.4		
[CC-N]	OD–OH state line	1.2–41.1	39.9		
[CC-YB]	Ben. Hbr. yard line	0–1.6	(1.6)		
[DTM-Y1D]	In Battle Creek	90.9–93.9	(3.0)		
[DTM-Y2D]	In Marshall	77.0–77.5	(0.5)		
[DTM-Y3D]	In Battle Creek	89.9–90.4	(0.5)		
[GR&I-S]	Ft. Wyn.–Gr. Rpds.	146.4–234.0	87.6		
[GR&I-N]	Gr. Rpds.–Mack.Cty.	234.0–459.8	225.8		
[GR&I-M]	Walker–Musk.	10.0–39.3	29.3		
[GR&I-T]	Walton Jct.–Trav. Cty.	0–26.0	26.0		
[GR&I-YG]	Plaster Creek Branch	3.1+0.8	(3.9)		
[GR&I-YM]	Musk. Heights Branch	38.0–39.3	(1.3)		
[GR&I-Y1M]	Musk. Jct.–Kinney	2.6–7.4	(4.8)		
[LS-A]	Toledo OH–Clayton	307.9–339.7	31.8		
[LS-A]	Osseo–Elkhart IN	356.3–424.1	67.8		
[LS-J]	Lenawee Jct.–Clinton	0–13.6	13.6		
[LS-Y1J]	In Jackson	40.1–42.1	(2.0)		
[LS-M]	Ida–Lenawee Jct.	9.5–29.3	19.8		
[LS-Y1M]	In Monroe	0–2.1	(2.1)		
[LS-YM]	In Monroe	0–1.1	(1.1)		
[LS-F]	Grosvenor–Morenci	0–18.6	18.6		
[LS-D]	D&M Jct.–Toledo	3.3–54.5	51.2		
[LS-Y]	Ypsi.–Saline	0.4–11.2	10.8		
[LS-Y]	Brooklyn–Cement Cty.	34.2–40.2	6.0		
[LS-Y]	N. Adams–Bankers	53.3–65.6	12.3		
[LS-S]	In Sturgis	27.4–29.5	(2.1)		
[LS-L]	Jonesville–Hillsdale	0.6–6.9	6.3		
[LS-L]	In Homer	13.4–13.9	(0.5)		
[LS-Y6L]	Albion–Springport	21.9–33.1	11.2		
[LS-Y3L]	In Eaton Rapids	41.8–42.4	(0.6)		
[LS-Y2L]	In Lans.	57.5–58.8	(1.3)		
[LS-Y1L]	In Lans.	59.7–61.2	(1.5)		
[LS-G]	White Pigeon	0.7+0.4–95.0	95.3		

[LS-GA]	Three Rivers bypass	68.2–69.9	1.7
[LS-W]	OD–Ft. Wyn. IN	1.1–44.7	43.6
[LS-Y1W]	In Jackson	0.4–1.1	(0.7)
[MC-Z]	Det. River Tunnel	226.3–227.7	1.4
[MC-E]	Det.–Jackson	1.2–75.4	74.2
[MC-Y1E]	In Det.	0–1.2	(1.2)
[MC-YP]	Ypsi. Belt	Line	(1.1)
[MC-YJ]	Jackson Belt	Line	(1.3)
[MC-YDE]	Exposition Spur	Line	(1.2)
[MC-YDF]	Exp. Spur extension	Line	(0.6)
[MC-YDD]	Delta Spur	Line	(1.0)
[MC-YDB]	Det. Belt Line	Line	(4.4)
[MC-YDC]	Det. Belt Extension	Line	(1.9)
[MC-YDM]	Det. Manufacturers	Line	(1.3)
[MC-Y1DD]	DD&D Line	Line	(1.3)
[MC-DZ]	Junction Yard Br.	0–4.2	4.2
[MC-T]	W. Det.–Toledo	2.7–49.5	46.8
[MC-B]	Bay Cty. Jct.–Munger	2.2–101.1	98.9
[MC-Y1B]	Water St.Jct.–Bay Cty. ES	106.1–108.9	(2.8)
[MC-YBL]	Bay Cty. Belt Line	Line	(3.1)
[MC-YBS]	S. Water St. Spur	Line	(1.6)
[MC-YBN]	N. Water St. Spur	Line	(2.5)
[MC-YBH]	Hecla Belt	Line	(3.5)
[MC-BS]	Denmark Jct.–Sag.	4.8–20.7	15.9
[MC-BC]	Caro Jct.–Bach	0.4–28.3	27.9
[MC-A]	Jackson Jct.–OD	0–0.8	0.8
[MC-A]	Haires–Three Rivers	4.8–68.8	64.0
[MC-Y1A]	In Niles	102.8–104.0	(1.2)
[MC-Y2A]	In Three Rivers	69.5–70.9	(1.4)
[MC-N]	Niles–S. Bend IN	0–5.8	5.8
[MC-C]	Jackson–Niles	75.4–191.9	116.5
[MC-YF]	Fort Custer Spur	Line	(1.7)
[MC-H]	Kal.–S. Haven	0.2–39.6	39.4
[MC-Y1K]	In Battle Creek	0.8–1.3	(0.6)
[MC-J]	In St. Joseph	35.1–37.0	1.9
[MC-JB]	Ben. Hbr. Spur	0–1.6	1.6
[MC-W]	Niles–Chi. IL	191.9–222.7	30.8
[MC-WB]	Lee & Porter Track	Line	(1.9)
[MC-G]	Pearl St.–Gr. Rpds.	0.2–94.4	94.2
[MC-YG]	In Gr. Rpds.	Line	(2.7)
[MC-YLT]	Lans. Transit	Line	(0.8)
[MC-YLM]	Lans. Manufacturers	Line	(5.2)
[MC-S]	Rives Jct.–Bay Cty. WS	10.6–114.6	104.0
[MC-L]	BC&BC Jct.–Midland	1.7–19.7	18.0
[MC-YM1]	Dow Chemical Spur	Line	(3.0)
[MC-YM2]	Midland Yard	Line	(0.6)
[MC-M]	Bay Cty. ES–Mack. Cty.	0–182.6	182.6
[MC-MR]	Portage Lk. Br.	0–5.6	5.6
[MC-Y1P]	In Pinconning	0–0.6	(0.6)
[PRR-A]	Carleton–Ecorse Jct.	116.4–137.1	20.7
[PRR-YF]	Foreman Wye	0–0.2	(0.2)
[PRR-YO]	Oakman Spur	0–1.5	(1.5)
[PRR-YU]	Union Belt	0–5.8	(5.8)

1968/2/1   CK&S=17.9   CC=66.3   DTM=0   GR&I=368.7   LS=390.0   MC=934.5   PRR=20.7   PC=1798.1

DATE	ACT	LINE	END POINTS	MP	CHANGE	SOURCE	NOTE
1968/9/1	X	[LS-L]	Albion–Springport	23.8–33.1	–9.3		
9/1	Y	[LS-L]	In Albion (to Y4L)	21.9–23.8	(1.9)		
ca.	X	[MC-Y2A]	In Three Rivers		(–0.7)		
1968		CK&S=17.9 CC=66.3 DTM=0 GR&I=368.7 LS=378.8 MC=934.5 PRR=20.7 PC=1786.9					
1969	X	[LS-Y]	Ypsi.–Pittsfield Jct.	0.4–4.8	–4.4		
	S	[LS-Y]	Pittsfield Jct.–Saline	4.8–11.2	–6.4		
1969		CK&S=17.9 CC=66.3 DTM=0 GR&I=368.7 LS=368.0 MC=934.5 PRR=20.7 PC=1776.1					
1970	X	[CK&S-A]	Kal.–MP 0.3	0–0.3	–0.3		
	X	[LS-Y]	Brooklyn–Cement Cty.	34.2–40.2	–6.0		
	X	[LS-Y1M]	In Monroe	1.5–2.1	(–0.6)		
1970 ca.	X	[MC-YG]	In Gr. Rpds.		(–2.7)		
1970		CK&S=17.6 CC=66.3 DTM=0 GR&I=368.7 LS=362.0 MC=934.5 PRR=20.7 PC=1769.8					
1972	X	[MC-Y1E]	In Det.		(–0.3)		
/5	X	[LS-A]	Hillsdale–Osseo	356.3–360.6	–4.3		
	X	[LS-G]	N. Yard–Plainwell	39.5–46.8	–7.3		
	Y	[LS-G]	In Kal.(to Y1G)	36.8–39.5	(2.7)		
	X	[LS-Y]	Hillsdale–N. Adams	60.4–53.3	–7.1		
	Y	[LS-Y]	In Hillsdale(to Y1Y)	60.4–61.1	(0.7)		
1972		CK&S=17.6 CC=66.3 DTM=0 GR&I=368.7 LS=339.9 MC=934.5 PRR=20.7 PC=1747.7					
1973/3/1	X	[MC-J]	In St. Joseph		–1.9		
3/1	X	[MC-JB]	Ben. Hbr. Extension		–1.6		
3	X	[LS-A]	Adrian–Clayton	333.6–339.7	–6.1		
6/15	X	[LS-W]	Ft. Wyn. Jct.–Bankers	25.3–31.1	–5.8		
6/15	X	[LS-W]	Haires–Horton	5.1–10.5	–5.4		
7/1	X	[MC-BC]	Bach–Colling		–5.9		
9/1	X	[MC-H]	Kal.–S. Haven		–37.7		
9/1	Y	[MC-H]	In Kal. (to MC-Y1H)		(1.7)		
1973		CK&S=17.6 CC=66.3 DTM=0 GR&I=368.7 LS=322.6 MC=885.7 PRR=20.7 PC=1681.6					
1974 ca.	X	[MC-YBH]	Hecla Belt Line		(–3.5)		
1974		CK&S=17.6 CC=66.3 DTM=0 GR&I=368.7 LS=322.6 MC=885.7 PRR=20.7 PC=1681.6					
1975 ca.	X	[MC-N]	In S. Bend IN		–2.1		
	X	[LS-Y1L]	In Lans.	59.7–60.4	(–0.7)		
	X	[LS-Y3L]	In Eaton Rapids	41.8–42.4	(–0.6)		
	X	[LS-Y4L]	In Albion	23.6–23.8	(–0.2)		
	X	[LS-Y6L]	In Homer	13.4–13.9	(–0.5)		
1975		CK&S=17.6 CC=66.3 DTM=0 GR&I=368.7 LS=322.6 MC=885.7 PRR=20.7 PC=1681.6					
1976	X	[GR&I-T]	In Trav. Cty.	25.2–26.0	–0.8		
	X	[PRR-YO]	Oakman Spur	0–1.5	(–1.5)		
1976/4/1		CK&S=17.6 CC=66.3 DTM=0 GR&I=367.9 LS=322.6 MC=885.7 PRR=20.7 PC=1680.8					

On 1 April 1976 part of this company was conveyed to Conrail, and part retained by the trustees of Penn Central. The lines were:

LINE DESIG.	END POINTS	MP	MI MAIN	SOURCE	NOTE
PC-[CK&S-A]	Kal.–Richland Jct.	1.9–9.2	7.3		1
PC-[CK&S-[DTM]]	Richland–Hooper	0–8.7	8.7		1
PC-[CK&S-YH]	In Hastings	30.0–30.9	(0.9)		2

PC-[CC-N]	MP 4.3–OH state line	4.3–41.1	36.8	
CNR-[CC-M]	Ben. Hbr.–Niles	0–26.4	26.4	
CNR-[CC-YB]	In Ben. Hbr.	0–1.6	(1.6)	
CNR-[CC-Y1N]	In Jackson	1.2–4.3	(3.1)	
CNR-[CK&S-YA]	In Kal.	0.3–1.9	(1.6)	
CNR-[CK&S-YK]	In Kal.	1.3–2.6	(1.3)	
CNR-[CK&S-YS]	In Kal.	0–1.3	(1.3)	
CNR-[DTM-Y1D]	In Battle Creek	90.9–93.9	(3.0)	
CNR-[DTM-Y2D]	In Marshall	77.0–77.5	(0.5)	
CNR-[DTM-Y3D]	In Battle Creek	89.9–90.4	(0.5)	
CNR-[GR&I-Y1S]	In Sturgis	146.4–150.6	(4.2)	
PC-[GR&I-S]	N. Sturgis–Vicksburg	150.6–173.0	22.4	
CNR-[GR&I-S]	Vicksburg–Gr. Rpds.	173.0–234.0	61.0	
CNR-[GR&I-YG]	Plaster Creek Branch	3.1+0.8	(3.9)	
CNR-[GR&I-Y1M]	Musk. Jct.–Kinney	2.6–7.4	(4.8)	
PC-[GR&I-M]	Walker–Musk.	10.0–39.3	29.3	
PC-[GR&I-YM]	Musk. Heights Branch	38.0–39.3	(1.3)	
CNR-[GR&I-N]	Gr. Rpds.–Comstock Park	234.0–239.5	5.5	
PC-[GR&I-N]	Comstock Park–Mack.Cty.	239.5–459.8	220.3	
PC-[GR&I-T]	Walton Jct.–Trav. Cty.	0–25.2	25.2	
CNR-[LS-A1]	OH state line–Riga	307.9–315.5	7.6	
PC-[LS-A]	Riga–W of Adrian	315.5–333.6	18.1	4
PC-[LS-A]	Hillsdale–Quincy	360.6–376.6	16.0	5
CNR-[LS-A5]	Quincy–IN state line	376.6–424.1	47.5	
CNR-[LS-Y1M]	In Monroe	0–1.5	(1.5)	
CNR-[LS-YM]	In Monroe	0–1.1	(1.1)	
PC-[LS-M]	Ida–Lenawee Jct.	9.5–29.3	19.8	4
PC-[LS-F]	Grosvenor–Morenci	0–18.6	18.6	4
PC-[LS-Y]	Hillsdale–Bankers	61.1–65.6	4.5	4
PC-[LS-Y1Y]	In Hillsdale	60.4–61.1	(0.7)	5
PC-[LS-W]	Horton–Ft Wayne Jct	10.5–25.3	14.8	5
CNR-[LS-Y1W]	In Jackson	0.4–1.1	(0.7)	
CNR-[LS-W3]	OD–Haires	1.1–5.1	4.0	
PC-[LS-W]	Bankers–IN state line	31.1–44.7	13.6	5
CNR-[LS-D]	D&M Jct–OH state line	3.3–54.5	51.2	
CNR-[LS-J]	Lenawee Jct.–Clinton	0–13.6	13.6	
CNR-[LS-Y1J]	In Jackson	40.1–42.1	(2.0)	
PC-[LS-L]	Jonesville–Litchfield	0.6–6.9	6.3	5
CNR-[LS-Y4L]	In Albion	21.9–23.6	(1.7)	
CNR-[LS-Y2L]	In Lans.	57.5–58.8	(1.3)	
CNR-[LS-Y1L]	In Lans.	60.4–61.2	(0.8)	
CNR-[LS-G]	Wh. Pi. Jct.–N. Yard	0–36.8	37.1	
CNR-[LS-Y1G]	In Kal.	36.8–39.5	(2.7)	
CNR-[LS-G2]	Plainwell–Otsego	46.8–52.7	5.9	
PC-[LS-G]	Otsego–Lamar	52.7–91.6	38.9	
CNR-[LS-GA]	Three Rivers bypass	Line	1.7	
CNR-[LS-G]	Lamar–Gr. Rpds.	91.6–95.0	3.4	
CNR-[LS-Y1S]	In Sturgis	27.4–29.5	(2.1)	
CNR-[MC-Z]	Det. River Tunnel	226.3–227.7	1.4	
CNR-[MC-E]	Det.–Jackson	1.2–75.4	74.2	
CNR-[MC-Y1E]	In Det.	0.3–1.2	(0.9)	
CNR-[MC-YP]	Ypsi. Belt	Line	(1.1)	
CNR-[MC-YJ]	Jackson Belt	Line	(1.3)	
CNR-[MC-YDE]	Exposition Spur	Line	(1.2)	

CNR-[MC-YDF]	Exp. Spur extension	Line	(0.6)
CNR-[MC-YDD]	Delta Spur	Line	(1.0)
CNR-[MC-YDB]	Det. Belt Line	Line	(4.4)
CNR-[MC-YDC]	Det. Belt Extension	Line	(1.9)
CNR-[MC-YDM]	Det. Manufacturers	Line	(1.3)
CNR-[MC-DZ]	Junction Yard Br.	Line	4.2
CNR-[MC-Y1DD]	Part of Jct.Yd. Br.	2.0–3.3	(1.3)
CNR-[MC-T]	W. Det.–Toledo	2.7–49.5	46.8
CNR-[MC-B]	Bay Cty. Jct.–Rays Pit	2.2–28.2	26.0
PC-[MC-B]	Millington–Munger	79.3–101.1	21.8
PC-[MC-Y1B]	Water St Jct.–Bay Cty. ES	106.1–108.9	(2.8)
PC-[MC-YBL]	Bay Cty. Belt Line	Line	(3.1)
PC-[MC-YBS]	S. Water St. Spur	Line	(1.6)
PC-[MC-YBN]	N. Water St. Spur	Line	(2.5)
PC-[MC-BC]	Caro Jct–Colling	0.4–22.4	22.0
PC-[MC-BS]	At Denmark Jct.	4.8–6.0	1.2
CNR-[MC-A]	Jackson Jct.–OD	0–0.8	0.8
CNR-[MC-A]	Haires–Three Rivers	4.8–68.8	64.0
CNR-[MC-Y1A]	In Niles	102.8–104.0	(1.2)
CNR-[MC-Y2A]	In Three Rivers	69.5–70.9	(1.4)
CNR-[MC-N]	Niles–S. Bend IN	0–5.8	5.8
CNR-[MC-C]	Jackson–Kal.	75.4–145.0	69.6
PC-[MC-C]	Kal.–Niles	145.0–191.9	46.9
PC-[MC-W]	Niles–Chi. IL	191.9–222.7	30.8
CNR-[MC-YF]	Fort Custer Spur	Line	(1.7)
CNR-[MC-Y1K]	In Battle Creek	0.8–1.3	(0.5)
CNR-[MC-Y1H]	In Kal.	0.2–1.9	(1.7)
CNR-[MC-G]	Rives Jct.–Eaton Rapids	10.6–24.8	14.2
PC-[MC-G]	Eaton Rapids–Dutton	24.8–88.0	63.2
CNR-[MC-G]	Dutton–Gr. Rpds.	88.0–94.4	6.4
CNR-[MC-YLT]	Lans. Transit	Line	(0.8)
CNR-[MC-YLM]	Lans. Manufacturers	Line	(5.2)
CNR-[MC-S]	Jackson–N. Lans.	0.2–39.7	39.5
PC-[MC-S]	N. Lans.–Bay Cty. WS	39.7–114.6	74.9
PC-[MC-L]	BC&BC Jct.–Midland	1.7–19.7	18.0
PC-[MC-YM1]	Dow Chemical Spur	Line	(3.0)
PC-[MC-YM2]	Midland Yard	Line	(0.6)
PC-[MC-M]	Bay Cty. E.S.–Mack.	0–182.6	182.6
PC-[MC-MR]	Grayling–Rasmus	0–5.6	5.6
PC-[MC-Y1P]	In Pinconning	0–0.6	(0.6)
CNR-[PRR-A]	Carleton–Ecorse Jct.	116.4–137.1	20.7
CNR-[PRR-YF]	Foreman Wye	0–0.2	(0.2)
CNR-[PRR-YU]	Union Belt	0–5.8	(5.8)

1976/4/1 from PC: CK&S=17.6   CC=66.3   GR&I=367.9   LS=322.6   MC=885.7   PRR=20.7   TOTAL=1680.8
1976/4/1 to CNR: from CK&S=1.6   CC=29.5   GR&I=70.7   LS=172.0   MC=352.9   PRR=20.7   TOTAL=647.4
1976/4/1 to PC: from CK&S=16.0   CC=36.8   GR&I=297.2   LS=150.6   MC=532.8   PRR=0   TOTAL=1033.4
1976/4/1to: CNR=647.4   PC=1033.4   TOTAL=1680.8

On 1 April 1976 the property retained by the trustees of Penn Central was:

LINE	END POINTS	MP	MI MAIN	NOTE
PC-[CK&S-A]	Kal.–Richland Jct.	1.9–9.2	7.3	
PC-[CK&S-[DTM]]	Richland–Hooper	0–8.7	8.7	
PC-[CK&S-YH]	In Hastings	30.0–30.9	(0.9)	

PC-[CC-N]	MP 4.3–OH state line	4.3–41.1	36.8
PC-[GR&I-S]	N. Sturgis–Vicksburg	150.6–173.0	22.4
PC-[GR&I-M]	Walker–Musk.	10.0–39.3	29.3
PC-[GR&I-YM]	Musk. Heights Branch	38.0–39.3	(1.3)
PC-[GR&I-N]	Comstock Park–Mack.	239.5–459.8	220.3
PC-[GR&I-T]	Walton Jct–Trav. Cty.	0–25.2	25.2
PC-[LS-A]	Riga–W. of Adrian	315.5–333.6	18.1
PC-[LS-A]	Hillsdale–Quincy	360.6–376.6	16.0
PC-[LS-M]	Ida–Lenawee Jct.	9.5–29.3	19.8
PC-[LS-F]	Grosvenor–Morenci	0–18.6	18.6
PC-[LS-Y]	Hillsdale–Bankers	61.1–65.6	4.5
PC-[LS-Y1Y]	In Hillsdale	60.4–61.1	(0.7)
PC-[LS-W]	Horton–Ft Wayne Jct	10.5–25.3	14.8
PC-[LS-G]	Otsego–Lamar	52.7–91.6	38.9
PC-[LS-W]	Bankers–IN state line	31.1–44.7	13.6
PC-[LS-L]	Jonesville–Litchfield	0.6–6.9	6.3
PC-[LS-G]	Otsego–Lamar	52.7–91.6	38.9
PC-[MC-B]	Rays Pit–Munger	28.2–101.1	72.9
PC-[MC-Y1B]	Water St Jct.–Bay Cty. ES	106.1–108.9	(2.8)
PC-[MC-YBL]	Bay Cty. Belt Line	Line	(3.1)
PC-[MC-YBS]	S. Water St. Spur	Line	(1.6)
PC-[MC-YBN]	N. Water St. Spur	Line	(2.5)
PC-[MC-BC]	Caro Jct–Bach	0.4–22.4	22.0
PC-[MC-BS]	Denmark Jct.–Sag.	4.8–20.7	15.9
PC-[MC-C]	Kal.–Niles	145.0–191.9	46.9
PC-[MC-W]	Niles–Chi. IL	191.9–222.7	30.8
PC-[MC-WB]	Lee & Porter Track	Line	(1.9)
PC-[MC-G]	Eaton Rapids–Bowen	24.8–88.0	63.2
PC-[MC-S]	N. Lans.–Bay Cty. WS	39.7–114.6	74.9
PC-[MC-L]	BC&BC Jct.–Midland	1.7–19.7	18.0
PC-[MC-YM1]	Dow Chemical Spur	Line	(3.0)
PC-[MC-YM2]	Midland Yard	Line	(0.6)
PC-[MC-M]	Bay Cty. ES–Mack. Cty.	0–182.6	182.6
PC-[MC-MR]	Grayling–Rasmus	0–5.6	5.6
PC-[MC-Y1P]	In Pinconning	0–0.6	(0.6)
1976/4/1	CK&S=16.0 CC=36.8 DTM=0 GR&I=297.2 LS=150.6 MC=532.8 PRR=0 PC=1033.4		

DATE	ACT	LINE	END POINTS	MP	CHANGE	NOTE
1976	X	[CC-N]	MP 4.3–OH state line	4.3–41.1	–36.8	
	X	[GR&I-S]	Nottawa–Wasepi	157.9–159.4	–1.5	
	S1	[GR&I-M]	Walker–Musk.	10.0–39.3	[29.3]	to GTW-[GR&I-M]
	S1	[GR&I-YM]	Musk. Heights Br.	38.0–39.3	[(1.3)]	to GTW-[GR&I-YM]
	X	[LS-M]	Ida–Lenawee Jct.	9.5–29.1	–19.6	
	Y	[LS-M]	At Lenawee Jct.	29.1–29.3	(0.2)	to PC-[LS-Y2M]
	X	[LS-W]	Horton–Jonesville	10.5–24.1	–13.6	
	X	[LS-G]	Otsego–Lamar	52.7–91.6	–38.9	
	X	[MC-B]	Rays Pit–Oxford	28.2–42.2	–14.0	
	S1	[MC-B]	At Oxford	42.2–45.0	[2.8]	to GTW-[MC-Y2B]
	X	[MC-B]	Oxford–Lapeer	45.0–58.4	–13.4	
	S1	[MC-B]	At Lapeer	58.4–60.3	[1.9]	to GTW-[MC-Y3B]
	X	[MC-B]	Lapeer–Millington	60.3–79.3	–19.0	
	S1	[MC-Y1B]	Water St. Jct.–Bay Cty. ES	106.1–108.9	[(2.8)]	to GTW-[MC-Y1B]
	S1	[MC-BS]	Richville–Sag.	6.0–20.7	[14.7]	to GTW-[MC-BS]
	S1	[MC-YBL]	Bay Cty. Belt Line	Line	[(3.1)]	to GTW-[MC-YBL]
	S1	[MC-YBS]	S. Water St. Spur	Line	[(1.6)]	to GTW-[MC-YBS]

	S1	[MC-YBN]	N. Water St. Spur	Line	[(2.5)]	to GTW-[MC-YBN]
	S3	[MC-C]	Kal.–Niles	145.0–191.9	[46.9]	to AMK-[MC-C]
	S3	[MC-W]	Niles–Porter IN	191.9–222.7	[30.8]	to AMK-[MC-W]
	X	[MC-WB]	Lee & Porter Track	Line	(–1.9)	
	X	[MC-G]	Eaton Rapids–Charlotte	24.8–32.0	–7.2	
	S1	[MC-G]	At Charlotte	32.0–35.4	[3.4]	to GTW-[MC-Y2G]
	X	[MC-G]	Charlotte–Vermontville	35.4–46.1	–10.7	
	X	[MC-S]	N. Lans.–Owosso	39.7–61.1	–21.4	
	S1	[MC-S]	At Owosso	61.1–64.2	[3.1]	to GTW-[MC-Y1S]
	X	[MC-S]	At Swan Creek	91.3–91.8	–0.5	
	S1	[MC-S]	Swan Creek–Sag.	91.8–101.2	[9.4]	to GTW-[MC-Y2S]
	S1	[MC-S]	Sag.–Bay Cty. WS	101.2–114.6	[13.4]	to GTW-[MC-S]
	S1	[MC-L]	BC&BC Jct.–Midland	1.7–19.7	[18.0]	to GTW-[MC-L]
	S1	[MC-YM1]	Dow Chemical Spur	Line	[(3.0)]	to GTW-[MC-YM1]
	S1	[MC-YM2]	Midland Yard	Line	[(0.6)]	to GTW-[MC-YM2]
	S1	[MC-M]	Bay Cty. ES–Bay Cty. WS	0–0.7	[0.7]	to GTW-[MC-Y2M]
	S1	[MC-M]	Bay Cty. WS–Kawkawlin	0.7–5.0	[4.3]	to GTW-[MC-M]
	S4	[MC-M]	Kawkawlin–Linwood	5.0–10.8	[5.8]	to D&M-[MC-M1]
	S4	[MC-M]	Salling–Mack. Cty.	115.8–182.6	[66.8]	to D&M-[MC-M2]
1976			CK&S=16.0 CC=0 DTM=0 GR&I=266.4 LS=78.3 MC=224.6 PRR=0 PC=585.3			
1977	X	[GR&I-S]	Mendon–Vicksburg	164.1–171.9	–7.8	
	S1	[GR&I-S]	In Vicksburg	171.9–173.0	[1.1]	
1977			CK&S=16.0 GR&I=257.5 LS=78.3 MC=224.6 PC=576.4			
1978	X	[CK&S-A]	Kal.–Richland Jct	1.9–9.2	–7.3	1
	X	[CK&S-[DTM]]Richland–Hooper		0–8.7	–8.7	1
	X	[LS-A]	In Hillsdale	360.6–361.0	–0.4	
1978			CK&S=0 GR&I=257.5 LS=77.9 MC=224.6 PC=560.0			
1979	X	[LS-A]	In Adrian	332.9–333.6	–0.7	
1979			GR&I=257.5 LS=77.2 MC=224.6 PC=559.3			
1980/9	S2	[MC-M]	Linwood–Sallings	10–8.115.8	[105.0]	8
9	S2	[MC-Y1P]	In Pinconning	0–0.6	[(0.6)]	8
	X	[MC-MR]	Grayling–Rasmus	0–5.6	–5.6	
1980			GR&I=257.5 LS=77.2 MC=114.0 PC=448.7			
1982/4/1	X	[MC-G]	Vermontville–Caledonia	46.1–79.0	–32.9	2
	X	[CK&S-YH]	In Hastings	30.0–30.9	(–0.9)	2
	X	[GR&I-S]	N. Sturgis–Nottawa	150.6–157.9	–7.3	
	X	[GR&I-S]	Wasepi–Mendon	159.4–164.1	–4.7	
	S2	[LS-A]	Riga–Lenawee Jct.	315.5–325.5	[10.0]	
	X	[LS-F]	W. of Grosvenor–Weston	1.7–11.4	–9.7	
	X	[LS-Y1Y]	In Hillsdale	60.4–61.1	(–0.7)	
1982			GR&I=245.5 LS=57.5 MC=81.5 PC=384.1			
1983	X	[MC-G]	Caledonia–Bowen	79.0–88.0	–9.0	2
1983 TOTAL			GR&I=245.5 LS=57.5 MC=72.1 PC=375.1			
1984/2/15	S2	[GR&I-N]	Comstock Park–Petoskey	239.5–426.0	[186.5]	3
2/15	S2	[GR&I-T]	Walton Jct.–Trav.Cty.	0–25.2	[25.2]	3
2/15	S2	[LS-A]	Lenawee Jct.–Adrian	325.5–332.9	[7.4]	4
2/15	S2	[LS-A]	Hillsdale–Quincy	361.0–376.6	[15.6]	5
2/15	S2	[LS-M]	At Lenawee Jct.	29.1–29.3	[(0.2)]	4

2/15	S2	[LS-F]	At Grosvenor	0–1.7	[1.7]	4
2/15	S2	[LS-F]	Weston–Morenci	11.4–18.6	[7.2]	4
2/15	S2	[LS-Y]	Hillsdale–Bankers	61.1–65.6	[4.5]	5
2/15	S2	[LS-Y1Y]	In Hillsdale	60.4–61.1	[(0.7)]	5
2/15	S2	[LS-L]	Jonesville–Litchfield	0.6–6.9	[6.3]	5
2/15	S2	[LS-W]	In Jonesville	24.1–25.3	[1.2]	5
2/15	S2	[LS-W]	Bankers–IN state line	31.1–44.7	[13.6]	5
2/15	S2	[MC-B]	Millington–Munger	79.3–101.1	[21.8]	6
2/15	S2	[MC-BC]	Caro Jct.–Colling	0.4–22.4	[22.0]	6
2/15	S2	[MC-BS]	Denmark Jct.–Richville	4.8–6.0	[1.2]	6
2/15	S2	[MC-S]	Owosso–Swan Creek	64.2–91.3	[27.1]	7

1984 TOTAL   GR&I=33.8   LS=0   MC=0   PC=33.8

ca.1988	X	[GR&I-N]	Mack.Cy–Alanson	459.8–434.9	–24.9	9
	L	[GR&I-N]	Petoskey–Alanson	426.0–434.9		9

1988 TOTAL   GR&I=8.9   LS=0   MC=0   PC=8.9

ca.1992	XL	[GR&I-N]	Petoskey–Alanson	426.0–434.9		
	X	[GR&I-N]	Petoskey–Alanson	426.0–434.9	–8.9	

1992 TOTAL   CK&S 0   CC=0   DTM=0   GR&I=0   LS=0   MC=0   PRR=0   PC=0

OWNERSHIP

1976   Penn Central

Act Column Key

  L   Leased to Alanson & Petoskey
 S1   Sold to Grand Trunk Western
 S2   Sold to State of Michigan
 S3   Sold to Amtrak
 S4   Sold to Detroit & Mackinac
  X   Abandoned
 XL   Lease to Alanson & Petoskey canceled

Notes

1. This property was operated by Conrail under State of Michigan contract from 1 April 1976, until abandonment in 1978.
2. This property was operated by Conrail beginning 1 April 1976, under State of Michigan contract, and beginning 15 July 1979, by Kent–Barry–Eaton Connecting, until abandonment.
3. This property was operated by Michigan Northern beginning 1 April 1976, under State of Michigan contract, and by Tuscola & Saginaw Bay beginning 1 October 1984 until conveyed to the state.
4. This property was operated by Conrail beginning 1 April 1976, under State of Michigan contract until part abandoned in 1979, and by Lenawee County beginning 1 October 1979 until conveyed to the state.
5. This property was operated by Hillsdale County beginning 1 April 1976, under State of Michigan contract, until conveyed to the state.
6. This property was operated by Conrail beginning 1 April 1976, under State of Michigan contract, and by Tuscola & Saginaw Bay beginning 1 October 1977, until conveyed to the state.
7. This property was operated by Conrail beginning 1 April 1976, under State of Michigan contract, by Michigan Interstate beginning 1 October 1977, and by Tuscola & Saginaw Bay beginning 1 October 1982, until conveyed to the state.
8. This property was operated by Detroit & Mackinac beginning 1 April 1976, under State of Michigan contract.
9. Between 1984 and 1988 Michigan Northern apparently had a contract with Penn Central to operate between Petoskey and Mackinaw City.

Pennsylvania

MAIN LINE (PRR-A)

	MILEAGE	COUNTY	CROSSINGS, JUNCTIONS, ETC.
	[Mansfield OH]		
Carleton	116.4	Monroe	J/PM-T 105.2
Ash	119.2	Wayne	
Brownstown	125.0	"	
Bro	125.5	"	
Lurmet	126.5	"	
Penford	129.4	"	X/DTI-D 6.0
Garfield	133.0	"	
Cicotte	133.9	"	
Lincoln Yard	134.4	"	aka Lincoln Park
Melvindale	134.6	"	
Coolidge	135.6	"	C/WAB-A 6.5
Ecorse Jct.	137.1	"	J/WAB-A 5.6
(Det., via WAB)	142.4	"	

CONSTRUCTION/ABANDONMENT

DATE	ACT	END POINTS	MP	CHANGE	MAIN	SOURCE	NOTE
1922	B	Carleton–Ecorse Jct.	116.3–136.8	+20.7	20.7	1	

OWNERSHIP

1922	Pennsylvania–Detroit (B), controlled by Pennsylvania
1923/1/1	Pennsylvania, leased Pennsylvania–Detroit
1924/7/1	Pennsylvania, Ohio & Detroit, merger of Pennsylvania–Detroit
1926	Pennsylvania, leased Pennsylvania, Ohio & Detroit
1968/2/1	Penn Central, merger of Pennsylvania
1976/4/1	Conrail, purchased Penn Central
1999/6/1	Conrail, jointly owned by CSX Transportation and Norfolk Southern

FOREMAN WYE (PRR-YF)

	MILEAGE	COUNTY	CROSSINGS, JUNCTIONS, ETC.
(Junction)	0	Wayne	J/WAB-A 4.8
(Junction)	0.2	"	J/PM-F 5.5

CONSTRUCTION/ABANDONMENT

DATE	ACT	END POINTS	MP	CHANGE	MAIN	SOURCE	NOTE
1923	B	Line	0–0.2	(+0.2)	0	1	
1997/2	S	Line	0–0.2	(–0.2)	0		

OWNERSHIP

1922	Pennsylvania–Detroit (B), of segment, controlled by Pennsylvania
1923/1/1	Pennsylvania, leased Pennsylvania–Detroit
1924/7/1	Pennsylvania, Ohio & Detroit, merger of Pennsylvania–Detroit
1926	Pennsylvania, leased Pennsylvania, Ohio & Detroit
1968/2/1	Penn Central, merger of Pennsylvania
1976/4/1	Conrail, purchased Penn Central
1997/2	Norfolk Southern, purchased Conrail line

OAKMAN SPUR (PRR-YO)

	MILEAGE	COUNTY	CROSSINGS, JUNCTIONS, ETC.
(Jct.)	0	Wayne	J/PM-D 8.1
(Oakman Boulevard	0.6	"	X/DSR-OM 7.54
(Kingsley Ave.)	1.0	"	C/DT-A 1.6
(End)	1.5	"	

CONSTRUCTION/ABANDONMENT

DATE	ACT	END POINTS	MP	CHANGE	MAIN	SOURCE	NOTE
1923	B	Line	0–1.5	(+1.5)	0	1	
1976	X	Line	0–1.5	(–1.5)	0		

OWNERSHIP

1922	Pennsylvania–Detroit (B), of segment, controlled by Pennsylvania
1923/1/1	Pennsylvania, leased Pennsylvania–Detroit
1924/7/1	Pennsylvania, Ohio & Detroit, merger of Pennsylvania–Detroit
1926	Pennsylvania, leased Pennsylvania, Ohio & Detroit
1968/2/1	Penn Central, merger of Pennsylvania

UNION BELT (PRR-YU)

	MILEAGE	COUNTY	CROSSINGS, JUNCTIONS, ETC.
(Jct.)	0	Wayne	J/PM-D 8.8
(Warren Ave.)	0.5	"	X/DSR-X 11.55
Fullerton Yard	2.5	"	
Fullerton	3.0	"	X/PM-DW 5.2
(Grand Riv. Ave.)	3.3	"	X/DSR-R 7.90, (X/DUR-L 4.2)
(Junction, Livernois Ave.)	5.8	"	J/DT 6.1

CONSTRUCTION/ABANDONMENT

DATE	ACT	END POINTS	MP	CHANGE	MAIN	SOURCE	NOTE
1923	B	Line	0–5.8	(+5.8)	0	1	

OWNERSHIP

1922	Pennsylvania–Detroit (B), controlled by Pennsylvania
1923/1/1	Pennsylvania, leased Pennsylvania–Detroit
1924/7/1	Pennsylvania, Ohio & Detroit, merger of Pennsylvania–Detroit
1926	Pennsylvania, leased Pennsylvania, Ohio & Detroit
1968/2/1	Penn Central, merger of Pennsylvania
1976/4/1	Conrail, purchased Penn Central
1999/6/1	Conrail, jointly owned by CSX Transportation and Norfolk Southern

The Pennsylvania also held trackage rights on the Wabash, Detroit Union Railroad Station, and Fort Street Union Depot Company between Ecorse Junction and Detroit; on PM-D from MP 5.5 to MP 8.8 to reach PRR-O and PRR-U from PRR-F; and on PM-T and AA-A from Toledo, Ohio to Carleton.

ACQUISITION/DISPOSITION RECORD

DATE	ACT	PRR–	END POINTS	CHANGE	MI MAIN
1922	B	A	Carleton–Ecorse Jct.	+20.7	20.7
1923	B	YF	Foreman Wye	(+0.2)	
	B	YO	Oakman Spur	(+1.5)	
	B	YU	Union Belt	(+5.8)	20.7

On 1 February 1968 this company was conveyed to Penn Central. Its Acquisition/Disposition Record is continued in two places: under Pennsylvania and under Penn Central.

| 1976 | X | YO | Oakman Spur | (−1.5) | 20.7 |

On 1 April 1976 Penn Central was conveyed to Conrail. Its Acquisition/Disposition Record is continued in two places: under Pennsylvania and under Conrail.

| 1997/2 | S | YF | Foreman Wye | (−0.2) | 20.7 |

Act Column Key

B	Built by Pennsylvania
S	Sold to Norfolk Southern
X	Abandoned

Sources

1. Burgess & Kennedy, *Pennsylvania Railroad.*

Pere Marquette

TOLEDO DIVISION (PM-T)

	MILEAGE	COUNTY	CROSSINGS, JUNCTIONS, ETC.
Sag.	0	Sag.	J/PM-L 0, J/PM-B 0, J/PM-S 0, f. E. Sag.
(Tuscola St.)	1.1	"	B/MUR-E 12.95
Hoyt	2.18	"	X/MC-BS 18.1, f. Sag. Cty. Jct.
(Jct.)	2.6	"	J/PM-Q 2.6, PM-YSS 0
Standard Mine	4.1	"	
(Genesee St.)	6.1	"	B/MUR-E 20.18
Bridgeport	6.28	"	
Blackmar	12.15	"	
Smiths	13.1	"	
Birch Run	15.47	"	
County Line	18.0	"	
Clio	21.28	Genesee	
Pine Run	22.1	"	later moved and renamed Clio
(Bridge)	23.4	"	B/MUR-E 37.7
Mount Morris	26.10	"	
Horton	28.6	"	J/PM-F 4.7, f. Flint River Jct.
McGrew Jct.	29.5	"	J/PM-FB 29.5, old 28.70
N. Flint	31.89	"	
(Hamilton Ave.	33.2	"	X/FLCL-1 2.85
Flint	33.31	"	X/GTW-YF 270.0
(Court St.	33.95	"	X/FLCL-3 0.52
(Bridge)	34.6	"	B/GTW-C 269.3
Thread	35.1	"	
(Sag. St.)	35.6	"	X/FLCL-1 0.58
Atwood Jct.	38.36	"	J/PM-FB 37.7
Grand Blanc	40.63	"	
Stony Run		Oakland	f. S. Grand Blanc
Newark	45.05	"	f. Belford
Holly	50.15	"	X/GTW-D 46.3
Rose Center	54.76	"	
Clyde	58.24	"	
Highland	61.27	"	
Milford	65.06	"	
Wixom	70.34	"	X/GTW-A 50.7

Lincoln	70.6	"	
Novi	74.54	"	
(Bridge)	78.1	Wayne	B/DUR-LF 22.28
Northville	78.51	"	
Hospital Spur	79.6	"	
Waterford	80.1	"	
(Bridge)	81.0	"	B/DUR-JP 11.7
Plymouth	82.03	"	X/PM-D 24.6, f. Plymouth Jct.
(Main St.)	82.4	"	X/DUR-JP 7.95
Plymouth (old)	82.5	"	
(A.A. Trail)	83.1	"	B/DUR-JP 9.0
Canton	86.46	"	
National Block	86.6	"	
(Michigan Ave.)	90.0	"	X/DUR-J 13.27
Wayne	90.17	"	X/MC-E 18.2
Romulus	93.84	"	X/WAB-A 19.0
Barrett Track	95.2	"	
New Boston	97.93	"	
Willow	101.2	"	
Belden		"	
Waltz	102.4	"	
Carleton	105.16	Monroe	X/DT&I-M 24.2, J/PRR-A 116.3
Grafton	106.8	"	
Steiner	109.98	"	
Toledo Jct.	111.7	"	J/PM-TZ 0
Monroe	115.15	"	X/LS-M 1.5
Winchester	119.5	"	
Erie	125.37	"	
Ottawa Yard		"	
(MI–OH state line)	130.1		
Alexis OH	130.35	Lucas OH	

CONSTRUCTION/ABANDONMENT

DATE	ACT	END POINTS	MP	CHANGE	MI MAIN	SOURCE	NOTE
1862/1/20	B1	Sag.–Mt. Morris	0–26.1	+26.1	26.1	5	
1863/12/8	B1	Mt. Morris–Flint	26.1–33.3	+7.2	33.3	5	1
1864/11/1	B2	Flint–Holly	33.3–50.1	+16.8	50.1	5	
1871/5/30	B8	Wayne–Northville	90.2–78.5	+11.7		5	9
1871/11/6	B8	Northville–Holly	78.5–50.1	+28.4	90.2	5	
1872/1/1	B8	Wayne–Toledo Jct.	90.2–111.7	+21.5	111.7	5	
1896/11/15	B38	Toledo Jct.–Alexis	111.7–130.3	+18.6	130.1	5	42
1970	X	In Flint	32.7–33.4	–0.7			
1970	Y	In Flint (as PM-Y1T)	29.5–32.7	(3.2)			
1970	Y	In Flint (as PM-Y2T)	33.4–38.4	(5.0)	121.2		

OWNERSHIP

1862	Flint & Pere Marquette Railway (B1)
1864	Flint & Holly (B2), of segment
1868/5/30	Flint & Pere Marquette Railway, bought Flint & Holly
1871	Holly, Wayne & Monroe (B8)
1872/2/1	Flint & Pere Marquette Railway, merger of Holly, Wayne & Monroe
1880/8/24	Flint & Pere Marquette Railroad, reorganize Flint & Pere Marquette Railway
1896	Monroe & Toledo (B38), controlled by Flint & Pere Marquette Railroad

1897/8/27	Flint & Pere Marquette Railroad, bought Monroe & Toledo
1899/12/6	Pere Marquette Railroad, merger of Flint & Pere Marquette Railroad
1917/3/12	Pere Marquette Railway, reorganize Pere Marquette Railroad
1929/5	Chesapeake & Ohio, control of Pere Marquette Railroad
1947/4/1	Chesapeake & Ohio, merger of Pere Marquette Railroad
1987/9/2	CSX Transportation, merger of Chesapeake & Ohio

MONROE BRANCH (PM-TZ)

	MILEAGE	COUNTY	CROSSINGS, JUNCTIONS, ETC.
Toledo Jct.	0	Monroe	J/PM-T 111.7
Warner		"	
(Junction)	2.5	"	J/LS-D 39.1

CONSTRUCTION/ABANDONMENT

DATE	ACT	END POINTS	MP	CHANGE	MAIN	SOURCE	NOTE
1872/1/1	B8	Line	0–2.5	+2.5	2.5	5	13
1905 ca.	X	Line	0–2.5	–2.5	0		

OWNERSHIP

1871	Holly, Wayne & Monroe (B8)
1872/2/1	Flint & Pere Marquette Railway, merger of Holly, Wayne & Monroe
1880/8/24	Flint & Pere Marquette Railroad, reorganize Flint & Pere Marquette Railway
1899/12/6	Pere Marquette Railroad, merger of Flint & Pere Marquette Railroad

FOSTORIA BRANCH (FLINT RIVER BRANCH) (PM-F)

	MILEAGE	COUNTY	CROSSINGS, JUNCTIONS, ETC.
	[Flint]		
Horton	4.7	Genesee	J/PM-T 28.6
Genesee	8.32	"	
Jeffrey	8.9	"	
Shoecraft	9.8	"	
Bayer Brice Pit	9.9	"	
Genesee Gravel Co.	10.2	"	
Rogersville	10.71	"	
Otisville Gravel Co.	13.9	"	
Otisville	14.54	"	
Catsman Pit	17.6	"	
Branch Siding	17.8	"	
Otter Lk.	19.1	Lapeer	X/MC-B 73.6
N. Lk. Crossing	20.8	"	
Stewarts	22.2	"	
Fostoria	24.3	Tuscola	

CONSTRUCTION/ABANDONMENT

DATE	ACT	END POINTS	MP	CHANGE	MAIN	SOURCE	NOTE
1872/10/8	B10	Horton–Otter Lk.	4.7–19.1	+14.4	14.4	5	
1881/12/19	B24	Otter Lk.–Fostoria	19.1–24.3	+5.2	19.6	5	
1933	X	Otisville–Fostoria	14.5–24.3	–9.8	9.8	6	
———							
1972	X	Horton–Otisville	5.5–14.5	–9.0		4	
1972	Y	At Horton (as PM-Y1F)	4.7–5.5	(0.8)	0		

OWNERSHIP

1872	Flint River (B10)
1872/2/1	Flint & Pere Marquette Railway, merger of Flint River

1880/8/24	Flint & Pere Marquette Railroad, reorganize Flint & Pere Marquette Railway
1899/12/6	Pere Marquette Railroad (B24), merger of Flint & Pere Marquette Railroad
1917/3/12	Pere Marquette Railway, reorganize Pere Marquette Railroad
1929/5	Chesapeake & Ohio, control of Pere Marquette Railroad
1947/4/1	Chesapeake & Ohio, merger of Pere Marquette Railroad

FLINT BELT (PM-FB)

	MILEAGE	COUNTY	CROSSINGS, JUNCTIONS, ETC.
	[Saginaw]		
McGrew Jct.	29.5	Genesee	J/PM-T 29.5
Kearsley	32.9	"	X/GTW-YF 272.5
(Crossing)	33.6	"	X/GTW-C 271.8
(Bridge)	34.7	"	B/DUR-F 52.8
Atwood Jct.	37.7	"	J/PM-T 38.4

CONSTRUCTION/ABANDONMENT

DATE	ACT	END POINTS	MP	CHANGE	MAIN	SOURCE	NOTE
1923/6/5	B49	Line	29.5–37.7	+8.2	8.2	6	

OWNERSHIP

1923	Flint Belt, owned by Pere Marquette Railway
1955/11/30	Chesapeake & Ohio, merger of Flint Belt
1987/9/2	CSX Transportation, merger of Chesapeake & Ohio

BAY CITY BRANCH (PM-B)

	MILEAGE	COUNTY	CROSSINGS, JUNCTIONS, ETC.
Sag.	0	Sag.	J/PM-L 0, PM-T 0
Loop Line Switch	1.54	"	J/PM-YSL 0
Crow Island	2.1	"	J/PM-B3 0
Fifield	4.8	"	
(Junction)	5.7	"	J/PM-B2 0
Fitch	7	Bay	
Cheboyganing	7.61	"	
McGraws Siding	9.5	"	
S. Bay Cty.	10.05	"	
(Junction)	10.2	"	J/PM-YBS 0
26th St.	10.9	"	X/MC-YBL 5.8
23rd St.	11.1	"	J/PM-BP 11.1
(Farragut St.)	11.4	"	X/BYCL-5 1.18
(Tuscola Rd.)	12.6	"	
Center St.	13.2	"	X/MC-B 107.2, X/DCS 1.9
Hampton Yard	13.5	"	
(Woodside Ave.	14.8	"	X/BYCL-7 2.38
Foss	15.15	"	J/D&M-S 0, X/MC-YBN 1.9
N. Water St. Jct.	16.5	"	X/MC-YBN 0.4
Woodside	16.7	"	X/MC-M 0.2
(1st St.)	16.8	"	X/BYCL-7 0.43
Bay Cty.	16.95	"	J/PM-BP 12.5

CONSTRUCTION/ABANDONMENT

DATE	ACT	END POINTS	MP	CHANGE	MAIN	SOURCE	NOTE
1867/11/1	B4	Sag.–23rd St.	0–11.1	+11.1	11.1	5	
1891	B36	23rd St,–N.Water St.Jct.	11.1–16.5	+5.4	16.5	5	
1905	B43	N.Water St.Jct.–Bay Cty.	16.5–17.0	+0.5	17.0		

OWNERSHIP

1867	Bay City & East Saginaw (B4)
1872/2/1	Flint & Pere Marquette Railway, merger of Bay City & East Saginaw
1880/8/24	Flint & Pere Marquette Railroad (B24), reorganize Flint & Pere Marquette Railway
1899/12/6	Pere Marquette Railroad, merger of Flint & Pere Marquette Railroad
1917/3/12	Pere Marquette Railway, reorganize Pere Marquette Railroad
1929/5	Chesapeake & Ohio, control of Pere Marquette Railroad
1947/4/1	Chesapeake & Ohio, merger of Pere Marquette Railroad
1987/9/2	CSX Transportation, merger of Chesapeake & Ohio

OLD LINE TO BAY CITY (PM-BP)

	MILEAGE [Sag.]	COUNTY	CROSSINGS, JUNCTIONS, ETC.
23rd St.	11.1	Bay	J/PM-B 11.1
Columbus Ave.	11.9	"	X/BYCL-5 0.11
Bay Cty.	12.5	"	J/PM-B 17.0

CONSTRUCTION/ABANDONMENT

DATE	ACT	END POINTS	MP	CHANGE	MAIN	SOURCE	NOTE
1867/11/1	B4	Line	11.1–12.5	+1.4	1.4	5	
1905	X	Line	11.1–12.5	−1.4	0		53

OWNERSHIP

1867	Bay City & East Saginaw (B4)
1872/2/1	Flint & Pere Marquette Railway, merger of Bay City & East Saginaw
1880/8/24	Flint & Pere Marquette Railroad (B24), reorganize Flint & Pere Marquette Railway
1899/12/6	Pere Marquette Railroad, merger of Flint & Pere Marquette Railroad

HURON & WESTERN (PM-BH)

	MILEAGE [Foss]	COUNTY	CROSSINGS, JUNCTIONS, ETC.
N. Bay Cty.	1.1	Bay	J/D&M-S 3.0
(Patterson Rd.)	1.7	"	X/BYCL-2 2.65
Bangor St.	2.0	"	
Henry St.	2.9	"	
(Crossing)	3.3	"	X/MC-M 2.1
(Junction)	3.9	"	J/MC-M 2.7
Millers Crossing	5.8	"	
Arnold	6.6	"	
Felton	7.7	"	
Seven Mile Rd.	8.8	"	
(Junction)	9.0	"	J/PM-YBH2 0
Wolverine Mine #3	11.0	"	

CONSTRUCTION/ABANDONMENT

DATE	ACT	END POINTS	MP	CHANGE	MAIN	SOURCE	NOTE
1903	B45	Line	1.1–11.0	+9.9	9.9	5	
1930	X	MP 3.3–MP 3.9	3.3–3.9	−0.6	9.3	1	
1941	X	West end of line	3.9–11.0	−7.1		6	
1941	X	Near Bay Cty.	2.7–3.3	−0.6			
1941	Y	MP 1.1–MP 2.7 (as PM-YBH)	1.1–2.7	(1.6)	0		

OWNERSHIP

1903	Huron & Western (B45)
1903	Pere Marquette Railroad, leased Huron & Western
1917/3/12	Pere Marquette Railway, reorganize Pere Marquette Railroad
1929/5	Chesapeake & Ohio, control of Pere Marquette Railroad
1947/4/1	Chesapeake & Ohio, merger of Pere Marquette Railroad
1987/9/2	CSX Transportation, merger of Chesapeake & Ohio

WOLVERINE MINE #2 BRANCH (PM-BH2)

	MILEAGE	COUNTY	CROSSINGS, JUNCTIONS, ETC.
(Jct.)	0	Bay	J/PM-YBH 9.0
Wolverine Mine #2	1.4	"	

CONSTRUCTION/ABANDONMENT

DATE	ACT	END POINTS	MP	CHANGE	MAIN	SOURCE	NOTE
1903	B45	Line	0–1.4	+1.4	1.4	5	
1941	X	Line	0–1.4	−1.4	0	6	

OWNERSHIP

1903	Huron & Western (B45)
1903	Pere Marquette Railroad, leased Huron & Western
1917/3/12	Pere Marquette Railway, reorganize Pere Marquette Railroad
1929/5	Chesapeake & Ohio, control of Pere Marquette Railroad

SOUTH BAY CITY SPUR (PM-YBS)

	MILEAGE	COUNTY	CROSSINGS, JUNCTIONS, ETC.
(Jct.)	0	Bay	J/PM-B 10.15
(Jct.)	0.6	"	J/MC-YBS 2.7
(End)	1.9	"	

CONSTRUCTION/ABANDONMENT

DATE	ACT	END POINTS	MP	CHANGE	MAIN	SOURCE	NOTE
1895	B36	Line	0–1.9	(1.9)	0	3	

OWNERSHIP

1895	Bay City Belt Line (B36)
no date	Flint & Pere Marquette Railroad, acquired Bay City Belt Line
1899/12/6	Pere Marquette Railroad, merger of Flint & Pere Marquette Railroad
1917/3/12	Pere Marquette Railway, reorganize Pere Marquette Railroad
1929/5	Chesapeake & Ohio, control of Pere Marquette Railroad
1947/4/1	Chesapeake & Ohio, merger of Pere Marquette Railroad
1987/9/2	CSX Transportation, merger of Chesapeake & Ohio

ESSEXVILLE SPUR (PM-YBE)

	MILEAGE	COUNTY	CROSSINGS, JUNCTIONS, ETC.
(Jct.)	0	Bay	J/PM-B 14.9
(Crossing)	0.7	"	X/MC-YBL 0.3
(End)(Consumers Power Co.)	2.4	"	

CONSTRUCTION/ABANDONMENT

DATE	ACT	END POINTS	MP	CHANGE	MAIN	SOURCE	NOTE
??	B36	MP 0–MP 0.9	0–0.9	(+0.9)	0		50
??	B43	MP 0.9–MP 2.4	0.9–2.4	(+1.5)	0		

OWNERSHIP

1895	Bay City Belt Line (B36)
no date	Flint & Pere Marquette Railroad, acquired Bay City Belt Line
1899/12/6	Pere Marquette Railroad, merger of Flint & Pere Marquette Railroad
1917/3/12	Pere Marquette Railway, reorganize Pere Marquette Railroad
1929/5	Chesapeake & Ohio, control of Pere Marquette Railroad
1947/4/1	Chesapeake & Ohio, merger of Pere Marquette Railroad
1987/9/2	CSX Transportation, merger of Chesapeake & Ohio

WHATCHEER MINE BRANCH (PM-B2)

	MILEAGE	COUNTY	CROSSINGS, JUNCTIONS, ETC.
(Jct.)	0	Sag.	J/PM-B 5.7
(Crossing)	0.05	"	X/MUR-E 7.20
Houseback	1.9	"	
Krabbe	2.3	"	
Betts	2.8	"	
Whatcheer Mine	3.7	Bay	

CONSTRUCTION/ABANDONMENT

DATE	ACT	END POINTS	MP	CHANGE	MAIN	SOURCE	NOTE
1904	B43	Line	0–3.7	+3.7	3.7	1	
1928	X	Line	0–3.7	–3.7	0	1	

OWNERSHIP

1904	Pere Marquette Railroad (B43)
1917/3/12	Pere Marquette Railway, reorganize Pere Marquette Railroad

CROW ISLAND BRANCH (PM-B3)

	MILEAGE	COUNTY	CROSSINGS, JUNCTIONS, ETC.
Crow Island	0	Sag.	J/PM-B 2.1
Crow Island Mine	1.6	"	

CONSTRUCTION/ABANDONMENT

DATE	ACT	END POINTS	MP	CHANGE	MAIN	SOURCE	NOTE
1893	B24	Line	0–1.6	+1.6	1.6	5	
1905 ca.	X	Line	0–1.6	–1.6	0	5	

OWNERSHIP

1893	Flint & Pere Marquette Railroad (B24)
1899/12/6	Pere Marquette Railroad, merger of Flint & Pere Marquette

LUDINGTON DIVISION (PM-L)

	MILEAGE	COUNTY	CROSSINGS, JUNCTIONS, ETC.
Sag.	0	Sag.	J/PM-S 0, PM-T 0
Washington Ave.	0.1	"	J/PM-B 0.1
Mershon	0.68	"	X/GTW-S 40.6, X/MC-S 102.2
(Carrollton Rd.)	0.70	"	X/MUR-EW 11.79
Lawndale	5.92	"	f. Drissels
Freeland	11.03	"	
Smiths Crossing	15.43	Midland	
Dibble	16.59	"	
Bluffs		"	
Dean (new)	18.2	"	
Dean (old)	18.50	"	J/MC-YM1 3.0, aka Randall Branch–J/PM-YM1

(Junction)	18.9	"	J/MC-YM2 0.6
Bay Cty. Rd.	19.2	"	
Midland	20.05	"	
Anderson	22.1	"	
Averill	25.90	"	
Sanford	28.29	"	
N. Bradley	34.23	"	
Alamando	36.6	"	f. Dorr
Coleman	39.87	"	J/PM-LG 0, J/PM-LM 0
Loomis	44.72	Isabella	f. Buchtell
Herrick	46.9	"	f. Lans.
Clare	50.34	Clare	X/AA-B 178.8, J/PM-LH 0
Harrison Jct.	52.7	"	J/PM-LH 2.6+0.1
Farwell	55.04	"	
Remwick	60	"	
(Junction)	61.9	"	J/PM-LJS 0
Lk.	62.47	"	J/PM-LJN 0
Lk. Ice House	64.5	"	
Robinsons	65.2	"	
Chippewa	68.20	Osceola	
Manley	70.3	"	
Sears	72.11	"	f. Orient
Evart	75.94	"	
Evart Gravel Pit	79.1	"	
Wings Jct.	79.8	"	X/MRRL 0.2
Noble	80.95	"	
Brazil	82.6	"	X/MRCC 0.5
Hersey Gravel Co.	84.6		
Pere Marq. Pit	84.9	"	
Hersey	85.68	"	
Reed Cty.	89.20	"	X/GR&I-N 302.7
Olivers	93.03	Lk.	
Chase	95.90	"	
Summitville	98.0	"	
Nirvana	99.82	"	
Idlewild	102.43	"	f. Ungers
Forman	104.4	"	
Baldwin (old)	106.9	"	
Baldwin (new)	107.27	"	X/PM-P 73.8
Wingleton (old)	109.5	"	J/PM-LS 0
Wingleton (new)	111.12	"	
Stearns	112.7	"	
Sweetwater Tank	114.6	"	J/PM-LWX 0
(Crossing)	115.5	"	X/LAC 0.2
Branch	116.78	Mason	
(Crossing)	120.0	"	X/NBSR 0.5
Walhalla	120.61	"	J/PM-M 0, J/PM-LB 0, f. Manistee Jct, th. Merritt
Weldon Creek	123.1	"	
Custer	128.80	"	f. Black Creek
Scottville	128.71	"	
Amber	130.8	"	
Harding	131.7	"	
Conrad	133.9	"	
Lud. Yard	134.98	"	

(Junction)	135.3	"	J/PM-YL2 0	
(Junction)	135.7	"	J/PM-YL1 0	
Lud. (old)	136.63	"		
Lud. (new)	137.2	"		
Lud. Docks	137.6	"		

CONSTRUCTION/ABANDONMENT

DATE	ACT	END POINTS	MP	CHANGE	MAIN	SOURCE	NOTE
1867/12/1	B1	Sag.–Midland	0–20.0	+20.0	20.0	5	
1868/10/20	B1	Midland–Averill	20.0–25.8	+5.8	25.8	5	
1870/11	B1	Averill–Clare	25.8–50.4	+24.6		5	
1870/12/29	B1	Clare–Lk.	50.4–62.5	+12.1	62.5	5	
1871/9	B1	Lk.–Evart	62.5–75.9	+13.4		5	
1871/11	B1	Evart–Reed Cty.	75.9–89.2	+13.3	89.2	5	
1874/12/1	B1	Reed Cty.–Ludington	89.2–137.6	+48.4	137.6	5	
1987/11	X	Evart–Clare	75.7–52.0	−23.7	113.9	4	
1988/6/1	S7	In Clare	52.0–49.4	−2.6	111.3		
1988 ca.	X	Evart–Baldwin	75.7–107.3	−31.6	79.7		
1989/4/3	X	Midland–Clare	21.0–49.4	−28.4	51.3	4	

OWNERSHIP

1862	Flint & Pere Marquette Railway (B1)
1880/8/24	Flint & Pere Marquette Railroad, reorganize Flint & Pere Marquette Railway
1899/12/6	Pere Marquette Railroad, merger of Flint & Pere Marquette Railroad
1917/3/12	Pere Marquette Railway, reorganize Pere Marquette Railroad
1929/5	Chesapeake & Ohio, control of Pere Marquette Railroad
1947/4/1	Chesapeake & Ohio, merger of Pere Marquette Railroad
1987/9/2	CSX Transportation, merger of Chesapeake & Ohio

4TH WARD BRANCH (PM-YL1)

	MILEAGE	COUNTY	CROSSINGS, JUNCTIONS, ETC.
(Junction)	0	Mason	J/PM-L 135.7
(End)	2.2	"	J/LUN-A 1.4+0.2

CONSTRUCTION/ABANDONMENT

DATE	ACT	END POINTS	MP	CHANGE	MAIN	SOURCE	NOTE
1900	B43	Line	0–2.2	(+2.2)	0	5	

OWNERSHIP

1900	Pere Marquette Railroad (B43)
1917/3/12	Pere Marquette Railway, reorganize Pere Marquette Railroad
1929/5	Chesapeake & Ohio, control of Pere Marquette Railroad
1947/4/1	Chesapeake & Ohio, merger of Pere Marquette Railroad
1987/9/2	CSX Transportation, merger of Chesapeake & Ohio

DEVELOPMENT BRANCH (PM-YL2)

	MILEAGE	COUNTY	CROSSINGS, JUNCTIONS, ETC.
(Junction)	0	Mason	J/PM-L 135.3
(End)	2.1	"	

CONSTRUCTION/ABANDONMENT

DATE	ACT	END POINTS	MP	CHANGE	MAIN	SOURCE	NOTE
1900	B43	Line	0–2.1	(+2.1)	0	5	

OWNERSHIP

1900	Pere Marquette Railroad (B43)
1917/3/12	Pere Marquette Railway, reorganize Pere Marquette Railroad
1929/5	Chesapeake & Ohio, control of Pere Marquette Railroad
1947/4/1	Chesapeake & Ohio, merger of Pere Marquette Railroad
1987/9/2	CSX Transportation, merger of Chesapeake & Ohio

MANISTEE BRANCH (PM-M)

	MILEAGE	COUNTY	CROSSINGS, JUNCTIONS, ETC.
Walhalla	0	Mason	J/PM-P 120.61
Tallman	2.87	"	
Batchelor	4.5	"	
Fountain	8.11	"	
Gun Lk. Switch	10.4	"	
Freesoil	12.94	"	
Marsh	18.95	Manistee	
(Bridge)	19.3	"	B/M&GR-A 7.8
Stronach (old)	20.9	"	
Stronach (new)	23.0	"	
(Crossing)	23.6	"	X/M&L
E. Lk.	23.74	"	
(Parkdale Ave.)	25.45	"	X/MACL-B 1.35
M. & N. E. Jct.	25.6	"	J/M&NE-A 1.0
(Junction)	26.2	"	J/M&NE-A 0.4
Manistee	26.83	"	

CONSTRUCTION/ABANDONMENT

DATE	ACT	END POINTS	MP	CHANGE	MAIN	SOURCE	NOTE
1880	B24	Walhalla–Tallman	0–2.9	+2.9	2.9	5	22
1881/12/31	B27A	Tallman–Manistee	2.9–26.8	+23.9	26.8	5	

OWNERSHIP

1880	Flint & Pere Marquette Railroad (B24)
1881	Manistee Railroad (B27A), controlled by Flint & Pere Marquette
1888/11/2	Flint & Pere Marquette Railroad, merger of Manistee Railroad
1899/12/6	Pere Marquette Railroad, merger of Flint & Pere Marquette Railroad
1917/3/12	Pere Marquette Railway, reorganize Pere Marquette Railroad
1929/5	Chesapeake & Ohio, control of Pere Marquette Railroad
1947/4/1	Chesapeake & Ohio, merger of Pere Marquette Railroad
1987/9/2	CSX Transportation, merger of Chesapeake & Ohio

BUTTERS BRANCH (PM-LB)

	MILEAGE	COUNTY	CROSSINGS, JUNCTIONS, ETC.
Walhalla	0	Mason	J/PM-L 120.6, f. Butters Jct.
Peltman	3.2	"	

CONSTRUCTION/ABANDONMENT

DATE	ACT	END POINTS	MP	CHANGE	MAIN	SOURCE	NOTE
1880	B24	Walhalla–Peltman	0–3.2	+3.2	3.2	5	
1882 ca.	X	Walhalla–Peltman	0–3.2	–3.2	0	3	

OWNERSHIP

    1880   Flint & Pere Marquette Railroad (B24)

MOUNT PLEASANT BRANCH (PM-LM)

	MILEAGE	COUNTY	CROSSINGS, JUNCTIONS, ETC.
Coleman	0	Midland	J/PM-L 39.9
Wise	3.60	Isabella	
Denver	5.2	"	
Delwin	6.47	"	
Leaton	9.01	"	
Jordan	10.3	"	
Isabella	11.7	"	
Mt. Pl.	14.4	"	
(End)	14.7	"	J/AA-B 164.2

CONSTRUCTION/ABANDONMENT

DATE	ACT	END POINTS	MP	CHANGE	MAIN	SOURCE	NOTE
1879/12/15	B20	Line	0–14.7	+14.7	14.7	5	21
1979	X	Line	0.8–12.4	−11.6			
1979	Y	In Coleman (as PM-Y2LM)	0–0.8	(0.8)			
1979	Y	In Mt. Pl. (as PM-Y1LM)	12.4–14.7	(2.3)	0		

OWNERSHIP

    1879   Saginaw & Mt. Pleasant (B20), controlled by Flint & Pere Marquette
 1888/11/2   Flint & Pere Marquette Railroad, merger of Saginaw & Mt. Pleasant
 1899/12/6   Pere Marquette Railroad, merger of Flint & Pere Marquette Railroad
 1917/3/12   Pere Marquette Railway, reorganize Pere Marquette Railroad
   1929/5   Chesapeake & Ohio, control of Pere Marquette Railroad
  1947/4/1   Chesapeake & Ohio, merger of Pere Marquette Railroad

BEAVERTON (COLEMAN) BRANCH (PM-LG)

	MILEAGE	COUNTY	CROSSINGS, JUNCTIONS, ETC.
Coleman	0	Midland	J/PM-L 39.9
(Junction)	2.5	"	J/PM-LG2 0 (sec 8 T16N R2W)
Coal Kilns	2.9	"	
Lyle	5.9	Gladwin	
Beaverton	11.09	"	

CONSTRUCTION/ABANDONMENT

DATE	ACT	END POINTS	MP	CHANGE	MAIN	SOURCE	NOTE
1888	B24	Coleman–MP 7.8	0–7.8	+7.8	7.8	5	34
1889	B24	MP 7.8–Beaverton	7.8–11.1	+3.3	11.1	1	
1943	X	Line	0–11.1	−11.1	0		

OWNERSHIP

    1888   Flint & Pere Marquette Railroad (B24)
 1899/12/6   Pere Marquette Railroad, merger of Flint & Pere Marquette Railroad
 1917/3/12   Pere Marquette Railway, reorganize Pere Marquette Railroad
   1929/5   Chesapeake & Ohio, control of Pere Marquette Railroad

BRANCH TO CURTIS (PM-LG2)

	MILEAGE	COUNTY	CROSSINGS, JUNCTIONS, ETC.
(Junction)	0	Midland	J/PM-LG 2.5
Curtis	5.1	"	

CONSTRUCTION/ABANDONMENT

DATE	ACT	END POINTS	MP	CHANGE	MAIN	SOURCE	NOTE
1895 ca.	B24	Line	0–5.1	+5.1	5.1		
1901 ca.	X	Line	0–5.1	−5.1	0		

OWNERSHIP

1895   Flint & Pere Marquette Railroad (B24)

1899/12/6   Pere Marquette Railroad, merger of Flint & Pere Marquette Railroad

HARRISON BRANCH (PM-LH)

	MILEAGE	COUNTY	CROSSINGS, JUNCTIONS, ETC.
Clare	0	Midland	J/PM-L 50.4
(Jct.)	2.6	Clare	J/conn. to Harrison Jct. on PM-L, 0.1 mis.
Moores Siding	4.2	"	
Atwoods Siding	7.8	"	
Galliver	8.02	"	
Hatton	9.15	"	J/PM-LH2 0
Manns Siding	12.33	"	
Harrison	16.84	"	
(Junction)	17.8	"	J/PM-LL 0
Arnold Lk.	22.0	"	
Hackley	23	"	
Levington	25.1	"	
Frost	26.0	"	
Eyke	28.0	"	
Meredith	31.7	"	
(End)	38.0	Gladwin	

CONSTRUCTION/ABANDONMENT

DATE	ACT	END POINTS	MP	CHANGE	MAIN	SOURCE	NOTE
1879	B19	Harrison Jct.–MP 11.4	2.6–11.4 + 0.1	+8.9	8.9	5	35
1880/9/30	B19	MP 11.4–Harrison	11.4–18.0	+6.6	15.5	5	
1883/11/22	B19	Harrison–Meredith	18.0–32.4	+14.4	29.9	5	
1887	B19	Clare–MP 2.6	0–2.6	+2.6			30
1887	X	Harrison Jct.–MP 2.6	0–0.1	−0.1	32.4		30
1896	X	Meredith–Frost	32.4–25.4	−7.0	25.4	5	
1916 ca.	X	Frost–MP 17.8	25.4–17.8	−7.6	17.8		
1944	X	Clare–MP 17.8	0–17.8	−17.8	0	1	

OWNERSHIP

1879   Saginaw & Clare County (B19), controlled by Flint & Pere Marquette Railroad

1888/11/2   Flint & Pere Marquette Railroad, merger of Saginaw & Clare County

1899/12/6   Pere Marquette Railroad, merger of Flint & Pere Marquette Railroad

1917/3/12   Pere Marquette Railway, reorganize Pere Marquette Railroad

1929/5   Chesapeake & Ohio, control of Pere Marquette Railroad

BRANCH OFF HARRISON BRANCH (PM-LH2)

	MILEAGE	COUNTY	CROSSINGS, JUNCTIONS, ETC.
Hatton	0	Clare	J/PM-LH 9.1
(Jct.)	6.6	"	
Mostetlers Siding	8.4	"	
Dodge	9.8	"	
(End)	11.5	"	(sec18 T19N R3W)

CONSTRUCTION/ABANDONMENT

DATE	ACT	END POINTS	MP	CHANGE	MAIN	SOURCE	NOTE
1891 ca.	B24	Line	0–11.5	+11.5	11.5		41
1901 ca.	X	Line	0–11.5	–11.5	0		

OWNERSHIP

1891	Flint & Pere Marquette Railroad (B24)
1899/12/6	Pere Marquette Railroad, merger of Flint & Pere Marquette Railroad

LEOTA BRANCH (PM-LL)

	MILEAGE	COUNTY	CROSSINGS, JUNCTIONS, ETC.
(Jct.)	0	Clare	J/PM-LH 17.8
(Jct.)	1.9	"	
Leota	8.8	"	
(End)	9.9	"	

CONSTRUCTION/ABANDONMENT

DATE	ACT	END POINTS	MP	CHANGE	MAIN	SOURCE	NOTE
1891 ca.	B24	Line	0–8.8	+8.8	8.8		
1922 ca.	X	Line	0–8.8	–8.8	0	1	

OWNERSHIP

1891	Flint & Pere Marquette Railroad (B24)
1899/12/16	Pere Marquette Railroad, merger of Flint & Pere Marquette Railroad
1917/3/12	Pere Marquette Railway, reorganize Pere Marquette Railroad

TOWN LINE LAKE BRANCH (PM-LTX) (LINE NOT LOCATED)

	MILEAGE	COUNTY	CROSSINGS, JUNCTIONS, ETC.
(Jct.)	0		
(End)	2.4		

CONSTRUCTION/ABANDONMENT

DATE	ACT	END POINTS	MP	CHANGE	MAIN	SOURCE	NOTE
1900	B43	Line	0–2.4	+2.4	2.4	5	41
1905 ca.	X	Line	0–2.4	–2.4	0	5	41

OWNERSHIP

1900	Pere Marquette Railroad (B43)

HOYTS NORTH BRANCH (PM-LJN)

	MILEAGE	COUNTY	CROSSINGS, JUNCTIONS, ETC.
Lk.	0	Clare	J/PM-L 62.5
(Jct.)	0.9	"	J/PM-LJN2 0 (sec 14 T17N R6W)
(Jct.)	2.4	"	J/PM-LJN3 0 (sec 12 T17N R6W)
(Jct.)	2.7	"	J/PM-LJN4 0 (sec 12 T17N R6W)
(End)	4.8	"	(sec36 T18N R8W)

CONSTRUCTION/ABANDONMENT

DATE	ACT	END POINTS	MP	CHANGE	MAIN	SOURCE	NOTE
??		Line					36

OWNERSHIP

1891	Flint & Pere Marquette Railroad (B24)
1899/12/16	Pere Marquette Railroad, merger of Flint & Pere Marquette Railroad

BRANCH OFF HOYTS NORTH BRANCH (PM-LJN2)

	MILEAGE	COUNTY	CROSSINGS, JUNCTIONS, ETC.
(Jct.)	0	Clare	J/PM-LJN 0.9
(End)	0.5	"	(sec14 T17N R6W)

CONSTRUCTION/ABANDONMENT

DATE	ACT	END POINTS	MP	CHANGE	MAIN	SOURCE	NOTE
??		Line					36

OWNERSHIP

1891	Flint & Pere Marquette Railroad (B24)
1899/12/16	Pere Marquette Railroad, merger of Flint & Pere Marquette Railroad

BRANCH OFF HOYTS NORTH BRANCH (PM-LJN3)

	MILEAGE	COUNTY	CROSSINGS, JUNCTIONS, ETC.
(Jct.)	0	Clare	J/PM-LJN 2.4
(End)	0.7	"	(sec12 T17N R6W)

CONSTRUCTION/ABANDONMENT

DATE	ACT	END POINTS	MP	CHANGE	MAIN	SOURCE	NOTE
??		Line					36

OWNERSHIP

1891	Flint & Pere Marquette Railroad (B24)
1899/12/16	Pere Marquette Railroad, merger of Flint & Pere Marquette Railroad

BRANCH OFF HOYTS NORTH BRANCH (PM-LJN4)

	MILEAGE	COUNTY	CROSSINGS, JUNCTIONS, ETC.
(Jct.)	0	Clare	J/PM-LJN 2.7
(End)	3.9	"	(sec33 T18N R6W)

CONSTRUCTION/ABANDONMENT

DATE	ACT	END POINTS	MP	CHANGE	MAIN	SOURCE	NOTE
??		Line					36

OWNERSHIP

1891	Flint & Pere Marquette Railroad (B24)
1899/12/16	Pere Marquette Railroad, merger of Flint & Pere Marquette Railroad

HOYTS SOUTH BRANCH (PM-LJS)

	MILEAGE	COUNTY	CROSSINGS, JUNCTIONS, ETC.
(Jct.)	0	Clare	J/PM-L 61.9
(Jct.)	1.3	"	J/PM-LJS2 0 (sec 26 T17N R6W)
(End)	1.8	Isabella	(sec2 T16N R6W)

CONSTRUCTION/ABANDONMENT

DATE	ACT	END POINTS	MP	CHANGE	MAIN	SOURCE	NOTE
??		Line					36

OWNERSHIP

1891	Flint & Pere Marquette Railroad (B24)
1899/12/16	Pere Marquette Railroad, merger of Flint & Pere Marquette Railroad

BRANCH OFF HOYTS SOUTH BRANCH (PM-LJS2) (LINE NOT LOCATED)

	MILEAGE	COUNTY	CROSSINGS, JUNCTIONS, ETC.
(Jct.)	0	Clare	J/PM-LJS 1.3

CONSTRUCTION/ABANDONMENT

DATE	ACT	END POINTS	MP	CHANGE	MAIN	SOURCE	NOTE
??		Line					36

OWNERSHIP
?? Flint & Pere Marquette Railroad (B24)

STAR LAKE BRANCH (PM-LS)

	MILEAGE	COUNTY	CROSSINGS, JUNCTIONS, ETC.
Wingleton (old)	0	Lk.	J/PM-L 109.5
(Jct.)	3.3	"	J/PM-LS2 0 (sec 19 T17N R13W)
(End–Star Lk.)	4.6	"	(sec25 T17N R14W)

CONSTRUCTION/ABANDONMENT

DATE	ACT	END POINTS	MP	CHANGE	MAIN	SOURCE	NOTE
1891	B24	Line	0–4.6	+4.6	4.6	5	37
1898 ca.	X	Line	0–4.6	−4.6	0	5	

OWNERSHIP
1891 Flint & Pere Marquette Railroad (B24)

BRANCH OFF STAR LAKE BRANCH (PM-LS2)

	MILEAGE	COUNTY	CROSSINGS, JUNCTIONS, ETC.
(Jct.)	0	Lk.	J/PM-LS 3.3
(Jct.)	2.6	"	J/PM-LS2A 0, J/PM-LS2B 0 (sec 32 T17N R13W)
(End)	7.4	Newaygo	(sec20 T16N R13W)

CONSTRUCTION/ABANDONMENT

DATE	ACT	END POINTS	MP	CHANGE	MAIN	SOURCE	NOTE
1891	B24	Line	0–7.4	+7.4	7.4	5	37
1898 ca.	X	Line	0–7.4	−7.4	0	5	

OWNERSHIP
1891 Flint & Pere Marquette Railroad (B24)

BRANCH OFF STAR LAKE BRANCH (PM-LS2A)

	MILEAGE	COUNTY	CROSSINGS, JUNCTIONS, ETC.
(Jct.)	0	Lk.	J/PM-LS2 2.6
(End)	1.5	"	(sec31 T17N R13W)

CONSTRUCTION/ABANDONMENT

DATE	ACT	END POINTS	MP	CHANGE	MAIN	SOURCE	NOTE
1891	B24	Line	0–1.5	+1.5	1.5	5	
1898 ca.	X	Line	0–1.5	−1.5	0	5	

OWNERSHIP
1891 Flint & Pere Marquette Railroad (B24)

BRANCH OFF STAR LAKE BRANCH (PM-LS2B)

	MILEAGE	COUNTY	CROSSINGS, JUNCTIONS, ETC.
(Jct.)	0	Lk.	J/PM-LS2 2.6
(End)	1.5	"	(sec34 T17N R13W)

CONSTRUCTION/ABANDONMENT

DATE	ACT	END POINTS	MP	CHANGE	MAIN	SOURCE	NOTE
1891	B24	Line	0–1.5	+1.5	1.5	5	
1898 ca.	X	Line	0–1.5	−1.5	0	5	

OWNERSHIP

1891   Flint & Pere Marquette Railroad (B24)

SWEETWATER BRANCH (PM-LWX) (LINE NOT LOCATED)

	MILEAGE	COUNTY	CROSSINGS, JUNCTIONS, ETC.
Sweetwater	0	Lake	J/PM-L 114.6

CONSTRUCTION/ABANDONMENT

DATE	ACT	END POINTS	MP	CHANGE	MAIN	SOURCE	NOTE
1900	B43	Line	0–5.4	+5.4	5.4	5	41
1903 ca.	X	Line	0–5.4	−5.4	0	5	41

OWNERSHIP

1900   Pere Marquette Railroad (B43)

RANDALL BRANCH (PM-YM1)

	MILEAGE	COUNTY	CROSSINGS, JUNCTIONS, ETC.
Dean	0	Midland	J/PM-L 18.50
(End)	1.9	"	(sec29 T14N R2E)

CONSTRUCTION/ABANDONMENT

DATE	ACT	END POINTS	MP	CHANGE	MAIN	SOURCE	NOTE
??		Line	0–1.9				50

OWNERSHIP

?? Pere Marquette Railroad
1917/3/12   Pere Marquette Railway, reorganize Pere Marquette Railroad

SAGINAW–BAD AXE LINE (PM-S)

	MILEAGE	COUNTY	CROSSINGS, JUNCTIONS, ETC.
Sag.	0	Sag.	J/PM-T 0, J/PM-L 0
Donald	1.5	"	X/MUR-E 11.58
Stephen	3.9	"	
Creens	4.92	"	aka Greens
Uncle Henry Mine	6.1	"	
Manning	6.84	"	
Arthur	9.20	"	
Reese	12.48	Tuscola	X/MC-B 94.5
Stone	13.7	"	
Dewar	14.3	"	
Van Patten	15.4	"	
Gilford	16.74	"	
Kintner	19.0	"	
Fairgrove	21.61	"	
(Crossing)	24.4	"	X/DCS 19.2

Akron	24.74	"	
Woodway	27.4	"	f. Woodman
Unionville	31.00	"	
Robert Gage Coal	31.5	"	J/PM-SR 0
Kemps	33.2	"	
Sebewaing	36.95	Huron	
Rose Island	39.5	"	
Tarry	42	"	
Weale	42.67	"	
Bart	44.62	"	J/PM-SB 0, f. Bay Port Jct.
Quarry	46.12	"	
Quarry (Jct.)	47.2	"	J/PM-SQ 0
Pigeon	50.05	"	X/GTW-P 91.8, f. Berne Jct.
Rosevear	52.4	"	
Elkton	54.56	"	f. Oliver
Grassmere	57.56	"	f. Robinsons, th. Goodman
Longs	60.06	"	
Sandy	60.6	"	
Bad Axe Pit	63.0	"	
(Junction)	63.9	"	J/PM-N 70.7

CONSTRUCTION/ABANDONMENT

DATE	ACT	END POINTS	MP	CHANGE	MAIN	SOURCE	NOTE
1882/4/4	B28	Sag.–Sebewaing	0–37.0	+37.0	37.0	5	
1884/6/15	B28	Sebewaing–Bart	37.0–44.6	+7.6	44.6	5	
1886/7/1	B28	Bart–Bad Axe	44.6–63.9	+19.3	63.9	5	
1986/3/27	S4	MP 62.6–MP 63.9	62.6–63.9	−1.3	62.6		
1988/12/22	S4	MP 4.1–MP 62.6	4.1–62.6	−58.5			
1988	Y	Sag.–MP 4.1 (as PM-Y1S)	0–4.1	(4.1)	0		
1996	S4	MP 1.1–MP 4.1	1.1–4.1	[Y]−3.0	0		

OWNERSHIP

1882	Saginaw, Tuscola & Huron (B28)
1903/5/6	Pere Marquette Railroad, purchased Saginaw, Tuscola & Huron
1917/3/12	Pere Marquette Railway, reorganize Pere Marquette Railroad
1929/5	Chesapeake & Ohio, control of Pere Marquette Railroad
1947/4/1	Chesapeake & Ohio, merger of Pere Marquette Railroad
1987/9/2	CSX Transportation, merger of Chesapeake & Ohio

BAY PORT BRANCH (PM-SB)

	MILEAGE	COUNTY	CROSSINGS, JUNCTIONS, ETC.
Bart	0	Huron	J/PM-S 44.62
Bay Port	1.39	"	

CONSTRUCTION/ABANDONMENT

DATE	ACT	END POINTS	MP	CHANGE	MAIN	SOURCE	NOTE
1884/6/15	B28	Line	0–1.4	+1.4	1.4	5	
1973	X	North end of line	0.9–1.4	−0.5			
1973	Y	South end of line (as PM-Y2SB)	0–0.9	(0.9)	0		
1988/12/22	S4	South end of line (PM-Y2SB)	0–0.9	(−0.9)	0		

OWNERSHIP

1884	Saginaw, Tuscola & Huron (B28)
1903/5/6	Pere Marquette Railroad, purchased Saginaw, Tuscola & Huron
1917/3/12	Pere Marquette Railway, reorganize Pere Marquette Railroad
1929/5	Chesapeake & Ohio, control of Pere Marquette Railroad
1947/4/1	Chesapeake & Ohio, merger of Pere Marquette Railroad
1987/9/2	CSX Transportation, merger of Chesapeake & Ohio

QUARRY SPUR (PM-SQ)

	MILEAGE	COUNTY	CROSSINGS, JUNCTIONS, ETC.
Quarry Jct.	0	Huron	J/PM-S 47.2
Bayport Quarry	0.8	"	

CONSTRUCTION/ABANDONMENT

DATE	ACT	END POINTS	MP	CHANGE	MAIN	SOURCE	NOTE
??		Line					50

OWNERSHIP

1884	Saginaw, Tuscola & Huron (B28)
1903/5/6	Pere Marquette Railroad, purchased Saginaw, Tuscola & Huron
1917/3/12	Pere Marquette Railway, reorganize Pere Marquette Railroad
1929/5	Chesapeake & Ohio, control of Pere Marquette Railroad
1947/4/1	Chesapeake & Ohio, merger of Pere Marquette Railroad
1987/9/2	CSX Transportation, merger of Chesapeake & Ohio

ROBERT GAGE COAL CO. SPUR (PM-SR)

	MILEAGE	COUNTY	CROSSINGS, JUNCTIONS, ETC.
(Junction)	0	Tuscola	J/PM-S 31.5
Robert Gage Coal Co.	2.2	"	(sec34 T15N R6E)

CONSTRUCTION/ABANDONMENT

DATE	ACT	END POINTS	MP	CHANGE	MAIN	SOURCE	NOTE
??	B43	Line	0–2.2	(+2.2)	0		50
1948 ca.	X	Line	0–2.2	(–2.2)	0		

OWNERSHIP

??	Pere Marquette Railroad (B43)
1917/3/12	Pere Marquette Railway, reorganize Pere Marquette Railroad
1929/5	Chesapeake & Ohio, control of Pere Marquette Railroad
1947/4/1	Chesapeake & Ohio, merger of Pere Marquette Railroad

PORT HURON–PORT AUSTIN (PM-N)

	MILEAGE	COUNTY	CROSSINGS, JUNCTIONS, ETC.
Pt. Hur. (Court St.)	0	St. Clair	J/PM-Q 90.1
Thomas St.	1.3	"	J/GTW-H 59.1+0.3
Pine Grove Ave.	1.60	"	X/PHCL-1 2.83
Poplar St.	1.74	"	X/GTW-H 58.7
Twelfth St.	1.8	"	
Harker St. Siding	2.2	"	
(Elmwood St.)	2.3	"	X/PHCL-4 0.26
Canal Bridge	3.9	"	
Gardendale	6.10	"	
Gratiot Center	6.88	"	
N. St.	8.91	"	
Balkwell	10.40	"	f. Eighty Foot Grade

Atkins	11.66	"	
Kingsley	11	"	
Zion	12.82	"	J/PM-NZ 12.8, f. Balmers, th. Sag. Jct.
Blaine	15.30	"	
Jeddo	17.71	"	
Amadore	20.97	Sanilac	
Croswell	26.64	"	
Odlam	28	"	
Lewis Siding	30.7	"	
Applegate	32.40	"	f. Anderson
Packs Mills	34.6	"	
Packs Siding	34.8	"	
Carsonville	37.56	"	
Poland	38.97	"	J/PM-NS 0
Bridgehampton	41.2	"	f. Wilbur Rd.
McGregor	43.16	"	
Downington	45.28	"	f. Downing
Deckerville	46.25	"	
Brotherton	49.0	"	
Marion	49.3	"	
Cooley Rd.	50.3	"	f. Cedardale
Palms	52.23	"	J/PM-NH 0
Tyre	59.81	"	
Krohns Siding	62	Huron	
Ubly	62.84	"	
Wadsworth	66.36	"	
Huron	69.6	"	J/GTW-B 18.1+0.4
Bad Axe	70.12	"	
(Jct.)	70.7	"	J/PM-S 63.9
Scully Siding		"	
Rapsons Siding	73.6	"	
Clarks	75.6	"	
Filion	76.56	"	
Creevy Siding	77.6	"	
Kinde	79.57	"	
Johnson	82.58	"	
Port Austin	86.82	"	
Pointe Aux Barques	89.15	"	
Eagle Bay	90.86	"	
Grindstone Cty.	92.14	"	

CONSTRUCTION/ABANDONMENT

DATE	ACT	END POINTS	MP	CHANGE	MAIN	SOURCE	NOTE
1879/5/12	B21	Pt. Hur.–Croswell	0–26.6	+26.6	26.6	5	20
1880/3/8	B21	Croswell–Carsonville	26.6–37.6	+11.0		5	20
1880/7/5	B21	Carsonville–Deckerville	37.6–46.3	+8.7		5	20
1880/8/9	B21	Deckerville–Palms	46.3–52.2	+5.9	52.2	5	20
1882/12/11	B21	Palms–Port Austin	52.2–86.8	+34.6	86.8	5	20
1892/7/31	B24	Pt Austin–Grindstone Cty.	86.8–92.1	+5.3	92.1	5	20
1933	X	Pt Austin–Grindstone Cty.	86.9–92.1	–5.2	86.9	1	
1972	X	Pt. Hur.–MP 24.7	0.1–24.7	–24.6	62.3	4	
1984	X	In Pt. Hur.	0–0.1	–0.1			
1984	X	Port Austin–Kinde	86.9–79.5	–7.4	54.8	4	
1986/3/27	S4	Kinde–Croswell	79.5–24.7	–54.8	0		

OWNERSHIP

1879	Port Huron & Northwestern (B21)
1889/4/1	Flint & Pere Marquette Railroad (B24), bought Port Huron & Northwestern
1899/12/6	Pere Marquette Railroad, merger of Flint & Pere Marquette Railroad
1917/3/12	Pere Marquette Railway, reorganize Pere Marquette Railroad
1929/5	Chesapeake & Ohio, control of Pere Marquette Railroad
1947/4/1	Chesapeake & Ohio, merger of Pere Marquette Railroad
1987/9/2	CSX Transportation, merger of Chesapeake & Ohio

ZION–YALE LINE (PM-NZ)

	MILEAGE	COUNTY	CROSSINGS, JUNCTIONS, ETC.
	[Pt. Hur.]		
Zion	12.8	St. Clair	J/PM-N 12.8
Gravel Siding	15	"	
Fargo	17.3	"	
Green Corners	20.5	"	
Lutz Siding	22.0	"	
Yale	24.9	"	J/PM-Q 66.1

CONSTRUCTION/ABANDONMENT

DATE	ACT	END POINTS	MP	CHANGE	MAIN	SOURCE	NOTE
1881/1/17	B21	Zion–Yale	12.8–24.9	+12.1	12.1	5	24
1891	X	Zion–Yale	12.8–24.9	−12.1	0	5	

OWNERSHIP

1881	Port Huron & Northwestern (B21)
1889/4/1	Flint & Pere Marquette Railroad, bought Port Huron & Northwestern

SANDUSKY BRANCH (PM-NS)

	MILEAGE	COUNTY	CROSSINGS, JUNCTIONS, ETC.
Poland	0	Sanilac	J/PM-N 39.0
Scranton	1.6	"	
Berkshire	3.71	"	
Sandusky	7.08	"	
(Jct.)	7.4	"	J/DCS 57.6

CONSTRUCTION/ABANDONMENT

DATE	ACT	END POINTS	MP	CHANGE	MAIN	SOURCE	NOTE
1903/6/1	B44	Line	0–7.1	+7.1	7.1	5	
1986/3/27	S4	Line	0–7.1	−7.1	0		

OWNERSHIP

1903	Sanilac Railroad (B44)
1903/6/1	Pere Marquette Railroad, bought Sanilac Railroad
1917/3/12	Pere Marquette Railway, reorganize Pere Marquette Railroad
1929/5	Chesapeake & Ohio, control of Pere Marquette Railroad
1947/4/1	Chesapeake & Ohio, merger of Pere Marquette Railroad

HARBOR BEACH BRANCH (PM-NH)

	MILEAGE	COUNTY	CROSSINGS, JUNCTIONS, ETC.
Palms	0	Sanilac	J/PM-N 52.3
Minden Cty.	4.17	"	
Ruth	7.72	Huron	f. Adams Corners
Helena	12.7	"	old 12.48

Harbor Beach	18.33	"	f. Sand Beach
Hobson	20.7	"	
Atherton	22.35	"	
Port Hope	25.66	"	
(End)	26.1	"	

CONSTRUCTION/ABANDONMENT

DATE	ACT	END POINTS	MP	CHANGE	MAIN	SOURCE	NOTE
1880/8/9	B21	Palms–Minden Cty.	0–4.2	+4.2		5	20
1880/9/13	B21	Minden Cty.–Harbor Beach	4.2–18.3	+14.1	18.3	5	20
1903/10	B46	Harbor Beach–Port Hope	18.3–26.1	+7.8	26.1	5	
1982	X	Port Hope–Harbor Beach	26.1–19.0	–7.1	19.0	4	
1986/3/27	S4	Harbor Beach–Palms	19.0–0	–19.0	0		

OWNERSHIP

1881	Port Huron & Northwestern (B21)
1889/4/1	Flint & Pere Marquette Railroad, bought Port Huron & Northwestern
1899/12/6	Pere Marquette Railroad, merger of Flint & Pere Marquette Railroad
1903	Harbor Beach & Port Hope (B46), controlled by Pere Marquette; sold to Pere Marquette 21 December 1903
1917/3/12	Pere Marquette Railway, reorganize Pere Marquette Railroad
1929/5	Chesapeake & Ohio, control of Pere Marquette Railroad
1947/4/1	Chesapeake & Ohio, merger of Pere Marquette Railroad

SAGINAW–PORT HURON (PM-Q)

	MILEAGE [Sag.]	COUNTY	CROSSINGS, JUNCTIONS, ETC.
(Jct.)	2.6	Sag.	J/PM-T 2.6
Brewer	2.8	"	
Arndt	5.0	"	
Kulmback	7.14	"	
Gera	11.15	"	f. Frankenmuth
Tuscola	14.98	Tuscola	
Haines	17.2	"	
Vassar	19.37	"	
(Crossing)	19.7	"	X/MC-B 86.0
McHale	21.6	"	
Great Lakes Sand	22.1	"	
Wampson	22.52	"	
Frank	25.3	"	
Juniata	25.41	"	
Juniata Gravel Pit	25.5	"	
Mayville	31.22	"	
Harbin	32.9	"	
Silverwood	36.64	"	f. Silver Creek
Clifford	39.94	Lapeer	X/GTW-P 54.7
Marlette	45.18	Sanilac	
Reagan	46.2	"	
Wilson	48.4	"	
Index	50.6	Lapeer	
Brown Cty.	54.21	Sanilac	
Valley Center	58.23	"	f. Yorks
Melvin	60.88	"	
Merrillsville	64.8	St. Clair	
Yale	66.15	"	J/PM-NZ 24.9, f. Brockway Center

Avoca	73.49	"	
Abbottsford	77.74	"	old 77.54
Bruce	78.8	"	
Wadhams	82.9	"	
Westover	85.62	"	J/DCS 97.3
(Crossing)	86.1	"	X/GTW-C 332.1
Tappan	86.14	"	X/GTW-H 55.6, J/PM-NA 4.0
(Crossing)	87.3	"	X/PHD 0.6
Upton Works	87.9	"	
Tunnel Station	88.10	"	
16th St.	88.2	"	
Military St.	89.1	"	X/PHCL-1 0.65
(Griswold St.)	89.6	"	J/conn. to GTW-C 335.0, 0.1 miles
Pt. Hur. (Court St.)	90.12	"	

CONSTRUCTION/ABANDONMENT

DATE	ACT	END POINTS	MP	CHANGE	MAIN	SOURCE	NOTE
1881/1/17	B21	Yale–Marlette	66.2–45.2	+21.0		5	24
1881/9/21	B21	Marlette–Mayville	45.2–31.2	+14.0		5	24
1881/12/1	B21	Mayville–Vassar	31.2–19.4	+11.8	46.8	5	24
1882/2/21	B21	Vassar–Hoyt	19.4–2.6	+16.8		5	24,27
1882/10/3	B30	Pt. Hur.–Tappan	90.1–86.1	+4.0	67.6	5	28
1889	B24	Tappan–Yale	86.1–66.2	+19.9	87.5	5	
1989	X	Avoca–W of Tappan	73.5–83.3	–9.8	77.7		
1998/4/28	S8	Hoyt–Brown Cty.	2.6–54.3	–51.7			58
1998 ca.	S9	Brown Cty.–Avoca	54.3–73.5	–19.2	6.8		57
1998	Y	W of Tappan–Pt. Hur.(PM-YP)	83.3–90.1	(6.8)	0		

OWNERSHIP

1881	Port Huron & Northwestern (B21)
1882	Port Huron & South Western (B30), controlled by Port Huron & Northwestern
1882/9/13	Port Huron & Northwestern, merger of Port Huron & South Western
1889/4/1	Flint & Pere Marquette Railroad (B24), bought Port Huron & Northwestern
1899/12/6	Pere Marquette Railroad, merger of Flint & Pere Marquette Railroad
1917/3/12	Pere Marquette Railway, reorganize Pere Marquette Railroad
1929/5	Chesapeake & Ohio, control of Pere Marquette Railroad
1947/4/1	Chesapeake & Ohio, merger of Pere Marquette Railroad
1987/9/2	CSX Transportation, merger of Chesapeake & Ohio

ALMONT BRANCH (PM-NA)

	MILEAGE [Pt. Hur.]	COUNTY	CROSSINGS, JUNCTIONS, ETC.
Tappan	3.98	St.Clair	J/PM-Q 86.1
Almont Jct.	4.8	"	
Sweet Siding	4.9	"	
Pound Hill	6.4	"	
Kimball	8.55	"	
Burns	10.78	"	
Wales	14.15	"	
Lamb	15.83	"	
Shanahan	18.7	"	
Memphis	19.68	"	
Martin	22–1/2	"	
Doyle	23.33	"	

Berville	25.58	"	
Allenton	28.91	"	f. Smith
Hopkins Rd.	31.60	Lapeer	
Almont	34.04	"	
(End)	34.1	"	

CONSTRUCTION/ABANDONMENT

DATE	ACT	END POINTS	MP	CHANGE	MAIN	SOURCE	NOTE
1882/10/3	B30	Tappan–Almont	4.0–34.1	+30.1	30.1	5	28
1942	X	Tappan–Almont	4.0–34.1	−30.1	0	1	

OWNERSHIP

1882	Port Huron & South Western (B30), controlled by Port Huron & Northwestern
1882/9/13	Port Huron & Northwestern, merger of Port Huron & South Western
1889/4/1	Flint & Pere Marquette Railroad, bought Port Huron & Northwestern
1899/12/6	Pere Marquette Railroad, merger of Flint & Pere Marquette Railroad
1917/3/12	Pere Marquette Railway, reorganize Pere Marquette Railroad
1929/5	Chesapeake & Ohio, control of Pere Marquette Railroad

SAGINAW BELT LINE (PM-YSB)

	MILEAGE	COUNTY	CROSSINGS, JUNCTIONS, ETC.
	[Mershon]		
(Jct.)	0.7	Sag.	J/PM-L 1.3
(S. wye switch)	0.9	"	
State Rd.	1.5	"	
(Genesee Ave.)	1.6	"	X/SACL-4 1.10
Court St. W. S.	2.6	"	X/SACL-7 0.55
Gratiot Rd.	3.4	"	X/SACL-8 0.17
Fordney	3.9	"	X/MC-S 98.9
Mich. Ave.	4.1	"	X/SACL-6 2.58
(Jct.)	5.4	"	J/PM-YSS 3.7

CONSTRUCTION/ABANDONMENT

DATE	ACT	END POINTS	MP	CHANGE	MAIN	SOURCE	NOTE
1888	B24	MP 0.7–MP 5.4	0.7–5.4	(+4.7)	0	5	
1960 ca.	X	MP 5.4–MP 4.5	5.4–4.5	(−0.9)	0		

OWNERSHIP

1888	Flint & Pere Marquette Railroad (B24)
1899/12/6	Pere Marquette Railroad, merger of Flint & Pere Marquette Railroad
1917/3/12	Pere Marquette Railway, reorganize Pere Marquette Railroad
1929/5	Chesapeake & Ohio, control of Pere Marquette Railroad
1947/4/1	Chesapeake & Ohio, merger of Pere Marquette Railroad
1987/9/2	CSX Transportation, merger of Chesapeake & Ohio

LOOP LINE (PM-YSL)

	MILEAGE	COUNTY	CROSSINGS, JUNCTIONS, ETC.
(Jct.)	0	Sag.	J/PM-B 1.5, aka Loop Line Switch
(Jct.)	1.3	"	J/PM-T 0.4

CONSTRUCTION/ABANDONMENT

DATE	ACT	END POINTS	MP	CHANGE	MAIN	SOURCE	NOTE
1891	B24	MP 0–MP 1.3	0–1.3	(+1.3)	0	5	

OWNERSHIP

1891	Flint & Pere Marquette Railroad (B24)
1899/12/6	Pere Marquette Railroad, merger of Flint & Pere Marquette Railroad
1917/3/12	Pere Marquette Railway, reorganize Pere Marquette Railroad
1929/5	Chesapeake & Ohio, control of Pere Marquette Railroad
1947/4/1	Chesapeake & Ohio, merger of Pere Marquette Railroad
1987/9/2	CSX Transportation, merger of Chesapeake & Ohio

ZILWAUKEE SPUR (PM-YSZ)

	MILEAGE	COUNTY	CROSSINGS, JUNCTIONS, ETC.
Mershon	0	Sag.	J/PM-L 0.8
(Crossing)	0.2	"	X/MC-S 102.4
(End)	6.1	"	

CONSTRUCTION/ABANDONMENT

DATE	ACT	END POINTS	MP	CHANGE	MAIN	SOURCE	NOTE
1888	B24	Mershon–MP 1.8	0–1.8	(+1.8)	0	5	
1889	B24	MP 1.8–MP 2.5	1.8–2.5	(+0.7)	0	5	
1891	B24	MP 2.5–MP 5.3	2.5–5.3	(+2.8)	0	5	
1892	B24	MP 5.3–MP 6.1	5.3–6.1	(+0.8)	0	5	
1905 ca.	X	MP 6.1–MP 5.0	6.1–5.0	(–1.1)	0	5	
1930 ca.	X	MP 5.0–MP 1.4	5.0–1.4	(–3.6)	0		

OWNERSHIP

1888	Flint & Pere Marquette Railroad (B24), of segment
1899/12/6	Pere Marquette Railroad, merger of Flint & Pere Marquette Railroad
1917/3/12	Pere Marquette Railway, reorganize Pere Marquette Railroad
1929/5	Chesapeake & Ohio, control of Pere Marquette Railroad
1947/4/1	Chesapeake & Ohio, merger of Pere Marquette Railroad
1987/9/2	CSX Transportation, merger of Chesapeake & Ohio

WEST SIDE BRANCH (PM-YSW)

	MILEAGE	COUNTY	CROSSINGS, JUNCTIONS, ETC.
Mershon	0	Sag.	J/PM-L 0.7
(Genesee Ave.)	0.7	"	X/SACL-4 0.35
(Crossing)	1.0	"	X/GTW-S 39.6
(Crossing)	1.2	"	X/MC-BS 20.5
(Remington St.)	1.6	"	X/SACL-10 0.14
(Jct.)	1.7	"	J/MC-S 100.7
—via MC-S—			
(Jct.)	2.9	"	J/MC-S 99.5
(Sag. Manufacturing)	3.1	"	

CONSTRUCTION/ABANDONMENT

DATE	ACT	END POINTS	MP	CHANGE	MAIN	SOURCE	NOTE
1888	B24	Mershon–MP 1.7	0–1.7	(+1.7)	0	5	
??	??	MP 2.9–MP 3.1	2.9–3.1	(+0.2)	0		50

OWNERSHIP

1888	Flint & Pere Marquette Railroad (B24)
1899/12/6	Pere Marquette Railroad, merger of Flint & Pere Marquette Railroad
1917/3/12	Pere Marquette Railway, reorganize Pere Marquette Railroad
1929/5	Chesapeake & Ohio, control of Pere Marquette Railroad
1947/4/1	Chesapeake & Ohio, merger of Pere Marquette Railroad
1987/9/2	CSX Transportation, merger of Chesapeake & Ohio

WATER STREET SPUR (PM-YSG)

	MILEAGE	COUNTY	CROSSINGS, JUNCTIONS, ETC.
Washington St.	0	Sag.	J/PM-L 0.1
(Carroll St.)	0.3	"	
(Genesee Ave.)	0.6	"	X/SACL-4 0.06
(Crossing)(Thompson St.)	1.0	"	X/GTW-S 37.8
(Crossing)(Meredith St.)	1.2	"	X/MC-BS 20.3
(End)(Holland St.)	1.8	"	

CONSTRUCTION/ABANDONMENT

DATE	ACT	END POINTS	MP	CHANGE	MAIN	SOURCE	NOTE
??		Line					48

OWNERSHIP

??	Flint & Pere Marquette Railroad (B24)
1899/12/6	Pere Marquette Railroad, merger of Flint & Pere Marquette Railroad
1917/3/12	Pere Marquette Railway, reorganize Pere Marquette Railroad
1929/5	Chesapeake & Ohio, control of Pere Marquette Railroad
1947/4/1	Chesapeake & Ohio, merger of Pere Marquette Railroad

SOUTH SAGINAW LINE (PM-YSS)

	MILEAGE	COUNTY	CROSSINGS, JUNCTIONS, ETC.
(Jct.)	0	Sag.	J/PM-T 2.6, J/PM-Q 2.6
Genesee Ave.	0.7	"	X/SACL-1 1.77
(Sheridan Ave.)	1.5	"	X/GTW-S 37.8
Washington Ave.	1.9	"	X/SACL-2 1.66
S. Sag.	2.8	"	
(Fordney St.)	3.1	"	X/SACL-8 1.27
Centre St.	3.5	"	
(Jct.)	3.7	"	J/PM-YSB 5.4
(End)	4.2	"	

CONSTRUCTION/ABANDONMENT

DATE	ACT	END POINTS	MP	CHANGE	MAIN	SOURCE	NOTE
1880	B24	MP 0–Centre St.	0–3.5	(+3.5)	0	3	23
1882	B24	Centre St.–MP 4.2	3.5–4.2	(+0.7)	0	5	

OWNERSHIP

1880	Flint & Pere Marquette Railroad (B24)
1899/12/6	Pere Marquette Railroad, merger of Flint & Pere Marquette Railroad
1917/3/12	Pere Marquette Railway, reorganize Pere Marquette Railroad
1929/5	Chesapeake & Ohio, control of Pere Marquette Railroad
1947/4/1	Chesapeake & Ohio, merger of Pere Marquette Railroad
1987/9/2	CSX Transportation, merger of Chesapeake & Ohio

SPUR (PM-YSV)

	MILEAGE	COUNTY	CROSSINGS, JUNCTIONS, ETC.
(Jct.)(McCoskry St.)	0	Sag.	J/MC-BS 19.9
(Crossing)	0.25	"	X/SACL-10 0.70
(Crossing)	0.45	"	X/GTW-S
(Jct.)	0.8	"	J/PM-YSS 1.7

CONSTRUCTION/ABANDONMENT

DATE	ACT	END POINTS	MP	CHANGE	MAIN	SOURCE	NOTE
??		Line				49,50	

OWNERSHIP

1888	Flint & Pere Marquette Railroad (B24)
1899/12/6	Pere Marquette Railroad, merger of Flint & Pere Marquette Railroad
1917/3/12	Pere Marquette Railway, reorganize Pere Marquette Railroad
1929/5	Chesapeake & Ohio, control of Pere Marquette Railroad
1947/4/1	Chesapeake & Ohio, merger of Pere Marquette Railroad
1987/9/2	CSX Transportation, merger of Chesapeake & Ohio

SAGINAW–EDMORE–HOWARD CITY (PM-V)

	MILEAGE [Sag.]	COUNTY	CROSSINGS, JUNCTIONS, ETC.
Paines	7.72	Sag.	J/MC-S 95.6
Mentz	9.28	"	
Calvin	9.9	"	
Swan Creek	10.6	"	
Sand Ridge	11.22	"	
Graham	12.27	"	
Graylock	14.22	"	
Hemlock	17.33	"	
Potters	20.4	"	
Merrill	22.34	"	f. Greene
Eaton	24.33	Gratiot	f. Meridian, th. Doyle
Wheeler	27.79	"	
Breckenridge	29.82	"	
St. Louis	36.27	"	J/PM-VO 36.3
(Crossing)	37.0	"	X/AA-O2 8.4
Detroiter Mobile	37.2	"	
(Jct.)	39.6	"	J/PM-VT 0
(Crossing)	39.9	"	X/AA-B 145.1
Alma	40.2	"	old 40.0
(Jct.)	41.0	"	J/PM-VO 40.7
Elwell	44.53	"	
Seville		"	
Boyers	46.53	"	
Riverdale	49.15	"	
Vestaburg	53.07	Montcalm	
Cedar Lk.	56.86	"	
Edmore (new)	59.5	"	J/PM-G 59.5
Edmore (old)	59.71	"	X/PM-J 58.7
Osin	62.3	"	
Six Lakes	65.24	"	
Town Line	67	"	
Belvidere		"	
Lakeview	71.71	"	
Amble	77.76	"	
Howard Cty.	82.52	"	J/GR&I-N 268.0, J/PM-I 64.3

CONSTRUCTION/ABANDONMENT

DATE	ACT	END POINTS	MP	CHANGE	MAIN	SOURCE	NOTE
1873/1/1	B13	Paines–St. Louis	7.7–36.3	+28.6	28.6	5	15
1875/8/15	B15	MP 41.0–Riverdale	41.0–49.2	+8.2		5	

1875/12/1	B15	Riverdale–Cedar Lk.	49.2–56.9	+7.7	44.5	5	
1878/10/1	B15	Cedar Lk.–Edmore	56.9–59.7	+2.8	47.3	5	
1879/3	B22	St. Louis–MP 40.0	36.3–40.0	+3.7		5	
1879/8/1	B15	Edmore–Lakeview	59.7–71.7	+12.0	63.0	5	
1883	B22	MP 40.0–MP 41.0	40.0–41.0	+1.0	64.0	5	29
1886/8	B32	Lakeview–Howard Cty.	71.7–82.5	+10.8	74.8	5	
1943	X	Howard Cty.–Lakeview	82.5–71.7	−10.8	64.0	1	
1974	X	Lakeview–Edmore	71.7–59.7	−12.0	52.0	4	
1987/12/18	S6	Paines–Elwell	7.7–44.5	−36.8	15.2		
1988/6/16	X	Elwell–Edmore	44.5–59.7	−15.2	0		

OWNERSHIP

1873	Saginaw Valley & St. Louis (B13)
1875	Chicago, Saginaw & Canada (B15), of segment
1879	Saginaw & Grand Rapids (B22), controlled by Saginaw Valley & St. Louis
1883/6/5	Saginaw & Western (B32), reorganize Chicago, Saginaw & Canada
1897/1/1	Detroit, Grand Rapids & Western, merger of Saginaw Valley & St. Louis, Saginaw & Western, and Saginaw & Grand Rapids
1899/12/7	Pere Marquette Railroad (B43), merger of Detroit, Grand Rapids & Western
1917/3/12	Pere Marquette Railway, reorganize Pere Marquette Railroad
1929/5	Chesapeake & Ohio, control of Pere Marquette Railroad
1947/4/1	Chesapeake & Ohio, merger of Pere Marquette Railroad
1987/9/2	CSX Transportation, merger of Chesapeake & Ohio

ST. LOUIS–ALMA ORIGINAL LINE (PM-VO)

	MILEAGE	COUNTY	CROSSINGS, JUNCTIONS, ETC.
	[Sag.]		
St. Louis	36.3	Gratiot	J/PM-V 36.3
(Crossing)	36.7	"	X/AA-O2A 9.0
(Jct.)	37.2	"	J/AA-O2 9.3
Alma (old)	40.0	"	
(Jct.)	40.3	"	J/AA-O2 12.4
(Jct.)	40.7	"	J/PM-V 41.0

CONSTRUCTION/ABANDONMENT

DATE	ACT	END POINTS	MP	CHANGE	MAIN	SOURCE	NOTE
1875/8/15	B15	Line	36.3–40.7	+4.4	4.4	5	17
1883	X	Line	36.3–40.7	−4.4	0		

OWNERSHIP

| 1875 | Chicago, Saginaw & Canada (B15) |
| 1883/6/5 | Saginaw & Western, reorganize Chicago, Saginaw & Canada |

ALMA–ITHACA (PM-VT)

	MILEAGE	COUNTY	CROSSINGS, JUNCTIONS, ETC.
(Jct.)	0	Gratiot	J/PM-V 39.6
(Jct.)	0.4	"	J/AA-B 144.9
Ithaca	6.7	"	

CONSTRUCTION/ABANDONMENT

DATE	ACT	END POINTS	MP	CHANGE	MAIN	SOURCE	NOTE
1882/12/28	B31	Line	0–6.7	+6.7	6.7	5	
1897	S1	Line	0.4–6.7	−6.3	5		
1897	Y	In Alma (as PM-Y1VT)	0–0.4	(0.4)	0		

OWNERSHIP

1882	Ithaca & Alma (B31)
1882	Saginaw Valley & St. Louis, operated line
1897	Detroit, Grand Rapids & Western, bought Ithaca & Alma
1899/12/7	Pere Marquette Railroad (B43), merger of Detroit, Grand Rapids & Western
1917/3/12	Pere Marquette Railway, reorganize Pere Marquette Railroad
1929/5	Chesapeake & Ohio, control of Pere Marquette Railroad
1947/4/1	Chesapeake & Ohio, merger of Pere Marquette Railroad
1987/9/2	CSX Transportation, merger of Chesapeake & Ohio

WEST DETROIT BRANCH (PM-DW)

	MILEAGE	COUNTY	CROSSINGS, JUNCTIONS, ETC.
W. Det.	0	Wayne	J/MC-E 2.9
(Mich. Ave.)	0.8	"	X/DSR-M 3.62
(Warren Ave.)	1.8	"	X/DSR-X 8.75
W. Chicago Blvd.	3.2	"	X/DT 4.1
(Northlawn Ave.)	3.4	"	X/DSR-OM 4.35
Fullerton	5.2	"	X/PRR-YU 3.0
Greenfield	5.9	"	f. Town Line
Oak	7.9	"	J/PM-D 13.1

CONSTRUCTION/ABANDONMENT

DATE	ACT	END POINTS	MP	CHANGE	MAIN	SOURCE	NOTE
1871/6/30	B9	W. Det.–Oak	0–7.9	+7.9	7.9	5	10

OWNERSHIP

1871	Detroit, Lansing & Lake Michigan (B9)
1876/12/21	Detroit, Lansing & Northern, reorganize Detroit, Lansing & Lake Michigan
1896/11/30	Detroit, Grand Rapids & Western, reorganize Detroit, Lansing & Northern
1899/12/7	Pere Marquette Railroad, merger of Detroit, Grand Rapids & Western
1917/3/12	Pere Marquette Railway, reorganize Pere Marquette Railroad
1929/5	Chesapeake & Ohio, control of Pere Marquette Railroad
1947/4/1	Chesapeake & Ohio, merger of Pere Marquette Railroad
1987/9/2	CSX Transportation, merger of Chesapeake & Ohio

DETROIT DIVISION (PM-D)

	MILEAGE	COUNTY	CROSSINGS, JUNCTIONS, ETC.
(Detroit)		Wayne	
—via Fort St. Union Depot and Detroit Union Railroad Sta.		"	
Delray	4.60	"	J/DURS 4.5, J/WAB-A 4.4
(Dearborn Rd.)	4.6	"	X/DSR-DR 0.65
Fort St.	5.5	"	J/PRR-YF 0.2
Rougemere (new)	6.6	"	B/DSR-MR 1.29
(Jct.)	6.9	"	J/DT&I-D 15.3
Rougemere (old)	7.06	"	
(Bridge)	7.1	"	B/MC-E 5.6
Michigan Ave.	7.84	"	X/DT 0.6, B/DUR-J 0.78, B/DSR-M 6.16
(Oakman Boulevard)	8.0	"	B/DSR-OM 8.16
(Jct.)	8.1	"	J/PRR-YO 0
(Jct.)	8.8	"	J/PRR-YU 0
(Warren Ave.)	9.5	"	X/DSR-X 12.00
Oak	13.12	"	J/PM-DW 7.9, f. Redford, th. Redford Jct.
Birrel	15.1	"	
Koenig Spur	15.3	"	
Beech	16.14	"	f. Fishers

Norton	16.9	"	f. Elmwood
Elm	17.99	"	f. McKinneys
Stark	20.46	"	f. Livonia?
(Mill St.)	24.3	"	X/DUR-JP 10.41
Plymouth	24.5	"	
Plymouth Jct.	24.64	"	X/PM-T 82.0
Beck	27.0	"	
Turkey	27.51	"	
Dehoco	27.7	"	
Salem	30.98	Washtenaw	f. Dicksons
S. Lyon	36.16	Oakland	J/AA-S 60.4, X/GTW-A 69.0
Green Oak	39.5	Livingston	
Island Lk.	42.04	"	
Brighton	45.24	"	
Genoa	48.5	"	
Canwell	51.09	"	f. Summit
Ann Pere	52.92	"	X/AA-A 72.0, f. Howell Jct.
Howell	54.24	"	
Fleming	57.87	"	
Fowlerville	62.53	"	
Webberville	67.73	Ingham	f. Leroy
Dana	72.3	"	
Williamston	73.40	"	
Meridian	77.59	"	
Okemos	81.27	"	
College Farm	83.4	"	
Trowbridge	84.85	"	X/GTW-C 223.5, J/PM-YEL 0, f. Chi. Cross.
Lans.	87.43	"	J/MC-S 36.9
—via MC-S—			
N. Lans.	88.33	"	J/MC-S 37.8
(Bridge)	88.7	"	B/MUR-NS 1.57
Turner St.	88.8	"	J/LS-L 61.3
Ensel	89.94	"	
State Warehouse	91.42	Clinton	
Delta	94.21	"	
Ingersolls	96	"	f. Daniells
Gr. Ledge	99.35	Eaton	
W. Gr. Ledge	100.1	"	J/PM-I 0.8
Clay	103.10	"	
Mulliken	107.18	"	
Sunfield	112.24	"	
Woodbury	116.31	"	J/CK&S-A 44.2
Lk. Odessa	120.12	"	
Clarksville	126.41	"	
Elmdale	130.39	Kent	X/PM-G 110.5
Alto	133.96	"	
Brannin	135.26	"	
McCords	137.33	"	
Cascade	141	"	
Fox	142.50	"	
E. Paris	144.4	"	
Seymour (new)	148.1	"	
Seymour (old)	148.53	"	J/PM-DR 0, f. Oakdale Park
(Madison Ave.)	149.7	"	X/GRCL-3 1.65
(Division Ave.)	150.1	"	X/GRCL-1 2.52

Pleasant St.	151.5	"			X/GR&I-S 233.2, X/MC-G 93.7, J/PM-DZ 151.5		
Wealthy St.	151.8	"			J/PM-C 0.4		
(Gr. Rpds.	152.05)	"					

CONSTRUCTION/ABANDONMENT

DATE	ACT	END POINTS	MP	CHANGE	MAIN	SOURCE	NOTE
1869/11/18	B5	N. Lans.–W. Gr. Ledge	88.3–100.1	+11.8	11.8	5	4
1871/6/30	B9	Beech–Plymouth	13.1–24.6	+11.5		5	
1871/7/31	B9	Plymouth–Brighton	24.6–45.2	+20.6		5	
1871/7/31	B9	Lans.–Williamston	87.4–73.4	+14.0		5	
1871/8/31	B9	Brighton–Williamston	45.2–73.4	+28.2	86.1	5	
1888/8	B35	W. Gr. Ledge–Wealthy St.	100.1–151.8	+51.7	137.8	5	
1893/1/22	B24	Delray–Oak	4.5–13.1	+8.6	146.4	5	39
1996	T1	Lans.–N. Lans.	87.4–88.3	+0.9	147.3		

OWNERSHIP

1869	Ionia & Lansing (B5)
1871/3/16	Detroit, Lansing & Lake Michigan (B9), merger of Ionia & Lansing
1876/12/21	Detroit, Lansing & Northern, reorganize Detroit, Lansing & Lake Michigan
1888	Grand Rapids, Lansing & Detroit (B35), controlled by Detroit, Lansing & Northern
1896/11/30	Detroit, Grand Rapids & Western, reorganize Detroit, Lansing & Northern
1893	Flint & Pere Marquette Railroad (B24)
1897/1/1	Detroit, Grand Rapids & Western, merger of Grand Rapids, Lansing & Detroit
1899/12/7	Pere Marquette Railroad, merger of Flint & Pere Marquette and Detroit, Grand Rapids & Western.
1917/3/12	Pere Marquette Railway, reorganize Pere Marquette Railroad
1929/5	Chesapeake & Ohio, control of Pere Marquette Railroad
1947/4/1	Chesapeake & Ohio, merger of Pere Marquette Railroad
1987/9/2	CSX Transportation, merger of Chesapeake & Ohio

COLLEGE SPUR (PM-YEL)

	MILEAGE	COUNTY	CROSSINGS, JUNCTIONS, ETC.
Trowbridge	0	Ingham	J/PM-D 84.8
(End)	1.5	"	

CONSTRUCTION/ABANDONMENT

DATE	ACT	END POINTS	MP	CHANGE	MAIN	SOURCE	NOTE
1880 ca.	B16	Line	0–1.5	(+1.5)	0		

OWNERSHIP

1880	Detroit, Lansing & Northern (B16)
1896/11/30	Detroit, Grand Rapids & Western, reorganize Detroit, Lansing & Northern
1899/12/7	Pere Marquette Railroad, merger of Detroit, Grand Rapids & Western
1917/3/12	Pere Marquette Railway, reorganize Pere Marquette Railroad
1929/5	Chesapeake & Ohio, control of Pere Marquette Railroad
1947/4/1	Chesapeake & Ohio, merger of Pere Marquette Railroad
1987/9/2	CSX Transportation, merger of Chesapeake & Ohio

IN GRAND RAPIDS (PM-DZ)

	MILEAGE [Det.]	COUNTY	CROSSINGS, JUNCTIONS, ETC.
Pleasant St.	151.5	Kent	J/PM-D 151.5
(Grandville Ave.)	151.8	"	X/GRCL-9 0.66
Sunnyside	151.9	"	J/PM-C 0.7

CONSTRUCTION/ABANDONMENT

DATE	ACT	END POINTS	MP	CHANGE	MAIN	SOURCE	NOTE
1888 ca.	B35	Line	151.5–151.9	+0.4	0.4		31

OWNERSHIP

1888	Grand Rapids, Lansing & Detroit (B35), controlled by Detroit, Lansing & Northern
1897/1/1	Detroit, Grand Rapids & Western, merger of Grand Rapids, Lansing & Detroit
1899/12/7	Pere Marquette Railroad, merger of Detroit, Grand Rapids & Western
1917/3/12	Pere Marquette Railway, reorganize Pere Marquette Railroad
1929/5	Chesapeake & Ohio, control of Pere Marquette Railroad
1947/4/1	Chesapeake & Ohio, merger of Pere Marquette Railroad
1987/9/2	CSX Transportation, merger of Chesapeake & Ohio

REEDS LAKE BRANCH (PM-DR)

	MILEAGE	COUNTY	CROSSINGS, JUNCTIONS, ETC.
Oakdale Park	0	Kent	J/PM-D 148.53
(Kal. Ave.)	1.1	"	
Reeds Lk.	2.5	"	

CONSTRUCTION/ABANDONMENT

DATE	ACT	END POINTS	MP	CHANGE	MAIN	SOURCE	NOTE
1888/8	B35	Line	0–2.5	+2.5	2.5	5	
1934	X	East end of line	1.4–2.5	−1.1		1	
1934	Y	West end of line	0–1.4	(1.4)	0	1	52

OWNERSHIP

1888	Grand Rapids, Lansing & Detroit (B35), controlled by Detroit, Lansing & Northern
1897/1/1	Detroit, Grand Rapids & Western, merger of Grand Rapids, Lansing & Detroit
1899/12/7	Pere Marquette Railroad, merger of Detroit, Grand Rapids & Western
1917/3/12	Pere Marquette Railway, reorganize Pere Marquette Railroad
1929/5	Chesapeake & Ohio, control of Pere Marquette Railroad
1947/4/1	Chesapeake & Ohio, merger of Pere Marquette Railroad

EDMORE–ELMDALE–FREEPORT (PM-G)

	MILEAGE [Sag.]	COUNTY	CROSSINGS, JUNCTIONS, ETC.
Edmore (new)	59.5	Montcalm	J/PM-V 59.5
(Jct.)	59.9	"	J/PM-J 58.3
Woods Mill		"	
McBrides	63.5	"	
Slaghts Track	65.7	"	J/PM-J2 0
Stanton	67.9	"	J/PM-I 50.3
Sidney	72.6	"	
Moeller	75.5	"	
Martha	77.8	"	
N. Greenville	80.3	"	J/PM-I 45.8, X/GTW-M 40.4
Greenville	81.4	"	
Kidd	86.5	Ionia	J/PM-I 39.6, f. Kiddville
Belding	88.2	"	
Otisco		"	
Smyrna	92.2	"	
Moseley	96.6	Kent	f. LaGrange
Vergennes		"	
Fernald		"	
Lowell	104.1	"	

Malta	104.9	"	X/GTW-D 139.0
Pratt Lk.	107	"	
Hillcrest	108.2	"	
Elmdale	110.5	"	X/PM-D 130.4
Elkerton	111.6	"	
Logan	113.3	"	
Freeport	116.8	Barry	
(End)	117.1	"	

CONSTRUCTION/ABANDONMENT

DATE	ACT	END POINTS	MP	CHANGE	MAIN	SOURCE	NOTE
1870/9	B5	Kidd–Greenville	86.5–81.4	+5.1	5.1	5	
1871/9/30	B9	Greenville–N. Greenville	81.4–80.3	+1.1	6.2	5	
1872/Aut.	B9	Kidd–Belding	86.5–88.2	+1.7	7.9	5	14
1878/1	B9	Stanton–McBrides	67.9–63.5	+4.4		5	
1878/9	B9	McBrides–MP 59.9	63.5–59.9	+3.6	15.9	5	
1887/12	B34	Lowell–Freeport	104.1–117.1	+13.0	28.9	5	
1900/1/1	B42	Lowell–Belding	104.1–88.2	+15.9	44.8	5	
1901	B43	N. Greenville–Stanton	80.3–67.9	+12.4	57.2	5	
1903 ca.	B48	Edmore–MP 59.9	59.5–59.9	+0.4	57.6		44
1935	X	Freeport–Elmdale	117.1–110.5	−6.6	51.0	1	
———————							
1987/12/18	S6	Elmdale–N. Greenville	110.5–78.5	−32.0	19.0		
1988	X	Edmore–N. Greenville	59.5–78.5	−19.0	0	4	

OWNERSHIP

1870	Ionia & Lansing (B5)
1871/3/16	Detroit, Lansing & Lake Michigan (B9), merger of Ionia & Lansing
1876/12/21	Detroit, Lansing & Northern (B16), reorganize Detroit, Lansing & Lake Michigan
1887	Lowell & Hastings (B42)
1896/11/30	Detroit, Grand Rapids & Western, reorganize Detroit, Lansing & Northern
1899/5/1	Grand Rapids, Belding & Saginaw (B43), bought Lowell & Hastings
1899/12/7	Pere Marquette Railroad (B43), merger of Detroit, Grand Rapids & Western
1903/5/6	Pere Marquette Railroad, bought Grand Rapids, Belding & Saginaw
1917/3/12	Pere Marquette Railway (B44), reorganize Pere Marquette Railroad
1929/5	Chesapeake & Ohio, control of Pere Marquette Railroad
1947/4/1	Chesapeake & Ohio, merger of Pere Marquette Railroad
1987/9/2	CSX Transportation, merger of Chesapeake & Ohio

IONIA SPUR (PM-Y1G)

	MILEAGE	COUNTY	CROSSINGS, JUNCTIONS, ETC.
Malta	104.9	"	
Pratt Lk.	107	"	
Hillcrest	108.2	"	
Elmdale	110.5	"	J/PM-D 130.4

CONSTRUCTION/ABANDONMENT

DATE	ACT	END POINTS	MP	CHANGE	MAIN	SOURCE	NOTE
1999	P3	Elmdale–Malta	110.5–104.9	(+5.6)	0		

OWNERSHIP

1999	CSX Transportation

GRAND LEDGE–IONIA–HOWARD CITY (PM-I)

	MILEAGE	COUNTY	CROSSINGS, JUNCTIONS, ETC.
	[Gr. Ledge]		
W. Gr. Ledge	0.8	Eaton	J/PM-D 100.1
Eagle	4.27	Clinton	
Danby	8.8	Ionia	
Portland	12.05	"	
Stebbins	16.4	"	f. Orange, th. Stebbinsville
Collins	17.36	"	
Webber	19.63	"	
Lyons	20.75	"	J/PM-I2 0
(Crossing)	25.4	"	X/GTW-D 124.2
Ionia	26.13	"	
Warden	27.6	"	
Haynor	30.36	"	J/PM-J 30.4, f. Stanton Jct.
Sangsters	33.7	"	
Orleans	34.66	"	f. Palmers
Chadwick	37.50	"	
Kidd	39.61	"	J/PM-G 86.5, f. Kiddville
—via PM-G—			
N. Greenville	45.84	Montcalm	J/PM-G 80.7, X/GTW-M 40.4
Gowen	50.75	"	f. Kaywood
Trufant(s)	55.91	"	
Maple Valley	58.0	"	
Coral	59.99	"	
Howard Cty.	64.3	"	J/GR&I-N 268.0, J/PM-V 82.5

CONSTRUCTION/ABANDONMENT

DATE	ACT	END POINTS	MP	CHANGE	MAIN	SOURCE	NOTE
1869/11/18	B5	W. Gr. Ledge–Portland	0.8–12.1	+11.3		5	
1869/12	B5	Portland–Ionia	12.1–26.1	+14.0	25.3	5	
1870/9	B5	Ionia–Kidd	26.1–39.6	+13.5		5	
1871/9/30	B9	N. Greenville–Gowen	45.8–50.8	+5.0		5	
1871/11/30	B9	Gowen–Howard Cty.	50.8–64.3	+13.5	57.3	5	
1942	X	Warden–Kidd	27.6–39.6	−12.0	45.3	6	
1943	X	N. Greenville–Howard Cty.	45.8–64.3	−18.5	26.8	6	
1972	X	Ionia–Warden	26.1–27.6	−1.5	25.3	4	
1983	S3	MP 24.9–Ionia	24.9–26.1	−1.2			
1983	X	Portland–MP 24.9	11.9–24.9	−13.0	11.1		
1986 ca.	X	Portland–Eagle	11.9–4.3	−7.6	3.5		

OWNERSHIP

1869	Ionia & Lansing (B5)
1871/3/16	Detroit, Lansing & Lake Michigan (B9), merger of Ionia & Lansing
1876/12/21	Detroit, Lansing & Northern, reorganize Detroit, Lansing & Lake Michigan
1896/11/30	Detroit, Grand Rapids & Western, reorganize Detroit, Lansing & Northern
1899/12/7	Pere Marquette Railroad, merger of Detroit, Grand Rapids & Western
1917/3/12	Pere Marquette Railway, reorganize Pere Marquette Railroad
1929/5	Chesapeake & Ohio, control of Pere Marquette Railroad
1947/4/1	Chesapeake & Ohio, merger of Pere Marquette Railroad
1987/9/2	CSX Transportation, merger of Chesapeake & Ohio

LYONS SPUR (PM-I2)

	MILEAGE	COUNTY	CROSSINGS, JUNCTIONS, ETC.
Lyons	0	Ionia	J/PM-20.75
(End)	1.0	"	

CONSTRUCTION/ABANDONMENT

DATE	ACT	END POINTS	MP	CHANGE	MAIN	SOURCE	NOTE
1900	B43	Line	0–1.0	+1.0	1.0	5	
1983	X	Line	0–1.0	−1.0	0		

OWNERSHIP

1900	Pere Marquette Railroad (B43)
1917/3/12	Pere Marquette Railway, reorganize Pere Marquette Railroad
1929/5	Chesapeake & Ohio, control of Pere Marquette Railroad
1947/4/1	Chesapeake & Ohio, merger of Pere Marquette Railroad

IONIA–BIG RAPIDS (PM-J)

	MILEAGE [Gr. Ledge]	COUNTY	CROSSINGS, JUNCTIONS, ETC.
Haynor	30.36	Ionia	J/PM-I 30.36, f. Stanton Jct.
Higbee	32.2	"	
Henderson	32.8	"	
Woods Corners	34.8	"	
Shiloh	36.81	"	
Fenwick	39.95	Montcalm	
Sheridan	44.40	"	X/GTW-M 31.1
Wagers		"	
Fish Creek Branch	47.3	"	
Colby	48.2	"	
Stanton	50.36	Montcalm	J/PM-G 67.9
—via PM-G—			
(Jct.)	58.3	"	J/PM-G 59.9
Edmore (old)	58.74	"	X/PM-V 59.7
Wyman	61.93	"	
Remick	63.3	Isabella	
Murphy	64.87	"	
Rand	66.0	"	
Blanchard	67.71	"	
Millbrook	70.30	Mecosta	
Midland Gravel Co.	71.1	"	
Remus	74.30	"	
Rem	74.6	"	J/PM-JW 0.3
Mec	78.2	"	J/PM-JB 0.6
Mecosta	78.81	"	
Martiny	82.2	"	
Rodney	85.12	"	J/PM-JC 0, X/MEC 6.2
Marshfield	87.3	"	
(Crossing)	92.2	"	X/C&BR 0.9
(Crossing)	93.3	"	X/GR&I-N 290.6
Big Rapids	93.65	"	J/PM-R 51.2

CONSTRUCTION/ABANDONMENT

DATE	ACT	END POINTS	MP	CHANGE	MAIN	SOURCE	NOTE
1873/2	B9	Haynor–Stanton	30.4–50.4	+20.0	20.0	5	
1879/1	B16	Edmore–Blanchard	58.3–67.7	+9.4	29.4	5	
1880/7/4	B16	Blanchard–Big Rapids	67.7–93.7	+26.0	55.4	5	
1933	X	Haynor–Stanton	30.4–50.4	−20.0	35.4	6	
1943	X	Rem–Big Rapids	74.6–93.7	−19.1	16.3	6	
1943 ca.	X	MP 58.3–Edmore	58.3–58.7	−0.4	15.9		
1981	X	MP 58.3–Rem	58.7–74.6	−15.9	0		

OWNERSHIP

1873	Detroit, Lansing & Lake Michigan (B9)
1876/12/21	Detroit, Lansing & Northern (B16), reorganize Detroit, Lansing & Lake Mich.
1896/11/30	Detroit, Grand Rapids & Western, reorganize Detroit, Lansing & Northern
1899/12/7	Pere Marquette Railroad, merger of Detroit, Grand Rapids & Western
1917/3/12	Pere Marquette Railway, reorganize Pere Marquette Railroad
1929/5	Chesapeake & Ohio, control of Pere Marquette Railroad
1947/4/1	Chesapeake & Ohio, merger of Pere Marquette Railroad

HEMMINGWAYS SPUR (PM-J2)

	MILEAGE	COUNTY	CROSSINGS, JUNCTIONS, ETC.
Slaghts Track	0	Montcalm	J/PM-G 65.7
Hemmingway	1.4	"	

CONSTRUCTION/ABANDONMENT

DATE	ACT	END POINTS	MP	CHANGE	MAIN	SOURCE	NOTE
1878/1	B16	Line	0–1.4	+1.4	1.4	5	
1880	X	Line	0–1.4	−1.4	0	5	

OWNERSHIP

1878	Detroit, Lansing & Northern (B16)

BARRYTON BRANCH (PM-JB)

	MILEAGE	COUNTY	CROSSINGS, JUNCTIONS, ETC.
	[Mecosta]		
Mec	0.6	Mecosta	J/PM-J 78.2
Hughes	3.2	"	
McKay	4.3	"	
Moiles	6.6	"	
Chatterton	7.8	"	
Hogan		"	
Barryton	11.73	"	

CONSTRUCTION/ABANDONMENT

DATE	ACT	END POINTS	MP	CHANGE	MAIN	SOURCE	NOTE
1894/11	B16	Line	0.6–11.7	+11.1	11.1	5	
1943	X	Line	0.6–11.7	−11.1	0	6	

OWNERSHIP

1894	Detroit, Lansing & Northern (B16)
1896/11/30	Detroit, Grand Rapids & Western, reorganize Detroit, Lansing & Northern
1899/12/7	Pere Marquette Railroad, merger of Detroit, Grand Rapids & Western
1917/3/12	Pere Marquette Railway, reorganize Pere Marquette Railroad
1929/5	Chesapeake & Ohio, control of Pere Marquette Railroad

CHIPPEWA LAKE BRANCH (PM-JC)

	MILEAGE	COUNTY	CROSSINGS, JUNCTIONS, ETC.
Rodney	0	Mecosta	J/PM-J 85.12
Maynards	3.2	"	
Chippewa Lk.	5.2	"	

CONSTRUCTION/ABANDONMENT

DATE	ACT	END POINTS	MP	CHANGE	MAIN	SOURCE	NOTE
1883/6	B16	Line	0–5.2	+5.2	5.2	5	
1906	X	Line	0–5.2	−5.2	0		

OWNERSHIP

1883	Detroit, Lansing & Northern (B16)
1896/11/30	Detroit, Grand Rapids & Western, reorganize Detroit, Lansing & Northern
1899/12/7	Pere Marquette Railroad, merger of Detroit, Grand Rapids & Western

WEIDMAN BRANCH (PM-JW)

	MILEAGE	COUNTY	CROSSINGS, JUNCTIONS, ETC.
	[Remus]		
Rem	0.3	Mecosta	J/PM-J 74.6
Millers	2.3	"	
Stirling	4.2	Isabella	
Foster	5.6	"	f. Mansfield
Bundy	8.1	"	
Drew	11.2	"	
Weidman	13.29	"	

CONSTRUCTION/ABANDONMENT

DATE	ACT	END POINTS	MP	CHANGE	MAIN	SOURCE	NOTE
1894/9	B16	Line	0.3–13.3	+13.0	13.0	5	
1944	X	Line	0.3–13.3	−13.0	0	6	

OWNERSHIP

1894	Detroit, Lansing & Northern (B16)
1896/11/30	Detroit, Grand Rapids & Western, reorganize Detroit, Lansing & Northern
1899/12/7	Pere Marquette Railroad, merger of Detroit, Grand Rapids & Western
1917/3/12	Pere Marquette Railway, reorganize Pere Marquette Railroad
1929/5	Chesapeake & Ohio, control of Pere Marquette Railroad

CHICAGO DIVISION (PM-C)

	MILEAGE	COUNTY	CROSSINGS, JUNCTIONS, ETC.
Gr. Rpds. (old)	0	Kent	
Williams St.	0.3	"	C/GR&I-S 233.7 to Gr. Rpds. Union Sta.
Wealthy St.	0.4	"	J/PM-D 151.6
Sunnyside	0.7	"	J/PM-DZ 0.4, J/PM-P 0
(Grandville Ave.)	0.6	"	X/GRCL-9 0.56
Godfrey Ave.	0.8	"	J/GR&I-YG 2.2
(Bridge)	1.0	"	B/MC-YG 0.8 (B/MUR-W 48.3)
Plaster Creek (new)	1.8	"	
Wyoming	2.51	"	
Plaster Creek (old)	3.0	"	
Lamar	3.51	"	X/LS-G 91.1
Ivanrest	4.9	"	
Grandville	5.99	"	
Jenison	7.2	Ottawa	f. Jenisonville

Hudsonville	11.76	"	
Vriesland	16.33	"	
Zeeland	20.69	"	
Veneklaasen	22.4	"	
Waverly	24.46	"	J/PM-AO 0
(Junction)	24.73	"	J/PM-A2 23.56
(Bridge)	25.15	"	B/GRHC-A 25.50
Holland	25.31	"	X/PM-A 22.98
Graafschap	28?	Allegan	
Boyd	29.99	"	
E. Saugatuck	32.98	"	f. State Rd.
Richmond	35.4	"	
New Richmond	36.27	"	
Manlius	37.2	"	
Fennville	40.51	"	
Wells	42.4	"	
Pearl(e)	43.6	"	old 44.09, f. Clyde
Bravo	46.09	"	f. Sherman
Pullman	48.16	"	f. Hoppertown
Lee	50.4	"	f. Black River
Grand Jct.	53.80	Van Buren	X/MC-H 29.2
Horner	54.8	"	
Breedsville	57.73	"	
Bangor	60.64	"	
Gross	61.7	"	old 61.41
Thomas	62	"	
McDonald	64.76	"	f. Deerfield
(Crossing)	68.5	"	X/PM-H 15.8
Hartford	68.81	"	
Kirk	71.4	"	
Watervliet	73.84	Berrien	
(Bridge)	75.9	"	B/BHSJ-A 11.6
Coloma	76.25	"	
(Jct.)	76.4	"	J/PM-CP 0
Vrooman	79.1	"	
Riverside	80.14	"	
Hagar	82.0	"	
Waldo	83.7	"	
Ben. Hbr.	85.98	"	J/PM-U 0, J/CC-M 0
Planks Tavern	87	"	
(Drawbridge)	87.5	"	
(Jct.)	87.7	"	J/MC-J 39.5
St. Joseph	87.86	"	
Summit	90.5	"	f. Hilltop
Vine	92.03	"	
Lincoln	92.4	"	
Glenlord	92.8	"	
Stevensville	94.93	"	f. Stevens
Livingston	98.3	"	f. Morris
Bridgman	100.16	"	
Oakhill	103.3	"	f. Browns
Sawyer	104.63	"	f. Troy
Harbert	106.8	"	
Chickaming	107.8	"	
Lakeside	109.2	"	f. Wilkinson, old 109.99

Union Pier	111.08	"	J/PM-CO 111.08, f. Town Line
(Bridge)	113.1	"	B/MC-W 217.2
New Buffalo (new)	115.1	"	old 114.86
Alfred	116.2	"	J/PM-W 34.2
(MI–IN state line)	117.9		
Merrick IN	119.90	LaPorte IN	
Mich. Cty.	125.26	"	
Doran	131.49	Porter IN	
Porter IN	136.6	"	J/LS

CONSTRUCTION/ABANDONMENT

DATE	ACT	END POINTS	MP	CHANGE	MI MAIN	SOURCE	NOTE
1870/2/2	B7	St. Joseph–Union Pier	87.9–111.1	+23.2	23.2	5	5
1871/2/28	B7	St. Joseph–Grand Jct.	87.9–53.8	+34.1		5	
1871/6/30	B7	Grand Jct.–Waverly	53.8–24.5	+29.3	86.6	5	
1872/1/1	B7	Waverly–Gr. Rpds.	24.5–0	+24.5	111.1	5	12
1903/12/15	B47	Union Pier–Porter IN	111.1–136.6	+25.2	117.9	5	43

OWNERSHIP

1870	Chicago & Michigan Lake Shore (B7)
1878/12/20	Chicago & West Michigan Railroad, reorganize Chicago & Michigan Lake Shore
1881/7/16	Chicago & West Michigan Railway, merger of Chicago & West Michigan Railroad
1899/12/7	Pere Marquette Railroad, merger of Chicago & West Michigan Railway
1903	Pere Marquette Railroad of Indiana (B47)
1907/8/12	Pere Marquette Railroad, merger of Pere Marquette of Indiana
1917/3/12	Pere Marquette Railway, reorganize Pere Marquette Railroad
1929/5	Chesapeake & Ohio, control of Pere Marquette Railway
1947/4/1	Chesapeake & Ohio, merger of Pere Marquette Railway
1987/9/2	CSX Transportation, merger of Chesapeake & Ohio

OLD CHICAGO DIVISION (PM-CO)

	MILEAGE [Gr. Rpds.]	COUNTY	CROSSINGS, JUNCTIONS, ETC.
Union Pier	111.08	Berrien	J/PM-C 111.08
New Buffalo (old)	114.8	"	J/MC-W 219.0, J/PM-W 36.2

CONSTRUCTION/ABANDONMENT

DATE	ACT	END POINTS	MP	CHANGE	MAIN	SOURCE	NOTE
1870/2/2	B7	Line	111.1–114.8	+3.7	3.7	5	5
1903	X	Line	111.1–114.8	–3.7	0		43

OWNERSHIP

1870	Chicago & Michigan Lake Shore (B7)
1878/12/20	Chicago & West Michigan Railroad, reorganize Chicago & Michigan Lake Shore
1881/7/16	Chicago & West Michigan Railway, merger of Chicago & West Michigan Railroad
1899/12/7	Pere Marquette Railroad, merger of Chicago & West Michigan Railway

LA CROSSE BRANCH (PM-W)

	MILEAGE	COUNTY	CROSSINGS, JUNCTIONS, ETC.
(End)	0.3	LaPorte IN	
LaCrosse IN	0	"	X/PRR
Meadow	0.3	"	X/C&O
Machler	2.0	"	
Thomaston	6.13	"	X/NKP

Hanna	8.94	"	X/PRR
Chambers	11.9	"	
Wellsboro	15.05	"	X/B&O, X/GTW-C
Magee	17.46	"	X/WAB
LaPorte	23.12	"	X/LS
Hilt	24.6	"	
Belfast	26.50	"	X/NKP
Youngs	29.9	"	
(Bridge)	30.0	"	B/CSSSB
Ackerman IN	31.9	"	
(IN–MI state line)	33.0		
Alfred	34.2	Berrien	X/PM-C 116.2
(Bridge)	34.9	"	B/MC-W 220.3
New Buffalo (old)	36.2	"	J/PM-CO 114.8, J/MC-W 219.0

CONSTRUCTION/ABANDONMENT

DATE	ACT	END POINTS	MP	CHANGE	MI MAIN	SOURCE	NOTE
1882/5/24	B26	LaPorte IN–New Buffalo	23.1–36.2	+13.1		5	
1882/11/12	B26	LaCrosse IN–LaPorte	−0.3–23.1	+23.4	3.2	5	
1903	X	Alfred–New Buffalo	34.2–36.2	−2.0	1.2		43
1988	X	Alfred–Wellsboro IN	34.2–16.8	−17.4	0		

OWNERSHIP

1882	Chicago & West Michigan Railway, built by Indiana & Michigan (B27)
1899/12/7	Pere Marquette Railroad, merger of Chicago & West Michigan Railway
1917/3/12	Pere Marquette Railway, reorganize Pere Marquette Railroad
1929/5	Chesapeake & Ohio, control of Pere Marquette Railway
1947/4/1	Chesapeake & Ohio, merger of Pere Marquette Railway
1987/9/2	CSX Transportation, merger of Chesapeake & Ohio

SOUTH HAVEN BRANCH (PM-H)

	MILEAGE	COUNTY	CROSSINGS, JUNCTIONS, ETC.
S. Haven	0	Van Buren	J/MC-H 39.7
(Crossing)	0.1	"	X/MC-H 39.8
Cableton	1.04	"	
Fruitland	2.81	"	
Roosevelt Hills	5.33	"	f. Packard
Hills Siding	7.0	"	
Covert	7.95	"	
Toquin	11.20	"	J/KLSC-P 0
Hartford	15.3	"	X/PM-C 68.5
Lawrence	21.7	"	
Kirby	24.5	"	
Lk. Cora	25.2	"	
Wildeys	26.1	"	
Benway	26.7	"	
Barrison	26.9	"	
Paw Paw	29.9	"	
(Jct.)	30.0	"	J/spur to old station, 0.4 miles
Lawton	33.4	"	J/KLSC-A 16.0, J/MC-C 160.6

CONSTRUCTION/ABANDONMENT

DATE	ACT	END POINTS	MP	CHANGE	MAIN	SOURCE	NOTE
1867/9	B3	Lawton–Paw Paw	33.4–30.0+0.4	+3.8	3.8	5	2
1877/10/1	B17	Paw Paw–Lawrence	30.0–21.7	+8.3		5	18
1877 ca.	X	In Paw Paw	0.4 miles	−0.4	11.7		19
1878/3/8	B33	Lawrence–Hartford	21.7–15.3	+6.4	18.1	5	18
1887/7/27	B33	Hartford–S. Haven	15.3–0	+15.3	33.4	5	18
1910/1/24	L2	S. Haven–Lawton	0–33.4	−33.4	0	5	
1916/5/31	XL	S. Haven–Lawton	0–33.4	+33.4	33.4	5	
1941	X	Lawton–Paw Paw	30.4–33.4	−3.0	30.4	1	
1971	X	S. Haven–Cableton	0–1.0	−1.0	29.4	4	
1986/8/4	S5	Paw Paw–near Hartford	30.4–17.3	−13.1			
1986	X	Hartford–Cableton	1.0–15.3	−14.3	2.0	4	
1990/2	S5	In Hartford	15.7–17.3	−1.6			
1990/2	Y	In Hartford (to Y1H)	15.3–15.7	(0.4)	0		

OWNERSHIP

1867	Paw Paw (B3)
1877	Van Buren Division of Toledo & South Haven (B17)
1886/9/9	Toledo & South Haven (B33), renaming of Van Buren Division of T&SH
1887/3/7	Toledo & South Haven, merger of Paw Paw
1894/5/18	South Haven & Eastern, reorganize Toledo & South Haven
1903/4/1	Pere Marquette Railroad, purchase of South Haven & Eastern
1910/1/24	Kalamazoo, Lake Shore & Chicago leased entire line
1916/5/31	Kalamazoo, Lake Shore & Chicago lease canceled
1917/3/12	Pere Marquette Railway, reorganize Pere Marquette Railroad
1929/5	Chesapeake & Ohio, control of Pere Marquette Railway
1947/4/1	Chesapeake & Ohio, merger of Pere Marquette Railway

PAW PAW LAKE BRANCH (PM-CP)

	MILEAGE	COUNTY	CROSSINGS, JUNCTIONS, ETC.
(Jct.)	0	Berrien	J/PM-C 76.4
(Coloma)	0.15	"	
(Jct.)	0.8	"	J/BHSJ-B 12.2
Maplewood	1.4	"	
Pleasantview	1.6	"	
Paw Paw Lk.	2.7	"	

CONSTRUCTION/ABANDONMENT

DATE	ACT	END POINTS	MP	CHANGE	MAIN	SOURCE	NOTE
1896	B39	Line	0–2.7	+2.7	2.7	5	
1907/3/23	L	Line	0–2.7	−2.7	0	5	45

OWNERSHIP

1896	Benton Harbor, Coloma & Paw Paw Lake Train Railway (B39)
1903/5/7	Pere Marquette Railroad, purchase of Benton Harbor, Coloma & Paw Paw Lake Train Railway
1907/3/23	Property leased to Benton Harbor, St. Joe Railway & Light Co.

BENTON HARBOR BRANCH (PM-U)

	MILEAGE	COUNTY	CROSSINGS, JUNCTIONS, ETC.
Ben. Hbr.	0	Berrien	J/PM-C 86.0
(Mich. Ave.)	0.4	"	X/BHCL-4 0.3
Bankers	1	"	
(Bridge)	1.6	"	B/CC-M 1.6

Napier	3.2	"	
Nickerson	4	"	
Scotdale	5.74	"	
(Bridge)	5.9	"	B/SOM 28.9
Carl		"	
Royalton	7.76	"	
Hinchman	10.92	"	
Stemms	12.27	"	
Berrien Springs	16.11	"	
Jaquay	19.6	"	
Bainton	21.5	"	
Wenatchee	22.61	"	
Buchanan	26.00	"	
(Jct.)	26.1	"	J/MC-W 198.6

CONSTRUCTION/ABANDONMENT

DATE	ACT	END POINTS	MP	CHANGE	MAIN	SOURCE	NOTE
1881/9/1	B27	Buchanan–Berrien Springs	26.1–16.1	+10.0	10.0	5	25
1897/8/24	B40	Ben. Hbr.–Berrien Sprs	0–16.1	+16.1	26.1	5	
1925 ca.	X	Ben. Hbr.–Buchanan	2.7–26.1	−23.4		1	46
1925 ca.	Y	In Benton Hbr.(as PM-Y1U)	0–2.7	(2.7)	0	1	
1980 ca.	X	In Ben. Hbr. (PM-Y1U)	0–2.7	(−2.7)	0		

OWNERSHIP

1881	St. Joseph Valley Railroad (B27)
1889/7/29	St. Joseph Valley Railway, reorganize St. Joseph Valley Railroad
1897/4/6	Milwaukee, Ben. Hbr. & Columbus (B40), merger of St. Joseph Valley Railway
1903/5/6	Pere Marquette Railroad, purchased Milwaukee, Benton Harbor & Columbus
1917/3/12	Pere Marquette Railway, reorganize Pere Marquette Railroad
1929/5	Chesapeake & Ohio, control of Pere Marquette Railway
1947/4/1	Chesapeake & Ohio, merger of Pere Marquette Railway

ALLEGAN–MUSKEGON–PENTWATER LINE (PM-A)

	MILEAGE	COUNTY	CROSSINGS, JUNCTIONS, ETC.
Allegan	0	Allegan	
(Junction)	1.0	"	J/spur to LS-G 61.8 and DTM 132.9, 0.8 mi.
Mill Grove	4.16	"	
Dunningville	8.38	"	f. Dunning
Gilcrist	9.8	"	
Brick Yard	11.7	"	
Hamilton	13.28	"	f. Rabbit River
Filmore	17.12	"	
May	20.0	"	
Holland	22.98	Ottawa	X/PM-C 25.3
Cronje	24.3	"	
Cronje	24.53	"	X/PM-AM 0, J/PM-A2 24.5
N. Holland	28.0	"	
Harlem	29.17	"	
Farmers	32.6	"	f. Pigeon (River)
W. Olive	33.09	"	
Consumers Power	33.6	"	J/Consumers Power private industrial road
Marble	34.9	"	
Agnew	36.38	"	f. Johnsville

Oconto	38.5	"	
Beech Tree	39.6	"	
Rosymound	41.0	"	
Bottje	41.5	"	
Bakers	43.4	"	f. Sheldon
(Crossing)	43.8	"	X/GRGHM-B 30.4
(Jct.)	43.9	"	J/PM-YGH1 0
Gr. Hav.	43.97	"	J/PM-YGH2 0
(Jct.)	44.2	"	J/GTW-D 187.7
—via GTW-D—			
Ferrysburg	44.78	"	J/GTW-D 187.1
(Crossing)	44.9	"	X/GTW-DA 187.1
Kirk	46.62	"	J/PM-AZ 0, f. Kirks Jct.
Musk. Stone Co.	48.3	Musk.	
Fruitport Siding	48.9	"	
Stone Siding	50.2	"	
Lk. Harbor	52.72	"	f. Black Lk.
Mona Lk.	53.5	"	
(Sanford St.)	54.1	"	X/MUCL-3 2.56
Musk. Heights	54.15	"	
(Crossing)	54.3	"	X/GTW-MR 2.3
(Crossing)	54.9	"	X/GR&I-YM 38.5
(Crossing)	56.1	"	X/GR&I-M 39.1
(Western Ave.)	56.2	"	X/MUCL-1 2.34
Western Ave.	56.2	"	X/GTW-M 95.9
(Jct.)	56.3	"	J/PM-YM1 0
Musk. (new)	56.51	"	
Third St.	56.8	"	f. Musk. (old)
N. Yard	57.8	"	J/PM-AO 35.6
Lakeside	59	"	
Sand Pit	59.3	"	
(Jct.)	59.5	"	J/PM-YM3 0
Berry	61.63	"	J/PM-R 0, f. Big Rapids Jct.
Dalton	63.2	"	
Calif	65.0	"	
Lakewood	66.26	Musk.	f. Sweet?
Nielson	68.6	"	
White Lk. Jct.		"	
Whitehall	71.7	"	old 71.35
Montague	72.17	"	
Rothbury	78.39	Oceana	f. Greenwood
Bunker Lk.	79.5	"	
Blackmarrs	79.8	"	
Cooks Switch	81.5	"	
New Era	82.08	"	
Ford	83.3	"	
Shelby	86.17	"	f. Barnett
Rankin	87.2	"	
Crossmans	87.7	"	
Bender	88.1	"	
E. Golden	89.3	"	
Collins	90.7	"	
(Jct.)	91.62	"	J/PM-AH 91.6, f. Mears Jct.
Mears	91.8	"	
Hart	93	"	
Pentwater	98.96	"	

CONSTRUCTION/ABANDONMENT

DATE	ACT	END POINTS	MP	CHANGE	MAIN	SOURCE	NOTE
1869/12	B6	Ferrysburg–N. Yard	44.8–57.8	+13.0	13.0	5	3
1870/8/29	B6	Allegan–Gr. Hav.	0–44.2	+44.0	58.0	5	6,7
1871/6/30	B7	N. Yard–Montague	57.8–72.2	+14.4	71.4	5	
1872/1/1	B7	Montague–Pentwater	72.2–99.0	+26.8	98.2	5	
1881 ca.	Y	Holland–MP 23.8 (as PM-YH1)	23.0–23.8	(0.8)			26
1881 ca.	X	MP-23.8–Cronje	23.8–24.3	–0.5	96.9		26
1933 ca.	X	Pentwater–Mears	99.0–92.2	–6.8	90.1	6	
1973/11/15	X	Allegan–Hamilton	0–12.0	–12.0	78.1	4	
1977/7/6	P	Ferrysburg–Gr. Hav.	44.2–44.8	+0.6	78.7		
1981	X	Mears–Montague	72.3–92.2	–19.9	58.8	4	
1983	X	In Hamilton	12.0–12.9	–0.9	57.9		
1997/10/1	X	Berry–Montague	62.1–72.3	–10.2	47.7		

OWNERSHIP

1869	Michigan Lake Shore (B)
1871	Chicago & Michigan Lake Shore (B7)
1878/9/21	Grand Haven Railroad, reorganize Michigan Lake Shore
1878/12/20	Chicago & West Michigan Railroad, reorganize Chicago & Michigan Lake Shore
1881/7/16	Chicago & West Michigan Railway, merger of Chi & West Michigan Railroad and Grand Haven Railroad
1899/12/7	Pere Marquette Railroad, merger of Chicago & West Michigan Railway
1917/3/12	Pere Marquette Railway, reorganize Pere Marquette Railroad
1929/5	Chesapeake & Ohio, control of Pere Marquette Railroad
1947/4/1	Chesapeake & Ohio, merger of Pere Marquette Railroad
1987/9/2	CSX Transportation, merger of Chesapeake & Ohio

NEW ALLEGAN–MUSKEGON LINE IN HOLLAND (PM-A2)

	MILEAGE	COUNTY	CROSSINGS, JUNCTIONS, ETC.
	[Allegan]		
(Jct.)	23.56	Ottawa	J/PM-C 24.73
(W. wye switch)	23.8	"	J/PM-AM 0.2
Cronje	24.53	"	J/PM-A 24.53, J/PM-AM 0

CONSTRUCTION/ABANDONMENT

DATE	ACT	END POINTS	MP	CHANGE	MAIN	SOURCE	NOTE
1881 ca.	B26	Line	23.6–24.5	+0.9	0.9		26

OWNERSHIP

1881	Chicago & West Michigan Railway (B26)
1899/12/7	Pere Marquette Railroad, merger of Chicago & West Michigan Railway
1917/3/12	Pere Marquette Railway, reorganize Pere Marquette Railroad
1929/5	Chesapeake & Ohio, control of Pere Marquette Railroad
1947/4/1	Chesapeake & Ohio, merger of Pere Marquette Railroad
1987/9/2	CSX Transportation, merger of Chesapeake & Ohio

OLD HOLLAND–MUSKEGON LINE (PM-AO)

	MILEAGE	COUNTY	CROSSINGS, JUNCTIONS, ETC.
Waverly	0	Ottawa	J/PM-C 24.5
New Holland	4.1	"	
Blendon	6.6	"	
Olive Center	8.2	"	f. Olive
Ottawa	9.7	"	
Robinson(ville)	13.3	"	

Spoonville	17.2	"	
Nunica	19.9	"	X/GTW-D 179.5
Fruitport	25.2	Musk.	
Pickand	26.4	"	J/PM-AZ 3.8
(Bridge)	27.3	"	B/GRGHM-A 28.2
Norton	30.6	"	
Fruitport Jct.	32.6	"	X/GR&I-M 36.0, f. Kanitz
Toledo Crossing	33.4	"	X/GTW-M 93.4, now Simpson
(Ottawa St.)	35.5	"	X/MUCL-1 1.01
N. Yard	35.6	"	J/PM-A 57.8

CONSTRUCTION/ABANDONMENT

DATE	ACT	END POINTS	MP	CHANGE	MAIN	SOURCE	NOTE
1870	B7	Nunica–N. Yard	19.9–35.6	+15.7	15.7	5	8
1871/6/30	B7	Waverly–Nunica	0–19.9	+19.9	35.6	5	
1881	X	Waverly–Fruitport	0–25.2	−25.2	10.4	5	
1934	X	Fruitport–MP 31.3	25.2–31.3	−6.1		6	
1934	Y	No. Yard–MP 31.3(as PM-YM2)	31.3–35.6	(4.3)	0		

OWNERSHIP

1870	Chicago & Michigan Lake Shore (B7)
1878/12/20	Chicago & West Michigan Railroad, reorganize Chicago & Michigan Lake Shore
1881/7/16	Chicago & West Michigan Railway, merger of Chicago & West Michigan Railroad
1899/12/7	Pere Marquette Railroad, merger of Chicago & West Michigan Railway
1917/3/12	Pere Marquette Railway, reorganize Pere Marquette Railroad
1929/5	Chesapeake & Ohio, control of Pere Marquette Railway
1947/4/1	Chesapeake & Ohio, merger of Pere Marquette Railway
1987/9/2	CSX Transportation, merger of Chesapeake & Ohio

HART BRANCH (PM-AH)

	MILEAGE [Allegan]	COUNTY	CROSSINGS, JUNCTIONS, ETC.
(Jct.)	91.6	Oceana	J/PM-A 91.6
Charcoal Kilns	92.2	"	
Cockell	93.9	"	
(Junction)	94.5	"	J/industrial spur, 1.2 miles
Hart	95.2	"	

CONSTRUCTION/ABANDONMENT

DATE	ACT	END POINTS	MP	CHANGE	MAIN	SOURCE	NOTE
1880/7/1	B18	Line	91.6–94.8	+3.2	3.2	5	
1902 ca.	B43	In Hart	94.8–95.2	+0.4	3.6	5	
1981	X	Line	91.6–95.2	−3.6	0	4	

OWNERSHIP

1880	Chicago & West Michigan Railroad (B18)
1881/7/16	Chicago & West Michigan Railway, merger of Chicago & West Michigan Railroad
1899/12/7	Pere Marquette Railroad, merger of Chicago & West Michigan Railway
1917/3/12	Pere Marquette Railway, reorganize Pere Marquette Railroad
1929/5	Chesapeake & Ohio, control of Pere Marquette Railroad
1947/4/1	Chesapeake & Ohio, merger of Pere Marquette Railroad

MACATAWA BEACH BRANCH (PM-AM)

	MILEAGE	COUNTY	CROSSINGS, JUNCTIONS, ETC.
Cronje	0	Ottawa	J/PM-A 24.5, f. Macatawa Jct.
Fort Howard	1	"	
Ottawa Beach	6.3	"	

CONSTRUCTION/ABANDONMENT

DATE	ACT	END POINTS	MP	CHANGE	MAIN	SOURCE	NOTE
1890	B26	Line	0–6.3	+6.3	6.3	5	32
1928 ca.	X	W. end of line	1.6–6.3	−4.7			
1928 ca.	Y	E. end of line(as PM-YH2)	0–1.6	(1.6)	0		

OWNERSHIP

1890	Chicago & West Michigan Railway (B26)
1899/7/16	Pere Marquette Railroad, merger of Chicago & West Michigan Railway
1917/3/12	Pere Marquette Railway, reorganize Pere Marquette Railroad
1929/5	Chesapeake & Ohio, control of Pere Marquette Railroad
1947/4/1	Chesapeake & Ohio, merger of Pere Marquette Railroad
1987/9/2	CSX Transportation, merger of Chesapeake & Ohio

KIRK–PICKAND (PM-AZ)

	MILEAGE	COUNTY	CROSSINGS, JUNCTIONS, ETC.
	[Allegan]		
Kirk	46.62	Ottawa	J/PM-A 46.62
Pickand	50.36	Musk.	J/PM-AO 26.4

CONSTRUCTION/ABANDONMENT

DATE	ACT	END POINTS	MP	CHANGE	MAIN	SOURCE	NOTE
1881	B26	Line	46.6–50.4	+3.8	3.8	5	
1934	X	Line	46.6–50.4	−3.8	0	6	55

OWNERSHIP

1881	Chicago & West Michigan Railway (B26)
1899/12/7	Pere Marquette Railroad, merger of Chicago & West Michigan Railway
1917/3/12	Pere Marquette Railway, reorganize Pere Marquette Railroad
1929/5	Chesapeake & Ohio, control of Pere Marquette Railroad

SOUTH HORN (PM-YM1)

	MILEAGE	COUNTY	CROSSINGS, JUNCTIONS, ETC.
(Jct.)	0	Musk.	J/PM-A 56.3
(Crossing)	0.1	"	X/GTW-YMA 96.0
(Crossing)(11th St.)	0.2	"	X/GR&I-M 39.3
(Crossing)(McCracken Ave.)	2.2	"	X/GTW-MR spur 56.2
Port Sherman	4.0	"	
(End)	6.0	"	

CONSTRUCTION/ABANDONMENT

DATE	ACT	END POINTS	MP	CHANGE	MAIN	SOURCE	NOTE
1881	B6	Line	0–4.7	(+4.7)	0	5	
1882	B6	Extend west end of line	4.7–6.0	(+1.3)	0	5	

OWNERSHIP

1881	Muskegon Lake Railroad (B25)
1900/10/1	Pere Marquette Railroad, bought Muskegon Lake
1917/3/12	Pere Marquette Railway, reorganize Pere Marquette Railroad

1929/5   Chesapeake & Ohio, control of Pere Marquette Railroad
1947/4/1 Chesapeake & Ohio, merger of Pere Marquette Railroad
1987/9/2 CSX Transportation, merger of Chesapeake & Ohio

NORTH HORN (PM-YM3)

	MILEAGE	COUNTY	CROSSINGS, JUNCTIONS, ETC.
(Jct.)	0	Muskegon	J/PM-A 59.5
(End)	2.2	"	

CONSTRUCTION/ABANDONMENT

DATE	ACT	END POINTS	MP	CHANGE	MAIN	SOURCE	NOTE
1890	B2	Line	0–2.2	(+2.2)	0	5	
1895 ca.	X	West end of line	1.0–2.2	(–1.2)	0	5	
1981	X	East end of line	0–1.0	(–1.0)	0		

OWNERSHIP

1890	Chicago & West Michigan Railway (B26)
1899/7/16	Pere Marquette Railroad, merger of Chicago & West Michigan Railway
1917/3/12	Pere Marquette Railway, reorganize Pere Marquette Railroad
1929/5	Chesapeake & Ohio, control of Pere Marquette Railroad
1947/4/1	Chesapeake & Ohio, merger of Pere Marquette Railroad

GRAND HAVEN YARD–LAKE SHORE SPUR (PM-YGH1)

	MILEAGE	COUNTY	CROSSINGS, JUNCTIONS, ETC.
(Jct.)	0	Ottawa	J/PM-A 43.9
(End)	0.6	"	

CONSTRUCTION/ABANDONMENT

DATE	ACT	END POINTS	MP	CHANGE	MAIN	SOURCE	NOTE
1871 ca.	B6	Line	0–0.6	(+0.6)	0		11
1970 ca.	X	Line	0–0.6	(–0.6)	0		

OWNERSHIP

1870	Michigan Lake Shore (B6)
1878/9/21	Grand Haven Railroad, reorganize Michigan Lake Shore
1881/7/16	Chicago & West Michigan Railway, merger of Grand Haven Railroad
1899/12/7	Pere Marquette Railroad, merger of Chicago & West Michigan Railway
1917/3/12	Pere Marquette Railway, reorganize Pere Marquette Railroad
1929/5	Chesapeake & Ohio, control of Pere Marquette Railroad
1947/4/1	Chesapeake & Ohio, merger of Pere Marquette Railroad

GRAND HAVEN YARD – EAST SPUR (PM-YGH2)

	MILEAGE	COUNTY	CROSSINGS, JUNCTIONS, ETC.
(Jct.)	0	Ottawa	J/PM-A 43.97
(Crossing)	0.3	"	X/GRGHM-B 29.8
(End)	1.3	"	

CONSTRUCTION/ABANDONMENT

DATE	ACT	END POINTS	MP	CHANGE	MAIN	SOURCE	NOTE
??	B?	Line	0–1.3	(+1.3)	0		11

OWNERSHIP

1870	Michigan Lake Shore (B6)
1878/9/21	Grand Haven Railroad, reorganize Michigan Lake Shore
1881/7/16	Chicago & West Michigan Railway, merger of Grand Haven Railroad
1899/12/7	Pere Marquette Railroad, merger of Chicago & West Michigan Railway
1917/3/12	Pere Marquette Railway, reorganize Pere Marquette Railroad
1929/5	Chesapeake & Ohio, control of Pere Marquette Railroad
1947/4/1	Chesapeake & Ohio, merger of Pere Marquette Railroad
1987/9/2	CSX Transportation, merger of Chesapeake & Ohio

BIG RAPIDS BRANCH (PM-R)

	MILEAGE	COUNTY	CROSSINGS, JUNCTIONS, ETC.
Berry	0	Musk.	J/PM-A 61.6, f. Big Rapids Jct.
Spires	3.0	"	
Twin Lk.	6.4	"	
Linderman	7.4	"	
Evenwood	10.9	"	
Holton	12.3	"	
Emens	13.4	"	
Brunswick	14.7	"	f. County Line
Reeman	16.4	Newaygo	f. Bailies
Fremont Lk.	18.2	"	
Fremont	19.6	"	f. Fremont Center
Wooster	25.0	"	f. Worcester Hill, th. Worcester
Ryerson	26.1	"	
Alleytown	29.8	"	
White Cloud	31.0	"	X/PM-P 47.2, f. Morgan
Progress Dam	33	"	
Eastman	33.7	"	
White River Club	33.9	"	
Harroun	35.2	"	
Field	36.0	"	f. Fields Crossing
Kinney	37.0	"	
Wilcox	37.4	"	
Swains Crossing	37.9	"	
Cardinal Jct.	38.5	"	
Hayes Siding	38.7	"	
Woodville	40.2	"	J/PM-RX1 0, f. Cooks Station, th. Trav. Roads
Lumberton	42.2	"	
Hungerford	44.0	"	f. Norwich
Bakers	45.5	"	
Trumbulls Siding	45.9	"	
Big Rapids	51.1	Mecosta	J/PM-J 93.6

CONSTRUCTION/ABANDONMENT

DATE	ACT	END POINTS	MP	CHANGE	MAIN	SOURCE	NOTE
1873/7/21	B7	Berry–Big Rapids	0–51.1	+51.1	51.1	5	16
1926	X	White Cloud–Big Rapids	31.0–51.1	−20.1	31.0	1	54
1963	X	Fremont–White Cloud	21.0–30.2	−9.2		4	
1963	Y	In White Cloud (to PM-Y1R)	30.2–31.0	(0.8)	21.0		

OWNERSHIP

1871	Chicago & Michigan Lake Shore (B7)
1878/12/20	Chicago & West Michigan Railroad, reorganize Chicago & Michigan Lake Shore

1881/7/16	Chicago & West Michigan Railway, merger of Chicago & West Michigan Railroad
1899/12/7	Pere Marquette Railroad, merger of Chicago & West Michigan Railway
1917/3/12	Pere Marquette Railway, reorganize Pere Marquette Railroad
1929/5	Chesapeake & Ohio, control of Pere Marquette Railroad
1947/4/1	Chesapeake & Ohio, merger of Pere Marquette Railroad
1987/9/2	CSX Transportation, merger of Chesapeake & Ohio

MUSKEGON RIVER BRANCH (PM-RX1) (LINE NOT LOCATED PRECISELY)

	MILEAGE	COUNTY	CROSSINGS, JUNCTIONS, ETC.
Woodville	0	Newaygo	J/PM-R 40.2
(End)	17.0	"	

CONSTRUCTION/ABANDONMENT

DATE	ACT	END POINTS	MP	CHANGE	MAIN	SOURCE	NOTE
1880	B18	Woodville–MP 13.1	0–13.1	+13.1	13.1	5	
1881	B26	MP 13.1–MP 17.0	13.1–17.0	+3.9	17.0	5	
1883	X	MP 17.0–MP 8.0	17.0–8.0	–9.0	8.0	5	
1884	X	MP 8.0–MP 5.5	8.0–5.5	–2.5	5.5	5	
1888	X	MP 5.5–Woodville	5.5–0	–5.5	0	5	

OWNERSHIP

| 1880 | Chicago & West Michigan Railroad (B18) |
| 1881/7/16 | Chicago & West Michigan Railway (B26), merger of Chicago & West Michigan Railroad |

PETOSKEY DIVISION (PM-P)

	MILEAGE	COUNTY	CROSSINGS, JUNCTIONS, ETC.
Sunnyside	0	Kent	J/PM-C 0.7, J/PM-DZ 0.4
Front St.	0.3	"	X/MUR-W 48.5
(Fulton St.)	0.6	"	X/GRCL-7 0.65
Winter St.	0.87	"	X/GR&I-N 234.7 & C/to G. Rpds. Union Sta.
(Lk. Mich. Drive)	0.9	"	X/LS-G 95.0
Bridge St. (W. Gr. Rpds.)	1.2	"	
Fourth St.	1.5	"	
(Leonard St.)	2.2	"	X/GRCL-18 0.37
Fuller	3.00	"	X/GTW-D 158.9
Park	4.9	"	
Soldier's Home	5.1	"	
Comstock Park	5.5	"	X/GR&I-N 239.2
O'Brien	6.9	"	
Alpine	8.61	"	
Englishville	11.66	"	
Sparta	14.86	"	
Sag. Crossing	15.2	"	X/GTW-M 65.3
Kent Cty.	20.00	Musk.	f. Tyrone, th. Ball Creek, old 20.5
Casnovia	22.52	"	
Voss	24.1	"	
Moon	24.5	"	f. Trent
Bailey	25.86	"	f. County Line
Ashland	27.7	Newaygo	
Grant	29.78	"	old 31.0?
Brooks	31.4	"	
Hess Lk.	33.4	"	
Simmonds	35.3	"	
Newaygo	36.23	"	
Erwin	39.5	"	J/PM-P2 0, J/Cons. Power private road,

			f. Croton, th. McCool
Drew	40.9	"	old 40.61
Newaygo Lakes	41.7	"	
Ray	42.4	"	
Gilbert	43.9	"	f. Uhl, old 43.72
White Cloud	47.28	"	X/PM-R 31.0, f. Morgan
Pattersons	49.6	"	
Ruckel	51.53	"	
Ramona	52.2	"	f. Diamond Loch, old 51.95
Narrow Gauge Crossing	53.4	"	
Norths Siding	53.9	"	
Park Cty.	54.3	"	
Reeves	55.2	"	
Jacksons Crossing	57.2	"	
Brohman	57.8	"	f. Otia, old 58.04
Kopje	58.6	"	
Camp 8	60.0	"	
Brookings (Lk.)	60.5	"	
W. Troy Jct.	61.7	"	J/PM-P3 0
Bitely	63.30	"	
Lilley	65.1	"	
Lilley Jct.	65.5	"	J/PM-P4 0
Nassons	66.6	"	
Alderson	67.5	"	f. Pickerel Creek
Marlboro(ugh)	71.1	Lk.	f. Roby's Jct.
Rainbow	71.6	"	
Baldwin	73.65	"	
(Crossing)	73.8	"	X/PM-L 107.3
Wolf Lk.	81.81	"	
Conley	82	"	
Peacock	84.96	"	X/M&GR-A 31.2
Peters	85.6	"	X/M&L
Little Manistee	88.41	"	
Irons	91.62	"	
Florence	94.4	Manistee	
Dublin	94.85	"	f. Doubling
Wellston	97.71	"	
High Bridge	102.28	"	f. Corfu
Brethren	105.2	"	old 105.68
Conger	108.2	"	X/M&NE-3 1.7
Kaleva	110.12	"	X/M&NE-A 19.9
State Rd.	114.0	"	
Henry	116.98	"	X/A&BR 17.8, X/M&NE-1 4.4
Thom.	120.94	Benzie	X/AA-C 270.4
Gerber	124.2	"	J/PM-P5 0
Wallin	125.27	"	
Clary	128.17	"	J/PM-P6 0
Bendon	130.46	"	f. Inland
Interlochen	134.18	Gr.Trav.	X/M&NE-A 44.0
Grawn	138.02	"	
Beitners	141.1	"	
Sabin	143.4	"	
S. Trav. Cty.	146.1	"	
Boardman (Jct.)	147.21	"	J/PM-YTC 147.21
Trav. Cty. (new)	147.70	"	

Kerry	147.77	"	X/GR&I-T 25.6
Mitchell	150.2	"	
E. Bay	151.5	"	
Acme	153.25	"	
Bates	156.86	"	
Williamsburg	158.72	"	J/PM-PE 0
Mable	160.9	"	
Tunk	162.0	"	
Barker Creek	163.79	Kalkaska	
Rapid Cty.	168.54	"	J/PM-K 0, f. VanBuren
Alden	171.72	Antrim	
Helena	172.2?	"	
Lull	176	"	
Comfort	178.86	"	J/PM-P8, f. Aabee?, th. Lk. Forest
Fishermans Paradise	181.8	"	f. Indian Landing
Bellaire	183.55	"	J/EJ&S-A 18.0
Snowflake	188.7	"	
Cameron	190.8	"	
Central Lk.	191.56	"	
Dix	194.6	"	J/PM-P9 0
Harper	196.59	"	
Ellsworth	198.27	"	
Phelps	202.60	Charlevoix	f. Ballous Siding
Cherrie (new)	207.10	"	J/PM-P10 0
Cherrie (old)	208.0	"	
Belvedere	209.37	"	
Charlevoix	209.80	"	
Burgess	214.9	"	
Superior	216	"	
KawCaChewIng	216.9	"	
Bayshore	218.25	"	
Bells Landing	220	Emmet	
Carpenter	219.2?	"	
Lamson	221.84	"	
Petoskey	225.24	"	
Bay View	226.23	"	J/GR&I-N 425.7

CONSTRUCTION/ABANDONMENT

DATE	ACT	END POINTS	MP	CHANGE	MAIN	SOURCE	NOTE
1872/5/9	B11	Winter St.–Sparta	0.9–14.9	+14.0		5	
1872/6	B11	Sparta–Casnovia	14.9–22.5	+7.6		5	
1872/9/11	B11	Casnovia–Newaygo	22.5–36.2	+13.7	35.3	5	
1875/9/24	B11	Newaygo–White Cloud	36.2–47.3	+11.1	46.4	5	
1880/4/1	B23	White Cloud–Ramona	47.2–52.2	+5.0	51.4	5	
1881/12	B23	Ramona–Brookings	52.2–60.5	+8.3	59.7	5	
1882/6/1	B29	Sunnyside–Winter St.	0–0.9	+0.9		5	
1882/12	B23	Brookings–W. Troy Jct.	60.5–61.7	+1.2	61.8	5	
1883/12/8	B23	W. Troy Jct.–Baldwin	61.7–73.8	+12.1	73.9	5	
1890	B26	Baldwin–Boardman	73.8–147.2	+73.4	147.3	5	
1892/1/3	B37	Boardman–Williamsburg	147.2–158.7	+11.5	158.8	5	
1892/7/17	B37	Williamsburg–Bay View	158.7–226.2	+67.5	226.2	5	
1946/6/21	—	In Gr. Rpds.					56
1956	X	Baldwin–Kaleva	73.8–110.1	−36.3	189.9	6	
1982	X	Kaleva–Grawn	110.1–136.4	−26.3		4	

1982/2/19	S2	Grawn–Williamsburg	136.4–159.1	–22.7			
1982	X	Williamsburg–Charlevoix	159.1–209.7	–50.6			4
1982/2/19	S2	Charlevoix–Bay View	209.7–226.2	–16.5	73.8		

OWNERSHIP

1872	Grand Rapids, Newaygo & Lake Shore (B11)
1880	White River (B23)
1881/7/16	Chicago & West Michigan Railway (B26), merger of Grand Rapids, Newaygo & Lake Shore
1882	Grand Rapids Transfer & Junction (B29), owned by Chicago & West Michigan
1884/2/7	Chicago & West Michigan Railway, bought White River
1892	Chicago & North Michigan (B37), owned by Chicago & West Michigan
1899/11/3	Chicago & West Michigan Railway, bought Chicago & North Michigan
1899/12/7	Pere Marquette Railroad, merger of Chicago & West Michigan Railway
1917/3/12	Pere Marquette Railway, reorganize Pere Marquette Railroad
1929/5	Chesapeake & Ohio, control of Pere Marquette Railroad
1947/4/1	Chesapeake & Ohio, merger of Pere Marquette Railroad
1982/2/19	State of Michigan, bought part of line
1987/9/2	CSX Transportation, merger of Chesapeake & Ohio

IN TRAVERSE CITY (PM-YTC)

	MILEAGE	COUNTY	CROSSINGS, JUNCTIONS, ETC.
	[Sunnyside]		
Boardman	147.21	Gr.Trav.	J/PM-P 147.21
Trav. Cty. (old)	147.78	"	
(Jct.)(Bay St.)	148.5	"	J/M&NE-A 69.8, J/M&NE-NT 1.0

CONSTRUCTION/ABANDONMENT

DATE	ACT	END POINTS	MP	CHANGE	MAIN	SOURCE	NOTE
1890	B26	Boardman–Trav. Cty.	147.2–147.8	+0.6	0.6	5	33
1892 ca.	B26	Trav. Cty.–Bay St.	147.8–148.5	+0.7	1.3		38
1926 ca.	Y	Line (as PM-YTC)	147.2–148.5	(1.3)	0		47
1982/2/19	S2	Line	147.2–148.5	(–1.3)	0		

OWNERSHIP

1890	Chicago & West Michigan Railway (B26)
1899/12/7	Pere Marquette Railroad, merger of Chicago & West Michigan Railway
1917/3/12	Pere Marquette Railway, reorganize Pere Marquette Railroad
1929/5	Chesapeake & Ohio, control of Pere Marquette Railroad
1947/4/1	Chesapeake & Ohio, merger of Pere Marquette Railroad
1982/2/19	State of Michigan, bought line

ELK RAPIDS BRANCH (PM-PE)

	MILEAGE	COUNTY	CROSSINGS, JUNCTIONS, ETC.
Williamsburg	0	Gr.Trav.	J/PM-P 158.72
Angell	4.35	"	
Elk Rapids	8.68	Antrim	
(End)	9.4	"	

CONSTRUCTION/ABANDONMENT

DATE	ACT	END POINTS	MP	CHANGE	MAIN	SOURCE	NOTE
1892/1/3	B37	Line	0–9.4	+9.4	9.4	5	
1979	X	Line	0–9.4	–9.4	0	4	

OWNERSHIP

1892	Chicago & North Michigan (B37), owned by Chicago & West Michigan
1899/11/3	Chicago & West Michigan Railway, bought Chicago & North Michigan
1899/12/7	Pere Marquette Railroad, merger of Chicago & West Michigan Railway
1917/3/12	Pere Marquette Railway, reorganize Pere Marquette Railroad
1929/5	Chesapeake & Ohio, control of Pere Marquette Railroad
1947/4/1	Chesapeake & Ohio, merger of Pere Marquette Railroad

BRANCH TO MARL LAKE (PM-P2)

	MILEAGE	COUNTY	CROSSINGS, JUNCTIONS, ETC.
Erwin	0	Newaygo	J/PM-P 39.5
Marl Lk.	2.0	"	(sec6 T12N R 12W)

CONSTRUCTION/ABANDONMENT

DATE	ACT	END POINTS	MP	CHANGE	MAIN	SOURCE	NOTE
??		Line	0–2.0				50

BRANCH TO WEST TROY (PM-P3)

	MILEAGE	COUNTY	CROSSINGS, JUNCTIONS, ETC.
W. Troy Jct.	0	Newaygo	J/PM-P 61.7
W. Troy	3.9	"	

CONSTRUCTION/ABANDONMENT

DATE	ACT	END POINTS	MP	CHANGE	MAIN	SOURCE	NOTE
1883 ca.	B23	Line	0–3.9	+3.9	3.9		
1895	X	Line	0–3.9	–3.9	0	5	

OWNERSHIP

1883	White River (B23), of segment
1884/2/7	Chicago & West Michigan Railway, bought White River

BRANCH TO SISSONS (PM-P4)

	MILEAGE	COUNTY	CROSSINGS, JUNCTIONS, ETC.
Lilley Jct.	0	Newaygo	J/PM-P 65.5
Sissons	2.4	"	

CONSTRUCTION/ABANDONMENT

DATE	ACT	END POINTS	MP	CHANGE	MAIN	SOURCE	NOTE
1884	B26	Line	0–2.4	+2.4	2.4	5	
1895	X	Line	0–2.4	–2.4	0	5	

OWNERSHIP

1884	Chicago & West Michigan Railway (B26)

GERBER SPUR (PM-P5)

	MILEAGE	COUNTY	CROSSINGS, JUNCTIONS, ETC.
Gerber	0	Benzie	J/PM-P 124.2
King	1.7	"	
Colfax	2.1	"	
Bye	2.6	"	
Alpha	3.8	"	
W. End	4.6	"	
(End)	5.3	"	

CONSTRUCTION/ABANDONMENT

DATE	ACT	END POINTS	MP	CHANGE	MAIN	SOURCE	NOTE
1900	B43	Gerber–MP 3.4	0–3.4	+3.4	3.4	5	
1903 ca.	B43	MP 3.4–MP 5.3	3.4–5.3	+1.9	5.3	5	
1911	X	Gerber–MP 5.3	0–5.3	–5.3	0	5	

OWNERSHIP

1900　Pere Marquette Railroad (B43)

TURTLE LAKE BRANCH (PM-P6)

	MILEAGE	COUNTY	CROSSINGS, JUNCTIONS, ETC.
Clary	0	Benzie	J/PM-P 128.17
Blake	1.2	"	
Hull	1.5	"	
Turtle Lk.	2.7	"	f. Kehoe
Carters	4.2	"	
Case	7.0	"	
Platte River	7.5	"	
Honor	9.1	"	
(Jct.)	9.6	"	J/M&NE-E 11.1

CONSTRUCTION/ABANDONMENT

DATE	ACT	END POINTS	MP	CHANGE	MAIN	SOURCE	NOTE
1895	B26	Clary–Honor	0–9.6	+9.6	9.6	5	
1918	X	Carters–Honor	4.5–9.6	–5.1	4.5	6	
1921	X	Clary–Carters	0–4.5	–4.5	0	6	

OWNERSHIP

1895　Chicago & West Michigan Railway (B26)
1899/12/7　Pere Marquette Railroad, merger of Chicago & West Michigan Railway
1917/3/12　Pere Marquette Railway, reorganize Pere Marquette Railroad

FINCH CREEK BRANCH (PM-P8)

	MILEAGE	COUNTY	CROSSINGS, JUNCTIONS, ETC.
Comfort	0	Antrim	J/PM-P 178.86
Tindall	0.7	"	
Wells Branch	1.3	"	J/PM-P8A 0
Webb	1.9	"	
Norfolk	3.1	"	
(End)	4.9	"	

CONSTRUCTION/ABANDONMENT

DATE	ACT	END POINTS	MP	CHANGE	MAIN	SOURCE	NOTE
1900	B43	Comfort–MP 4.9	0–4.9	+4.9	4.9	5	
1905 ca.	X	Norfolk–MP 4.9	3.1–4.9	–1.8	3.1	5	
1911	X	Comfort–Norfolk	0–3.1	–3.1	0	5	

OWNERSHIP

1900　Pere Marquette Railroad (B43)

WELLS BRANCH (PM-P8A)

	MILEAGE	COUNTY	CROSSINGS, JUNCTIONS, ETC.
Wells Branch	0	Antrim	J/PM-P8 1.3
Gilletts	0.3	"	
Wells	0.8	"	

Fork	1.5	"	
Blosser	2.7	"	

CONSTRUCTION/ABANDONMENT

DATE	ACT	END POINTS	MP	CHANGE	MAIN	SOURCE	NOTE
1905 ca.	B43	Wells Branch–Blosser	0–2.7	+2.7	2.7	5	.
1911 ca.	X	Wells Branch–Blosser	0–2.7	–2.7	0	5	

OWNERSHIP

1905   Pere Marquette Railroad (B43)

ESSEX BRANCH (PM-P9)

	MILEAGE	COUNTY	CROSSINGS, JUNCTIONS, ETC.
Dix	0	Antrim	J/PM-P 194.6
Essex	2.7	"	

CONSTRUCTION/ABANDONMENT

DATE	ACT	END POINTS	MP	CHANGE	MAIN	SOURCE	NOTE
1900	B43	Dix–Essex	0–2.7	+2.7	2.7	5	
1915 ca.	X	Dix–Essex	0–2.7	–2.7	0	5	

OWNERSHIP

1900   Pere Marquette Railroad (B43)

IRONTON BRANCH (PM-P10)

	MILEAGE	COUNTY	CROSSINGS, JUNCTIONS, ETC.
Cherrie	0	Charlevoix	J/PM-P 207.1
Ironton	4.1	"	

CONSTRUCTION/ABANDONMENT

DATE	ACT	END POINTS	MP	CHANGE	MAIN	SOURCE	NOTE
1892/9/26	B37	Cherrie–Ironton	0–4.1	+4.1	4.1	5	
1905 ca.	X	Cherrie–Ironton	0–4.1	–4.1	0		

OWNERSHIP

1892   Chicago & North Michigan (B37), of segment
1899/11/3   Chicago & West Michigan Railway, bought Chicago & North Michigan
1899/12/7   Pere Marquette Railroad, merger of Chicago & West Michigan Railway

KALKASKA BRANCH (PM-K)

	MILEAGE	COUNTY	CROSSINGS, JUNCTIONS, ETC.
Rapid Cty.	0	Kalkaska	J/PM-P 168.54
Clearwater	1.8	"	
Ricker	3.4	"	
Rugg	5.5	"	
Leiphardt	6.9	"	
Mahan	9.1	"	J/PM-K2 0
Kalkaska	11.1	"	X/GR&I-N 371.5
Saunders	15.6	"	
Eastman	18	"	
Spencer	18.4	"	
(Crossing)	19.5	"	X/M&NE-R 56.1
Sands	22.3	"	
Sharon	23.2	"	
Naples	27.0	"	J/PM-K3 0

Halsted	29.0	"
Dempsey	30	"
Butcher	30.8	"
Stratford	32.8	Missaukee
(End)	32.9	"

CONSTRUCTION/ABANDONMENT

DATE	ACT	END POINTS	MP	CHANGE	MAIN	SOURCE	NOTE
1898/1/10	B41	Rapid Cty.–Stratford	0–32.9	+32.9	32.9	5	
1915	X	Spencer–Stratford	19.2–32.9	–13.7	19.2	6	
1918	X	Kalkaska–Spencer	11.5–19.2	–7.7	11.5	6	
1921 ca.	X	Rapid Cty.–Kalkaska	0–11.5	–11.5	0	6	

OWNERSHIP

1898	Grand Rapids, Kalkaska & Southeastern (B41)
1898	Chicago & West Michigan Railway, lease of Grand Rapids, Kalkaska & Southeastern
1903	Chicago & West Michigan Railway, control of Grand Rapids, Kalkaska & Southeastern
1899/12/7	Pere Marquette Railroad, merger of Chicago & West Michigan Railway
1917/3/12	Pere Marquette Railway, reorganize Pere Marquette Railroad

MAHAN BRANCH (PM-K2)

	MILEAGE	COUNTY	CROSSINGS, JUNCTIONS, ETC.
Mahan	0	Kalkaska	J/PM-K 9.1
Lewis Branch	4.1	"	
Soules	4.8	"	

CONSTRUCTION/ABANDONMENT

DATE	ACT	END POINTS	MP	CHANGE	MAIN	SOURCE	NOTE
1898 ca.	B41	Mahan–Soules	0–4.8	+4.8	4.8		
1915 ca.	X	Mahan–Soules	0–4.8	–4.8	0		

OWNERSHIP

1898	Grand Rapids, Kalkaska & Southeastern (B41)
1898	Chicago & West Michigan Railway, lease of Grand Rapids, Kalkaska & Southeastern
1903	Chicago & West Michigan Railway, control of Grand Rapids, Kalkaska & Southeastern
1899/12/7	Pere Marquette Railroad, merger of Chicago & West Michigan Railway

NAPLES BRANCH (PM-K3)

	MILEAGE	COUNTY	CROSSINGS, JUNCTIONS, ETC.
Naples	0	Kalkaska	J/PM-K 27.0
(End)	2.7	"	(sec36 T25N R7W)

CONSTRUCTION/ABANDONMENT

DATE	ACT	END POINTS	MP	CHANGE	MAIN	SOURCE	NOTE
1898 ca.	B41	Line	0–2.7	+2.7	2.7		
1915 ca.	X	Line	0–2.7	–2.7	0		

OWNERSHIP

1898	Grand Rapids, Kalkaska & Southeastern (B41)
1898	Chicago & West Michigan Railway, lease of Grand Rapids, Kalkaska & Southeastern
1903	Chicago & West Michigan Railway, control of Grand Rapids, Kalkaska & Southeastern
1899/12/7	Pere Marquette Railroad, merger of Chicago & West Michigan Railway

WALKERVILLE–ST. THOMAS LINE (PM-EW)

	MILEAGE	COUNTY	CROSSINGS, JUNCTIONS, ETC.
Walkerville ON	0	Essex ON	
Walkerville Jct.	3.0	"	
Pelton	6.2	"	
Oldcastle	7.7	"	
Paquette	10.7	"	
McGregor	13.3	"	
New Canaan	15.3	"	
Fosters	16.7	"	
Marshfield	18.4	"	
Harrow	21.1	"	
Arner	25.9	"	
Kingsville	30.4	"	
Ruthven	34.2	"	
Leamington Gravel Pit	36.0	"	
Leamington	38.0	"	
Piggots Siding	42.8	"	
Wheatley	46.0	"	
Renwick	50.6	Kent ON	
Sutherland Innes Co. Siding	51.4	"	
Coatsworth	52.9	"	
Meredith Siding		"	
Stevenson	55.1	"	
Glenwood	57.6	"	
Merlin	61.0	"	
Ouvry	64.6	"	
Sandison	66.6	"	
Cedar Springs	70.8	"	
Blenheim Gravel Pit	73.4	"	
Blenheim Jct.	73.9	"	
Wilkie	78.3	"	
Ridgetown	84.1	"	
Highgate	89.6	"	
Muirkirk	91.9	"	
Taylor	94.7	Elgin ON	
Rodney	97.8	"	
Kerr Siding	100.1	"	
W. Lorne	102.4	"	
Dutton	109.1	"	
Iona	114.8	"	
Shedden	118.7	"	
Middlemarch	123.1	"	
St. Thomas Jct. ON	127.0	"	

CONSTRUCTION/ABANDONMENT

DATE	ACT	END POINTS	MP	CHANGE	MAIN	SOURCE	NOTE
1888	B51	Walkerville–Ridgetown	0–84.1	+84.1			
1893 ca.	B52	Ridgetown–St. Thomas Jct.	84.1–127.0	+42.9			40

OWNERSHIP

1888	Lake Erie, Essex & Detroit River (B51)
1891/7/31	Lake Erie & Detroit River (B52), to rename Lake Erie, Essex & Detroit River
1903/12/17	Pere Marquette Railroad, leased Lake Erie & Detroit River
1917/3/12	Pere Marquette Railway, reorganize Pere Marquette Railroad

1929/5	Chesapeake & Ohio, control of Pere Marquette Railroad
1947/4/1	Chesapeake & Ohio, merger of Pere Marquette Railroad
1987/9/2	CSX Transportation, merger of Chesapeake & Ohio

SARNIA LINE (PM-ES)

	MILEAGE	COUNTY	CROSSINGS, JUNCTIONS, ETC.
Sarnia ON	0	Lambton ON	
Sarnia Yard	0.8	"	
Wawanosh	4.5	"	
Corunna	6.2	"	
Mooretown	9.9	"	
Courtright	11.1	"	
M. C. R. R. Jct.	11.6	"	
Watson	14.9	"	
Sombra	18.9	"	
Port Lambton	22.3	"	
Whitebread	25.7	Kent ON	
Clancy Siding		"	
Wallaceburg	31.1	"	
Tupperville	37.0	"	
Dresden	41.7	"	
Ennett	44.2	"	
Eberts	47.5	"	
Darrell	49.1	"	
Chatham	54.9	"	
Chatham Jct.	55.9	"	
Richardson	58.8	"	
Fargo	63.2	"	
Blenheim Jct.	65.8	"	
Blenheim	66.6	"	
Shrewsbury	"		
Erieau ON	73.6	"	f. Rond Eau

CONSTRUCTION/ABANDONMENT

DATE	ACT	END POINTS	MP	CHANGE	MAIN	SOURCE	NOTE
1883/9	B50	Erieau–Wallaceburg	73.6–31.1	+42.5			
1886/9	B50	Wallaceburg–Sarnia	31.1–0	+31.1			
1974	X	Erieau–Blenheim	73.6–66.6	−7.0			

OWNERSHIP

1883	Erie & Huron (B50)
1898/1/1	Lake Erie & Detroit River, merger of Erie & Huron
1903/12/17	Pere Marquette Railroad, leased Lake Erie & Detroit River
1917/3/12	Pere Marquette Railway, reorganize Pere Marquette Railroad
1929/5	Chesapeake & Ohio, control of Pere Marquette Railroad
1947/4/1	Chesapeake & Ohio, merger of Pere Marquette Railroad
1987/9/2	CSX Transportation, merger of Chesapeake & Ohio

The dates shown in this record are the completion of the segment by its owner, and not the date of amalgamation into the Pere Marquette system of companies.

ACQUISITION/DISPOSITION RECORD

DATE	ACT	PM–	END POINTS	CHANGE	MI MAIN	NOTE
1862/1/20	B1	T	Sag.–Mt. Morris	+26.1	26.1	
1863/12/8	B1	T	Mt. Morris–Flint	+7.2	33.3	1
1864/11/1	B2	T	Flint–Holly	+16.8	50.1	
1867/9	B3	H	Lawton–Paw Paw	+3.8		2
11/1	B4	B,BP	Sag.–Bay Cty.	+12.5		
12/1	B1	L	Sag.–Midland	+20.0	86.4	
1868/10/20	B1	L	Midland–Averill	+5.8	92.2	
1869/2	B6	A	Ferrysburg–N. Yard	+13.0		3
11/18	B5	D,I	N. Lans.–Portland	+23.1		4
12	B5	I	Portland–Ionia	+14.0	142.3	
1870/2/2	B7	C,CO	St. Joseph–New Buffalo	+26.9		5
8/29	B6	A	Allegan–Gr. Hav.	+44.0		6,7
9	B5	I,G	Ionia–Greenville	+18.6		
11	B1	L	Averill–Clare	+24.6		
12/29	B1	L	Clare–Lk.	+12.1		
	B7	AO	Nunica–N. Yard	+15.7	284.2	8
1871/2/28	B7	C	St. Joseph–Grand Jct.	+34.1		
5/30	B8	T	Wayne–Northville	+11.7		9
6/30	B9	DW,D	W. Det.–Plymouth	+19.4		10
6/30	B7	C	Grand Jct.–Waverly	+29.3		
6/30	B7	A	N. Yard–Montague	+14.4		
6/30	B7	AO	Waverly–Nunica	+19.9		
7/31	B9	D	Plymouth–Brighton	+20.6		
7/31	B9	D	Lans.–Williamston	+14.0		
8/31	B9	D	Brighton–Williamston	+28.2		
9	B1	L	Lk.–Evart	+13.4		
9/30	B9	G,I	Greenville–Gowen	+6.1		
11	B1	L	Evart–Reed Cty.	+13.3		
11/6	B8	T	Northville–Holly	+28.4		
11/30	B9	I	Gowen–Howard Cty.	+13.5		
ca.	B6	YGH1	Lk. Shore Spur (Gr. Hav.)	(+0.6)		11
?	B6	YGH2	E. Spur (Gr. Hav.)	(+1.3)	550.5	11
1872/1/1	B7	C	Waverly–Gr. Rpds.	+24.5		12
1/1	B7	A	Montague–Pentwater	+26.8		
1/1	B8	T,TZ	Wayne–Monroe	+24.0		13
5/9	B11	P	Gr. Rpds.–Sparta	+14.0		
6	B11	P	Sparta–Casnovia	+7.6		
9/11	B11	P	Casnovia–Newaygo	+13.7		
Fall	B9	G	Kidd–Belding	+1.7		14
10/8	B10	F	Horton–Otter Lk.	+14.4	677.2	
1873/1/1	B13	V	Paines–St. Louis	+28.6		15
2	B9	J	Haynor–Stanton	+20.0		
7/21	B7	R	Berry–Big Rapids	+51.1	776.9	16
1874/12/1	B1	L	Reed Cty.–Ludington	+48.4	825.3	
1875/8/15	B15	VO,V	St. Louis–Riverdale	+12.6		17
9/24	B11	P	Newaygo–White Cloud	+11.1		
12/1	B15	V	Riverdale–Cedar Lk.	+7.7	856.7	
1877/10/1	B17	H	Paw Paw–Lawrence	+8.3		18
ca.	X	H	In Paw Paw	–0.4	864.6	19
1878/1	B16	J2	Hemmingways Spur	+1.4		
1	B9	G	Stanton–McBrides	+4.4		
3/8	B33	H	Lawrence–Hartford	+6.4		18

9	B9	G	McBrides–Edmore	+3.6		
10/1	B15	V	Cedar Lk.–Edmore	+2.8	883.2	
1879/1	B16	J	Edmore–Blanchard	+9.4		
3	B22	V	St. Louis–Alma	+3.7		
5/12	B21	N	Pt. Hur.–Croswell	+26.6		20
8/1	B15	V	Edmore–Lakeview	+12.0		
12/15	B20	LM	Coleman–Mt. Pleasant	+14.7		21
	B19	LH	Harrison Jct–Manns Siding	+8.9	958.5	
1880/3/8	B21	N	Croswell–Carsonville	+11.0		20
4/1	B23	P	White Cloud–Ramona	+4.9		
7/1	B18	AH	Mears–Hart	+3.2		
7/4	B16	J	Blanchard–Big Rapids	+26.0		
7/5	B21	N	Carsonville–Deckerville	+8.7		20
8/9	B21	N	Deckerville–Palms	+5.9		20
8/9	B21	NH	Palms–Minden Cty.	+4.2		20
9/13	B21	NH	Minden Cty.–Harbor Beach	+14.1		20
9/30	B19	LH	Manns Siding–Harrison	+6.6		
	B18	RX1	Musk. River Br.	+13.1		
ca.	B16	YEL	College Spur	(+1.5)		
	X	J2	Hemmingways Spur	−1.4		
	B24	M	Walhalla–Tallman	+2.9		22
	B16	MXX	Manistee Br. (unlocated)	+0.3		
	B24	LB	Butters Br.	+3.2		
	B24	YSS	In Sag.	(+3.5)	1061.2	23
1881/1/17	B21	Q,NZ	Zion–Marlette	+33.1		24
9/1	B27	U	Buchanan–Berrien Springs	+10.0		25
9/21	B21	Q	Marlette–Mayville	+14.0		24
12	B23	P	Ramona–Brookings	+8.3		
12/1	B21	Q	Mayville–Vassar	+11.8		24
12/19	B24	F	Otter Lk.–Fostoria	+5.2		
12/31	B27A	M	Walhalla–Manistee	+23.9		
ca.	B26	A2	In Holland	+0.9		26
ca.	Y	A	In Holland (to YH1)	(0.8)		26
ca.	X	A	In Holland	−0.5		26
	X	AO	Waverly–Fruitport	−25.2		
	B26	AZ	Kirk–Pickand	+3.8		
	B6	YM1	S. Horn (in Musk.)	(+4.7)		
	B26	RX1	Musk. River Br.	+3.9	1149.6	
1882/2/21	B21	Q	Vassar–Hoyt	+16.8		24,27
4/4	B28	S	Sag.–Sebewaing	+37.0		
5/24	B26	W	LaPorte IN–New Buffalo	+13.1	[+3.2]	
6/1	B29	P	In Gr. Rpds.	+0.9		
10/3	B30	Q,NA	Pt. Hur.–Almont	+34.1		28
11/12	B26	W	LaCrosse IN–LaPorte IN	+23.4		
12	B23	P	Brookings–W. Troy Jct.	+1.2		
12/11	B21	N	Palms–Port Austin	+34.6		20
12/28	B31	VT	Alma–Ithaca	+6.7		
	B27A	M	In Manistee	+1.2		
	B6	YM1	S. Horn (in Musk.)	(+1.3)		
ca.	X	LB	Butters Br.	−3.2	1280.9	
1883/6	B16	JC	Rodney–Chippewa Lk.	+5.2		
·9	B50	ES	Erieau ON–Wallaceburg ON	+42.5		
11/22	B19	LH	Harrison–Meredith	+14.4		
12/8	B23	P	W. Troy Jct.–Baldwin	+12.1		
	X	RX1	Musk. River Br.	−9.0		

ca.	B23	P3	W. Troy Jct.–W. Troy	+3.9		
	B22	V	In Alma	+1.0		29
	X	VO	St. Louis–Alma	−4.4	1304.1	
1884/6/15	B28	S	Sebewaing–Bart	+7.6		
6/15	B28	SB	Bay Port Br.	+1.4		
	X	RX1	Musk. River Br.	−2.5		
	B26	P4	Lilley Jct.–Sissons	+2.4	1313.0	
1886/7/1	B28	S	Bart–Bad Axe	+19.3		
8	B32	V	Lakeview–Howard Cty.	+10.8		
9	B50	ES	Wallaceburg ON–Sarnia ON	+31.1	1343.1	
1887/7/27	B33	H	Hartford–S. Haven	+15.3		18
12	B34	G	Lowell–Freeport	+13.0		
	B19	LH	Clare–Harrison Jct.	+2.6		30
	X	LH	At Harrison Jct.	−0.1	1373.9	30
1888/8	B35	D	Gr. Ledge–Gr. Rpds.	+51.7		
8	B35	DR	Reeds Lk. Br.	+2.5		
	B51	EW	Walkerville ON–Ridgetown ON	+84.1		
	X	RX1	Musk. River Br.	−5.5		
ca.	B35	DZ	In Gr. Rpds.	+0.4		31
	B24	LG	Coleman Br.	+7.8		
	B24	YSB	Sag. Belt Line	(+4.7)		
	B24	YSZ	Zilwaukee Spur	(+1.8)		
	B24	YSW	W. Side Br.	(+1.7)	1430.8	
1889/	B24	LG	Coleman Br.	+3.3		
	B24	YSZ	Zilwaukee Spur	(+0.7)		
	B24	Q	Tappan–Yale	+19.9	1454.0	
1890/	B26	P	Baldwin–Boardman	+73.4		
	B26	AM	Cronje–Ottawa Beach	+6.3		32
	B2	YM3	N. Horn (in Musk.)	(+2.2)		
	B26	YTC	In Trav. Cty.	+0.6	1534.3	33
1891/	B24	LS	Star Lk. Br.	+4.6		
	B24	LS2	Off Star Lk. Br.	+7.4		
	B24	LS2A	Off Star Lk. Br.	+1.5		
	B24	LS2B	Off Star Lk. Br.	+1.5		
ca.	B24	LH2	Off Harrison Br.	+11.5		41
ca.	B24	LL	Harrison–Leota	+8.8		
	B24	YSZ	Zilwaukee Spur	(+2.8)		
	B36	B	23rd St.–N. Water St. Jct.	+5.4		
	X	NZ	Zion–Yale	−12.1		
	B24	LGXX	Coleman Br. (unlocated)	+3.8		34
	B24	LHXX	Harrison Br. (unlocated)	+34.8		35
	B24	LJXX	Hoyts N & S Br. (unlocated)	+20.5		36
	B24	LMXX	Manistee Br. (unlocated spur)	+5.0		22
	B24	LXSS	Star Lk. Br. (unlocated)	+5.0		37
	B24	YSL	In Sag.	(+1.3)	1632.0	
1892/1/3	B37	P	Boardman–Williamsburg	+11.5		
1/3	B37	PE	Williamsburg–Elk Rapids	+9.4		
7/17	B37	P	Williamsburg–Bay View	+67.5		
7/31	B24	N	Port Austin–Grindstone Cty.	+5.3		20
9/26	B37	P10	Ironton Br.	+4.1		
ca.	B37	YTC	In Trav. Cty.	+0.7		38
	B24	YSZ	Zilwaukee Spur	(+0.8)		
	B24	LGXX	Coleman Br. (unlocated)	+4.1		34
	X	LHXX	Harrison Br. (unlocated)	−2.0		35
	X	LSXX	Star Lk. Br. (unlocated)	−2.6	1730.0	37

1893/1/22	B24	D	Delray–Oak	+8.6		39
	B24	B3	Crow Island Br.	+1.6		
ca.	B52	EW	Ridgetown ON–St. Thomas Jct.ON	+42.9		40
	B24	LGXX	Coleman Br. (unlocated)	+0.3		34
	X	LHXX	Harrison Br. (unlocated)	−8.4	1732.1	35
1894/9	B16	JW	Remus–Weidman	+13.0		
11	B16	JB	Mecosta–Barryton	+11.1		
	B24	LGXX	Coleman Br. (unlocated)	+0.6		34
	X	LHXX	Harrison Br. (unlocated)	−22.7		35
	B24	MXX	Manistee Br. (unlocated)	+3.4		22
	B24	LSXX	Star Lk. Br. (unlocated)	+4.2	1741.9	37
1895	B36	YBS	S. Bay Cty. Spur	(+1.9)		
	X	YM3	N. Horn (in Musk.)	(−1.2)		
	X	P3	W. Troy Jct.–W. Troy	−3.9		
	X	P4	Lilley Jct.–Sissons	−2.4		
	B26	P6	Clary–Honor	+9.6		
ca.	B24	LG2	Br. to Curtis	+5.1		
	B24	LGXX	Coleman Br. (unlocated)	+2.1		34
	X	LH2	Harrison Br. (unlocated)	−11.5		41
	X	MXX	Manistee Br. (unlocated)	−5.1		22
	B24	LSXX	Star Lk. Br. (unlocated)	+2.1	1737.7	37
1896/11/15	B38	T	Toledo Jct.–Alexis	+18.6	(+18.4)	42
	B39	CP	Coloma–Paw Paw Lk.	+2.7		
	X	LH	Frost–Meredith	−7.0		
	X	LJXX	Hoyts N & S Br. (unlocated)	−2.2	1749.6	36
1897/8/24	B40	U	Ben. Hbr.–Berrien Springs	+16.1		
	S	VT	Alma–Ithaca	−6.3		
	Y	VT	In Alma	(0.4)	1759.0	
1898/1/10	B41	K	Rapid Cty.–Stratford	+32.9		
ca.	B41	K2	Mahan Br.	+4.8		
ca.	B41	K3	Naples Br.	+2.7		
ca.	X	LS	Star Lk. Br.	−4.6		
ca.	X	LS2	Off Star Lk. Br.	−7.4		
ca.	X	LS2A	Off Star Lk. Br.	−1.5		
ca.	X	LS2B	Off Star Lk. Br.	−1.5		
ca.	B24	YSJ	Jamestown Spur	(+5.3)		
	X	LJXX	Hoyts N & S Br. (unlocated)	−18.3		36
	X	MXX	Manistee Br. (unlocated)	−3.6		22
	X	LSXX	Star Lk. Br. (unlocated)	−8.7	1753.8	37
1900/1/1	B42	G	Lowell–Belding	+15.9		
	B43	I2	Lyons Spur	+1.0		
	B43	P5	Gerber–Alpha	+3.4		
	B43	P8	Finch Creek Br.	+4.9		
	B43	P9	Essex Br.	+2.7		
	B43	YL1	4th Ward Br.	(+2.2)		
	B43	YL2	Development Br.	(+2.1)		
	B43	LTX	Town Line Lk. Br.	+2.4		41
	B43	LWX	Sweetwater Br.	+5.4	1789.5	41
1901	B43	G	N. Greenville–Stanton	+12.4		
ca.	X	LG2	Br. to Curtis	−5.1	1796.8	
1902 ca.	B43	AH	In Hart	+0.4	1797.2	
1903 6/1	B44	NS	Poland–Sandusky	+7.1		
10	B46	NH	Harbor Beach–Port Hope	+7.8		
12/15	B47	C	Union Pier–Porter IN	+25.2	(+6.8)	43
	B45	BH	Hecla & Western	+9.9		

	B45	BH2	Wolverine Mine #2 Br.	+1.4		
	X	CO	Union Pier–New Buffalo	−3.7		43
	X	W	Alfred–New Buffalo	−2.0		43
ca.	B48	G	In Edmore	+0.4		44
ca.	B43	P5	Gerber Spur	+1.9		
ca.	X	LWX	Sweetwater Br.	−5.4	1825.1	41
1904	B43	B2	Whatcheer Mine Br.	+3.7	1828.8	
1905	B43	B	N. Water St. Jct.–Bay Cty.	+0.5		
ca.	X	BP	In Bay Cty.	−1.4		53
ca.	X	TZ	Toledo Jct.–Monroe	−2.5		
ca.	X	P8	Finch Creek Br.	−1.8		
ca.	B43	P8A	Wells Br.	+2.7		
ca.	X	P10	Ironton Br.	−4.1		
ca.	X	LTX	Town Line Lk. Br.	−2.4		41
ca.	X	YSZ	Zilwaukee Spur	(−1.1)		
ca.	X	B3	Crow Island Br.	−1.6		
	X	LGXX	Coleman Br. (unlocated)	−7.9	1806.6	34
1906	X	JC	Rodney–Chippewa Lk.	−5.2		
	X	LGXX	Coleman Br. (unlocated)	−3.0	1798.4	34
1907 3/23	L1	CP	Coloma–Paw Paw Lk.	−2.7	1795.7	45
1910/1/4	L2	H	S. Haven–Lawton	−33.4	1762.3	
1911	X	P5	Gerber Spur	−5.3		
ca.	X	P8	Finch Creek Br.	−3.1		
ca.	X	P8A	Wells Br.	−2.7	1751.2	
1915	X	K	Spencer–Stratford	−13.7		
ca.	X	P9	Essex Br.	−2.7		
ca.	X	K2	Mahan Br.	−4.8		
ca.	X	K3	Naples Br.	−2.7	1727.3	
1916/5/31	XL	H	S. Haven–Lawton	+33.4		
	X	LH	Frost–Harrison	−7.6		
	X	LHXX	Harrison Br. (unlocated)	−1.7	1751.4	35
1918	X	P6	Carters–Honor	−5.1		
	X	K	Kalkaska–Spencer	−7.7	1738.6	
1921	X	P6	Clary–Carters	−4.5		
ca.	X	K	Rapid Cty.–Kalkaska	−11.5	1722.6	
1922 ca.	X	LL	Harrison–Leota	−8.8	1713.8	
1923/6/5	B49	FB	Flint Belt	+8.2	1722.0	
1924 ca.	Y	U	In Ben. Hbr. (PM-Y1U)	(2.7)		
ca.	X	U	Ben. Hbr.–Buchanan	−23.4	1695.9	46
1925 ca.	X	YSJ	Jamestown Spur	(−4.3)	1695.9	
1926 ca.	Y	YTC	In Trav. Cty.	(1.3)		47
	X	R	White Cloud–Big Rapids	−20.1	1674.5	54
1928	X	B2	Whatcheer Mine Br.	−3.7		
	Y	AM	At Cronje (as PM-YH2)	(1.6)		
ca.	X	AM	Cronje–Ottawa Beach	−4.7	1664.5	
1930	X	B2	Near Bay Cty.	−0.6		
ca.	X	YSZ	In Sag.	(−3.6)	1663.9	
1933 ca.	X	A	Pentwater–Mears	−6.8		
	X	F	Otisville–Fostoria	−9.8		
	X	N	Port Austin–Grindstone Cty.	−5.2		
	X	J	Haynor–Stanton	−20.0	1622.1	
1934	X	AO	Fruitport–Kanitz	−6.1		
	Y	AO	In Musk. (as PM-YM2)	(4.3)		
	X	DR	Oakdale Park–Reeds Lk.	−1.1		52
	Y	DR	In Gr. Rpds. (as PM-Y1DR)	(1.4)		

	X	AZ	Kirk–Pickand	–3.8	1605.4	55
1935	X	G	Elmdale–Freeport	–6.6	1598.8	
1941 ca.	X	H	Lawton–Paw Paw	–3.0		
	X	BH	Hecla & Western	–7.7		
	Y	BH	Hecla & Western (as PM-YBH)	(1.6)		
	X	BH2	Wolverine Mine #2 Br.	–1.4	1585.1	
1942 ca.	X	NA	Tappan–Almont	–30.1		
	X	I	Warden–Kidd	–12.0	1543.0	
1943	X	I	N. Greenville–Howard Cty.	–18.5		
	X	JB	Mecosta–Barryton	–11.1		
	X	J	In Edmore	–0.4		
	X	J	Remus–Big Rapids	–19.1		
	X	V	Lakeview–Howard Cty.	–10.8		
	X	LG	Coleman–Beaverton	–11.1	1472.0	
1944	X	JW	Remus–Weidman	–13.0		
	X	LH	Clare–Harrison	–17.8	1441.2	

On 1 April 1947 this company was merged into Chesapeake & Ohio. Its Acquisition/Disposition Record is continued in two places: under the name of the former company and under the name of the new company. The Michigan lines conveyed were:

LINE DESIG.	END POINTS	MP	MAIN	SOURCE	NOTE
PM-T	Sag.–Toledo OH	0–130.1	130.1		
PM-F	Horton–Otisville	4.7–14.5	9.8		
PM-FB	Flint Belt	29.5–37.7	8.2		
PM-B	Sag.–Bay Cty.	0–17.0	17.0		
PM-YBH	Huron & Western	1.1–2.7	(1.4)		
PM-YBS	S. Bay Cty. Spur	0–1.9	(1.9)		
PM-YBE	Essexville Spur	0–2.4	(2.4)		
PM-L	Sag.–Ludington	0–137.6	137.6		
PM-YL1	4th Ward Branch, Lud.	0–2.2	(2.2)		
PM-YL2	Development Branch, Lud.	0–2.1	(2.1)		
PM-M	Walhalla–Manistee	0–26.8	26.8		
PM-LM	Coleman–Mt. Pl.	0–14.7	14.7		
PM-S	Sag.–Bad Axe	0–63.9	63.9		
PM-SB	Bay Port Branch	0–1.4	1.4		
PM-SR	Robert Gage Coal Spur	0–2.2	(2.2)		
PM-N	Pt. Hur.–Port Austin	0–86.9	86.9		
PM-NS	Poland–Sandusky	0–7.1	7.1		
PM-NH	Palms–Harbor Beach	0–26.1	26.1		
PM-Q	Sag.–Pt. Hur.	2.6–90.1	87.5		
PM-YSB	Sag. Belt Line	0.7–5.4	(4.7)		
PM-YSL	Loop Line, Sag.	0–1.3	(1.3)		
PM-YSZ	Zilwaukee Spur, Sag.	0–1.4	(1.4)		
PM-YSW	W. Side Branch, Sag.	0–1.7 & 2.9–3.1	(1.9)		
PM-YSS	S. Sag. Line, Sag.	0–4.2	(4.2)		
PM-V	Paines–Lakeview	7.7–71.7	64.0		
PM-Y1VT	In Alma	0–0.4	(0.4)		
PM-D	Delray–Wealthy St., G. R.	4.6–151.8	146.4		
PM-YEL	In E. Lans.	0–1.5	(1.5)		
PM-DZ	Pleasant St.–Sunnyside	151.5–151.9	0.4		
PM-YDR	Reeds Lk. Br., Gr. R.	0–1.4	(1.4)		
PM-G	Edmore–Elmdale	59.5–110.5	51.0		
PM-I	Gr.Ledge–Ionia	0.8–27.6	26.8		
PM-I2	Lyons Spur	0–1.0	1.0		
PM-C	Gr. Rpds.–Porter IN	0–117.9	117.9		

PM-W	New Buffalo–LaCrosse IN	34.2–0	1.2	
PM-H	S. Haven–Paw Paw	0–30.4	30.4	
PM-Y1U	In Ben. Hbr.	0–2.7	(2.7)	
PM-A	Allegan–Holland	0–23.0		
	And Cronje–Mears	24.5–92.2	90.1	
PM-A2	Waverly–Cronje	23.6–24.5	0.9	
PM-Y1H	In Holland	23.0–23.8	(0.8)	
PM-AM	Mears–Hart	91.6–95.2	3.6	
PM-YM1	S. Horn, Musekgon	0–6.0	(6.0)	
PM-YM2	In Musk.	31.3–35.6	(4.3)	
PM-YM3	N. Horn, Musk.	0–1.0	(1.0)	
PM-YGH1	In Gr. Hav.	0–0.6	(0.6)	
PM-YHG2	In Gr. Hav.	0–1.3	(1.3)	
PM-R	Berry–White Cloud	0–31.0	31.0	
PM-P	Sunnyside–Bay View	0–226.2	226.2	
PM-YTC	In Trav. Cty.	147.2–148.5	(1.3)	
PM-PE	Williamsburg–Elk Rapids	0–9.4	9.4	
		TOTAL	1441.2	

DATE	ACT	PM–	END POINTS	MI CHANGE	MAIN	NOTE
1956	X	P	Baldwin–Kaleva	–36.3	1404.9	
1960 ca.	X	YSB	In Sag.	(–0.9)	1404.9	
1963	X	R	White Cloud–Fremont	–9.2		
	Y	R	In White Cloud (as PM-Y1R)	(0.8)	1394.9	
1970 ca.	X	YGH1	In Gr. Hav.	(–0.6)		
	Y	T	In Flint (as PM-Y1T & Y2T)	(8.2)		
	X	T	In Flint	–0.7	1386.0	
1971	X	H	S. Haven–Cableton	–1.0		
	X	ES	Erieau–Blenheim	–7.0	1385.0	
1972	X	I	Ionia–Warden	–1.5		
	X	F	Horton–Otisville	–9.0		
	Y	F	In Horton (as PM-Y1F)	(0.8)		
	X	N	Pt. Hur.–Croswell	–24.6		
	X	NH	Port Hope–Harbor Beach	–7.1	1342.0	
1973/11/15	X	A	Allegan–Hamilton	–12.0		
	Y	SB	Bay Port Br. (as PM-Y2SB)	(0.9)		
	X	SB	In Bay Port	–0.5	1328.6	
1974	X	V	Edmore–Lakeview	–12.0	1316.6	
1977/7/6	P1	A	Ferrysburg–Gr. Hav.	+0.6	1317.2	
1979	X	PE	Williamsburg–Elk Rapids	–9.4		
	X	LM	Coleman–Mt. Pl.	–11.6		
	Y	LM	In Mt. Pl. (as PM-Y2LM)	(2.3)		
	Y	LM	In Coleman (as PM-Y1LM)	(0.8)	1293.1	
1981	X	A	Mears–Montague	–19.9		
	X	AH	Mears–Hart	–3.6		
	X	YM3	N. Horn, Musk.	(–1.0)		
	X	I	Edmore–Remus	–15.9	1253.7	
1982/2/19	S2	P	Grawn–Williamsburg	–22.7		
2/19	S2	P	Charlevoix–Bay View	–16.5		
	S2	YTC	In Trav. Cty.	(–1.3)		
	X	P	Kaleva–Grawn	–26.3		
	X	P	Williamsburg–Charlevoix	–50.6	1137.6	
1983	X	A	In Hamilton	–0.9		
	S3	I	In Ionia	–1.2		
	X	I	Portland–Ionia	–13.0		

	X	I2	Lyons Spur	−1.0	
/1/26	P1	[GTW-YMG]In Greenville		(+0.6)	1121.5
1984	X	N	Port Austin–Kinde	−7.4	
	X	N	In Pt. Hur.	−0.1	1114.0
1986/3/27	S4	S	In Bad Axe	−1.3	
3/27	S4	N	Kinde–Croswell	−54.8	
3/27	S4	NH	Palms–Harbor Beach	−19.0	
3/27	S4	NS	Poland–Sandusky	−7.1	
8/14	S5	H	Paw Paw–Hartford	−13.1	
	S	H	Cableton–Hartford	−14.3	
ca.	S	I	Eagle–Portland	−7.6	
	X	Y1U	In Ben. Hbr.	(−2.7)	996.8
1987/11	X	L	Evart–Clare	−23.7	
12/18	S6	G	Elmdale–N. Greenville	−32.0	
12/18	S6	V	Paines–Elwell	−36.8	
12/18	S6	[GTW-YMG]In Greenville		(−0.6)	904.3
1988/6	S7	L	In Clare	−2.6	
ca.	S	L	Clare–Baldwin	−31.6	
12/22	S4	S	Sag.–Bad Axe	−58.5	
12/22	S4	YSB	Bay Port Br.	(−0.9)	
	Y	S	In Sag. (as PM-Y1S)	(4.1)	
	X	G	N. Greenville–Edmore	−19.0	
	X	V	Elwell–Edmore	−15.2	
	X	Q	Avoca–W of Tappan	−9.8	
	X	W	Alfred–Wellsboro IN	−1.2	762.3
1989/4/3	X	L	Midland–Clare	−28.4	733.9
1990/2	S5	H	In Hartford	−1.6	
2	Y	H	In Hartford (as PM-Y1H)	(0.4)	731.9
1996	S4	Y1S	In Sag.	(−3.0)	
	T1	D	Lans.–N. Lans.	+0.9	732.8
1997/10/1	X	A	Berry–Montague	−10.2	722.6
1998/4/28	S8	Q	Hoyt–Brown Cty.	−51.7	59
	S9	Q	Brown Cty.–Avoca	−19.2	58
	Y	Q	W of Tappan–Pt. Hur. (as PM-YP)	(6.8)	644.9
1999	P3	G	Elmdale–Ionia	+5.6	650.5

Act Column Key

A	Adjust mileage
B1	Built by Flint & Pere Marquette Railway
B2	Built by Flint & Holly
B3	Built by Paw Paw
B4	Built by Bay City & East Saginaw
B5	Built by Ionia & Lansing
B6	Built by Michigan Lake Shore
B7	Built by Chicago & Michigan Lake Shore
B8	Built by Holly, Wayne & Monroe
B9	Built by Detroit, Lansing & Lake Michigan
B10	Built by Flint River
B11	Built by Grand Rapids, Newaygo & Lake Shore
B12	Built by Muskegon & Big Rapids
B13	Built by Saginaw Valley & St. Louis
B14	Built by East Saginaw & St. Clair
B15	Built by Chicago, Saginaw & Canada
B16	Built by Detroit, Lansing & Northern
B17	Built by Van Buren Division of Toledo & South Haven

B18 Built by Chicago & West Michigan Railroad
B19 Built by Saginaw & Clare County
B20 Built by Saginaw & Mount Pleasant
B21 Built by Port Huron & Northwestern
B22 Built by Saginaw & Grand Rapids
B23 Built by White River
B24 Built by Flint & Pere Marquette Railroad
B25 Built by Muskegon Lake
B26 Built by Chicago & West Michigan Railway
B27 Built by Indiana & Michigan
B27A Built by Manistee
B28 Built by Saginaw, Tuscola & Huron
B29 Built by Grand Rapids Transfer & Junction
B30 Built by Port Huron & Southwestern
B31 Built by Ithaca & Alma
B32 Built by Saginaw & Western
B33 Built by Toledo & South Haven
B34 Built by Lowell & Hastings
B35 Built by Grand Rapids, Lansing & Detroit
B36 Built by Bay City Belt Line
B37 Built by Chicago & North Michigan
B38 Built by Monroe & Toledo
B39 Built by Benton Harbor, Coloma & Paw Paw Lake
B40 Built by Milwaukee, Benton Harbor & Columbus
B41 Built by Grand Rapids, Kalkaska & Southeastern
B42 Built by Grand Rapids, Belding & Saginaw
B43 Built by Pere Marquette Railroad
B44 Built by Sanilac
B45 Built by Hecla & Western
B46 Built by Harbor Beach & Port Hope
B47 Built by Pere Marquette Railroad of Indiana
B48 Built by Pere Marquette Railway
B49 Built by Flint Belt
B50 Built by Erie & Huron
B51 Built by Lake Erie, Essex & Detroit River
B52 Built by Lake Erie & Detroit River
L1   Leased to Benton Harbor–St Joe Railway & Light
L2   Leased to Kalamazoo, Lake Shore & Chicago
P1   Purchased from Grand Trunk Western
P2   Purchased line of Port Huron & Detroit
P3   Purchased from Mid-Michigan
S1   Sold to Ann Arbor Railroad
S2   Sold to State of Michigan for operation by other companies
S3   Sold to Grand Trunk Western
S4   Sold to Huron & Eastern
S5   Sold to Southwestern Michigan Railroad (operated under name of Kalamazoo, Lake Shore & Chicago)
S6   Sold to Mid-Michigan
S7   Sold to Tuscola & Saginaw Bay
S8   Sold to Saginaw Valley
S9   Sold to Detroit Edison Co.
T1   Leased from Consolidated Rail
X   Abandonment
XL   Lease canceled
Y   Converted main to yard/industrial track

Change Column Key

[Y]   Change shown affects yard mileage, not main track mileage.

( )   Mileage shown is conversion from main track to yard/industrial track mileage.

Sources

1.   ICC, *Finance Dockets.*
2.   Ivey, Pere Marquette Railroad Company
3.   Michigan, Commissioner of Railroads, *Annual Reports,* 1873.
4.   MDOT records.
5.   Michigan Railroad Commission, *Aids, Gifts, Grants.*
6.   Underwood, "Survey of the C&O."

Notes

1.   This date is taken from Source 5. Source 3 has the year 1862.
2.   This line was converted from standard to narrow gauge in ca.1878 and converted to standard gauge in 1898.
3.   Work on this segment was begun by the Muskegon & Ferrysburg and conveyed to Michigan Lake Shore before completion. The north end of this construction is not known with certainty. Source 5 gives the mileage as 15.0, but it is unlikely that the work extended north of North Yard.
4.   Trains used Michigan Central line MC-S between North Lansing and Lansing.
5.   Passenger trains were operated on Michigan Central line MC-W from New Buffalo to Chicago.
6.   The original construction was 43.8 miles and the southern terminus at the Lake Shore & Michigan Southern station. The date of construction to the station in downtown Allegan is not known but probably was not until the late 1870's. Mileage given here is the distance to the downtown Allegan location.
7.   The company also held trackage rights over the Grand River drawbridge on Grand Trunk Western line GTW-D.
8.   The mileage shown is to North Yard.
9.   Passenger trains were operated, until about 1893, from Wayne into Detroit over Michigan Central line MC-E.
10.   The company also held trackage rights between West Detroit and Detroit on Michigan Central line MC-E.
11.   This completion date is assumed given the completion of line PM-A.
12.   Work on this segment was begun by the Grand Rapids & Holland, and was merged before completion.
13.   The company also held trackage rights between Monroe and Toledo on Lake Shore & Michigan Southern line LS-D.
14.   Source 5 states that this segment was partially completed by the Patterson Railroad, donated on 18 July 1872, and finished on the date shown.
15.   The company also held trackage rights between Paines and Mershon on Michigan Central line MC-S.
16.   Work on this segment was begun by the Muskegon & Big Rapids and conveyed before completion.
17.   This segment was located north of the Pine River and on the north side of Alma.
18.   This segment was built as narrow gauge and converted to standard gauge in 1898.
19.   The abandonment was to the station in Paw Paw on St. Joseph Street and coincided with the completion of the segment from Paw Paw to Lawrence.
20.   This segment was built as narrow gauge and converted to standard gauge in 1898.
21.   This segment was built as narrow gauge and converted to standard gauge in 1884.
22.   The construction of all segments of the Manistee Branch, or spurs off that branch, cannot be identified. The unidentified annual changes are reported only the Acquisition/Disposition Record with the line designation PM-MXX and are as given in Sources 3 and 5.
23.   Source 5 gives the completion date as 1874. Between 1890 and 1905 Sources 3 and 5 report construction and abandonment changes annually. Most of this later work appears to have been industrial tracks that did not alter the length of the line.
24.   This segment was built as narrow gauge and converted to standard gauge in 1889.
25.   This segment was built as narrow gauge. Operations were suspended by order of Railroad Commissioners in 1886, and operations resumed and the segment converted to standard gauge in 1889. Operations were again suspended between 15 July 1893, to 4 October 1897.
26.   The date of this alteration is assumed given the abandonment of line PM-AO and the merger of the Grand Haven into the Chicago & West Michigan.
27.   Between Vassar and Hoyt this segment apparently used a grade of the projected Cass River Railroad. Source

3 infers that this segment also used some or all of line PM-YSS to a station in Saginaw approximately at Washington Street

28. This segment was built as narrow gauge. East of Tappan it was converted to standard gauge in 1884; the remainder was converted to standard gauge in 1903.

29. This construction is assumed given the abandonment of line PM-VO.

30. This construction and the abandonment of the short segment to Harrison Junction were made coincident with the construction of Ann Arbor line AA-B in 1887.

31. This construction is assumed given the completion of line PM-D as well as the close working relationship between this company and the Chicago & West Michigan which owned line PM-C.

32. Source 5 states this line was completed as given, withdrawn from service in 1891, and service restored in 1896.

33. This construction is assumed, given the location of the original Traverse City passenger station, which remained in service until about 1926.

34. The construction of all segments of the Coleman Branch, or spurs off that branch, cannot be identified. The unidentified annual changes are reported only the Acquisition/Disposition Record with the line designation PM-LGXX and are as given in Sources 3 and 5.

35. The construction of all segments of the Harrison Branch, or spurs off that branch, cannot be identified. The unidentified annual changes are reported only the Acquisition/Disposition Record with the line designation PM-LHXX and are as given in Sources 3 and 5.

36. The construction of all segments of the Hoyt's North and South Branches, or spurs off those branches, cannot be identified. The unidentified annual changes are reported only the Acquisition/Disposition Record with the line designation PM-LJXX and are as given in Sources 3 and 5.

37. The construction of all segments of the Star Lake Branch, or spurs off that branch, cannot be identified. The unidentified annual changes are reported only the Acquisition/Disposition Record with the line designation PM-LSXX and are as given in Sources 3 and 5.

38. This construction is assumed. It provided a connection to Manistee & North Eastern line M&NE-A which was completed into Traverse City in 1892.

39. Trains operated between Delray and Detroit on tracks of Fort Street Union Depot and Detroit Union Railway Station Cos.

40. This segment also held trackage rights over the Canada Southern east of St. Thomas Jct.

41. The construction and abandonment dates are from Source 5, but the line has not been located precisely.

42. This segment also held trackage rights on the Ann Arbor and on the Toledo Terminal south of Alexis.

43. This construction replaced the original main line between Union Pier and New Buffalo, which is assumed to have been abandoned. Also it is assumed that that part of line PM-W between Alfred and New Buffalo was abandoned at the same time.

44. This construction on the south side of Edmore is assumed, based on the acquisition of the Grand Rapids, Belding & Saginaw and the need to facilitate through movements between Grand Rapids and Saginaw.

45. This property was subsequently abandoned on 31 August 1928, by the lessee.

46. A section of this line was retained in Benton Harbor as line PM-Y1U, and a section in Buchanan was sold to the Michigan Central as an industrial track. The ICC *Finance Docket* also required the PM to build a connection to the Southern Michigan at Berrien Springs and convey its tracks there to the Southern Michigan.

47. The date of this change is assumed given the completion of the new passenger station.

48. No construction or abandonment dates could be found, but it appears that this segment was built by 1880 and abandoned during the 1960's.

49. No construction date could be found, but it appears that this segment was built soon after 1890.

50. The date of construction and/or abandonment could not be determined, and therefore is not included in the mileage shown in the Acquisition/Disposition Record.

51. Sources 3 and 5 report alterations to this line between 1890 and 1905. Most of this work appears to have been industrial tracks that did not alter the length of the line.

52. A section was retained west of Kalamazoo Avenue as industrial track. Passenger service ended Fall of 1932.

53. This date is assumed given the completion of the new Bay City passenger station. It is probable that some of this segment was retained as industrial track for a time, but the date of the final disposition can not be determined.

54. Source 1 states the last service between Woodville and Big Rapids was operated on 1 November 1923.

55. The ICC *Finance Docket* authorizing abandonment states no trains operated over this line since at least 1919.

56. Trackage rights over the Grand Rapids & Indiana line GR&I-N between Grand Rapids Union Station and Fuller were authorized on the date shown.

57. This segment was sold to Detroit Edison Co. and railbanked by that company for future use.

58. Trackage rights over Grand Trunk Western between Tappan and Flint were substituted for this line upon its sale.

Peters Manistee Train Railway

MAIN LINE (PMTR)

	MILEAGE	COUNTY	CROSSINGS, JUNCTIONS, ETC.
Line not located			

OWNERSHIP

1883   Peters Manistee Train Railway.

Peters Train Railway

MAIN LINE (PTRY)

	MILEAGE	COUNTY	CROSSINGS, JUNCTIONS, ETC.
Line not located			

OWNERSHIP

1883   Peters Train Railway.

Port Huron & Detroit

MAIN LINE (PH&D-A)

	MILEAGE [GTW–Pt Huron]	COUNTY	CROSSINGS, JUNCTIONS, ETC.
(Jct., crossing)	0.6	St. Clair	J/GTW-C 333.3, X/PM-Q 87.3
(Military St.)	3.0	"	X/DUR-R 63.11
Marysville (old)	3.4	"	
(River Rd.)	3.6	"	X/DUR-R 62.28
Marysville (new)	4.6	"	
St. Clair	10.8	"	
(Jct.)	11.6	"	J/PH&D-YSC 0
Belle River	15.2	"	
Mar. Cty.	18.2	"	
(Jct.)	18.8	"	J/DUR-R 46.26
(End)	19.1	"	J/ATR 0

CONSTRUCTION/ABANDONMENT

DATE	ACT	END POINTS	MP	CHANGE	MAIN	SOURCE	NOTE
1901	B1	Pt. Hur.–Marysville	0.6–3.4	+2.8	2.8	1	
1918/8/1	B2	Marysville–Mar. Cty.	3.4–19.1	+15.7	18.5	1	

OWNERSHIP

1901	Port Huron Southern (B1)
1918	Port Huron & Detroit (B2)
1923 ca.	Port Huron & Detroit, merger of Port Huron Southern
1984/12	Chesapeake & Ohio, purchase of Port Huron & Detroit
1997/9/2	CSX Transportation, merger of Chesapeake & Ohio

ST. CLAIR SPUR (PH&D-YSC)

It appears that the Port Huron & Detroit acquired about 1 mile of the Michigan Central line MC-DM in about 1932 as an industrial track to reach industries in St. Clair.

ACQUISITION/DISPOSITION RECORD

See record above

Act Column Key

B1	Built by Port Huron Southern
B2	Built by Port Huron & Detroit

Sources

1. Michigan Railroad Commission, *Aids, Gifts, Grants.*

Rapid River & Eastern

	MILEAGE	COUNTY	CROSSINGS, JUNCTIONS, ETC.
Line not located			

OWNERSHIP

1892	Rapid River & Eastern

Notes

GENERAL No details could be found of the construction or abandonment of this company. It may have been constructed about 1892 between Rapid City and Kalkaska, as proposed, and subsequently transferred either its line or its grade to the Grand Rapids, Kalkaska & Southeastern in about 1898, but no transfer of record could be found.

Saginaw Valley

For arrangement of stations, construction record, and prior ownerships, see Pere Marquette line PM-Q.

ACQUISITION/DISPOSITION RECORD

DATE	ACT	SGVY–	END POINTS	MP	CHANGE	MAIN
1998/4/28	P1	[PM-Q]	Hoyt–Brown Cty.	2.6–54.3	+51.7	51.7

OWNERSHIP

1998	Saginaw Valley, wholly-owned subsidiary of RailAmerica.

Act Column Key

P1	Purchased from CSX.

St. Helens Lake & Southern

MAIN LINE (SHL&S-A) (LINE NOT LOCATED)

	MILEAGE	COUNTY	CROSSINGS, JUNCTIONS, ETC.
St. Helens (End)	0	Roscommon	J/MC-M 64.4

CONSTRUCTION/ABANDONMENT

DATE	ACT	END POINTS	MP	CHANGE	MAIN
1883	B				
1890 ca.	X				

OWNERSHIP

1883	St. Helens Lake & Southern.

Act Column Key

B Built by St. Helens Lake & Southern
X Abandoned

Notes

GENERAL This company was incorporated in 1883 under the General Railroad Law, but served principally as a logging road for Henry Stephens & Co. and had little common carrier use.

Shelby & Detroit

MAIN LINE (S&D)

	MILEAGE	COUNTY	CROSSINGS, JUNCTIONS, ETC.
Utica	0	Macomb	
(7 Mile Rd.)	13	Wayne	

CONSTRUCTION/ABANDONMENT

DATE	ACT	END POINTS	MP	CHANGE	MAIN	SOURCE
1839/9	B	Line	0–13	+13.0	13.0	1
1844	X	Line	0–13	−13.0	0	1

OWNERSHIP

1839	Shelby & Detroit

ACQUISITION/DISPOSITION RECORD

See mileage record above. This road is not included in the mileage table in chapter 2.

Notes

GENERAL This shadowy company apparently was built and operated for the period shown above based on statements in Source 1. Although the northern terminus is given as Utica, the southern terminus is given as "to within five miles of Gratiot Road." It appears that it used only horses for motive power during its operating life.

Act Column Key

B Built by Shelby & Detroit
X Abandoned

Sources

1. Farmer, *Detroit and Wayne County.*

Sweet Line Railroad

MAIN LINE (SWL-A)

For arrangement of stations, construction record, and prior ownerships, see Grand Trunk Western line GTW-M.

ACQUISITION/DISPOSITION RECORD

DATE	ACT	END POINTS	MP	CHANGE	MAIN	SOURCE	NOTE
1984/8?	P	Middleton–Carson City	12.0–19.3	+7.3	(7.3)		

OWNERSHIP

1984   Sweet Line Railroad

Act Column Key

P   Purchased from Grand Trunk Western.

Notes

General   Sweet Line Railroad is owned for exclusive use by area shippers and is not a common carrier.

Tuscola & Saginaw Bay

The Tuscola & Saginaw Bay operated the following lines under contract with the State of Michigan which had acquired ownership of the lines or had contractual arrangements with trustees of Penn Central, the prior owner. See also page for Michigan, State of.

For arrangement of stations, construction record, and prior ownerships, see Ann Arbor lines AA-A, AA-B, AA-C, and AA-F; Grand Rapids & Indiana lines GR&I-N and GR&I-T; Michigan Central lines MC-S, MC-B, MC-BS, and MC-BC; and Pere Marquette lines PM-P, PM-L and PM-YTC.

ACQUISITION/DISPOSITION RECORD

DATE	ACT	TSBY–	END POINTS	MP	CHANGE	MICHIGAN DES.OPR. MAIN	OWNED MAIN	NOTE
1977/10/1	C	[MC-B]	Millington–Munger	79.3–101.1	+21.8			1
10/1	C	[MC-BS]	Denmark Jct.–Richv.	4.8–6.0	+1.2			1
10/1	C	[MC-BC]	Caro Jct.–Colling	0.4–22.4	+22.0	45.0		1
1981/5/1	P1	[MC-BS]	Richville–Harger	6.0–15.5	+9.5	45.0	9.5	
1982/10/1	C	[AA-A]	A.A.–Pitt	47.5–93.9	+46.4			2
10/1	C	[AA-B]	Ashley–Alma	128.3–145.4	+17.1			2
10/1	C	[MC-S]	Owosso–Swan Creek	64.2–91.3	+27.1	135.6	9.5	2
1984/5/6	C	[AA-B]	Alma–Cadillac	145.4–227.1	+81.7			3
5/6	C	[AA-C]	Cadillac–Frankfort	227.1–292.4	+65.3			3
5/6	C	[AA-F]	Frankfort–Boat Land.	290.3–291.8	+1.5			3
8	P1	[GTW-M]	Ashley–Middleton	0–12.0	+12.0			
10/1	C	[GR&I-N]	Reed Cty.–Petoskey	302.0–426.0	+124.0			3
10/1	C	[GR&I-T]	Walton Jct.–Trav. Cty.	0–25.2	+25.2			3
10/1	C	[PM-P]	Grawn–Williamsburg	158.1–180.8	+22.7			3,4
10/1	C	[PM-P]	Charlevoix–Bay View	231.4–248.0	+16.5			3,4
10/1	C	[PM-YTC]	In Trav. Cty.		(+1.3)	472.5	21.5	
1988 ca.	E	[PM-P]	Charlevoix–Bay View	231.4–248.0	–16.5			

ca.	E	[AA-C]	Thompsonv.–Frankfort	271.2–292.4	–21.2			
ca.	E	[AA-F]	to Boat Landing	0–1.5	–1.5			
ca.	E	[GR&I-S]	Reed Cty.–Cadillac	302.0–333.1	–31.1			
6/1	P2	[PM-L]	In Clare	49.4–52.0	(+2.6)	402.2	21.5	
1991/1/22	T	[MC-B]	Millington–Munger	79.3–101.1	–21.8			5
1/22	T	[MC-BS]	DenmarkJct.–Richv.	4.8–6.0	–1.2			5
1/22	T	[MC-BC]	Caro Jct.–Colling	0.4–22.4	–22.0			5
1/22	S1	[MC-BS]	Richville–Harger	6.0–15.5	–9.5	357.2	12.0	

OWNERSHIP

Titles to lines operated by this company remained with the State of Michigan or with the trustees of Ann Arbor or Penn Central, the prior owners, unless stated otherwise.

Act Column Key

C   Operated under Designated Operator contract with State of Michigan
E   Designated Operator contract ended
P1   Purchased from Grand Trunk Western
P2   Purchased from CSX Transportation
S1   Sold to Huron & Eastern
T   Designated Operator contract ended and transferred to another operator

Source

MDOT records

Notes

1.   Company succeeded Conrail as designated operator.
2.   Company succeeded Michigan Interstate as designated operator.
3.   Company succeeded Michigan Northern as designated operator.
4.   Mile posts shown are C&O renumbered locations and are 21.7 miles higher than shown for line PM-P.
5.   Operations were transferred to Huron & Eastern, which see.

Wabash

MAIN LINE (WAB-A)

	MILEAGE [Detroit]	COUNTY	CROSSINGS, JUNCTIONS, ETC.
Delray	4.4	Wayne	J/DURS 4.5, J/WAB-W 2.5
(Dearborn Rd.)	4.4	"	X/DSR-DR 0.65
(Jct.)	4.8	"	J/PRR-F 0
River Rouge	5.2	"	J/DTSL 47.0
Ecorse Jct.	5.6	"	J/MC-DZ 0.9, J/PRR-A 136.8, B/DUR-T 0.87
(Jct.)	6.7	"	J/WAB-YD 0
Oakwood	7.0	"	
Oakwood Jct.	8.7	"	X/DTI-D 10.3
Hand	12.4	"	
Romulus	19.0	"	X/PM-T 93.8
French Landing	21.3	"	
Belleville	23.8	"	
Willis	28.6	Washtenaw	
Whittaker	31.5	"	
Milan	37.3	Monroe	X/AA-A 30.9
Cone	42.7	"	
Britton	46.7	Lenawee	X/DTM 9.4, f. Balch

Holloway	52.4	"		
Raisin Center	54.8	"	X/LS-J 2.1	
(Bridge)	58.7	"	B/LS-A2 31.2, B/T&W-A 36.1	
Adrian	58.8	"		
WB	59.0	"	X/LS-A 328.3	
Page	59.8	"	X/DTI-A 44.3, f. South Adrian	
Stan	61.2	"		
Madison	61.7	"		
Sand Creek	65.6	"		
Leaf	68.4	"	J/DTI-A 36.0, f. Lima Jct.	
Seneca	70.2	"	f. Ennis	
N. Morenci	73.2	"		
Munson	79.5	"	f. N. Fayette	
(MI/OH state line)	80.2			
Franklin OH	84.7	Williams OH		
Alvordton	85.7	"		
Kunkle	89.8	"		
Mode	93.7	"		
East Yard	96.0	"		
Montpelier OH	96.9	"		

CONSTRUCTION/ABANDONMENT

DATE	ACT	END POINTS	MP	CHANGE	MI MAIN	SOURCE	NOTE
1881/8/15	B1	Delray–Montpelier	4.4–96.9	+92.5	75.8	1	1

OWNERSHIP

1881	Detroit, Butler & St. Louis (B1)
1881/6/13	Wabash, St. Louis & Pacific, merger of Detroit, Butler & St. Louis
1889/2/19	Detroit & State Line Wabash, to reorganize Detroit, Butler & St. Louis
1889/5/23	Wabash Railroad, merger of Detroit & State Line Wabash
1915/10/22	Wabash Railway, to reorganize Wabash Railroad
1941/12/31	Wabash Railroad, to reorganize Wabash Railway
1964/10/16	Norfolk & Western leased Wabash Railroad
1980/7/23	Norfolk Southern, control of Norfolk & Western

TECUMSEH BRANCH (WAB-[DTI-A])

For stations see Detroit, Toledo & Ironton line DTI-A, Page–Tecumseh (MP 44.3–MP 55.4).

OWNERSHIP

1979	Wabash Railroad, leased to Norfolk & Western
1980/7/23	Norfolk Southern, control of Norfolk & Western

WEST DETROIT BRANCH (WAB-W)

	MILEAGE	COUNTY	CROSSINGS, JUNCTIONS, ETC.
W. Det.	0	Wayne	J/GTW-H 0, J/MC-E 2.9
(Vernor Hwy.)	0.7	"	X/DSR-A 12.69
(Fort St.)	1.6	"	B/DSR-F 0.63
Delray	2.5	"	J/PM-D 4.5, J/WAB-A 4.4

CONSTRUCTION/ABANDONMENT

DATE	ACT	END POINTS	MP	CHANGE	MAIN	SOURCE	NOTE
1881	B1	W. Det.–Delray	0–2.5	+2.5	2.5		

OWNERSHIP

1881	Detroit, Butler & St. Louis (B1)
1881/6/13	Wabash, St. Louis & Pacific, merger of Detroit, Butler & St. Louis
1889/2/19	Detroit & State Line Wabash, to reorganize Detroit, Butler & St. Louis
1889/5/23	Wabash Railroad, merger of Detroit & State Line Wabash
1915/10/22	Wabash Railway, to reorganize Wabash Railroad
1941/12/31	Wabash Railroad, to reorganize Wabash Railway
1964/10/16	Norfolk & Western leased Wabash Railroad
1980/7/23	Norfolk Southern, control of Norfolk & Western

DETROIT SPUR (WAB-YD)

	MILEAGE	COUNTY	CROSSINGS, JUNCTIONS, ETC.
(Jct.)	0	Wayne	J/WAB-A 6.7
(Crossing)	0.6	"	X/MC-DZ 1.7
(End of track)	1.1	"	

CONSTRUCTION/ABANDONMENT

DATE	ACT	END POINTS	MP	CHANGE	MAIN	SOURCE	NOTE
1908	B2	Line	0–1.1	(+1.1)	0		

OWNERSHIP

1908	Detroit & Western (B2)
1915/10/22	Wabash Railway, acquired control of Detroit & Western
1941/12/31	Wabash Railroad, to reorganize Wabash Railway
1964/10/16	Norfolk & Western leased Wabash Railroad
1980/7/23	Norfolk Southern, control of Norfolk & Western

ACQUISITION/DISPOSITION RECORD

DATE	ACT	WAB–	END POINTS	CHANGE	MI MAIN	NOTE
1881/8/15	B1	A	Delray–Montpelier OH	+75.8		1
1881	B1	W	W. Det.–Delray	+2.5	78.3	
1908	B2	YD	Det. spur	(+1.1)	78.3	

On 16 October 1964 this company was conveyed to Norfolk & Western. Its Acquisition/Disposition Record is continued in two places: under the name of the former company and under the name of the new company. The lines conveyed were:

LINE DESIG.	END POINTS	MP	MI MAIN	SOURCE	NOTE
N&W-					
[WAB-A]	Delray–OH state line	4.4–80.2	75.8		
[WAB-WD]	W. Det.–Delray	0–2.5	2.5		
[WAB-YD]	Det. spur	0–1.1	(1.1)		
		TOTAL	78.3		

Act Column Key

B1	Built by Detroit, Butler & St Louis
B2	Built by Detroit & Western

Sources

1. Michigan Railroad Commission, *Aids, Gifts, Grants.*

Notes

1. The original Detroit terminal was in the vicinity of West Grand Boulevard on the present Fort Street Union Depot line at MP 1.9. The property east of Delray was conveyed to FSUD in 1883 when Fort Street Station was completed.

West Branch & Moorestown

LINE (WB&M)

Line not located

CONSTRUCTION/ABANDONMENT

DATE	ACT	END POINTS	MP	CHANGE	MAIN	SOURCE	NOTE
1882/7	B	Main line	?	+10.5		1	
1882/7	B	Branch	?	+0.7	11.2	1	
1885	X	Branch	?	−0.7	10.5	1	
1887	X	Main line	?	−10.5	0	1	

OWNERSHIP
1882   West Branch & Moorestown

Act column
B   Built by West Branch & Moorestown
X   Abandoned

Sources
1.   Michigan, Commissioner of Railroads, *Annual Reports*, 1885, 1887.

West Michigan

MAIN LINE (WM-A)
For arrangement of stations, construction record, and prior ownerships, see Pere Marquette line PM-H.

ACQUISITION/DISPOSITION RECORD

DATE	ACT	END POINTS	MP	CHANGE	MAIN	SOURCE	NOTE
1995/9/11	P	Paw Paw–Hartford	30.4–15.7	+14.7	14.7		

OWNERSHIP
1995   West Michigan.

Act Column Key
P   Purchased from Kalamazoo, Lake Shore & Chicago Division, Southern Michigan Railroad, at bankruptcy.

Notes
GENERAL   West Michigan Railroad is a wholly owned subsidiary of Pioneer Railcorp.

Wyandotte Southern

CONSTRUCTION/ABANDONMENT

DATE	ACT	END POINTS	MP	CHANGE	MAIN	SOURCE	NOTE

OWNERSHIP
1901   Pennsalt Railroad
1908/8/17   Wyandotte Southern, renamed Pennsalt

Notes

GENERAL   This company is a terminal switching road and not an intercity carrier. Its mileage is not included the Michigan mileage table in chapter 2. The road was built about 1908 and was abandoned in 1992.

Wyandotte Terminal

CONSTRUCTION/ABANDONMENT

DATE	ACT	END POINTS	MP	CHANGE	MAIN	SOURCE	NOTE

OWNERSHIP

1905		Wyandotte Terminal					

Notes

GENERAL   This company is a terminal switching road and not an intercity carrier. Its mileage is not included the Michigan mileage table in chapter 2. The line was built in June 1905 and abandoned, but the abandonment date could not be determined.